# Ramism and the Reformation of Method

# OXFORD STUDIES IN HISTORICAL THEOLOGY

*Series Editor*
Richard A. Muller, Calvin Theological Seminary

*Founding Editor*
David C. Steinmetz †

*Editorial Board*
Robert C. Gregg, Stanford University
George M. Marsden, University of Notre Dame
Wayne A. Meeks, Yale University
Gerhard Sauter, Rheinische Friedrich-Wilhelms-Universität Bonn
Susan E. Schreiner, University of Chicago
John Van Engen, University of Notre Dame
Robert L. Wilken, University of Virginia

THE REGENSBURG ARTICLE 5 ON JUSTIFICATION
*Inconsistent Patchwork or Substance of True Doctrine?*
Anthony N. S. Lane

AUGUSTINE ON THE WILL
*A Theological Account*
Han-luen Kantzer Komline

THE SYNOD OF PISTORIA AND VATICAN II
*Jansenism and the Struggle for Catholic Reform*
Shaun Blanchard

CATHOLICITY AND THE COVENANT OF WORKS
*James Ussher and the Reformed Tradition*
Harrison Perkins

THE COVENANT OF WORKS
*The Origins, Development, and Reception of the Doctrine*
J. V. Fesko

RINGLEADERS OF REDEMPTION
*How Medieval Dance Became Sacred*
Kathryn Dickason

REFUSING TO KISS THE SLIPPER
*Opposition to Calvinism in the Francophone Reformation*
Michael W. Bruening

FONT OF PARDON AND NEW LIFE
*John Calvin and the Efficacy of Baptism*
Lyle D. Bierma

THE FLESH OF THE WORD
*The* extra Calvinisticum *from Zwingli to Early Orthodoxy*
K. J. Drake

JOHN DAVENANT'S HYPOTHETICAL UNIVERSALISM
*A Defense of Catholic and Reformed Orthodoxy*
Michael J. Lynch

RHETORICAL ECONOMY IN AUGUSTINE'S THEOLOGY
Brian Gronewoller

GRACE AND CONFORMITY
*The Reformed Conformist Tradition and the Early Stuart Church of England*
Stephen Hampton

MAKING ITALY ANGLICAN
*Why the Book of Common Prayer Was Translated into Italian*
Stefano Villani

AUGUSTINE ON MEMORY
Kevin G. Grove

UNITY AND CATHOLICITY IN CHRIST
*The Ecclesiology of Francisco Suarez, S.J.*
Eric J. DeMeuse

CALVINIST CONFORMITY IN POST-REFORMATION ENGLAND
*The Theology and Career of Daniel Featley*
Gregory A. Salazar

RETAINING THE OLD EPISCOPAL DIVINITY
*John Edwards of Cambridge and Reformed Orthodoxy in the Later Stuart Church*
Jake Griesel

BEARDS, AZYMES, AND PURGATORY
*The Other Issues that Divided East and West*
A. Edward Siecienski

BISSCHOP'S BENCH
*Contours of Arminian Conformity in the Church of England, c.1674–1742*
Samuel Fornecker

JOHN LOCKE'S THEOLOGY
*An Ecumenical, Irenic, and Controversial Project*
Jonathan S. Marko

THEOLOGY AND HISTORY IN THE METHODOLOGY OF HERMAN BAVINCK
*Revelation, Confession, and Christian Consciousness*
Cameron D. Clausing

CHRIST, THE SPIRIT, AND HUMAN TRANSFORMATION IN GREGORY OF NYSSA'S *IN CANTICUM CANTICORUM*
Alexander L. Abecina

THE ZURICH ORIGINS OF REFORMED COVENANT THEOLOGY
Pierrick Hildebrand

RAMISM AND THE REFORMATION OF METHOD
*The Franciscan Legacy in Early Modernity*
Simon J. G. Burton

# Ramism and the Reformation of Method

*The Franciscan Legacy in Early Modernity*

SIMON J. G. BURTON

**OXFORD**
UNIVERSITY PRESS

Oxford University Press is a department of the University of Oxford. It furthers
the University's objective of excellence in research, scholarship, and education
by publishing worldwide. Oxford is a registered trade mark of Oxford University
Press in the UK and certain other countries.

Published in the United States of America by Oxford University Press
198 Madison Avenue, New York, NY 10016, United States of America.

© Oxford University Press 2024

All rights reserved. No part of this publication may be reproduced, stored in
a retrieval system, or transmitted, in any form or by any means, without the
prior permission in writing of Oxford University Press, or as expressly permitted
by law, by license, or under terms agreed with the appropriate reproduction
rights organization. Inquiries concerning reproduction outside the scope of the
above should be sent to the Rights Department, Oxford University Press, at the
address above.

You must not circulate this work in any other form
and you must impose this same condition on any acquirer.

Library of Congress Cataloging-in-Publication Data
Names: Burton, Simon J. G., author.
Title: Ramism and the reformation of method : the Franciscan legacy in
early modernity / Simon J. G. Burton.
Description: New York : Oxford University Press, 2024. |
Series: Oxford studies in historical theology |
Includes bibliographical references and index.
Identifiers: LCCN 2023049380 (print) | LCCN 2023049381 (ebook) |
ISBN 9780197516355 (hardback) | ISBN 9780197516379 (epub)
Subjects: LCSH: Ramus, Petrus, 1515–1572—Influence. | Franciscans—History.
Classification: LCC B785.L24 B87 2024 (print) | LCC B785.L24 (ebook) |
DDC 194—dc23/eng/20240117
LC record available at https://lccn.loc.gov/2023049380
LC ebook record available at https://lccn.loc.gov/2023049381

DOI: 10.1093/oso/9780197516355.001.0001

Printed by Integrated Books International, United States of America

*For Marilyn and Edward
with deepest love and gratitude*

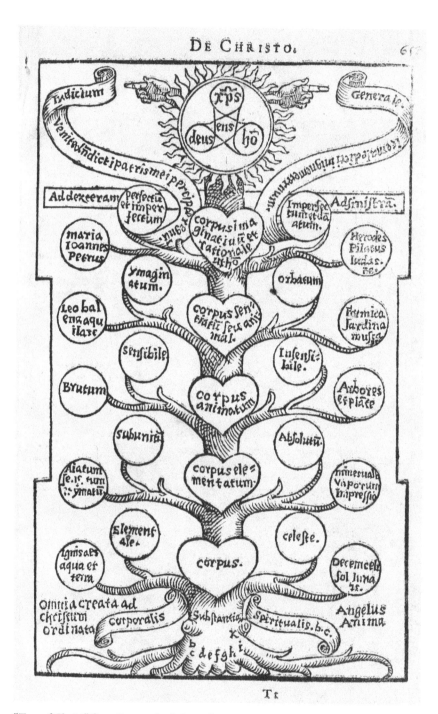

"Tree of Christ" from Bernardo de Lavinheta, *Opera Omnia*, ed. Johann Heinrich Alsted (Cologne, 1612), 657. This illustrates the symbolic conjunction of the Franciscan, Lullist, and Ramist-encyclopaedic traditions in early modernity. Reproducd by kind permission of the Bibliothèque Nationale de France.

# Contents

*Acknowledgements*     xiii
*Abbreviations*     xix

Introduction: The Franciscan Reformation of Method     1
    I.1. Augustinian and Franciscan Platonism     6
    I.2. Lullism     17
    I.3. Christian Humanism     22
    I.4. Reformed Scholasticism     31
    I.5. Ramist Itinerary     42

1. Divine Dialectic: Ramus, Method, and the Ascent to God     44
    1.1. Evangelical and Mystical Milieu     48
    1.2. Fabrist Formation     53
    1.3. Natural and Cusan Dialectic     54
    1.4. Mathematics, Dialectic, and the Mystical Ascent to God     58
    1.5. Rhetorical and Metaphysical Turn     62
    1.6. The Emerging Shape of Ramist Dialectic     64

2. Return to the Golden Age: Ramus and the Reform of Church and Society     79
    2.1. Reforming the University     81
    2.2. Mathematical and Evangelical Reform     87
    2.3. Return to the Golden Age     91
    2.4. Transforming Theological Method     95

3. Logics of Faith: Piscator, Herborn Ramism, and the Confessionalization of Method     105
    3.1. Ramism, Philippism, and Neo-Platonism     106
    3.2. The Ambiguities of Philippo-Ramism     110
    3.3. Olevian's Ramism     112
    3.4. Olevian and the Birth of Federal Theology     116
    3.5. Olevian and the Founding of the Herborn Academy     119
    3.6. Piscator's Ramist Conversion     122
    3.7. Piscator and the Reform of Ramism     125
    3.8. Logic, Exegesis, and Theology     128
    3.9. Herborn Ramism     132

## x  CONTENTS

4. Archetypal Reform: Richardson, Ames, and the Reduction of the Arts — 137
   - 4.1. The Character of Cambridge Ramism — 140
   - 4.2. Perkins' Ramism — 144
   - 4.3. Richardsonian Ramism — 146
   - 4.4. Exemplarism and Encyclopaedism — 159
   - 4.5. Archetype, Ectype, and the Logic of Scripture — 165
   - 4.6. Counter-Logic and Metaphysics — 169
   - 4.7. Towards the Logic of Faith — 171
   - 4.8. Living to God — 174

5. Catholic Symphony: Scaliger, Polanus, and the Reconfiguring of Ramism — 181
   - 5.1. Scaliger's Franciscan Logic and Metaphysics — 184
   - 5.2. Goclenius and Reformed Metaphysics — 188
   - 5.3. Polanus' Symphonic Method of Theology — 193
   - 5.4. Szegedinus' Trinitarian Method of Theology — 205
   - 5.5. Trinitarian and Transcendental Turn — 211

6. Christian Philosophy: Keckermann, Encyclopaedism, and the Return to Eden — 213
   - 6.1. Keckermann and German Ramism — 215
   - 6.2. Methodical Peripateticism — 221
   - 6.3. Christian Philosophy — 226
   - 6.4. Encyclopaedism and Eden — 231
   - 6.5. Towards a Trinitarian Philosophy — 234
   - 6.6. Therapeutic Theology and Architectonic Politics — 236

7. Philosophical Panacea: Alsted, Lullism, and Trinitarian Encyclopaedism — 242
   - 7.1. Between Ramism and Lullism — 245
   - 7.2. The Quest for a Lullist Key — 251
   - 7.3. Harmonic Philosophy and *Mathesis Universalis* — 257
   - 7.4. Towards a Triune Universal Method — 261
   - 7.5. Biblical Encyclopaedism — 266
   - 7.6. Scriptural and Scotist Metaphysics — 268
   - 7.7. Trinitarian and Apocalyptic Encyclopaedism — 272

8. Universal Harmony: Bisterfeld, Immeation, and Mystical Transformation — 280
   - 8.1. Bisterfeld's Formation — 282
   - 8.2. Trinitarian, Encyclopaedic, and Apocalyptic Reform — 286
   - 8.3. Trinitarian and Transcendental Metaphysics — 291
   - 8.4. Neo-Platonic and Mathematical Logic — 296
   - 8.5. Encyclopaedism, Meditation, and Ascent — 299
   - 8.6. Scriptural Method and the *Ars Concionandi* — 303

|  |  | 8.7. Theological Logic | 308 |
|---|---|---|---|
|  |  | 8.8. Trinity, Symbiotics, and Society | 312 |
| 9. |  | Pansophia: Comenius and the Quest for Human Omniscience | 319 |
|  |  | 9.1. Ramist and Lullist Formation | 321 |
|  |  | 9.2. Baconian and Campanellan Influence | 325 |
|  |  | 9.3. Millennialism and the Rosicrucian Furore | 330 |
|  |  | 9.4. Augustinian and Franciscan Encyclopaedism | 336 |
|  |  | 9.5. Pansophia, Anti-Socinianism, and the Coincidence of Opposites | 343 |
|  |  | 9.6. *Mathesis Universalis* | 348 |
|  |  | 9.7. *Consultatio Catholica* | 354 |

*Bibliography*   363
*Index*   403

# Acknowledgements

This book has been nearly ten years in the writing. It follows on from my previous monograph *The Hallowing of Logic*, which explored the Trinitarian method of Richard Baxter, the leading seventeenth-century English Reformed and Puritan theologian. Ramism played a major role in the development of Baxter's theological system, as is evident from the intricate trichotomous charts—his own answer to Ramus' dichotomies—which make up his monumental *Methodus Theologiae*. In Baxter's methodology Ramism combined into a fertile synthesis with Scotism and Lullism to form a new and distinctive Trinitarian method. In grappling with the mystery of the Trinity, he came to believe that God's utter transcendence of human reason meant that theology required its own, scriptural, "logic of faith"—a view with deep roots in late medieval, Nominalist, thought. Moreover, as I perhaps then only dimly perceived, Baxter's scriptural logic and Trinitarian method resonates with the Christian philosophy of Bonaventure and the Franciscans.

Baxter was my induction into the world of Ramism and Reformed scholasticism, and a better guide one could hardly wish to have. However, it was a postdoctoral fellowship at the Faculty of "*Artes Liberales*" in the University of Warsaw which first gave me the opportunity to pursue intensive research on Ramism and also introduced me to the fascinating world of universal reform. During my doctoral studies I had tended to see Baxter and his Trinitarian method as something of an outlier in the Reformed tradition. To discover the deep roots of his thought in the wider Ramist movement therefore came as an exciting surprise. It began to suggest to me the roots of Ramism itself in a Franciscan Reformation of method, connecting the innovations of the sixteenth and seventeenth centuries to a much longer history of reform.

Work on Ramism also dovetailed well with my wider research on Reformed scholasticism, which has focussed on the phenomenon of Reformed Scotism—something I have come to believe is also crucial to understanding Ramism. A final piece of the puzzle came with a growing fascination, nurtured during an earlier postdoctoral fellowship at McGill University, with the Christian Platonism of Nicholas of Cusa. The link between Ramism and Cusan thought is one I pursued backwards from Jan Amos Comenius, but hope now to have traced to its fountainhead in Ramus himself. Due to his birthplace in Cuts in Picardy, his friend and biographer, Nicholas Nancel, insisted Ramus should be called a Cusan. For very different reasons, I have found no other name to be more apt.

I have come to realize that, in many ways, the inspiration for this book goes back far beyond my doctoral studies at the University of Edinburgh or even my undergraduate studies at the University of Cambridge—where I first encountered Cusanus in a memorable seminar led by Eamon Duffy—to my childhood encounter with Christian Platonism and aestheticism in the works of C. S. Lewis and Dante Alighieri. In terms of Ramism itself, it was Perry Miller's spell-binding *New England Mind* which opened my mind to the fundamental Platonism and aestheticism of this movement. For all its brilliance, in my view, the work of his student Walter Ong—often taken as the definitive word on Ramism—fails to perceive its true spirit and thus get to the intellectual and theological beating-heart of this movement.

In writing this book I have incurred a considerable number of debts. I must express my thanks first of all to Richard Muller, my Series Editor. I well remember the pleasure with which I first encountered his *Post-Reformation Reformed Dogmatics*, and he is a towering scholar in the field. It is therefore an enormous privilege and delight to be accepted in the Oxford Studies of Historical Theology, the home of so many books I admire. I am grateful to Cynthia Read, Tom Perridge, Rada Radojicic, and all of the team at Oxford University Press for all their help and patience in producing this book. I am also profoundly grateful to the anonymous peer reviewers in both initial and final reviews for their invaluable advice and feedback, which I know has enriched this book. In particular, the advice to write an orienting Prologue to the work, to define the many—I hope not too many!—"-isms" which the reader will encounter in this work, and to engage further with Ramism's productive clash with a wider culture of erudition are insightful suggestions that I have truly benefited from. Discussion with Howard Hotson on Alsted and Bisterfeld has proved particularly enriching and helped to enhance the book.

I am grateful to Brill, Vandenhoeck & Ruprecht, Wydawnictwa Uniwersytetu Warszawskiego, and the Faculty of *"Artes Liberales"*, University of Warsaw for permissions to reproduce material from previous publications. I am also grateful to the Bibliothèque Nationale de France and the Syndics of Cambridge University Library for their permission to reproduce the images of Ramist and Lullist charts which illustrate the chapters. Specific acknowledgement for all these sources can be found in the text of the book. I am also grateful to all the libraries and archives I have used or consulted including the Bodleian Library, British Library, the National Library of Scotland, the Library of Trinity College Dublin, the Library of the University of Leiden, the Main Library and Special Collections of the University of Edinburgh, and above all to Christine Love-Rodgers and the staff of New College Library, where I currently have the honour of being Curator. I am also indebted to the project GA ČR 19-02938S, "Early Modern Encyclopaedism in the Centre and on the Peripheries: Lavinheta, Apáczai Csere,

Comenius, Leibniz" funded by the Czech Science Foundation and based at the Institute of Philosophy, Czech Academy of Sciences, for their valuable support. Finally, I must extend my special gratitude to the Royal Collections Trust for permission to reuse the wonderful image of Jan Brueghel the Elder's painting *Adam and Eve in the Garden of Eden*, which can be found hanging in the Cumberland Withdrawing Room of Hampton Court Palace.

In mapping out the many ramifications of Ramism, the works of Howard Hotson have proved a constant guide, and I am profoundly indebted to him and to Vladimír Urbánek, Piotr Wilczek, Michał Choptiany, Petr Pavlas, Zsombor Tóth, Dolf te Velde, and Matthew Payne for helping me engage with Ramism and the universal reformation in its multiple guises. My first introduction to Reformed scholasticism and Puritanism came from my doctoral supervisor Susan Hardman Moore, and I am deeply grateful to her for her ongoing support and encouragement. The late and much missed Willem van Asselt was my early mentor in Reformed scholastic studies and I will always remember his kindness, hospitability, and encouragement. It was through Willem, as well as Antonie Vos and Andreas Beck, that I was introduced to Reformed Scotism, and I remain greatly indebted to them, as well as to Philip Fisk, who generously shared some of his own current research. Some of my earliest and most memorable discussions on Scotism and Reformed scholasticism were with Andrew Leslie, and they continue to shape and inform my work. While there is little of Scotland in this current book apart from Scotus himself, the work of Alexander Broadie and Giovanni Gellera on Scottish Scotism has been deeply enriching to me and I am grateful to them for many hours spent discussing this over the years. More recent connections with Ueli Zahnd, Richard Cross, and Arthur Huiban through the project "A Disregarded Past—Medieval Scholasticism and Reformed Thought" hosted by the Institut d'histoire de la Réformation in Geneva have only enhanced that conversation further.

In terms of Christian Platonism I owe much to Torrance Kirby, James Bryson, Eric Parker, and Joshua Hollmann, all friends made at McGill. Ota Pavlíček long ago pointed me to the Scotist underpinnings of late medieval Realism, and his work on Wyclif and Hus has proved highly relevant to my own. Bill Hyland has also been an excellent companion in Cusanus studies, as have Il Kim and David Albertson—the latter of whose book on Cusa opened my eyes to an important mathematical and Neo-Pythagorean dimension within Ramism. In similar vein, the work of my friend and colleague Richard Oosterhoff on the Fabrists has been an inspiration to me. I also must extend my enormous gratitude to him for his reading and engaging with early drafts of this book, as well as his helping in the early shaping of this project.

While begun in Warsaw, much of the writing of this book took place at the School of Divinity in the University of Edinburgh, my own doctoral school, to which I was delighted to return in 2017. Here I must thank the Laing Foundation for their ongoing support of my current position, the John Laing Senior Lectureship in Reformation History. I am delighted to be supported by an organization which shares my own evangelical Christian values. I am also grateful to my colleagues there for their support and encouragement in writing this book, especially as this turned out to be a much longer process than envisaged. I have already expressed my thanks to Susan Hardman Moore and Richard Oosterhoff, but I also owe a deep debt to my other colleagues during this time, especially to Jay Brown, Sara Parvis, Paul Parvis, Kirsty Murray, Russell Newton, and Nathan Hood in the History of Christianity, to James Eglinton and David Fergusson in Divinity, to Thomas Ahnert in History, and most recently to my new colleagues Felicity Loughlin and Salam Rassi.

One of the great pleasures of being back at Edinburgh has been having my own PhD and postgraduate students, many of whom share my passion for late medieval and early modern theology. Wider discussions with Emma Mavin, Chuck Williams, Chun Tse, and Qiu Yuhau have proved highly stimulating. In some cases our work has more directly overlapped and I am grateful to Caleb Kobosh, Jaekook Lee, Sam Musgrave, Sean Duncan, Sergiej Slavinski, Bo van Broekhoven, Zachary Seals, and Takayuki Yagi for discussions on Ramism and Reformed scholasticism. Above all in this regard I must express my thanks to Matt Baines. During the final stages of writing this book we had the opportunity to co-edit a book, *Reformation and Education*, together, which proved valuable for placing Ramism in a broader pedagogical landscape. However, above all I owe him gratitude for his meticulous reading of this book and for many deeply stimulating conversations on Ramism and Reformed Scotism. I look forward with great anticipation to the fruition of his own exciting endeavours in this regard.

Finally, I owe the greatest thanks to my family and friends, without whose support the writing of this book simply would not have been possible. For Tom West, Matthew Firth, and Tim Cutts this is the book I have long been writing. I hope it does not prove too dry! For my cousin Robert Wainwright this is at least a foretaste of the book I promised to write. For my parents-in-law Alan and Sandra Oldfield I am hugely grateful for the ongoing love and generosity you have shown to me. For my brother and sister and their families, Matthew, Ali, Imogen, Esther, and Anna Burton and Emma, Hugh, Zach, Zeph, Caleb, and Nathaniel Wells, my deepest gratitude and affection. The keystone of the Franciscan vision of the world is the love of the Triune God and I owe some of my earliest and deepest intuitions of it to my parents, David and Hilary Burton. Their unfailing love and kindness have been a rock to me my whole life long. They shared the dedication of my previous book but I know will understand if I now extend the dedication of this book to my wonderful wife, Marilyn, and little son, Edward, with the deepest love and affection that words can express. Marilyn has spent countless hours discussing the contents of this book and agonizing over them with me, and her sacrificial love, encouragement, and extraordinary sense of fun have continually buoyed me up, especially in the times I thought I might never finish it. She has also helped enormously in the formatting and proofing of the book and preparation of the tables. It will be a long time before Edward can understand this book, but his presence in my life has left me continually surprised by joy, reminding me of the things that matter most.

Clermiston Mains, Edinburgh<br>May 2023

# Abbreviations

| | |
|---|---|
| *BOO* | Bonaventure of Bagnoregio. *Doctoris Seraphici S. Bonaventurae Opera Omnia*. 10 vols. Quaracchi, 1882. |
| *BR* | Bisterfeld, Johann Heinrich. *Bisterfeldius Redivivus seu Operum Joh. Henrici Bisterfeldi Magni Theologi ac Philosophi, Posthumorum*. Edited by Adriaan Heereboord. 2 vols. The Hague, 1661. |
| *DC* | Ramus, Petrus. *P. Rami Dialectica, Audomari Talaei Praelectionibus Illustrata*. Cologne, 1573. |
| *DI* | Bonner, Anthony, and Eve Bonner. *Doctor Illuminatus: A Ramon Llull Reader*. Princeton, NJ: Princeton University Press, 1993. |
| *DID* | Agricola, Rudolph. *De Inventione Dialectica*. Cologne, 1527. |
| *DJAK* | Comenius, Jan Amos. *Dílo Jana Amose Komenského*. Edited by Antonín Škarka. Prague: Academia, 1969–. |
| *DLD* 1566 | Ramus, Petrus. *P. Rami Dialecticae Libri Duo*. Cologne, 1566. |
| *DLD* 1572 | Ramus, Petrus. *Dialecticae Libri Duo*. Edited by Sebastian Lalla and Karlheinz Hülser. Paris, 1572; Stuttgart: Frommann-Holzboog, 2011. |
| *Exercitationes* | Scaliger, Julius Caesar. *Iulii Caesaris Scaligeri Exotericarum Exercitationum Liber Quintus Decimus, De Subtilitate ad Hieronymum Cardanum*. Paris, 1557. |
| *NCOO* | Cusa. Nicholas of. *Nicolai de Cusa Opera Omnia*. Edited by Raymond Klibansky et al. Hamburg: Felix Meiner, 1932–. |
| *ODNB* | Oxford Dictionary of National Biography. https://www.oxforddnb.com/. |
| *Ord.* | Scotus, John Duns. *Ordinatio*. In Vatican, I–XIV. |
| *PL* | Migne, Jacques-Paul, ed. *Patrologia Latina Cursus Completus*, 221 Vols. Paris, 1844–55. |
| *PP* | Keckermann, Bartholomäus. *Praecognitorum Philosophicorum Libri Duo*. Hanau, 1612. |
| *PRRD* | Muller, Richard A. *Post-Reformation Reformed Dogmatics: The Rise and Development of Reformed Orthodoxy, ca. 1520 to ca. 1725*. Grand Rapids, MI: Baker Academic, 2006. |
| *PTT* | Ames, William. *The Philosophical and Theological Treatises of William Ames*. Edited by Lee Gibbs. Lewiston, NY: Edwin Mellen Press, 2013. |
| *Rep. 1A* | Scotus, John Duns. *The Examined Report of the Paris Lecture: Reportatio 1A*. Edited by Allan B. Wolter, OFM and Oleg V. Bychkov. St Bonaventure, NY: Franciscan Institute, 2004. |
| *ROL* | Lull, Ramon. *Raimundi Lulli Opera Latina*. Edited by Friedrich Stegmüller et al. Turnhout: Brepols, 1975–. |

ST         Aquinas, Thomas. *Summa Theologiae. Blackfriars English Translation*. 60 vols. London/New York: McGraw-Hill, 1964–1976.
STC        Polanus von Polansdorf, Amandus. *Syntagma Theologiae Christianae*. 2 vols. Hanau, 1609.
Vatican    Scotus, John Duns. *Opera Omnia*. Edited by Charles Balić et al. Rome: Typis Polyglottis Vaticanis, 1950–.
WA         Luther, Martin. *D. Martin Luthers Werke: Abteilung 1 Schriften*. 72 vols. Weimar, 1883–2009.

# Introduction

## The Franciscan Reformation of Method

Ramism was the system of thought and logic pioneered in the sixteenth century by Peter Ramus, the brilliant and controversial Huguenot philosopher and reformer. Consecrated by his martyrdom in the St Bartholomew's Day massacre of 1572, Ramism spread rapidly through Protestant Europe, playing an essential role in the development and systematization of Reformed theology, the growth of early modern encyclopaedism, and the wider reform of Church and society.[1] While bitterly opposed by elitist humanist and scholastic philosophers, and even barred from many prestigious universities, Ramus' own logical, rhetorical, and other works still managed to go through hundreds of editions by the end of the seventeenth century—a testament to their lasting popularity and influence.[2] Within a generation what had begun as a protest movement and a radical alternative to Aristotelianism and scholasticism had become part of the mainstream of European intellectual and cultural life, and soon was to make its mark on the New World as well.[3] Ramus certainly had many devoted followers, but his influence was felt far beyond these circles. Figures as important and diverse as William Shakespeare, Philip Sidney, John Milton, Francis Bacon, René Descartes, Gottfried Wilhelm Leibniz, and Jonathan Edwards all felt the tug and attraction of Ramism—in some cases even despite themselves.[4]

---

[1] For detailed accounts of Ramism see Walter J. Ong, *Ramus, Method, and the Decay of Dialogue: From the Art of Discourse to the Art of Reason* (Chicago, IL: University of Chicago Press, 2004) and Howard Hotson, *Commonplace Learning: Ramism and its German Ramifications, 1543–1630* (Oxford: Oxford University Press, 2007).

[2] See Walter J. Ong, *Ramus and Talon Inventory: A Short-Title Inventory of the Published Works of Peter Ramus, (1515–1572) and of Omer Talon, (ca. 1510–1562)* (Cambridge, MA: Harvard University Press, 1958).

[3] Perry Miller, *The New England Mind: The Seventeenth Century* (Cambridge, MA: Harvard University Press, 1982), 64–238.

[4] For these influences see variously Paolo Rossi, *Logic and the Art of Memory: The Quest for a Universal Language*, trans. Stephan Clucas (London: Athlone Press, 2000); Michael Wainwright, *The Rational Shakespeare: Peter Ramus, Edward de Vere, and the Question of Authorship* (Cham: Springer International, 2018); Harris Francis Fletcher, *The Intellectual Development of John Milton: Volume II, The Cambridge University Period, 1625–32* (Urbana IL: University of Illinois Press, 1981); Leroy E. Loemker, "Leibniz and the Herborn Encyclopedists", *Journal of the History of Ideas* 22.3 (1961): 323–38; and David Hill Scott, "From Boston to the Baltic: New England, Encyclopedics, and the Hartlib Circle" (PhD Dissertation, University of Notre Dame, 2003).

## 2  RAMISM AND THE REFORMATION OF METHOD

To offer a comprehensive history of Ramism and its manifold influences is a task well beyond the scope of this book, and is, in any case, unnecessary given the outstanding work of Howard Hotson.[5] Instead, the focus of this work is at once much narrower and far broader: namely method, and especially the Reformation of method that Ramism set in train. For Ramism was at the epicentre of a methodological revolution which came to profoundly impact every sphere of early modern thought. Understood in terms of a logical and systematic ordering of thought, and ideas, and expressed graphically in the neat, branching dichotomous charts which became ubiquitous in early modernity, Ramist method was far more than a mere principle of organization. Rather, for its devotees it became the hallmark of all true philosophy and theology, the divine pattern of all of reality, and the heavenly blueprint of Church and society.[6] While earlier Reformers such as Luther and Calvin had sought a Reformation of Church and doctrine, those influenced by Ramism sought nothing less than a universal reform "of all people, in all things, and in all ways".[7] It was obvious to them that such a Reformation must proceed according to a divine model or "idea".[8] Indeed, as one seventeenth-century universal reformer neatly expressed this, God's method "promises the highest form of light in the end".[9]

Fundamental to Ramist method therefore, as well as the movement of universal reform which followed in its wake, was a dynamic convergence of ontology, epistemology, and theology. While influenced by a wide variety of intellectual and philosophical currents, Ramism was at its heart a Platonic method, grounded on the central insight that the temporal and changing must always be modelled on the eternal and unchanging.[10] In fact, central to Ramism was the notion of exemplarism—the understanding that all of reality mirrors and participates in the divine reality of God himself. Of almost equal importance to Ramism was the connected notion of Realism, the view, opposed to Nominalism,

---

[5] For the full narrative arc see Hotson, *Commonplace Learning* and Howard Hotson, *The Reformation of Common Learning: Post-Ramist Method and the Reception of the New Philosophy, 1618–c. 1670* (Oxford: Oxford University Press, 2020).

[6] For the connection of Ramism to the movement of universal reform see Howard Hotson, *Johann Heinrich Alsted, 1588–1638* (Oxford: Oxford University Press, 2000) and "The Instauration of the Image of God in Man: Humanist Anthropology, Encyclopaedic Pedagogy, Baconianism and Universal Reform", in *The Practice of Reform in Health, Medicine and Science, 1500–2000: Essays for Charles Webster*, ed. Margaret Pelling and Scott Mandelbrote (Aldershot: Ashgate, 2005), 1–21.

[7] Jan Amos Comenius, *Panorthosia*, 1.8 in *De Rerum Humanarum Emendatione Catholica Consultatio: Editio Princeps*, ed. Otokar Chlup et al., 2 vols. (Prague: Academia, 1966), II.212. References to the *Consultatio* are in page numbers rather than column numbers throughout. For a paraphrased and abbreviated translation of this work see *Panorthosia or Universal Reform*, trans. A. M. O. Dobbie, 2 vols. (Sheffield: Sheffield Academic Press, 1993–95). Volume I of Dobbie's translation covers chapters 19–26 and volume II covers chapters 1–18 and 27.

[8] Comenius, *Panorthosia*, 5.5, in *Consultatio*, II.242.

[9] Comenius, *Panorthosia*, 2.9, in *Consultatio*, II.217.

[10] For Ramism's connections to the Platonic tradition see Nelly Bruyère, *Méthode et dialectique dans l'oeuvre de la Ramée: Renaissance et Age Classique* (Paris: J. Vrin, 1984).

that our universal concepts such as whiteness and humanity have a real existence outside the human mind, even if inseparable from the individuals in which they exist and to which they give existence. For Ramists, as well as other Realists, it was important that such universal concepts should be taken to reflect and participate in God's own divine ideas. Indeed, following a long Platonic tradition, many Ramists held that such ideas illuminated the human mind, flooding it with light, and were thus essential for all true and certain knowledge.[11]

Within the Western tradition it was Augustine of Hippo who first gave expression to that nexus of Realism, exemplarism, and illumination that was later to prove so fundamental to Ramism. Yet it was his Franciscan disciples of the Middle Ages who took up and developed his scattered insights into a new Christian methodology and philosophy, against the forces of an encroaching Aristotelianism which they believed threatened the very foundations of Christendom.[12] In the Franciscan theologian Bonaventure and his later follower Ramon Lull, this new method was to flower into a far-reaching scriptural and Trinitarian encyclopaedism which sought to harmonize philosophy and theology, marking the antithesis of the radical Aristotelian attempt to separate them.[13] The victory of these Christian Augustinians in 1277 was to have a profound and lasting effect on the whole of medieval philosophy and theology, rippling through to the Reformation and beyond. While it had perhaps never truly abated, the conflict between Platonists and Aristotelians waged at the end of the thirteenth century was renewed with vigour in the Renaissance of the fifteenth century. At stake was nothing less than the true method of Christian philosophy.[14] If anything, such disputes were only further intensified by the raging contemporary battles between Realists and Nominalists in the medieval schools, and the emergence of humanism on the international stage as a rival to scholasticism.

In his own conflicts with Aristotelian scholasticism in the sixteenth century, Ramus proved an heir to all these movements, becoming one of the most important early modern champions of Christian philosophy. Indeed, it is the principal thesis of this book that Ramism represents a revival of the Christian Platonism of Augustine and his medieval and Renaissance followers, including supremely the Franciscans and Lullists who systematized his insights into a new and abiding Christian method. In its bare outlines, such a thesis is not entirely new, yet the extent to which Ramism itself represents a Franciscan Reformation of method

---

[11] For the disputes between Realists and Nominalists in the context of Platonism see Alain de Libera, *La querelle des universaux: De Platon à la fin du Moyen Age* (Paris: Points, 2014).

[12] For discussion of this see Etienne Gilson, *The Philosophy of St Bonaventure* (London: Sheed & Ward, 1938), 23–34.

[13] See Christopher M. Cullen, *Bonaventure* (New York: Oxford University Press, 2006) and Jocelyn N. Hillgarth, *Ramon Lull and Lullism in Fourteenth-Century France* (Oxford: Clarendon Press, 1971).

[14] See James Hankins, *Plato in the Italian Renaissance*, 2 vols. (Leiden: Brill, 1991).

has scarcely been realized.[15] Indeed, seen from the perspective of Ramism, the Reformation itself becomes simply an episode—albeit a highly important one—within a much broader and longer narrative of universal reform stretching back to at least the thirteenth century and forward into the eighteenth century and beyond. In fact, rooted in eternity and inspired by the Franciscan quest to recover an Edenic perfection, the twin movements of Ramism and universal reform increasingly came to see themselves as part of the apocalyptic climax of history itself.[16]

It will be clear to many that such an account contrasts sharply with prevailing narratives of modernity, which follow Max Weber in arguing that the Protestant Reformation ushered in a profound movement of "disenchantment", paving the way for modern, secularized society.[17] Thus major studies by Hans Blumenberg, John Milbank, Louis Dupré, Charles Taylor, Michael Allen Gillespie, Hans Boersma, and Brad Gregory have all argued forcefully that Franciscan thought, both Scotist and Nominalist, undermined the participationist metaphysics of the High Middle Ages, destabilizing the worldview on which medieval Christendom was founded and preparing the way for the Reformation's remaking of the world.[18] Indeed, it is no surprise that Milbank and his Radical Orthodoxy school have recently sought to co-opt Ramism into this wider narrative of disintegration, viewing it as the very nadir of the new Protestant "Nominalizing" approach to reality.[19]

By contrast, this book follows Richard Cross, Daniel Horan, Garrett Smith, and others in challenging such a narrative of decline.[20] Over a number of decades now,

---

[15] Kent Emery Jr., "Introduction", in *Renaissance Dialectic and Renaissance Piety: Benet of Canfield's Rule of Perfection* (Binghamton, NY: Medieval and Renaissance Texts and Studies, 1987), 39 notes the affinities of Ramus and Bonaventure. See also Frances Yates, *The Art of Memory* (London: Pimlico, 2008), 234–35; Rossi, *Logic and the Art of Memory*, 97–129; and Miller, *New England Mind*, 111–206.

[16] For aspects of this Edenic theme see Hotson, "Instauration", 1–21. For the important valence of Eden in late medieval and early modern culture, science, and theology see Alastair Minnis, *From Eden to Eternity: Creations of Paradise in the Later Middle Ages* (Philadelphia: University of Pennsylvania Press, 2016) and Peter Harrison, *The Fall of Man and the Foundations of Science* (Cambridge: Cambridge University Press, 2007).

[17] Max Weber, *The Protestant Ethic and the Spirit of Capitalism*, trans. Stephen Kalberg (Hoboken: Taylor and Francis, 2013), 60.

[18] See Hans Blumenberg, *The Legitimacy of the Modern Age*, trans. Robert M. Wallace (Cambridge, MA: MIT Press, 1983); John Milbank, *Theology and Social Theory: Beyond Secular Reason* (Oxford: Blackwell, 2006); Louis K. Dupré, *Religion and the Rise of Modern Culture* (Notre Dame, IN: University of Notre Dame Press, 2008); Charles Taylor, *A Secular Age* (Cambridge, MA: Harvard University Press, 2007), 90–99, 774; Michael Allen Gillespie, *The Theological Origins of Modernity* (Chicago, IL: University of Chicago Press, 2008), 19–43; Hans Boersma, *Heavenly Participation: The Weaving of a Sacramental Tapestry* (Grand Rapids, MI: Eerdmans, 2011), 68–89; and Brad S. Gregory, *The Unintended Reformation: How a Religious Revolution Secularized Society* (Cambridge, MA: Harvard University Press, 2012), 34–47.

[19] Catherine Pickstock, "Spacialisation: The Middle of Modernity", in *The Radical Orthodoxy Reader*, ed. John Milbank and Simon Oliver (Abingdon: Routledge, 2009), 158–59.

[20] See, for example, Richard Cross, "Where Angels Fear to Tread: Duns Scotus and Radical Orthodoxy", *Antonianum* 76 (2001): 7–41; Daniel P. Horan OFM, *Postmodernity and Univocity: A Critical Account of Radical Orthodoxy and John Duns Scotus* (Minneapolis, MN: Fortress Press, 2014);

the pioneering work of Richard Muller, Willem van Asselt, Carl Trueman, and other scholars has convincingly demonstrated a fundamental methodological—and to some degree metaphysical—continuity between medieval and Reformed theology, underlying more obvious doctrinal discontinuities.[21] This work offers an amplification and reconsideration of this continuity, highlighting the nature of method as a contested philosophical and theological battleground in early modernity.[22] In particular, it seeks to give much-needed attention to the methodological distinctives of Ramism in relation to the broader culture of Protestant scholasticism. In offering such a comprehensive integration of philosophy and theology, and in doing so along broadly Franciscan and Scotist lines, Ramism stood as an important bulwark against disenchantment. Indeed, Ramists offered their Reformed coreligionists potent weapons in their ongoing struggle against the rationalizing and secularizing forces of advancing modernity.[23] That such a Realist Renaissance could occur in the heartlands of Protestant Reform and Puritanism, among some of the stoutest defenders of radical Augustinianism and Calvinism, suggests the pressing need to readdress the metaphysical contours not only of Ramism but also of the Reformation itself.[24]

Of course, like all great intellectual and theological movements, Ramism must be seen in the context of its own time. Yet before doing so it is necessary to grasp more fully the "idea of reform"—to borrow Gerhart Ladner's compelling phrase—which Ramism inherited from the Renaissance and Middle Ages. For while ideas certainly change and develop over time, Ladner was right to recognize that there is yet something of the timeless about them, exercising a powerful

---

and Garrett R. Smith, "The Analogy of Being in the Scotist Tradition", *American Catholic Philosophical Quarterly* 93.4 (2019): 633–73.

[21] For the methodological continuity see Richard A. Muller, *Post-Reformation Reformed Dogmatics: The Rise and Development of Reformed Orthodoxy, ca. 1520 to ca. 1725*, 4 vols. (Grand Rapids, MI: Baker Academic, 2006) [hereafter PRRD], 1.1–84 and Carl R. Trueman, *The Claims of Truth: John Owen's Trinitarian Theology* (Carlisle: Paternoster, 1998). For contrasting accounts of the metaphysical continuity see Richard A. Muller, "Not Scotist: Understandings of Being, Univocity, and Analogy in Early-Modern Reformed Thought", *Reformation and Renaissance Review* 14.2 (2012): 127–50 and Willem J. van Asselt, J. Martin Bac, and Roelf T. te Velde (eds.), *Reformed Thought on Freedom: The Concept of Free Choice in Early Modern Reformed Theology* (Grand Rapids, MI: Baker Academic, 2010).

[22] For the Renaissance and early Reformation roots of this conflict over method see Erika Rummel, *The Confessionalization of Humanism in Reformation Germany* (Oxford: Oxford University Press, 2000).

[23] For the Reformed conflict with Cartesian and Socinian rationalism see Muller, PRRD, 1.140–46; Aza Goudriaan, *Reformed Orthodoxy and Philosophy, 1625–1750: Gisbertus Voetius, Petrus van Mastricht, and Anthonius Driessen* (Leiden: Brill, 2006); and Sergiej S. Slavinski, "Polemic and Piety in Francis Cheynell's *The Divine Trinunity* (1650)" (PhD Dissertation, University of Edinburgh, 2022).

[24] The need to re-interrogate the metaphysical roots of the Reformation has recently been eloquently put forward in Silvianne Aspray, *Metaphysics in the Reformation: The Case of Peter Martyr Vermigli* (Oxford: Oxford University Press, 2021). Aspray's argument for both analogical-participationist and univocal elements of Protestant metaphysics bears some parallels with this work.

and perennial sway over the march of the centuries.[25] Many influences went into shaping Ramist method, but for our purposes the most important of these were those highlighted above: Augustinian and Franciscan Platonism, Lullism, Christian humanism, and Reformed Scholasticism. Indeed, the wellsprings of Ramist method are to be found in the convergence and confluence of these four great intellectual streams.

## I.1. Augustinian and Franciscan Platonism

Augustine of Hippo's theology has well been described as "ancient thought baptised", but for us what is most important is his profound engagement with Platonism.[26] Believing that Plato had glimpsed the mysteries of the Trinity and Christ from afar, he sought to transfigure Platonism into a new Christian methodology.[27] Rejecting Plato's account of a separate, transcendent realm of eternal Forms, he reconceived these as ideas in the mind of God. For Augustine, these became the divine blueprint for all of creation.[28] Seeing Christ as the consummation of the divine ideas and the Holy Spirit as the one who impressed their patterns on creation, he also recognized a Trinitarian dynamic at the heart of creation.[29] Indeed, for Augustine all creatures could be seen as "footsteps of the

---

[25] Gerhart B. Ladner, *The Idea of Reform: Its Impact on Christian Thought and Action in the Age of the Fathers* (Cambridge, MA: Harvard University Press, 2014). Quentin Skinner, "Meaning and Understanding in the History of Ideas", *History and Theory* 8.1 (1969): 3–53 has been highly critical of this kind of approach to the history of ideas. However, while Skinner's emphasis on contextualization is well taken, Francis Oakley, *Omnipotence, Covenant and Order: An Excursion in the History of Ideas from Abelard to Leibniz* (Ithaca, NY: Cornell University Press, 1984) has offered a spirited defence of the continuity of ideas through intellectual history. In Gerald Christianson, Thomas M. Izbicki, and Christopher M. Bellitto (eds.), *The Church, The Councils and Reform: The Legacy of the Fifteenth Century* (Washington, DC: Catholic University of America Press, 2008) Ladner's methodology is successfully applied to late medieval reform. By viewing ideas in context this study seeks to extend this kind of methodology into the early modern period.

[26] John M. Rist, *Augustine: Ancient Thought Baptised* (Cambridge: Cambridge University Press, 1994). For discussion on Augustine's Platonism see Robert Crouse, "*Paucis Mutatis Verbis*: St Augustine's Platonism", in *Augustine and His Critics: Essays in Honour of Gerald Bonner*, ed. Robert Dorado and George Lawless (London: Taylor and Francis Library, 2005), 37–50 and Lewis Ayres, *Augustine and the Trinity* (Cambridge: Cambridge University Press, 2010), 13–20.

[27] Augustine of Hippo, *Confessions*, trans. R. S. Pine-Coffin (London: Penguin, 1961), 7.9–10, 20 (pp. 144–47, 154–55). For the early influence of Platonism on Augustine see Carol Harrison, *Rethinking Augustine's Early Theology: An Argument for Continuity* (Oxford: Oxford University Press, 2005).

[28] Augustine of Hippo, *Eighty-Three Different Questions*, trans. David L. Mosher (Washington, DC: Catholic University of America Press, 2002), q. 46 (pp. 79–81).

[29] Augustine of Hippo, *Unfinished Literal Commentary on Genesis*, 16.57–60, in *On Genesis*, trans. Edmund Hill OP (Hyde Park, NY: New City Press, 2006), 147–50; *The Literal Meaning of Genesis*, 1.6.12–8.14, 15.29, in *On Genesis*, 173–74, 181–82. See further Simo Knuuttila, "Time and Creation in Augustine", in *The Cambridge Companion to Augustine*, ed. David Vincent Meconi SJ and Eleonore Stump (Cambridge: Cambridge University Press, 2014), 81–97.

Trinity" (*vestigia Trinitatis*) leading to God, with the human soul imaging the Trinity directly in its faculties of memory, understanding and will.[30]

Drawing on the Christian and Platonic symbolism of light, Augustine held that the light of God is manifest in all creation and illuminates the human mind. It is in the light of the "immutable Truth which is above our minds" that we come to see the truth.[31] For Augustine, this light is that of the divine ideas themselves as they continually radiate into the human mind.[32] He was insistent that all human arts and sciences participate in this eternal light. It is through recognizing the divine order imprinted on all things that the soul fashions the various liberal arts as steps to ascend to God.[33] Within this ascent mathematics was of particular importance. Augustine loved to quote the Book of Wisdom which held that God has created all things according to "number, measure and weight".[34] Paralleling the divine ideas, he held that God's "divine numbers" were the exemplars of the created numbers which structured every level of reality.[35] Indeed, Augustine could even recognize here a clear parallel with the Trinity.[36]

Augustine's most programmatic statement of the relationship between Scripture and the disciplines was to be found in his *De Doctrina Christiana*, a work which exercised a profound influence on the whole of medieval thought.[37] Augustine's desire was to institute a "Christian philosophy", and elsewhere he famously spoke of this in terms of a "spoiling of the Egyptians"—taking the best insights of pagan philosophers and consecrating them for a Christian purpose.[38]

---

[30] Augustine of Hippo, *The Trinity: De Trinitate*, trans. Edmund Hill OP (Hyde Park, NY: New City Press, 1991), 9.1–3.17; 10.1.1–4.18; 15.1–50 (pp. 270–83, 286–99, 495–535) and *De Civitate Dei Contra Paganos Libri Viginti Duo*, 11.24–25, in Jacques-Paul Migne (ed.), *Patrologia Latina Cursus Completus*, 221 Vols. (Paris, 1844–55) [hereafter *PL*], 41 col. 337–39.

[31] Augustine, *Confessions*, 12.25 (pp. 301–3) and *The Trinity*, 15.50 (pp. 534–35). For Augustine's doctrine of illumination see Lydia Schumacher, *Divine Illumination: The History and Future of Augustine's Theory of Knowledge* (Chichester: Wiley-Blackwell, 2011), 25–65. My own reading would emphasize more the nature of illumination as a continual irradiation in line with the Franciscan school.

[32] Augustine, *Eighty-Three Different Questions*, q. 46 (p. 80).

[33] Augustine of Hippo, *On Order: St Augustine's Cassiciacum Dialogues*, trans. Michael P. Foley (New Haven, CT: Yale University Press, 2021), 2.14.39 (pp. 85–86). See further Harrison, *Rethinking Augustine's Early Theology*, 35–73.

[34] Augustine, *De Civitate Dei*, 11.30 (*PL*, 41. col. 343–44); *On Order*, 2.14.39–19.51 (pp. 85–97). For Augustine's citation see Book of Wisdom, 11:20.

[35] Augustine, *On Order*, 2.14.39–16.44 (pp. 85–89); *Augustinus: De Musica*, ed. Martin Jacobson (Berlin: De Gruyter, 2017), 6.9.19–17.57 (pp. 207–32).

[36] Augustine of Hippo, *On Christian Teaching*, trans. R. P. H. Green (Oxford: Oxford University Press, 2008), 1.5.5 (p. 10). See David Albertson, *Mathematical Theologies: Nicholas of Cusa and the Legacy of Thierry of Chartres* (New York: Oxford University Press, 2014), 68–80 for discussion of Augustine's mathematical Trinitarianism.

[37] Augustine, *On Christian Teaching*, 2.39.58 (p. 63) warns Christian students "do not venture without due care into any branches of learning which are pursued outside the church of Christ". For Augustine's medieval influence see Edward D. English (ed.), *Reading and Wisdom: The "De Doctrina Christiana" of Augustine in the Middle Ages* (Notre Dame, IN: University of Notre Dame Press, 1995).

[38] For Augustine's "Christian philosophy" see Ann Blair, "Mosaic Physics and the Search for a Pious Natural Philosophy in the Late Renaissance", *Isis* 91.1 (2000): 34. For his account of spoiling the Egyptians see *On Christian Teaching*, 2.42.63 (p. 67).

Here he went even further showing how Scripture both contains the disciplines and is unfolded through them. For Augustine, there is an intimate reciprocity between the Bible and the arts and sciences, grounded exemplaristically in their relation to eternal truth and the divine ideas—a notion he often expressed in terms of the harmony of the Two Books of God's Word and his works.[39] Thus logic, which is of "paramount importance" for understanding Scripture, can be seen as both "built into the permanent and divinely instituted system of things" and embodied in Scripture itself.[40] The same is true for all the other disciplines, and Augustine could even hint at a Trinitarian structure to this nascent scriptural encyclopaedia, holding that physics, ethics, and dialectic mirrored the relation of Father, Son, and Holy Spirit.[41]

Up until the end of the twelfth century this Augustinian Platonism remained dominant in the West. Yet by the thirteenth century it was increasingly under threat from the rise of Aristotelianism.[42] For a massive translation movement had made the logic and metaphysics of Aristotle accessible to the Latin West, stimulating the growth of scholasticism in newly founded universities in Bologna, Paris, Oxford, and elsewhere.[43] Theologians now rushed to reconstitute their discipline as an Aristotelian science grounded on first principles and expressed logically in syllogistic form as a chain of deductions. Aristotelian logic, metaphysics, and psychology became the stock-in-trade of scholastic theologians, contributing to a new level of sophistication and systematization in theology as a discipline.[44]

Right at the vanguard of this new movement of Christian Aristotelianism was the Dominican theologian Thomas Aquinas. Of course, Aquinas' theology was not straightforwardly Aristotelian. Indeed, following Augustine and Plato, he still retained an important place for exemplarism.[45] Thus in his 1259 *De Veritate*

---

[39] Augustine, *On Order*, 2.14.39–19.51 (pp. 85–97); *Confessions*, 10.9–17 (pp. 216–24); and *On Christian Teaching*, 2.1.1–42.63 (pp. 30–67). For Augustine and the Two Books see Augustine of Hippo, *Enarrationes in Psalmos*, 45 (*PL*, 36 col. 518).
[40] Augustine, *On Christian Teaching*, 2.31.49–32.50 (pp. 58–59).
[41] Augustine, *De Civitate Dei*, 11.25 (*PL*, 41 col. 338–39).
[42] For the Platonic character of the twelfth-century Renaissance and the influence of Augustine see Marie-Dominique Chenu, *Nature, Man and Society in the Twelfth Century: Essays on New Theological Perspectives in the Latin West* (Toronto: University of Toronto Press, 1997), 1–98. Chenu makes clear that this Augustinian Platonism was refined by encounter with Boethius, Dionysian Platonism, Plato's *Timaeus*, and Jewish and Islamic Neo-Platonism.
[43] See Bernard G. Dod, "*Aristoteles Latinus*", in *The Cambridge History of Later Medieval Philosophy*, ed. Norman Kretzmann, Anthony Kenny, Jan Pinborg, and Eleonore Stump (Cambridge: Cambridge University Press, 2008), 43–79.
[44] For an excellent account of the rise of scholastic theology see Ulrich G. Leinsle, *Introduction to Scholastic Theology*, trans. Michael G. Miller (Washington, DC: Catholic University of America Press, 2010).
[45] See, for example, Thomas Aquinas, *Summa Theologiae*, 1a q. 15–16, 84 art. 5 [hereafter *ST*] and *De Veritate*, q. 1, 3. For Aquinas' exemplarism see Gregory T. Doolan, *Aquinas on the Divine Ideas as Exemplar Causes* (Washington, DC: Catholic University of America Press, 2008). For his important debt to Christian Platonism and to Augustine see Fran O'Rourke, *Pseudo-Dionysius and the Metaphysics of Aquinas* (Leiden: Brill, 1992) and Michael Dauphinais, Barry David, and

he maintained that God was the efficient, exemplar, and final cause of all things, holding that all things exist through participation in the divine ideas.[46] Likewise, in his early *Sentences* commentary, and perhaps even his later *Summa Theologiae*, he constituted his theology according to a Neo-Platonic and Dionysian pattern of emanation, manation, and remanation.[47] Aquinas' celebrated metaphysics of participation also drew deeply on Platonic models, while reconfiguring them in light of an overarching Aristotelian metaphysics of act and potency.[48]

Nevertheless, although deeply influenced by Augustine, Aquinas departed markedly from his attempt to institute a Christian philosophy on a Platonic foundation.[49] For Aquinas, following Aristotle, illumination became simply a natural and intrinsic dimension of human reason.[50] Similarly, while he could speak eloquently of converting the water of philosophical reasoning into the wine of Christian truth, in practice he sharply demarcated philosophy from theology.[51] Finally, despite holding to the *vestigia Trinitatis* he tended to eschew any attempt to develop a Trinitarian method or metaphysics, and, following what is often taken to be a broader Dominican trend, showed little appetite for a scriptural encyclopaedism or logic.[52]

---

Matthew Levering (eds.), *Aquinas the Augustinian* (Washington, DC: Catholic University of America Press, 2007).

[46] Aquinas, *De Veritate*, q. 1 art. 4.
[47] See Marie-Dominique Chenu, *Aquinas and His Role in Theology* (Collegeville, MN: Liturgical Press, 2002), 98, 137–38.
[48] See, for example, John F. Wippel, *Metaphysical Themes in Thomas Aquinas II* (Washington, DC: Catholic University of America Press, 2011), 272–90.
[49] For Aquinas' Christian Aristotelianism and his eschewal of the Christian Platonic project see Denys Turner, *Thomas Aquinas: A Portrait* (New Haven, CT: Yale University Press, 2014).
[50] Aquinas, *ST*, 1a q. 86 art. 5 states that "the intellectual light which is in us, is nothing else than a participated likeness of the uncreated light, in which are contained the eternal types". In 1a q. 86 art. 6 Aquinas also assimilates Augustinian illumination to Aristotle's active intellect. Robert Pasnau, "Divine Illumination", *Stanford Encyclopedia of Philosophy* (https://plato.stanford.edu/entries/illumination/; accessed 27/11/2021) rightly contrasts this with Augustine and the Franciscans.
[51] Frederick Christian Bauerschmidt, *Thomas Aquinas: Faith, Reason and Following Christ* (Oxford: Oxford University Press, 2013), 61. For Aquinas' sharp demarcation of the two disciplines see Gilson, *Philosophy*, 27–31. As Gilson summarizes, for Bonaventure "the philosophy of St. Albert and St. Thomas was of necessity in error because, while it situated Christ in the centre of theology, it did not situate him in the centre of philosophy" (p. 31). In similar vein, Lydia Schumacher, *Early Franciscan Theology: Between Authority and Innovation* (Cambridge: Cambridge University Press, 2019), 27 insightfully contrasts the Franciscan top-down approach to reality from Aquinas' bottom-up approach.
[52] Aquinas, *ST*, 1a q. 32 art. 1 sharply differentiates the Trinity from the sphere of natural reason and philosophy. Roger French and Andrew Cunningham, *Before Science: The Invention of the Friars' Natural Philosophy* (Abingdon: Routledge, 2016), 212–18 notes the marked difference between Dominican and Franciscan encyclopaedism, with the latter far more oriented towards Scripture and contemplation. Mary Franklin-Brown, *Reading the World: Encyclopedic Writing in Scholasticism* (Chicago, IL: University of Chicago Press, 2012), 35–92 does draw attention to an implicit scriptural impulse evident in the Dominican encyclopaedist Vincent of Beauvais, but this is still less pronounced than in the Franciscan tradition. Likewise, Andrew Davison, *Participation in God: A Study in Christian Doctrine and Metaphysics* (Cambridge: Cambridge University Press, 2019), 47–50

While Aristotle quickly came to dominate the thirteenth-century schools, many pious Christians were deeply alarmed by the influx of his thought and profoundly sceptical of the possibilities of attaining a Christian Aristotelianism. The situation was only exacerbated by the existence of radical Aristotelians, called Averroists, who were accused of teaching a doctrine of double truth—the understanding that something can be true in philosophy but false in theology. Spearheading the campaign against resurgent Aristotelianism was Bonaventure of Bagnoregio, the celebrated Franciscan theologian and Minister General. Indeed, it was his own followers who first attacked the Dominican publicly and who masterminded the subsequent 1277 condemnations of Aristotelianism in both Paris and Oxford—a concerted attack which came within a whisker of earning Aquinas a papal condemnation and stoked tensions between the Dominicans and Franciscans for centuries afterwards.[53]

Despite his own appreciation for Aristotelian philosophy, Bonaventure believed that a Christian Aristotelianism was effectively a contradiction in terms. In his 1273 *Collationes in Hexaemeron*, his own mature programme for a Christian philosophy, he attacked Aristotle mercilessly for his neglect of exemplarism.[54] In Neo-Platonic fashion, he held instead that all of metaphysics was summed up in emanation, exemplarism, and consummation.[55] Of course, such an intuition was scarcely foreign to Aquinas and other medieval theologians, and Fernand van Steenberghen is right to claim exemplarism as near universal in the thirteenth century.[56] Yet nonetheless it is important to make a clear distinction between the *doctrine* of exemplarism shared by all, and the *method* of exemplarism pioneered especially by the Franciscans.[57]

---

insightfully identifies an implicit Trinitarian metaphysic in Aquinas, but still concedes that this is more muted than in Bonaventure and the Franciscans.

[53] Gilson, *Philosophy*, 23–34. Joseph Ratzinger, *The Theology of History in St Bonaventure*, trans. Zachary Hayes OFM (Chicago, IL: Franciscan Herald Press, 1971), 137–38 argues that Bonaventure was opposed to Aquinas' Aristotelian view of the soul without wishing to attack Aquinas personally. For the implicit inclusion of Aquinas in the papal condemnations see John F. Wippel, "Thomas Aquinas and the Condemnation of 1277", *Modern Schoolman* 72.2–3 (1995): 233–72.

[54] Bonaventure of Bagnoregio, *Collationes in Hexaemeron*, 6.2–4, in Bonaventure of Bagnoregio, *Doctoris Seraphici S. Bonaventurae Opera Omnia*, 10 vols. (Quaracchi, 1882) [hereafter *BOO*], V.360–61; cf. Cullen, *Bonaventure*, 71–77. The notion of Bonaventure's "Christian philosophy" derives from Gilson, *Philosophy*, 30–31, 139–41.

[55] Bonaventure, *Collationes*, 1.17 (*BOO*, V.332); cf. Cullen, *Bonaventure*, 60 and Gilson, *Philosophy*, 139–41.

[56] Fernand van Steenberghen, *The Philosophical Movement in the Thirteenth Century* (Edinburgh: Nelson, 1955), 68–73. Ratzinger, *Theology of History*, 124–34 points to an important distinction between the wider exemplaristic culture and the specific Franciscan approach to Christian philosophy.

[57] This method is well summed up in Bonaventure of Bagnoregio, *Legenda Sancti Francisci*, 9.1 (*BOO*, VIII.530).

Following the lead of earlier Christian Augustinians, such as Hugh of St Victor and Robert Grosseteste, Bonaventure's own philosophy represents a powerful systematization of Augustine's doctrines of exemplarism and illumination.[58] Indeed, Bonaventure was insistent that Augustine provided the perfect paradigm for a Christian approach to philosophy, coupling Aristotle's emphasis on sensible cognition with Plato's insistence on eternal, intelligible light, and thus correcting the deficiencies in both.[59] Contrary to Aquinas he held that the continual irradiation of light from the divine ideas was necessary for all knowledge of truth, and expressed this in terms of a shared concurrence of divine and human causality.[60]

Like Grosseteste, Bonaventure also combined this Augustinian approach with a profound attention to the Neo-Platonic metaphysics of light, which was so popular among Franciscans of his age.[61] While adhering strongly to a doctrine of creation out of nothing, this traced the emanation of all things from the divine wellspring of light within the Trinity, offering a comprehensive explanation of all things according to a gradation of spiritual, intelligible, and material light.[62] Following Augustine's own precedent this was frequently elaborated, as in Grosseteste and Bonaventure, according to a hexameral treatment of the six days of creation in the Genesis narrative, sparking an important and enduring "Mosaic physics" and scriptural philosophy.[63] Through the influence of Pseudo-Dionysius—a sixth-century Syrian Platonist universally believed at this time to be the disciple of the Apostle Paul—it increasingly took on a triadic and Trinitarian structure.[64]

---

[58] For Bonaventure's Augustinian philosophy and his debt to Hugh of St Victor and Robert Grosseteste see Bonaventure of Bagnoregio, *St Bonaventure's On the Reduction of Arts to Theology* (St Bonaventure, NY: Franciscan Institute, 1996), n. 5 (pp. 43-45; BOO, V.321) and Cullen, *Bonaventure*, 4, 8, 20, 30, 48, 77, 127, 165.

[59] Bonaventure of Bagnoregio, *"Christus Unus Omnium Magister"*, n. 8-10, 18-19 (BOO, V.569-70, 572).

[60] Bonaventure of Bagnoregio, *Quaestiones Disputatae de Scientia Christi*, q. 4 *"Conclusio"* (BOO, V.22-23). See Suzanne Metselaar, "Are the Divine Ideas Involved in Making the Sensible Intelligible? The Role of Knowledge of the Divine in Bonaventure's Theory of Cognition", *Recherches de théologie et philosophie médiévales* 79.2 (2012): 339-72. For Bonaventure's doctrine of illumination and concurrence see Cullen, *Bonaventure*, 70-71, 77-87 and Gilson, *Philosophy*, 341-403.

[61] French and Cunningham, *Before Science*, 202-68. Lucia Miccoli, "Two Thirteenth-Century Theories of Light: Robert Grosseteste and St. Bonaventure", *Semiotica* 136.1 (2001): 69-84 traces the thought of both back to a Neo-Platonic metaphysics of light.

[62] Robert Grosseteste, "Robert Grosseteste's *On Light*: An English Translation", trans. Neil Lewis, in *Robert Grosseteste and His Intellectual Milieu: New Editions and Studies*, ed. John Flood, James R. Ginther and Joseph W. Goering (Toronto: Pontifical Institute of Medieval Studies, 2013), 239-47; cf. James McEvoy, *The Philosophy of Robert Grosseteste* (Oxford: Clarendon Press, 1986), 149-62 and French and Cunningham, *Before Science*, 230-55.

[63] See Augustine, *The Literal Meaning of Genesis*, 1.3.7-17.35 (pp. 170-85); Robert Grosseteste, *On the Six Days of Creation*, trans. C. F. J. Martin (Oxford: Oxford University Press, 1999); and Bonaventure, *Collationes* (BOO, V.327ff.). French and Cunningham, *Before Science*, 230-31 emphasizes the hexameral foundation of this Franciscan metaphysics of light.

[64] French and Cunningham, *Before Science*, 218-24 emphasizes the central influence of Pseudo-Dionysius on the Franciscan tradition. For Pseudo-Dionysius' triadism see Paul

In his *De Reductione Artium ad Theologiam* Bonaventure followed Augustine and Hugh of St Victor in offering a programmatic outline of a scriptural encyclopaedia.[65] Regarding Scripture as taking its origin from an "inflowing of the most Blessed Trinity" he explained how this and all the other disciplines descend from God the "Father of Lights" in a chain of divine illuminations.[66] Going well beyond Aquinas' "handmaid" model, he sought to show how all the arts and sciences could be "reduced" to Scripture.[67] Dividing all of philosophy into its natural, rational, and moral branches, and elaborating these according to a series of triads, he sought to show their relation to both Christ and the Trinity.[68] For Bonaventure, all of knowledge is a circle centred on and returning to God: the pattern of emanation, exemplarism, and consummation so dear to his heart.[69]

In his *Itinerarium Mentis in Deum* Bonaventure took up and systematized this Trinitarian exemplarism into a ladder of mystical ascent patterned on Francis of Assisi's celebrated vision on Mount Alverna of a six-winged Crucified Seraph.[70] In this the soul ascends first through the created *vestigia Trinitatis*, marked out especially by the dynamic imprint of God's Power, Wisdom, and Love.[71] Following Augustine, the soul then turns within to contemplate itself as the image of God, both in its natural powers of memory, understanding, and will and in their gracious restoration through faith, hope, and charity.[72] Finally, the soul comes to contemplate God in his Unity and Trinity, as well as Christ as the Centre and Circumference of all reality, ascending by the ladder of the Cross to union with God. In this the mind comes to realize how God transcends all reason and intellect in the paradoxical "touching" of unity and multiplicity within his being.[73]

Indeed, elsewhere Bonaventure can claim that Scripture has its own logic which transcends the syllogistic logic of the Aristotelians.[74] This Franciscan critique of Aristotelian logic launched an important tradition of the "logic of faith"

---

Rorem, *Pseudo-Dionysius: A Commentary on the Texts and an Introduction to Their Influence* (New York: Oxford University Press, 1993), 52–84.

[65] Bonaventure, *Reduction*, n. 1–8 (pp. 37–47; *BOO*, V.319–21). See Hugh of St Victor, *The Didascalion of Hugh of St Victor: A Medieval Guide to the Arts*, trans. Jerome Taylor (New York: Columbia University Press, 1961), "Preface", 2.1–3, 17–18 (pp. 43–45, 60–63, 71–73).
[66] Bonaventure of Bagnoregio, *Breviloquium*, trans. Dominic V. Monti (Saint Bonaventure, NY: Franciscan Institute Press, 2005), "Prologue" 1–2 (pp. 1–2; *BOO*, V.201–2); *Reduction*, n. 1–4 (*BOO*, V.319–20).
[67] Bonaventure, *Reduction*, n. 8, 26 (pp. 47–61; *BOO*, V.321, 325).
[68] Bonaventure, *Reduction*, n. 8–26 (pp. 47–61; *BOO*, V.321–25); Bonaventure of Bagnoregio, *Itinerarium*, 3.6 (*BOO*, V.305).
[69] Bonaventure, *Reduction*, n. 6–8 (pp. 45–47; *BOO*, V.321–22).
[70] Bonaventure, *Itinerarium*, "Prologue" 1–3; 1.1–6; 2.1 (*BOO*, V.295–97, 299–300).
[71] Bonaventure, *Itinerarium*, 1.10 (*BOO*, V.298).
[72] Bonaventure, *Itinerarium*, 3.1, 4.1–8 (*BOO*, V.303, 306–8); cf. Augustine, *Confessions*, 10.6–8 (pp. 211–16).
[73] Bonaventure, *Itinerarium*, 5.1–8, 6.3–7, 7.1–6 (*BOO*, V.308–13).
[74] Bonaventure, *Breviloquium*, "Prologue" 3 (pp. 3–4; *BOO*, V.201–2).

in the Late Middle Ages and fed into the scriptural logic of the Wyclifites and Hussites.[75] Expressed as a "coincidence of opposites" it also influenced Nicholas of Cusa's remarkable claim that God transcends not only Aristotelian logic but also the principle of non-contradiction itself—the cornerstone of all scholastic method.[76] The thirst to develop other methods beyond that of syllogistic logic also led to a mathematical Renaissance among the Franciscans of the thirteenth century.[77] Thus Bonaventure himself was clear that numbers were the "highest exemplars" of all reality and Roger Bacon, his fellow Franciscan, saw mathematics as a new key to universal knowledge.[78]

For both Bonaventure and Bacon this biblical and mathematical encyclopaedism was linked to an "Edenic paradigm" of knowledge and an attempt to recover the pristine, unfallen knowledge of Adam and Eve.[79] While Richard Southern rightly claims this as a common inheritance of scholasticism, it was especially pronounced among the Franciscans.[80] Indeed, under the influence of the prophetic eschatology of Joachim of Fiore, many Franciscans, including to a degree Bonaventure, became convinced that their Order would inaugurate the final age of the world and the Millennial Kingdom of Christ and his Saints, in which philosophy and theology would unite and a "perfect system of knowledge" would be attained, realized according to its heavenly pattern.[81] Such an idealistic and eschatological paradigm of reform marched through the Wyclifites and Hussites of the Later Middle Ages and came to exercise a profound influence on the universal reformers of the seventeenth century.[82]

---

[75] For this broad trajectory see Giuseppe Mazzotta, "Dante's Franciscanism", in *Dante and the Franciscans*, ed. Santa Casciani (Leiden: Brill, 2006), 192–98; Hester Goodenough Gelber, "Logic and the Trinity: A Clash of Values in Scholastic Thought, 1300–1335" (PhD Dissertation, University of Wisconsin, 1974); Michael H. Shank, *"Unless You Believe, You Shall Not Understand": Logic, University, and Society in Late Medieval Vienna* (Princeton, NJ: Princeton University Press, 1988), 57–138; and Ian Christopher Levy, *John Wyclif: Scriptural Logic, Real Presence, and the Parameters of Orthodoxy* (Milwaukee, WI: Marquette University Press, 2003).

[76] Nicholas of Cusa, *De Docta Ignorantia*, 1.4.11–12, in Nicholas of Cusa, *Nicolai de Cusa Opera Omnia*, ed. Raymond Klibansky et al. (Hamburg: Felix Meiner, 1932–) [hereafter *NCOO*], I.10–11. For the Franciscan dimensions of this see Ewert H. Cousins, "The Coincidence of Opposites in the Christology of Saint Bonaventure", *Franciscan Studies* 28 (1968): 27–45.

[77] French and Cunningham, *Before Science*, 230–50.

[78] Bonaventure, *Itinerarium*, 2.10 (*BOO*, V.303); Roger Bacon, *The Opus Maius of Roger Bacon*, ed. John Henry Bridges, 2 vols. (Oxford: Clarendon Press, 1897), 4 d. 1 c. 1 (I.97–98). For Bacon's project see also French and Cunningham, *Before Science*, 237–43 and Amanda Power, *Roger Bacon and the Defence of Christendom* (Cambridge: Cambridge University Press, 2013).

[79] Bonaventure, *Itinerarium*, 4.2; 7.2 (*BOO*, V.306, 312); Bacon, *Opus Maius*, 2 c. 1, 8–9; 4 d. 1 c. 1 (I.33–34, 44–45, 97–98).

[80] Richard W. Southern, *Scholastic Humanism and the Unification of Europe, Volume 1: Foundations* (Oxford: Blackwell, 1995), 4–5 cited from Jens Zimmermann, "The Cultural Context for Re-Envisioning Christian Humanism", in *Re-Envisioning Christian Humanism: Education and the Restoration of Humanity*, ed. Jens Zimmermann (Oxford: Oxford University Press, 2017), 149.

[81] For Bonaventure's apocalyptic perspective see Ratzinger, *Theology of History*, 9–19.

[82] See, for example, Levy, *John Wyclif* and Vilém Herold, "Platonic Ideas and 'Hussite Philosophy'", *Bohemian Reformation and Religious Practice* 1 (1994): 13–17.

Following the 1277 condemnations we find John Duns Scotus taking up and refining the Christian Augustinianism of the Franciscan School. At first sight, such a claim might seem strange, for Scotus has often been roundly blamed for the collapse of Augustinian illuminationism and the radical decline of a metaphysics of participation.[83] Yet while there can be no doubt that Scotus played a major role in instigating a new covenantal and contingent understanding of reality—in which creation becomes bound together as much by the divine will as by the divine ideas—this should not be seen as antithetical to an emphasis on participation and illumination.[84] Indeed, we will see later in this book a growing and important convergence of the two "Franciscan methods" of participation and covenant.

Taking up the mantle of Grosseteste and Bonaventure, Scotus thus reconfigured the Franciscan metaphysics of light into a new and pioneering "mathematized" ontology.[85] According to this, the light emanating from the Trinity into all creation is manifest supremely in being and its transcendental affections of unity, truth, and goodness. Like Bonaventure, and unlike Aquinas, he linked these directly to the Trinity and saw them as the supreme example of the *vestigia Trinitatis*.[86] Going beyond Bonaventure, he sought to develop a universal transcendental framework of philosophy and theology—his own version of Christian philosophy—in which God and creatures could be encompassed under a common, univocal concept of being (i.e. one that signifies according to an identical meaning and not only a related, analogical, meaning as in Aquinas and others).[87] Comparing degrees of being to mathematical degrees of intensity

---

[83] For this prominent critique of Scotus see Catherine Pickstock, "Duns Scotus: His Historical and Contemporary Significance", *Modern Theology* 21 (2005): 543–74 and Milbank, *Theology and Social Theory*.

[84] For Scotus' initiation of a covenantal and contingency revolution see Simo Knuuttila, "Time and Modality in Scholasticism", in *Reforging the Great Chain of Being: Studies of the History of Modal Theories*, ed. Simo Knuuttila (Dordrecht: Reidel, 1981), 163–257; Antonie Vos, *The Philosophy of John Duns Scotus* (Edinburgh: Edinburgh University Press, 2006); Michael Sylwanowicz, *Contingent Causality and the Foundations of Duns Scotus' Metaphysics* (Leiden: Brill, 1996); and Steven E. Ozment, *The Age of Reform (1250–1550): An Intellectual and Religious History of Late Medieval and Reformation Europe* (New Haven, CT: Yale University Press, 1980), 33–36.

[85] John Duns Scotus, *Ordinatio* [hereafter *Ord.*], 1 d. 3 p. 1 q. 1–2 n. 58, 62; 1 d. 8 p. 1 q. 3 n. 84; this can be found in John Duns Scotus, *Opera Omnia*, ed. Charles Balić et al. (Rome: Typis Polyglottis Vaticanis, 1950–) [hereafter Vatican], III.40; IV.192; cf. Peter King, "Scotus on Metaphysics", in *The Cambridge Companion to Duns Scotus*, ed. Thomas Williams (Cambridge: Cambridge University Press, 2003), 27–33. Grosseteste, "On Light", 240, 246–47 derives all the mathematical proportions governing the universe from the infinite expansion of light.

[86] Scotus, *Ord.*, 1 d. 3 p. 2 q. un (Vatican, III.173–200). Jan A. Aertsen, *Medieval Philosophy as Transcendental Thought: From Philip the Chancellor (ca. 1225) to Francisco Suárez* (Leiden: Brill, 2012), 452–53 notes that the intimate bond between the Trinity and transcendentals is a Franciscan distinctive. Trent Pomplun, "Notes on Scotist Aesthetics in Light of Gilbert Narcisse's 'Les Raisons de Dieu'", *Franciscan Studies* 66.1 (2008): 254–56 places the transcendentals in the context of Scotus' broader Trinitarian exemplarism. For the link between the Trinity, metaphysics of light and inner emanation see Sylwanowicz, *Contingent Causality*, 130.

[87] John Duns Scotus, *Philosophical Writings: A Selection*, trans. Allan Wolter OFM (Indianapolis, IN: Hackett Publishing Company, 1987), 19–30; cf. Aertsen, *Medieval Philosophy*, 371–432. The

of light, Scotus yet insisted that the infinite being of God was radically distinct from the finite being of his creatures.[88] For Scotus, the fact that all being was radiant and lit from within by the light of the Trinity meant that he no longer saw any need for an extrinsic divine illumination.[89] Yet his departure from Augustine should not be construed—as it too often has been—as a rejection of an exemplaristic account of all human truth as participating in the higher light of divine truth.[90]

The fourteenth century saw a new emphasis on the individual in what Heiko Oberman has memorably called a "hunger for reality".[91] Scotus played a major role in this emphasizing both the ontological priority of the individual and the direct, intuitive contact of the mind with reality—emphases soon to be taken up and radicalized by his fellow Franciscan William of Ockham.[92] Unlike Ockham, however, Scotus was not a Nominalist and was insistent on the real existence of universal concepts outside the mind, and the key metaphysical role of universals in constituting individual reality.[93] He thus preserved exemplarism in the face of a rising Nominalist tide.[94] In fact, as Maarten Hoenen suggests, the Scotists came to be seen as the most Platonic of the medieval schools of thought.[95]

---

reading of Scotus in terms of Christian philosophy is my own, although influenced by Oleg Bychkov, "What Does Beauty Have to Do with the Trinity? From Augustine to Duns Scotus", *Franciscan Studies* 66.1 (2008): 197–212 and Pomplun, "Scotist Aesthetics", 247–68. For Aquinas' view on analogy see *ST*, 1a q. 13. Significantly, John Duns Scotus, *The Examined Report of the Paris Lecture: Reportatio 1A*, ed. Allan B. Wolter OFM and Oleg V. Bychkov (St Bonaventure, NY: Franciscan Institute, 2004) [hereafter *Rep. 1A*], d. 3, q. 1 n. 41–46 (I.196–97).does not see his doctrine of univocity as contradicting either an analogy of being or a metaphysics of participation.

[88] Scotus, *Ord*. 1 d. 3 p. 1 q. 1–2 n. 58, 62 (Vatican, III.40).

[89] Scotus, *Philosophical Writings*, 96–132 offers a detailed critique of the Augustinian theory of extrinsic illumination as found in Henry of Ghent.

[90] Scotus, *Philosophical Writings*, 103–6, 113, 123–30 places his own epistemology squarely in an Augustinian, exemplaristic context. Andrew Leslie, *The Light of Grace: John Owen on the Authority of Scripture and Christian Faith* (Göttingen: Vandenhoeck & Ruprecht, 2015), 71–77 highlights the "structural parallel" in Scotus between God and the mind. Pace Schumacher, *Divine Illumination*, 181–216 who traces a simple decline in Augustinian illumination after Duns Scotus. I am grateful to Andrew Leslie and Matthew Baines for discussion of this point.

[91] Heiko A. Oberman, "The Shape of Late Medieval Thought: The Birthpangs of the Modern Era", in *The Pursuit of Holiness in Late Medieval and Renaissance Religion: Papers from the University of Michigan Conference*, ed. Charles Trinkaus and Heiko A. Oberman (Leiden: Brill, 1972), 13.

[92] Scotus, *Ord*. 2 d. 3 p. 2 q. 2 n. 319–21 (Vatican, VII.552–53). For Scotus' revolutionary account of intuitive cognition see Katherine H. Tachau, *Vision and Certitude in the Age of Ockham: Optics, Epistemology and the Foundations of Semantics, 1250–1345* (Leiden: Brill, 1987), 68–85.

[93] Universal concepts are those such as humanity and whiteness which all humans and all white objects are understood to exemplify, instantiate, and participate in according to a Realist metaphysical framework.

[94] For Scotus' and Ockham's contrasting account of universals see Paul Vincent Spade (ed.), *Five Texts on the Mediaeval Problem of Universals: Porphyry, Boethius, Abelard, Duns Scotus, Ockham* (Indianapolis, IN: Hackett Publishing Company, 1994), 57ff.

[95] Maarten Hoenen, "Scotus and the Scotist School: The Tradition of Scotist Thought in the Medieval and Early Modern Period", in *John Duns Scotus (1265/6–1308): Renewal of Philosophy: Acts of the Third Symposium organised by the Dutch Society for Medieval Philosophy Medium Aevum (May 23 and 24 1996)*, ed. Egbert Bos (Amsterdam: Rodopi, 1998), 209.

Fundamental to this was Scotus' own notion of the formal distinction and it was not for nothing that the Scotists became known as "formalizers" (*formalizantes*) in the later Middle Ages.[96] The seed of this notion was present in Bonaventure himself, who argued for the need for an intermediate distinction between a real distinction, such as exists between two separable things (at least in principle), and a purely rational distinction, such as the mind makes subjectively.[97] Notably, Scotus found inspiration for his own, intermediate, formal distinction from the Franciscan metaphysics of light, and specifically from the Dionysian concept of "unitive containment", which held that all beings are contained within God but not in such a way as to impair or compromise his divine unity and simplicity.[98]

For Scotus, two things could be said to be formally distinct if they were identical and inseparable even by God's infinite power but yet still differed in definition.[99] Importantly, he used the formal distinction to characterize the distinction of persons in the Trinity, of the divine attributes and ideas, of the powers in the human soul, and of the transcendental affections of being, thus shaping a comprehensive Trinitarian metaphysics of being.[100] He also used it to explain how universals are formally distinct from the individuals in which they inhere, grounding a much stronger Realism than any to be found in Aquinas.[101] Finally, as Trent Pomplun argues, Scotus' formal distinction allowed a direct map, or isomorphism, between reality and the mind of God.[102] It was this that proved particularly attractive to the Ramists, who stood in a long line of medieval "formalizers" in using Scotus' distinction to coordinate their logic, metaphysics, and theology.

---

[96] Hoenen, "Scotus", 201–2, 208–9.

[97] For the Bonaventuran origins of the formal distinction see Christian Kappes, "Foreword", in J. Isaac Goff, *Caritas in Primo: A Historical-Theological Study of Bonaventure's Quaestiones Disputatae de Mysterio SS. Trinitatis* (New Bedford, MA: Academy of the Immaculate, 2015), xxiv–xxv. For Scotus' account of these distinctions see King, "Scotus on Metaphysics", 21–22. A classic example of a rational distinction which is often given is between Venus as the Morning and Evening Star.

[98] Jan A. Aertsen, "Being and One: The Doctrine of the Convertible Transcendentals in Duns Scotus", in Bos, *John Duns Scotus*, 24–26; *Medieval Philosophy*, 419–25.

[99] Scotus, *Ord*, 1 d. 8 q. 1 p. 4 n. 193 (Vatican, IV.261–62). See also Richard Cross, *Duns Scotus* (Oxford: Oxford University Press, 1999), 149.

[100] Scotus, *Ord.*, 1 d. 2 q. 2 p. 1–4 n. 389–90 (Vatican, II.349–50); *Rep. 1A* d. 8 p. 2 q. 4 n. 104–5; d. 33 q. 2 n. 56–67, 74 (I.362–63; II.327–32). See also Richard Cross, *Duns Scotus on God* (Aldershot: Ashgate, 2005), 107–11, 235–40; Sylwanowicz, *Contingent Causality*, 127–29, and Pomplun, "Scotist Aesthetics", 259.

[101] John Duns Scotus, "Six Questions on Individuation", in Spade, *Five Texts*, 106–7. For Aquinas' weaker Realism see Jeffrey E. Brower, "Aquinas on the Problem of Universals", *Philosophy and Phenomenological Research* 92.3 (2016): 715–35. Brower notes Aquinas' complex affinities to both Realist and Nominalist views of universals.

[102] Scotus, *Rep 1A*, d. 36 pars. 1 q.1–2 n. 74–75 (II.405) draws on Plato and Augustine to argue for a direct map between creation and its intelligible existence in the mind of God. See further Pomplun, "Scotist Aesthetics", 258–64.

## I.2. Lullism

Following Bonaventure and Scotus we find an important further stage in the Franciscan Reformation of method in their contemporary Ramon Lull. While Lull has been described as a man centuries ahead of his time, his thought had deep roots in the Franciscan tradition of his era.[103] Indeed, Lull's Art, which sought to provide both a universal key to all of knowledge and an apologetic tool for proving the truth of Christian doctrine to unbelievers, has been characterized by Mark Johnston as effectively a "massive amplification" of Bonaventure's *reductio*.[104] Certainly, he shared with the Seraphic Doctor a profound Trinitarian exemplarism, as well as a desire to trace the origins of all human knowledge back to its divine ground. In his pronounced Realism and his conviction that intrinsic distinctions within God can be mapped directly onto the created order, Lull has also been seen as adumbrating the univocal and formalizing approach to metaphysics found in Scotus himself.[105] Indeed, by the fifteenth century it had become common to read Lull's thought through the lens of Scotus' formal distinction.[106]

By his own account, Lull received his Art through a divine illumination which he received in 1274 on the slopes of Mount Randa in his native Majorca. Already, a number of years earlier Lull had expressed his desire to write the "best book in the world" against the "errors of the unbelievers".[107] Now, at last, his revelation on Mount Randa gave him the "form and method" of the book he had been seeking.[108] Lull's couching of his breakthrough in methodological terms is highly significant, for it gave to method a central role in the reform of knowledge. Indeed, while Lull's Art was to go through multiple recensions during his lifetime, its core methodological assumptions were always to remain fundamentally unchanged.[109]

---

[103] Charles Lohr, "Metaphysics", in *The Cambridge History of Renaissance Philosophy*, ed. Charles B. Schmitt, Eckhard Kessler and Quentin Skinner (Cambridge: Cambridge University Press, 2008), 538–43.

[104] Mark D. Johnston, *The Evangelical Rhetoric of Ramon Llull: Lay Learning and Piety in the Christian West around 1300* (New York: Oxford University Press, 1996), 18.

[105] Mark D. Johnston, *The Spiritual Logic of Ramon Llull* (Oxford: Clarendon Press, 1987), 159 and Anthony Bonner, *The Art and Logic of Ramon Llull: A User's Guide* (Leiden: Brill, 2007), 136 point to univocal elements in Lull's reasoning. For formalizing elements see Josep E. Rubio, "Llull's 'Great Universal Art'", in *A Companion to Ramon Llull and Lullism*, ed. Amy M. Austin and Mark D. Johnston (Leiden: Brill, 2019), 87–88 and Johnston, *Spiritual Logic*, 170.

[106] See Joseph M. Victor, "The Revival of Lullism at Paris, 1499–1516", *Renaissance Quarterly* 28.4 (1975): 517–20 and Stephan Meier-Oeser, "Von der Koinzidenz zur coincidentia oppositorum. Zum philosophiehistorischen Hintergrund des Cusanischen Koinzidenzgedankens", in *Die Philosophie im 14. und 15. Jahrhundert. In Memoriam Konstanty Michalski (1879–1947)*, ed. Olaf Pluta (Amsterdam: B. R. Grüner, 1988), 321–42.

[107] Ramon Lull, *Vita Coaetanea*, n. 5–7, in Ramon Lull, *Raimundi Lulli Opera Latina*, ed. Friedrich Stegmuller et al. (Turnhout: Brepols, 1975–) [hereafter *ROL*], 8.274–75.

[108] Lull, *Vita*, n. 14 (*ROL*, 8.280–81).

[109] Rubio, "Art", 81–82.

The fundamental insight grounding Lull's Art is that the dynamism of the divine nature becomes imprinted on all of being. As Charles Lohr suggests, Lull therefore vigorously rejects any static or "otiose" understanding of the Godhead, such as he saw in the prevailing Aristotelian and scholastic culture of his time.[110] Rather, he correlated the unfolding of all of reality with the inner emanation of the Godhead—a decidedly Neo-Platonic and Franciscan move.[111] In the final Ternary phase of the Art, so called due to its distinctive triadic character, Lull was able to offer an influential threefold expression of this according to what his Renaissance followers were later to designate as his absolute, relative, and correlative principles.[112]

Lull's absolute principles, also known as divine dignities, can be fruitfully compared to both the divine attributes and divine ideas. Grouped in three triads as Goodness, Greatness, and Eternity; Power, Wisdom, and Will; and Virtue, Truth, and Glory, they constitute the exemplar causes of creation. All things exist through participation in them. However, while distinct in identity they are by no means static, but rather are both convertible with each other and capable of dynamically combining with other principles—something Lull indicated graphically by placing these nine dignities around a circle centred on God (Figure I.1.a).[113] Regulating the mutual communication of the absolute principles with each other and their differential emanation, or diffusion, into creation are a corresponding set of nine relative principles of Difference, Concordance, and Contrariety; Beginning, Middle, and End; and Majority, Equality, and Minority. Notably, it is the combinatorial interaction of these which gives rise to the unity-in-diversity of creation, something Lull once again chose to express graphically with another circular figure (Figure I.1.b).[114] Finally, Lull's correlative principles (which he indicated by the suffixes *-tivum*, *-bile* and *-are*) are used to express the dynamic Trinitarian structure of all of reality. Conceived of, in Scotistic fashion, as intrinsic "moments of activity" they express an inner emanation, or unfolding, of being itself.[115] In this way, every creature—indeed, every aspect of every creature—is seen to mirror the Trinity, the least thing becoming a "living token of the presence of God".[116]

---

[110] Lohr, "Metaphysics", 537–39.

[111] Lohr, "Metaphysics", 540. For parallels with the Franciscans see Johnston, *Spiritual Logic*, 19–20.

[112] For the ternary phase of Lull's Art see Bonner, *Art and Logic*, 121–87. On pp. 130–33 he critiques this Renaissance division.

[113] Ramon Lull, *Ars Brevis*, 2.1, in *Doctor Illuminatus: A Ramon Llull Reader*, ed. and trans. Anthony and Eve Bonner (Princeton, NJ: Princeton University Press, 1993) [hereafter *DI*], 300–301; Johnston, *Spiritual Logic*, 20–21.

[114] Lull, *Ars Brevis*, 2.2 (*DI*, 301–4); Johnston, *Spiritual Logic*, 21–26.

[115] Lohr, "Metaphysics", 542. Lohr does not make the Scotist connection here. For Scotus' instants of nature see Scotus, *Rep.* 1A d. 39–40 q. 3 art. 3 n. 38–44 (II.475–77).

[116] Hillgarth, *Lull*, 10.

INTRODUCTION 19

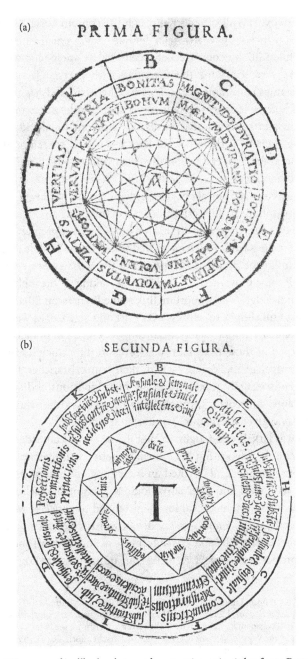

**Figure I.1** Diagram of Lull's absolute and respective principles from Bernardo de Lavinheta, *Opera Omnia*, ed. Johann Heinrich Alsted (Cologne, 1612), 40, 52. Reproduced by kind permission of the Bibliothèque Nationale de France.

Lull's attempt to explain all of reality through the combinatorial interaction of basic, universal principles gave his Art a definite encyclopaedic thrust from the beginning. While initially conceived of chiefly for its apologetic value in providing "necessary reasons" for the Christian faith derived from the divine attributes, or names, common to the Jewish, Christian, and Islamic religions, Lull very quickly came to see his art as a universal method—a *scientia generalis*—capable of allowing its practitioners to discourse on any topic and discover the truth of all questions.[117] Especially in its later recensions, therefore, the Art developed into an ambitious, encyclopaedic endeavour in which philosophy and theology became unified into a single synthesis. While Lull only rarely and tacitly expressed this as a scriptural encyclopaedism, his later followers were much more explicit in arguing for the scriptural basis of the entire Art.[118]

We may see this encyclopaedic dimension of Lull's Art supremely in his *Arbor Scientiae* of 1295–96, a work which circulated widely in the Middle Ages and had an important influence on the development of the Renaissance encyclopaedia and the wider Ramist movement.[119] In this work, taking up the biblical image of the "Tree of Knowledge"—an important link to the Franciscan Edenic paradigm of knowledge—Lull sought to express every art and science, as well as the entire structure of Church and society, according to a series of branching trees.[120] Significantly, each of these trees had their roots in the principles of the Art—indicating its universal applicability—with their trunk, branches, twigs, leaves, flowers, and fruits visually representing the main divisions and sub-divisions of each discipline. Moreover, through Lull's correlatives the whole Christian encyclopaedia was given a dynamic, Trinitarian structure.[121]

While Lull was largely self-taught, in later life he spent a considerable time in the Parisian schools, advocating his reform at both the university and French court. As a consequence, Lull devoted an increasing amount of time to developing his Art as a rival and alternative logic to Aristotelian scholasticism.[122] Following Peter of Spain, medieval logicians tended to conceive of their discipline as a *"scientia sermocinalis"*—a science of words or concepts. Aristotelian logic was thus centred on the analysis of terms (e.g. dog, animal) and their combination into propositions (e.g. "Every dog is an animal") and syllogisms ("Every

---

[117] Rubio, "Art", 83; Ramon Lull, *Ars Generalis Ultima*, "De Prologo" (*ROL*, 14.5–7).

[118] Ramon Lull, *Liber de Fine*, I.5 (*ROL*, 9.267) makes clear the tacit scriptural dimensions of the Art. For late medieval engagement between the Lullist Art and Scripture see Peter Casarella, *Word as Bread: Language and Theology in Nicholas of Cusa* (Münster: Aschendorff, 2017), 165–274.

[119] Mary Franklin-Brown, "Ramon Llull as Encyclopedist", in *A Companion to Ramon Llull and Lullism*, ed. Austin and Johnston, 364–96; Rossi, *Logic and the Art of Memory*, 5–6.

[120] Ramon Lull, *Arbor Scientiae*, "*Prooemium*", VII.I.1–VII.3; VIII.I.1–VII.3 (*ROL*, 24.4–10, 333–60; 25.377–484). See Franklin-Brown, "Ramon Llull", 389–90. The Edenic setting is also apparent in Ramon Lull, *The Book of the Gentile and the Three Wise Men*, "Prologue" (*DI*, 85–92).

[121] Lull, *Arbor Scientiae*, XV (*ROL*, 25.709); Franklin-Brown, "Ramon Llull", 389–90.

[122] Hillgarth, *Lull*, 135–85; Bonner, *Art and Logic*, 188–255.

dog is an animal", "Every animal is a creature": "Every dog is a creature") and spent much of its time developing rules for the analysis of abstract truth claims.[123] In these terms logic was often described as concerned with second intentions (broadly "concepts of concepts") and not first intentions (concepts immediately apprehended by the mind).[124]

Importantly, Scotus, and especially a number of his followers, had sought to bridge the gap between first and second intentions, arguing that some terms such as genus and species could function as both. For example, we might consider a genus like animal as present in an individual dog (first intention) or as known by a human mind (second intention).[125] Following this broader Franciscan concern to ground logic in extra-mental reality, Lull pressed towards what was effectively a logic of first intentions. For him, logic was concerned with the "nature of things" and not only with terms or words.[126] In his Art, the common scholastic distinction between logic and metaphysics is thus thoroughly broken down.[127]

Axiomatic to Lull's logic is the exact correspondence between reality and our conception of it. Philosophically, Lull has often been labelled an extreme or ultra-Realist due to his claim, going beyond Scotus, that not only logical terms but also propositions and syllogisms had a real existence outside the mind.[128] Lull expressed this in his distinctive metaphysical account of predication, which held that the relation between subject, predicate, and their bond (copula) in a proposition was mirrored exactly in the structure of reality.[129] Notably, as Johnston suggests, such a propositional Realism closely reflects that to be found in fourteenth-century philosophers like Walter Burley and Gregory of Rimini and has deep roots in the Augustinian and Franciscan tradition. Effectively it extends the parallel between divine ideas and created universals to divine propositions—conceived by Rimini as so-called *complexe significabile*—and created states of affairs.[130] Significantly, the combinatorial mechanism of his Art meant that the revolving of its wheels could be used to match a potentially infinite set of terms together, thus patterning all the logical and metaphysical relations capable of existing in reality.[131]

---

[123] See Alexander Broadie, *Introduction to Medieval Logic* (Oxford: Clarendon Press, 1993).
[124] For a detailed discussion of intentions see Christian Knudsen, "Intentions and Impositions", in *Cambridge History of Later Medieval Philosophy*, 479–95.
[125] Knudsen, "Intentions and Impositions", 485–86.
[126] Johnston, *Spiritual Logic*, 47–48.
[127] Bonner, *Art and Logic*, 18–19. Bonner is also quick to point out that Lull still retained a distinction between logic and metaphysics.
[128] Johnston, *Spiritual Logic*, 76–84, 105.
[129] Lull, *Ars Brevis*, 2.3 (*DI*, 305); cf. Bonner, *Art and Logic*, 219. In the proposition "x is y", "x" is the subject, "is" is the copula, and "y" is the predicate.
[130] Johnston, *Spiritual Logic*, 105. For a detailed discussion of Rimini's account of the *complexe significabile* see Pascale Bermon, *L'assentiment et son objet chez Grégoire de Rimini* (Paris: Vrin, 2007). In essence, the *complexe significabile* refers to a proposition designating a state of affairs knowable either by God or humans.
[131] Lull, *Ars Brevis*, 2.2–4; 5–8 (*DI*, 303–8, 316–24).

Ultimately, Lull sought to offer not only a natural, or ontological, logic but also a profoundly spiritual one. For logic, like all the other disciplines, becomes ultimately reducible to the interaction of his divine principles. Lullist logic thus proceeds by what Johnston terms "moralising arguments", which by means of the absolute, relative, and correlative principles, as well as his own distinctive logical operations, seeks to relate all things to their end in God.[132] Significantly, the imprint of the correlatives means that Lull's logic manifests a distinct Trinitarian structure and dynamic. This is evident not only in the structure of the syllogism itself, which he reconceives according to the mutual, generative relation of its terms, but also especially in his "logic of equivalence", which grounds logic on the mutual conversion of the divine dignities, offering a "logic of coessentiality" grounded on the Trinity.[133] In this sense, the Lullist Art already represents an important fulfilment of the Franciscan quest for a divine logic.

## I.3. Christian Humanism

For Charles Lohr, Thomas Leinkauf, and Maria Rosa Antognazza, the roots of the dynamic worldview of the Renaissance are to be found in Lull and his fifteenth-century disciple Nicholas of Cusa. For it is in their thought that we find the break from the static Aristotelian world to a Neo-Platonic conception of the dynamic parallel between God and his creation. This is especially manifest in the new, elevated position given to humans not only as interpreters but as makers and fashioners of their own reality.[134] Indeed, for Cusa man is a "human god" who freely creates conceptual worlds in imitation of God's own infinite creative power. Echoing Protagoras, Cusa can thus claim that man is the "measure of all things".[135] The encyclopaedic arts and sciences that humans develop can all be seen to mirror the infinite divine Art of God himself. Yet such a mirroring is not static but dynamic, capable of progressing infinitely towards a dual horizon of both the original, Edenic perfection of the arts and their promised eschatological flourishing.[136]

---

[132] Johnston, *Spiritual Logic*, 5–6, 16–18. This is the thesis of Johnston's whole work.
[133] Ramon Lull, *Liber de demonstratione per aequiparantiam*, "Prologus" (ROL, 9.216–18); cf. Johnston, *Spiritual Logic*, 101–6, 114–17.
[134] Lohr, *Metaphysics*, 538–58; Maria Rosa Antognazza, "Leibniz and the Post-Copernican Universe: Koyré Revisited", *Studies in History and Philosophy of Science* 34 (2003): 309–27; and Thomas Leinkauf, *Einheit, Natur, Geist: Beiträge zu metaphysischen Grundproblemen in Denken von Gottfried Wilhelm von Leibniz* (Berlin: Trafo, 2012), 15–50.
[135] Nicholas of Cusa, *Idiota de Mente*, 1.57; 3.72; 9.116 (NCOO, V.90–91, 108–10, 171–72); *De coniecturis*, 2.14.143–44 (NCOO, III.143–44). For parallels with Protagoras see Karsten Harries, *Infinity and Perspective* (Cambridge, MA: MIT Press, 2001), 184–200.
[136] Nicholas of Cusa, *Compendium*, 3.6–7; 6.16–7.19 (NCOO, XI/3.6–7, 11–16).

If Lull and Cusa must be seen as at the fountainhead of an influential stream of Renaissance Platonism—a movement caught up and quickly assimilated into the wider current of Classical and Christian Rebirth in fourteenth- and fifteenth-century Christendom—then it must be stressed that this was a thoroughly Franciscan Renaissance.[137] The influence of Franciscan thought on seminal Renaissance figures like Dante and Petrarch has long been known. Indeed, Dante's *Divine Comedy* is not only structured according to the Franciscan metaphysics of light but also, as Giuseppe Mazzotta has compellingly argued, according to the canons of Bonaventuran encyclopaedism.[138] Its culmination in an encounter with a God who transcends both reason and logic, memorably captured in the mathematical motif of squaring the circle, not only echoes Bonaventure but also points forward to Cusa's own coincidence of opposites.[139] In its own way Petrarch's epochal ascent of Mont Ventoux—an event which is often seen as marking the beginning of the modern age—recapitulated Francis' earlier ascent of Mount Alverna.[140]

Recently, Eugenio Garin has extended such a comparison to Marsilio Ficino and Pico della Mirandola, the two giants of Renaissance Platonism, pointing out their deep connections to the Franciscan and Scotist tradition.[141] Like Bonaventure, Ficino was convinced that the separation of philosophy and theology was the greatest problem of his age and was a strident opponent of the renascent Averroism taught in the Italian schools.[142] His response to this was to propose a new *Theologia Platonica* which in its pronounced exemplarism and illuminationism owes much to Augustine and Bonaventure.[143] Notably, Ficino offered a genealogy of this new Christian Platonism beginning with Augustine

---

[137] Eugenio Garin, *History of Italian Philosophy: Vol. 1*, trans. Giorgio Pinton (New York: Rodolphi, 2008), 114, 134–38, 248–49 and Hans Baron, *In Search of Florentine Civic Humanism, Volume 1: Essays on the Transition from Medieval to Modern Thought* (Princeton, NJ: Princeton University Press, 2014), 158–225.

[138] See Mazzotta, "Dante's Franciscanism", 192-98. For the wider context of this engagement see Nick R. Havely, *Dante and the Franciscans: Poverty and Papacy in the Commedia* (Cambridge: Cambridge University Press, 2009).

[139] Dante Alighieri, *The Comedy of Dante Alighieri The Florentine: Cantica III Paradise (Il Paradiso)*, trans. Dorothy L. Sayers and Barbara Reynolds (London: Penguin, 2004), 33.114–45 (pp. 346–47). For Dante's metaphysics of light see Christian Moev, *The Metaphysics of Dante's Comedy* (New York: Oxford University Press, 2005), 53–85.

[140] For the epochal character of Petrarch's ascent see Harries, *Infinity and Perspective*, 148–60. For the Franciscan parallels see Rodney Lokaj, "Petrarch vs. Gherardo: A Case of Sibling Rivalry inside and outside the Cloister" (PhD Dissertation, University of Edinburgh, 2001), 139–200.

[141] Garin, *History*, 134–38, 248–49.

[142] Marsilio Ficino, *De Religione Christiana* (Paris, 1559), "*Prooemium*"; c. 1–3 (pp. 1r–5v); *Epistolae* (Florence, 1494), XI.220r.

[143] For the Augustinian and Franciscan dimensions of his Platonic theology see Anthony Levi, "Ficino, Augustine and the Pagans", in *Marsilio Ficino: His Theology, His Philosophy, His Legacy*, ed. Michael J. B. Allen, Martin Davies, and Valery Rees (Leiden: Brill, 2002), 99–113 and Garin, *History*, 248–49. Lohr, "Metaphysics", 578 also notes how Ficino's Platonic theology countered fifteenth-century Thomism.

and Pseudo-Dionysius, proceeding through the Christian Augustinian Henry of Ghent and Duns Scotus, and concluding in his own time with Cusa—Aquinas is here conspicuous by his absence.[144] If anything, this Franciscan influence is even greater on Pico, who sought to engage Scotus' univocity of being and formal distinction with a metaphysics of coincidence profoundly indebted to Lull and Cusa.[145] In his celebrated 1486 *Oration on the Dignity of Man*, he follows Bonaventure by making the encyclopaedia central to the mystical ascent and transformation of the soul. Notably, logic plays a fundamental role in this ascent, both patterning and uncovering the dynamic relation of unity and multiplicity running through all of reality, which Pico elsewhere characterized according to Scotus' intrinsic reasons.[146]

It is within this broad and eclectic Neo-Platonic and Franciscan ambit that we must come to see the Renaissance dialectic of the fifteenth and sixteenth centuries, going from Valla and Agricola through to Melanchthon and Ramus himself. It is well known that Renaissance logic went through a distinctive "rhetorical turn", which in its attention to ordinary language use and techniques of persuasion marked a radical departure from the technical Aristotelian logic of the scholastics.[147] Notably, however, the roots of this split go back to Aristotle himself. For his *Organon* included not only his *Prior* and *Posterior Analytics*, in which he established a scientific logic of terms and syllogisms oriented towards necessary (apodictic) proof, but also the *Topics* in which he developed a new method oriented towards probable (dialectic) argumentation.[148] Importantly, this topical method was taken up and refined by Roman orators such as Cicero and Quintilian. While Cicero's works were well known in the Middle Ages, Quintilian's were rediscovered in the Renaissance and exerted an important stimulus on the development of topical logic.[149]

---

[144] Cited from Joseph M. Victor, *Charles de Bovelles, 1479–1553: An Intellectual Biography* (Geneva: Droz, 1978), 66. Ficino also includes Islamic and Jewish Platonists in this genealogy pointing forward to Pico's project of concord.

[145] Giovanni Pico della Mirandola, *Syncretism in the West: Pico's 900 Theses (1486): The Evolution of Traditional Religious and Philosophical Systems*, ed. and trans. S. A. Farmer (Tempe, AZ: Medieval & Renaissance Texts and Studies, 1998), 233–41, 402–3; cf. Garin, *History*, 135, 306–7. For Pico's complex Scotist and Cusan affinities see S. A. Farmer, "Introductory Monograph", in Pico, *Syncretism in the West*, 23–24, 55–56. For Pico's Lullism see Hillgarth, *Lull*, 281–84.

[146] Giovanni Pico della Mirandola, *Oration on the Dignity of Man: A New Translation and Commentary*, ed. and trans. Francesco Borghesi, Michael Papio, and Massimo Riva (Cambridge: Cambridge University Press, 2012), 149. On p. 79 the editors note the parallel with Bonaventure's *Itinerarium*. Pico, *Syncretism in the West*, 235, 237, 241 draws on Scotus and Francis of Meyronnes in their discussion of formalities, intrinsic respects, and haecceities.

[147] Marc Cogan, "Rodolphus Agricola and the Semantic Revolutions of the History of Invention", *Rhetorica* 2.2 (1984): 167–86.

[148] For Aristotle's logic see Christopher Shields, *Aristotle* (London: Routledge, 2014), 116–71.

[149] For a detailed account of Classical rhetoric and the topics see William J. Dominik and Jon C. R. Hall (eds.), *A Companion to Roman Rhetoric* (Oxford: Blackwell, 2007). Sara Rubinelli, *Ars Topica: The Classical Technique of Constructing Arguments from Aristotle to Cicero* (Dordrecht: Springer, 2009) argues for an intimate connection between Aristotle and Cicero. For the diffusion of Classical

As the name suggests, topical logic relates to topics or places (*loci*) rather than the terms of Aristotelian syllogistic logic. Topics are basically to be understood as classes of things—such as subject, adjunct, cause, effect, genus, species, similarity, difference, etc.—used by orators and rhetoricians to structure their arguments. Cicero thus described how orators could draw on the topics for discovering, or "inventing", arguments, "judging" their truth, and memorizing their content.[150] The term "place" (*locus*) refers to the way in which orators often conceived of the topics as a set of rooms in a house, with each room holding relevant arguments. By making use of such a "memory palace", trained orators could remember with ease long and complex speeches—establishing an early and important connection between topical logic and the art of memory.[151]

In his own *Topics* Aristotle's primary concern was to integrate this rhetorical account of topics into his complex machinery of syllogistic logic. In the Middle Ages Boethius continued this trend by seeking to offer a systematic account of topical logic, transforming the topics into an interconnected system of self-evident "maximal propositions", or maxims, under which a whole set of arguments could be classed. Indeed, for Boethius, the architecture of the topics, in its various divisions and sub-divisions, begins to reflect the metaphysical architecture of the universe itself, instituting an important topical Realism.[152] Yet Boethius' was by no means the only influential medieval account of the topics. Augustine himself had been deeply influenced by Ciceronian topical logic.[153] Bonaventure too was deeply attracted to the topics as offering a scriptural alternative to Aristotelian, scholastic notions of system. In his *Breviloquium* he offered a powerful description of this new method as using the topics to chart a route through the impenetrable forest of Scripture. This compelling notion of the topics as the path through a discipline was to become fundamental in articulating new Renaissance notions of method.[154]

---

Rhetoric in the Middle Ages and Renaissance see Peter Mack, *A History of Renaissance Rhetoric 1380–1620* (Oxford: Oxford University Press, 2011), 13–32.

[150] Cicero, *De Inventione*, I.22–28 and *Topica*, II–III, in *De Inventione, De Optimo Genere Oratorum, Topica*, trans. H. M. Hubbell (Cambridge, MA: Harvard University Press, 1956) (pp. 63–83, 387–91). For links to the art of memory see Yates, *Art of Memory*, 17–41.

[151] Yates, *Art of Memory*, 17–92; Rossi, *Logic and the Art of Memory*, 1–28.

[152] Boethius, *De Topicis Differentiis*, trans. Eleonore Stump (Ithaca, NY: Cornell University Press, 2018), 1173C-D, 1177C–1178B, 1184D (pp. 29–30, 35–36, 46). See also Eleonore Stump, *Dialectic and Its Place in the Development of Medieval Logic* (Ithaca, NY: Cornell University Press, 2020), 31–57.

[153] For Augustine's debt to Cicero in terms of rhetoric and the art of memory see Catherine Conybeare, "Augustine's Rhetoric in Theory and Practice", in *The Oxford Handbook of Rhetorical Studies*, ed. Michael J. MacDonald (Oxford: Oxford University Press, 2017), 301–10 and Yates, *Art of Memory*, 59–63.

[154] Bonaventure, *Breviloquium*, "Prologue" 6 (pp. 19–23; BOO, V.207–8). See Ong, *Ramus, Method, and the Decay of Dialogue*, 237.

One of the first to challenge the hegemony of scholastic logic was Lorenzo Valla in his 1439 *Repastinatio dialecticae et philosophiae*. Valla's "re-ploughing" or "weeding out" of Aristotelian logic and metaphysics was comprehensive.[155] Like the Franciscans of an earlier age Valla was especially concerned about the deleterious effect of Aristotle on theology, and his own renewed dialectic was dedicated to the reform of the "Christian republic".[156] He himself professed great admiration not only for Plato and Augustine but also for Franciscans such as Alexander of Hales, Bonaventure, and Scotus.[157] Valla achieved his ambitious aim not only through instituting a new "common-sense" philosophy, in which extravagant ontological claims were deflated through careful linguistic and philological analysis, but also through reconfiguring logic as a part of rhetoric itself.[158] Following Bonaventure, he conceived of logic as a teaching art.[159] Going beyond him, he suggested that it was merely preparatory to the higher art of rhetoric, establishing a body of arguments and topics to be further clothed and embellished.[160] Significantly, Valla drew on a broad Augustinian and Neo-Platonic framework of exemplarism and illuminationism, and he also subscribed to a loose and attenuated Realism—sometimes undermined by his sharp, linguistic critique.[161] What this meant for Valla was that logical terms such as universals, and even propositions and syllogisms, had some kind of existence outside the mind, and some of his discussion even hinted at a loose affiliation with Scotus' formal distinction.[162] Indeed, for Valla, the truth of a syllogism does not depend so much

[155] For Valla's comprehensive critique of Aristotelian scholasticism see Lodi Nauta, *In Defense of Common Sense: Lorenzo Valla's Humanist Critique of Scholastic Philosophy* (Cambridge, MA: Harvard University Press, 2009) and Peter Mack, *Renaissance Argument: Valla and Agricola in the Traditions of Rhetoric and Dialectic* (Leiden: Brill, 1993), 22–36.

[156] For Valla's critique of the influence of Aristotle on theology see Lorenzo Valla, *Dialectical Disputations*, ed. and trans. Brian P. Copenhaver and Lodi Nauta (Cambridge, MA: Harvard University Press, 2012), I "Proem"; c. 8 (I.11, 103). For his ideal of the Christian Republic see Salvatore I. Camporeale, "Lorenzo Valla's *Oratio* on the Pseudo-Donation of Constantine: Dissent and Innovation in Early Renaissance Humanism", *Journal of the History of Ideas* 57.1 (1996): 11, 15–16, 19–26.

[157] Lorenzo Valla, *Encomium for Thomas Aquinas*, in *Christianity, Latinity and Culture: Two Studies on Lorenzo Valla*, ed. and trans. Christopher S. Celenza and Patrick Baker (Leiden: Brill, 2013), 313; cf. Salvatore I. Camporeale, *Christianity, Latinity and Culture: Two Studies on Lorenzo Valla*, ed. and trans. Christopher S. Celenza and Patrick Baker (Leiden: Brill, 2013), 145–296.

[158] Valla, *Dialectical Disputations*, II "Proem" (II.3); Nauta, *Common Sense*, 13–47, 82–128 argues that Valla subscribes to a linguistic reductionism distinct from Nominalism and compatible with an attenuated Realism.

[159] Valla, *Dialectical Disputations*, I c. 2 (I.33–35); John Monfasani, "Lorenzo Valla and Rudolph Agricola", *Journal of the History of Philosophy* 28.2 (1990): 185.

[160] Valla, *Dialectical Disputations*, II "Proem" (II.5–7). Mack, *Renaissance Argument*, 83–87 points to the important if subsidiary role of the topics in Valla's dialectic.

[161] Valla, *Dialectical Disputations*, I c. 2; c. 14–15 (I.33–35, 221–25). For Valla's illuminism and Realism see John Monfasani, "The Theology of Lorenzo Valla", in *Humanism and Early Modern Philosophy*, ed. Jill Kraye and M. W. F. Stone (London: Routledge, 2000), 1–23 and Nauta, *Common Sense*, 17, 39–41.

[162] Valla, *Dialectical Disputations*, I c. 2; III c. 2; 3; 9 (I.35; II.229, 231–37, 267–71); Nauta, *Common Sense*, 135–36 implies that Valla's view of the soul's faculties hovers between an Augustinian-Scotist and Thomist one.

on the logical form of the argument—the Aristotelian and scholastic concern—but on the "natural" connection, or kinship, between its terms.[163]

Even more ambitious in scope was Rudolph Agricola's *De Inventione Dialectica* of 1479, the work which launched a far-reaching methodological revolution and had a profound impact not only on the sixteenth-century Reformation but especially, as we shall see in subsequent chapters, on the emerging movements of Ramism and universal reform.[164] Agricola's work is dedicated to dialectical invention—a sequel on dialectical judgement was never written—and his goal was to offer humanists a new logic suitable for the analysis of a wide range of texts, including poems and orations, and oriented towards practical use and application to other arts.[165] Agricola was the first to reunite the dialectical and rhetorical topics, which had been sundered since Boethius, and his desire was to offer a universal, topical logic.[166] This marked not only a dethroning of the syllogistic logic of the scholastics but also a blurring of Aristotle's sharp division between apodictic and dialectic. Indeed, Agricola was clearly committed to the view that dialectical arguments could carry the force of necessity—a link to an older, Neo-Platonic conception of dialectic grounded on the divine ideas.[167]

Like Valla, Agricola was profoundly impacted by the Franciscans, not only Bonaventure but also Scotus and Lull, who are the only two medieval sources he cites in the *De Inventione*.[168] For our purposes, he therefore represents a fusion of the new rhetorical orientation of humanism with the Platonism and Realism of the Franciscan schools. What Peter Mack has called Agricola's "extreme Realism" comes through clearly in his famous definition of dialectical topics or places, which is worth citing at length:

> All things which are either said for or against a thing cohere and are, as they say, conjunct by a certain society of nature. But things are immense in number and so immense also are their properties and differences. From this it follows that no discourse and no power of the human mind can comprehend individually all the relations in which individuals agree and differ. Yet there is in all, although they are discrete in their notes, a certain common habitude, and all things tend to similitude of nature. So everything has a substance of its own, all things arise from causes, and all things effect something. Therefore the cleverest

---

[163] Valla, *Dialectical Disputations*, III c. 2; 3; 9 (II.229, 231–37, 267–71).
[164] For the revolutionary impact of Agricola see Cogan, "Rodolphus Agricola", 163–64 and Mack, *Renaissance Argument*, 257ff.
[165] For Agricola's dialectic in the context of his life see Mack, *Renaissance Argument*, 117–29.
[166] Cogan, "Rodolphus Agricola", 167–86.
[167] Rudolph Agricola, *De Inventione Dialectica* [hereafter *DID*] (Cologne, 1527), II c. 2, 5 (pp. 156–57, 172–76); Mack, *Renaissance Argument*, 177–81, 185. Such a view is anticipated in Cicero, *De Inventione*, I.29 (pp. 83–84) and Boethius, *De Topicis Differentiis*, 1180C–1182B (pp. 40–42).
[168] Agricola, *DID*, I c. 27; II c. 1 (pp. 121, 146).

of men have chosen from that poured out variety of things, certain common heads, as substance, cause, event and the rest of which we shall speak shortly. So that when we turn our mind to consider any thing, following these, we at once go through every nature of a thing and its parts and through all things consentaneous and dissentaneous, and we are led thence to an argument accommodated to the proposed thing. Therefore these common things are therefore called places because just as whatever is able to be said concerning any thing so they contain all arguments inside them as if all instruments for making faith are reposed in a refuge or treasury. Therefore a place is nothing other than a certain common note of a thing by whose urging what is proveable/probable in whatever thing is able to be invented.[169]

For Agricola, it is clear that the various logical and propositional relations discovered by the mind really exist in the world. Topics are therefore not only convenient classes drawn on by orators to order their discourse but are "common notes" which belong to and inhere in individual things, and which can be employed to relate all things to each other.[170]

In fact, as Lodi Nauta has argued, Agricola himself subscribed to a broadly Scotistic Realism, and in both the *De Inventione* and other works we find tantalizing evidence that he conceived not only of universals but also of a whole range of topics in terms of Scotus' formal distinction.[171] In this, he may be seen as part of a wider fifteenth-century movement, seeking to connect Scotus' sophisticated logic and metaphysics to a broader topical framework.[172] In effect, the *De Inventione* transposes the Scotistic Realist understanding of universals characteristic of Agricola's earlier treatises onto a much broader topical framework more suitable for a humanist dialectic.[173] For Agricola, the topics, conceived of as Scotistic universals or intrinsic respects, thus map out the consentaneous and dissentaneous features of reality—the similarities and differences between things—exposing the complex set of interconnections which bind all things together.[174]

---

[169] Agricola, *DID*, I c. 2 (p. 8). Translation adapted from Mack, *Renaissance Argument*, 140. For Agricola's extreme Realism see p. 136 n. 20.
[170] Mack, *Renaissance Argument*, 139–42.
[171] Lodi Nauta, "From Universals to Topics: The Realism of Rudolph Agricola, with an Edition of His Reply to a Critic", *Vivarium* 50.2 (2012): 196–205 notes his broad Scotistic affinities.
[172] For Scotus' metaphysical and Realist treatment of the topics see Giorgio Pini, "Duns Scotus' Commentary on the Topics: New Light on His Philosophical Teaching", *Archives d'histoire doctrinale et littéraire du moyen âge* 66 (1999): 225–43. See also Nauta, "From Universals to Topics", 190–224.
[173] Nauta, "From Universals to Topics", 190–224 makes a similar argument but without connecting Agricola to a Scotist relational framework.
[174] Agricola, *DID*, I c. 27 (pp. 121–22) draws explicitly on Scotus in his understanding of relations or internal respects.

Reinforcing this Realist approach he can connect the topics both to the emanation and return of all things to the One, and to the mathematical progression of numbers from unity.[175] In Franciscan fashion he can even speak of the topics as following the "*vestigia*" of things themselves.[176] Notably, Agricola can also connect his Scotist version of topical Realism to a Lullist combinatorial worldview. His emanational account of the topics and his understanding of them as surrounding or "circumferencing" things and the human soul fits well with the dynamic framework of Lullist method.[177] Like Lull, Agricola also sought to develop an easy method (*via*) of invention, through finding what is effectively a "natural middle"—or metaphysical connection—between subject and predicate terms.[178] Indeed, Agricola himself developed a kind of combinatorial procedure of running through all the topics and comparing them together in order to locate the precise bond between two terms.[179] While not always uncritical of Lull, Agricola was clear about the definite overlap between Lull's Art and his own rhetorical logic, and deeply attracted to the capacity of Lullism to coordinate and systematize topical reasoning.[180]

Agricola was writing on the cusp of the Reformation and his thought had a marked influence on key figures such as Erasmus, Melanchthon, and supremely Ramus himself.[181] For Protestant Reformers especially, Agricola became important in offering a new topical logic for analysing biblical texts. In making his protest against the Catholic Church, Luther set himself resolutely against the Aristotelian scholasticism undergirding its theology.[182] While Luther was fully aware of the late medieval Nominalist tradition of a supernatural, biblical logic of faith transcending Aristotelian logic, he rejected this alternative in favour of an even more radical one: Scripture itself as our logic.[183] For Luther himself this may well have entailed something like Cusa's coincidence of opposites—certainly this

---

[175] Agricola, *DID*, I. c. 15, 28 (pp. 66, 136–37).
[176] Agricola, *DID*, I c. 22 (p. 92).
[177] Agricola, *DID*, I c. 1, 28 (pp. 2, 136–37).
[178] Cogan, "Rodolphus Agricola", 186–90; cf. Bonner, *Art and Logic*, 219–20. Cogan does not note any Lullist parallels here.
[179] Agricola, *DID*, II c. 21 (pp. 329–32)
[180] Agricola, *DID*, II c. 1 (pp. 146–47).
[181] Emery, "Introduction", 26–44.
[182] See extensively Martin Luther, *Disputation against Scholastic Theology*, in *Martin Luther's Works, Vol. 31: Career of the Reformer I*, ed. Harold J. Grimm and Helmut T. Lehmann (Philadelphia, PA: Muhlenberg Press, 1957), 3–16.
[183] Martin Luther, "Die Disputation de sententia: Verbum Caro Factum Est", in Martin Luther, *D. Martin Luthers Werke: Abteilung 1 Schriften*, 72 vols. (Weimar, 1883-2009) [hereafter *WA*], 39.II.4–5; *Disputation against Scholastic Theology*, 12. For Luther's complex relation to the logic of faith tradition see also Eric Leland Saak, *Luther and the Reformation of the Later Middle Ages* (Cambridge: Cambridge University Press, 2017), 130–53.

is what some early modern commentators believed.[184] For Melanchthon, it led to the writing of his revolutionary *Loci Communes* of 1521, in which the pattern of theology is intended to mirror through the topics the structure and dynamic of Scripture itself.[185]

In this work, the first Protestant systematic theology, we see the clear influence of Agricolan topical reasoning, and also of the entire tradition preceding it. Although, like Luther, Melanchthon was a convinced Nominalist in the question of universals, his own account of the topics betrays definite Neo-Platonic and exemplaristic assumptions.[186] His own understanding was that God had impressed on the human soul at creation innate principles which allowed the mind to uncover the ideal and mathematical patterns which structured all of reality. While as a Nominalist he did not believe that universals could be found in things themselves, he did hold that the mind could be awakened by the senses to recognize them as eternal exemplars in the mind of God.[187] As Günter Frank evocatively sums this up, "in these principles the human mind participates in the mind of God".[188] By means of them, logic thus comes to reflect a divine pattern, and is thus not only adequate but in some way connatural to the Bible itself. Like Bonaventure, Melanchthon believed that method was the path laid out by the topics through the dense thickets of Scripture, and that the arts were thus "itineraries" to eternal truth.[189]

---

[184] See Joshua Hollmann, "Nicholas of Cusa and Martin Luther on Christ and the Coincidence of Opposites", in *Nicholas of Cusa and the Making of the Early Modern World*, ed. Simon J. G. Burton, Joshua Hollmann, and Eric M. Parker (Leiden: Brill, 2019), 153–72. For early modern parallels between Lutheranism and the coincidence of opposites see Francis Turretin, *Institutes of Elenctic Theology: Volume One*, ed. James T. Dennison Jr. and trans. George Musgrave Giger (Phillipsburg, NJ: Presbyterian and Reformed Publishing Company, 1992), I q. 10 (pp. 32–34).

[185] Philipp Melanchthon, *Loci Communes 1521*, 64–65 (*Corpus Reformatorum*, vol. 21), ed. Heinrich Ernest Bindseil (Brunswick: C. A. Schwetschke et Filium, 1854), col. 82–83. Graham Ward, *How the Light Gets In: Ethical Life I* (Oxford: Oxford University Press, 2016), 88–114 points to Melanchthon's harnessing of a topical and scriptural method in a Neo-Platonic context.

[186] Philipp Melanchthon, *Erotemata Dialectices* (Wittenberg, 1555), 9–13, 198; *De Anima* (Leiden, 1542), 222–23. For Melanchthon's Neo-Platonism see Günter Frank, "Melanchthon and the Tradition of Neoplatonism", in *Religious Confessions and the Sciences in the Sixteenth Century*, ed. Jürgen Helm and Annette Winkelmann (Leiden: Brill, 2001), 3–18. Sandra Bihlmaier, *Ars et Methodus: Philipp Melanchthon's Humanist Concept of Philosophy* (Göttingen: Vandenhoeck & Ruprecht, 2018), 155, 162 also notes Melanchthon's Neo-Platonic account of the topics and its connection to the ontological structure of reality.

[187] Melanchthon, *De Anima*, 222–26; cf. Cusa, *Idiota de Mente*, 4.74–79 (*NCOO*, V.112–20). See also Andreas J. Beck, "Melanchthonian Thought in Gisbertus Voetius' Scholastic Doctrine of God", in *Scholasticism Reformed: Essays in Honour of Willem J. van Asselt*, ed. Maarten Wisse, Marcel Sarot, and Willemien Otten (Leiden: Brill, 2010), 105–26.

[188] Frank, "Melanchthon and the Tradition of Neoplatonism", 14.

[189] Melanchthon, *Erotemata Dialectices*, 247; cf. Ong, *Ramus, Method, and the Decay of Dialogue*, 237.

## I.4. Reformed Scholasticism

The movement of Protestant scholasticism was exactly contemporaneous with Ramism and formed a vital context for its emergence and development as a movement. While Luther had loudly proclaimed the victory of Scripture and Augustine over the anti-Christian theology of Aristotle and the schools, the later sixteenth and seventeenth centuries saw an important revival of Aristotelian and scholastic philosophy among Protestants of all confessions, but above all among the Reformed.[190] Fusing humanist and scholastic approaches, this new Reformed scholasticism played a fundamental role not only in establishing and defending the boundaries of Reformed orthodoxy but also in energizing a far-reaching movement for the "further Reformation" of academy, Church, and society.[191] Ramus himself wrote only at the beginnings of this movement and his own sympathies lay much more with Agricola, Melanchthon, and an earlier Renaissance humanism and Neo-Platonism. Yet Ramism itself profoundly shaped Reformed scholasticism, even as it was in turn deeply shaped by it.[192] Within the broader horizon of the unfolding Reformation of method, three features of this Reformed scholasticism clearly stand out: topical and biblical logic, Reformed Scotism, and Christian philosophy.

The Protestant impulse begun by Melanchthon to develop a new topical and biblical method, continued and accelerated among the Lutherans and Reformed of the sixteenth and seventeenth centuries, issuing in a whole series of ever-complexifying theological "commonplaces" ranged against the *summae* and *sententiae* of Catholic scholasticism. Although by no means unique to the Protestants, the use of *loci communes* became one of the key hallmarks of Reformation theology.[193] In this sense, as both Kent Emery and Graham Ward would remind us, the use of a topical, broadly Neo-Platonic, method to analyse Scripture and impress its intrinsic structure on the human mind and soul became fundamental to new Protestant dynamic and transformative understandings of method.[194] To the extent which Reformed theologians were consciously modelling themselves on Melanchthon, and imbibing their dialectic in a context moulded by Agricolan and Philippist influences, this understanding was particularly pronounced.[195] Muller thus notes the "close relationship between Calvin's

---

[190] For Luther's attitude see Carter Lindberg, *The European Reformations* (Oxford: Wiley-Blackwell, 2010), 63.
[191] Muller, *PRRD*, 1.27–84, 177–220.
[192] Muller, *PRRD*, 1.62–63, 181–84.
[193] Richard A. Muller, *The Unaccommodated Calvin: Studies in the Foundation of a Theological Tradition* (New York: Oxford University Press, 2001), 101–17; *PRRD*, 1.177–80; and Emery, "Introduction", 34.
[194] Emery, "Introduction", 26–35; Ward, *How The Light Gets In*, 88–114.
[195] Muller, *PRRD*, 1.177–80.

logic and the place-logic of the later Middle Ages and early Renaissance".[196] Likewise, the pedagogical works of Heinrich Bullinger and Andreas Hyperius show a profound engagement with Agricola in developing a topical and biblical approach to theology.[197] Indeed, in the wake of Nauta's pathbreaking research, a reassessment of the topical Realism of the wider Reformed tradition is necessary.[198]

The important and widespread influence of the Melanchthonian understanding of method on early Reformed systems has also been rightly highlighted by Muller. Framed as a route through the scriptural topics or *loci*, it allowed Reformed theologians to express the priority of a biblical ordering in governing systematic expression, without in any way becoming detached from logical or causal accounts of God's activity.[199] What was most important for the Reformed was that this represented the true biblical method or, as John Calvin neatly expressed this, the "right order of teaching".[200] The evolution of Calvin's *Institutes* from its early catechetical form to a pioneering and paradigmatic system of Reformed theology has been brilliantly charted by Muller.[201] At the heart of this transformation, as he notes, was Calvin's pregnant understanding of the *Institutes* as a "sum of religion in all its parts ... arranged in such an order, that if anyone rightly grasps it, it will not be difficult for him to determine especially what he ought to seek in Scripture, and to what end he ought to relate its contents". Echoing Melanchthon, Calvin held that in "paving" this road there was no longer any need to "undertake long disputations" or "wander about in the basic topics".[202] Taken up by Hyperius and others, this topical method of theology became standard in the Reformed tradition.[203]

While the use of the "commonplace" model remained prominent throughout the era of Reformed orthodoxy, the second-half of the sixteenth century saw an increasing recourse to scholastic definitions and distinctions, especially in the systematic elaboration of the individual *loci*. In this way, as Muller pointed out, Reformed scholasticism emerged from a distinctive blending of humanist and scholastic methods.[204] Throughout much of the fifteenth century, as Paul

---

[196] Muller, *Unaccommodated Calvin*, 110.
[197] Heinrich Bullinger, *Ratio Studiorum*, in *De Ratione Studiorum Opuscula Aurea*, ed. Johann Heinrich Heidegger (Zurich, 1670), 117–48, 155–56; Andreas Hyperius, *De Formandis Concionibus Sacris* (Basel, 1573); and Andreas Hyperius, *Methodi Theologiae Libri Tres* (Basel, 1567), "*Praefatio*", pp. 1–3, 21–22. See further Richard A. Muller, *After Calvin: Studies in the Development of a Theological Tradition* (Oxford: Oxford University Press, 2003), 106–7 and Mack, *Renaissance Rhetoric*, 265–66.
[198] Nauta, "From Universals to Topics", 190–224.
[199] Muller, *PRRD*, 1.177–181.
[200] Muller, *PRRD*, 1.178.
[201] Muller, *Unaccommodated Calvin*, 101–17.
[202] Muller, *Unaccommodated Calvin*, 104.
[203] Muller, *PRRD* 1.177–80.
[204] Muller, *After Calvin*, 32; *PRRD*, 1.189–208.

Kristeller has reminded us, humanism and scholasticism were often viewed as complementary methods and approaches, each with their own foci and distinctive languages.[205] Yet in both Valla and the Northern Renaissance the growing "confessionalization of humanism" and intensifying conflicts over the relation of philosophy and theology often saw humanism and scholasticism pitted against each other as rival methods, stoking a mounting tension to be unleashed in the Reformation.[206] As we will see, the early history of Ramism, as well as its subsequent development, bears ample testimony to the potency of this clash, especially as it tapped into older antagonisms between Platonism and Aristotelianism. However, Ramism in the end did little to halt the wider revival of scholasticism taking place in Protestant circles and, to varying degrees, Ramists quickly came to appropriate important aspects of this revival for themselves.

Ironically, for all his fervent attacks on medieval scholasticism, the roots of a truly Protestant scholasticism can be found in Melanchthon himself. For it was his revival of Aristotelian philosophy in the curriculum of Wittenberg that proved absolutely crucial for the subsequent movement. Through Melanchthon's role as *Praeceptor Germaniae* the Wittenberg curriculum became the inspiration for schools and universities across Germany. In studying his textbooks schoolchildren were exposed not only to Agricolan dialectic but to a purified Aristotelian logic. In the higher schools and universities this was then supplemented by complete courses in Aristotelian physics, ethics, and psychology, with metaphysics following later.[207] While Melanchthon exposed the Reformed to an Aristotelianism suffused with a definite Neo-Platonism, he was by no means the only conduit for Aristotelianism. In its repeated rescensions Calvin's *Institutes* clearly shows the growing influence of scholastic distinctions and devices in his handling of theological topics.[208] In his fellow Genevan Reformers Antoine de la Roche Chandieu and Theodore Beza we see the rise of a reinvigorated Aristotelian logic attuned to the subtleties of Scripture.[209] In the Italian Reformers Peter Martyr Vermigli and Girolamo Zanchi we see the fruits

---

[205] Paul Oskar Kristeller, *Renaissance Thought and Its Sources* (New York: Columbia University Press, 1979).
[206] James Overfield, *Humanism and Scholasticism in Late Medieval Germany* (Princeton, NJ: Princeton University Press, 2019); Rummel, *Confessionalization of Humanism*, 1–49.
[207] For Melanchthon's influence see Sachiko Kusukawa, *The Transformation of Natural Philosophy: The Case of Philip Melanchthon* (Cambridge: Cambridge University Press, 2009), 27–74, 201–10; Eckhard Kessler, "Psychology: The Intellective Soul", in *The Cambridge History of Renaissance Philosophy*, ed. Schmitt, Kessler, and Skinner, 516–18; and Lohr, "Metaphysics", 621–33.
[208] Muller, *Unaccommodated Calvin*, 39–61.
[209] Theodore G. Van Raalte, *Antoine de Chandieu: The Silver Horn of Geneva's Reformed Triumvirate* (New York: Oxford University Press, 2018), 149–204; Donald Sinnema, "Antoine de Chandieu's Call for a Scholastic Reformed Theology (1580)", in *Later Calvinism: International Perspectives*, ed. W. Fred Graham (Kirksville, MO: Sixteenth Century Journal Publishers, 1994), 173–79; and Muller, *PRRD*, 1.62.

of a rigorous Paduan training in Aristotelian logic and metaphysics applied to the study of Reformed theology.[210]

Throughout the rest of the sixteenth and seventeenth centuries, as Muller has brilliantly demonstrated, the development of Reformed scholasticism was propelled by two powerful forces. The first was the internal desire to systematize Reformed theology and teach it in an academic setting, thus going beyond the catechetical constraints of early Protestant systems. The second was the growing necessity of responding to external attacks and thus mounting a defence of Reformed orthodoxy.[211] At first, this was especially in relation to ever-more sophisticated Catholic and Lutheran attacks, but by the end of the sixteenth century there was also a pressing need to refute Anti-Trinitarians and Arminians as well.[212] The rise of Catholic Second Scholasticism especially, prompted a new depth and sophistication in Reformed logic and metaphysics, with the need to rebut formidable opponents such as Roberto Bellarmine and Francisco Suárez. Indeed, philosophical and theological conflict often proved the crucible for the testing and refining of new scholastic concepts and doctrines. Such that by the end of the seventeenth century elaborate Reformed systems of theology drawing extensively and explicitly on a whole range of medieval and early modern scholastic voices had become the norm.[213]

Recent years have seen renewed and intensified debate over the principal medieval influences on Reformed scholasticism, something especially relevant for our discussion of Ramism. While Muller's magisterial work pointed to a widespread eclecticism in Reformed scholasticism, recent debate has tended to polarize between a Calvinist Thomism and Reformed Scotism, with some acknowledgement of a broader Nominalist influence.[214] For our purposes it is important not to lose sight of a definite eclecticism, as well as an evident desire to harmonize the different schools. In part this harmonizing eclecticism stemmed from a wider late medieval and early modern Catholic enterprise to overcome the painful divisions of the fourteenth- and fifteenth-century *Wegestreit*, especially among Franciscans and Scotists keen not to be eclipsed by a resurgent Thomism; in part it reflected a marked debt to Renaissance Platonism and its wider project

---

[210] John Patrick Donnelly, *Calvinism and Scholasticism in Vermigli's Doctrine of Man and Grace* (Leiden: Brill, 1976); Luca Baschera, *Tugend und Rechtfertigung: Peter Martyr Vermiglis Kommentar zur Nikomachischen Ethik im Spannungsfeld von Philosophie und Theologie* (Zurich: Theologischer Verlag Zürich, 2008), 31–54.
[211] Muller, *PRRD*, 1.63.
[212] Muller, *PRRD*, 4.59–195; J. Martin Bac, *Perfect Will Theology: Divine Agency in Reformed Scholasticism as against Suárez, Episcopius, Descartes and Spinoza* (Leiden: Brill, 2010).
[213] Muller, *PRRD*, 1.63–67.
[214] For the eclecticism of the Reformed tradition see Muller, *After Calvin*, 28; *PRRD*, 1.67. For the polarization into opposing Thomist and Scotist camps see the discussion below. For a detailed discussion of Nominalist influence on the Reformed tradition see Simon J. G. Burton, *The Hallowing of Logic: The Trinitarian Method of Richard Baxter's Methodus Theologiae* (Leiden: Brill, 2012).

of conciliation.²¹⁵ Nevertheless, school divisions certainly remained and on certain flashpoint issues were arguably more intense than ever, as manifest in frequent conflicts between Jesuits, Dominicans, and Franciscans.²¹⁶

Of course, unlike Catholic religious orders, Protestant and Reformed thinkers owed no allegiance to any school and so their commitment to scholasticism must be conceptualized rather differently. Just like their Reformation forebears, the use of specific Thomist, Scotist, or Nominalist distinctions or devices could indeed be commensurate with a searching critique of Thomism, Scotism, or Nominalism as a whole.²¹⁷ However, in general, Reformed scholastics learned to admire both the piety and doctrine of many of their medieval counterparts.²¹⁸ Even more significantly, scholarship has pointed to loose but definite preferences among Reformed theologians for different medieval schools, so that the variety mirrored in early modern Catholic scholasticism is to some degree replicated among the Reformed—albeit within tight doctrinal and confessional constraints.²¹⁹ As Muller and others have rightly reminded us, we should be cautious of the anachronism of "-isms" of all kinds, yet used in an informed and qualified manner they can still be immensely valuable.²²⁰

One interesting way of gauging this is to look at the theologically freighted accounts of the development of scholasticism to be found in many Reformed theologians. Here it is notable that some of these espouse a "decline narrative" reminiscent of many modern scholars, in which Aquinas is seen as the zenith of scholasticism and late medieval developments are looked on with great suspicion, especially for their association with unbridled speculation and renewed Pelagianism.²²¹ By contrast, however, for other Reformed theologians, Aquinas

---

²¹⁵ The *Wegestreit* refers to the fracturing of scholasticism into rival schools, especially Realist and Nominalist. For a Scotist example of engagement with Aquinas see Johannes de Rada, *Controversiae Theologicae* (Cologne, 1620). For the Neo-Platonic dimension of harmonizing eclecticism, especially in the German context, see Christia Mercer, *Leibniz's Metaphysics: Its Origins and Development* (Cambridge: Cambridge University Press, 2001), 37–76.

²¹⁶ For examples of some of these conflicts relating to the doctrine of grace see Jordan J. Ballor, Matthew T. Gaetano, and David S. Sytsma (eds.), *Beyond Dordt and "De Auxiliis": The Dynamics of Protestant and Catholic Soteriology in the Sixteenth and Seventeenth Centuries* (Leiden: Brill, 2019).

²¹⁷ Muller, *After Calvin*, 25–46.

²¹⁸ See, for example, Richard Baxter, *A Treatise of Knowledge and Love Compared* (London, 1689), 9.

²¹⁹ Muller, *PRRD*, 1.51–52 holds that Thomist, Scotist, and Nominalist models were carried over into the Reformed tradition and represented by different theologians.

²²⁰ Richard A. Muller, "Scholasticism, Reformation, Orthodoxy, and the Persistence of Christian Aristotelianism", *Trinity Journal* 19.1 (1998): 83.

²²¹ Lambert Daneau, *In Petri Lombardi Episcopi Parisiensis Librum Primum Sententiarium Commentarius* (Geneva, 1580), "Prolegomena" offers a celebrated division of medieval scholasticism according to declining periods of *vetus*, *media*, and *nova*. Taking up this paradigm, Johann Heinrich Alsted, *Clavis Artis Lullianae et Verae Logicae Duos in Libellos Tributa* (Strasbourg, 1609), 10 is also critical of Scotus' corrupting influence on theology. See further Jordan J. Ballor, "Deformation and Reformation: Thomas Aquinas and the Rise of Protestant Scholasticism", in *Aquinas Among the Protestants*, ed. Manfred Svensson and David VanDrunen (Hoboken: Wiley, 2017), 27–48.

himself was too closely associated with Catholic doctrines such as transubstantiation and papal authority and they therefore looked more favourably to later medieval developments.[222] Indeed, in tune with an important endeavour of Protestant historiography, we even find Scotus and other fourteenth- and fifteenth-century theologians taken up as "forerunners of the Reformation".[223]

It is clear even from a cursory glance at Reformed systems of theology that their engagement with Aquinas is direct and extensive. However, it is equally evident that they interpreted Aquinas against the backdrop of centuries of debate and refinement. The Thomism encountered by the Reformed was a renewed system of doctrine codified by Johannes Capreolus and Thomas Cajetan in the fifteenth and sixteenth centuries. This sought to harmonize discrepancies between the *Summa Theologiae* and Aquinas' earlier, more Neo-Platonic, writings, ironing out ambiguities and integrating late medieval Augustinian readings.[224] In Vermigli we therefore see the influence of a Paduan Thomism shot through with important elements of the *schola Augustiniana moderna* of Rimini.[225] Similarly, in Zanchi we see the impact of a Thomism which has absorbed and assimilated important aspects of Scotism.[226] Much the same is true of Dominican theologians of the sixteenth century who were especially influenced by Thomas Bradwardine's fusion of Augustinian and Scotist conceptualities.[227] The seventeenth-century Reformed theologian John Owen engaged extensively

---

[222] See, for example, William Perkins, *The Problem of Forged Catholicism*, in *The Works of William Perkins*, ed. Joel R. Beeke and Derek W. H. Thomas, 10 vols. (Grand Rapids, MI: Reformation Heritage Books, 2014–20), 7.202, 242–43, 246–47, 254, 270, 283, 288, 298–302, 318, 321, 326, 333, 354, 376, 386–87, 398, 405–06, who while appreciative of Aquinas' anti-Pelagianism offers markedly positive citations of a whole range of late medieval theologians. See also Edward Leigh, *A Treatise of Religion and Learning and of Religious and Learned Men* (London, 1656), 96, 320 for his praise of Scotus as the "wittiest of all the schoolmen" and with Burley, Ockham, Bradwardine, and others as one of the "great lights of Europe".

[223] Samuel Rutherford, *The Due Right of Presbyteries* (London, 1644), 233 remarks that "Occam, Gerson, Scotus, in most poynts were not papists".

[224] Denis Janz, *Luther and Late Medieval Thomism: A Study in Theological Anthropology* (Waterloo: Wilfrid Laurier University Press, 1983) highlights late medieval Augustinian influences on Thomism.

[225] Frank A. James III, "Peter Martyr Vermigli: At the Crossroads of Late Medieval Scholasticism, Christian Humanism and Resurgent Augustinianism", in *Protestant Scholasticism: Essays in Reassessment*, ed. Carl Trueman and R. S. Clark (Carlisle: Paternoster, 1999), 62–78; Simon J. G. Burton, "Peter Martyr Vermigli on Grace and Free Choice: Thomist and Augustinian Perspectives", *Reformation and Renaissance Review* 15.1 (2013): 37–52.

[226] Dolf te Velde, *Paths Beyond Tracing Out: The Connection of Method and Content in the Doctrine of God, Examined in Reformed Orthodoxy, Karl Barth, and the Utrecht School* (Delft: Eburon, 2010), 33 n. 64 points to a "remarkable Scotist influence" evident in Zanchi's voluntarism.

[227] For Bradwardine's close connection to the Dominicans see Jean-François Genest, *Prédétermination et liberté créée à Oxford au XIVe siècle: Buckingham contre Bradwardine* (Paris: Vrin, 1992), 168–71. For his distinctive fusion of Thomist and Scotist conceptualities see Robert C. Sturdy, *Freedom from Fatalism: Samuel Rutherford's (1600-1661) Doctrine of Divine Providence* (Göttingen: Vandenhoeck & Ruprecht, 2021), 205–10 and Sylwanowicz, *Contingent Causality*, 210–20.

with Aquinas, but this did not prevent him from appreciating Scotus and other late medieval theologians.[228]

The myth of an unadulterated Thomism therefore needs to be firmly quashed.[229] Yet this is by no means to deny the importance and significance of "Calvinist Thomism".[230] For many of the Reformed, including the Ramists, Aquinas' analogical and exemplaristic account of reality was deeply attractive. Indeed, this has even led Muller and others to claim that the Reformed espoused not only a Thomist *analogia entis* but also the metaphysics of participation that undergirded it—although there are significant reasons for caution here.[231] Aquinas' nuanced and sophisticated Christian Aristotelianism frequently proved valuable to the Reformed in their elaboration of doctrine. Many were also drawn by his sharper distinction of faith and reason, which acted as a definite brake on unwarranted speculation into the Godhead.[232] In this way, his apophatic expression of the divine simplicity could certainly act as a counter to what was seen as the over-confidence of the Scotists in peering into the mystery of God and the Trinity—exposing a surprising affinity here between Thomism and Nominalism.[233] Appeal to Aquinas' account of God as pure act and as the "unmoved mover" behind every created motion was prominent among the Reformed, dovetailing well with their shared anti-Pelagian doctrines of grace and predestination.[234] In questions of ethics, Thomist accounts of virtue and natural law proved highly significant, albeit often interpreted through an Augustinian matrix.[235]

---

[228] Leslie, *The Light of Grace*, 41–42, 85, 157–60. For Owen's marked Thomism see Christopher Cleveland, *Thomism in John Owen* (Aldershot: Ashgate, 2013).

[229] Andreas J. Beck, *Gisbertus Voetius (1589-1676) on God, Freedom, and Contingency: An Early Modern Reformed Voice* (Leiden: Brill, 2021), 480.

[230] For an influential formulation of this thesis see John Patrick Donnelly, "Calvinist Thomism", *Viator* 7 (1976): 441–55. For an important recent discussion of Aquinas' influence see Svensson and VanDrunen (eds.), *Aquinas Among the Protestants*.

[231] For Thomist views of analogy see Muller, "Not Scotist", 127–50. For a Thomistic account of participation in the Reformed tradition see Paul Anthony Dominiak, *Richard Hooker: The Architecture of Participation* (London: T&T Clark, 2021). See below for the reasons for caution.

[232] Muller, *PRRD*, 4.151–57; cf. Aquinas, *ST*, 1a q. 12 art. 13.

[233] Muller, *PRRD*, 3.287–89. For an important seventeenth-century example of Thomist-Nominalist convergence see John Davenant, *De Praedestinatione et Reprobatione in Dissertationes Duae* (Cambridge, 1650), 108, 209. For an attack on Scotist speculation see Richard Baxter, *Richard Baxter's Catholick Theologie* (London, 1675), II. 44.

[234] Richard A. Muller, *Divine Will and Human Choice: Freedom, Contingency and Necessity in Early Modern Reformed Thought* (Grand Rapids, MI: Baker Academic, 2017), 271–72, 286; Ballor, Gaetano, and Sytsma (eds.), *Beyond Dordt and "De Auxiliis"*.

[235] While admitting eclecticism, Stephen J. Grabill, *Rediscovering the Natural Law in Reformed Theological Ethics* (Grand Rapids, MI: William B. Eerdmans, 2006) has a dominant Thomist reading. For an Augustinian reading see Simon J. G. Burton, "Between Aristotle and Augustine: Peter Martyr Vermigli and the Development of Protestant Ethics", *Studies in Medieval and Renaissance History* 11 (2014): 225–60.

Arguably, the Reformed encounter with Scotism started earlier and went deeper than their rapprochement with Thomism.[236] While vexed debates continue over Calvin's scholastic inheritance, above all his relation to the Scottish theologian John Mair, it seems clear that he was exposed to the *via moderna* scholasticism which was flourishing at the University of Paris during his time as an undergraduate there.[237] Certainly, this accounts for the distinctive blend of Scotism and Nominalism which many commentators have found throughout his *Institutes*.[238] Indeed, this debt seemed so extensive to Heiko Oberman that he even went so far as to call him "more Scotist than Scotus".[239] In the case of Huldrych Zwingli there is no need to speculate for we know that his teachers at the University of Basel, Thomas Wyttenbach, and Antonius Beck inducted him into a flourishing Scotist tradition. Indeed, Zwingli's extensive annotations on the works of Scotus, Stephen Brulefer and Conrad Summenhart still survive and, as Daniel Bolliger has convincingly argued, demonstrate his deep affinity with Scotist philosophy and theology.[240] In Wolfgang Musculus, one of the most important early Reformed systematizers, we also see a definite inheritance of medieval Franciscan and Scotist theology.[241] Chandieu likewise held Scotus in high esteem, drawing on him in support of some of his key doctrinal moves.[242] By the time we come to the seventeenth century, evidence of a profound engagement with Scotus and the Scotist school abounds. In important Reformed theologians such as William Ames, William Twisse, Samuel Rutherford, Gisbertus Voetius, Melchior Leydecker, James Sibbald, and Richard Baxter we find a distinctive

---

[236] Beck, *Voetius*, 480–81 and Ueli Zahnd, "Calvin, Calvinism, and Medieval Thought", in *The Oxford Handbook of Calvin and Calvinism*, ed. Bruce Gordon and Carl R. Trueman (Oxford: Oxford University Press, 2021), 26–42.

[237] For the classic statement of this see Karl Reuter, *Das Grundverständnis der Theologie Calvins* (Neukirchen: Verlag des Erziehungsvereins, 1963). For a cautious but positive evaluation of Calvin's relation to Mair and the Scotist tradition see John T. Slotemaker, "John Calvin's Trinitarian Theology in the 1536 *Institutes*: The Distinction of Persons as a Key to his Theological Sources", in *Philosophy and Theology in the Long Middle Ages: A Tribute to Stephen F. Brown*, ed. Kent Emery, Russell Friedman and Andreas Speer (Leiden: Brill, 2011), 781–810. For Calvin's wider relation to late medieval Scotism see Zahnd, "Calvin", 29–31.

[238] For Scotism in Calvin see Richard Muller, "Scholasticism in Calvin: A Question of Relation and Disjunction", in Wilhelm Neuser and Brian Armstrong (eds.), *Calvinus Sincerioris Religionis Vindex: Calvin as Protector of the Purer Religion* (Kirksville, MO: Sixteenth Century Journal Publishers, 1997), 247–65; Heiko Oberman, *Initia Calvini: The Matrix of Calvin's Reformation* (Amsterdam: Koninklijke Nederlandse Akademie van Wetenschappen, 1991), 10–19; and François Wendel, *Calvin: The Origins and Development of His Religious Thought*, trans. Philip Mairet (New York: Harper & Row, 1963), 127–29, 176, 231, 344–45.

[239] Cited from Oberman, *Initia Calvini*, 17–19.

[240] Daniel Bolliger, *Infiniti Contemplatio: Grundzüge der Scotus- und Scotismusrezeption im Werk Huldrych Zwinglis* (Leiden: Brill, 2003).

[241] Muller, *PRRD*, 1.51.

[242] Zahnd, "Calvin", 34–36.

Reformed Scotism, albeit one shaped by pertinent Thomist and Nominalist critiques.[243]

Axiomatic to the Reformed was the late medieval, Scotistic, principle of *finitum non capax infiniti*. Indeed, their entire theology was structured on the radical disjunction between finite and infinite, something they held to be supremely embodied in Christ.[244] For this reason it is no surprise that Richard Cross has identified Reformed Christology as basically Scotist in character.[245] Emphasis on the infinity and transcendence of God went hand-in-hand with emphasis on the infinite freedom of God. The Reformed therefore shared with Scotus the view of the contingency of the created order, underscoring the sheer gratuity of divine grace.[246] A definite commitment to a Scotist and voluntaristic ethics of freedom could also lead to a Scotistic reconfiguring of the natural law.[247] As Antonie Vos, Willem van Asselt, and others have claimed, many of the Reformed also shared Scotus' revolutionary account of synchronic contingency.[248] According to this, both the present moment of time and the undivided "moment" of eternity could be analysed according to a sequence of logical instants of nature, correlating closely with the decretal structure of Reformed theology.[249]

Drawing on this Scotist understanding importantly allowed the Reformed to hold together the divine predestination and predetermination of all things and the freedom and contingency of the human will.[250] It also fostered an important covenantal understanding of reality and a decisively practical account of theology as supremely oriented to the love of God.[251] For the Reformed, as for Scotus and the Franciscan tradition, the roots of divine freedom and covenant

---

[243] See Bac, *Perfect Will Theology*; Beck, *Voetius*; Burton, *Hallowing of Logic*; Takayuki Yagi, *A Gift from England: William Ames and His Polemical Discourse against Dutch Arminianism* (Göttingen: Vandenhoeck & Ruprecht, 2020); and Jean-Pascal Anfray, "Scottish Scotism? The Philosophical Theses in the Scottish Universities, 1610–1630", *History of Universities* 29.2 (2017): 96–120.

[244] Muller, *PRRD*, 1.222–25; 3.288; Stephen Tipton, "Defining 'Our Theology'", *Journal of Reformed Theology* 10.4 (2016): 291–313.

[245] Richard Cross, *Communicatio Idiomatum: Reformation Christological Debates* (Oxford: Oxford University Press, 2019); *Christology and Metaphysics in the Seventeenth Century* (Oxford: Oxford University Press, 2022), 149–66. Cross does suggest that this mediation may be indirect through Vermigli and Paduan Scotism.

[246] See, for example, Sturdy, *Freedom from Fatalism*.

[247] Simon J. G. Burton, "Samuel Rutherford's Euthyphro Dilemma: A Reformed Perspective on the Scholastic Natural Law Tradition", in *Reformed Orthodoxy in Scotland*, ed. Aaron C. Denlinger (London: Bloomsbury, 2015), 123–40. Rutherford suggests such an attitude was more widespread among the Reformed.

[248] Antonie Vos, "Scholasticism and Reformation", in *Reformation and Scholasticism: An Ecumenical Enterprise*, ed. Willem J. van Asselt and Eef Dekker (Grand Rapids: Baker, 2001), 99–119; Willem J. van Asselt, J. Martin Bac, and Roelf T. te Velde (eds.), *Reformed Thought on Freedom: The Concept of Free Choice in Early Modern Reformed Theology* (Grand Rapids, MI: Baker Academic, 2010); and Bac, *Perfect Will Theology*.

[249] Vos, *Philosophy*, 245–49.

[250] This is the principal thesis of Van Asselt, Bac, and Te Velde, *Reformed Thought on Freedom*.

[251] Muller, *PRRD*, 1.340–55.

were to be found in the Trinity itself.[252] While generally more cautious than late medieval and early modern Scotists, there were certainly prominent Reformed theologians for whom Scotus' formal distinction was fundamental for offering a metaphysical account of all reality from the Trinity downwards, buttressing a strong Realism and exemplarism.[253]

Similarly, although more of a minority report, there were also Reformed and Ramist theologians who followed Scotus in holding a logical, univocal core to analogical predication.[254] Moreover, whether or not they affirmed univocity, there can be no doubt that Scotus' transcendental account of being ran deep in the Reformed tradition, with many Reformed metaphysicians rejecting Aquinas' hallmark doctrine of essence-existence composition in creatures.[255] Likewise, Giovanni Gellera has detected a broad and eclectic Scotism running through Reformed metaphysics and epistemology.[256] Overall, on the basic criteria for medieval Scotism set out by Maarten Hoenen and others—namely espousing univocity, the formal distinction, synchronic contingency, and instants of nature—many of the Reformed score highly with some even meeting the much higher bar set by early modern Scotists.[257]

In the final analysis it must be said that what bound the Reformed tightly together, whether Calvinist Thomist, Reformed Scotist, or Nominalist, was an overarching commitment to an Augustinian and biblical pattern of theology. Of course, there is no question that this came from a profound encounter with Augustine's own works, but their reading of Augustine was also undoubtedly

---

[252] For Trinity and covenant in the Reformed tradition see Willem J. van Asselt, *The Federal Theology of Johannes Cocceius (1603–1669)* (Leiden: Brill, 2001) and John V. Fesko, *The Covenant of Redemption: Origins, Development, and Reception* (Göttingen: Vandenhoeck & Ruprecht, 2016). For late medieval resonances see Samuel Rutherford, *The Covenant of Life Opened* (Edinburgh, 1655), 24, 306–7 and Burton, *Hallowing of Logic*, 79–87.

[253] Muller, *PRRD*, 3.295–96; 4.170; Beck, *Voetius*, 263.

[254] Beck, *Voetius*, 235–39; Burton, *Hallowing of Logic*, 213–14; Giovanni Gellera, "Univocity of Being, the *Cogito* and Idealism in Johannes Clauberg (1622–1655)", in *Cognitive Issues in the Long Scotist Tradition*, ed. Daniel Heider and Claus A. Andersen (Basel: Schwabe-Verlag, 2023), 417–46. It is worth noting that Reformed attacks on univocity were usually on a metaphysical plane and so it is possible that more were open to Scotus' logical account of univocity than may appear at first sight.

[255] See Ludger Honnefelder, *Scientia transcendens: Die formale Bestimmung der Seiendheit und Realität in der Metaphysik des Mittelalters und der Neuzeit (Duns Scotus, Suárez, Wolff, Kant, Peirce)* (Hamburg: Felix Meiner, 1990) for a discussion of the important Scotist and transcendental impulse of early modern metaphysics. For important examples of Reformed attacks on essence-existence composition see Giovanni Gellera, "Natural Philosophy in the Graduation Theses of the Scottish Universities in the First Half of the Seventeenth Century" (PhD Dissertation, University of Glasgow, 2012), 41–43. See also below.

[256] Giovanni Gellera, "Reformed Scholastic Philosophy in the Seventeenth-Century Scottish Universities", in *Scottish Philosophy in the Seventeenth Century*, ed. Alexander Broadie (Oxford: Oxford University Press, 2020), 94–110; "Univocity of Being", 417–46; and "Natural Philosophy".

[257] For the essential criteria of Scotism see Hoenen, "Scotus and the Scotist School", 197–210 and Burton, *Hallowing of Logic*, 12. For more maximalist criteria relating to early modern Scotism see Anfray, "Scottish Scotism?", 96–120.

shaped by both the medieval systematization of Augustinian theology and the recent conflict, renewed and intensified at the Reformation, between Augustinians and "modern Pelagians".[258] Yet, arguably, the intense focus on the Reformed reception of the Augustinian doctrine of grace and predestination has detracted from a wider engagement with Christian Augustinianism in its rich Neo-Platonic, exemplaristic, and illuminationist dimensions. Likewise, the possibility of a broader engagement with Augustinian and Franciscan currents of theology, not least with Bonaventure, has been generally neglected.[259] For all the necessary and valuable focus on Christian Aristotelianism and scholasticism, it is important to reconsider the Platonic inheritance of the Reformed tradition. Platonism—at least Christian Platonism—and Reformed theology were by no means antithetical as Muller and others have sometimes suggested, and there was a definite legacy of Reformed Platonism, above all in the Ramist tradition.[260]

One important aspect of this, highlighted by Ann Blair and David Sytsma, was the Reformed commitment to a Christian or Mosaic philosophy, which owed much to Augustine, as well as a wider patristic and medieval tradition of hexameral thought.[261] Once again Melanchthon stands at the fountainhead of this important Protestant tradition. For, as Sachiko Kusukawa has insightfully argued, creatively correlating the Lutheran dichotomy of Law and Gospel with philosophy and theology enabled him to argue the need for a far-reaching scriptural transformation of philosophy.[262] Significantly, Melanchthon followed the medieval Augustinians and Franciscans in highlighting Aristotle's major departures from Scripture.[263] He also drew deeply on Neo-Platonic and Neo-Pythagorean understandings, holding that mathematics and mathematical proportions revealed the divine footsteps throughout all creation.[264] Going

---

[258] For the classic account of the Reformation and late medieval Augustinianism see Heiko A. Oberman, *The Dawn of the Reformation: Essays in Late Medieval and Early Reformation Thought* (Edinburgh: T&T Clark, 1986), 39–83. For late medieval Augustinian influence on the wider Reformed tradition see Frank A. James III, *Peter Martyr Vermigli and Predestination: The Augustinian Inheritance of an Italian Reformer* (Oxford: Clarendon Press, 1998); Sturdy, *Freedom from Fatalism*, 205–10; and Ueli Zahnd, "The Early John Calvin and Augustine: Some Reconsiderations", *Studia Patristica* 87 (2017): 193–94.

[259] Muller, *PRRD*, 1.319, 336, 385 gives some attention to Bonaventure's influence but this is disproportionately much less than his discussion of the influence of Aquinas and Scotus.

[260] Muller, *PRRD*, 1.67–68, 144–45. Muller, "Not Scotist", 145 does point to a Platonising tendency among a minority of the Reformed. Dewey Wallace Jr., *Shapers of English Calvinism, 1660-1714: Variety, Persistence and Transformation* (Oxford: Oxford University Press, 2011) and Eric M. Parker, "Cambridge Platonism(s): John Sherman and Peter Sterry", in *Revisioning Cambridge Platonism: Sources and Legacy*, ed. Douglas Hedley and David Leech (Dordrecht: Springer, 2020), 31–46 give fresh attention to this Reformed Platonism.

[261] Blair, "Mosaic Physics", 32–58; David S. Sytsma, "Calvin, Daneau and the 'Physica Mosaica': Neglected Continuities at the Origins of an Early Modern Tradition", *Church History and Religious Culture* 95.4 (2015): 457–76.

[262] Kusukawa, *Transformation*, 27ff.

[263] Kusukawa, *Transformation*, 43–44.

[264] Philipp Melanchthon, *Melanchthon: Orations on Philosophy and Education*, ed. Sachiko Kusukawa and trans. Christine F. Salazar (Cambridge: Cambridge University Press, 1999), 91–92.

beyond this Melanchthon delighted in following Augustine in *De Doctrina Christiana* in tracing the origin of all arts and sciences back, through Moses and the Patriarchs, to God and an Edenic paradigm of knowledge.[265]

Notably, we find similar notions in Calvin for whom the whole universe was a theatre of God's glory and an image and mirror of the Power, Wisdom, and Goodness of the Trinity.[266] Calvin likewise praised Plato above other philosophers and could be sharply critical of the unbiblical character of Aristotelian philosophy.[267] In espousing an Augustinian framework of illumination and affirming the origin of all the arts in God we can therefore certainly speak of him, as Pekka Kärkkäinen has done, as championing a Christian philosophy.[268] While in Lambert Daneau and Zanchi the Mosaic philosophy entered a more Aristotelian phase, its Augustinian critique of the excesses of Aristotelian philosophy is still clear.[269] Taken up into the Ramist movement this Augustinian and Neo-Platonic dimension of Reformed scriptural philosophy was once again to become dominant and definitive.

## I.5. Ramist Itinerary

In Ramus, the Reformation met the Franciscan Reformation of method. Indeed, in the movement that he birthed we see the convergence of the Middle Ages, Renaissance, and Reformation at a vital crossroads in European history. Inheriting the methodological revolution of Agricola and Melanchthon, Ramus combined their insights with important Neo-Platonic and mystical elements from his native French reform to fashion a new divine dialectic capable of revealing the truth not only of Scripture but also of all the arts and sciences.[270] In doing so, he constructed a new Christian philosophy grounded on Neo-Platonic, Realist, and exemplaristic principles and resonating profoundly with the Augustinian and Franciscan ideals of a previous age.

---

[265] Melanchthon, *Orations*, 239, 246.

[266] John Calvin, *Institutes of the Christian Religion*, trans. Henry Beveridge (Grand Rapids, MI: Eerdmans, 1989), 1.5.3; 1.6.2–3; 1.13.18. See further Susan E. Schreiner, *The Theater of His Glory: Nature and the Natural Order in the Thought of John Calvin* (Durham, NC: Labyrinth Press, 1991).

[267] Pekka Kärkkäinen, "Philosophy Among and in the Wake of the Reformers: Luther, Melanchthon, Zwingli, and Calvin", in *The Routledge Companion to Sixteenth Century Philosophy*, ed. Henrik Lagerlund and Benjamin Hill (New York: Routledge, 2016), 198.

[268] Calvin, *Institutes*, 1.7.5; 2.2.14–16; Sytsma, "Calvin", 464; and Kärkkäinen, "Philosophy", 198. Kärkkäinen only makes a general link to Augustine here.

[269] Muller, *PRRD*, 1.137–38; Kusukawa, *Transformation*, 205–7.

[270] For connections with Agricola and Melanchthon see Ong, *Ramus, Method, and the Decay of Dialogue*, 236–39.

While Ramus' Platonic dialectic came under heavy attack from Aristotelians and scholastics across Europe, its Realist and exemplaristic desire to frame method according to a divine and objective order of reality proved deeply attractive to many, dovetailing with the topical Realism of the Agricolan tradition. At the same time, Ramus' relation to Aristotelianism was complex, and the malleability and flexibility of his dialectic proved to be one of its greatest strengths, able to assimilate the variety of humanist and scholastic logics under the overarching canopy of his method. In this Ramism took on an eclectic shape, albeit one profoundly shaped by Franciscan and Scotist thought. Ramism flourished most among the Reformed philosophers and theologians who are the focus of this book, but its presence in Lutheran and even Catholic thought is testimony to its broader appeal. Indeed, the fact that we find the same Bonaventuran and Scotist themes recurring in Reformed, Lutheran, and Catholic contexts only serves to confirm the deep affinities which contemporaries perceived between Ramist and Franciscan method.[271]

True to its turbulent origins, Ramism itself never stood still. In the century following Ramus' own dramatic death it went through an important process of confessionalization and transformation, combining successively with Philippist (Melanchthonian), scholastic, Lullist, and covenantal methods in order to achieve a Trinitarian and scriptural reconfiguration of all of knowledge, and a comprehensive reform of Church and society. At a time when Christendom was fracturing into deep and enduring faultlines, Ramism held up a compelling vision of the transcendent unity of all truth in God. While Ramus may have proven the only martyr for his art, many willingly faced opposition to follow in his footsteps. For them it was a journey which promised to lead not only back to Eden itself but also forward to the very dawn of a new Heaven and Earth. It is to the story of this Ramist itinerary that we now turn.

---

[271] For Franciscan themes in the Catholic Ramist and mystic Benet of Canfield see Emery, "Introduction", 39–44. For Franciscan and Scotist themes in the Lutheran Bishop and Ramist Brynjolf Sveinsson see Gunnar Hardarson, "The Method of Exposition in Brynjolf Sveinsson's 'Commentary' (1640) on the *Dialecticae* of Petrus Ramus", in *Ramus, Pedagogy and the Liberal Arts: Ramism in Britain and the Wider World*, ed. Steven J. Reid and Emma Annette Wilson (Aldershot: Ashgate, 2011), 197–98.

# 1
# Divine Dialectic
## Ramus, Method, and the Ascent to God

In his own day, Peter Ramus was surrounded by a storm of controversy. As the son of a poor charcoal-burner who rose to become Regius Professor and Dean at the University of Paris and one of Europe's leading intellectuals, it was unsurprising that he should attract so much attention. Regarded by some as a heretic and radical who sought to dismantle everything sacred in Church and society, he was hailed by others as a hero and a martyr for the cause of Reformation. Ramus' contested reputation stems from his strident attack on Aristotelian logic right at the beginning of his career, as well as his own bold claim to have rediscovered and revived a dialectical method which went back not only to Plato but also through Moses and the Patriarchs to the very dawn of the human race. Compounding all this, Ramus' later conversion to Protestantism, in the midst of early modern Europe's bloodiest wars of religion, raised the stakes considerably. For it connected his developing methodology to a frontal assault on Catholic scholasticism and its philosophical moorings.[1] To do this in Paris, the home of scholasticism, must have appeared either the height of boldness or reckless audacity, and it is no surprise that Ramus' views polarized his contemporaries, almost as much as the religious controversies of the day. In fact, arguably they did so all the more due to his own profound entwining of method and reform.[2]

Nearly four hundred years later, Ramus' legacy continues to be divisive. Since the pioneering work of Walter Ong and Perry Miller, few can really doubt his significance or his influence, but the reasons for this remain hotly debated.[3] For decades, Ong's landmark study *Ramus, Method, and the Decay of Dialogue* has proved absolutely fundamental in gauging the reasons behind his success. In a brilliant piece of deconstruction, he argued that Ramism itself was a facile and superficial movement of logical simplification whose true significance lay not in

---

[1] James Skalnik, *Ramus and Reform: University and Church at the End of the Renaissance* (Kirksville, MO: Truman State University Press, 2002), 92 notes that "nothing did his reputation among Catholics more damage than his repeated attacks on Aristotle".
[2] See Ong, *Ramus, Method, and the Decay of Dialogue*, 214–24 for an account of Ramus' most prominent opponents.
[3] Miller, *New England Mind*, 64–238 and Ong, *Ramus, Method, and the Decay of Dialogue*, 295–320.

*Ramism and the Reformation of Method*. Simon J. G. Burton, Oxford University Press. © Oxford University Press 2024.
DOI: 10.1093/oso/9780197516355.003.0002

its intellectual content, which according to him was negligible, but in its relation to the printing and educational revolution of early modernity. Ramus' "spatialization" of logic, as witnessed by his famous dichotomous charts which became so ubiquitous in early modernity, proved ideally suited to the layout of the printed page, fuelling the rise of the mass-produced, mass-market textbook. Yet, for Ong, Ramus' topical approach represented a radical oversimplification of logic, the supreme triumph of method over content.[4]

Despite Wilhelm Risse's more sympathetic assessment, scholars such as Jennifer Ashworth, Anthony Grafton, and Lisa Jardine have all concurred with this judgement, seeing in Ramism the nadir of early modern logic and the precipitous decline from humanism to the humanities.[5] Siding with Ong, as well as Ramus' many contemporary Parisian critics, Ashworth can only see in Ramism the utter debasement of Aristotelian and scholastic logic, stripping it of any worth for precise, technical argumentation. For her, Ramism marks the culmination of a Renaissance collapse of logic into rhetoric before its later sixteenth- and seventeenth-century revival under second scholasticism.[6] Going beyond Ashworth, and here siding with Ramus' humanist critics, Grafton and Jardine argue that Ramus' overriding concern for the methodization and systematization of knowledge undermined the humanist goal of a unified pursuit of knowledge, reducing it into a loose plurality of disciplines neatly packaged for classroom consumption.[7]

Taking this further, others such as Mordechai Feingold detach Ramism from the wider culture of Renaissance humanism, effectively writing him out of the Republic of Letters that Grafton has done so much to reconstruct.[8] Indeed, the view that, for Ramus, pedagogy trumps scholarship has become widespread, with Feingold, Dmitri Levitin, and Jonathan Sheehan all holding that Ramism was essentially foreign to the early modern culture of erudition and pursuit of ancient wisdom.[9] Even Ramus' much-vaunted Platonism, memorably reconstructed by

---

[4] Ong, *Ramus, Method, and the Decay of Dialogue*, 149–213.

[5] Wilhelm Risse, *Die Logik der Neuzeit: 1. Band. 1500–1640* (Stuttgart-Bad Canstatt: Friedrich Frommann Verlag, 1964), 122–200; E. J. Ashworth, *Language and Logic in the Post-Medieval Period* (Dordrecht: Springer Netherlands, 2012), 15–17; and Anthony Grafton and Lisa Jardine, *From Humanism to the Humanities: Education and the Liberal Arts in Fifteenth- and Sixteenth-Century Europe* (London: Duckworth, 1986), 161–200.

[6] Ong, *Ramus, Method, and the Decay of Dialogue*, 24, 208–12 and Ashworth, *Language and Logic*, 15–17.

[7] Grafton and Jardine, *Humanism*, 161–200.

[8] Mordechai Feingold, "English Ramism: A Reinterpretation", in *The Influence of Petrus Ramus: Studies in Sixteenth and Seventeenth Century Philosophy and Sciences*, ed. Mordechai Feingold, Joseph S. Freedman, and Wolfgang Rother (Basel: Schwabe & Co., 2001), 156–59 seeks to defend the claim that "Ramus can not be truly regarded as a humanist according to the expansive discernment of the ideal by his contemporaries". While more balanced, Hotson, *Commonplace Learning*, 52–68 comes to a similar conclusion.

[9] Feingold, "English Ramism", 127–76; Dmitri Levitin, *Ancient Wisdom in the Age of the New Science: Histories of Philosophy in England, c. 1640–1700* (Cambridge: Cambridge University Press,

Nelly Bruyère, has been subjected to a searching critique by Erland Sellberg.[10] Following Ong, Sellberg seeks to detach Ramism from any transcendent moorings, claiming it ultimately for a Nominalist, individualizing view of reality.[11] For all these scholars, Ramism becomes associated with a narrative of watering-down, fragmentation, or dissolution—the "end of the Renaissance" as much as the end of the Middle Ages.[12]

Much more positive accounts of Ramus' influence have been offered by both Howard Hotson and James Skalnik. In particular, Hotson has deftly pointed to the way in which the encyclopaedic and transformative dimensions of Ramism proved attractive to many and helped to fuel Reformed confessionalization.[13] Likewise, Skalnik has highlighted an important idealistic and theological component to Ramism, seen especially in Ramus' drive to recreate a lost, golden age of civilization, whether Christian or Classical in character.[14] Following the trajectory established by Ong, both thinkers rightly emphasise the importance of Ramism as a movement of pedagogical simplification and utility.[15] For Skalnik, this relates especially to the social consequences of his reform, above all the attempt to preserve a meritocratic society and egalitarian Church in the face of the looming twin threats of *Ancien Régime* France and Presbyterian Geneva.[16]

Without discounting in any way the social or pedagogical dimensions of Ramist reform, this chapter offers a rather different account of the significance of Ramus and his method. For its fundamental claim—building on that of the previous chapter—is that Ramus' logic and method belongs to a long tradition of Neo-Platonic, Realist, and exemplaristic reflection, with deep roots in Augustinian and Franciscan theology, but which came to full fruition in the Lullist and Cusan reform of Jacques Lefèvre d'Étaples and the Fabrist circle. Such a claim resonates with Perry Miller's insights into the medieval origins of Ramism, and fits closely with narratives of the methodological continuity between Lullism and Ramism put forward variously by Frances Yates, Paolo Rossi,

---

2015), 150; and Jonathan Sheehan, "From Philology to Fossils: The Biblical Encyclopedia in Early Modern Europe", *Journal of the History of Ideas* 64.1 (2003): 43–48.

[10] Ernand Sellberg, "Petrus Ramus", *Stanford Encyclopedia of Philosophy*, https://plato.stanford.edu/entries/ramus is critical of Bruyère's claim. See further Nelly Bruyère, *Méthode et dialectique dans l'oeuvre de La Ramée: Renaissance et âge classique* (Paris: J. Vrin, 1984).

[11] Ong, *Ramus, Method, and the Decay of Dialogue*, 199–210, 306–18, Bruyère, *Méthode et Dialectique*, 255–65, and Sellberg, "Petrus Ramus" all associate Ramus with Nominalism.

[12] Skalnik, *Ramus and Reform* positions Ramus at the "end of the Renaissance" but in an opposite sense to Grafton and Jardine.

[13] See Hotson, "Instauration"; and *Commonplace Learning*, 153–273.

[14] Skalnik, *Ramus and Reform*, 88–115, 148–58. Robert Goulding, *Defending Hypatia: Ramus, Savile, and the Renaissance Rediscovery of Mathematical History* (Dordrecht: Springer, 2010), 35–56 also emphasizes this aspect of Ramus' reform.

[15] The pragmatic dimension of Ramism is emphasized in Hotson, *Commonplace Learning*, 25–37.

[16] Skalnik, *Ramus and Reform*, 35–87, 116–47.

Kent Emery, and Grazia Olivieri.[17] It also connects to recent studies by Robert Goulding, Giovanna Cifoletti, and Timothy Reiss, which have rightly insisted on the mathematical and combinatorial dimensions of Ramist logic.[18] While the Neo-Pythagorean revival of the fifteenth and sixteenth centuries has been brilliantly mapped out by David Albertson and Richard Oosterhoff, the deeper roots of Ramism in the Fabrist and Cusan tradition have not yet been plumbed, nor its profound connection to the Franciscan Reformation of method.[19]

In seeking to explore the connections between Ramus and the Fabrists, one of the principal goals of this chapter is to reconnect Ramism to the evangelical and mystical milieu in which it had its genesis. It has become too easy to forget that Ramus was educated at a university which had undergone profound changes as a result of the Fabrist influence and in which Lullism was still very much "in the air".[20] Indeed, one need only look at a contemporary work like Rabelais' *Pantagruel*, whose earliest publication post-dates Ramus' matriculation at Paris, to gauge just how deeply Neo-Platonism and Lullism still registered in Parisian intellectual culture.[21] The Fabrist influence on religious culture was, if anything, even more pronounced. Ramus' early education took place in the wake of the abortive evangelical reforms of the Fabrist circle. As Jonathan Reid has argued, the influence of Lefèvre and the Fabrists continued to be deeply felt in France long after the failure of their endeavours and it would be surprising, to say the least, to find Ramus untouched by it.[22]

For Ramus and his many followers, his method was at the vanguard of the Reformed quest to remake the world. However, to truly understand or appreciate

---

[17] Miller, *New England Mind*, 111–206; Yates, *Art of Memory*, 234–35; Rossi, *Logic and the Art of Memory*, 97–129; Emery, "Introduction", 26–44; and Grazia Tonelli Olivieri, "Ideale Lulliano e Dialettica Ramista: Le 'Dialecticae Institutiones' del 1543", *Annali della Scuola Normale Superiore di Pisa* 22.3 (1992): 885–929.

[18] Goulding, *Defending Hypatia*, 19–33; Giovanna Cifoletti, "From Valla to Viète: The Rhetorical Reform of Logic and Its Use in Early Modern Algebra", *Early Science and Medicine* 11.4 (2006): 390–423; Timothy J. Reiss, "From Trivium to Quadrivium: Ramus, Method and Mathematical Technology", in *The Renaissance Computer: Knowledge Technology in the First Age of Print*, ed. Neil Rhodes and Jonathan Sawday (London: Routledge, 2000), 43–56; and *Knowledge, Discovery and Imagination in Early Modern Europe: The Rise of Aesthetic Rationalism* (Cambridge: Cambridge University Press, 1997), 108–18. The Fabrist dimension of this project is acknowledged by Cifoletti, "From Valla to Viète", 399–400.

[19] See Albertson, *Mathematical Theologies* and Richard J. Oosterhoff, *Making Mathematical Culture: University and Print in the Circle of Lefèvre d'Étaples* (Oxford: Oxford University Press, 2018). Emery, "Introduction", 39 touches on Ramus' link to Franciscanism.

[20] Olivieri, "Ideale Lulliano", 914 calls Lullism a "fundamental component" of sixteenth-century French culture.

[21] See John Lewis, "Rabelais and the Reception of the 'Art' of Ramón Lull in Early Sixteenth-Century France", *Renaissance Studies* 24.2 (2010): 260–80 and Victor, "The Revival of Lullism at Paris, 1499–1516".

[22] Jonathan Reid, *King's Sister, Queen of Dissent: Marguerite of Navarre (1492–1549) and Her Evangelical Network*, 2 vols. (Leiden: Brill, 2009), I.249ff. and II.379ff. chart the fortunes of Marguerite of Navarre's evangelical network, which was closely entwined with the Fabrist network, from the disaster at Meaux to the Wars of Religion.

Ramism's reforming impulse we first need to uncover its deeper metaphysical and theological presuppositions. It is only then that the true social consequences of Ramism will become fully apparent. In many ways, this chapter is therefore the pivot on which the rest of the book turns. Its principal focus is on Ramus' dialectic, and especially his *Institutiones Dialecticae* of 1543, his first major work and the one in which, as all commentators are agreed, the Neo-Platonic character of Ramus' thought shines through most clearly. However, while scholars have been nearly unanimous in arguing for a major break between the 1543 dialectic and all subsequent editions, this chapter argues for an important continuity of Neo-Platonic and exemplaristic themes even in Ramus' mature thought. Throughout it maintains that Ramus' pioneering account of method must be seen in the light of the Franciscan quest for a Christian philosophy. At the same time, it presents his revolutionary new understanding of dialectic and method as part of an unfolding Cusan and Fabrist movement of reform.

## 1.1. Evangelical and Mystical Milieu

When Ramus arrived at the University of Paris as a young undergraduate in the late 1520s he encountered a university culture profoundly shaped by both scholastic and humanist thought. Throughout much of the Middle Ages Paris had reigned supreme as the queen of scholasticism. At its height in the thirteenth and fourteenth centuries, Aquinas, Bonaventure, and Scotus had all taught there, not to mention a host of other eminent philosophers and theologians. While by the fifteenth and sixteenth centuries, Paris' crown was no longer undisputed, it still remained a thriving centre of scholasticism. Indeed, the university saw a major flowering of scholastic logic during this period under a succession of eminent professors such as Thomas Bricot, Stephen Brulefer, Pierre Tartaret, and above all John Mair. While Mair himself was a Nominalist, he was profoundly influenced by Scotism, and by all accounts this remained the dominant school in the early sixteenth century.[23]

At the same time, Paris also became the home of a new and vibrant French humanist movement. While this had its roots in Jean Gerson and native currents of French reform, it was deeply touched by the spirit of the Italian Renaissance and Neo-Platonism, with the Habsburg-Valois wars at the end of the fifteenth century intensifying the cultural exchange between France and Italy.[24] It was also influenced by the wider streams of Christian humanism, mysticism, and

---

[23] Cited from Oosterhoff, *Making Mathematical Culture*, 68.
[24] Augustin Renaudet, *Préréforme et humanisme à Paris pendant les premieres guerres d'Italie (1494-1517)* (Paris: Librairie Ancienne Honoré Champion, 1916), 114–59 and Guy Bedouelle, *Lefèvre d'Étaples et l'intelligence des écritures* (Geneva: Droz, 1976), 7–12.

the *devotio moderna* characteristic of the Northern Renaissance. Through the influence of Bartholomew Latomus, Desiderius Erasmus, and Johannes Sturm the new Agricolan logic penetrated deeply into Parisian humanism. Latomus' commentary on Agricola's *De Dialectica Inventione* was widely read in Paris and formed the "immediate prelude" to Ramus' own innovations.[25] Sturm, Ramus' own teacher, made Agricola's dialectic the centrepiece of his model gymnasium in Strasbourg.[26] In Erasmus we find Agricola's topical logic marshalled into an even more ambitious programme of reform, offering a new dialectical approach to theology against the rigid syllogistic logic of the scholastics.[27]

In Lefèvre d'Étaples and the Fabrist circle we see the confluence of all these movements, combined with an intense evangelical and mystical drive for further reform. Methodologically, the Fabrists were supreme innovators and their attempts to harness logic, metaphysics, and mathematics into a coordinated encyclopaedic and theological system were truly groundbreaking, paving the way for Ramus' own impressive breakthroughs. Indeed, it is important to remember that Lefèvre first came to prominence, as Oosterhoff has well reminded us, as an educational pioneer and writer of innovative textbooks. Covering the whole corpus of Aristotle, as well as a whole range of philosophical and theological topics, the Fabrist textbooks were landmarks of accessibility and became immensely popular among Parisian students.[28] Marking a decisive shift from the scholastic culture of disputation, they initiated a new humanist culture of textbook pedagogy. Replete with indices and organized according to keywords, sub-headings, tables, and diagrams, they were designed entirely with the convenience of students in mind.[29] They also played a crucial role in the genesis of method, enabling the structure of an entire discipline from its "broadest headings down to [its] narrowest subcategories" to be seen at almost a single glance.[30] For the Fabrists, method came to be seen as a "conceptual map" providing a route through all the different disciplines—a notion prominent in Melanchthon and with deep roots in the medieval topical tradition.[31]

---

[25] Ong, *Ramus, Method, and the Decay of Dialogue*, 126–30.
[26] Ong, *Ramus, Method, and the Decay of Dialogue*, 232–36. Hotson, *Reformation of Common Learning*, 271 identifies Sturm as Ramus' teacher.
[27] See R. J. Schoeck, "Agricola and Erasmus: Erasmus' Inheritance of Northern Humanism", in *Rodolphus Agricola Phrisius 1444-1485: Proceedings of the International Conference at the University of Groningen 28-30 October 1585*, ed. Fokke Akkerman and Arjo J. Vanderjagt (Leiden: Brill, 1988), 181–88.
[28] For full documentation of their impressive publication record see Jacques Lefèvre d'Étaples, *The Prefatory Epistles of Jacques Lefèvre d'Étaples and Related Texts*, ed. Eugene F. Rice Jr. (New York: Columbia University Press, 1972).
[29] Oosterhoff, *Making Mathematical Culture*, 86–87, 111–21.
[30] Oosterhoff, *Making Mathematical Culture*, 98–111. The quote is from figure 4.3.
[31] Oosterhoff, *Making Mathematical Culture*, 113, 179. See further Ong, *Ramus, Method, and the Decay of Dialogue*, 237.

Some of the earliest of these textbooks were in logic and in these Lefèvre sought to reframe Parisian Scotism and terminism according to new humanist priorities.[32] Following the wider Agricolan turn, Lefèvre organized his own dialectic according to an overarching pattern of *proloquia*, judgement and invention, which he parsed in terms of the classification of reality, the formation of propositions and the fitting of subject matter to argument.[33] For Lefèvre, it was important that logic should correspond to the underlying structure of reality.[34] In Charles de Bovelles, his close friend and collaborator, we find this conviction expressed according to a nascent Realist and Scotist understanding.[35] It was therefore only natural for the Fabrists to regard logic as a gateway to the entire encyclopaedia, providing the definitions, divisions and rules according to which all the other arts and sciences are structured and organized.

Following in a long Augustinian and Franciscan tradition the Fabrists attempted their own comprehensive fusion of philosophy and theology. While Lefèvre championed the "sacred philosophy" of Aristotle, his own approach to this was often intensely Neo-Platonic in character. In 1492, before embarking on his Parisian career, Lefèvre made a celebrated journey to Italy in which he met the great Florentine Platonists Ficino and Pico.[36] Their influence on his early thought was profound and undoubtedly influenced his encyclopaedic turn. Like Pico, he was soon seeking a "concord" of Aristotle and Plato, and a new scriptural philosophy.[37] For Lefèvre, all philosophical truth could be seen as a kind of divine revelation or illumination.[38] Contrasting sharply the divine Sun of biblical revelation with the broad and diffuse light of pagan thought,[39] he sought a new Christian approach to philosophy. Augustine was of great importance to such a quest, of course, but of even greater importance was Pseudo-Dionysius, whom Lefèvre still believed—despite the doubts of Valla—to be the disciple of the Apostle Paul and the greatest exponent of his theology.[40] For the Fabrists the "highest reading of Dionysius' theology" was made by the "seraphic

---

[32] Lefèvre, *Prefatory Epistles*, 190–91.
[33] Richard J. Oosterhoff, "Jacques Lefèvre d'Étaples", *Stanford Encyclopedia of Philosophy*, https://plato.stanford.edu/entries/lefevre-etaples/.
[34] For Lefèvre's Realism see Oosterhoff, "Jacques Lefèvre d'Étaples".
[35] Victor, *Charles de Bovelles*, 75 stresses the convergence of logic and metaphysics in Bovelles.
[36] Bedouelle, *Lefèvre d'Étaples*, 11–16.
[37] Lefèvre, *Prefatory Epistles*, 21. Bedouelle, *Lefèvre d'Étaples*, 15–16 argues that Pico had a deeper impression on Lefèvre's theological formation. The central role of Pico in the Fabrist circle is also made clear in Emmanuel Faye, "Nicolas de Cues et Charles de Bovelles dans le manuscrit 'Exigua pluvia' de Beatus Rhenanus", *Archives d'Histoire Doctrinale et Littéraire du Moyen Âge* 65 (1998): 418–20.
[38] Lefèvre, *Prefatory Epistles*, 4.
[39] Lefèvre, *Prefatory Epistles*, 60–61; cf. Bedouelle, *Lefèvre d'Étaples*, 41–43.
[40] Oosterhoff, *Making Mathematical Culture*, 43–44.

commentaries" of Bonaventure as well as the "sublime philosophy" of Cusa,[41] and to these august names we can surely add that of Lull, whom Lefèvre regarded as one of the greatest Christian mystics.[42]

Viewed from this Dionysian and Franciscan vantage-point it made complete sense to the Fabrists to see Aristotle's thought as a connected and tightly knit system, and its various disciplines as rungs on a mystical ladder enabling ascent from sensibles to intelligible and divine things.[43] In Neo-Platonic fashion logic could be viewed as the "parent of all other arts", the wellspring from which they all flowed and the radiant light from which they emanated.[44] Transcending logic, however, Lefèvre could also speak of a "hidden and secret analogy" which binds together and "animates" the whole encyclopaedia.[45] The search for this analogy was to occupy the Fabrists for many years but, as Oosterhoff has revealed, they came to develop an expansive mathematical understanding of it as a kind of "art of arts" capable of connecting the trivium and quadrivium together in a powerful synthesis.[46]

Notably, Lull's own Art, with its dynamic combinatorial character, became vital to the Fabrists in expressing this new mathematical encyclopaedism. For Lefèvre, its attraction lay especially in its claim to be a universal method, capable of expressing and ordering that Neo-Platonic dialectic of unity and multiplicity, according to which "singulars diverge to infinity and universals truly collect themselves to unity".[47] A similar conviction is evident in Bovelles' 1510 *Ars Oppositorum*, which employs Lullist methodology to elicit the "concordances" and "differences" of all things.[48] For Bovelles, this art of opposites mediates between unity and multiplicity by arranging all things hierarchically in terms of genus, species, and individual. As a student of Tartaret, he characterized these implicitly according to Scotus' formal distinction.[49] In Realist and exemplaristic fashion, logic and all the other arts are therefore intended to mirror the intrinsic structure of reality, such that "every discipline begins from genus and is terminated in species".[50] Indeed, Bovelles could even set out at the beginning

---

[41] Beatus Rhenanus, *Briefwechsel des Beatus Rhenanus*, ed. Adalbert Horawitz and Karl Hartfelder (Nieuwkoop: B. de Graaf, 1966), 576–77: "*Quare si post altissimam Dionysianae theologiae lectionem, post sublimem Cusani de sacris philosophiam, Seraphicique Bonaventurae commentarios*".
[42] Lefèvre, *Prefatory Epistles*, 141–43.
[43] Lefèvre, *Prefatory Epistles*, 4–5.
[44] Lefèvre, *Prefatory Epistles*, 79–80.
[45] Lefèvre, *Prefatory Epistles*, 6.
[46] Lefèvre, *Prefatory Epistles*, 10; cf. Oosterhoff, *Making Mathematical Culture*, 78–88.
[47] Lefèvre, *Prefatory Epistles*, 76.
[48] Charles de Bovelles, *Ars oppositorum*, in *Que Hoc Volumine Continetur: Liber de Intellectu, Liber de Sensu, Liber de Nichilo, Ars Oppositorum, Liber de Generatione, Liber de Sapiente, Liber de Duodecim Numeris, Epistole Complures* (Paris, 1511), "*Epistola Dedicatoria*" and "*Formula*" (pp. 77r–78v).
[49] Bovelles, *Ars Oppositorum*, 79r–80r. Victor, *Charles de Bovelles*, 47, 60 notes the deep influence of Scotus on Bovelles.
[50] Bovelles, *Ars Oppositorum*, 93v–94v.

of the work a table of the disciplines in which the generic structure of each one is mapped out mathematically according to a pattern of dichotomous opposites.[51] An even more impressive venture in Lullist encyclopaedism can be found in Bernardo de Lavinheta, the Spanish Fabrist who offered a popular series of lectures on Lull's Art at the Sorbonne in 1514–16. For in his *Explanatio Compendiosa* of 1523 he offered a comprehensive Scotist and Lullist treatment of the entire encyclopaedia. This he conceived, following Bonaventure and Lull, as a circle centred on Christ and unfolding in a Trinitarian and correlative dynamic.[52]

For the Fabrists, the most potent combination of Lullist, mathematical, and mystical methodology was to be found in Nicholas of Cusa. By the beginning of the sixteenth century, it is clear from their works that they were reading Cusa intensively. Indeed, by as early as 1507, Lefèvre was engaged in tirelessly tracking down manuscripts of Cusa's works, a labour of love which culminated in the celebrated 1514 Paris edition of his *Opera*, meticulously indexed and beautifully illustrated in the best Fabrist style.[53] For Lefèvre and Bovelles, Cusa was a master of "theology and holy and supramundane philosophy".[54] He was also a person who had profoundly "penetrated" the mathematical disciplines, seeking to touch things—such as the squaring of the circle—that "none of our great mathematicians have yet attained".[55] Most important was the way Cusa used mathematics to provide "most beautiful and worthy contemplations of God". Cusa's mathematics thus provided "divine anagogies, assurections and elevations", and by the analogical use of geometrical figures he enabled an ascent to God and the realm of the intellect.[56] Ultimately, the Fabrists could hold that such an ascent transcended both reason and logic itself. As Lefèvre expressed this in his *Theologia Vivificans* of 1499, in divine philosophy" the "affirmations and negations of dialectic" no longer have repugnance, but in fact coincide with

---

[51] Bovelles, *Ars Oppositorum*, "Formula" (pp. 77v–78v).

[52] Mark D. Johnston, "The Reception of the Lullian Art, 1450–1530", *The Sixteenth Century Journal* 12.1 (1981): 39–40. Bernardo de Lavinheta, *Opera Omnia*, ed. Johann Heinrich Alsted (Cologne, 1612), 57: "*Christum benedictum: qui est punctus quem quaerimus: in quo omnia tamquam in speculo relucent*". See also p. 658 where Lavinheta holds that Christ is the point in which every line converges. For Lavinheta's Trinitarian and Scotist treatment of being see Chapter 7.

[53] Nicholas of Cusa, *Haec Accurata Recognitio Trium Voluminum Operum Clariss. P. Nicolai Cusae Card.*, ed. Jacques Lefèvre d'Étaples (Paris, 1514). For an account of this see Lefèvre, *Prefatory Epistles*, 342–48.

[54] Lefèvre, *Prefatory Epistles*, 344–45.

[55] Lefèvre, *Prefatory Epistles*, 345.

[56] Lefèvre, *Prefatory Epistles*, 345: "*Neque quisquam putet mathematicum laboriosum sciendi genus inutile esse, quandoquidem in eo divina maxime relucet; et quae qui ignoraverit, pulcherrimas et dignissimas de Deo contemplationes, quas manuductiones, assurrectiones et divina paradigmata dicere possumus ... quos ipse vir divinus divinis anagogis, assurrectionibus elevationibusque per mathematica respersit*".

each other.[57] Cusa's coincidence of opposites becomes a way of transcending all created opposition, expressing the ultimate unity of all things in God.

## 1.2. Fabrist Formation

By the time he finished his undergraduate career, Ramus had grown thoroughly disillusioned with the Aristotelian and scholastic logic he had been steeped in from his youth. Although, by his own testimony, he had at first been addicted to terminist logic, he had soon tired of what he came to see as its sophistic and disputatious character.[58] By contrast, there is good evidence that Ramus was early attracted to the fresh logical and mathematical approaches of the Fabrists. Indeed, Ramus had a direct connection to the Fabrists through Oronce Fine, his own tutor in mathematics who had been a close friend of Bovelles.[59] Ramus himself was clearly an admirer of Bovelles and later paid homage to him in his own geometrical works.[60] In fact, Ramus' own abiding passions in mathematics—squaring the circle and doubling the cube—were those on which Bovelles himself had written, in works later republished by Fine.[61]

While Ramus admittedly could be somewhat dismissive of Lefèvre's logical works,[62] other evidence actually suggests his profound appreciation for Lefèvre's dialectic. Most important here is the testimony of Nicholas Nancel, his friend, collaborator, and biographer, that Ramus had once told him that "from the beginning" he had taken Lefèvre, along with the Agricolans Sturm and Latomus, as "reliable methodological guides"[63]—a rare admission from one who guarded his contemporary sources so jealously. Scholarship has long known of the intimate connection between Ramus' method and the Agricolan logic which flourished

---

[57] Cited from Stephan Meier-Oeser, *Die Präsenz des Vergessenen: Zur Rezeption der Philosophie des Nicolaus Cusanus vom 15. bis zum 18. Jahrhundert* (Münster: Aschendorff, 1989), 38.

[58] Skalnik, *Ramus and Reform*, 31.

[59] For Ramus' link with Oronce Fine see Petrus Ramus, *P. Rami Professoris Regii Prooemium Mathematicum* (Paris, 1567), 128; Nicholas Nancel, "Nicholas Nancelius, 'Petri Rami Vita'. Edited with an English Translation", trans. Peter Sharratt, *Humanistica Lovaniensia* 24 (1975): 236–37, 255; Goulding, *Defending Hypatia*, 50–51; Cifoletti, "From Valla to Viète", 399–402; and Reiss, "From Trivium to Quadrivium", 50. Nancel notes that Ramus and Fine were close friends and not only co-workers. Ramus himself records his shared astronomical interests with Fine. Reiss, *Knowledge, Discovery and Imagination*, 108–18 makes clear the conceptual links between Ramus, Fine, and Bovelles.

[60] See Bruyère, *Méthode et Dialectique*, 363–64.

[61] Nancel, "'Petri Rami Vita'", 203; cf. Victor, *Charles de Bovelles*, 44. Victor notes Fine's desire, stemming from Bovelles, to extend mathematics into the study of the wider liberal arts curriculum. Fine's republication of his short epistle on this topic in 1551 significantly dates from his association with Ramus.

[62] Petrus Ramus, *Aristotelicae Animadversiones* (Paris, 1543 facsimile edition Stuttgart: Friedrich Frommann Verlag, 1964), 29v.; Ramus here sharply distinguishes his own dialectic from that of Titelmans, Trebizond, Caesarius, and Lefèvre.

[63] Nancel, "'Petri Rami Vita'", 223.

at Paris during his years of study,[64] but the close ties now known to exist between Lefèvre, Sturm, and Rhineland humanism suggest a pressing need to place Ramus' Agricolan inheritance in a broader and richer context.[65]

Taking up his first teaching job in 1536 only reinforced Ramus' conviction of both the inadequacy of Aristotelian logic and its unsuitability for young and impressionable minds, leading him in urgent search of an alternative.[66] The 1543 *Institutiones Dialecticae*, the fruit of intensive methodological reflection, was his own answer to this need. Coupled with its companion piece the *Aristotelicae Animadversiones*—a scorching attack on contemporary scholastic logic—it marked an attempt at dialectical reform of a scope and ambition which had not been seen in Paris since the Fabrists themselves, but which went far beyond them in its strident critique of Aristotle. Yet in this, as we shall now turn to, we may also recognize profound affinities with Cusanus' own attacks on the *via Aristotelica* a century earlier and his corresponding championing of a natural and mathematical dialectic on Neo-Platonic and Neo-Pythagorean grounds.

## 1.3. Natural and Cusan Dialectic

Writing in the *Institutiones Dialecticae* Ramus held that there are two kinds of philosophers wedded to two very different methods of inquiry. The first kind are those who place "truth before all things". These are "born to freedom", and their mind becomes polished through the study of the liberal arts. The second kind are those who prefer to rely on authority and remain in "pertinacious opinion" rather than seeking out the truth for themselves. They become blinded, even to the point where they prefer to hold their eyes shut rather than gaze upon the "naked" light of truth.[67] In the *Animadversiones*, Ramus amplifies the point, linking the two kinds of people to the two rival dialectical schools in the University of Paris: his own revived Platonic method of natural dialectic and his opponents,

---

[64] Ong, *Ramus, Method, and the Decay of Dialogue*, 123–30, 196–97, 230–40; Bruyère, *Méthode et Dialectique*, 303–8; and Peter Mack, "Agricola and the Early Versions of Ramus' Dialectic", in *Autour de Ramus: Texte, théorie, commentaire*, ed. Kees Meerhoff and Jean-Claude Moisan (Québec: Nuit Blanche, 1997), 17–35.

[65] For Lefèvre's links to Alsatian humanism see Oosterhoff, *Making Mathematical Culture*, 61. Philip Edgcumbe Hughes, *Lefèvre: Pioneer of Ecclesiastical Renewal in France* (Grand Rapids, MI: Eerdmans, 1984), 182–83, 187–88 notes Sturm's keen interest in the Fabrist and evangelical reform movements in France.

[66] Ramus, *Animadversiones*, 8r notes the damaging impact of Aristotle on young students. Ong, *Ramus, Method, and the Decay of Dialogue*, 41–45 has an excellent summary of Ramus' own account of his development.

[67] Petrus Ramus, *Institutiones Dialecticae* (Paris, 1543 facsimile edition Stuttgart: Friedrich Frommann Verlag, 1964), 32v; cf. Ramus, *Animadversiones*, 2r.

the Aristotelian scholastic and terminist logicians who have turned away from nature and become hopelessly entangled in the inventions of their own minds.[68]

Echoing in Ramus' words we are no doubt right to detect the voices of generations of humanists preceding him. Yet in pitting truth against authority so pointedly, and especially in seeking to recall humanity to natural dialectic, we are reminded even more of the celebrated opening of Cusa's *Idiota* trilogy of 1450. Responding to the learned orator, the *idiota* argues that he has been held back from true wisdom due to his love of authority and written learning, becoming like a horse who "by nature is free" but "by art"—a loaded term in the context—"is bound with a halter to its manger so that it eats nothing but what is served to it". He then urges the orator not to look for wisdom in the books of men but in "God's books" which are written with his finger and which are present everywhere in the world. Challenged to provide a practical example of this, he points to the acts of numbering, weighing, and measuring taking place in the forum, going on to demonstrate their ultimate origin in God.[69]

In many ways this passage serves as a programmatic outline for Ramus' *Institutiones*. While Goulding has suggested that Ramus was the first to "look beyond the walls of the university and find natural dialectic in the world around him", in fact we can see that Cusa preceded him.[70] Ramus' exhortation in the *Institutiones* that to learn true logic we should interrogate those who are closest to nature, such as agricultural workers and vine-dressers, whose uncultivated minds reveal most brightly the mind's natural light, clearly resonates with Cusa finding wisdom in the Roman forum.[71] Indeed, in a later work, Ramus offers an account of walking through the streets of Paris and seeing the workings of natural dialectic in artisans and shopkeepers.[72] Oosterhoff powerfully connects Ramus' natural dialectic to the Parisian intellectual context of Ramus' day, profoundly shaped as it was by the legacy of the Fabrists, but the passage reads almost as a transplanting of Cusanus' *idiota* into the France of the middle of the sixteenth century.[73]

Like Cusa, Ramus also wanted to ground his dialectic on the books of God written with his finger. Indeed, he compares the three parts of his own early dialectic—nature, doctrine, and exercise—to "three books fruitful for every discipline". The first of these books is the human mind, which he holds has been

---

[68] Ramus, *Animadversiones*, 2r–5v.
[69] Nicholas of Cusa, *Idiota de Sapientia*, I.1–7 (*NCOO*, V.3–13).
[70] Goulding, *Defending Hypatia*, 21.
[71] Ramus, *Institutiones*, 6v; cf. Goulding, *Defending Hypatia*, 21.
[72] Ramus, *Prooemium Mathematicum*, 229–32; cf. Goulding, *Defending Hypatia*, 41–42. Goulding does not make the connection with Cusa.
[73] Richard J. Oosterhoff, "*Idiotae*, Mathematics and Artisans: The Untutored Mind and the Discovery of Nature in the Fabrist Circle", *Intellectual History Review* 24 (2014): 1–19. Heightening the comparison with Cusa, Ramus, *Prooemium Mathematicum*, 229 explicitly references the "Parisian forum". I am grateful to Richard Oosterhoff for discussion of this point.

impressed by God "with eternal characters". The second is fashioned as an "exemplar of these eternal notes" by the "diligent observer of nature" through imitation of the natural pattern found in the human mind. The third embraces a "copious" expression of these in all human acts and speech, thus fulfilling the principal humanist aspiration. For Ramus, the art of dialectic, expressed as doctrine or human teaching, is effectively "read" out of the book of nature. Since art must always imitate nature, the dialectician must therefore turn away from human authorities and seek to discover the innate workings of their own mind. In fact, as Ramus makes clear, the natural dialectic that he champions is nothing other than the mind itself.[74]

While the polyvalent notion of the "books of God" which Ramus drew on had deep roots in the Augustinian and Franciscan traditions, the notion of the book of the mind and its innate dialectical structure recalls most clearly Cusa and the Lullist Ramon de Sebonde.[75] For Ramus, the mind is a light "emulating the eternal and blessed light" and the "image of the parent of all things".[76] Crucially the mind images God precisely in his role as Creator, with the human act of logical analysis mirroring the divine act of creative genesis.[77] Indeed, this parallel between the divine and human mind is fundamental to the French philosopher and, in places, he can press this even further, referring to man as a "certain god" or a "certain mortal god"—phrases which recall Cusa, as well as the wider Renaissance trope of the "dignity of man".[78] Further evidence for his Sebondian and Cusan affinity can be seen in his affirmation that the natural dialectic of the mind is a "living exemplar" to which the art of dialectic itself must be progressively conformed. For both Sebonde and Cusa had emphasized the mind as the "living image" of God capable of conforming itself more and more to his reality.[79] For Ramus, this dynamism carries through in his comparison—echoing Cusa's

---

[74] Ramus, *Institutiones*, 5v–6r. Bruyère, *Méthode et dialectique*, 10 notes the implicit division of the *Institutiones* into three actual books corresponding to nature, doctrine, and exercise. Nevertheless, it is clear from the passage that Ramus is also comparing the mind to a book imprinted with eternal characters.

[75] For detailed discussion of Cusa's innovative notion of the "book of the mind" see Petr Pavlas, "The Book Metaphor Triadized: The Layman's Bible and God's Books in Raymond of Sabunde, Nicholas of Cusa and Jan Amos Comenius", in *Nicholas of Cusa and the Making of the Early Modern World*, ed. Simon J. G. Burton, Joshua Hollmann, and Eric M. Parker (Leiden: Brill, 2019), 384–416.

[76] Ramus, *Institutiones*, 6r: "*Naturalis autem dialectica, id est, ingenium, ratio, mens, imago parentis omnium rerum Dei, lux denique beatae illius, et aeternae lucis aemula, hominis propria est, cu[m] eoq. nascitur*".

[77] Petrus Ramus, *Arguments in Rhetoric against Quintilian: Translation and Text of Peter Ramus's Rhetoricae Distinctiones in Quintilianum*, ed. James J. Murphy and trans. Carole Newlands (Carbondale: Southern Illinois University Press, 2010), 158; *Institutiones*, 15r, 32r. The connection to divine creativity becomes more explicit in the later Ramist tradition.

[78] Ramus, *Institutiones*, 15v, 39r; cf. Cusa, *De Conjecturis*, 2.14.143 (*NCOO*, III.143–44).

[79] Ramus, *Institutiones*, 7r–8v, 42v–43r; cf. Ramon de Sebonde, *Theologia Naturalis* (Venice, 1581), c. 152, 155 (pp. 130v, 132v) and Cusa, *Idiota de Mente*, 5.85, 87; 7.106 (*NCOO*, V.127–29, 131, 158–60).

contrast between "living image" and "dead portrait"—of the logician to an artist painting an accurate picture of the "lively dialectic" of the mind.[80] Read in this light, Ramus' dichotomous charts of the disciplines can be seen as "maps" of the mind and the dialectician as an intellectual cartographer, evoking the celebrated map-maker analogy of Cusa's 1463 *Compendium*.[81]

Fundamental to Ramus is the understanding that dialectic should match the natural progression of the ideas from God as discovered in the world and the human mind. To illustrate this, he draws on Plato's *Philebus* and the important understanding that even those things which are "eternal and perpetual", namely the ideas, correspond to the one and the many. What this means is that in them a "certain infinite force is ... comprehended and terminated in a certain manner".[82] For Ramus, art thus unfolds the infinite *vis* present in each idea. Since our mind cannot comprehend this infinity it must work through these generic ideas and the species contained within them sequentially, first following one idea and then another in turn, finally arriving at an "infinite multitude of individual parts".[83] Far from being just a static or "frozen" snapshot,[84] Ramus' early dialectic seems to view this process of subdivision—and thereby the charts that later came to represent it—as, in principle, infinitely extendable, capable of ever more precision in their anatomizing of the universe and its metaphysical structure. In all this we are again reminded not only of Cusa's contention that the mind itself as a living image, but also of the Sebondian account of the mind as an image of the divine infinity.[85] Indeed, as we shall see below, Ramus too can claim that the human mind is "greater than the universe" in its capacity to encompass all things.[86]

For Ramus, as a number of commentators have remarked, dialectic thus offers something of a God's-eye view of reality.[87] While he is clear that the logician is not like God in seeing "all causes as able to demonstrate their events", he does insist that dialectic grants access to all logical arguments and their "universal and eternal precepts"—holding, in other words, that, as far as possible, it should mirror the arts and sciences as they exist in the divine mind.[88] Echoing Aquinas'

---

[80] Ramus, *Institutiones*, 7r–8v, 42v–43r; cf. Cusa, *Idiota de Mente*, 13.148–49 (*NCOO*, V.203–5).

[81] Ong, *Ramus, Method, and the Decay of Dialogue*, 190; cf. Nicholas of Cusa, *Compendium*, 8.22–24 (*NCOO*, XI/3.17–20). Ong points to the Cambridge satirical play *The Pilgrimage to Parnassus*, which draws explicitly on the notion of Ramism providing a "map of the mind".

[82] Ramus, *Institutiones*, 27v–28r: "*in quibus terminata quaedam, et infinita rursus quodammodos vis est comprehensa*".

[83] Ramus, *Institutiones*, 27v–28r.

[84] Goulding, *Defending Hypatia*, 27 speaks of mathematics as "a frozen snapshot of the real dialectical structure of the human and divine minds and the world". Goulding misses the implicit dynamism of Ramus' understanding but his treatment is nonetheless highly insightful.

[85] Cusa, *Idiota de Mente*, 13.149 (*NCOO*, V.204–5); cf. Sebonde, *Theologia Naturalis*, c. 6 (p. 8r).

[86] Ramus, *Institutiones*, 40v: "*Mathesis liberat, seu potius hominem hac mundi universitate maiorem reddit*".

[87] See especially Craig Walton, "Ramus and Socrates", *Proceedings of the American Philosophical Society* 114.2 (1970): 122 and Goulding, *Defending Hypatia*, 27.

[88] Ramus, *Institutiones*, 32r.

famous Boethian account of God eternally looking down at the world as though from a high tower, he can hold that dialectic, as if from a "perpetual summit", exposes all things before the eyes of the mind.[89] It is the "Platonic science" which traces the proceeding and flowing out of one idea from God into many singulars and then follows them back again as they return to their head and fountain.[90] In this we are reminded vividly of Pico's famous *Oration on the Dignity of Man*, which speaks of the mind being prepared through the art of discourse or reason, in other words through dialectic, to move up and down the ladder of nature, so that "at one time we shall descend, dismembering with titanic force the 'unity' of the 'many', like the members of Osiris; at another time, we shall ascend, recollecting those same members, by the power of Phoebus, into their original unity".[91] We also see more clearly what it means for the mind to image God as the "parent of all things". Imitating God, the mind goes out with him from the one into the many and then returns back to the original unity. It is no wonder that Ramus could see dialectic as a "golden chain" reaching down from the throne of God in heaven to earth and binding together all things.[92]

## 1.4. Mathematics, Dialectic, and the Mystical Ascent to God

Ramus was deeply influenced by the Franciscan vision that all philosophy must be oriented towards theology. For him the end of every human art and science must be the praise and worship of God. Not only dialectic but in fact all the arts—the entire encyclopaedia—must be modelled on the divine ideas as discovered in nature. Given this, it is no surprise that Emery has described Ramus' dialectical system as entailing a kind of Bonaventuran *reductio* of all the arts to theology.[93] For Ramus, as for Bonaventure, the encyclopaedia in its Neo-Platonic emanation and return is thus patterned exemplaristically on the mind, and art, of God. All this, of course, also resonates with Cusa's understanding of human arts as imaging, however imprecisely, the infinite divine art.[94] In his final works, as we will see below and in the next chapter, this notion attains a definite encyclopaedic expression in his quest for a universal method. More and more, we also find him connecting his encyclopaedic endeavours to both a mathematical and mystical

---

[89] Ramus, *Institutiones*, 34v; cf. Aquinas, *ST*, 1a q. 14.13.
[90] Ramus, *Institutiones*, 34v–35r.
[91] Giovanni Pico della Mirandola, *Oration on the Dignity of Man*, trans. A. Robert Caponigri (Chicago, IL: Gateway, 1956), 18–19.
[92] Ramus, *Animadversiones*, 2r–3v. Yates, *Art of Memory*, 240 notes the Neo-Platonic valence of this image and its importance in Ramus' wider system.
[93] Emery, "Introduction", 39.
[94] Cusa, *Idiota de Mente*, 13.148–49 (*NCOO*, V.203–5).

vision of reality, in which the arts—and supremely the mathematical arts of the quadrivium—pattern an ascent to theology and union with God.

From his earliest works onwards, Cusa had maintained that mathematics formed the most important bridge between the finite and infinite. By contrast, logic occupied a more lowly position in the hierarchy of disciplines, proving unable to penetrate to the "exemplars and ideas" of things.[95] Cusa therefore held that in order to reason theologically, logic must be transformed by mathematics.[96] Despite his profound debt to Cusa, Ramus had to dissent from this Cusan denigration of logic. For him, dialectic was itself a theological method, capable of calling back the mind "from the crass shadows of the senses" and revealing the "most bright ideas of eternal truth".[97] In both Realist and Platonic fashion, it liberates the "truth which is in things" from the "chains of body".[98] Crucially for Ramus, dialectic was not only the lowest rung on the ladder, as it had been for Cusa, the Fabrists, and even perhaps for Pico. Rather, dialectic itself *was* the ladder. There is no sense in which it is ever left behind to mount onto higher things. Yet, at the same time, Ramus was clearly deeply attracted to Cusa's fusion of dialectic and mathematics. Goulding thus insightfully notes the "two-way" traffic between dialectic and mathematics in the *Institutiones*, suggesting that for Ramus "mathematics was both perfected by dialectic and identical with dialectic". In these terms, mathematics thus validated "Ramus' metaphysics of art, tying together in the clearest way the action of the human mind, the world which confronted it, and the deity who was the source of both the world and the commensurate structure of the human intellect".[99]

While in his later works Ramus came to take with the utmost seriousness the Pythagorean notion that the world consisted entirely of numbers,[100] as early as his *Institutiones* he had sought to give expression to the fundamentally mathematical character of the human mind and human logic. Following Renaissance dialecticians like Agricola, and indeed like Lefèvre himself, Ramus analysed the processes of human reasoning according to two fundamental divisions: the invention of logical arguments and the judgement of truth arising from the combination of invented arguments.[101] Going somewhat beyond Agricola, however, he reconceived logical judgement explicitly as a mathematical operation, holding that, whenever an occasion of reasoning arises, nature excites in our souls

---

[95] Cusa, *Idiota de Mente*, 2.66 (*NCOO*, V.101–3).
[96] *De Conjecturis*, 2.2.86 (*NCOO*, III.83) and *De Aequalitate*, 12 (*NCOO*, X/1.16–17).
[97] Ramus, *Institutiones*, 42v–43r: "*Cum igitur hoc modo dialectica animum ab hisce crassis sensuum umbris avocaverit, omnesque philosophiae regiones peragraverit, in eis suo quibusque ordine descriptis ideas illius sempiternae veritatis . . . clarissimas demonstrabit*".
[98] Ramus, *Institutiones*, 19v.
[99] Goulding, *Defending Hypatia*, 24.
[100] Goulding, *Defending Hypatia*, 71.
[101] Ramus, *Institutiones*, "*Epistola Dedicatoria*" 3v, 8v, 19v–20v, 28v–29r, 53v.

"certain twin subtle and acute motions for inventing faith of doubtful things and for expressing and collocating of things by mode and number".[102] Reading on in the *Institutiones* we find that numerical, and indeed geometrical, order continues to play a vital role for Ramus in structuring logical reasoning. Thus, from the *Philebus* he draws on Plato's account of unity and multiplicity, which he conceives graphically as two lines framing a "dialectical continuum".[103] Even more significant is the way in which he can compare, again with the *Philebus* in mind, the emanation of ideas from the mind of God with the progression of number from unity towards multiplicity, and indeed infinity.[104]

In his *Idiota de Mente*, Cusa had emphasized Boethius' claim that "without the quadrivium no one can philosophise rightly".[105] Ramus would have agreed with this wholeheartedly. In all his curricular reforms, mathematics thus played a crucial role. While ostensibly he upheld the Augustinian-Platonic model of the encyclopaedia as encompassed in dialectic, physics, and ethics, in fact he "mathematicizes" all of these.[106] We may see this from his celebrated but controversial account of "third judgement", which Goulding has rightly highlighted as one of the most "dense and difficult" passages in his works.[107] In this he describes the way in which all the human arts correspond to their origin in God through a recounting of the famous myth of the cave in Plato's *Republic*, tracing an ascent from the shadowy cave-world of matter to the eternal and transcendent ideas blazing like the Sun.[108] Yet Ramus subtly offers a mathematical re-rendering of this which is ultimately much more Pythagorean, and indeed Cusan, in tone—qualifying somewhat Goulding's suggestion that Ramus only came to Pythagoras late in life—even as it recalls, and is perhaps modelled on, other contemporary encomia to mathematics, such as that of Melanchthon.[109]

Beginning from the linguistic arts of the trivium, Ramus charts the beginnings of a movement from "inchoate shadows" to "eternal and absolute ideas". However, it is dialectic which first forces the mind to confront itself as an "image of the divine mind" and realize its own divinity. This is quite literally a conversion, and,

---

[102] Ramus, *Institutiones*, 7r: "Excitat igitur in animis nostris natura (cum disceptationis occasio oblata est) geminos quosdam motus cum ad inveniendam rei dubie fidem subtiles, et acutos, tum ad exprimendam, et pro modo numeroque rerum collocandam, atque estimandam prudentes, et moderatos". It should be noted that Agricola, *DID*, I c. 28 1 (p. 136) does hint at a mathematical approach to the topics.

[103] Ramus, *Institutiones*, 28r; cf. Plato, *Philebus*, 16e–18b in *Plato: Complete Works*, ed. John M. Cooper (Cambridge: Hackett, 1997), 404–6. The notion of the "dialectical continuum" can be found in Ong, *Ramus, Method, and the Decay of Dialogue*, 196–213.

[104] Ramus, *Institutiones*, 28r.

[105] Cusa, *Idiota de Mente*, 10.127 (NCOO, V.179–80).

[106] Ramus, *Institutiones*, 36v.

[107] Goulding, *Defending Hypatia*, 22. It is called third judgement to distinguish it from the first judgement of propositions and the second judgement of syllogisms.

[108] Plato, *Republic*, VII (514a–517c), in *Plato: Complete Works*, ed. Cooper, 1132–35.

[109] Goulding, *Defending Hypatia*, 37–38, 50; cf. Melanchthon, *Orations*, 90–125.

like Augustine in his *Confessions*, Ramus finds both within and above his mind "unfailing treasures of wisdom".[110] Continuing in an Augustinian vein, he holds that the mind now returns from within itself to go out with confidence into the world, through physics tracing the "footsteps (*vestigia*) of this truth impressed in physical things" and tracking them back to their divine origin.[111] Yet it is mathematics—albeit, crucially, as ordered and illuminated by dialectic—which, in a kind of second conversion, finally breaks the prisoners' chains, liberating the mind from the body and allowing it to emerge from the cave and gaze upon the "aspect of the divine Sun"—namely on God himself. For Ramus, mathematics thus brings us to the vision of God. Indeed, it is through mathematics that we are restored to the "fatherlands of heaven"—a notion redolent of the early Augustine of the Cassiciacum dialogues.[112]

Offering a quite extraordinary account of the beatific vision which awaits Christians in the future, Ramus holds that in apophatic fashion it surpasses all human speech. The only way in which he can hope to capture this is through the sight of that "flowing sphere of the Pythagoreans, whose centre is everywhere and circumference nowhere"[113]—a kind of mathematical deification! Of all natural disciplines it is thus mathematics which offers the best intuition of the divine. Even in this life, Ramus seems to imply, mathematics renders man "greater than the universe" itself.[114] While the notion of God as a Pythagorean sphere can be sourced to *The Book of the Twenty-Four Philosophers* and is found in a host of medieval philosophers and theologians, not least in Bonaventure himself, it was above all Cusa's treatment of this in his 1440 *De Docta Ignorantia*, which captured the minds and hearts of Renaissance mathematicians and mystics alike.[115] Through Cusa, it deeply impacted the Fabrists, with the motif of God as infinite sphere playing a central role in a number of Bovelles' works and even making a celebrated appearance in the poetry of Marguerite of Navarre.[116] For them it expressed that fusion of mathematics and theology which was their highest ideal. For Ramus too, this evocative image—at once mathematical and transcending all mathematics—neatly captured his understanding of the mystical centring of all

---

[110] Ramus, *Institutiones*, 37r–37v; cf. Augustine, *Confessions*, 10.6.9–8.15.

[111] Ramus, *Institutiones*, 37v–38r: "*hac eadem via, in physicis rebus impressa veritatis illius vestigia persequetur*".

[112] Ramus, *Institutiones*, 38r–41r; cf. Augustine, *On Order*, 2.14.39–19.51 (pp. 85–97).

[113] Ramus, *Institutiones*, 41r–v: "*animis hic opus est, qui liberrima, et per omnes mundi partes aequabiliter fusam sphaeram illam Pythagoreorum speculentur: cuius centrum sit ubique, circumferentia nusquam*".

[114] Ramus, *Institutiones*, 40v–41r.

[115] For a detailed account of this, see Dietrich Mahnke, *Unendliche Sphäre und Allmittelpunkt: Beiträge zur Genealogie der mathematischen Mystik* (Halle: S. Niemeyer, 1937).

[116] Mahnke, *Unendliche Sphäre*, 46, 108ff. Oosterhoff, *Making Mathematical Culture*, 83–84 refers to this as Beatus Rhenanus' "favourite maxim".

things in God. It marked the fitting culmination of his own "journey of the mind into God", revealing the *Institutiones* to be as much *Itinerarium* as *Reductio*.

## 1.5. Rhetorical and Metaphysical Turn

In characterizing Ramist dialectic and its development, it has become entirely natural to see it as a continuation of the humanist, rhetorical pattern of logic instituted by Valla and developed and popularized by Agricola. In this sense, Ramism can be seen as part of the wider "rhetorical turn" undergone by Renaissance thought.[117] In similar vein, Kees Meerhof sees Ramism as very much the culmination of the humanist tradition of textual logic.[118] The links between Ramus and Agricola were very close, mediated especially through Sturm and the Parisian Agricolan tradition. Indeed, Ramus himself credited Agricola as the founder of an entirely new school of logical reflection:

> The true study of the genuine (*germanae*) logic was first awoken in Germany by one Agricola, and then by his followers and emulators in the whole world. But the University of Paris perceived firstly this fruit by the advent of Jacobus Omphalos, Bartholomaeus Latomus and especially Johannes Sturm, from whom the utility of the art of logic was more fully and richly expounded.[119]

Ramus also made no secret of his desire to complete the Agricolan project, by providing the missing account of logical judgement that Agricola himself always intended to write. There can be no doubt then that Agricola played a fundamental role in the genesis of Ramist dialectic.[120]

However, while it is absolutely right to see Ramus himself as part of the humanist, rhetorical refashioning of logic, to label his logic as straightforwardly "rhetorical" is actually a major misconception. There can be no doubt that Ramus

---

[117] For this rhetorical turn see Marco Sgarbi, *The Italian Mind: Vernacular Logic in Renaissance Italy (1540–1551)* (Leiden: Brill, 2014), 3. It receives a classic formulation in Cesare Vasoli, *La dialettica e la retorica dell'umanesimo: "Invenzione" e "metodo" nella cultura del XV e XVI secolo* (Milan: Feltrinelli, 1968). From pp. 353ff. Vasoli places Ramus as the culmination of his narrative.
[118] Kees Meerhoff, "Beauty and the Beast: Nature, Logic and Literature in Ramus", in *The Influence of Petrus Ramus*, ed. Feingold, Freedman and Rother, 200–14.
[119] Petrus Ramus, *P. Rami Dialectica, Audomari Talaei Praelectionibus Illustrata* (Cologne, 1573) [hereafter *DC*], 73–74: "*palam ab uno Agricola verum germanae logicae studium in Germania primum, tum per eius sectatores et aemulos, toto terrarum orbe excitatum esse. Percepit autem Parisiensis Academia primo fructum illum adventu Iacobii Omphalii, Bartholomaei Latomi: sed in primis Ioannis Sturmii, a quo Logicae artis utilitas plenius et uberius est exposita*". This edition contains annotations by Talon, but since it was originally published within Ramus' lifetime and under his name, no distinction will be made in this volume.
[120] Petrus Ramus, *P. Rami Scholae in Liberales Artes* (Basel, 1578), col. 426. For the connection between Agricola and Ramist method, see also Mack, *Renaissance Argument*, 334–55.

himself would have angrily rejected this charge. Again and again he makes clear in his works against Cicero and Quintilian that their biggest mistake was to subordinate dialectic to rhetoric—something he rather cheekily suggests they took over from Aristotle.[121] Following what was perhaps implicit in Agricola,[122] Ramus also rejects utterly the scholastic attempt to read Aristotle as endorsing a bipartite notion of logic as split between necessary (apodictic) and probable (dialectical) reasoning. For Ramus, such a distinction was illusory. In fact, although Aristotle had denied its very possibility, it was his dream to institute a single universal method of logic which would be valid in all circumstances and for every form of rational argumentation.[123] Indeed, this, much more than humanist affectation or even the pragmatic desire to meet the needs of his young charges, was the real reason that he chose to illustrate his Latin dialectical textbooks with copious examples taken from poets and orators such as Cicero, Virgil, Horace, and Catullus. For he resolved that if he could demonstrate his logic with such "alien" examples as these, he could demonstrate it in any circumstance.[124]

Seen in this light, Ramus' project may actually be seen as an emancipation of dialectic from rhetoric, an emancipation which importantly freed dialectic from its traditional lowly position in the trivium to take up a much more general and universal role, very much akin to that of metaphysics in the Aristotelian worldview. In fact, it is not at all wrong to see Ramist dialectic as a metaphysical logic and to describe Ramism as having undergone a metaphysical turn quite as much as—or actually rather more than—a rhetorical turn. At first sight, such a claim might seem both perplexing and astonishing. For it has become a commonplace that Ramism sought to overthrow metaphysics.[125] It is certainly true that Ramus had little but contempt for scholastic metaphysics. He only turned late and with considerable reluctance to writing a commentary on Aristotle's *Metaphysics*. However, his reason for this was not due to any lack of interest in metaphysical notions, but rather his conviction that his dialectic had rendered metaphysics as a separate discipline completely unnecessary.[126]

To Ramus' mind it was not Aristotle's metaphysics that was the true science of "being *qua* being", giving certain knowledge of the first principles or causes of the universe; rather it was his own dialectic. In fact, he even went one better

---

[121] Petrus Ramus, *Peter Ramus's Attack on Cicero: Text and Translation of Ramus's Brutinae Quaestiones*, ed. James J. Murphy and trans. Carole Newlands (Portland, OR: Hermagoras Press, 1992), 8 and *Arguments in Rhetoric*, 79–82.
[122] Mack, *Renaissance Argument*, 141–42.
[123] Ramus, *Scholae in Liberales Artes*, col. 338–40; cf. Aristotle, *Topics*, 1.1 (100a20–b24), in *The Complete Works of Aristotle: The Revised Oxford Translation*, ed. Jonathan Barnes, 2 vols. (Princeton, NJ: Princeton University Press, 1984), I.167–68.
[124] Ramus, *Institutiones*, 44r.
[125] Sellberg, "Petrus Ramus".
[126] Petrus Ramus, *P. Rami Professoris Regii Scholarum Metaphysicarum* (Paris, 1566), "*Praefatio*" expresses in no uncertain terms the utter superiority of logic over metaphysics.

than that, claiming that his logic was also a transcendental method common to both being and non-being.[127] Indeed, as Risse perceptively recognized, Ramism is a logic which transcends the fundamental scholastic distinction between metaphysical first intentions and logical second intentions, not only bridging, but in effect eliminating, the gulf between logic and metaphysics.[128] In this way, it not only has a Scotist flavour, but is also even more closely akin to Lullism, which also treated such distinctions with relative abandon, frequently shuttling back and forth between them. Indeed, Ramus' conviction in 1543 that his mathematico-dialectic should be seen as a kind of universal "art of arts" clearly resonates with the claims of Lull's *Ars Magna*.[129] Of course, this should scarcely surprise us, for Ramus could easily have imbibed such Lullist influence not only indirectly from Agricola but also much more directly from the Fabrists or even their master Cusa.

### 1.6. The Emerging Shape of Ramist Dialectic

#### 1.6.1. Invention

In order to see this, let us turn with fresh eyes to the fundamental threefold pattern of the mature dialectic: invention, judgement, and method—a pattern which quickly supplanted the 1543 one of invention, judgement, and use.[130] Ramus' understanding of topical invention not only as a method of sorting ideas and ordering discourse but also as a kind of key to unlock the structure of reality is clearly redolent of wider currents in the fifteenth-century reform of rhetoric.[131] It is well known that Ramus' "arguments", the building-blocks of his entire dialectical structure, derive directly from the topics and places (*loci*) of Classical rhetoric, and are indeed a kind of conflation of these. In his rhetorical works, Ramus criticized the proliferation of *loci* in Cicero and Quintilian.[132] His own desire was to simplify these and in doing so to isolate and identify those arguments which truly embodied the natural dialectic of the mind. Indeed, his interpretation of "arguing" as "showing" or "declaring" already places the emphasis on the role of logical arguments in disclosing reality.[133]

---

[127] Ramus, *Scholae in Liberales Artes*, 933–37, 942, 959.
[128] Risse, *Logik der Neuzeit*, 135 cited from Olivieri, "Ideale Lulliano", 891, 916.
[129] Olivieri, "Ideale Lulliano", 893; cf. Ramus, *Institutiones*, 35v.
[130] Ramus himself subsumes method under judgement in a nested dichotomy but the threefold pattern is more helpful here for illustration.
[131] Rossi, *Logic and the Art of Memory*, 1–28.
[132] See, for example, Ramus, *Arguments in Rhetoric*, 108–14, 121, 124.
[133] Ramus, *DC*, 22–24.

Ramus' arguments have an important relation not only to Ciceronian *loci* but also to Aristotelian categories. Where Aristotle famously identified ten fundamental categories of being, Ramus in his mature dialectic referenced ten basic arguments—causes, effects, subjects, adjuncts, opposites, comparisons, names, divisions, definitions, testimonies—which he pointedly referred to as his own "categories" (Figure 1.1).[134] Indeed, from as early as his *Animadversiones*, it is clear that he intended his arguments to entirely supplant Aristotle's categories.[135] For centuries logicians had debated the place of Aristotle's *Categories* in his wider logical project of the *Organon*. While to some, particularly those of a Nominalist persuasion, discussion of categories of being within logic seemed anomalously metaphysical, to others, especially those in the Scotist metaphysical tradition, they offered a charter for a Realist logic.[136]

Surprisingly, Ramus brushes aside with cavalier disregard the question, which he well knew to have been debated heatedly in the Paris of the fifteenth century, of whether the categories are real objects or names. He clearly had little desire to renew the conflict of Realists and Nominalists, which he remarks had led to such strife and even bloodshed, as well as a legacy of bitter division in the schools. Indeed, his own logic embraces both names and things—*realia* and *nomina* in late medieval terms—and as with Cusa and Lefèvre one gains a real sense that Ramus was seeking to transcend the damaging divides of the medieval schools.[137] Yet it is also clear that he, again like Cusa and Lefèvre, ultimately espoused a Realist account of reality. For there can be little doubt that, for all his attention to names and their logical and linguistic structure, Ramus saw his arguments not only as subsuming Aristotle's categories but also as mapping out the metaphysical structure of reality.[138]

Yet Ramus' desire to institute a "logic of being and non-being" meant that his arguments must also transcend Aristotle's categories of being and even the realm of being itself. In seeing Ramus as espousing a crude, physicalist rendering of reality, both Ramus' contemporary opponents and modern scholars like Ong have done him an injustice.[139] For Ramus is clear that when we use terms such as cause or place in logic these are not understood purely physically but rather as having a metaphysical, indeed a transcendent, extension. Thus, following Plato and Pythagoras—not to mention Bonaventure—we may speak of an intelligible

---

[134] Petrus Ramus, *P. Rami Scholarum Dialecticarum* (Frankfurt, 1594), 119. Ramus, *Arguments in Rhetoric*, 79 pointedly remarks that Aristotle missed the ten "general topics" necessary for the art of invention.
[135] Ramus, *Animadversiones*, 17r–20v.
[136] See Alessandro D. Conti, "Categories and Universals in the Later Middle Ages", in *Medieval Commentaries on Aristotle's Categories*, ed. Lloyd A. Newton (Leiden: Brill, 2008), 369–409.
[137] Ramus, *Scholae in Liberales Artes*, col. 398; *Scholarum Metaphysicarum*, 15v–16r.
[138] See Risse, *Logik der Neuzeit*, 124–25, 200. This is in stark contrast to Sellberg, "Petrus Ramus", who argues for Ramus' Nominalism.
[139] Ong, *Ramus, Method, and the Decay of Dialogue*, 205–6.

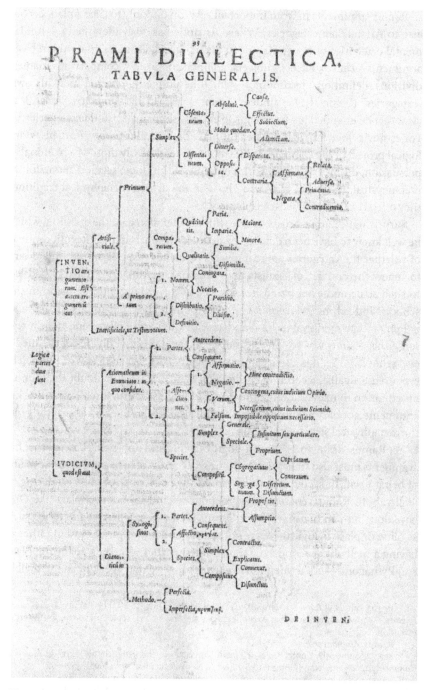

**Figure 1.1** Ramist chart of logic from Johann Thomas Freige, *P. Rami Professio Regia* (Basel, 1576), 95. The top half of the chart (under "*Inventio*") shows the sequence of Ramus' ten basic arguments (plus further subdivisions). Reproduced by kind permission of the Bibliothèque Nationale de France.

kind of matter as well as physical or sensible matter. Likewise, we must distinguish between place as it applies in the physical world and logical place which can be extended to the incorporeal realm and even to the infinite being of God himself.[140] He therefore seeks to extrapolate all of his logical arguments into the intelligible and even divine realm. Unfortunately, he does not enter into details about how this extrapolation is made, but there are hints that, like Scotus and Lull, he understood an analogical relation between God and creatures to be consistent with a shared univocal definition of being.[141] In fact, in their role as what we might call "divine topics", Ramus' arguments bear close relation to Lullist dignities, and there can be no doubt that like Lull he sought to institute a spiritual logic capable of discoursing on all of reality. As he expressed this, we cannot have a logic of being and non-being unless it also includes God in its scope.[142]

Key to Ramus is the inter-relation of his logical arguments, the pattern of which even in the later dialectic preserves implicitly the Neo-Platonic structure of the original 1543 dialectic. As "lights" or "founts", arguments can be seen to emanate or flow from each other. This is also evident from their fundamental division into "first" or "arising" arguments. Tacitly referencing Platonic light metaphysics, Ramus holds that the most general arguments are first in light and knowledge, while succeeding, subaltern arguments are "proximate in clarity".[143] Arguments therefore illuminate each other in a kind of gradually descending chain of lights.[144] Here we are already verging on the territory of method, but what is clear is that Ramus has not abandoned, even if he may well have reconfigured, the Neo-Platonic conceptuality of the earlier dialectic.

Yet while Ramus' arguments are intimately connected to an emanational understanding of reality, we must be careful not to reify them. For they also preserve a dynamic, relational structure characteristic of Lullism. In this way, they not only pattern the ordered progression of being, but also describe the network of relations connecting all beings together. Ramus holds that in every logical argument there is thus a "certain mutual affection of two things among themselves".[145] This is also reflected in his other fundamental division of arguments into consentaneous and dissentaneous, which map out in logical terms the

---

[140] Ramus, *DC*, 38–39, 58–62. For the Franciscan doctrine of spiritual matter see Michael B. Sullivan, "The Debate over Spiritual Matter in the Late Thirteenth Century: Gonsalvus Hispanus and the Franciscan Tradition from Bonaventure to Scotus" (PhD Dissertation, Catholic University of America, 2010).

[141] Ramus, *Scholae in Liberales Artes*, col. 376; cf. Scotus, *Ord.* 1 d. 3 p. 1 q. 1–2 n. 26 (Vatican, III.26). Ramus' account of this is undoubtedly cruder than Scotus'.

[142] Ramus, *DC*, 59.

[143] Petrus Ramus, *Dialecticae Libri Duo*, ed. Sebastian Lalla and Karlheinz Hülser (Paris, 1572; Stuttgart: Frommann-Holzboog, 2011), 132–33 [hereafter *DLD* 1572].

[144] Ramus, *Scholarum Dialecticarum*, 137.

[145] Ramus, *DC*, 22.

metaphysical pattern of unity and multiplicity, identity and distinction, which runs through all of reality.[146]

Very simply Ramus defines consentaneous arguments as those which agree with what is argued and dissentaneous arguments as those which dissent from it.[147] In the final recension of his dialectic, Ramus is clear that consentaneous arguments must be understood as the "first and simple founts" of all modes of unity and identity. Absolutely consentaneous arguments, such as cause and effect, display a greater degree of unity and identity, while consentaneous arguments "in a certain manner", such as subject and adjunct, show a lesser degree. By contrast, dissentaneous arguments are said of things which differ according to any mode.[148] Although he does not say it quite as plainly, they must therefore be the founts of all multiplicity and distinction. Indeed, recalling Bovelles' *Ars Oppositorum*, Ramus makes an important distinction between diverse arguments which differ only by reason and opposites which differ both really and by reason.[149]

For Ramus, as much as for Lull or Agricola, logic therefore provides a "ladder of concordance and contrariety", allowing its practitioners confidently to relate any being to any other in their identity or distinction.[150] The 1543 dialectic also expressed a dynamic, combinatorial understanding of the arguments and their use. Mack rightly links this to Agricola, but it is also clearly reminiscent of the Lullist dignities in their mutual informing of each other.[151] While this combinatorial dynamism is perhaps somewhat lacking in later editions, the progressive mathematization of Ramist dialectic, which we shall return to below, means that logical arguments are increasingly understood as somehow mathematical, or quasi-mathematical, in character. In this sense arguments can be compared not only to rhetorical places or Aristotelian categories of being but also, albeit rather more cautiously, to mathematical, or even algebraic, terms, which are capable of being combined with each other according to different logical patterns.[152]

---

[146] Ramus, *DLD* 1572, 6.
[147] Ramus, *DLD* 1572, 6, 28.
[148] Ramus, *DLD* 1572, 22, 28–30.
[149] Ramus, *DLD* 1572, 28–30; cf. Bovelles, *Ars Oppositorum*, "Praefatio", 79r–80r.
[150] See Lull, *Ars Brevis*, 2.2 (*DI*, 303).
[151] Mack, *Renaissance Argument*, 344–49 offers a helpful comparison of Ramus and Agricola noting their shared tendency to treat topics as "headings into which connections are sorted". He also notes in passing the link between Lull and Agricola on p. 136 n. 20. The Lullist, combinatorial dimensions of Ramism are discussed further in Olivieri, "Ideale Lulliano", 885–929.
[152] For parallels between mathematical terms and logic see Ramus, *DC*, 22; *Prooemium Mathematicum*, 370–407; and *Scholae in Liberales Artes*, col. 463–65, 480. Cifoletti, "From Valla to Viète", 393–420 places Ramus in what he calls the "French algebraic tradition" and highlights some of the Neo-Platonic and Fabrist aspects of this. Once again Fine appears as a mediating figure between Ramus and the Fabrists, as does his contemporary Jacques Peletier.

## 1.6.2. Judgement

Significantly, the greatest expression of this combinatorial drive is to be found in Ramus' account of logical judgement. While Ong holds that Ramus debases logical judgement by abstracting it from any viable theory of predication, it would seem better to see him as reconfiguring predication itself.[153] For Ramus, predication is not simply a relation between logical concepts, as in Nominalist logic, but it expresses metaphysical reality. Indeed, he actually dramatically expands the scope of predication to include all the logical arguments and not just the rigid scholastic template of subject and predicate. Language thus reflects the actual subtlety and complexity of the world, and is not merely an artificial imposition for the sake of human understanding. In fact, it is clear that language can be held to "track" reality, revealing not just its metaphysical structure but also the necessity and contingency of the bonds which tie words, concepts and things together.[154] There is undoubtedly a connection here to the "ordinary language" philosophy of Renaissance humanists such as Valla and Agricola, but as Lodi Nauta has convincingly demonstrated this was itself profoundly indebted to currents of late medieval Realism.[155]

If predication maps reality then it is also clear, *pace* Ong,[156] that for Ramus the different combinations, or permutations, of logical arguments, whether into propositions or syllogisms, become a criterion of truth itself. In fact, for Ramus, truth is to be defined as a transcendent operation which matches propositions to external reality. A proposition is thus said to be true "when it pronounces as a thing is".[157] In this we clearly see Ramus' Realism resurfacing for, unlike the Nominalists, he clearly does not wish to reduce truth to a purely logical operation in the mind. While it may be right to recognize a broad Stoic influence here,[158] such a position reflects even more closely the propositional Realism associated with the Augustinian, Franciscan, and Lullist schools of the Late Middle Ages.[159] Indeed, although Ramus—unlike his later

---

[153] Ong, *Ramus, Method, and the Decay of Dialogue*, 182–83.
[154] See Ramus, *DLD* 1572, 22–24, 28; *Scholae in Liberales Artes*, col. 463–66, 480. Cifoletti, "From Valla to Viète", 410–20 maps the intimate relation between Ramus' new dialectic and his algebra and mathematics. Petrus Ramus, *Algebra* (Paris, 1560) was an important short textbook on algebra.
[155] See Nauta, *In Defense of Common Sense*, 16–19 and "From Universals to Topics".
[156] Ong, *Ramus, Method, and the Decay of Dialogue*, 209.
[157] Ramus, *DLD* 1572, 92–96: "*Axioma deinde est verum aut falsum: verum quando pronuntiat uti res est: falsum, contra*".
[158] For an account of this see Sellberg, "Petrus Ramus" and Stephen Daniel, *George Berkeley and Early Modern Philosophy* (Oxford: Oxford University Press, 2021), 37–55. Daniel's reading of Ramus as a proto-Idealist is innovative and insightful but misses the medieval and Platonic context of his Realism.
[159] See Laurent Cesalli, "Le 'pan-propositionnalisme' de Jean Wyclif", *Vivarium* 43.1 (2005): 124–55; Alessandro D. Conti, "Wyclif's Logic and Metaphysics", in *A Companion to John Wyclif: Late Medieval Theologian*, ed. Ian Christopher Levy (Leiden: Brill, 2006), 67–125; and Johnston, *Spiritual Logic*, 105.

followers—does not seem to have believed that propositions exist outside the human mind, he plainly goes beyond Parisian Nominalists such as Buridan who believed that propositions only signify the sum total of their terms, namely individual substances and their accidents.[160] By contrast, Ramus holds that a proposition such as "fire burns" expresses the real relation of cause and effect existing between the two separate logical arguments "fire" and "burns" and their significations. In other words, it seems true to say that for Ramus propositions express "states of affairs" really existing in the world, a notion redolent of Rimini's *complexe significabile*.[161]

Borrowing his own conceptuality, we might even say that for Ramus the mind is the propositional "mirror" of reality.[162] In his 1555 *Dialectique* he argues that the mind has the power to know all things just as the eye has the natural power to see all colours. It does so through universal genera—a point we will return to below—which like a "certain mirror, represent to him the universal and general images of all things".[163] In the rest of the work Ramus continues to draw creatively on this Neo-Platonic light metaphysics in order to explain the mind's apprehension of both propositions and syllogisms. Thus the mind has an intuitive grasp of the truth of necessary propositions, which is compared to its apprehension of colours "visible through themselves". It is this light which subsequently illuminates the entire spectrum of the truth of all other propositions.[164] The same is true of syllogisms, which Ramus elsewhere identifies, with Aristotle, not as the "external symbol of reason" but as the "intimate reason of the soul".[165] It is the "twin light" of the major and minor proposition which reveals the truth of the conclusion.[166] For Ramus, the essence of logical judgement is thus the complex apprehension of the light of truth shining in and through all things—a notion that clearly resonates with an Augustinian and Franciscan epistemology of illumination, not to mention a Scotistic account of intuitive cognition.[167]

---

[160] Paul Vincent Spade, *Thoughts, Words and Things: An Introduction to Late Mediaeval Logic and Semantic Theory* (2007), 165–88, https://pvspade.com/Logic/docs/thoughts.pdf, accessed 07/10/2019.

[161] Ramus, *DLD* 1572, 96–98; cf. Gregory of Rimini, *Gregorii Ariminensis OESA Lectura Super Primum et Secundum Sententiarum*, ed. A. Damasus Trapp, OSA and Venicio Marcolino, 6 vols. (Berlin: Walter de Gruyter, 1981), Prologus q. 1 art. 1 (I.1–12). For a brief discussion of Rimini's doctrine and its link to propositional Realism see Conti, "Wyclif's Logic and Metaphysics", 78–86. Johnston, *Spiritual Logic*, 105 points to Lull's affinities with Rimini in this regard.

[162] The notion of the mind as a mirror was a common medieval and Renaissance view, but Victor, *Charles de Bovelles*, 156 rightly draws attention to its central place in Cusa and Bovelles.

[163] Petrus Ramus, *Dialectique de Pierre de la Ramee* (Paris, 1555), 68–69: "ces genres uniuerselz, comme quelque mirouër, luy representant les images uniuerselles & generalles de toutes choses".

[164] Ramus, *Dialectique*, 83–86.

[165] Ramus, *Scholae in Liberales Artes*, col. 459.

[166] Ramus, *Dialectique*, 113–14.

[167] For a concrete link with late medieval, Scotistic, accounts of intuitive cognition see Chapter 4.

### 1.6.3. Method

We come now finally to Ramus' notion of method, in the judgement of many his greatest and most influential contribution to logic. The origins and development of Ramist method have been dealt with extensively by both Ong and Neal Gilbert, who make clear that Ramus, like other Renaissance philosophers, drew deeply on thinkers such as Plato, Aristotle, and Galen. Indeed, Ramus' own quest for method clearly marks an attempt to synthesize the varying and pluriform accounts of method to be found in the medical, philosophical, and scientific traditions of antiquity into a single, unique method for acquiring, proving and organizing all of knowledge. Characteristic of Ramism, as other Renaissance exponents of method would frequently complain, was the overriding claim that the systematic organization of knowledge was the key to all proof and demonstration.[168]

Ramus' earliest exposure to method was likely through Sturm. For it was he who first brought method to prominence in a dialectical system, innovatively fusing Galenic and rhetorical conceptions of method into a new Platonic synthesis.[169] From the Classical rhetorician Hermogenes, Sturm derived the understanding of method as the "thought-structure" of a discipline.[170] He was then able to give this important but broad notion much needed precision through his engagement with the Platonist physician Galen, whose works were widely discussed in the Renaissance.[171] Drawing implicitly on Galen's *Medical Art*, Sturm identified a threefold method of teaching the arts, namely the method of division (dividing definitions into their parts), composition (proceeding from simple to more complex things), and resolution (proceeding from more complex to simple things).[172] Strikingly, Sturm drew on Plato's *Timaeus* to argue that method paralleled the divine ordering of the chaos of the elements in creation.[173] For him, resonating with a Scotistic understanding, method can thus be related to a progression from what is naturally prior to what is naturally posterior—or vice-versa.[174] Forging an important link with the existing topical tradition

---

[168] Neal W. Gilbert, *Renaissance Concepts of Method* (New York: Columbia University Press, 1960), 3–38, 129–44 and Ong, *Ramus, Method, and the Decay of Dialogue*, 230–40.

[169] Ong, *Ramus, Method, and the Decay of Dialogue*, 227–36. Gilbert, *Renaissance Concepts*, 123 points to Sturm's explicit Platonism. He also points out that Sturm is unlikely to have been the first in the humanist tradition to engage with method.

[170] Ong, *Ramus, Method, and the Decay of Dialogue*, 230–32.

[171] Ong, *Ramus, Method, and the Decay of Dialogue*, 238–39.

[172] Johannes Sturm, *Partitionum Dialecticarum Libri IIII* (Strasbourg, 1566), III c. 15 (pp. 199v–203r); cf. Ong, *Ramus, Method, and the Decay of Dialogue*, 233 and Gilbert, *Renaissance Concepts*, 123.

[173] Sturm, *Partitionum Dialectiarum*, III c. 15 (p. 200v).

[174] Sturm, *Partitionum Dialectiarum*, III c. 15 (pp. 200v–201v). Despite Sturm's Nominalistic-sounding treatment of genus and species as notions in I c.3 (pp. 8v–13r) it is clear from his linking of genus to "common nature" (p. 210v) that he is a Realist. This order of natural priority also relates to what Ong, *Ramus, Method, and the Decay of Dialogue*, 240–45 identifies as the Aristotelian "priorities" literature relating to the technical treatment of the syllogism.

he gave this important diagrammatic expression by linking Galen's threefold method to the ascent and descent of the Porphyrian tree of genus and species.[175]

While Sturm's influence on Ramus is beyond doubt, it was ironically his Parisian opponent Antonio de Gouveia who first stimulated his deeper reflections on method. For, as Ong notes, it was Gouveia's suggestion that second judgement relates to the "order in teaching the arts which the Greeks call method", and his explicit citation of Galen, which prompted Ramus' far-reaching revision of his dialectic to include method as its crown.[176] Yet in claiming that Ramist method owed its genesis to Gouveia, Ong is surely going too far. For as another of Ramus' opponents, Adrian Turnèbe, remarked of method as taught in the Parisian schools, "no word is more popular in our lectures these days, none more often heard".[177] Indeed, Ramus could have learned about it not only from Sturm but also from Melanchthon and the Rhineland humanist Johann Caesarius, from whom he was later to draw his celebrated three requirements for demonstrative method, namely that it should be valid per se, concerning all things, and universal.[178]

Yet while Ramus' account was clearly infused with a humanist and Neo-Platonic understanding, he insisted that his method was the "unique method of Aristotle" which had long been abandoned and which he alone had recovered and renewed.[179] Thus, while he never abandoned his assertion of the Platonic origins of his dialectic, his later works do show a definite rapprochement with Aristotle. Indeed, in what would surely have come as a great shock to his readers, Ramus now locates the *locus classicus* of method in the *Organon* itself. In particular, Ramus' famous three "laws of method" are drawn straight from a discussion of syllogistic in the *Posterior Analytics*, although he abstracts them from their original setting and transposes them onto a universal topical and dialectical framework.[180] While contemporary Aristotelians like Ramus' opponent Jacob Schegk struggled to make sense of and contain Aristotle's scattered and diverse discussions of method, it was Ramus' genius to unite them all into a single synthesis.[181]

For Ramus, the Aristotelian laws of method are holy and divine and express the "architectonic" structure of every art and science. Drawing on them, he gives a strict definition of method in terms of its conformity to the law of truth

---

[175] Ong, *Ramus, Method, and the Decay of Dialogue*, 232–36.
[176] Ong, *Ramus, Method, and the Decay of Dialogue*, 218–19.
[177] Cited from Ong, *Ramus, Method, and the Decay of Dialogue*, 228–29.
[178] Ong, *Ramus, Method, and the Decay of Dialogue*, 239–40.
[179] Ramus, *DLD* 1572, 131–32.
[180] Ramus, *Scholae in Liberales Artes*, col. 426–27.
[181] Ong, *Ramus, Method, and the Decay of Dialogue*, 229–30 points to Schegk identifiying twenty-four different kinds of Aristotelian method and another anti-Ramist, Everard Digby, utilizing as many as 110 different notions of method.

(everything in the art must be necessary and true), the law of justice (everything in the art is homogeneous and belongs to it and not to another art), and the law of wisdom (in every art general things must be handled generally and special things specially, so that method always descends from the highest genera through the middle to the lowest).[182] In his final dialectic he offered a celebrated example of the law of wisdom, asking his reader to imagine that all the definitions, distributions, and rules of grammar are written down on pieces of paper, scrambled up, and then placed in an urn. It is method which allows one to arrange the different parts of the art of grammar into their proper order. Moreover, this method is itself extendable to all the other arts and capable of illuminating their inner structure and their relation to each other in encyclopaedic fashion.[183]

Importantly, Ramus' understanding of method bears close affinity with the Fabrists. In fact, their championing of a methodical and Neo-Platonic reading of Aristotle offers an important but neglected context for reconceptualizing Ramus' own later Aristotelian turn and its hidden continuity with his earlier thought. While his desire to reconceive all the arts in apodictic fashion is perhaps more idiosyncratic, it clearly resonates with the Fabrist account of the mathematical, axiomatic structure of all the arts. In the case of the law of justice, Ramus' insistence from Aristotle that arithmetic must be handled arithmetically and geometry geometrically, and so forth, finds an almost exact verbatim parallel in Lefèvre's rule in his Aristotelian commentaries that every discipline must be handled according to its proper subject matter.[184]

Ramus' understanding of method as a universal template applicable to all disciplines also bears detailed comparison with Bovelles. Indeed, Bovelles' notion of the progressive unfolding of genus into species through a pattern of dichotomous opposition closely reflects Ramus' ideal of method, and has a strong claim to be its prototype. For both philosophers, method involves the "agglutination" or "conglutination" of opposites and can be compared to the mathematical progression of numbers from unity—as we saw for Ramus in the 1543 dialectic.[185] Ramus' championing of the dichotomy has often been attacked—both now and at the time—as a crude oversimplification of reality. At best, it is portrayed as a useful pedagogical or mnemonic tool.[186] Yet it is notable that Bovelles in his *Art of Opposites* also sought to express the entire encyclopaedia according to a nested series of dichotomies.[187] Ramus himself linked the

---

[182] Ramus, *Scholae in Liberales Artes*, col. 333–37.
[183] Ramus, *DLD* 1572, 134; cf. Goulding, *Defending Hypatia*, 22.
[184] Ramus, *Scholae in Liberales Artes*, col. 334; cf. Lefèvre, *Prefatory Epistles*, 5, 8, 12.
[185] Ramus, *Institutiones*, 27v–28r; cf. Bovelles, *Ars Oppositorum*, c. 12, 17 (pp. 88v–89v, 93v–95r). Bovelles' fourfold progression of number is different from Ramus but closely related to Cusa, *De Conjecturis*, 1.3.10–11 (*NCOO*, III.15–17).
[186] For a negative evaluation see Ong, *Ramus, Method, and the Decay of Dialogue*, 199–202.
[187] Bovelles, *Ars Oppositorum*, "*Formula*" (pp. 77v–78v).

dichotomy to a Platonic understanding, and the connection with Bovelles suggests that Ramist dichotomizing, whatever its faults, reflects a more subtle metaphysical engagement with reality than many have given him credit for.[188] In fact, as Ayelet Even-Ezra has convincingly demonstrated, the use of dichotomous method and the associated branching charts was by no means a Renaissance innovation, but rather has a long and proud medieval heritage, with no less a figure than Bonaventure using it to organize his systematic expositions of theology.[189]

Like Sturm's, Ramus' notion of method was intimately related to the celebrated Porphyrian tree of genus and species, ubiquitous in every logic textbook of his time. In line with his Platonic and Realist theory of language, Ramus had a twofold understanding of genus and species as both "notes" or "symbols" of logical arguments and as the "exemplary archetypes" to which these symbols pointed.[190] Ramus defined genus as a "whole essential to its parts", and it is clear that he understood this as expressing not just a logical, or conceptual, commonality but also a community of essence.[191] Indeed, while he eschewed "tortuous" scholastic discussions concerning universals, there is enough evidence to suggest that he upheld a broadly Scotistic position, quite in line with the Realist emphases we have observed elsewhere in his logic.[192]

In particular, Ramus stoutly maintained that individuals differ by their own "proper and individual forms". Against the Thomist position that individual humans are distinguished only accidentally and not essentially, he held that all individuals have their own proper form as well as exemplifying a common, ideal, form. Ramus insisted that "singulars alone subsist"—a view that is as much Scotist as Nominalist[193]—but his discussion makes clear that each individual can be distinguished into both genus (the common form) and species (the proper or individuating form). Furthermore, he distinguishes these according to different ideas, reasons or definitions existing within the same individual—an understanding which clearly recalls Scotus' formal distinction.[194] In one important passage this is made fully explicit:

---

[188] Ramus, *DC*, 150–54. Oosterhoff, *Making Mathematical Culture*, 120–21 notes how Ramus' earliest dichotomous chart in his *Institutiones* closely resembles the charts of the Fabrists.
[189] Ayelet Even-Ezra, *Lines of Thought: Branching Diagrams and the Medieval Mind* (Chicago, IL: University of Chicago Press, 2021). For the reference to Bonaventure see pp. 151–55.
[190] Ramus, *DC*, 173, 189.
[191] Ramus, *Scholae in Liberales Artes*, col. 371, 377–78. Ramus makes clear here that genus signifies a "common essence". For example, the genus "animal" is the common essence of man and a herd animal (*pecus*).
[192] Ramus, *Scholae in Liberales Artes*, col. 370–71 says that Porphyry should not have tortured his followers with questions about universals, but having done so should have answered them. Immediately after he expresses his view of genus as "common essence".
[193] Ong, *Ramus, Method, and the Decay of Dialogue*, 203–4 asserts a Nominalist background to this. He also seems to miss Ramus' language of common and proper form.
[194] Ramus, *Scholae in Liberales Artes*, col. 377–83; cf. Scotus, *Ord.*, 1 d. 8 q. 1 p. 4 n. 193 (Vatican, IV.261–62).

And although the same is perhaps able to be efficient and form and similar and accident, and others in the same manner, yet not therefore the reasons of singulars are not to be distinguished. The same is genus and species, yet reasons of genus and species are distinct: thus the reasons of end, form, efficient, matter and of others must be distinguished and defined.[195]

Here, recalling Agricola, the pattern of formal distinction seems to be extended from genus and species to a whole range of other arguments.[196]

Recalling Ramus' conviction that arguments map out modes of unity and identity, we may now discern an important connection between Scotist formalities and Ramus' arguments, confirming our suggestion that Ramist logic was intended to mirror the intricate metaphysical structure of reality. Of course, this is not to suggest that Ramus shares anything like the same kind of sophistication or nuance as Scotus. Rather, Ramus' idiosyncratic view that individuals are "most special species", pilloried mercilessly by Ong, should actually be seen as a reification of Scotus' more subtle understanding that genus and species are concepts which can only be applied analogically to individuals.[197] It is thus a kind of commonplace Scotism resembling the topical Scotism to be found in Agricola or the Fabrists, or the watered-down Realism which trickled through the Parisian schools.[198]

In the early dialectic this Realism clearly has an exemplaristic foundation, but in the later dialectic many have seen this as being completely undercut. Indeed, there is a general, almost unanimous, consensus that some time after 1543 Ramus dramatically tempered the Platonism and exemplarism of his early dialectic. For those following in the footsteps of Ong, of whom Mack and Sellberg are most prominent in this regard, such a shift is, of course, retrospective confirmation that Ramus' Platonism was only ever superficial and evanescent.[199] The reasons for maintaining such a claim are not difficult to find. In his mature

---

[195] Ramus, *Scholae in Liberales Artes*, col. 372: "*Et quamvis idem fortasse possit esse et efficiens et forma et simile et accidens, et e caeteris eodem modo, attamen non ideo rationes singulorum non sunt distinguendae. Idem genus est et species, rationes tamen generis et speciei distinctae sunt: sic finis, formae, efficientis, materiae, et caeterorum rationes distinguendae et definiendae fuerunt*".

[196] If there could be any doubt of this interpretation, see Ramus, *DC*, 214 where Ramus makes absolutely explicit that really identical things are still able to be distinct in terms of reasons and arguments.

[197] Ong, *Ramus, Method, and the Decay of Dialogue*, 203–4. For the Scotist account see Scotus, "Six Questions on Individuation", 106–7. For Scotus' view see Rosa Maria Perez-Teran Mayorga, *From Realism to "Realicism": The Metaphysics of Charles Sanders Peirce* (Lanham, MD: Lexington Books, 2009), 61.

[198] Nauta, "From Universals to Topics", 200–205 makes the point that Agricola's account of universals also blends logical and metaphysical understandings in a confusing and ambiguous manner and does not precisely reflect Scotus' own view. Richard Oosterhoff ("Jacques Lefèvre d'Étaples") makes a similar point about the difficulty in pinning down Lefèvre's moderate Realism.

[199] Ong, *Ramus, Method, and the Decay of Dialogue*, 205–6; Mack, "Agricola", 29; and Sellberg, "Petrus Ramus".

dialectic Ramus repeatedly attacks in no uncertain terms the Platonic doctrine of ideas as separate exemplars, maintaining steadfastly in its place the Aristotelian understanding that idea means nothing else apart from "logical genus" and is therefore inseparable from the thing itself.[200] Against the Platonic doctrine of separate ideas, Ramus arrays a battery of arguments including the famous "third man" argument from the *Parmenides* utilized to devastating effect in Aristotle's *Metaphysics*.[201] Even more seriously, in at least one place he also seems to cast aspersion on the divine ideas, holding that "some ancient logicians perversely philosophized that ideas are certain things fashioned separate *reipsa* from subject species, which consist in the divine mind as though certain images of things which God seeing [then] creates singulars".[202]

Despite this it would be mistaken to see Ramus as rejecting divine ideas *tout court*. Indeed, the thrust of Ramus' polemic is clearly against the *separate* nature of Platonic ideas.[203] This is made clear by his reference to a "most serious disputation in the schools" as to whether substances are in the mind of God—something he takes as refuted by the *Parmenides*—or whether they are only present as thought—his implied position.[204] Elsewhere, in fact, Ramus confirms his own view that there are "logical ideas" of all things in the divine mind.[205] This not only resembles Scotus' view of the divine ideas as "quiddities known to the divine mind",[206] but it also echoes Lefèvre's important distinction between the Platonists who affirm ideas and the Aristotelians who uphold instead "eternal divine reasons". It was Lefèvre's express desire to show the "great concordance and consent" between the two camps and we should remember that Ramus too wrote a lost work on the harmony of Plato and Aristotle.[207] In fact, Ramus was clear that his "logical" doctrine of divine ideas was as much Platonic as Aristotelian, and maintained a definite correspondence between a modified Platonic view of the ideas as "eternal models for the particular things created by God" and his own less "abstruse" view of ideas as "general and perfect notions of things".[208] His polemic was always directed against the Platonists, rather than Plato, and in this

---

[200] Ramus, *Scholae in Liberales Artes*, col. 383–84.
[201] Ramus, *Scholae in Liberales Artes*, col. 384. See Plato, *Parmenides*, 132a–b, in Plato, *Plato: Complete Works*, ed. Cooper, 366; Aristotle, *Metaphysics*, 1.9; 13.4 (990b17, 1079a13), in *Complete Works of Aristotle*, II.1566, 1706.
[202] Ramus, *DC*, 174: "*Quidam aut[em] Logici veteres perverse philosophati, ideas quasdam reipsa separata a subjectis speciebus comme[n]ti sunt, quae consisterent in mente divina, tamquam imagines quaedam rerum, quas Deus intuens, singularia crearet*".
[203] Bruyère, *Méthode et dialectique*, 255.
[204] Ramus, *Scholae in Liberales Artes*, col. 370.
[205] Ramus, *Scholarum Metaphysicarum*, 124v.
[206] *Rep. 1A* d. 36 pars. 1 q. 1–2 n. 74–75.
[207] Jacques Lefèvre d'Étaples, *Introductio in Metaphysicorum Libros Aristotelis* (Paris, 1493), "*Epistola Dedicatoria*"; cf. Nancel, "'Petri Rami Vita'", 222.
[208] Ramus, *Peter Ramus's Attack on Cicero*, 22; cf. Ramus, *DC*, 174–75.

sense can be seen like Bovelles who roundly attacked the *Platonici* while still retaining a fruitful account of divine exemplars.[209]

It is also plain from his final works that Ramus never lost his understanding either of the parallel between the divine and human minds or of logic as a ladder of ascent to eternal realities and truths. In this sense, Ong is simply wrong to claim that after 1543 the Platonic notion of the transcendent ceased to exercise its spell on Ramus.[210] Take, for example, this lyrical passage from the *Schola Dialecticae*:

> Indeed, truly the light of reason is far brighter and clearer than the light of the Sun. The light of the Sun only illuminates this corporeal world. The light of reason also wanders above the world through the supramundane regions of infinity. It beholds (*intuetur*) not only mortal bodies but divine and eternal minds. The light of the Sun is only visible in daytime, but the light of reason even shines in nocturnal shadows ... the art of dialectic by its precepts ought to propound and unfold this natural light of reason shining through all things.[211]

Despite appearances, it was thus never Ramus' desire to exorcise third judgement from logic. Rather, as transposed into method, it actually became ever more closely integrated into his dialectical system, ultimately to the point where it became indistinguishable from the whole. Even in his final works Ramus could still maintain that the supreme purpose of dialectic was the "conversion" of all the arts to God, just as ardently he had done in his 1543 *Institutiones*.[212]

Ramus also never lost his understanding of the mathematical character of method, even if his way of expressing this changed. It is true that one of the main reasons, and most likely the principal one, that Ramus chose to remove third judgement from later editions of his dialectic was due to his tight definition of method, now entailing that the arts should be separate in precepts but united in use. Yet the emancipation of dialectic from mathematics paradoxically also led to a deeper mathematization of dialectic itself, culminating, as Reiss suggests, in the 1572 dialectic in which method takes on an almost geometrical character.[213] Indeed, so pervasive was this mathematical understanding of method that it began to influence Ramus' understanding of all the arts. Thus in his 1549

---

[209] Victor, *Charles de Bovelles*, 162–63. A major difference may be that Bovelles understood the divine ideas as created.
[210] Ong, *Ramus, Method, and the Decay of Dialogue*, 189–90, 205–7.
[211] Ramus, *Scholae in Artes Liberales*, col. 336: "*Imo vero lux rationis luce solis longe clarior et illustrior. Lux solis mundu[m] duntaxat istu[m] corporeum illustrat: lux rationis etia[m] supra mundum per illas supramundanae infinitatis regiones pervagatur: neq[ue] mortalia tantu[m] corpora, sed mentes aeternas et divinas intuetur. Lux solis diurno tantum tempore nobis perspicua est: at lux rationis etiam in tenebris nocturnis pellucet ... naturalem hanc universae rationis per omnia resplendentis lucem ars Dialectica suis praeceptis proponere et explicare debebit*".
[212] Ramus, *Scholae in Liberales Artes*, col. 317–18.
[213] Reiss, "From Trivium to Quadrivium", 45–56.

*Rhetorical Distinctions in Quintilian* Ramus expressed his conviction that, by applying logical method, rhetoric could become an art "almost as fixed as arithmetic and geometry", with its precepts "as unchanging as Euclid's theorem of the plane and the line".[214] If this was the case for his rhetoric, then how much more so for dialectic itself! While the 1543 dialectic had somewhat clumsily sought to include mathematics within dialectic as its culmination, by the final 1572 edition mathematical patterns and proportions—but *not* mathematics as the distinct and separate art of number and figure—have become encoded into the very structure of logic itself.[215] Once again there is an important link here to the Fabrists, who, as Oosterhoff suggests, were pioneering in their use of mathematical analogy as a universal method capable of coordinating all the disciplines in the encyclopaedia, the trivium as much as the quadrivium.[216] Indeed, in many ways, Ramus' mature dialectic represents a fulfilment of the Fabrist quest for a mathematical method adequate to all reality.

---

[214] Ramus, *Arguments in Rhetoric*, 101.
[215] Reiss, "From Trivium to Quadrivium", 49–51.
[216] Oosterhoff, *Making Mathematical Culture*, 78–85.

# 2
# Return to the Golden Age
## Ramus and the Reform of Church and Society

Ramus expounded his new method in the midst of a turbulent age of nearly unprecedented civil and religious strife. When he arrived as a student in Paris at the end of the 1520s, the Fabrist circle had only recently been dispersed and the Affair of the Placards was less than a decade away. His early studies took place at a time when the university, and indeed the whole country, was convulsed by the emergence of the French reform party. This was a heady period when the Protestant Gospel was openly championed in the lecture halls and schools, by no less a figure than Nicolas Cop, the rector of the university. Many in the university, including some of Ramus' own teachers, retained links with the Fabrists, whether or not they shared their evangelical views. A smaller, but still significant, number had been members of Lefèvre's circle and maintained close connections with the royal court through Queen Marguerite of Navarre.[1]

In 1534, the most famous of these, John Calvin, fled from France in fear for his life. Despite his haste, Calvin made time to visit Lefèvre in his retirement at Nerac. In this symbolic meeting we see the final parting of ways of the old and new reform.[2] For only two years later, Lefèvre died and Calvin penned the first edition of his celebrated *Institutes of the Christian Religion*—a work that revolutionized Protestant theology. In the same momentous year, which was also that in which Ramus received his MA, Calvin took up residence in Geneva, where, together with Guillaume Farel, another former Fabrist, he launched a wave of second reformation which changed the face of Europe and of the Church forever.[3] The ensuing decades, in which Ramus was eagerly pursuing his own reform plans, saw the emergence of Reformed Geneva and the dramatic rise of the French Huguenot party. Ramus was hardly detached from these events, for

---

[1] For the Fabrist context of the early French reform see Reid, *King's Sister*, I.115–50 and Hughes, *Lefèvre*, 129ff. Surprisingly neither Skalnik, *Ramus and Reform*, 11–35 nor Ong, *Ramus, Method, and the Decay of Dialogue*, 18–21 touch on this aspect of Ramus' early education. Goulding, *Defending Hypatia*, 35–74 significantly places Ramus' later mathematical works in the context of the religious tumult of the age.

[2] Bruce Gordon, *Calvin* (New Haven, CT: Yale University Press, 2011), 38.

[3] Gordon, *Calvin*, 31–78; Skalnik, *Ramus and Reform*, 35. Gordon emphasizes that Calvin's conversion took place in the wider Fabrist context. For Farel's connection to the Fabrists see Reid, *King's Sister*, I.20–22, 268–74 and Hughes, *Lefèvre*, 94–96.

during all this time he enjoyed the patronage, and also apparently the friendship, of the powerful Guise family, the arch-opponents of French Protestantism.[4]

Ramus' conversion to Protestantism in the wake of the Colloquy of Poissy of 1561 opened a new chapter in his reform programme.[5] It also saw the onset of the French Wars of Religion, perhaps the most brutal of all sixteenth-century conflicts. The approach of war to the gates of Paris forced Ramus to flee three times from the university during the 1560s, finding shelter with the King and the royal family. In 1568–70 he took advantage of exile to make a celebrated tour of the German and Swiss heartlands of Reformed Christianity, during which he openly declared his allegiance to Protestantism for the first time.[6] This was a brave move, given the times, but one that was scarcely a surprise, for Ramus had long been suspected of harbouring Nicodemite views.[7] However, Ramus' reputation preceded him, meaning that many did not welcome him to the Reformed fold with open arms. Indeed, his final years were wracked by controversy as he became involved in Eucharistic and ecclesiological debates and fought the rising influence of Presbyterian Geneva among the Huguenot party.[8] Ramus' life ended, of course, in the bloodiest massacre of the Wars of Religion, a twist of history which led to both him and his method becoming consecrated by the sanctity of martyrdom.[9]

The entirety of Ramus' career must therefore be seen against the backdrop of the French Reform—a point which has been insufficiently recognized by scholarship. Jonathan Reid points out that both Calvin and Loyola, those two giants of Reformation and Counter-Reformation, passed their formative years in Paris during the 1530s.[10] Precisely the same is true of Ramus, and it would be surprising, to say the least, to find him untouched by this atmosphere of reform. In fact, while Skalnik is right to argue pragmatic motivations of Ramus' reform, there was also a profound connection between his dialectical and mathematical endeavours and the wider reform of university, Church, and society.[11] Aspects of this have been brilliantly illuminated by Goulding, but even he misses the immediate context of Ramus' programme in the converging mathematical,

---

[4] Ong, *Ramus, Method, and the Decay of Dialogue*, 19; Skalnik, *Ramus and Reform*, 31–33, 42, 99, 111.

[5] Skalnik, *Ramus and Reform*, 88–115.

[6] Skalnik, *Ramus and Reform*, 110–15. For a detailed account of this journey see Wolfgang Rother, "Ramus and Ramism in Switzerland", in *The Influence of Petrus Ramus*, ed. Feingold, Freedman, and Rother, 9–14.

[7] Skalnik, *Ramus and Reform*, 97–99.

[8] Skalnik, *Ramus and Reform*, 88–89, 110–15, 132–48.

[9] Ong, *Ramus, Method, and the Decay of Dialogue*, 28–29. For contemporary Protestant views of Ramus as a martyr see Roland McIlmaine, *The Logike of the Most Excellent Philosopher P. Ramus Martyr* (London, 1574).

[10] Reid, *King's Sister*, I.2. Skalnik, *Ramus and Reform*, 29–30, notes that both Ramus and Calvin came from Picardy, a region well known for its fostering of religious reform.

[11] Skalnik, *Ramus and Reform*, 63–87.

encyclopaedic, and evangelical reforms of the Fabrists.[12] If Ramus truly was moving in the orbit of the Fabrists during these years—and all the signs indicate that this was so—then it is not surprising that he should slowly gravitate towards the centre of their reform in their vision for a renewed Christendom, even if his close association with the Guise family prevented this from being anything like a rapid motion.[13]

Scholarship on both Calvin and the French Reformation has tended to drive a wedge between the Fabrists and the French Reformers, although the work of Philip Hughes, Henry Heller, and more recently Reid has gone some way to remedying this.[14] Building on this, this chapter argues that in Ramus, we see an important bridge between the two worlds. While he later became linked to the most radical and iconoclastic of the French Huguenots, becoming a thorn in the flesh of no less a figure than Calvin's lieutenant Theodore Beza himself, his own theological programme is more conservative and, in many ways, more conciliatory than this, appealing to the principles that animated the heart of the early Fabrist reform before it became polarized and split irrevocably.[15] In this sense, we might even say that Ramus strove to hold together what had proved impossible for Calvin and Beza and many others to preserve—the unity of the old and new reform.[16]

## 2.1. Reforming the University

Since Ong, it has become common to depreciate Ramus' religious motivations and to argue that he was only ever a late and superficial advocate of theological reform.[17] In fact, nothing could be further from the truth. From the very

---

[12] Goulding, *Defending Hypatia*, 154–55 only briefly touches upon Lefèvre in relation to the wider Parisian mathematical context.

[13] Skalnik, *Ramus and Reform*, 99, 111 emphasizes Ramus' desire to justify his conversion to his former patron Cardinal of Lorraine.

[14] Henry Heller, "The Evangelicalism of Lefèvre d'Étaples: 1525", *Studies in the Renaissance* 19 (1972): 42–77; Hughes, *Lefèvre*, 60–64, 97–98; and Reid, *King's Sister*, I.2, 11–13, 28–33, 81–84. In II.550–63 Reid highlights the early intimate links between Calvin, Marguerite of Navarre, and the Fabrists, but also traces the "dynamics of separation" back to the Nicodemite crisis.

[15] Skalnik, *Ramus and Reform*, 148–58 reveals Ramus' failed attempt to preserve the "congregational character of the French Reform" in the face of Bezan Presbyterianism. He also insightfully highlights the wider Platonic context of his politics and ecclesiology.

[16] Gordon, *Calvin*, 31–46 emphasizes the important but transitional nature of Calvin's engagement with Fabrist reform. Recently Preston Hill, "Feeling Forsaken: Christ's Descent into Hell in the Theology of John Calvin" (PhD Dissertation, University of St Andrews, 2021) has argued for a much deeper influence of Lefèvre's theology on Calvin than previously thought, opening the way to a reassessment of his Fabrist connections.

[17] Ong, *Ramus, Method, and the Decay of Dialogue*, 32–33 claims that before he wrote his *Commentariorum de Religione Christiana* "he had never touched theology". Skalnik, *Ramus and Reform*, 123 also notes this wider tendency.

beginning, dialectical reform entailed theological reform. We have already explored at length the connection between the *Institutiones* and theology. Much less noticed is the fact that the 1543 dialectic contains *in nuce* a remarkable summary of the reform programme Ramus was to pursue throughout the rest of his career. Beginning with the study of grammar, rhetoric, and logic in youth (first judgement), this moves on to the methodological mastery of the precepts of all the other arts in maturity (second judgement), and concludes with the study of religion in old age (third judgement).[18] This not only parallels impressively the subsequent publishing history of Ramus and his circle,[19] but also points to his growing awareness of the need to place third judgement at the end, and not the start, of his programme of study—another clue to its apparent disappearance from the dialectic. For it is only after the other arts have been mastered that it becomes possible to see their relation to God, and thus to realize explicitly what was always implicit from the very beginning.

In many ways all of Ramus' subsequent efforts to reform the university should be seen as attempts to further this encyclopaedic vision of education and, as Skalnik rightly suggests, to make it accessible to all.[20] Ramus' programmatic desire to unite philosophy and eloquence, cemented by his triumphant appointment to a Regius Professorship in 1551, reversing the ignominy of a 1544 ban on teaching and publishing philosophy,[21] spoke to a general aspiration which had been present in French humanism from its beginnings under Guillaume Fichet, and surely reached back even further to Gerson's rhetorical reform programme.[22] However, his concern for promoting a mathematical and encyclopaedic approach to the curriculum clearly marks a continuation of the wider reforms pioneered by the Fabrists. Such an approach was already anticipated in the theoretical framework of the 1543 dialectic, but Ramus devoted much of his career to bringing this to practical fruition. It was a programme that he was later forced to defend to the hilt in his celebrated battle with Jacques Charpentier over the Regius chair of mathematics in 1565–66.[23] For, as Goulding astutely points out, the ramifications of this were much wider than a mere squabble between

---

[18] Ramus, *Institutiones*, 54r–v.
[19] For a brief account of this and its different phases see Ong, *Ramus, Method, and the Decay of Dialogue*, 29–35.
[20] Skalnik, *Ramus and Reform*, 63–87.
[21] The ban was orchestrated by Ramus' opponent Gouveia. For discussion of this see Ong, *Ramus, Method, and the Decay of Dialogue*, 23–25.
[22] Ong, *Ramus, Method, and the Decay of Dialogue*, 25–27. Donald Geoffrey Charlton, *France: A Companion to French Studies* (London: Methuen, 1983), 26 sees Ramus as Fichet's heir in combining philosophy and eloquence. For Fichet and fifteenth-century French humanism see George Kennedy, "The 'Rhetorica' of Guillaume Fichet (1471)", *Rhetorica* 5.4 (1987): 411–18 and Renaudet, *Préréforme et humanisme*, 78–89. For Gerson's rhetorical reform programme see Isabel Iribarren, "Le Paradis retrouvé: L'utopie linguistique de Jean Gerson", *Revue de l'histoire des religions* 231.2 (2014): 223–51.
[23] For detailed discussion of this and its consequences see Goulding, *Defending Hypatia*, 35–74.

academic rivals might suggest. At stake was nothing less than Ramus' own vision to remake the University of Paris as a "Platonic and Pythagorean academy" and a preeminent centre of Christian reform.[24]

Ramus' reform programme is set out at length in a series of important orations and works that he wrote over the course of his career. It is too easy to see Ramus as a lone voice, but it is important to remember that he was backed by a group of collaborators at his College of Presles who were just as committed to advancing curricular reform.[25] Despite the setback of the early royal ban on his works, for much of his career he could also count on the support of the King and the Guise family, remaining an established royal favourite right through to his untimely death.[26] His most comprehensive reform work, the *Advertisements sur la réformation de l'Université de Paris* of 1562, was in fact the fruit of a royal commission.[27] In later years, as Dean of the Regius Professors, Ramus exercised powerful sway in the university. King François I, who had established the Regius Professorships, had originally desired to establish them as a separate College, rivalling the Sorbonne, to promote his own humanist vision of reform.[28] Significantly, Ramus was able to present his own radical reforms as simply a renewing of this project, as well as a defence and propagation of the university "reformation" initiated by Cardinal d'Estouteville in the fifteenth century, which we should remember had first opened the way for French humanism and the Fabrist programme.[29]

Ramus shared the Fabrist conviction that all education should be directed towards the formation and transformation of the human soul.[30] The whole programme of the liberal arts is therefore intended to care for the soul and is directed to the "true piety of religion" as well as the government of the nation. In support of this, Ramus cited not only expected Classical precedents like Plato and Aristotle but also, rather more surprisingly, the ancient Druids, whom he saw, much like the Fabrists, as representing an idealized Platonic society in which education and piety were fully integrated into a mathematized,

---

[24] Robert Goulding, "Pythagoras in Paris: Petrus Ramus Imagines the Pre-History of Mathematics", *Configurations* 17 (2009): 76; cf. Petrus Ramus, *Petri Rami Scholarum Mathematicarum Libri Unus et Triginta* (Frankfurt, 1599). Goulding downplays the Platonic aspect of this, but it is clearly evident in Ramus' own texts.

[25] See Skalnik, *Ramus and Reform*, 35–62. Nancel, "'Petri Rami Vita'", 255 lists some of these friends and collaborators.

[26] Ong, *Ramus, Method, and the Decay of Dialogue*, 25 points to the fact that Ramus was killed against the express order of Charles IX and his mother Queen Catherine de Medici. Yates, *Art of Memory*, 237 suggests that Ramism was even taught to Mary, Queen of Scots.

[27] Skalnik, *Ramus and Reform*, 65–68.

[28] Ong, *Ramus, Method, and the Decay of Dialogue*, 25–27; Skalnik, *Ramus and Reform*, 63–87.

[29] Petrus Ramus, *Oratio Pro Philosophica Parisiensis*, in *Scholae in Liberales Artes* (Basel, 1578), col. 1085; *Prooemium Reformandae Parisiensis Academiae*, in *Petri Rami Professoris Regii, et Audomari Talaei Collectaneae* (Paris, 1577), 475.

[30] Ramus, *Pro Philosophica*, col. 1075–76; cf. Oosterhoff, *Making Mathematical Culture*, 25–55.

proto-encyclopaedic curriculum.[31] Claiming patriotically that the glories of Greece had their origins in Gaul, he held up the educational programme of the Druids as a mirror to the defects of the modern university.[32] As well as invoking the ancient precedent of the *prisca philosophia*, Ramus could also appeal to Christian models such as the Carolingian Renaissance, during which, as tradition claimed, the University of Paris had itself been founded, and above all the humble "school" of the Apostles convened under Christ and the Holy Spirit. For him, as for the Fabrists, this represented the supreme example of *idiotae* who have received the gifts of philosophy and eloquence through divine inspiration.[33]

In appealing to all these examples, Ramus clearly desired to go back to a time before Christian education had been corrupted by Aristotelian scholasticism, when it represented a purer biblical and Platonic pedagogy grounded on divine illumination. It is no surprise then that, like Lefèvre, Ramus should also appeal to the "divine light" which has come from Greece through Italy to France to banish the "shadows" of the scholastics.[34] While Ong suggested that Ramus gained little from Italian humanism and Neo-Platonism,[35] his own writings give a rather different impression. For he singles out the leading Renaissance humanists Cardinal Bessarion, George of Trebizond and Jean Lascaris as inaugurators of a new age whose mantle he desires to take up,[36] and upholds the New Academy of Ficino and the Florentine Neo-Platonists as an exemplar of the kind of educational reform he desired to institute.[37] All these humanist aspirations are neatly summed up in Ramus' desire to remove the "whole dregs of barbarous men" and to introduce "purer and more serious authors of philosophy"—a wholesale change he instituted at Presles by sweeping away the standard scholastic authors and commentators, the mainstay of the Parisian curriculum, and replacing them with study of the best Classical orators and poets.[38]

In Ramus' mature advocacy for a Neo-Platonized reading of Aristotle and his concern for a methodolgically oriented, interconnected and streamlined curriculum, we begin to see even closer parallels to the Fabrist programme. Indeed,

---

[31] Ramus, *Pro Philosophica*, col. 1064–65. For his approbation of the Druids and their education system see Petrus Ramus, *Liber de Moribus Veterum Gallorum* (Frankfurt, 1584). Johann Thomas Freige, *P. Rami Professio Regia* (Basel, 1576), 215, also makes clear the Platonic character of Druid society according to Ramus. For the Fabrist admiration of the Druids see D. P. Walker, *The Ancient Theology: Studies in Christian Platonism from the Fifteenth to the Eighteenth Century* (London: Duckworth, 1972), 73–79 and Victor, *Charles de Bovelles*, 29.
[32] Skalnik, *Ramus and Reform*, 152–55.
[33] Ramus, *Pro Philosophica*, col. 1086–92.
[34] Petrus Ramus, *Oratio de Studiis Philosophiae et Eloquentiae Conjungendis*, in *Collectaneae*, 305; *Pro Philosophica*, col. 1087.
[35] Ong, *Ramus, Method, and the Decay of Dialogue*, 48–49.
[36] Ramus, *Pro Philosophica*, col. 1087.
[37] Ramus, *Prooemium Mathematicum*, "Praefatio ad Catherinam Mediceam".
[38] Ramus, *Prooemium Reformandae*, in *Collectaneae* 475: "repudiarunt totam illam hominum barbarorum faecem, puriores et graviores Philosophiae authores recepere".

Ramus' attention to Classical sources was no mere repristination of the humanist move *ad fontes*. Rather, he insisted that all of these authors must now be read through a new methodological lens.[39] Clearly, Ramus envisaged that this reformed curriculum was to be taught by the new, Ramist, textbooks being authored by him and his circle. Both Ong and Oosterhoff point to the way in which these, with their easy-to-use tables and their celebrated dichotomous charts, reflected the earlier pioneering efforts of Lefèvre and his coworkers.[40] While Ramus, perhaps, does not capitalize on these charts as much as his successors, we only need to glance at the 1576 *Professio Regia* of his disciple Johann Thomas Freige to realize the enormous potential of displaying the entire curriculum in tabular form (Figure 2.1).[41] In the Fabrists, as we will recall, these tables not only served as important pedagogical and mnemonic aids, but also recalled a Neo-Platonic and exemplaristic understanding of the harmonious interconnection of all the disciplines.[42] Precisely the same is true of Ramus, and we have already seen the connection of his charts to Bovelles and the wider Lullist-Cusan tradition.

Ong saw the "spatial" turn of Ramism as symptomatic of an early modern "atomizing" and fragmenting of the world, coming in the wake of Nominalism. In fact, the intimate connection between Ramus and the Fabrists suggests precisely the opposite.[43] Ramus was convinced that all the arts, and the virtues they give rise to, are connected together in the "highest society" by a "certain natural bond".[44] His watchword, which could have been taken straight from the Fabrists, was the "common utility" of all the arts.[45] While he separated the arts quite sharply in terms of their individual precepts, he always combined them in use. In fact, Ramus envisages a kind of chain in which the lower arts can be applied successively to the higher arts in a cumulative fashion.[46] Unsurprisingly, running through the whole of natural and moral philosophy is dialectic as a kind of common bond of all the arts.[47] Likewise, for every art, including mathematics, Ramus emphasizes the importance of practising logical analysis and genesis. This is not only so the arts can be committed to memory, although this is of great

---

[39] Meerhoff, "Beauty and the Beast".
[40] Ong, *Ramus, Method, and the Decay of Dialogue*, 75–79 and Oosterhoff, *Making Mathematical Culture*, 120–21.
[41] See the charts throughout Freige, *Professio Regia*, which present a prototypical Ramist encyclopaedia. For Freige's Ramism see Rother, "Ramus and Ramism in Switzerland", 16–21.
[42] Oosterhoff, *Making Mathematical Culture*, 86–121.
[43] Ong, *Ramus, Method, and the Decay of Dialogue*, 199–210, 306–18. Walton, "Ramus and Socrates", 125 also points out that Ramus taught the "inter-relatedness of all things" in Platonic fashion.
[44] Ramus, *Pro Philosophica*, col. 1079.
[45] Ramus, *Institutiones*, "*Epistola Dedicatoria*", 2v; cf. Lefèvre, *Prefatory Epistles*, 5.
[46] Ramus, *Pro Philosophica*, col. 1074–76.
[47] Ramus, *Pro Philosophica*, col. 1070–73.

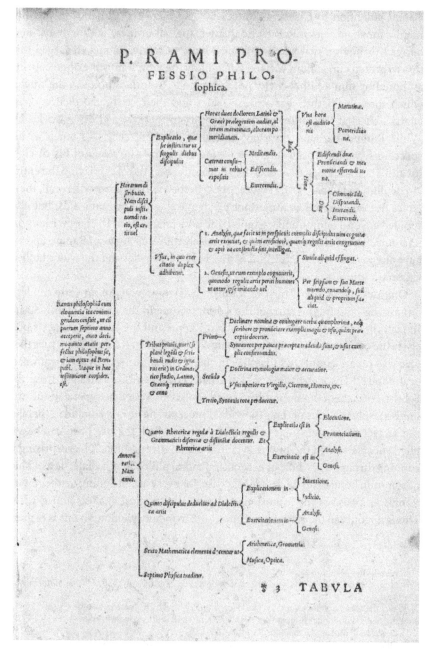

**Figure 2.1** Ramist division of the arts from opening of Johann Thomas Freige, *P. Rami Professio Regia* (Basel, 1576). Reproduced by kind permission of the Bibliothèque Nationale de France.

importance, but also, and perhaps even more importantly, so that all the arts can be traced back like rivulets to their original fonts.[48] It is through the methodological combining of all the arts that the soul becomes formed and perfected in their unified image, thus fulfilling the aspirations for an encyclopaedic curriculum.[49]

## 2.2. Mathematical and Evangelical Reform

Ramus' championing of mathematical reform to the Parisian curriculum is another clear link with the Fabrists. Despite the best efforts of the Fabrists, and their followers like Fine, mathematics at Paris was at a low ebb by the mid-sixteenth century. In an unguarded moment, Ramus' opponent Charpentier, who had recently taken over the Regius chair of mathematics, even admitted to being "*ageometrikos*". If this was the case with the professors, it is scarcely surprising that many arts students graduated without having studied any mathematics at all. The problem, as Ramus saw it, was that the original Parisian statutes gave "no separate honour or place" to mathematics.[50] The reform statutes of d'Estouteville had made some improvements, but did not specify books or hours of study, leaving many free to ignore them.[51] Ramus' goal, which quickly became a consuming passion, was to rectify this state of affairs. He desired to make Paris a veritable palace of the mathematical arts.[52]

For Ramus, mathematics was the "most ancient and primary" of the liberal arts "without which the rest of philosophy is blind".[53] Like the Fabrists, Ramus saw mathematics as a key to understanding the universe. For it reveals the symmetry and proportion running through all things, as well as the pattern of "concordance and discordance" which structures them.[54] Indeed, in his earliest mathematical work, his 1549 edition of Euclid, mathematics, and not only dialectic, can be described as a golden chain binding all truth together.[55] Although mathematics had to later firmly cede place to dialectic, and undergo its own methodological reworking at Ramus' hands,[56] it continued to occupy a fundamental role in his encyclopaedic curriculum. In particular, it is mathematics which serves

---

[48] Ramus, *Pro Philosophica*, col. 1081. For the intimate connections between Ramism and the art of memory see Yates, *Art of Memory*, 228–38 and Rossi, *Logic and the Art of Memory*, 97–102.
[49] Ramus, *Pro Philosophica*, col. 1076.
[50] Ramus, *Prooemium Reformandae*, in *Collectaneae*, 476.
[51] Ramus, *Pro Philosophica*, col. 1074.
[52] Petrus Ramus, *Tres Orationes*, in *Collectaneae*, 276–77.
[53] Ramus, *Prooemium Reformandae*, in *Collectaneae*, 476: "*quae tamen liberalium artium antiquissimae et primariae . . . sine quibus reliquia Philosophia caeca est*".
[54] Ramus, *Tres Orationes*, in *Collectaneae*, 279, and *Prooemium Reformandae*, in *Collectaneae*, 476.
[55] Petrus Ramus, *Petri Rami Mathematicae Praefationes: Prima*, in *Collectaneae*, 167.
[56] See Goulding, *Defending Hypatia*, 28–33.

as the gateway not only to physics but also to ethics, politics, and all the higher disciplines including theology.[57]

Theology itself is also a principal target of Ramus' reforms. From the beginning of the Reformation the Faculty of Theology had led the attack against Protestants as well as Catholic Reformers such as Erasmus and Lefèvre. It prided itself on being a bastion of orthodoxy and had come to view the new humanist programme of biblical study as dangerous and in itself tantamount to heresy.[58] It is no wonder then that Ramus can complain that Parisian theologians "alone of all mortals" do not read or meditate on the Bible in the original languages but instead devote themselves to "biting questions" drawn unskilfully from the philosophy of Plato and Aristotle.[59] They take away the "holy and divine science of true religion" and introduce into the schools "inextricable sophistics".[60]

Ramus' attack on scholastic theology is two-pronged and relates to defects in both the matter and the form. In material terms he is clear that theology has become corrupted by the influence of pagan philosophy, and argues for the need to return to questions taken from Scripture rather than dictated by Aristotle or Plato. While, in line with his own methodological principles, he advocates the treatment of philosophy philosophically and theology theologically, this should not be read as him advocating the wholesale removal of philosophy from theology. In fact, echoing Bonaventure and the Fabrists, he actually champions a renewed "Christian philosophy" against the pagan philosophy taught in the Parisian schools.[61]

Ramus' desire is for a new dawn in which the "heavenly and divine suns"—the Old Testament in Hebrew and the New Testament in Greek—now eclipsed, may rise again and cast their beams over the Parisian schools.[62] Crucially his model for such a revival is François Vatable, a collaborator with Lefèvre and a pioneer of the new approach to biblical studies.[63] Advocating an evangelical programme of reformation, his hope is that Moses and Paul will "live again" in the theological schools. Sharing the conviction of generations of reformers that scholastic theology has become divorced from piety, he champions the "eupraxia" of theology

---

[57] Ramus, *Prooemium Mathematicum*, 218–20. Goulding, *Defending Hypatia*, 41 notes the methodological proximity of mathematics and theology in Ramus' later works.

[58] Renaudet, *Préréforme et humanisme*, 488ff., examines the different reform trajectories of Erasmus and Lefèvre in Paris.

[59] Ramus, *Prooemium Reformandae*, in *Collectaneae*, 488: "At Theologi Parisienses soli omnium mortalium questionarios mordicus retinent".

[60] Ramus, *Prooemium Reformandae*, in *Collectaneae*, 481: "proque sancta et divina scientia ad verae religionis cultum a Deo hominibus oblata, sophisticam inextricabilem in Theologiae scholas induxerunt".

[61] Ramus, *Prooemium Reformandae*, in *Collectaneae*, 488.

[62] Ramus, *Prooemium Reformandae*, in *Collectaneae*, 488, 507.

[63] Ramus, *Prooemium Reformandae*, in *Collectaneae*, 485. For Vatable's link with Lefèvre see Reid, *King's Sister*, I.120–21.

as expressed in "Christian life and holy and incorrupt morals".[64] Ethics should be taught from the Gospels, and theologians should dedicate themselves to sermons and declamations rather than disputations, in line with d'Estouteville's reforms. In Gersonian fashion, Ramus clearly wishes to combine theology and eloquence and to have theologians preach a public programme of reformation, thus nurturing a new culture of evangelical piety.[65]

If the matter of scholastic theology is "most alien", then Ramus thinks the form is "infinitely more alien".[66] In place of the old *summae* and *sententiae* he advocates for the new theological commonplaces championed by Protestant and humanist reformers.[67] For Ramus, theology has a "sacred order" and the instauration and reformation of this order is required. Scholastic syllogistic, which he views as tautologous, is thus to be replaced with his own dialectical principles. At the same time, Ramus argues for a root-and-branch reform of the entire theological curriculum: the learning of biblical languages, application of all the liberal arts to theology in encyclopaedic fashion, detailed study of the Old and New Testaments in their original languages, and the revolving and comparing of biblical interpretation with the decrees of the Councils and the entire history and polity of the Church.[68] By following this methodological and evangelical programme of reform—which Ramus sees as a continuation of that of Charles IX and the Regius Professors, but which is really more radical than that—he holds that the "splendour and dignity" of theological order will rise again so that from France rivers of blessing will flow out and irrigate the whole of Europe, making Paris the "academy of the whole world".[69]

Such a vision is notably taken up in his *Prooemium Mathematicum* of 1567, which Nancel fittingly described as his swan-song.[70] Written at the beginning the Wars of Religion, while he was sheltering under the King's protection as royal librarian at Fontainebleau, it sets out a grand and sweeping narrative of mathematical and theological reform.[71] Dedicated to Queen Catherine of Medici, the work implores her son King Charles IX to establish Plato and Pythagoras at the University of Paris.[72] Correlating the "commigration of disciplines" with the "commigration of peoples", Ramus also seeks to trace the reception of mathematics from antiquity to the present day.[73] According to Ramus it is among the

---

[64] Ramus, *Prooemium Reformandae*, in *Collectaneae*, 484, 490, 495.
[65] Ramus, *Prooemium Reformandae*, in *Collectaneae*, 490–92. For Gerson's combining of theology and eloquence see Iribarren, "Le Paradis retrouvé", 223–51.
[66] Ramus, *Prooemium Reformandae*, in *Collectaneae*, 495.
[67] Ramus, *Prooemium Reformandae*, in *Collectaneae*, 489–90.
[68] Ramus, *Prooemium Reformandae*, in *Collectaneae*, 494–95, 504–6.
[69] Ramus, *Prooemium Reformandae*, in *Collectaneae*, 506–9.
[70] Nancel, "'Petri Rami Vita'", 203.
[71] Goulding, *Defending Hypatia*, 35–38.
[72] Ramus, *Prooemium Mathematicum*, "Praefatio", 48–50.
[73] Ramus, *Prooemium Mathematicum*, 2.

Germans especially that mathematics is flourishing. Indeed, in a move calculated to appeal to the King, he links German military prowess and wealth directly to the founding of mathematical academies. Emphasizing the practical utility of mathematics, Ramus appeals to German mathematicians of his own day such as Melanchthon, Dürer, and Copernicus, but above all Regiomontanus, the "glory of Vienna".[74] Ramus' correspondent John Dee had seen Cusa as the origin of a new practical and experimental approach to mathematics,[75] but Ramus preferred to valorize Cusa's friend Regiomontanus instead.[76] In doing so, he self-consciously championed a straightforward mathematical understanding according to which "God created all things in number, measure and weight, that is according to arithmetic and geometrical rule" over what he viewed as the mystification of a Pythagorean theology "enveloped in mathematical veils".[77]

In writing the *Prooemium*, Ramus' desire was to reverse the late medieval exodus from Paris to the German universities, which he held had begun in the fourteenth century with Henry of Langenstein, and to restore the honour of French mathematics, not to mention that of the French exchequer and army.[78] However, it is also much more than that. For despite his emphasis on the use of mathematics for waging war, Ramus' larger aim is to use mathematics to institute a pan-European movement for peace.[79] In effect, by combining the German dialectic of Agricola and Sturm, who earns a special mention in the *Prooemium*,[80] with the German mathematics of Regiomontanus he hopes to initiate an educational and methodological revolution in the universities and academies of Christendom which will unite them in a common goal for the restoration of divine and human studies.[81]

---

[74] Ramus, *Prooemium Mathematicum*, 216, 266–301.

[75] John Dee, "To the Unfained Lovers of Truthe", in Euclid, *The Elements of Geometrie of the Most Aunciente Philosopher Euclide of Megara*, trans. H. Billingsley (London, 1570), Aiiiv. I am very grateful to Richard Oosterhoff for this reference. For Ramus' correspondence with Dee see Ramus, *Collectaneae*, 204–5. Notably this concerns ancient mathematical manuscripts which Ramus may have used in the final edition of the *Prooemium*.

[76] Goulding, *Defending Hypatia*, 36, 57n. mentions Ramus' admiration for Regiomontanus and his reliance on his celebrated Paduan oration for constructing his own history of mathematics.

[77] Ramus, *Prooemium*, 220: "*Theologia paganorum mathematicis velamentis tota involuta est: Christianam theologiam potius intueor et considero in qua Deus creat omnia in numero, mensura, pondere*". James Steven Byrne, "A Humanist History of Mathematics? Regiomontanus's Paduan Oration in Context", *Journal of the History of Ideas* 67.1 (2006): 56 makes clear that Regiomontanus did mention Cusa in his Paduan oration as an important "patron of mathematics", making Ramus' omission of him from the *Prooemium* seem more pointed. It is likely that by this stage he saw Cusa as too implicated in the mystical and numerological approach to mathematics that he was seeking to break away from. Petrus Ramus, *Scipionis Somnium* (Paris, 1550), 23–35 makes clear his early rejection of Pythagorean number mysticism as "false" and "superstitious".

[78] Ramus, *Prooemium Mathematicum*, 273. For the exodus from Paris see Shank, "Unless You Believe", 6–7.

[79] Ramus, *Prooemium Mathematicum*, 291.

[80] Ramus, *Prooemium Mathematicum*, 302–3.

[81] Ramus, *Prooemium Mathematicum*, "*Praefatio*", 284–301.

Throughout the *Prooemium* Ramus makes his appeal to the Kings and Princes of Europe to sponsor such an effort, but his most passionate appeal is to Pope Pius V himself.[82] He argues that, as the "lord of all academies", he should show a singular care for establishing mathematical studies.[83] Referencing the divine character of mathematics, Ramus hopes that the Pope will "fill Rome with the heroes of all sciences and doctrines", drawing the best teachers in theology, law, medicine, mathematics, and languages to the eternal city. Summing up his twin evangelical and mathematical aspirations, he says that this should combine Moses and Paul with Plato and Pythagoras, handling all disciplines in encyclopaedic fashion, with theology as their consummation. If the Pope does this, Ramus promises him that Rome will be the "mistress and queen of all academies" and that he himself will enjoy a "golden pontificate" which all peoples shall embrace.[84] Method and mathematics, as Goulding suggests, become potent means for healing all the "rifts in Christendom"—a bold and staggering vision of universal reform.[85]

## 2.3. Return to the Golden Age

In the annals of the French reform, the Colloquy of Poissy of 1561 marks an irrevocable turning point, forever remembered due to its failure to prevent the onset of the Wars of Religion. It is highly significant then that it should also mark the moment of Ramus' conversion. In a bold and remarkable letter written to his former patron the Cardinal of Lorraine, the leader of the papal party in France, Ramus tells of having glimpsed at Poissy the vision of a lost "golden age" of Christianity. Ironically, Ramus told Guise that it was his own speech, which spoke eloquently of the growing corruption that had infected the Church in the fifteen centuries since its birth—a common complaint of both Catholic and Protestant reformers—which first set him to a make a critical comparison between the Church of the first century and the Church of his own day. With the choice set down so starkly before him, Ramus says he resolved to "choose the golden age".[86] It was a brave choice and one which not only severed him from Guise but ultimately led to his untimely death. However, having made it, Ramus never looked back.

---

[82] Ramus, *Prooemium Mathematicum*, "*Praefatio*", 482–88.
[83] Ramus, *Prooemium Mathematicum*, 483–84.
[84] Ramus, *Prooemium Mathematicum*, 487–88: "*Romam expleto heroibus omnium scientiarum atque doctrinarum ... fateanturque Romam academarium omnium dominam reginamque academiam ess ... Romam tum denique vere triumphantem omnes confitebuntur, laetisque animis praedicabunt, hunc aureum pontificatum omnes mortales complectentur*".
[85] Goulding, *Defending Hypatia*, 40, 48.
[86] Skalnik, *Ramus and Reform*, 90; cf. Ramus, *Collectaneae*, 257.

It is not surprising that Ramus should feel the allure of such a vision of reform. While inadvertently inspired by Guise, it actually fit far more closely the Fabrist programme of biblical reformation. According to Carlos Eire, Lefèvre too located the "golden age" of Christianity in the New Testament era and from this standpoint offered a strong scriptural critique of contemporary Catholic ritual and practice—much stronger indeed than anything Guise could ever countenance.[87] The drive towards the primitive had been strong since the fifteenth century, especially within circles influenced by the *devotio moderna*, but it was the Fabrists who truly harnessed it to a scriptural reform of Church and theology. Even before his conversion, his biographer Theophilus Banosius had described Ramus as admonishing Parisian monks to seek a "purer theology" from the Gospel, leaving behind the "relicts of the sophists".[88] We have already seen the extent to which he envisaged a wholesale reform of theology. Ramus knew that he would be accused of heresy by the Parisian theologians for his attempts at reformation.[89] While it is unclear whether or not he had actually converted by the time he published the *Advertisements* in 1562, its evangelical tone is at least indicative of the direction he was moving in after Poissy.[90]

Significantly, the notion of a lost age of perfection also resonated with the "metaphysical narrative" of history that Ramus had been developing for nearly twenty years.[91] In terms of dialectic this is evident from as early as the *Animadversiones* of 1543. Here, drawing once again on Plato's *Philebus*, Ramus compared the true dialectic to the "celestial fire" that Prometheus brought down from the gods to men. Indeed, Ramus interpreted this famous myth quite literally, holding that the real Prometheus was that "most ancient philosopher" who first formulated the principles of dialectic, through whom they were subsequently handed down to Zeno and then to Plato.[92] The figure of Prometheus was prominent in the Renaissance and was often imbued with Christian symbolism.[93] In fact, both Lefèvre and Bovelles refer prominently to Prometheus' theft of the "holy fire" from heaven. Moreover, Bovelles' identifying of Promethean fire with the gift of

---

[87] Carlos Eire, *War against the Idols: The Reformation of Worship from Erasmus to Calvin* (Cambridge: Cambridge University Press, 1986), 172. See also Hughes, *Lefèvre*, 65.

[88] Theophilus Banosius, *Petri Rami Vita*, in Petrus Ramus, *Commentariorum de Religione Christiana Libri Quattuor* (Frankfurt, 1576).

[89] Ramus, *Prooemium Reformandae*, in *Collectaneae*, 463.

[90] Skalnik, *Ramus and Reform*, 90–115 discusses the problems of dating Ramus' conversion. He argues, however, that Poissy should be seen as the major turning point.

[91] Goulding, *Defending Hypatia*, 7 refers to this in relation to Proclus, but it clearly fits his wider claims about Ramus as well.

[92] Ramus, *Animadversiones*, 2r-v: "Prometheum antiquissimum philosophum quaedam circa dialecticam principia movisse: brevibusque monitis mirabiles sapientiae fontes aperuisse: unde Vulcani, Minervaeque artificiosam pariter cum igne sapientiam de coelo clepisse dictus est"; cf. Plato, Philebus, 16c-3 (p. 404). See also Ramus, *Institutiones*, 27v-28r.

[93] Bruyère, *Méthode et dialectique*, 196, 285–89, 410–11n.

divine wisdom enabling intellectual ascent to God suggests a Fabrist context for Ramus' own understanding.[94]

Ramus agreed enthusiastically with Aristotle that the "arts are of eternal and immutable things" but that their fortune, like stars, rises and sets.[95] In other words, the arts are continually in need of rediscovery and continually at risk of decline and decay. In his early writings Ramus can even envisage this ongoing process of discovery and rediscovery as a collective process of Platonic reminiscence, through which humanity gains access to the eternal exemplars impressed on the soul.[96] In his later writings Ramus offered an alternative Christian explanation for this, transposing the biblical pattern of creation, fall and redemption onto the history of the liberal arts, so that each takes on the "shape of the story of sacred history" itself.[97] Notably, in such a paradigm Ramism itself clearly takes on a redemptive role in history, becoming a kind of eschatological vehicle for the divine purposes for humanity.

In his mature works the heavenly origins of dialectic are pushed all the way back to humanity's first parents, Adam and Eve. Prometheus is now identified no longer just as a great philosopher but as the biblical patriarch Noah himself, the "restorer of humankind after the flood".[98] While Plato's key role in the dialectical succession is preserved, the original of invention and judgement is located in the Bible itself, specifically with the mysterious Urim and Thummim of the High Priest's Ephod which conveyed the will of God to the people of Israel.[99] For Ramus, perhaps drawing on Jewish mysticism or the Cabala, these could be taken as symbolizing "brightness of the mind" and "exactness of judgement" and thus as patterning both a biblical and natural dialectic.[100]

Precisely the same process is evident in Ramus' account of the divine origin of mathematics. Like other Renaissance mathematicians, he was deeply influenced by Josephus' discussion of this. Indeed, as early as 1544 he had followed him in identifying Adam, Seth, and Noah as the first discoverers of mathematics. According to Ramus, the extraordinary age of the antediluvian patriarchs was

---

[94] Lefèvre *Prefatory Epistles*, 60–66 and Charles de Bovelles, *Liber de Sapiente*, in *Que Hoc Volumine Continetur*, 121v–122r.

[95] Goulding, *Defending Hypatia*, 38; cf. Ramus, *Prooemium Mathematicum*, 2.

[96] Ramus, *Mathematicae Praefationes: Prima*, in *Collectaneae*, 167–68; cf. Goulding, *Defending Hypatia*, 28–29.

[97] Goulding, *Defending Hypatia*, 32–33.

[98] Ramus, *Scholae in Liberales Artes*, col. 312.

[99] Ramus, *Scholae in Liberales Artes*, col. 311–13. Bruyère, *Méthode et dialectique*, 292–93 points out that Ramus' source for this was his opponent Jacob Schegk.

[100] Kees Meerhof, "Bartholomew Keckermann and the Anti-Ramist Tradition at Heidelberg", in *Späthumanismus und reformierte Konfession: Theologie, Jurisprudenz und Philosophie in Heidelberg an der Wende zum 17.Jh*, ed. Christoph Strohm, Joseph S. Freedman, and Herman Selderhuis (Tübingen: Möhr Siebeck, 2006), 195. Cabala refers to the Jewish mystical method centred on the divine names or attributes popular in the Renaissance and resonating with Franciscan and Lullist thought.

gifted by God for the purpose of contemplation and their results were inscribed on two huge columns for the remembrance of posterity.[101] In the *Prooemium* the brief outline sketched in the mathematical prefaces is expanded on considerably, into a grand and sweeping account of the divine origin of mathematics and its transmission through Hebrew, Egyptian, Greek, and Roman thought into Christendom. Ramus now gives particular weight to the legend of the two columns, holding that Adam and the first humans had inscribed their knowledge of mathematics and the other encyclopaedic arts on these pillars in order that their knowledge should survive the approaching Flood and the conflagration at the end of the world.[102] Once again, he therefore seeks to integrate his account of the arts into a providential, and indeed eschatological, narrative of history.

Ramus' later identification of Prometheus and Noah fused together his two distinct narratives of mathematics and dialectic, giving further weight to his claim for their divine origin.[103] Indeed, giving a certain priority to mathematics, he can even argue that, since God gave mathematics to the Hebrews, we cannot doubt the "logical faculty of the soul . . . to be divinely inspired".[104] In this way, both dialectic and mathematics become inscribed within the drama of revelation and salvation history. In earlier works Ramus had demurred on precisely which arts could be considered as divinely inspired and which arose naturally. Even in the *Prooemium* he had singled out mathematics alone as *directly* revealed by God, holding that grammar, dialectic, and rhetoric were all natural in character.[105] In his final work, in what might be seen as a reaffirmation of the Franciscan encyclopaedism of his youth, he expresses a more expansive view. God is the "God of sciences", and not only mathematics but all the liberal arts are "gifts of God" whose purpose is to sustain life and to "illuminate holy letters".[106]

Ultimately, Ramus' primitivism reaches back not only to the golden age of the New Testament Church but right back to the first golden age in history—the lost perfection of the Garden of Eden. While Goulding is perhaps right to suggest that Ramus, unlike other figures of his age, does not speculate on the original perfection of Adam,[107] this does not mean that that the Edenic paradigm has no grip

---

[101] Ramus, *Mathematicae Praefationes: Prima*, in *Collectaneae*, 168; cf. Goulding, *Defending Hypatia*, 26, 29.
[102] Ramus, *Prooemium Mathematicum*, 2–5.
[103] The significance of this fusion is highlighted by Bruyère, *Méthode et dialectique*, 290–92.
[104] Ramus, *Scholae in Liberales Artes*, col. 313: "*Cum mathemata Deo ipso pene docente Hebraeis tradita legeres in Iosepho utrum dubitares facultatem logicam animali ipsi quod Deus logicum fecisset, divinitus esse inspiratam*".
[105] Goulding, *Defending Hypatia*, 39–41.
[106] Ramus, *Commentariorum*, 326: "*Itaque Iehova Deus est scientiarum, 1 Samuel 2. Geometriaque et Physica sicuti reliquiae liberales artes dona Dei sunt, non solum ad humanam vitam sustenendam utilia, sed ad sanctas literas illustrandum*".
[107] Goulding, *Defending Hypatia*, 29 notes that Ramus did not hold that Adam had a "superlative" knowledge of all the sciences.

on him. Indeed, the *Prooemium* affirms it as an "especial duty" to restore and establish the "singular and excellent theology of the first men".[108] Elsewhere Ramus describes the disastrous impact of the Fall on logic as itself a "fall into sophistry", implying the need to recover the original pure logic gifted to humanity.[109]

Perhaps the most powerful example, however, is to be found as early as the *Animadversiones*. For here, Ramus pictures the renewed dialectic as being like the mythical Garden of the Hesperides. Confirming the parallel, we find, in the very middle of this garden, logic as though a tree of life.[110] Following Lull's celebrated *Arbor Scientiae*, it had become common among both his followers and other encyclopaedists to draw on the imagery of the tree of science (Figure 2.2). Ramus was no exception, and both his name—meaning "branch" or "bough" in Latin—and his dichotomous branching charts made this comparison particularly apt.[111] Surrounding the fence of the paradisal garden of Ramist logic and always trying to encroach upon it we find fearsome Aristotelian monsters such as the infamous syllogistic rules *dici de omni* and *dici de nullo*.[112] The task of the dialectician is to drive off these monsters and to restore humanity's access to the garden. Once again the clash between scholastic and Ramist logic takes on both cosmic and eternal significance. Despite his own rapprochement with Aristotle, it was a conflict that Ramus was to renew with vigour in the final years of his life in the battle over theological method.

## 2.4. Transforming Theological Method

In 1567, the same year that the *Prooemium Mathematicum* was finished, Ramus also published his monumental Basel compilation, the *Scholae in Liberales Artes*. In this work Ramus brought together for the first time his reflections on all the liberal arts. In doing so, he offered a complete Ramist curriculum or encyclopaedia, paralleling but also tacitly superseding the *cursus Fabri* of fifty years earlier. In the *Scholae*, Ramus reiterated his continuing desire for the "conversion" of all the arts.[113] Having never abandoned his aspiration to relate all the arts to their origin in God, it was natural for him to now turn his mind to

---

[108] Ramus, *Prooemium Mathematicum*, 485: "*Illa primorum hominum, ut antea docui, theologia singularis et eximia fuit, quam restituere et stabilire tuae authoritatis imprimis fuerit*".

[109] Ramus, *Commentariorum*, 185: "*Itaque cum primus homo verax logicus a Deo factus esset, peccata suo in mendacem sophistam degeneravit*".

[110] Ramus, *Animadversiones*, 34v, 64v. Specifically, Ramus compares his three species of syllogisms to three fruitful trees.

[111] Reiss, *Knowledge, Discovery and Imagination*, 107 makes a direct link between Ramist charts and the Lullist trees found in the works of the Fabrists. Reinforcing this comparison, Ramus, *Animadversiones*, 64v refers to the "twin" branches of each logical tree.

[112] Ramus, *Animadversiones*, 64v.

[113] Ramus, *Scholae in Liberales Artes*, col. 317–18.

**Figure 2.2** Lullist diagram of the "Tree of Sciences" from the opening of Bernardo de Lavinheta, *Practica Compendiosa Artis Raymundi Lulli* (Paris, 1523). Reproduced by kind permission of the Syndics of Cambridge University Library.

producing a Ramist theology, so completing the ambitious programme he had set out for himself right at the start of his career.[114] The work that resulted, the *Commentariorum de Religione Christiana*, was published posthumously in 1576 with the Wechel press of Frankfurt after having been rescued "as if from the flames" from among his manuscripts.[115] It was accompanied by an adulatory life of Ramus by Banosius, emphasizing his credentials as a Protestant Reformer, and the whole was dedicated to Sir Philip Sidney, that redoubtable champion of the international Reformed cause.[116]

In the *Commentariorum* we see Ramus' own attempt to bring about the methodological reform of theology he had already advocated for in his *Advertisement*. From the start, Ramus contrasts the popular exposition of theology that he hopes to give, accessible to all, to that proceeding by "spiny" scholastic questions which diminishes the splendour of the "sacred science".[117] In this of course Ramus shares common cause with many of the Protestant Reformers. Indeed, in inspiration his own *Commentariorum* clearly conforms to the broader rhetorical model of the *loci communes* which Melanchthon had initiated and which an entire subsequent generation of Protestant theologians had refined and developed further.[118] Importantly, it also appeals to an older catechetical model, prominent in Augustine and medieval theology and renewed by Protestantism, of structuring theology around the Apostles' Creed, Lord's Prayer, and Ten Commandments.[119]

Where Ramus' originality lay was in applying his own dialectic to the very structure and dynamic of theological discourse. Ramus held that there were as many methods of theology as there were doctors of theology. This had dire consequences, for the lack of a single, universal method had called theological judgement into question, resulting only in "conjectures and the opinion of men".[120] Ramus' new method—his own dialectic of course—was intended to bring a "singular light for seeing clearly and perspicuously all the parts of theology".[121] Going beyond the rhetorical pattern of previous Protestant theology, he sought an order patterned solely on dialectical and mathematical principles:

---

[114] Ramus, *Commentariorum*, 326 notably places the *Commentariorum* itself in the context of theological encyclopaedism.

[115] Banosius, *Vita*.

[116] Banosius, *Vita*.

[117] Ramus, *Commentariorum*, 1–2.

[118] For discussion of the Reformed appropriation of the *loci communes* model see Muller, *After Calvin*, 23–46.

[119] For this structure see the "*Index*" of the *Commentariorum*. Muller, *PRRD*, 1.58, 104, 110, 199, 210–11 emphasizes the importance of the catechetical model for Reformed theology.

[120] Ramus, *Commentariorum*, 3.

[121] Ramus, *Commentariorum*, 3–4: "*Itaque qui primus hanc methodum ad Theologiae informationem attulerit, accendet lumen singulare ad omnes Theologiae partes clare et perspicue pervidendum*".

I have chosen the most abundant elenchum constructed not in an alphabetical order but a methodical one, by which all the greatest, middle and least precepts, examples or whichever other arguments of the whole of Scripture there are, should be referred to the singular heads of Christian doctrine, allowing that the most ample and wide wood of so many and such things should yet be comprehended artificially and by brief and compendiary notes of numbers.[122]

In other works, Ramus had spoken of his desire that all the arts should have a mathematical structure; now, significantly, he extends this to theology itself. While he did not go nearly as far as the Fabrists in this direction, there remains an important sense in which he too sought a mathematical theology.

Ramus' dream was thus to develop a methodologically ordered body, or system, of Christian doctrine in which the interconnection of every truth to every other was made evident. In the *Commentariorum* he was well aware that he was only doing this in a provisional fashion. Recalling a prominent trope of his 1543 *Institutiones*, he speaks of having provided only a rough outline to be polished by others and filled in with "living colours".[123] Indeed, while later Ramist systems of theology were to apply a branching dichotomous pattern through the whole of theology, the *Commentariorum* explicitly extends this principle only to the major divisions of the work. According to Ramus, all of theology can be divided into doctrine and discipline—a notably Reformed statement. Doctrine itself consists of faith and the works of faith—books I and II of the *Commentariorum*—while discipline is expressed in prayer and sacraments, or praxis and polity—books III and IV.[124] For Ramus what is paramount is that this methodical unfolding of Christian truth itself precisely conforms to the creedal and catechetical pattern which he views as fundamental to all of theology. This is scarcely surprising given that Ramus has already positioned his method as a divine dialectic, encoded in the very text of Scripture itself.

For Ramus there was a direct connection between the renewal of method and the desire to recapture the golden age of the Apostolic Church. Following his conversion, during his time as a royal librarian, Ramus had made an intense study of patristic thought.[125] His conviction was that ancient light dispels new shadows,[126]

---

[122] Ramus, *Commentariorum*, 5: "optarem . . . elenchum locupletissimum, non alphabetice, sed methodico ordine constructum, quo omnia totius scripturae, et maxima, et mediocra, et minima sive praecepta, sive exempla, sive alia quaevis argumenta essent, ad singula illa doctrinae Christianae capita refferentur, sylvaque tot tantarumque rerum licet amplissima latissimaque, tamen brevibus compendiariisque; numerorum notis artificiose comprehenderetur".

[123] Ramus, *Commentariorum*, 4: "hactenus placuit ad istam tractationis methodique speciem tibi rudia quaedam doctrinae Christianae lineamenta ducere, quae tu polito limatoque judicio polires et limares, vivisque coloribus exprimeres"; cf. Ramus, *Institutiones*, 19r.

[124] Ramus, *Commentariorum*, 3.

[125] Banosius, *Vita*.

[126] Ramus, *Commentariorum*, 2: "Quapropter antiquam lucem novis eiusmodi tenebris longissime rejectis revocandam censeo".

and the *Commentariorum* clearly promotes the scriptural and Platonic theology of the Church Fathers against the Aristotelian and scholastic theology which he felt had corrupted it. Locating his theology in the "more elegant and urbane philosophy", he thus draws on Greek Fathers such as Justin Martyr, Clement, and Cyril and Latin Fathers like Arnobius, Lactantius, and Augustine.[127] Ramus believed Aristotle to overthrow the divine creation and administration of the world and bind everything in necessity—a charge anticipated centuries earlier by Bonaventure and other Christian Augustinians—but warmly cited Anaxagoras and Plato in favour of the free government of the world by the divine mind.[128] Ramus was also clearly an advocate of the Mosaic theology, holding that Plato not only had knowledge of the creation of the world but glimpsed the Trinity, as expressed in his famous triad of God, Mind, and World Soul[129]—perhaps the closest that he ever comes to espousing the analogical, Trinitarian method of the Fabrists.[130]

Ramus' championing of an older, Platonic theology against a newer Aristotelianism clearly placed the *Commentariorum* on a very different trajectory from the renascent scholasticism increasingly espoused by many of his Reformed brethren.[131] Importantly, it connects his methodology to a different tradition stretching back into the Renaissance of the Quattrocento and beyond to that of the twelfth century.[132] For it shows Ramus very much trying to develop a *prisca theologia* in conjunction with the *prisca philosophia* which animated his arts encyclopaedism. Indeed, Ramus specifically says that he combines the Church Fathers with the best Classical writers in the *Commentariorum*, in order to demonstrate that Christian theology is not abstruse or remote from the senses, but rather that a certain "natural light" illuminates all people and "invites and allures" them to divine studies.[133]

---

[127] Ramus, *Commentariorum*, 2.
[128] Ramus, *Commentariorum*, 19–20, 26–27; cf. Bonaventure, *Collationes*, 6.2–4 (*BOO*, V.360–61).
[129] Ramus, *Commentariorum*, 19–20, 74. On p. 99 Ramus openly espouses Platonic philosophy as Christian.
[130] Bruyère, *Méthode et dialectique*, 410n. rightly points out Ramus' distinction from Bovelles on this point. Nevertheless, the early Ramus was not immune to triadic thinking, as we see from the repeated pattern of threes in the *Institutiones*—three parts of dialectic, three degrees of judgement, etc.
[131] See Muller, *PRRD*, 1.33ff. Muller himself tends to downplay the Platonic influence on early modern Reformed theology, although rightly points out the ways in which medieval Aristotelianism absorbed Platonic influences (*PRRD*, 1.71–73, 285, 362, 369).
[132] For the Platonism of the Italian Renaissance see Hankins, *Plato in the Italian Renaissance*. For the Platonic character of the twelfth-century Renaissance see Chenu, *Nature, Man and Society*, 1–98. Ramus, *Commentariorum*, 316, 339 shows knowledge of some of the great twelfth-century theological debates and of the work of the Irish Neo-Platonist Eriugena. See also Paul Lobstein, *Petrus Ramus als Theologe: Ein Beitrag zur Geschichte der protestantischen Theologie* (Strasbourg, 1878), 22–23 who notes Ramus' affection for Bede, Eriugena, Ratramnus, and Bernard of Clairvaux. On p. 86 he argues that Ramus' main thrust is to connect the Reformation to humanism in the service of evangelical truth.
[133] Ramus, *Commentariorum*, 2.

Discounting his strident anti-Aristotelianism, his theology also actually displays a notable harmonizing tendency reminiscent of the broader tradition of Christian Platonism:

> And this elenchum of things, with all loci of the same genus having been compared everywhere, should not only place before our eyes in order a universal sentence concerning whatever thing of the whole Scriptures, but by that comparison should elicit and unfold the truth; and should effect the true concordance of discordant opinions concerning holy letters.[134]

Ramus' abiding concern is thus for his method to offer a *concordia discors*. In this we are reminded of the watchword not only of twelfth-century Platonists or systematicians such as Alan of Lille and Gratian but also of Lull, Pico, and above all Cusa himself.[135] Indeed, it was Lefèvre who in his *Quincuplex Psalterium* upheld the *concordia* of all the Scriptures as methodological justification for his own Christocentric approach to theology.[136]

For Ramus, theology is the "doctrine of living well".[137] From the beginning, and following a definite Franciscan trajectory, he espouses a thoroughly practical understanding of theology. As he insisted, the "greatest and nearly sole virtue of reasoning is in exercise".[138] While all the other arts teach how to excel in one aspect of life—to speak well, to reason well, to number well, to measure well, etc.—theology teaches the art of living well, which encompasses them all. To live well is to "live congruently and fittingly to God the fount of all goods".[139] It is not something which can be attained by one's own strength, as the ethics of the pagans taught, but only through grace. Indeed, although Ramus retains an important place for natural light, he insists that theology is divinely given to men and comprehended in the revelation of Scripture. Outside of Scripture there can be no true theology. It is the Word of God which is a light both to us and within

---

[134] Ramus, *Commentariorum*, 5: "*At hic rerum elenchus, comparatis undique locis eiusdem generis omnibus, non solum ordine subjiceret ante oculus universam quaque de re totius scripturae sententiam, sed ipsa comparatione verum . . . eliceret et explicaret: veramque discordantium de sacris literis opinionum concordantiam efficeret*".

[135] For twelfth-century references see Gratian's *Concordia Discordantium Canonum* and Alan of Lille, *The Complaint of Nature*, trans. Douglas M. Moffat (New York, 1908), "Prose III" (https://sourcebooks.fordham.edu/basis/alain-deplanctu.asp; accessed 25/11/2021). Lohr, "Metaphysics", 542–43, 557, 582 emphasizes the importance of *concordantia* in Lull, Cusa, and Pico. Nicholas of Cusa, *The Catholic Concordance*, ed. and trans. Paul E. Sigmund (Cambridge: Cambridge University Press, 2003), 1.2.12 (p. 9; NCOO, XIV.36) draws on this principle explicitly.

[136] See Guy Bedouelle, *Le Quincuplex Psalterium de Lefèvre d'Étaples: Un guide de lecture* (Geneva: Droz, 1979), 109–13.

[137] Ramus, *Commentariorum*, 6.

[138] Ramus, *Institutiones*, 3v, 4v, 44r: "*Summa igitur, ac prope sola disserendi virtus est in exercitatione*".

[139] Ramus, *Commentariorum*, 6.

us.[140] Ramus' theology is thus a harmonizing of both natural and scriptural illumination, and in this way the whole of the *Commentariorum* becomes bathed in the radiance of divine light.

The subject of the entirety of Scripture is Christ and supremely his sacrificial death on the Cross for remission of sins. Indeed, all theology must be directed to Christ the way, the truth, and the life.[141] Like the Fabrists, Ramus clearly has an evangelical understanding of theology. The whole of theology is summed up in faith in Christ. Faith gives understanding of the Bible, and it is faith—understood as trust (*fiducia*)—which converts the shadowy virtues of pagan philosophy into living colours.[142] Moreover, echoing Lefèvre, Ramus can describe Christ as the supreme "exemplar" and "archetype" of the Christian life.[143]

In Ramus' theology we also find an important convergence of the mathematical and mystical currents characteristic of Fabrist thought. While the Bible reveals to us who God is and his name, it does not do so in any way that defines him. For the name of God, the tetragrammaton, is ineffable. Drawing on Exodus 33, he argues that God does not reveal to us his face, his essential majesty, as this is inscrutable and incomprehensible to us. Rather, God reveals to us only his posterior, that is his works, or to put it in logical terms his effects and adjuncts. While God can be known logically to us, to accurately define him it is necessary to have the "logic of God himself".[144] It is not clear whether Ramus knew the late medieval tradition of the *logica fidei*, but there is a definite affinity here.[145] Certainly he is highly critical of applying Aristotelian logic to theology, saying "if only Christian men had never taught the logic of Aristotle" then theology would not have been corrupted.[146] Likewise, it is clear that he views his logic as a kind of divine dialectic, patterned on Scripture and perfectly suited for analysing God's revelation of himself to humanity. In this sense, Ramist dialectic is the closest we can get to the logic of God's own being, even though this always remains beyond our grasp.

For Ramus, as for Cusa, there seems to be a real sense in which God transcends all human logic. Admittedly, this is only implicit in the *Commentariorum*, but there are some tantalizing hints, not least in the distinction between God's own logic and human logic. It is also striking that Ramus' discussion of Aristotelian and Platonic approaches to theology culminates in an assertion of that "high and sublime wisdom" which is the "learned ignorance of a pious soul".[147] Ramus

---

[140] Ramus, *Commentariorum*, 1–10, 18.
[141] Ramus, *Commentariorum*, 6–7, 9–10.
[142] Ramus, *Commentariorum*, 9–10.
[143] Ramus, *Commentariorum*, 309. For parallels with Lefèvre see Bedouelle, *Quincuplex*, 143–47.
[144] Ramus, *Commentariorum*, 15.
[145] Interestingly he does cite Henry of Langenstein in *Prooemium*, 273 but this is in rather a different context.
[146] Ramus, *Commentariorum*, 329.
[147] Ramus, *Commentariorum*, 28.

warns explicitly against the attempt to become a "scrutiniser of the divine majesty" and counsels instead to "descend rather into yourself and in those things which you judge yourselves to know recognise your own ignorance".[148]

Significantly, Ramus' espousal of learned ignorance links him to a long Christian tradition going back through Bonaventure to Augustine and Pseudo-Dionysius.[149] However, it was Cusa's account of learned ignorance which became paradigmatic for the Renaissance, especially the distinctive mathematical expression he gave to it and its consummation in the coincidence of opposites.[150] Thus while Ramus links this notion to Augustine,[151] who was also, it must be remembered, an important source for Cusa,[152] it is highly significant that two of the principal demonstrations of this learned ignorance come from mathematics: the infinity of numbers and the squaring of the circle.[153] Likewise, Ramus also tacitly invokes the coincidence of opposites when he indexes his account of the paradoxical coinciding of divine election and human freedom to the "learned ignorance of the Christian philosopher".[154] In this, we find a striking parallel with Lefèvre who, exactly like Ramus, drew on Cusa to affirm the coincidence of God's immutable decree of election with his omnisalvific will.[155]

Final confirmation of Ramus' intimate connection to a Fabrist and Cusan vision of theology comes from his discussion of God's infinity and his presence in the world. Citing the magnificent Psalm 139 in support of his claim that the "infinity of divinity is diffused through all times and places", he comes to a surprising mathematical conclusion:

> God is present in all times and places and fills all things with his perpetual virtue, but is not anywhere or ever filled. Rightly that philosopher said God to be a sphere whose centre is everywhere and circumference nowhere.[156]

Truly, we have come full circle and returned again to that fusion of mathematical and theological conceptualities which is the very summit of his 1543 *Institutiones*. For Ramus, all theology must therefore ultimately end in learned ignorance, exclaiming with the Apostle, "O, the altitude of the riches of the wisdom of God".[157]

---

[148] Ramus, *Commentariorum*, 27–28.
[149] Nicholas of Cusa, *Apologia Doctae Ignorantiae*, 17–18 (*NCOO*, II.12–14); Cullen, *Bonaventure*, 185.
[150] Cusa, *De Docta Ignorantia*, 1.4.11–12, 11.30–32 (*NCOO* I.10–11, 22–24).
[151] Ramus, *Commentariorum*, 326.
[152] Cusa, *Apologia*, 17–18 (*NCOO*, II.12–14).
[153] Ramus, *Commentariorum*, 26–28, 326.
[154] Ramus, *Commentariorum*, 28–33.
[155] Meier-Oeser, *Die Präsenz des Vergessenen*, 42.
[156] Ramus, *Commentariorum*, 13.
[157] Ramus, *Commentariorum*, 32–33 citing Romans 11:33.

On reading the *Commentariorum* one could almost be forgiven for thinking that the Reformation had never happened. Certainly, as Paul Lobstein notes, Ramus opposes in no uncertain terms keystones of both Lutheran and Roman Catholic doctrine—images, transubstantiation, and ubiquity—yet he does so virtually without a single mention of any theologian of his own day.[158] Indeed, Skalnik is right to connect Ramus to a more irenic Erasmian tradition, as much as to the Strasbourg and Zurich theology.[159] Nevertheless, as we have sought to demonstrate, Ramus shows an even greater proximity to the evangelical Catholicism of Lefèvre and the Meaux Circle. This becomes evident not only in his theological method but also, and perhaps above all, in his desire for the unity and concord of the Church. For it is here that we truly see in Ramus the converging of the old and new reform.

Evidence of this comes from a passionate and poignant appeal for Christian unity written by Ramus just days before his own violent death. In this he exhorts all Christians to return to the "age of the apostles", which was truly a "golden age of religion", in comparison to which our own is "scarcely . . . an age of iron". Referring to the "discord" which Satan has spread among Christians and which has taken hold in the Church, resulting in the "ruin of cities" and the "devastation of provinces"—something we must remember that he had likely witnessed firsthand—he counsels instead that

> God the author of agreement and the moderator of concord should be invoked and beseeched, to enlighten the minds of men who rule his church, so that they will perceive the truth and bring a peaceful settlement to the Christian people both in public and in private, to remove completely stubbornness and obstinacy, and enkindle in our hearts nothing but the desire and love for piety and truth.[160]

In providing a "concordance of discordant" scriptures, method serves a fundamental irenic and ecumenical purpose. Indeed, as we have seen throughout this chapter, method is intended to be a reflection of the divine order of reality, and theological method itself is patterned on the harmony of divine revelation. It has its origin, as the 1543 *Institutiones* made clear, in the unity of God and is thus intended to lead everything back to that unity. Its ultimate goal therefore is surely nothing less than to restore that "communion of the saints" which Ramus described from the Church Father Cyprian as many rays making up one light, many branches one tree, many streams one fount, and all united in Christ.[161]

---

[158] Lobstein, *Ramus*, 35–41.
[159] Skalnik, *Ramus and Reform*, 116–47; Lobstein, *Ramus*, 36–37, 41–48. On p. 125 n. 33 Skalnik points out that Vermigli, Bucer, and Tremellius are the only modern theologians cited.
[160] Nancel, "'Petri Rami Vita'", 261.
[161] Ramus, *Commentariorum*, 82–83.

Unity is also a mathematical concept, and Skalnik has unearthed compelling evidence that Ramus believed the unity of the Church to be best expressed in the arithmetical and geometrical harmony of its members—a notion which parallels not only Jean Bodin but much more significantly the *De Concordantia Catholica* of Cusa himself.[162] For Ramus, both Church and society are intended to mirror that unity and concordance which has its origin in God himself and which becomes expressed in the mathematical harmony that runs through and connects all of reality. If he cannot, unlike Cusa and the Fabrists, ever quite bring himself to connect the Trinity to this mathematical and concordant vision of reality, the connection is at least implicit in its realization as the "unity of the Spirit in the bond of peace".[163] Ramus was never to enjoy that peace, but its pursuit was at the heart of all his methodological endeavours, from his very first to his very last.

---

[162] Skalnik, *Ramus and Reform*, 155–57. For the Cusan connection to this see Cusa, *Catholic Concordance*, 2.33.242–46 (pp. 188–92; *NCOO*, XIV.286–89).
[163] Nancel, "'Petri Rami Vita'", 261.

# 3
# Logics of Faith

Piscator, Herborn Ramism, and
the Confessionalization of Method

Well before Ramus' tragic death in the St Bartholomew's day massacre of 1572, Ramism—the system of thought that he bequeathed—was spreading throughout Europe. Yet his followers inherited a dilemma, for Ramus' thought was pulling them in two directions. On the one hand, Ramism was clearly a product of the Renaissance "rhetorical turn" in logic. The new understanding of dialectic as encompassing both necessary and probable reasoning meant that, in principle, any form of speech or written discourse could now be subject to logical analysis. In this sense, as Kees Meerhof suggests, Ramist logic itself is best understood as the culmination of the humanist quest for a versatile method capable of analysing the nuances of Classical texts and revealing their hidden structural depths.[1] On the other hand, as we have argued, this rhetorical turn was also connected to a wider metaphysical turn. As becomes particularly apparent from Ramus' *Scholae*, Ramist logic is now intended to replace Aristotelian metaphysics as the science of "being *qua* being".[2] As we may also see from his *De Religione Christiana*, Ramus clearly intended his logic to replace scholasticism as the method of theological discourse.[3]

It thus fell to Ramus' followers, in both Britain and Continental Europe, to find ways of uniting these two divergent aspects of Ramism—the rhetorical and metaphysical—and to develop out of them new encyclopaedic and theological patterns of reform. Significantly, the first steps in achieving this were taken by Ramus' German followers. Ramism quickly established an important foothold in Germany. Many of the most important Ramist pioneers were German, and in Germany Ramism became institutionalized to an extent unparalleled anywhere else in Europe, and only to be rivalled in the seventeenth century by the Puritan colonies in New England.[4]

---

[1] Meerhof, "Beauty and the Beast".
[2] Ramus, *Scholae in Liberales Artes*, 933–37, 942, 959.
[3] Petrus Ramus, *De Religione Christiana* (Frankfurt, 1583), 3–5.
[4] Miller, *New England Mind*, 64–238.

Of course, Ramism's success should not be exaggerated. Even at its height its heartland was to be found in the numerous Reformed academies and gymnasia scattered across the country, and in Germany, as elsewhere in Europe, Ramists often found the gates of prestigious universities barred against them. Moreover, even in these academies Ramism sometimes struggled to establish itself, contending against rival scholastic and humanist pedagogies. In a sense, therefore, Hotson is right to suggest that Ramism, for all its undoubted successes, remained a movement of the peripheries.[5] Nevertheless, the championing of Ramism by leading German Reformed voices, both philosophers and theologians, points to the way in which Ramism spoke to concerns central to the age. Certainly, there can be no doubt that Ramism was ultimately to make deep inroads into the intellectual and theological culture of Germany and Central Europe.[6]

In this chapter we will consider the origins and early development of this German Ramism, especially as it took root in the famous Herborn Academy, where from its inception Ramism attained an impressive dominance in the curriculum of studies. As Hotson has suggested, it was often necessary for Ramism to adapt in order to survive and, we may say, in order to thrive.[7] This was certainly true of German Ramism, which quickly merged with Melanchthonian currents of thought to form a distinctive Philippo-Ramist synthesis. Marking a return to Ramus' earlier Platonism, this also prompted renewed attention to the therapeutic role of logic. It also received a new covenantal expression, marking the beginning of an important alliance between Ramism and federal theology. As taken up and developed by the Herborn school, this newly conceived Philippo-Ramism gradually became reconfigured into a powerful tool for analysing and systematizing scriptural *loci*, thus laying the foundation for the next stage of Ramism's ongoing transformation.

## 3.1. Ramism, Philippism, and Neo-Platonism

The spread of Ramism in Germany from around the middle of the sixteenth century onwards was undoubtedly governed by an important pedagogical dynamic. Due to the combined opposition of humanists and Aristotelians, Ramism was unable to gain a secure foothold in prestigious universities and academies, but it flourished in smaller Reformed schools and gymnasia. For in these schools the Ramist promise of an efficient, streamlined curriculum proved irresistible.

---

[5] Hotson, *Commonplace Learning*, 36–37.
[6] See Hotson, *Commonplace Learning*, 38ff.
[7] Hotson, *Commonplace Learning*, 227–30.

Of these gymnasia, Dortmund proved especially important, and the curriculum of the Dortmund academy early went through an extensive Ramist overhaul under the rectorships of Johann Lambach and Friedrich Beurhaus. In Hotson's words, it became the "major early seedbed of Ramism" in this region, and within a matter of decades Ramist academies had been planted throughout Rhineland-Westphalia, with major centres established at Korbach, Marburg, and Lemgo.[8] It was no surprise therefore that Beurhaus noted in a letter to Johann Freige that in "our Westphalia" students "read Ramus and Ramists with the greatest eagerness in almost all the schools".[9]

If we ask why North-Western Germany, in particular, proved such a fertile ground for the expansion of Ramism, then Hotson has an important answer to offer us: "The starting point for understanding the avid reception of Ramism in north-western Germany is the recognition that Ramism, in a sense, derived from that region".[10] For the Ramist dialectical system was profoundly indebted to an earlier tradition of German humanism, whose key representatives were Agricola, Sturm, and Melanchthon. Ramus himself was well aware of this connection, even though he proved unable to exploit it successfully during his visit to Germany in 1569–70.[11] While his pleas for the fundamentally Agricolan character of his logic largely fell on deaf ears at the University of Heidelberg, that proud bastion of scholastic Aristotelianism, they gained much more receptive hearers in the gymnasia where Agricola's dialectic was already strongly rooted. This was all the more true in the many schools touched by the educational revolution initiated by Sturm and Melanchthon, the *praeceptor Germaniae*.[12]

Notably, the proliferation of Ramism also coincided with a broader exodus of Philippists from the Lutheran universities of East Germany into the Protestant universities and academies of West Germany and the Rhineland. This stimulated the combining of their systems into a new "Philippo-Ramist" synthesis.[13] At first sight, any cooperation might seem surprising. For while Ramus had praised Melanchthon as the German Plato, Melanchthon had been openly dismissive of Ramus for his "foolish statements" and long-windedness, even predicting that there would be little demand for his logic![14] It has thus been easy to see this merging of Ramism and Philippism as something of a marriage of convenience. Indeed, Hotson seeks to argue this, demonstrating how in many schools and

---

[8] Hotson, *Commonplace Learning*, 25–30.
[9] Cited from Hotson, *Commonplace Learning*, 27.
[10] Hotson, *Commonplace Learning*, 26, 68.
[11] See Hotson, *Commonplace Learning*, 71; cf. Ramus, *DC*, 75.
[12] Hotson, *Commonplace Learning*, 71.
[13] For Melanchthon's negative attitude to Ramism see Joseph S. Freedman, "Melanchthon's Opinion of Ramus and the Utilization of Their Writings in Central Europe", in *The Influence of Petrus Ramus*, ed. Feingold, Freedman, and Rother, 70–71. For Philippo-Ramism in Germany see Hotson, *Commonplace Learning*, 102–26.
[14] Freedman, "Melanchthon's Opinion of Ramus", 69–71.

gymnasia Ramus was used for teaching the lower classes, but the upper classes added Melanchthon or Aristotle.[15] For example, we see this attitude clearly in the statutes of Uppsala, which held that Ramism was "enough for beginners" but "for the more learned and those who endeavour to get a sound knowledge of logic, it is not satisfactory".[16] Perhaps more surprisingly, the same pattern is also evident in Steinfurt, a daughter school of Herborn, where Ramism was not taught at the highest levels of the school and not intended to be employed at all in the teaching of advanced subjects such as ethics, physics, astronomy, jurisprudence, and theology.[17] Even in Bremen, where the teaching of Ramism dated back to Ramus' own lifetime, its hold on the upper curriculum proved fragile, with Melanchthon and Aristotle jostling with Ramus for dominance.[18] Given the two logics were so often unequally yoked, in Hotson's view the main reason for combining the two was thus wholly pragmatic: "since Ramus was easier but Melanchthon on many points sounder, the best foundation for ... pedagogy was a Ramism emended by reference to Melanchthon".[19]

Yet, while this clearly was the attitude of some Ramist educators, it was importantly not the attitude of the most prominent Philippo-Ramists themselves—men such as Paul Frisius, Johannes Rigerius, Michael Sonleutner, and Heizo Buscher, who carried out a systematic comparison and harmonization of the Ramist and Philippist dialectical systems. In his evocatively named *Harmoniae Logicae Philipporamae Libri Duo* of 1596, Buscher, formerly the rector of the Hanover gymnasium, speaks of his desire to "conjoin the perspicuity of Philipp with the wonderful brevity of Ramus".[20] Yet he also holds that Melanchthon's logic must be renewed and perfected according to the "canon" of Ramus' method.[21] The same pattern is evident in Johann Bilsten, who published in the same year the *Syntagma Philippo-Rameum Artium Liberalium*, the first Philippo-Ramist encyclopaedia. For he speaks of Ramus as having, by a "most perfect compendiary way", perfected Aristotle's three laws. In doing so he has achieved the "arts disposed by divine method", in other words, the ideal pattern of the encyclopaedia. For him, it is therefore Ramus, more than Melanchthon, who is the perfecter of the arts and the restorer of the divine light of logic, originally

---

[15] Hotson, *Commonplace Learning*, 104–7.
[16] Cited from Hotson, *Commonplace Learning*, 106 n. 23.
[17] Joseph S. Freedman, "Ramus and the Use of Ramus at Heidelberg within the Context of Schools and Universities in Central Europe, 1572–1622", in *Späthumanismus und reformierte Konfession*, ed. Strohm, Freedman, and Selderhuis, 104–5.
[18] Thomas Elsmann, "The Influence of Ramism on the Academies of Bremen and Danzig: A Comparison", in *The Influence of Petrus Ramus*, ed. Feingold, Freedman, and Rother, 54–62; Hotson, *Commonplace Learning*, 105.
[19] Hotson, *Commonplace Learning*, 104.
[20] Heizo Buscher, *Harmoniae Logicae Philipporamae Libri Duo* (Lemgo, 1597), "Praefatio ad Lectorem".
[21] Buscher, *Harmoniae*, "Praefatio ad Lectorem".

given to man in his innocency and subsequently darkened by the Fall. Ultimately, Ramism can be seen as both redemptive and revelatory in character.[22]

Bilsten's references to "divine method" are an important reminder that the Philippo-Ramists had powerful philosophical and theological motivations, as well as purely pragmatic or pedagogical ones, for desiring to combine the two dialectical systems. Indeed, as Sandra Bihlmaier has argued, the reason that these Philippo-Ramists were able to combine Ramism and Philippism so readily was due to their appreciation of the shared Neo-Platonic character of both systems. She argues that what unites Ramus and Melanchthon, despite their important differences, is a Platonic focus on natural dialectic. Fundamental to both logicians was their shared conviction that the human mind mirrors its divine archetype in both the structure and dynamics of its reasoning. For Melanchthon, this is realized through "inborn notions" (*notiones insitae*) which God impresses on the soul, and which as true and self-evident principles irradiate the mind with a divine light of certainty. For Ramus, it is evident in his exemplarism, and the dynamic convergence of the divine and human intellect through the bond of ideas. Crucially, for both thinkers this divine light of logic is mathematical in character and, for Ramus especially, it offers absolute certainty. In what Bihlmaier identifies, following Risse, as a profoundly un-Aristotelian move, logic thus becomes expounded *more geometrico* and—by implication, we might add—*more divino*.[23]

Importantly, as Bihlmaier suggests, we find these same kind of Neo-Platonic resonances in the Philippo-Ramists themselves. Thus Paul Frisius hailed Melanchthon and Ramus as the Plato of Germany and the Plato of France, and, like Bilsten, emphasized the divine origins of their dialectic.[24] Bilsten himself defined art as relating to the ordering of eternal precepts,[25] and Philippo-Ramists regularly appealed to the "natural order" of logic, which they identified with the Ramist pattern of a "descent from universals".[26] Moreover, the topical Realism which both Ramism and Philippism shared implied an important conformity between the structure of logic and the structure of reality.[27] Indeed, the German Ramists of the sixteenth century were frequently accused by their opponents of

---

[22] Johannes Bilsten, *Syntagma Philippo-Rameum Artium Liberalium* (Basel, 1596), "*Epistola Dedicatoria*".

[23] Sandra Bihlmaier, "Platonism in Humanist Logic Textbooks of the Sixteenth Century: Melanchthon, Ramus, and the Philippo-Ramists", *Acta Comeniana* 29 (2015): 14–26; Risse, *Logik der Neuzeit*, 105; Frank, "Melanchthon and the Tradition of Neo-Platonism"; and Bruyère, *Méthode et dialectique*.

[24] Paul Frisius, *Comparationum Dialecticarum Libri Tres* (Frankfurt, 1590), 13; cf. Bihlmaier, "Platonism", 28–32.

[25] Bilsten, *Syntagma*, 1.

[26] Bihlmaier, "Platonism", 30, 32, 34.

[27] Bihlmaier, "Platonism", 30.

trying to construct a "metaphysical logic" of first intentions, in opposition to the instrumental Aristotelian logic of second intentions.[28]

Notably, Bihlmaier makes no mention of the way that the Philippo-Ramists took up the parallel between mathematics and logic. Yet if we turn to Buscher's popular Ramist textbook of mathematics, the *Arithmeticae Libri Duo* of 1597, we find many of these assumptions paraded explicitly, even extravagantly.[29] Conceiving the arts in therapeutic terms, as divinely ordained "medicines of souls"—something which had been a particular emphasis of Melanchthon[30]— Buscher holds that mathematics should not be given the "last place". Instead, he argues that it is the "faculty of numbering" that distinguishes men from beasts, implying its contiguity to the image of God. Drawing on Plato's *Phaedrus*, he thus sees logic and mathematics as two "wings" of the mind, allowing it to ascend to contemplate invisible and heavenly natures. Developing the theme of the divine nature of mathematics, he holds that it is indispensable for all the other arts, including theology and the right ordering of society. Strikingly, he also suggests that the "first, antique and unique method of perpetually progressing from universals to singulars", i.e. the Ramist method, has as much place in mathematics and logic. Buscher therefore holds that the gift of combining the mathematical and logical order has been gifted by God to a "languishing age" through Ramus, who has restored the true order of the arts and revealed to us a "divine treasury".[31]

## 3.2. The Ambiguities of Philippo-Ramism

Of course, not all German Ramists were Philippo-Ramists. Indeed, there were some like Beurhaus, the above-mentioned rector of the gymnasium at Dortmund, who were rather resistant to the fusion of Ramism and Philippism. While they had great respect for Melanchthon, they were also concerned about the ambiguities in Philippist logic and the incompatibilities with Ramus' own pattern of dialectic. This becomes clear from Beurhaus' meticulous philosophical comparison of Ramus' *Dialecticae Libri Duo* and Melanchthon's *Dialecticae Libri Quatuor*—a defining work for sixteenth-century German Ramism.[32]

---

[28] Riccardo Pozzo, "Ramus' Metaphysics and Its Criticism by the Helmstedt Aristotelians", in *The Influence of Petrus Ramus*, ed. Feingold, Freedman, and Rother, 96–106.
[29] Heizo Buscher, *Arithmeticae Libri Duo Logica Methodo Conformati et Conscripti* (Hamburg, 1597), "*Dedicatio*", 1. The Ramist character of this work is made explicit in the dedicatory epistle and is clear from the definition of arithmetic as "*ars bene numerandi*".
[30] See Bihlmaier, "Platonism", 21.
[31] Buscher, *Arithmeticae Libri Duo*, "*Dedicatio*".
[32] Pozzo, "Ramus' Metaphysics", 101.

It is important to understand that as a "pure" Ramist, Beurhaus shared many of the same basic convictions as the Philippo-Ramists. Like Bilsten he daringly parallels God's plan of redemption and his progressive revelation of logic and the other arts.[33] He emphasizes also that the art of logic is of a "nearly divine dignity" and, following Ramus, that its pattern is revealed by God in the Urim and Thummim of the Old Testament. Dialectic itself is the "image of the natural use of reason expressed" and the faculty of reasoning on which it depends is "divinely impressed on the mind as though by the light of wisdom".[34] Put succinctly, natural dialectic is therefore the "archetype of art", and art should always follow the footsteps of nature as though following God himself. Following Melanchthon, he also holds that we have within us innate "seeds" of the arts, especially in the "ingenerate light" of logic, arithmetic, and geometry.[35] Overall, it is therefore little surprise that Beurhaus, much like the Philippo-Ramists, was viewed by his Aristotelian opponents as a "crypto-Platonist" seeking to institute a metaphysical logic.[36]

Nevertheless, despite this common ground, Beurhaus was emphatic that Melanchthon subverted the "natural order" of Ramist dialectic. His express purpose in comparing the two "dissimilar" systems of dialectic was therefore very simply to "see where Melanchthon departs from this order and recall him back to it".[37] For Beurhaus, Melanchthon's pattern of logic subverts the true Ramist order of the three laws of method. While he concedes that Melanchthon does follow a "natural progress from simple things to more complex", he sees his refusal to anchor the whole of logic in the natural ordering of invention and judgement as highly problematic.[38] Even more serious for him is Melanchthon's Nominalistic account of the relation of logic and reality. Beurhaus insists that universals are really existent outside the mind and manifest a "real communion" of essences and individuals which is then "conceived by common terms and genera". Like Ramus he clearly assumes an isomorphism between mind and reality, and his distinctive Ramist insistence that generic structure extends to individuals as "most special species" seems to imply a broad Scotism to be ranged against Melanchthon's pronounced Ockhamism.[39] In fact, Beurhaus may well have recognized that the Philippist emphasis on innate knowledge as revealing the ideal pattern of

---

[33] Friedrich Beurhaus, *P. Rami Dialecticae Libri Duo et His e Regione Comparati Philippi Melanchthonis* (Frankfurt, 1588), "Prooemium"; *De P. Rami Dialecticae Praecipius Capitibus Disputationes Scholasticae* (Dortmund, 1581), "Praefatio ad Lectorem".

[34] Beurhaus, *Disputationes Scholasticae*, "Praefatio ad Lectorem".

[35] Beurhaus, *Disputationes Scholasticae*, "Prooemium", 1–10.

[36] Pozzo, "Ramus' Metaphysics", 102–3.

[37] Beurhaus, *P. Rami Dialecticae Libri Duo*, "Prooemium".

[38] Beurhaus, *P. Rami Dialecticae Libri Duo*, "Prooemium", 21–22, 58, 62, 64, 70; cf. Bihlmaier, "Platonism", 14–15.

[39] Beurhaus, *P. Rami Dialecticae Libri Duo*, 23–34. For Melanchthon's Nominalism see Risse, *Logik der Neuzeit*, 90–93.

reality obviates the need for Realism with respect to the external world.[40] In this, he differs from Philippo-Ramists like Buscher, who tended to elide the difference between Melanchthon's Nominalism and Ramus' Realism, while tacitly upholding the latter.[41]

Importantly, the reflections of Beurhaus and the Philippo-Ramists are almost exactly contemporary with another Ramist movement that was emerging in North-Western Germany at this time: the Herborn school instituted by Caspar Olevian and Johannes Piscator. Confronting the extremes of contemporary Ramism and Philippism, they developed a more nuanced account of Realism and particularly of the grounding of logic in extra-mental reality. Upholding the broader Philippo-Ramist notion of a redemptive parallel between philosophy and theology, they also sought to resolve some of its ambiguities. For although some German Ramists followed Melanchthon in affirming an innate knowledge of God, others, like Beurhaus and his followers, seem to have assumed a radical disjunction between philosophy and theology.[42] For the Herborn theologians, Ramism becomes reintegrated, under grace, into every theological endeavour. Increasingly, if still rather inchoately, Ramist logic is perceived not simply as a tool for analysing texts, or even a natural dialectic, but rather as an intrinsic aspect of the structure of divine revelation itself. In this way, as Hotson has brilliantly illuminated, the Herborn school marked a significant step towards the Reformed confessionalization of Ramism—something that Buscher especially hotly opposed.[43]

## 3.3. Olevian's Ramism

Caspar Olevian was an exact contemporary of Beurhaus and like him he belonged to the broader Philippo-Ramist milieu.[44] However, while Beurhaus

---

[40] Riccardo Pozzo, "Logic and Metaphysics in German Philosophy from Melanchthon to Hegel", in *Approaches to Metaphysics*, ed. William Sweet (Dordrecht: Springer, 2005), 61–74 points to the ambiguity of modern accounts of Melanchthon's philosophy which polarize between Nominalist and Neo-Platonic readings.

[41] Buscher, *Harmoniae*, 172–75.

[42] See Friedrich Beurhaus, *Defensio P. Rami Dialecticae* (Erfurt, 1588), "Epistola". A Dortmund theological disputation from around 1610 attacked Bartholomäus Keckermann for his supposed assertion that "all that is true in philosophy is true in theology". This is bound in with a copy of Rudolph Goclenius, *Collegium Philosophico-Theologicum* (Marburg, 1610) to be found in New College Library, Edinburgh (Shelfmark—W5.280/1).

[43] Hotson, *Commonplace Learning*, 108–14. For Buscher see below.

[44] Olevian's Ramism has been the topic of some controversy. Jürgen Moltmann, "Zur Bedeutung des Petrus Ramus für Philosophie und Theologie in Calvinismus", *Zeitschrift für Kirchengeschichte* 68 (1957): 295–318 saw Olevian's Ramism as an important front against Theodore Beza and the emergent Protestant scholasticism. Such a view has been rightly refuted by Lyle D. Bierma, "The Covenant Theology of Caspar Olevian" (PhD Dissertation, Duke University, 1980), 230–38, R. Scott Clark, *Caspar Olevian and the Substance of the Covenant: The Double Benefit of Christ* (Grand Rapids, MI: Reformation Heritage Books, 2005), 39–71, and Muller, *PRRD*, 1.183. However, while Bierma

attained some celebrity as a philosopher, this paled into insignificance when compared with Olevian, who was an internationally renowned Reformed theologian, celebrated for his involvement in the Heidelberg Catechism and his pioneering role in the development of federal theology.[45]

In order to understand the roots of Olevian's Ramism we must go right back to his early education at Trier, likely in an Agricolan and Philippist mode, which instilled in him a vision of education as a sacred vocation capable of recalling people back to the paradise forfeited through sin.[46] Proceeding to the Universities of Orléans and Bourges, Olevian received a thorough education in "legal humanism" and possibly an induction to Ramism from his teacher François Hotman, one of the most celebrated jurists of the age.[47] It was also at this time that he converted to Protestantism, leading him to enrol in 1557 in the Genevan Academy under Theodore Beza, who became an important mentor and friend. Inspired by the fiery Guillaume Farel, Olevian returned to his native Trier in 1559, where he hoped to ignite a city-wide Reformation.[48] Significantly, he began his campaign in the schools, lecturing on the Latin dialectic of Melanchthon, and using him to preach Christ to his students—another important reminder of the close ties between logic, theology, and reform in this age.[49]

While Olevian's attempts to introduce Reformation in Trier proved abortive, they did bring him to the attention of the Elector Frederick III, whose son he had befriended at Bourges.[50] In 1560 the Elector appointed him to teach at the prestigious *Collegium Sapientiae* in Heidelberg, and in 1561 he was appointed Professor of Theology. Here he played a major role, along with his friend Zacharias Ursinus, in spearheading the attempt to introduce a Calvinist Church order into the Palatinate, and engaged in remodelling the school system. He also helped Ursinus to draft the Heidelberg Catechism, which he later promoted in his

---

denies outright that Olevian was a Ramist ("Covenant Theology", 232–35), Clark offers the more nuanced view that Olevian "mixed obviously Aristotelian substance with Ramist presentation" ("The Authority of Reason in the Later Reformation: Scholasticism in Caspar Olevian and Antoine de la Faye", in *Protestant Scholasticism*, ed. Trueman and Clark, 120; Clark, *Caspar Olevian*, 59). Our own reading is much closer to that of Clark but avoids any problematic dichotomy of form and content.

[45] For Olevian's federal theology see Clark, *Caspar Olevian*.
[46] Caspar Olevian, *An Exposition of the Symbole of the Apostles*, trans. John Fielde (London, 1581), "To the Youth Addicted to True Godlinesse", 36–39.
[47] Clark, *Caspar Olevian*, 51. For Hotman's friendship with Ramus and his intellectual debt to him see Donald Kelley, *François Hotman: A Revolutionary's Ordeal* (Princeton, NJ: Princeton University Press, 1973), 21, 57, 232.
[48] Clark, *Caspar Olevian*, 19 points out that although historically a second-generation reformer, Olevian experienced the same kind of challenges as the first-generation reformers.
[49] Johannes Piscator, *Kurzer Bericht vom Leben und Sterben Herrn Gasparis Oleviani* (Herborn, 1587); cf. Bierma, "Covenant Theology", 4. Piscator's mention of this seems particularly significant, given how little detail he gives on other aspects of Olevian's career.
[50] Clark, *Caspar Olevian*, 11. Olevian even (unsuccessfully) risked his life to save the young nobleman from drowning.

celebrated theological works *Vester Grundt* and *Expositio Symboli Apostolici*.[51] In 1569 he befriended Ramus during his visit to Heidelberg, defending his appointment to the faculty in the teeth of considerable opposition, including that of Ursinus, who just a year later pointedly published a treatise against the use of Ramus' logic and rhetoric in school instruction.[52] After Ramus left, Olevian continued to correspond with him through their common friend Immanuel Tremellius, the Professor of Old Testament at Heidelberg, by this time having become a devotee of his method.[53]

Following his expulsion from Heidelberg in 1576 by the new Lutheran Elector Ludwig VI, Olevian found shelter with Count Ludwig I of Wittgenstein at Berleburg, where he tutored the Count's sons, taught in the school, and led a Calvinist reorganization of the Church in the Wetterau counties. It was here that Olevian wrote some of his most important biblical commentaries, which offered important logical and theological analyses of Scripture, paving the way for Piscator's more famous logical commentaries.[54] Here also he published his two handbooks of dialectic, the *Fundamenta Dialecticae* of 1581 and *De Inventione Dialecticae* of 1583. The latter particularly provides an important record of his classes at Berleburg. It is replete with theological examples and reveals his intent to teach logic's "use and institution in the fear of the Lord".[55]

Indeed, in the *De Inventione* logic and theology become actually entwined, each informing the other. We may see this from the important therapeutic role that Olevian ascribed to his theological logic, surpassing medicine in its restoration of souls to eternal life and not merely physical health.[56] We may also see it in Eustace Vignon's preface to the work, which compares the scholastic logicians, with their "intricate questions", to bad doctors who harm more than they heal. For Vignon, the true logician must return to the "founts of nature"—thus going a step beyond the humanist return *ad fontes*. Advocating Ramus' natural dialectic, he holds that we have the principles of reasoning well, speaking well, numbering well, singing well, etc. "from our origin". The true dialectic, in the tradition of Pythagoras, Socrates, Plato, and Aristotle, thus follows the Ramistic pattern of nature, precepts, and use.[57] Vignon's clear implication is that Olevian's own work,

---

[51] Clark, *Caspar Olevian*, 27.
[52] Freedman, "Melanchthon's Opinion of Ramus", 81.
[53] Hotson, *Commonplace Learning*, 103 n. 6.
[54] Clark, *Caspar Olevian*, 34. See, for example, Caspar Olevian, *In Epistolam D. Pauli Apostoli ad Romanos Notae* (Geneva, 1584), "*Epistola Dedicatoria*", which praises the Apostle's method for taking the straight path and avoiding the labyrinth—a typical Ramist point. Despite this it would be rather a stretch to call them Ramist commentaries.
[55] See throughout Caspar Olevian, *De Inventione Dialecticae Liber e Praelectionibus Gasparis Oleviani Excerpti* (Geneva, 1583).
[56] Olevian, *De Inventione Dialecticae*, 18.
[57] Eustace Vignon, "*Typographus Candidus Lectoribus*", in Olevian, *De Inventione Dialecticae*.

which he notes for its brevity, method, and usefulness, has realized this natural dialectic.[58]

Importantly, such a goal is clearly in harmony with *both* Melanchthon's and Ramus' express purpose. Indeed, a close reading of the *De Inventione* places it in the Philippo-Ramist school, revealing a common debt to the Ciceronian-Agricolan pattern of dialectic. The title *De Inventione Dialecticae* is itself a tribute to both Cicero and Agricola. Likewise, Olevian's definition of dialectic as an "art, the mistress of wisdom and of the distinction of true from false", is derived from Cicero, and he praises Agricola's precepts highly in the work.[59] The interleaving of Ramist and Philippist method is also seen right from the start of the work. While it begins from Melanchthon's Ciceronian account of simple and composite questions, as representing respectively the two defining aspects of dialectic—wisdom and discernment of truth, or invention and judgement—it swiftly moves on to elaborate these according to Ramus' "ten lights"—his topical arguments.[60] Likewise, although Olevian, unlike Ramus, retains an important place for the predicaments and predicables, these are not given their controlling role at the beginning of dialectical system as in Aristotelian or Philippist logic. Rather, Olevian clearly assimilates the predicaments to his "ten lights" of arguments, as we may see from the Ramist charts he employs to illustrate their structure.[61]

Crucially, Olevian's Philippo-Ramist method plays a key role in mediating between his logic and theology. Referring to Melanchthon's method of questions, he points out that such questions may be formed by running through all the places of dialectic—the Ramist arguments. This, he suggests, provides a "wonderful treasury" allowing for systematic investigation of the Word of God.[62] Like Ramus, Olevian also gives a central place to causes in his logic, remarking that the "cognition of causes" is the "fount of every solid wisdom and of the distinction of true from false".[63] It is therefore highly significant that he directly parallels the causal structure of his logic with the causal structure of the divine mind:

> This order of causes arises from God the fount of every wisdom. For God acts according to a certain end since he is most wise. And the end in the divine mind precedes in order the efficiency or action of God, [and] then he gives matter and form to things, by which he constitutes things.[64]

---

[58] Vignon, "*Typographus Candidus Lectoribus*", in Olevian, *De Inventione Dialecticae*.
[59] Olevian, *De Inventione Dialecticae*, 1, 16.
[60] Olevian, *De Inventione Dialecticae*, 1–5.
[61] Olevian, *De Inventione Dialecticae*, 164–68.
[62] Olevian, *De Inventione Dialecticae*, 3.
[63] Olevian, *De Inventione Dialecticae*, 5.
[64] Olevian, *De Inventione Dialecticae*, 13: "*Hic causarum ordo a Deo fonte omnis sapientiae oritur. Deus enim agit ad certum finem, cum sit sapientissimus: et finis in mente divina efficientiam sive actionem Dei ordine praecedit, deinde materiam et formam dat rebus, per quas res constituit*".

Here we see the way in which the divine mind serves Olevian as an archetypal model for a new kind of natural dialectic.

Indeed, there is a sense in which Olevian is able to unfold the whole of his theology through his logic. From the nexus of causes in the Triune God "from whom, in whom, to whom are all things", he thus elaborates an account of creation and providence, including reflections on the Fall and human sinfulness.[65] The teleological correspondence of form and end is then used to reveal God's creation of humanity in his image and the mission of his Son to restore that image and gather a Church of the elect.[66] Significantly, the discussion of causes also encompasses the will of God, his decrees, and the grounding of his covenantal action.[67] Finally, throughout the *De Inventione*, the Ramist category of "use" reinforces the practical and therapeutic dimensions of his logic, always pointing the reader to salvation through the working of the Trinity and for his glory.[68] This is by no means to suggest that Olevian saw theology as a deductive system. Rather, it is to suggest that in both logic and theology he perceived parallel dynamics of revelation, such that the Triune God could be seen as the archetype of both—an understanding which clearly resonated with his Philippo-Ramist worldview, and, as we shall see, anticipated important later developments in the Ramist movement.

## 3.4. Olevian and the Birth of Federal Theology

From the *De Inventione* it was but a short step to working out a fully developed covenantal theology, and this Olevian was to produce just two years later in his celebrated *De Substantia Foederis* of 1585. The connection between Ramism and covenant theology has long been a topic of controversy. While Jürgen Moltmann's sharp dichotomizing of a Ramist-federal and Aristotelian-scholastic stream of Reformed theology has rightly been discredited, there can be no denying an important early alliance between Ramist and covenantal theologians.[69] Although Olevian was by no means the first Reformed covenantal theologian, he marks the beginning of a new, Ramist, phase of its development.[70]

---

[65] Olevian, *De Inventione Dialecticae*, 7–37.
[66] Olevian, *De Inventione Dialecticae*, 57.
[67] Olevian, *De Inventione Dialecticae*, 22–23, 39.
[68] See, for example, Olevian, *De Inventione Dialecticae*, 5.
[69] Moltmann, "Zur Bedeutung des Petrus Ramus". Wilhelm Neuser, "Die Calvinistischen Ramisten", in *Handbuch der Dogmen- und Theologiegeschichte*, ed. Carl Andresen, 3 vols. (Göttingen: Vandenhoeck & Ruprecht, 1980), 2.328–47 echoes Moltmann's claims in a less polemically freighted context.
[70] David A. Weir, "*Foedus Naturale*: The Origins of Federal Theology in Sixteenth-Century Reformation Thought" (PhD Dissertation, University of St Andrews, 1984), 161–66 follows Bierma in seeing Olevian as instituting a new personal phase of covenant theology but misses the systematizing dimension.

The origins of Reformed federal theology have been traced back to Switzerland and especially to the Zurich theologians Huldrych Zwingli and Heinrich Bullinger, with whom Ramus maintained a close connection.[71] While reflecting both a biblical pattern and an eclectic patristic and medieval inheritance, it had particularly deep roots, as we touched on above, in Scotist and Nominalist theology.[72] For it was Scotus who was the inaugurator of the covenantal turn of the Late Middle Ages, leading to covenant becoming the central motif of fourteenth- and fifteenth-century theology.[73] While the precise channels linking early Reformed and late medieval theology remain hotly debated,[74] Bolliger argues that Zwingli's own profound debt to Scotism shaped his understanding of God's gracious covenanting as a means of bridging the infinite gulf between Creator and creature.[75] Bullinger too was exposed to both the *via antiqua* and *via moderna* and is known to have engaged with Franciscan theology.[76] For Calvin too, his whole theology is given covenantal shape by a Scotistic dialectic of finite and infinite and thereby driven by a relentless "finalism", in which God's will becomes the ultimate ground of the physical, moral and salvific order, and all of history a covenantal unfolding of his eternal decrees.[77]

The new covenant theology subsequently received an important systematizing impulse from Ursinus, Olevian's close colleague and friend at Heidelberg. In line with a broader "Heidelberg Scotism",[78] Ursinus' theology had a markedly

---

[71] Skalnik, *Ramus and Reform*, 122–47.

[72] See J. Wayne Baker, *Heinrich Bullinger and the Covenant: The Other Reformed Tradition* (Athens: Ohio University Press, 1980), 1–25. While Baker argues that "the nominalist idea of 'pact' seems to have had little if any direct influence on the development of the Reformed covenant idea" (p. 24), John V. Fesko, *The Covenant of Works: The Origins, Development, and Reception of the Doctrine* (New York: Oxford University Press, 2020), 12–17 rightly acknowledges the important influence of Scotus and late medieval theology. Intriguingly, he also draws attention to Aquinas' Christological account of covenant. David P. Henreckson, *The Immortal Commonwealth: Covenant, Community, and Political Resistance in Early Reformed Thought* (Cambridge: Cambridge University Press, 2019), 16–48 also offers a valuable account of Thomist and intellectualist influences on Reformed covenant theology, although he tends to downplay too much the importance of the Scotist moderate voluntarist tradition.

[73] William J. Courtenay, "Nominalism and Late Medieval Religion", in *Covenant and Causality in Medieval Thought: Studies in Philosophy, Theology and Economic Practice*, ed. William J. Courtenay (London: Variorum Reprints, 1984), 26–58; Ozment, *Age of Reform*, 33–36.

[74] Stephen Strehle, *Calvinism, Federalism and Scholasticism: A Study of the Reformed Doctrine of the Covenant* (Bern: Peter Lang, 1988) argued for a late medieval, Scotistic, influence on early modern Reformed covenant theology. While by no means unproblematic, his overall argument is nevertheless worth revisiting.

[75] Bolliger, *Infiniti Contemplatio*; Georg Plasger, "Covenantal Theology: Risks and Chances of a Controversial Term", in *Covenant: A Vital Element of Reformed Theology. Biblical, Historical and Systematic-Theological Perspectives*, ed. Hans Burger, Gert Kwakkel, and Michael Mulder (Leiden: Brill, 2022), 386.

[76] Strehle, *Calvinism, Federalism and Scholasticism*, 146.

[77] Oberman, *Initia Calvini*, 10–19; cf. Calvin, *Institutes*, 3.23.2 where he claims in Scotist fashion that the "will of God is the supreme rule of righteousness, so that everything which he wills must be held to be righteous by the mere fact of his willing it".

[78] I have borrowed this phrase with permission from Arthur Huiban, whose own study of the Heidelberg Reformed tradition promises to reveal its deep Scotist presuppositions.

practical orientation, culminating in covenant as an expression of the gracious, reconciling love between God and humanity realized supremely in the Incarnate Christ—a Christological vision resonating with the Franciscans.[79] Indeed, as David Weir has argued, Ursinus was the first to extrapolate the federal pattern of God's dealings with Israel and the Church to a pre-Fall compact between God and Adam.[80] The effect of this should not be underestimated for, as Weir argues, it made covenant "the primary overarching vehicle" by which God relates to humanity, propelling it to the centre of Reformed theology.[81]

While Ursinus himself was strongly opposed to Ramism, his covenant theology proved deeply attractive to Olevian, already primed by Ramism to realize its practical and therapeutic potential. In the *De Substantia* itself we see this Ramist pattern in the overarching dichotomy between the substance of the covenant and its administration, which structures the work and gives it its dynamic trajectory from the eternal to the temporal. For substance refers to the promises of God rooted in the eternal decrees of the Trinity and administration to its manifestation over time in the visible Church.[82] Indeed, Olevian conceives the whole of the *De Substantia* as a "deduction" of the covenant through all the articles of faith, which he significantly refers to as an "unfolding" of the "universal substance of the covenant".[83]

While this gives the work its creedal structure, we also see a convergence with the logical pattern of the *De Inventione* in analysing the divine decrees according to a pattern of end and means. In particular, the twofold end of glorifying God and providing us eternal peace of conscience becomes expressed according to different logical stages in the divine willing—something subsequent Reformed theologians would link explicitly with Scotus and his instants of nature.[84] At the same time, running through the work we find the dynamic tension between the "legal covenant" which obliges humanity to perfect obedience to the law as an "eternal norm of justice in the divine mind" and the "gratuitous covenant" founded on the "eternal and immutable decree of God to adopt us in his Son".[85] In this Olevian adumbrates, even more clearly than Ursinus, the twofold distinction

---

[79] Zacharias Ursinus, *The Commentary of Dr Zacharias Ursinus on the Heidelberg Catechism*, trans. G. W. Williard (Cincinnati, OH: T. P. Bucher, 1861), 96–97. For Ursinus' practical and experiential theology see Lyle D. Bierma, "Theology and Piety in Ursinus' *Summa Theologiae*", in *Church and School in Early Modern Protestantism: Studies in Honor of Richard A. Muller on the Maturation of a Theological Tradition*, ed. Jordan J. Ballor, David Sytsma, and Jason Zuidema (Leiden: Brill, 2013), 295–305. Bierma does not draw out the medieval background to this, but Muller, *PRRD*, 1.340–54 notes an important Augustinian and Scotist context to the wider Reformed discussion.
[80] Weir, "*Foedus Naturale*", 116–36.
[81] Weir, "*Foedus Naturale*", 75.
[82] Caspar Olevian, *De Substantia Foederis Gratuiti inter Deum et Electos* (Geneva, 1585), 2–3.
[83] Olevian, *De Substantia*, 4.
[84] Olevian, *De Substantia*, 14–15, 28–29. For Scotus' instants of nature see Scotus, *Rep.* 1A d. 39–40 q. 3 art. 3 n. 38–44 (II.475–77).
[85] Olevian, *De Substantia*, 13, 28.

between the covenant of works and covenant of grace soon to be taken up and systematized by the British Ramist tradition.[86] In doing so, he reveals a budding nexus between Ramism, Scotism, and the emerging federal theology.[87] Indeed, following a long-established Franciscan pattern, Olevian is clear in understanding covenant as the self-giving of the Triune God to his elect people rooted in his gracious will.[88]

## 3.5. Olevian and the Founding of the Herborn Academy

Within a year of finishing writing the *De Inventione*, Olevian was called on to employ his expertise in logic and theology in pioneering the curriculum for the newly founded Reformed academy at Herborn. The founder of the Herborn academy, Count Johann VI of Nassau-Dillenberg, and Olevian's patron, Count Ludwig of Wittgenstein, were close friends and allies in the "Calvinization" of the Wetterau counties. The founding of a new academy was intended to serve as a Reformed bulwark against the hostile Catholic territories surrounding the Wetterau and the increasingly aggressive Lutheran Palatinate. Count Johann was also the brother of William, Prince of Orange, and one of the principal motivations for advancing the project was to establish a common Orange-Nassau academy for the education of the Reformed nobility, clergy, and civil servants to help promote their shared dynastic and confessional ambitions in the Netherlands and Germany.[89] Moreover, since the Peace of Augsburg of 1555 had given no official recognition to the Reformed Church, the founding of Herborn marked something of a bid for legitimation, playing into Emperor Maximilian II's moves towards toleration.[90]

Olevian's stellar reputation as a theologian and his role in advancing Reformed confessionalization in Heidelberg and the Wetterau made him a rather obvious

---

[86] For links between Ramism and federal theology see Neuser, "Die Calvinistischen Ramisten", 2.328–47. Fesko, *Covenant of Works*, 33–44 traces the covenant of works back to Robert Rollock, the noted Scottish Ramist theologian, and also notes its contemporaneous presence in other Ramists such as William Perkins and Dudley Fenner.

[87] Aaron C. Denlinger, *Omnes in Adam ex pacto Dei: Ambrogio Catarino's Doctrine of Covenantal Solidarity and Its Influence on Post-Reformation Reformed Theologians* (Göttingen: Vandenhoeck & Ruprecht, 2011), 74–76, 223–25 240, traces the Reformed covenant of works back to the Catholic theologian Ambrogio Catharinus who was deeply influenced by Scotist theology.

[88] Olevian, *De Substantia*, 4–12 emphasizes the Trinitarian foundation of the covenant. Bonaventure of Bagnoregio, *St Bonaventure's Life of Our Lord and Saviour Jesus Christ* (New York: P. J. Kenedy and Sons, 1881), 11–17 follows Bernard of Clairvaux in dramatizing redemption in terms of a pious dispute between the divine attributes of justice, truth, and mercy. Notably, Bonaventure interprets this explicitly in terms of an agreement between the Father, Son, and Holy Spirit.

[89] Hotson, *Alsted*, 15–24 and Gerhard Menk, *Die Hohe Schule Herborn in ihrer Frühzeit (1584–1660): Ein Beitrag zum Hochschulwesen des deutschen Kalvinismus im Zeitalter der Gegenreformation* (Wiesbaden: Historische Kommission für Nassau, 1981), 22–33, 43–45.

[90] See Menk, *Hohe Schule*, 22–33, 43–45 and Hotson, *Alsted*, 15–24.

choice for Count Johann. At least since 1577, around the time of Count Johann's open conversion to the Reformed faith, he had been closely involved in planning for the academy's foundation.[91] In Heidelberg and especially Berleburg, Olevian had had the opportunity to interact closely with the new Reformed gymnasia that were spreading throughout North-Western Germany. As Hotson argues, the runaway success of the Ramist pedagogical model with its efficient, streamlined approach to the curriculum must have been immediately apparent both to him and Count Johann.[92] At the same time, surely no less attractive to Olevian was the capacity of Ramism to engender a transformative, theological vision of education. Indeed, from his own written reflections, it is plain that the pious Count Johann entirely shared Olevian's appreciation of the spiritual benefits of a Ramist education for his subjects.[93]

It is therefore no surprise that when Olevian took charge of Herborn in 1584 the new foundation quickly took on a strongly Ramist character. A clear Philippo-Ramist approach is already enshrined in the Herborn statutes of 1585, the *Leges Scholae Herbornensis*, which mandated the teaching of both Ramist and Philippist dialectic in the public school. This was then continued by further grounding in Ramist dialectic in the first and second classes as well as a comprehensive introduction to Ramist rhetoric through the texts of Ramus' own collaborator Omer Talon. Supplementing the study of these dialectical and rhetorical texts was an intensive study of Classical texts and Scripture in the original languages, giving the students ample opportunity to practise their Ramist skills of analysis and genesis. In the third, upper, class the study of Ramus' dialectic continued, but was now combined with Melanchthon's dialectic and a reading of selected epistles from Sturm, thus reinforcing the overall Agricolan pedagogy.[94] Throughout the *Leges* there is an emphasis on the importance of combining theology and piety within a methodological framework. Theology is intended to be taught directly from the Bible as well as from Calvin's *Institutes*. Alongside other lessons there were also regular catechetical classes, as well as a weekly disputation on different theological *loci* to hone systematizing skills.[95] Going beyond other Reformed academies, Ramism was thus taught consistently at all levels of the Herborn academy, and not only as an introductory text at the lower levels.[96]

---

[91] Menk, *Hohe Schule*, 32–33.
[92] Hotson, *Commonplace Learning*, 28–33.
[93] See Andreas Mühling, "Anmerkungen zur Theologenausbildung in Herborn", in *The Formation of Clerical and Confessional Identities in Early Modern Europe*, ed. Wim Janse and Barbara Pitkin (Leiden: Brill, 2006), 83.
[94] Johannes Piscator, *Leges Scholae Herbornensis* (Neustadt, 1585), "*Index Lectionum Scholae Herbornensis*"; cf. Hotson, *Commonplace Learning*, 103.
[95] Piscator, *Leges*, "*Index Lectionum*".
[96] Freedman, "Ramus and the Use of Ramus", 101 n. 35. Elsmann, "Influence of Ramism", 55 suggests that Herborn was the exception in Germany.

Confirming the dominance of Ramism at Herborn is the early pattern of appointments. For, as Gerhard Menk emphasizes, from the beginning Olevian and Count Johann pursued a clear strategy of employing Ramist teachers.[97] For a brief time Rudolph Goclenius the Elder—the preeminent German philosopher of his age and, at this time, a noted Ramist—was employed at Herborn, but he soon returned to Marburg, where there was much more scope for his metaphysical and Lullistic talents.[98] More successful was the appointment of three Ramists from Korbach in 1586—Heinrich Crantz, Lazarus Schöner, and Hermann Germberg. Korbach was known for its strong Ramism, and the very fact that three prominent teachers were persuaded to stay, even if only for a time, is testimony to Herborn's own perceived Ramist orientation. Jacob Alsted, an early teacher in dialectic and the father of the celebrated Johann Heinrich Alsted, was also inclined towards Ramism, and became one of Olevian's closest friends and confidants.[99] However, undoubtedly, Olevian's most important appointment was that of his friend Johannes Piscator, who became rector of the Herborn school, and who was, in fact, chiefly responsible for composing the 1585 *Leges*. For, especially following Olevian's death in 1587, it was Piscator who was responsible, with the express support of Count Johann himself, for preserving the Philippo-Ramist character of the curriculum and for implementing a comprehensive Ramist programme of theological education.[100]

Yet even at Herborn Ramism did not go entirely unchallenged. In the very year of his appointment Piscator faced a considerable crisis when the Philippo-Ramist synthesis "threatened to disintegrate" due to the open rift between Lazarus Schöner, the Professor of Philosophy, and Jodocus Nahum, the new Professor of Theology.[101] While Schöner championed pure Ramism, the newcomer Nahum wished to replace the textbooks of Ramus entirely with those of Melanchthon. It was only the intervention of Count Johann which saved the situation and prevented wider division in the academy.[102] Although Menk quips that this was a "Solomonic solution", Hotson seems right to suggest that it rather reflects the desire of the Count and the founders that Ramism should not be taught at Herborn without reference to Aristotle.[103] It is thus notable that the teaching of the Scottish Aristotelian Gilbert Jack met with considerable applause in the Herborn schools, leading one commentator to write that "the discipline of Aristotle which for a long time the students had despised as supercilious now began to please them".[104]

---

[97] Menk, *Hohe Schule*, 38.
[98] Menk, *Hohe Schule*, 38; cf. Hotson, *Alsted*, 34, 56–58.
[99] Menk, *Hohe Schule*, 38–41.
[100] Menk, *Hohe Schule*, 210–13.
[101] Hotson, *Commonplace Learning*, 104.
[102] Menk, *Hohe Schule*, 210.
[103] Hotson, *Commonplace Learning*, 104.
[104] Menk, *Hohe Schule*, 211 n. 50.

From what we can discern at Herborn its scholasticism was eclectic, as elsewhere, and shaped by definite methodological priorities. In its insistence on closely aligning God's power and wisdom, David Henreckson has argued for an important intellectualist, even Thomistic, dimension to Herborn scholasticism.[105] Yet such a restrained voluntarism is by no means inconsistent with Scotism, as Alexander Broadie would remind us.[106] In fact, we find definite Scotist accents in the Herborners' approach to both divine and natural law.[107] Since this voluntaristic and covenantal approach is found combined with a strong Realism and exemplarism, we may feel justified in speaking of an important Scotist current at Herborn.[108] Such was, of course, consistent with the wider Ramist and Agricolan character of the pedagogy. Yet to understand the precise shape of this we must turn to Piscator, who did most to shape the teaching of Ramism in Herborn.

### 3.6. Piscator's Ramist Conversion

The connections between Piscator and Olevian go back well before the founding of the Herborn Academy. Indeed, as Piscator was later to tell Olevian's son Paul, in the preface to his *Animadversiones*, Olevian had played a major role in his own philosophical development, catalysing his own turn to Ramism. Born in Strasbourg in 1546, Piscator attended as a schoolboy the famous gymnasium of Johannes Sturm, where, in his own words, he was "nourished in the precepts of Aristotle". Piscator's Aristotelianism was only reinforced by study at the University of Tübingen where he came under the influence of Jacob Schegk, a fervent anti-Ramist, and was, by his own confession, "consumed by his study of Aristotelian logic".[109] From Tübingen, Piscator received in 1574 a prestigious appointment to a professorship at Heidelberg, only to shock everyone by resigning it a year later to take up the much humbler post of rector of the Heidelberg *Paedagogium*, the city's Latin preparatory school. Like Olevian and his own teacher Sturm, Piscator clearly felt a divine vocation as a teacher, dedicating himself to grounding his students in the knowledge of languages and the arts "necessary for the understanding and explanation of Christian doctrine".[110]

---

[105] Henreckson, *Immortal Commonwealth*, 28–30.
[106] Alexander Broadie, *The Shadow of Scotus: Philosophy and Faith in Pre-Reformation Scotland* (Edinburgh: T&T Clark, 1995), 19–34.
[107] Grabill, *Rediscovering the Natural Law*, 146 n. 46 notes the Scotism of Althusius in this regard. A similar doctrine is evident in Matthias Martinius, *Christianae Doctrinae Summa Capita* (Herborn, 1603), 133–34.
[108] Matthias Martinius, *Methodus Theologiae*, 132–33, 217, 226, in *Christianae Doctrinae Summa Capita*.
[109] Johannes Piscator, *Animadversiones Ioan. Piscatoris. Arg. In Dialecticam P. Rami* (2nd ed.; Frankfurt, 1582), 4–5.
[110] Hotson, *Alsted*, 20–21.

By this time, his attitude to Ramism had begun to shift quite markedly. Indeed, later he recorded in strikingly religious terms how "a clearer light began to shine on me" on reading Ramus' *Dialectica* for the first time.[111] However, it was only through Olevian visiting his classes and bullying and exhorting him to make an in-depth study of Ramus' logic that he experienced the full dawn of Ramist method. Newly convinced of the merits of Ramus, Piscator also began to turn a critical eye to the Philippist Aristotelianism he had been teaching, finding it especially wanting in the discussion of "places of argument"—the traditional territory of logical invention and judgement.[112] In true Philippo-Ramist style, Piscator resolved to combine the best of Melanchthon and Ramus. The result was an overhauling of his entire teaching of dialectic, such that, as Hotson has aptly put it, while he "began his lectures by making Ramist emendations to Melanchthon he finished them making Melanchthonian emendations to Ramus".[113]

Expelled from Heidelberg in 1577 by the new Lutheran Elector, Piscator first found employment with Olevian's patron Count Ludwig I of Wittgenstein before being appointed Professor of Theology at Neustadt and then co-rector of the gymnasium at Mörs.[114] At Mörs he offered Ramist readings of Cicero's *De Officiis* and Horace's complete epistles, in which he carried out detailed grammatical, logical, and rhetorical analysis of these texts—a pattern which would later serve him well in his commentaries on Scripture.[115] It was here also in 1580 that he published his first commentary on Ramus' dialectic, the *Animadversiones*. His inspiration for this was Olevian's own dialectical textbook, the *Fundamenta Dialectica*, from which he confessed to having borrowed "not a few examples". Dedicating this to Paul Olevian was thus a fitting way of restoring his patrimony to him.[116] In retrospect, Piscator had also evidently come to see his formation in the Agricolan humanism of Sturm's academy as an important propaedeutic to Ramism. For the first thing included in his *Animadversiones* is a copy of Sturm's famous letter to Heinrich Schorus, in which he defended Ramus, placing him in a venerable line of descent from Aristotle and Agricola. At the same time, of course, Piscator was also tacitly asserting his own right to adapt and modify Ramus' system as he chose.[117] Indeed, as we shall see, the liberties that Piscator took with Ramus' text, and his own retention of many Philippist tenets, proved an offence to purer Ramists.

---

[111] Piscator, *Animadversiones*, 5–6.
[112] Piscator, *Animadversiones*, 5–7.
[113] Hotson, *Commonplace Learning*, 101–4.
[114] See Cuno, "Piscator, Johannes", in *Allgemeine Deutsche Biographie* 26 (1888): 180–81 (https://www.deutsche-biographie.de/).
[115] See, for example, Johannes Piscator, *Analysis Logica Epistola Horatii Omnium* (Speyer, 1595), which offers Horace's text, its structure of argumentation, and a detailed logical analysis using Ramist arguments.
[116] Piscator, *Animadversiones*, 8.
[117] Piscator, *Animadversiones*, 3.

Such was the nature of Piscator's Ramist conversion. By the time he published his *Animadversiones*, he had become a fully fledged, if unusually critical, Ramist. However, this was by no means the end of his development as a Ramist. Between 1581 and 1583 Piscator devoted considerable time to making an extensive analysis and emendation of Ramus' *Scholae* on grammar, rhetoric, dialectic, physics, and metaphysics. Just a year later, in 1584, he received his call to take up the position of Professor of Theology at Herborn. Thus, as Hotson suggests, his reworking of Ramus' *Scholae* proved important preparation for preparing with Olevian the new curriculum here.[118] We have already seen the shape of this as codified in the *Leges* of 1585, which he published as Rector. From the preface to this we may see that he fully shared Olevian's convictions of the importance of Ramism for advancing Reformed confessionalization. According to Piscator, the proliferation of Reformed academies and schools in Germany is dealing an important blow to Antichrist's Kingdom. Key for him, in waging this struggle, is the Herborn integration of the "study of languages and the arts" with "sincere religion and integrity of life"[119]—something which Ramism was uniquely well placed to deliver.

Significantly, the year 1585 also marked the publication of the *Exercitationes*, Piscator's second extensive commentary on Ramus. In this work, Piscator clearly felt able to respond to many of the criticisms that had been made of his earlier commentary. Indeed, between the publication of the two commentaries he had been engaged in important philosophical debates with both the young English Reformed philosopher William Temple and the eminent German natural philosopher Wilhelm Adolf Scribonius. Both Temple and Scribonius were devoted Ramists, and both were critical—to different degrees—of Piscator's modified Ramism. In responding to Temple in a famous letter of 1583 and to Scribonius in the 1585 *Exercitationes*, Piscator was forced to reflect on and defend his own philosophical assumptions at great length. While on the surface this did little to change his precise views, Piscator emerged out of these discussions newly confident in his own methodology and ready to put it to good use both in his reforms of the Herborn academy, which he had taken over following Olevian's death in 1587, and in his grand vision of commenting on the whole of Scripture, which began to take root in the late 1580s and 1590s. It is to these discussions with Temple and Scribonius we now turn in order to discover some of the deep connections between Piscator's logic and his exegetical theology.

---

[118] Hotson, *Commonplace Learning*, 103.
[119] Piscator, *Leges*, "*Epistola Dedicatoria*".

## 3.7. Piscator and the Reform of Ramism

We do not have to look very far in Piscator's logical works to find evidence that he, like Olevian, had been profoundly touched by the new metaphysical and Realist tenor of German Ramism. Frequently in his *Exercitationes*, Piscator emphasizes that logic does not properly consider terms, which he calls the "symbols and notes of things", but rather the things signified by the terms.[120] While the scholastics had upheld logic as a *"scientia sermocinalis"*—a science of words—Piscator was adamant that logic looks not to words but to their signification. Indeed, he makes clear that the scope of logic is both being and non-being—the traditional territory of metaphysics.[121] In this, he follows not only Ramus but also Olevian, who stated clearly at the beginning of his *De Inventione* that the scope of dialectic is the "knowledge or truth of whichever thing". For Piscator, just as Ramist logic had an expanded rhetorical scope in considering every form of argument, it also had an expanded metaphysical scope, in considering real beings and not only "beings of reason".[122]

Yet Piscator's was not a straightforward or simplistic Realism like that which he discerned in Scribonius or Ramus himself. In fact, his logic embodied a more complex and subtle relation between mind and reality, which in its sophistication seems closer in spirit to the medieval Realist tradition, even if it has not yet attained the scholastic precision found in later Ramist theologians. This may be seen in his controversy with Scribonius and Temple over the nature of Ramus' arguments. All were agreed on the basic Realist position that logical arguments reflected objective features of the external world, yet they differed over precisely how this was to be understood. For Ramus, Temple, and Scribonius, an argument was seemingly a stand-alone feature of the world. In their understanding, every argument possessed an independent and intrinsic power to argue.[123] While Scribonius, unlike Temple, also conceived of arguments in relational terms, he still sought to distinguish the argument itself as absolute from its context-dependent mode of arguing.[124]

Piscator responded to this by insisting that "arguments are not able to be or be understood without that which is argued".[125] To his mind, Scribonius' distinction between the argument and its mode of arguing made no sense

---

[120] Johannes Piscator, *Exercitationum Logicarum Libri II* (1585), 16–18, 89.
[121] Piscator, *Exercitationum*, 96–98; cf. Ashworth, *Language and Logic*, 38. Despite the manifold differences, Ong, *Ramus, Method, and the Decay of Dialogue*, 171 sees Peter of Spain's quantified and topical logic as an important background influence on Ramus.
[122] Olevian, *De Inventione Dialecticae*, 1.
[123] Petrus Ramus, *P. Rami Dialecticae Libri Duo* (Cologne, 1566), 14–20 [hereafter *DLD* 1566]; William Temple, *Gulielmi Tempelli Philosophi Cantabrigiensis Epistola de Dialectica P. Rami* (London, 1583), 7–9; and Wilhelm Adolf Scribonius, *Triumphus Logicae Rameae* (Basel, 1587), 5–6.
[124] Cf. Piscator, *Exercitationum*, 21–22.
[125] Piscator, *Animadversiones*, 22.

whatsoever.[126] As he also made plain, especially against Temple, arguments are not to be considered as absolute but rather as relative.[127] For him there are no "nude arguments", but all must be placed in relation with each other. Illustrating what he meant, Piscator gave the common Ramist example of the proposition "fire burns". Unlike Ramus, Scribonius, and Temple, he resisted the temptation to analyse this into two arguments of "fire" and "burns" as cause and effect. Instead, pushing even closer to the Augustinian doctrine of the *complexe significabile* than Ramus himself had done, he held that taken alone "fire" and "burns" do not argue anything, and it is only when the two are combined that they can be seen as mutually entailing logical arguments in a proposition really reflecting reality.[128]

Another excellent example of Piscator's understanding can be seen in his dispute with Scribonius over the Aristotelian predicaments. Going somewhat against the Ramist grain, Scribonius had sought to retain the predicaments in his logic, by equating them rather simplistically with Ramus' own arguments—such that substance stood for subject, accident for adjunct, and so on.[129] Piscator's response to this is instructive. Following Ramus he held that the predicaments were the highest "genera of things" and, as such, alien to logic. However, siding with Scribonius, he agreed that they could be included under Ramist arguments, with substance representing a species of subject and accidents a species of adjunct. Defined independently substance stood alone, but defined in relation to the accidents/adjuncts inhering in it meant it took on the logical character of a subject.[130] Here it is important not to be misled. In defining an argument as a reason or relation, Piscator was by no means denying its status as a mind-independent reality. Rather he manifests considerable sympathy for Scribonius' inchoate view that an argument is to be considered as both "an affection of a thing" and a "certain thing" in its own right.[131] Indeed, he affirms that all names or terms when considered as Ramist arguments are not merely to be considered in Aristotelian fashion as "symbols or notes of signified things" but as real beings (*onta*). His precise meaning is unclear, but his discussion strongly implies the Realist position that arguments are both relations and beings in their own right, and is suggestive of a broadly Scotist view of reality.[132]

It may perhaps be wondered what the relevance is of Piscator's subtle Realism for his theology and exegesis. Firstly, Piscator's critique of Ramus' notion of argument led him to a quite fundamental revision in his approach to logic. As he

---

[126] Piscator, *Exercitationum*, 22.
[127] Johannes Piscator, *Responsio*, in Temple, *Epistola*, 36–37.
[128] Piscator, *Exercitationum*, 16–18; cf. Rimini, *Lectura*, Prologus q. 1 art. 1 (I.1–12).
[129] Scribonius, *Triumphus*, 6.
[130] Piscator, *Exercitationum*, 15.
[131] Piscator, *Exercitationum*, 15–18.
[132] Piscator, *Exercitationum*, 18. See the Scotist parallel concerning the understanding of intentions in Tachau, *Vision and Certitude*, 62–68.

points out as early as his *Animadversiones*, Ramus' own understanding of argument is both confused and ambiguous. For he uses it "not only to prove or demonstrate the truth of some affirmation or denial . . . but to explain or declare the true nature of whichever thing without any syllogism".[133] In claiming that arguments argue independently and per se Ramus and his followers thus miss the crucial distinction between declaration (as applying to simple terms) and demonstration (as applying to propositions and syllogisms).[134] In doing so they risk missing, or worse, misinterpreting, the nuances of the statements that they analyse. While this is of less moment in analysis of a secular text—such as a speech of Cicero—it is much more problematic when it comes to the analysis of the sacred text of Scripture, when salvation may well hinge on properly understanding the logic of biblical passages. Indeed, Piscator insisted that the distinction between declaration and demonstration is the "great light of the doctrine of invention", missed by his fellow Ramists because of their "poverty of words".[135] Following Melanchthon, he was thus insistent that logic as the "art of teaching"— a definition hotly opposed by Temple and Scribonius—must proceed by a careful process of question and answer, always refusing to collapse demonstration into declaration.[136]

The second reason why Piscator's Realist stance might be considered relevant for his theology is only hinted at in his works, but it attains great importance when viewed in the context of the developing Ramist tradition and the nascent currents of "universal reformation. It may be seen in his desire to add a fourth law to Ramus' famous three laws of method. This law, he says, would be a true "law of wisdom" by contrast to Ramus' own law of wisdom, which he says is better called a law of brevity. He then adds, wisdom belongs to method since "the highest wisdom is discerned in the legitimate order and disposition of things, just as the wisdom of God is perceived in the order of the parts of the world and of the species in the world".[137] Here we see his realization that the art of logic, in reflecting the order of nature, also reflects the divine wisdom. As we have seen, this was by no means a new claim for a Ramist to make, yet with Piscator it attained a new and vital theological resonance.

For the claim that logic embodies the divine wisdom coincided in Piscator with the first efforts to apply the Ramist logical analysis to Scripture. It had long

---

[133] Piscator, *Animadversiones*, 20: "*Arguere enim authori significat non solum veritatem alicuius affirmationis aut negationis probare seu demonstrare . . . verum etiam rei cuiuspam naturam declarare seu explicare absque ullo syllogismo*".
[134] Piscator, *Animadversiones*, 20.
[135] Piscator, *Animadversiones*, 21.
[136] Piscator, *Exercitationum*, 8–13; *Animadversiones*, 21; cf. Temple, *Epistola*, 6–7; Scribonius, *Triumphus*, 1–3.
[137] Piscator, *Exercitationum*, 167: "*Sane nomen sapientiae, legi methodi potius deberi videtur. Nam in legitimo ordine ac dispositione rerum, summa sapientia cernitur, sicut et sapientia Dei, in ordine partium mundium et specierum in mundo, a sapientibus perspicitur*".

been a critique of Ramus that his logic was illustrated solely by examples taken from pagan poets and orators. In such a context the theological import of his appeals to divine wisdom was somewhat nullified. When Piscator remodelled Ramist logic for the Reformed academy, he significantly turned chiefly to scriptural examples. As he expressed this in his *Exercitationes*, he drew not on Homer to illustrate his syllogisms but on the "eternal Word and Wisdom of the Heavenly Father".[138] In doing so he not only initiated what Hotson describes as the "confessionalization" of Ramist logic, but also forged a vital link between logic and the divine wisdom as displayed in both the world and the Word, a connection which was to prove immensely fruitful in the works of future Ramists and universal reformers.[139] Indeed, implicitly he made the claim of a particular fit between Ramist logic and method and the logic of Scripture—a claim which he of course went on to justify on a grand scale through his comprehensive logical analysis of the entire text of Scripture. Moreover, it was not hard for future generations to couple Piscator's sophisticated defence of logic as a *habitus* of the mind—made in the teeth of stiff opposition by both Temple and Scribonius—with Olevian's vivid picture of logic and the other arts as divine medicines. From here to the claim made by Keckermann and Alsted, and echoed by numerous English Ramists, that logic represented a remedy to the Fall of man and a sanctification of the human mind, was but a short step indeed.[140]

## 3.8. Logic, Exegesis, and Theology

Important as it was in binding the reflections of the human mind to an external objective order, which itself mirrored the higher order of the divine Wisdom, Piscator's Realism remains largely implicit in his exegesis and theology. In both the *Animadversiones* and the *Exercitationes*, Piscator's most extensive logical treatment of Scripture occurs in the context of his discussion of testimony. The category of testimony had been introduced into logic by Renaissance logicians as part of their general strategy of rhetorically refashioning logic. Since logicians now sought persuasive arguments as well as strictly necessary ones, it made sense that testimony should be incorporated into invention as representing one of the primary weapons in an orator's arsenal—arguments from authority. Ramus himself had offered an important twofold division of testimony into human and divine, and his treatment of this division constituted the starting point for

---

[138] Piscator, *Exercitationum*, 206.
[139] Hotson, *Commonplace Learning*, 108–14.
[140] See Piscator, *Responsio*, in Temple, *Epistola*, 19–23.

Piscator's own reflection on testimony and the basis for his later dispute with Scribonius over divine testimony.[141]

While Piscator upheld the basic features of Ramus' discussion of testimony, he disagreed strongly with some of its fundamental presuppositions. In particular, it was his conviction that Ramus and Scribonius had not posed a sharp enough disjunction between human and divine testimony, reading them too much in parallel. Ramus' own assimilation of Scripture into a broader category of divine testimony including the "oracles of the gods" and "responses of the prophets and soothsayers" and illustrated from Cicero was for Piscator a case of his Classicizing tendencies having gone too far. By contrast, he sharply distinguished true divine testimony as deriving immediately or mediately from God with the false testimony of demons, sharply rebuking Ramus and Scribonius for intermingling Christian prophecy with pagan oracles.[142] He also attacked Ramus for allotting divine testimony, along with other forms of testimony, the weakest probative force and thus relegating it to the lowest place in his hierarchy of arguments.[143] While Piscator seems to have been in agreement with respect to human testimony, he followed Aquinas in utterly inverting this order with respect to divine testimony.[144] Drawing on a longstanding theological axiom, he insisted that scriptural arguments had the greatest probative force possible, beyond that of any other of Ramus' arguments. Moreover, Piscator was also adamant, in line with the developing Reformed doctrine of *autopistia*, that divine testimony was self-authenticating.[145]

In suggesting this, Piscator completely overturned the standard Ramist definition of testimony. For Ramus and Temple, testimony was an "inartificial argument" and thus distinguished from those "artificial" arguments" which argued "from themselves".[146] Piscator strenuously disagreed, holding that only divine testimony is properly a per se argument since it rests on its own authority while all other arguments argue only in relation to each other.[147] In denying this, he held that Temple and Scribonius risked treating divine and human testimony according to the same reason—a dangerous category mistake—implying that God is only to be believed in so far as the human mind and reason are able to judge of the truth of his testimonies. By contrast, Piscator held that divine testimony was

---

[141] Ramus, *DLD* 1566, 114–24.
[142] Piscator, *Animadversiones*, 114–15, 120–21; *Exercitationum*, 132–45; cf. Ramus, *DLD* 1566, 114–24.
[143] See Petrus Ramus, *The Logike of the Most Excellent Philosopher P. Ramus Martyr* (London, 1581), 65–66. In *DLD* 1566, 117, Ramus points out that testimony does not have the "greatest strength of proof" but has faith, although he adds that divine testimony is adhered to with the "greatest faith".
[144] See Aquinas, *ST*, 1a q. 1 art. 8. It should be noted that Piscator does not cite Aquinas for this principle.
[145] Piscator, *Exercitationum*, 138–40. For discussion of this see Muller, *PRRD*, 2.265–67.
[146] Ramus, *DLD* 1566, 114–17; Temple, *Epistola*, 8.
[147] Piscator, *Exercitationum*, 138–40.

transcendent and absolute in character. It could not therefore be reduced to the level of human testimony or even that of the other arguments. In fact, the logical claim that divine testimony possessed the highest probative force was a clear corollary of the theological claim that faith had the highest certainty, beyond that of reason itself.[148]

That scriptural testimony could not be reduced to the level of other arguments did not mean, however, that it could not be expressed according to these same arguments. While Piscator clearly believed Scripture to have its own intrinsic logic, he does not seem to have believed that this differed in any other way, save in eloquence and probative force, from the ordinary pattern of Ramist logic.[149] We do not find in him, as we find more or less explicitly in other Ramists, that echo of the late medieval doctrine of the logic of faith, according to which Scripture was seen as possessing its own supernatural pattern of logic.[150] What this meant was that scriptural testimony could be analysed into its component arguments in a similar fashion to any kind of rational discourse, even if its authority did not finally rest on these underlying arguments.[151] Indeed, this was manifestly the purpose of Piscator's biblical commentaries which together present a sophisticated analysis of every verse of the Bible drawing on the full range of Ramus' arguments.

Unfortunately, Piscator has not left us a detailed account of the way that he applied his logic to Scripture. However, he has left us some important indications in the preface to his early *Commentary on Matthew*. Significantly, these also provide further illumination of the important connection that he recognized existing between logic, exegesis, and theology. As Piscator explains, his commentary consists of three conceptual layers. These he designates as logical analysis, scholia, and observations on the places of doctrine—the celebrated *loci communes*. Obviously, he found this to be a successful method, for he faithfully followed it in commenting on every book of the Old and New Testament. Indeed, in one of his rare acknowledgements of the novelty of what he was doing Piscator says that "these parts which by most others are expounded indiscriminately and confusedly, are handled by me distinctly and, as I believe, in a just order". For this reason Piscator suggests that what his commentary offers over others is brevity and perspicuity—two of the watchwords of the Ramist tradition.[152]

---

[148] Piscator, *Exercitationum*, 132–45; *Animadversiones*, 61, 114–30. Compare with Temple, *Epistola*, 14–15 and Scribonius, *Triumphus*, 106–14.

[149] Johannes Piscator, *Analysis Logica Epistolae Pauli ad Romanos* (Herborn, 1595), "Praefatio" speaks of the "divine method" of Paul's logic, but is explicit that as logic is a general art it can be applied to divine things as well as human things.

[150] See Chapter 4.

[151] See, for example, Johannes Piscator, *Admonitio Johannis Piscatoris de Exercitationibus Heizonis Buscheri* (Herborn, 1594), 4–7.

[152] Johannes Piscator, *Commentarii in Omnes Libros Novi Testamenti* (Herborn, 1638), 2.

Piscator's discussion of the three different aspects of his commentary and their connection is brief and to the point. Logical analysis of Scripture on a verse-by-verse basis comes first, since it is through this that we attain to the "genuine sense of Scripture". Without this we cannot either understand or use Scripture, and so this first step is understood by Piscator as absolutely indispensable for exegesis. Once the genuine sense has been grasped and the "summary of the matter" perceived, we are able to move on to the scholia. These have the purpose of removing any impediments to understanding Scripture and offering a more detailed linguistic study of any important points. Finally, when our understanding of the text has been refined to the point of perfection, we may turn to the "uses" of the text. These uses are indicated by observations on the places of doctrine. Drawing on 2 Timothy 3:16 and Romans 15, Piscator summarizes these uses as teaching doctrine, refuting errors, correcting fellow Christians, instruction in righteousness, and consolation. To these he adds the polemical category of vindicating Scripture from false consequences, and thus purging the Church of false dogmas, and the apologetic task of solving doubts and reconciling apparent contradictions in Scripture.[153]

Of course, in applying logic to Scripture so thoroughly, Piscator was hardly original, but rather stood in a long line of medieval exegetes reaching back to Augustine's *De Doctrina Christiana* and beyond.[154] This also closely reflects the topical and biblical priorities of the Reformers and early Reformed.[155] Nevertheless, Piscator was a genuine pioneer in developing Ramism as a sophisticated exegetical and theological tool. In his commentaries, Ramism thus not only guides the exposition of each conceptual level, but coordinates and unifies the three levels into a methodical unfolding of the genuine sense of the whole of Scripture. For it was his grand vision to connect the argument of every verse not only to the argument of a single chapter or even an entire book, but to the argument of the entire Bible.

We may see this in his commentary on Matthew, which opens with a single logical syllogism which he drew out from his analysis of the text and saw as summing up the message of the whole book. The proposition of the syllogism—note the distinctive Ramist terminology—is the testimony of all the Old Testament prophets, the assumption is warranted by the testimony of the book of Matthew itself, which he affirms as self-authenticating (*autopistos*) in character, and the complexion is the proof that Jesus is the Christ, the Saviour of the world, which is

---

[153] Piscator, *Commentarii in Omnes Libros Novi Testamenti*, 2.
[154] See Augustine, *On Christian Teaching*, 2.31.48–37.55 (pp. 58–61); cf. Gillian Evans, *The Language and Logic of the Bible: The Road to Reformation* (Cambridge: Cambridge University Press, 1985).
[155] Muller, *Unaccommodated Calvin*, 108–12 and *PRRD*, 1.177–84.

to be received by faith and leads to eternal life.[156] In this analysis, Piscator clearly attempts to capture through his Ramist logic something of the living dynamism of Scripture. The whole Bible becomes seen as a "methodical" text patterned according to a coherent set of Ramist arguments. Both exegete and believer are invited to participate in the transcendent pattern of divine revelation, and theology itself then flows out of this engagement with the logical texture and structure of Scripture. Ultimately, the purpose of Ramist method in theology, and an important clue to its elusive significance in Reformed dogmatics, is thus the transposition of the logic of Scripture onto the entire body of doctrine.[157]

## 3.9. Herborn Ramism

Ramism thus served a vital purpose for Piscator in drawing the *loci communes* gathered from exegesis into an organized, methodical system. In this, as in so much else, Olevian proved a vital inspiration. The curriculum at Herborn prescribed that theology in the public school should be taught from Calvin's *Institutes*. This was a course that Olevian had taught after the opening of the academy, and in order to aid students, as well as to have a chance of completing his survey in the allotted time, he prepared an epitome of the whole *Institutes*. However, Olevian died in the middle of giving his lecture course, leaving Piscator to take over from him. Since many of the Herborn students did not require training in polemical theology, Piscator prepared, at their express request, a new epitome of the *Institutes*, recast in the form of aphorisms and organized according to the canons of Ramist method.[158] Importantly, Piscator's *Aphorismi* was not just a simple summary, or condensing, of the *Institutes*, but rather, as Heber Carlos de Campos argues, was a methodological reconfiguring of the whole of Calvin's works into a system of connected common places structured according to a pattern of "Ramistic bifurcations". If desired, the whole work could be expressed as a Ramist chart, marking the next step in the efforts of Calvin and earlier Reformers to achieve a methodical pattern of theology.[159]

---

[156] Piscator, *Commentarii*, 3. Ramus preferred the Ciceronian terminology of proposition, assumption, and complexion to the Aristotelian and scholastic terminology of major, minor, and conclusion.

[157] This develops Richard Muller's important insight that the "Agricolan method freed rhetoric from the procrustean bed of logical forms and Aristotelian categories and allowed logic to follow out, in high discursive style, the patterns and implications inherent in the materials of debate" (*Unaccommodated Calvin*, 109).

[158] Johannes Piscator, *Aphorismi Doctrinae Christianae ex Institutione Calvini Excerpti* (Herborn, 1589), "Praefatio", 1–2, 12–13. Throughout the *Aphorismi* we find frequent emphasis on the "use" of doctrine as well. See also Heber Carlos de Campos Jr., "Johannes Piscator's (1546-1625) Interpretation of Calvin's *Institutes*", in *Church and School in Early Modern Protestantism*, 274–75.

[159] For Piscator's adaptation of Calvin see Campos, "Interpretation", 275–82.

The *Aphorismi* show the use of Ramism in developing a basic systematic theology, but Piscator was also able to develop his method into an important polemical tool. While Ursinus had attacked Ramism as too simplistic for theological disputation—saying that he might as well teach his pupils to fly without feathers as to argue without Aristotle[160]—its sophisticated use in the Herborn school and in other German academies demonstrates that Ramism was not just intended for theological beginners. We may see this in Piscator's heated debate with the Lutheran Buscher over the nature of Christ's presence in the Eucharist, which reveals the deep connections between method, logic, and confessionalization.

The trigger for the debate was Piscator's claim during his rhetorical lectures at Herborn that the biblical phrase "this is my body" is a trope or metaphor. This quickly led to an angry response from Buscher in his *De Ratione Solvendi Sophismata* of 1593. In this he rather cleverly sought to kill two birds with one stone. Many charged, he said, that Ramus' logic was imperfect, especially as it did not teach how to solve logical sophisms. They also held that Ramus' logic was the "mother of Calvinistic error" and the cause of introducing heresy into the German schools. By demonstrating the sophistical nature of Piscator's arguments, Buscher thus sought to rescue Ramism from the Calvinists and simultaneously show how it supported the true Lutheran theology.[161]

In demonstrating this, Buscher developed a comprehensive Ramist theory of sophisms. He also accused Piscator of mixing disciplines—a cardinal sin for a Ramist—in confusing rhetorical tropes with a logical account of predication. Where Piscator had argued that bread and the body of the Lord are disparate arguments and so could only be united in topical fashion, Buscher drew on the Ramist arguments of genus and species in order to defend a Realist account of Christ's presence in the Eucharist.[162] Even more strikingly he also pressed towards a logic of faith, arguing that "since theology far exceeds the grasp of human reason, it often transcends the rules of logic".[163] While Buscher conceded that disparates are not usually allowed to be predicated of disparates, he followed Melanchthon in arguing for a special category of "unusual predications" to be found in Scripture in which this rule is broken due to the "most narrow presence and real conjunction" of the predicates—a Christological pattern of logic pointing towards the Lutheran coincidence of opposites.[164]

---

[160] Cited from Hotson, *Alsted*, 25.
[161] Heizo Buscher, *De Ratione Solvendi Sophismata Solide et Perspicue ex P. Rami Dialectica Deducta et Explicata Libri Duo* (Lemgo, 1593), 2–7.
[162] Buscher, *De Ratione Solvendi Sophismata*, 113–20.
[163] Buscher, *De Ratione Solvendi Sophismata*, 109–10: "*Cum enim Theologia longe excedat humanae rationis captum, saepeq. transcendat logicas regulas*".
[164] Buscher, *De Ratione Solvendi Sophismata*, 109–12. See especially his table of examples on p. 122. For the connection with Melanchthon see Melanchthon, *Erotemata Dialectices*, 20–21.

Piscator responded with a series of works in which he sought to vindicate his own Ramistic account of predication, and, consequently, Reformed Christology and Eucharistic doctrine. Recalling Luther's famous response to Zwingli at the 1529 Colloquy of Marburg, Buscher and another Lutheran theologian had accused Piscator of using reason—in this case his analysis of tropes—to subvert the mystery of the Trinity and the two natures of Christ. In his *Admonitio*, Piscator responded with an appeal to the logic of Scripture and an emphatic rejection of the logic of faith, arguing that although the "mysteries of the Spirit" are "unusual" and beyond human understanding, yet they are expressed in the Bible according to "usual predications"—a point he buttresses from Beza—and not the "unusual predications" of the Lutherans.[165] In his responses to Buscher, he importantly offered an exhaustive defence of his own Philippo-Ramist account of predication—and an alternative theory of sophisms. He also confronted directly Buscher's arguments from genus and species. Thus, turning the tables on Buscher, Piscator sought to use the distinctive Ramist argument that the "individual is the most special species" to illustrate the infinite disjunction between the divine and human nature, and thus ultimately defend the Reformed doctrine of the spiritual presence in the Eucharist.[166] In doing so, he reminded Buscher, rather airily it must be said, that he was simply applying the precepts of Ramus which both of them extolled.[167]

The Piscator-Buscher conflict shows the central role that Ramism could play at the highest level of theological debate. It also exposes important underlying tensions between Reformed and Lutheran understandings of reason and logic, and the massive part that this played in contemporary confessional conflict. Importantly, we also find many Ramist academies at this time becoming engaged in this "confessionalization of logic". For example, the theological disputations at Dortmund, presided over by Beurhaus, show clear evidence of Ramist structure and argumentation. The whole of one disputation on the mystery of the Trinity is patterned on the Ramist syllogistic pattern of proposition, assumption, and complexion and directed explicitly against the Anti-Trinitarians. Another 1608 disputation on the image of God is arranged and analysed according to Ramist dichotomies and divisions. In both cases the Ramist character of the argumentation is reinforced by further Ramist theses or corollaries on dialectic and the other liberal arts, as well as open attacks on the philosophical and theological dangers of an Anti-Ramist stance.[168] In a thesis disputed under Goclenius at the

---

[165] Piscator, *Admonitio*, 4–7.
[166] Piscator, *Admonitio*, 23–26.
[167] Johannes Piscator, *Responsio Johannis Piscatoris ad Elenchos Heizonis Buscheri* (Herborn, 1593), 189.
[168] Friedrich Beurhaus, *Disputatio Theologica et ex Parte Physica* (Dortmund, 1608); *De Sacro Sancta Trinitate, seu, De Tribus Deitatis Personis Disputatio Theologica* (Dortmund, 1608?). These are both to be found bound in the New College, Edinburgh copy of Goclenius, *Collegium Philosophico-Theologicum*.

Marburg academy, we even find a Ramist chart being used to illustrate the doctrine of Hell, showing just how ubiquitous this approach had become in polemical discourse and disputations.[169]

In Herborn too we find the same Ramist approach to polemical and systematic theology manifest in student disputations. In 1596 Piscator collected together, into a single volume, theses disputed at the Herborn school. In subsequent years a number of further volumes were printed. In these we see that the kind of systematic approach pioneered by Olevian and Piscator had clearly taken root in the schools.[170] While the *Theses* tended to mix scholastic and Ramist approaches, in the *Hypotyposis S.S. Theologiae* of 1611 we find clear evidence of Ramist systematization. In this compendium of theology, prepared under Piscator's supervision, his student employs Ramist dichotomies in order to structure a tightly knit pattern of common places.[171] In the same year, Piscator's colleague Hermann Ravensperger published his *Gemma Theologica*. This consists of yet another set of student disputations methodologically arranged into a set of *loci communes*. Notably longer and more sophisticated than the *Hypotyposis*, the whole of this work is structured according to a Ramist analysis of covenant.[172] In this we see an important unifying of the Ramist and federal strands of Olevian's theology, which Johannes Althusius and other Herborn Ramists were soon to develop on an even more impressive scale.[173]

The preface to the *Gemma* includes a laudatory poem by Piscator praising this "gem" from which the light of doctrine reaches the eyes of the mind and heals souls. In this he captures elegantly both the therapeutic character of Ramist logic and its fundamental role in distilling scriptural truth into a method or system. The same conviction is expressed, in even stronger mystical tones, in another dedicatory poem written by the Marburg theologian Raphael Iconius Egli. Situating Ramism again as a divine method, he compares Ravensperger's *Gemma* to the gems adorning the High's Priest's ephod and especially to the Urim and Thummim—universally understood in the Ramist tradition as the light of invention and judgement.[174]

Egli, a controversial champion of Lullist and Brunian method, was a close friend of Johannes Heinrich Alsted, Piscator's own former student and at this time a rising Professor of Theology at Herborn.[175] One of the disputations

---

[169] Goclenius, *Collegium Philosophico-Theologicum*, Disputation X.
[170] Johannes Piscator, *Volumen Thesium Theologicarum* (Herborn, 1596).
[171] Johannes Piscator, *Hypotyposis S.S. Theologiae ad Leges Methodi qua Popularis qua Scholasticae Delineata et Conformata* (Herborn, 1611).
[172] Hermann Ravensperger, *Gemma Theologica Hoc est Brevis et Facilis Locorum S.S. Theologiae Communium Institutio* (Herborn, 1611), 18–24.
[173] Menk, *Hohe Schule*, 39–40, 231–37, 257–65. In Althusius' case this was more political than theological.
[174] Ravensperger, *Gemma Theologica*, "In Luculentissimum".
[175] For a brief discussion of Egli see Hotson, *Alsted*, 59–65.

included in the *Gemma* was also defended by none other than the young Jan Amos Comenius, who had just recently arrived in Herborn.[176] In this work we therefore find a symbolic conjunction of Herborn reformers—the old joining hands with the new. For what Piscator did for exegesis and theology, his students Alsted and Comenius were to attempt for the entire cycle of knowledge.[177] In doing so, they took up not only the scriptural and therapeutic method of Olevian and Piscator, but also the Neo-Platonic and Neo-Pythagorean elements latent in the wider Philippo-Ramist tradition, and used these to fuse together the "sacred logics" of Ramism and Lullism into a new Trinitarian and encyclopaedic synthesis. In this brief snapshot we thus see the Herborn school poised between Ramism and universal reformation.

---

[176] Ravensperger, *Gemma Theologica*, 3–8.
[177] Hotson, *Commonplace Learning*, 118–19.

# 4
# Archetypal Reform
## Richardson, Ames, and the Reduction of the Arts

When William Temple wrote to Johannes Piscator in 1583, he was one of a rising generation of English enthusiasts for the logic of Petrus Ramus. Consecrated by Ramus' death as a Huguenot martyr and offering to restore the "only perfecte methode" of Plato and Aristotle,[1] the Ramist system quickly gained a following among Puritans eager for the further reform of the Church of England.[2] Following the pattern of their German coreligionists many saw the establishing of new academies and colleges as the way to achieve this. After a stellar career at Cambridge, Temple himself became provost of Trinity College Dublin, a newly founded Ramist institution intended to speed the conversion of Ireland.[3] A parallel movement was taking place in Scotland under Andrew Melville, a former pupil of Ramus, leading to a Ramist reformation of the Scottish universities.[4] By the end of the sixteenth century, Ramism had thus spread throughout Puritan and Reformed colleges in Britain and Ireland and was poised to spread across the Atlantic.

Temple's Cambridge was undoubtedly a key epicentre of this impressive expansion, and the Ramism that developed in Cambridge soon took on a distinctive character of its own. To state a generalization, while the Continental movement developed along the lines of Piscator's mixed Ramism, evolving into what Hotson has called a post-Ramist system, the British movement long retained a "purer" character.[5] Of course, to speak of "pure" Ramism is something of a misnomer. As we will see in this chapter, the system developed by the Cambridge Ramists was just as eclectic as that of the mixed and post-Ramists. Yet it remained truer

---

[1] See McIlmaine, *Logike*, 12. Donald McKim, *Ramism in William Perkins' Theology* (New York: Peter Lang, 1987), 37–39 points out that McIlmaine's work was the first English translation of Ramus' dialectic to appear.

[2] Feingold, "English Ramism", 141–43 points to Ramus' status as a martyr as an important factor in the spread of his logic.

[3] See Elizabethanne Boran, "Temple, Sir William (1554/5–1627)", *Oxford Dictionary of National Biography* [hereafter *ODNB*] and "Ramism in Trinity College, Dublin, in the Early Seventeenth Century", in *The Influence of Petrus Ramus*, ed. Feingold, Freedman, and Rother, 177–99.

[4] Steven J. Reid, *Humanism and Calvinism: Andrew Melville and the Universities of Scotland, 1560–1625* (Farnham: Ashgate, 2011). Reid tends to downplay the long-term significance of Scottish Ramism, but also does not discuss its deeper philosophical and theological foundations.

[5] See Hotson, *Commonplace Learning*, 101, 227–30.

to Ramus' original intention, and, much as we saw in Beurhaus and Temple, also marked a return to the more pronounced Realism and exemplarism of Ramus' early dialectical works.

In this chapter we will focus on the Cambridge Ramism developed especially by Alexander Richardson and William Ames in the decades after Temple's controversy with Piscator. Ever since Perry Miller's *New England Mind*, the Ramism of Richardson and Ames has attracted attention from scholars of Puritanism and Reformed theology alike, not least because of its profound influence on the intellectual and spiritual milieu of early America.[6] Miller especially emphasized the Realist and exemplaristic grounds of this "Richardsonian Ramism",[7] arguing that Richardson and Ames were indebted to a Neo-Platonic understanding according to which all the diverse human arts and sciences attain a unity as ideas in the mind of God—their celebrated theory of *technologia*. Moreover, through encoding praxis—or use—into the very pattern of the divine understanding, these Puritans were then able to relate every human endeavour to the glory of God. In other words, what Ramism offered to its Reformed devotees was a theocentric account of the whole of reality.[8]

Notably, Miller traced the origins of this back to thirteenth-century scholasticism and its appeal to the "unity of knowledge" in the mind of God. In particular, he understood Ramist encyclopaedism as a way of resisting the Nominalist fragmentation of the world, such that the early modern strife between Aristotelians and Ramists could be seen as nothing less than a renewal of the late medieval conflict over universals. For Miller, the Ramist championing of the Realist cause simply reflected their wider understanding of divine truth as reflected in God's Word and world.[9] In the words of Donald McKim, Ramism thus marked "an attempt to perceive the logical plan in the mind of God that expressed itself through the flow of the Scriptural material"[10]—a crucial insight which much of this chapter will be dedicated to exploring.

---

[6] For the principal works see Miller, *New England Mind*; Keith Sprunger, "Ames, Ramus, and the Method of Puritan Theology", *Harvard Theological Review* 59 (1966): 133–51; Keith Sprunger, *The Learned Doctor William Ames: Dutch Backgrounds of English and American Puritanism* (Chicago, IL: University of Chicago Press, 1972), 105–41; Lee W. Gibbs, "William Ames' Technometry", *Journal of the History of Ideas* 33.4 (1972): 615–24; John Adams, "Alexander Richardson's Puritan Theory of Discourse", *Rhetorica* 4.3 (1986): 255–74; John Adams, "Alexander Richardson's Philosophy of Art and the Sources of the Puritan Social Ethic", *Journal of the History of Ideas* 50.2 (1989): 227–47; McKim, *Ramism*, 119–33; Jan van Vliet, *The Rise of Reformed System: The Intellectual Heritage of William Ames* (Milton Keynes: Paternoster, 2013), 71–84; Baird Tipson, "Seeing the World through Ramist Eyes: The Richardsonian Ramism of Thomas Hooker and Samuel Stone", *The Seventeenth Century* 28.3 (2013): 275–92; and Baird Tipson, *Hartford Puritanism: Thomas Hooker, Samuel Stone, and Their Terrifying God* (New York: Oxford University Press, 2015).

[7] This useful designation can be found in Tipson, "Seeing the World", 275–92. It was Miller who had the first insight into Richardson's importance as a Ramist philosopher.

[8] Miller, *New England Mind*, 161–80.

[9] Miller, *New England Mind*, 145–47.

[10] McKim, *Ramism*, 74.

Yet in proving unable to integrate his Neo-Platonic and exemplaristic account of Ramism with his discussion of the budding federal theology developed in Puritan England and New England, Miller unwittingly weakened his own case. Indeed, his Nominalistic tendency to view covenant as merely a means of domesticating the arbitrary and "terrifying" God of the Puritans not only disconnected it from its definite exemplaristic moorings but also contributed to the very narrative of atomization and fragmentation that he elsewhere sought to counter.[11] In such light, it is no surprise that Ramism and federal theology have been able to be integrated so seamlessly into narratives of Protestant disintegration and disenchantment.[12] Feingold, who offers a frontal attack on its significance, sees English Ramism as fundamentally opposed to both scholastic and humanist cultures of erudition, offering an influential interpretation of it as a movement on the intellectual margins linked to the "democratizing" of the Church.[13] In similar vein, John Adams and Hugh Kearney have argued for Ramism's fundamentally iconoclastic character, as well as its frontal assault on the Elizabethan social order.[14] For many, Puritan Ramism has come to be seen as a powerful solvent dissolving the participationist glue that bound early modern Church and society together.

By contrast, this chapter will argue that Puritan Ramism contributed to an integrative reform of Church and society according to definite Neo-Platonic tenets. Building on Miller's important thesis, it shows how the Cambridge Ramists revisited—and, it must be said, reinvigorated—Ramus' bond between logic and the divine ideas. In doing so, they were able to articulate a far-reaching scriptural and exemplaristic method profoundly indebted to Augustinian and Franciscan Realism, as well as Thomist analogical reasoning. In this, logic itself became caught up in the Trinitarian dynamic of God's self-revelation, marking a return to the late medieval pattern of the *logica fidei*. This not only allowed Ramism to serve as a counter-logic and -metaphysics to Catholic Second Scholasticism—in line with Ramus' own assimilation of metaphysics into logic—but also instituted a new "rhetoric of reality", encoding speech and language into the very structure of being.

In this model of archetypal reform the Bible became the divine blueprint for all knowledge, setting in train a new movement of Christian philosophy

---

[11] Miller, *New England Mind*, 375–82. Tipson, *Hartford Puritanism*, 161–63 offers a valuable critique of Miller's Nominalist reading of New England federal theology.
[12] Pickstock, "Spacialisation", 158–59; Taylor, *A Secular Age*, 106, 155, 196. For a valuable critique of this kind of approach to Reformed federal theology see Henreckson, *Immortal Commonwealth*, 16–48.
[13] Feingold, "English Ramism", 127–76.
[14] Adams, "Richardson's Philosophy of Art", 227–47; Hugh Kearney, *Scholars and Gentlemen: Universities and Society in Pre-Industrial Britain, 1500–1700* (London: Faber, 1970), 46–47, 64.

and a comprehensive "reduction" of all the arts to theology. Significantly, covenant had a key role to play in this, transposing the ideal, logical order of the divine mind and decrees onto their contingent outworking in human history, giving everything a teleological unity and purpose. In integrating Ramism and federal theology the British Ramists ended up drawing even more deeply on a Scotist framework than their Continental cousins. While undoubtedly eclectic and harmonizing in their philosophy and theology, they thus pioneered a profound integration of a Franciscan metaphysics of exemplarism with a Franciscan dynamic of covenant—both of which they saw as entirely biblical. Far from contributing to disenchantment, the Puritan theology of the Word thus became the basis for a profound re-enchantment of every sphere of life.

## 4.1. The Character of Cambridge Ramism

The roots of Cambridge Ramism can be traced back to the humanist reforms of the sixteenth century, in which Agricolan dialectic replaced the old scholastic textbooks of logic.[15] The university statutes of 1535 and Trinity College statutes of 1560 prescribed the dialectical works of Agricola and Melanchthon, as well as the popular *Dialectica* of John Seton, which fused Agricolan and scholastic approaches and which had been specifically designed for the Cambridge curriculum. However, from the 1580s onwards Ramism became an important popular alternative with students, and Ramist works soon vied with Seton's dialectic for a place in the bookshops and studies of Cambridge.[16] As Lisa Jardine has argued, Ramism proved attractive to many students due to its clear and comprehensive character, its attention to the natural structure of discourse, and its definite flavour of the avant-garde. In particular, it is easy to see why students nurtured in the Agricolan tradition of Christian humanism might have been attracted to the practical and Realist claims of Ramism.[17]

---

[15] For helpful overview accounts see Wilbur Samuel Howell, *Logic and Rhetoric in England, 1500–1700* (Princeton, NJ: Princeton University Press, 1956), 173–246 and McKim, *Ramism*, 43–50. Scholastic elements persisted in the higher faculties as is clear from William Costello, *The Scholastic Curriculum at Early Seventeenth-Century Cambridge* (Cambridge, MA: Harvard University Press, 1954).

[16] Lisa Jardine, "The Place of Dialectic Teaching in Sixteenth-Century Cambridge", *Studies in the Renaissance* 21 (1974): 43–62. See also Lisa Jardine, "Humanism and the Sixteenth Century Cambridge Arts Course", *History of Education* 4.1 (1975): 16–31. The popularity of Ramism is also attested to by probate inventories; see Elizabeth Leedham-Green, *Books in Cambridge Inventories: Book Lists from Vice-Chancellor's Court Probate Inventories in the Tudor and Stuart Periods* (Cambridge: Cambridge University Press, 1996), 2.652–54. The probate inventory of one bookshop owner in 1588 records as many as 178 copies of Ramus' grammar and 233 copies of Temple's commentary on Ramus' dialectic (2.653).

[17] Jardine, "Place", 59–60 and Lisa Jardine, "Gabriel Harvey: Exemplary Ramist and Pragmatic Humanist", *Revue des sciences philosophiques et théologiques* 70.1 (1986): 36–48. For Agricola's Realism see Nauta, "From Universals to Topics", 190–224.

Of course, the new movement of Ramism did not go unchallenged in Cambridge, where scholasticism still dominated the curriculum up until the mid-seventeenth century.[18] As Feingold and Hotson have shown, the influx of Ramism quickly met opposition from an influential cadre of English scholars.[19] As early as the 1550s Roger Ascham, the leading English humanist, had criticized Ramus for his attacks on Aristotle and Cicero.[20] In the 1570s he was to complain bitterly about the Ramistic culture of simplifying and epitomizing that was challenging his own, more sophisticated and decidedly elitist, pedagogy.[21] Similar attacks were heard in Oxford, where the combined attacks of John Case and Richard Hooker effectively drove Ramism underground, only for it to resurface in the seventeenth century in prominent Reformed theologians and philosophers such as Edward Leigh and Theophilus Gale.[22]

In Cambridge the most prominent attack came from the Neo-Platonist Everard Digby, whose 1580 work, pointedly titled *De Duplici Methodo*, attacked the single method of Ramus in no uncertain terms. Like Ramus' Parisian opponents, Digby held that Ramist method rode rough-shod over the important Aristotelian distinction of that which is more known by nature and that which is more known to us—the foundation of his own twofold method.[23] Drawing on Aquinas and Albert the Great, he insisted on the difficult and arduous path to achieving method, inveighing against the Ramist culture of the short-cut.[24] While a Platonist himself, Digby also attacked the simplified Realism of Ramist method with what he saw as its cavalier disregard for the distinction between first and second intentions.[25]

Yet the complaints of Digby and other contemporary detractors concerning the epitomes flooding the Cambridge market and the marked drop in educational standards, should not blind us to the fact that Ramism was evidently

---

[18] For Cambridge scholasticism see Costello, *Scholastic Curriculum*.

[19] Feingold, "English Ramism", 156-76 and Hotson, *Commonplace Learning*, 63-64.

[20] Howell, *Logic and Rhetoric*, 173-75. Elsewhere, however, Ascham felt able to praise Ramus' methodological innovations.

[21] Hotson, *Commonplace Learning*, 163.

[22] For the attacks of Case and Hooker see McKim, *Ramism*, 43. For the claim that Ramism retreated from Oxford see Mordechai Feingold, "The Humanities", in *The History of the University of Oxford: Volume IV, Seventeenth-Century Oxford*, ed. Nicholas Tyacke (Oxford: Oxford University Press, 1997), 290-93. For Gale's Ramism see Theophilus Gale, *The Court of the Gentiles. Part IV. Of Reformed Philosophie. Wherein Plato's Moral and Metaphysic or Prime Philosophie is Reduced to An Useful Forme and Method* (London, 1677), "Preface". For Edward Leigh's praise of Ramus and Ramist philosophers and theologians see extensively in his *Treatise of Religion and Learning*. I am also grateful to Matthew Baines for discussion of Leigh's Ramism.

[23] Everard Digby, *De Duplici Methodo Libri Duo Unicam P. Rami Methodum Refutantes* (London, 1580), I c. 1 (p. Biiv). For the Aristotelian character of this distinction see Ong, *Ramus, Method, and the Decay of Dialogue*, 241.

[24] Digby, *De Duplici Methodo*, I c. 3; 5 (pp. Biiiiv, Bvv). Ong, *Ramus, Method, and the Decay of Dialogue*, 3 cites Hardin Craig calling Ramus "the greatest master of the short-cut the world has ever known".

[25] Digby, *De Duplici Methodo*, I c. 11.

extremely popular in Cambridge.[26] Although Feingold is surely right to criticize Wilbur Howell for over-exaggeration in calling Ramism the "prevailing logical system" in England during this era, he himself tends to radically downplay its importance and significance for English intellectual, and especially theological, culture.[27] In particular, Ramism was able to flourish at Cambridge by taking root in the Puritan colleges of the University, above all at Christ's and Emmanuel. That it endured at these Colleges well into the seventeenth century is evident from figures such as the theologian John Preston, the poet John Milton, the author of a decidedly Ramist work of logic, and the Cambridge Platonist Henry More, who lavishly praised Ramus' "most excellent dialectic".[28]

The first Cambridge Ramist that we know about is Laurence Chaderton, and it was largely due to Chaderton's influence that Ramism gained such a secure foothold in the university. As a fellow of Christ's from 1567 to 1584 he nurtured generations of Puritan students. Chaderton was famous for his teaching of logic, and during the 1570s he offered lectures on Ramism which "roused a great interest in that study through the university".[29] Through his "methodicall" sermons, preached for over fifty years, thousands of students were exposed to his pulpit Ramism.[30] With a number of friends, Chaderton also pioneered biblical conferences dedicated to discovering the linguistic, grammatical, logical, and theological analysis of Scripture. This served to demonstrate the central place of Ramism in theological endeavours.[31]

One of Chaderton's early pupils at Christ's was Gabriel Harvey. He became an enthusiast for Ramus, zealously defending his reputation against the obloquies of Thomas Nash. For Harvey, who later became Professor of Rhetoric, Ramism represented an indispensable method of analysing texts, as well as of inventing and disposing orations. Complementing Chaderton's logic lectures, in 1575–76 Harvey offered popular lectures on Ramist rhetoric, which were later published.[32] This was the time when Temple himself was a student at King's, and it is quite possible that he heard both Chaderton and Harvey lecture.[33] Temple gained celebrity from his youthful correspondence with Piscator

---

[26] McKim, *Ramism*, 40.
[27] See Feingold, "English Ramism", 134 for his critique of Howell.
[28] For Preston see Miller, *New England Mind*, 186–87. For Milton see Emma Annette Wilson, "Reading the 'unseemly logomachy': Ramist Method in Action in Seventeenth-Century English Literature", in *Ramus, Pedagogy and the Liberal Arts*, ed. Reid and Wilson, 69–88. For More's praise of Ramism and his prominent use of his logic see Henry More, *Enchiridion Metaphysicum* (London, 1671), 3.1 (p. 19). This complicates Feingold's claim that Ramism was dying out in Cambridge by the early seventeenth century ("English Ramism", 176).
[29] Cited from McKim, *Ramism*, 44.
[30] This was the epithet that Gabriel Harvey gave them (McKim, *Ramism*, 46).
[31] McKim, *Ramism*, 44–45.
[32] Jardine, "Gabriel Harvey", 36–39 and McKim, *Ramism*, 45.
[33] McKim, *Ramism*, 45.

and his defence of Ramism against the attacks of Digby, which sparked a pamphlet war.[34] The commentary he wrote on Ramus' dialectic, with its pronounced Realism and sharp anti-Aristotelian notes, quickly became a firm favourite among Cambridge students.[35] Through connections with Sir Philip Sidney, to whom Temple dedicated his commentary, Ramism gained an important hearing in both court and literary circles.[36] Indeed, the presence of Ramism in Sidney, Spenser, Shakespeare, Donne, and above all Milton reveals its role at this time in helping to foster a distinctively English culture of erudition.[37]

It is clear then that by the early 1580s, through the influence of Chaderton, Harvey and Temple, Ramism was in the ascendancy across the university. In 1584 Chaderton became Master of Emmanuel College, which had been newly founded by Sir Walter Mildmay to serve as a Puritan seminary.[38] Chaderton's and Mildmay's emphasis was on training biblical preachers to spearhead the reform of the English Church, and in this Ramism played a vital role.[39] We may see this from Richard Holdsworth's "Directions for a Student in the Universitie", dating from the 1620s, one of our most important sources for the Cambridge curriculum of the early seventeenth century. Holdsworth later became Master of Emmanuel and his "Directions" reveal the centrality of logical instruction in the College. For a large portion of a student's first year was to be devoted to in-depth study of logical systems, first those short methodical compendia produced by their tutors and then printed works. Drawing on those works—whether Ramist, Semi-Ramist or Aristotelian—students were then to effectively draw up their own systems of logic for use in the College.[40]

Mildmay's statutes were clear that all study of philosophy and the arts was to be subordinated to "sacred theology". The logic they learned was therefore to be

---

[34] Boran, Temple, Sir William (1554/5–1627)".
[35] Jardine, "Place", 51, 57–59 and "Humanism", 26–27. Interestingly, this Realism did not stop him from inveighing against "Scotist delirium" in William Temple, *Francisci Mildapetti Navarreni ad Everardum Digbeium* (London, 1580), 56. However, the context suggests something of a rhetorical move similar to that made by Ramus against his scholastic opponents.
[36] McKim, *Ramism*, 46. Temple subsequently served Sidney as secretary. Apart from Temple, the most prominent Ramist in Sidney's circle was Abraham Fraunce. For more on him see William Barker, "Fraunce [France], Abraham (1559?–1592/3?)", *ODNB* and Zenón Luis-Martínez, "Ramist Dialectic, Poetic Examples, and the Uses of Pastoral in Abraham Fraunce's *The Shepherds' Logic*", *Parergon* 33.3 (2016): 69–95.
[37] See Wainwright, *The Rational Shakespeare*; Luis-Martínez, "Ramist Dialectic"; Niranjan Goswami, "Refiguring Donne and Spenser: Aspects of Ramist Rhetoric", in *Spenser and Donne: Thinking Poets*, ed. Yulia Ryzhik (Manchester: Manchester University Press, 2021), Chapter 3; and Wilson, "Reading the 'Unseemly Logomachy' ", 69–88.
[38] Patrick Collinson, "Chaderton, Laurence (1536?–1640)", *ODNB*.
[39] See the probate inventories for John Cocke (1593) and Alexander Clugh (1621) in Leedham-Green, *Cambridge Inventories*. Cocke owns works by Ramus, Fenner, and Piscator, and Clugh owns two different copies of Ramus' dialectic, as well as Temple and Talaeus.
[40] Richard Holdsworth, "Directions for a Student in the Universitie", in Harris Francis Fletcher, *The Intellectual Development of John Milton: Volume II, The Cambridge University Period, 1625–32* (Urbana IL: University of Illinois Press, 1981), 634–37.

turned to the glory of God. That this happened was ensured by weekly theological disputations as well as regular "exercises" in the Word and even "prophesyings". In this way, Chaderton's logical pattern of private Bible study became institutionalized to an even greater extent than it had at Christ's.[41] Even more importantly, the close intellectual and spiritual ties meant that at Emmanuel, Christ's, and other Puritan colleges important godly networks were being established and cemented for the further reform of the Church of England and the establishing of churches in the New World.[42] So integrated was the study of logic and theology in these colleges that for many young students their conversion to Puritanism—and there were many conversions—must have practically coincided with their "conversion" to Ramism. In this way, Ramism became essential to the Puritan effort to defeat the forces of Anti-Christ and build a New Jerusalem.[43]

## 4.2. Perkins' Ramism

One of the most important products of this intensive Puritan and Ramist educational system was William Perkins, the leading English theologian of the sixteenth century. Perkins had entered Christ's as a pensioner in 1577, and from the start Chaderton served as his tutor. He became a Fellow of Christ's until 1594, when he married, and until his death in 1602 was one of Cambridge's most popular preachers. Referred to by Patrick Collinson as the "Prince of Puritan Theologians", he had both a national and international reputation.[44] In Thomas Fuller's celebrated words, Perkins "brought the schools into the Pulpit, and unshelling their controversies out of their hard school-terms, made thereof plain and wholsome meat for his people".[45] In this endeavour, as McKim has shown us, Ramism played a central role.[46] For it served to unify and coordinate his exegetical, systematic, and practical theology into a powerful synthesis, and then to impress its pattern on the human soul.

---

[41] Joan Ibish, "Emmanuel College: The Founding Generation, with a Biographical Register of Members of the College 1584–1604" (PhD Dissertation, Harvard University, 1985), 20–25. See also Francis J. Bremer, *Congregational Communion: Clerical Friendship in the Anglo-American Clerical Community, 1610–92* (Boston, MA: Northeastern University Press, 1994), 25–28.

[42] Bremer, *Congregational Communion*, 17–40.

[43] Bremer, *Congregational Communion*, 19. Bremer does not actually comment on Ramism, but many of the figures he discusses were prominent Ramists.

[44] Michael Jinkins, "Perkins, William (1558–1602)", *ODNB*.

[45] Thomas Fuller, *The Holy State* (Cambridge, 1642), 90.

[46] McKim, *Ramism*, 51ff. McKim illustrates Perkins' abiding legacy in terms of theology and ethics, education, preaching, the art of memory, and biblical interpretation. See further Simon J. G. Burton, "Reforging the Great Chain of Being: Ramism Reconsidered", in *Faith Working through Love: The Theology of William Perkins*, ed. Joel R. Beeke, Matthew N. Payne, and J. Stephen Yuille (Grand Rapids, MI: Reformation Heritage Books, 2022), 205–27 for discussion of many of the same themes as this chapter.

The first hint of this comes from Perkins' earliest Ramist work, the *Antidicsonus* of 1584. For this pits the Ramist art of memory against the "impious" memory art of Alexander Dickson, the foremost British disciple of Giordano Bruno. In his own day Ramus had challenged the contemporary *ars memoriae* directly, arguing that his own logic and method could be used to speedily commit to memory anything desired.[47] For Perkins too the true art of memory is based not on the stimulation of images, as for Bruno or Dickson, but on the logical and intelligible structure of the thing to be memorized. By mapping out this structure, logic can imprint it on the mind. Following the Ramist ordering of universal to particular it thus becomes easily possible to commit whole disciplines to memory. In this Ramist charts form an important aid, although Perkins' emphasis falls on the intellectual, even ideal, character of logic, as a counter to the sensory immersion of Dickson's Brunian methodology.[48]

In Perkins' subsequent works, Ramism abounds. It thus plays an important, if rather implicit, role in structuring the discourse of Perkins' many commentaries and sermons.[49] The importance of this method for Perkins is clearly seen from his 1607 *The Arte of Prophecying*, one of his most popular works. Here he not only suggests using logic and all the other arts in the analysis of Scripture but also recommends that he "who is to preach does diligently imprint in his mind by the help of disposition (either axiomatical, or syllogistical, or methodical) the severall doctrines of the place he means to handle, the several proofs and applications of the doctrines, the illustrations of the applications, and the order of them all".[50] In his *The Foundation of Christian Religion*, *Exposition of the Symbole*, and above all *A Golden Chaine*, Perkins pioneered his own Ramist system of theology.[51] While not the earliest Ramist theology in England—it was preceded by some five years by the 1585 *Sacra Theologia* of Dudley Fenner, another Cambridge man—it was undoubtedly one of the most influential, imparting a vital systematizing impulse to the next generation of Ramists, as we will return to below.[52]

Ramism also played a crucial role in fusing together Perkins' theology and ethics into a coherent system of Christian praxis. Indeed, the two were tightly bound together in the Ramist dichotomy of faith and works, according to which all theology must be directed towards practical use.[53] For Perkins, ethics was

---

[47] Yates, *Art of Memory*, 228–38.
[48] William Perkins, *Antidicsonus Cuiusdam Cantabrigiensis G. P.* (London, 1584), "*Epistola*", 29–30, 45, 48. See Yates, *Art of Memory*, 260–78 and McKim, *Ramism*, 51–58.
[49] McKim, *Ramism*, 69–73.
[50] William Perkins, *The Art of Prophesying*, c. 9 (*Works*, 10.348).
[51] See Muller, *PRRD*, 1.197–203 and McKim, *Ramism*, 63–64, 93. Richard A. Muller, "Perkins' *A Golden Chaine*: Predestinarian System or Schematized Ordo Salutis?", *The Sixteenth Century Journal* 9.1 (1978): 80 calls the *Symbole* a "true system of theology".
[52] McKim, *Ramism*, 49.
[53] William Perkins, *A Golden Chain*, c. 1 (*Works*, 6.11). At the same time Perkins' account of theology as the supreme science does resonate with Aquinas, *ST*, 1a 1.3, 5.

essentially understood as biblical casuistry, applying scriptural principles to solve myriad "cases of conscience". His conviction of the innate logical character of the human mind, led him to structure his casuistry along explicit Ramist lines, allowing him to knit together a multiplicity of diverse ethical questions into a unified, biblically-controlled system.[54] While deriving from the Aristotelian scholastic methodology of Beza and Zanchi, the contemporary Puritan vogue for the "practical syllogism", in which the truths of the Bible are applied logically to the state of the individual Christian, surely had much to do with its Ramist popularization.[55] Analysing, revealing, and imprinting the logical pattern of Scripture on the soul thus became the job not only of the theologian, preacher, or exegete but also of the ordinary Christian—an important clue to the central place of Ramism in the Puritan vision of the world.[56]

## 4.3. Richardsonian Ramism

While Perkins' works clearly illustrate the synthetic power of Ramist method, they only hint at its underlying metaphysical and theological presuppositions. In order to uncover these, we must instead turn to Richardson and Ames. Richardson is one of the unsung heroes of the English Puritan movement. He graduated from Queen's in 1584, the same year that Perkins wrote the *Antidicsonus*. Unlike Perkins, however, Richardson was never to become established in the university. Forced to leave due to his radical sentiments, Richardson started an academy in Barking to help graduates preparing for their MA examination. Here, according to George Walker, due to his "singular learning in Divinity, and all other learned Arts, and excellent knowledge in the originall tongues of holy Scripture, divers studious young men did resort from Cambridge ... to be directed in their study of Divinity, and other arts".[57] His pupils here included Ames himself as well as Thomas Hooker, Charles Chauncy, John Yates, and other leading Puritans. Richardson was revered by his pupils and the notes of his lectures were sought after far and wide. Following his death around 1621, his logical notes were gathered up and published in 1629 as *A Logicians School-Master*, which quickly became a bestseller. An expanded version was published in 1657,

---

[54] McKim, *Ramism*, 96–103.
[55] For Perkins' casuistry see James Keenan, "William Perkins (1558–1602) and the Birth of British Casuistry", *The Context of Casuistry*, ed. James Keenan and Thomas Shannon (Washington, DC: Georgetown University Press, 1995), 105–30. For the atomizing tendency of late medieval casuistry see James Keenan, "The Casuistry of John Mair, Nominalist Professor of Paris", in *The Context of Casuistry*, 93–97. For the Ramist character of Perkins' casuistry see McKim, *Ramism*, 96–103.
[56] Perkins, *Art of Prophesying*, c. 4 (*Works*, 10.301).
[57] George Walker, *A True Relation of the Chiefe Passages betweene Mr. Anthony Wooton, and Mr. George Walker* (London, 1642), 6.

which also contained Richardson's notes on the encyclopaedia.[58] His systematic theology survives in his pupil Yates' *Modell of Divinite* of 1623, which Yates admitted was drawn largely from Richardson's Ramist tables and annotations.[59]

Ames was the inheritor of the mantle of both Perkins and Richardson, and has thus been aptly called "the foremost seventeenth-century Puritan Ramist".[60] Ames arrived at Christ's in 1594 and was soon converted to Puritanism by Perkins' ardent preaching.[61] From 1601 to 1609 Ames was a fellow of Christ's, until he too was forced out for his uncompromising views. The date of his contact with Richardson is uncertain, but George Walker, who knew Richardson personally, was quite clear that Ames was one of his pupils at Barking.[62] In 1610 Ames left England, never to return. Making his home in the Netherlands, Ames quickly established a reputation there for his Anti-Arminianism. Having come to prominence as adviser to Johannes Bogerman, the president of the Synod of Dordt, Ames was finally appointed Professor of Theology at the University of Franeker in 1622.[63]

During Ames' time at Franeker, there were major divisions between the scholastic and Ramist parties among the faculty and students—conflicts which were surely exacerbated by his own uncompromising stance as well as that of his scholastic colleagues Sibrandus Lubbertus and Johannes Maccovius. Ames was the leader of the Ramist party and in 1626–27 served as *rector magnificus* of the university.[64] As such, he attempted to make important reforms, urging Ramism as an important means of uniting theological method and piety. Indeed, Ames' first ever speech at Franeker exhorted students to be "inundated" in dialectic and stressed the importance of logic for the study of theology—albeit not the Aristotelian logic of the "sophists".[65]

Following in the footsteps of Perkins, during his time at Franeker, Ames wrote both a systematic theology—the celebrated *Medulla Theologiae* of 1627— and a comprehensive work of casuistry—the *De Conscientia* of 1630.[66] He also published a number of commentaries on Scripture which, like those of Perkins, are structured according to a Ramist model. It is also from this time that Ames'

---

[58] For Richardson's life see Adams, "Richardson's Philosophy of Art", 229–31 and Roland Hall, "Richardson, Alexander (d. in or before 1621)", *ODNB*.

[59] See John Yates, "An Advertisement to the Reader", in *A Modell of Divinitie, Catechistically Composed* (London, 1622); cf. Increase Mather, "To the Reader", in James Fitch, *The First Principles of the Doctrine of Christ* (Boston, 1679).

[60] Sprunger, *Learned Doctor*, 15.

[61] Sprunger, *Learned Doctor*, 11–12.

[62] Walker, *True Relation*, 6. Sprunger, *Learned Doctor*, 14–15 assumes that Ames' only contact with Richardson was through the latter's popular notes.

[63] Sprunger, *Learned Doctor*, 27–70.

[64] Sprunger, *Learned Doctor*, 75, 79, 81–83.

[65] William Ames, *The Philosophical and Theological Treatises of William Ames* [hereafter *PTT*], ed. Lee Gibbs (Lewiston, NY: Edwin Mellen Press, 2013), 353.

[66] Sprunger, *Learned Doctor*, 77.

*Philosophemata* dates. Compiled based on Richardson's notes and a series of disputations over which he presided in Franeker, the *Philosophemata* ranks with the *Logicians School-Master* as the most important treatise on Ramism in the English tradition. It had a profound impact on the Puritans of England and especially New England. As well as Ames' reflections on Ramist logic and its philosophical underpinning, it contains important disputations against scholastic metaphysics and ethics and the outline sketch of a Ramist encyclopaedia.[67]

### 4.3.1. The Radiance and Rhetoric of Reality

For both Richardson and Ames, logic is the universal art which grounds all other disciplines. Without logic there could be no knowledge of anything else—physics, mathematics, law, medicine, theology, or any human pursuit whatsoever.[68] Their reason for making such a claim is their belief that both the human mind and the external reality that the mind perceives are intrinsically and inescapably logical. We none of us can avoid seeing the world according to logical categories.[69] Following in the lines of Ramus' natural dialectic, logic becomes the precondition of all human activity.

The art of logic teaches us to reason well. Its scope is therefore immensely broad, covering both created being and non-being. As Richardson explains, human reason is like the "eye of the mind", the object of whose sight is being itself. For if we are unable to perceive being then we can know nothing about ourselves or our world; our reason would therefore be useless, like a blind eye.[70] More precisely, Ames holds that logic has being (and non-being) as its material object and reason as its formal object. Logic is thus intended to reveal the "reason of things" (*ratio rerum*), the intelligible structure of all reality expressed in the different logical affections (*rationes*) of each created thing and their interrelation.[71] These it becomes clear correspond closely to the metaphysical parts of things as the source from which they are derived and originate.[72]

In an important allusion to the Neo-Platonic metaphysics of light, Richardson compared these logical affections, emanating from every individual thing to

---

[67] Sprunger, *Learned Doctor*, 81–83.
[68] Alexander Richardson, *The Logicians School-Master: or, A Comment upon Ramus Logick* (London, 1657), 13 and William Ames, *Theses Logicae*, 21 in *Guilielmi Amesii Magni Theologi ac Philosophi Acutissimi Philosophemata* (Cambridge, 1646). Note that references within *Philosophemata* refer to page numbers.
[69] Ames, *Theses Logicae*, 22.
[70] Richardson, *Logicians School-Master*, 1.
[71] Ames, *Theses Logicae*, 21–22.
[72] Ames, *Theses Logicae*, 22–23; Richardson, *Logicians School-Master*, 28, 47.

colours. Just as our eye only sees things as they are coloured, so reason, the eye of our mind, only sees things as they are "logically coloured".[73]

> [A]s the Sun beams coming through a red or blew glass, &c. will bring the colour of the glass with them to our sense: so doth the irradiation of Art from the thing bring the colour of the thing with it to our understanding, I mean that this irradiation doth bring the frame of the thing with it, according to which we see it.[74]

Surrounding (*to peri*) every being, God has therefore placed a kind of halo—a parhelion—revealing, and diffusing, their inmost character.[75] Reality is therefore radiant and suffused with intelligible light.

To draw on another sensory modality prominent in Richardson's writings, reality is also both active and vocal in its communication of itself to the human understanding.[76] A crucial component of understanding things is thus in learning to "hear" and distinguish the rich polyphony of their logical arguments. This rhetorical dimension is evident in Richardson especially. He is clear that the act by which things argue—note the active voice—has a double dimension. First, we have the logical notion itself, which he also refers to as "*logismos*"—the reasoning or thought. It is this which communicates the being to the mind of man. Intimately coupled to this is the "*eponymia*" of the word which communicates the act from man to man and is therefore embodied in language as a carrier of meaning, founding both grammar and rhetoric, speech and eloquence.[77]

In Ramist terms, these logical affections, or *logismoi*, clearly correspond to arguments.[78] The process of identifying and classifying them thus constitutes invention as the first part of logic. This is then followed by judgement as the second part of logic, which shows how arguments can be combined together. Following Ramus closely, they held that this allowed the judgement of the truth of different propositions through the arrangement of axioms and syllogisms.[79] Significantly, Ames claimed that axioms were not first in minds or words, but in the things themselves. In this way, truth could be understood as inhering in things themselves, as well as in the conformity of the thing to the intellect.[80] In this way not only the individual *logismoi* but also their inter-connection among themselves

---

[73] Richardson, *Logicians School-Master*, 10–11, 23, 57.
[74] Richardson, *Logicians School-Master*, 23.
[75] Adams, "Richardson's Philosophy of Art", 236; cf. Richardson, *Logicians School-Master*, 16.
[76] Richardson, *Logicians School-Master*, 10–11, 22–23. Light and sound are not the only sensory modalities Richardson uses to illustrate this. He also compares the emanation of science from being to the way in which flowers "spirate" a scent (p. 22).
[77] Richardson, *Logicians School-Master*, 10–11.
[78] William Ames, *Demonstratio Logicae Verae*, 4, in *Philosophemata*.
[79] Ames, *Theses Logicae*, 22.
[80] Ames, *Theses Logicae*, 41.

becomes understood as grounded in reality and accessible through invention and judgement. As Adams neatly expresses this, these two logical processes "reflect being insofar as being is made of discrete and composite aspects. Discrete aspects correspond to dialectical invention and composite aspects correspond to judgement".[81]

The culmination of both invention and judgement was to be found in method. So enthusiastic were the Cambridge Ramists about method—"a plaine and perfect way of handling anything"—that they effectively turned it into the third part of logic, threatening the Agricolan twofold division and relegating syllogisms to a "certaine frame of proving".[82] Drawing on a common Renaissance trope, they held that method signified the order of proceeding through the axioms. It was therefore intimately linked with the intellectual process of genesis and analysis—the building up of things from simples to composites and the breaking down of composites into simples.[83] Richardson further insisted that method as "the rule of order" must be understood as inhering in things in the same way that arguments, axioms, and syllogisms were understood as grounded in reality.[84] Together with invention and judgement, method thus yielded a kind of blueprint of reality—evidenced in the famous Ramist charts with their dichotomous organization—mapping out the logical and metaphysical relations pertaining to individual things or states of affairs. It was intended to help memory both through visual representation and by imprinting the intrinsic order of things on the mind, allowing the Ramist to see the whole and its parts together in one intuition. Method therefore allowed humanity the closest thing possible to a God's-eye view of reality.

### 4.3.2. Realism and Propositional Realism

Richardson's and Ames' conviction that logic mirrors the intelligible structure of reality clearly entails a strong commitment to Realism. While their works are not at all explicit on the sources of this Realism, they do give some indications. In particular, they point to an important Augustinian and Franciscan influence. In the *Logicians School-Master*, Richardson notes that it is a "great question" whether universals are real (*realia*) or only intentional (*intentionalia*). He himself emphatically denies the Nominalist position that universals are merely "phantasms" or mental abstractions, pointing out that "the universal still

---

[81] Adams, "Richardson's Puritan Theory of Discourse", 265.
[82] Dudley Fenner, *The Arts of Logike and Rethorike Plainlie Set Forth in the English Tounge* (Middelburg, 1584), II c. 4; cf. Sprunger, "Ames, Ramus, and the Method of Puritan Theology", 142.
[83] Richardson, *Logicians School-Master*, 47.
[84] Richardson, *Logicians School-Master*, 333–37; cf. Ames, *Theses Logicae*, 53.

remains a thing, though I thus consider it in my mind".[85] Indeed, it is axiomatic to Richardson that universals communicate their nature to individuals leading him to argue that cause, effect, and other Ramist arguments are also "real in nature".[86] In Ames, and also in Perkins, we find a similar claim in the argument that a universal such as genus exists outside the intellect although not outside its own species.[87] As Richardson summed this up, following the moderate Realism of Aquinas and Scotus, "every universal is subsistent in *singularibus*".[88]

From hints in both Richardson and Ames, we gain a clear sense that they construed this Realism according to a more Scotistic than Thomistic understanding. Echoing Scotus, Ames claims that the genus is nothing other than the "common nature" which is in various things.[89] Even more important is Richardson's discussion of individuation, in which he denies the Thomist view that "singulars . . . are distinct onely by a conflux of common accidents" and affirms the Scotistic understanding that every individual has its own "really distinct" form. Applied to humans, this means that the soul is not properly the form of the body, but that "the forms of the body and the soul make up the form of a man"—a clear assertion of the Franciscan plurality of forms.[90] Moreover, Richardson's discussion of the "hypostatical union" of genus and species—in which both remain distinct within the same individual—points toward Scotus' formal distinction.[91] Elsewhere he more or less affirms this, holding that terms such as "man" and "genus" are "really" distinct according to definition even though they characterize a single thing.[92] In this they were simply following Perkins, who upheld it as "a principle in logic that the genus is actually in all the species", and, like Scotus, maintained that the genus is naturally prior to its species.[93]

---

[85] Richardson, *Logicians School-Master*, 219.

[86] Richardson, *Logicians School-Master*, 218–19.

[87] Ames, *Theses Logicae*, 37 and Perkins, *Art of Prophesying*, c. 6 (*Works*, 10.331).

[88] Richardson, *Logicians School-Master*, 218–19.

[89] Ames, *Theses Logicae*, 37. Scotus' adaptation of the Avicennian notion of common nature is often seen as one of the most important distinctives in his account of Realism. For a discussion of Scotus' complex relation to Avicenna see Timothy Noone, "Universals and Individuation", in *The Cambridge Companion to Duns Scotus*, ed. Thomas Williams (Cambridge: Cambridge University Press, 2002), 102–12.

[90] Richardson, *Logicians School-Master*, 215–16. For a discussion of Aquinas' complex treatment of individuation see John F. Wippel, *The Metaphysical Thought of Thomas Aquinas: From Finite Being to Uncreated Being* (Washington, DC: Catholic University of America Press, 2000), 351–74. Maurice J. Grajewksi, *The Formal Distinction of Duns Scotus* (Washington, DC: Catholic University of America Press, 1944), 152–53 points out that strictly speaking the Scotist principle of individuation is not a form but a formality. I am grateful to Matthew Baines for this reference.

[91] Richardson, *Logicians School-Master*, 214.

[92] Richardson, *Logicians School-Master*, 57–59; cf. Scotus, *Ord.* 1 d. 8 p. 1 q. 3 n. 106–7 (Vatican, IV.201–2).

[93] William Perkins, *A Friendly Admonition to Alexander Dickson* (*Works*, 6.555) and *Art of Prophesying*, c. 6 (*Works*, 10.331); cf. Scotus, *Ord.* 2 d. 3 p. 1 q. 5–6 n. 187 (Vatican, VII.483). For the Scotist aspect of this see further Todd Bates, "Fine-Tuning Pini's Reading of Scotus's *Categories*", in *Medieval Commentaries on Aristotle's Categories*, ed. Lloyd A. Newton (Leiden: Brill, 2008), 271.

It is also significant that both Richardson and Ames index their views on the Realist foundation of logic according to the scholastic distinction between terms of first and second intention. Against what may be identified as a broadly Thomistic tendency to characterize logic as a discipline only involving second intentions, Richardson argues that this involves an overly sharp distinction between first and second intentions. For where Aquinas characterized second intentions as "concepts of concepts", Richardson is much closer to Scotus in arguing that the same term, such as "genus" can function as both a first and second intention, according to whether it is considered as rooted in the thing or apprehended by the human mind.[94] From this Richardson concludes that "we cannot sever the logical notion from the thing, because it is never but *in re*".[95] Ames' argument is terser and less sophisticated, but he is likewise clear in holding that not all logical notions are "second notions" but that some—like cause, effect, subject, adjunct, etc.—are "first notions", more rightly called arguments.[96]

While Scotus seems a likely source for Richardson's discussion of intentions, it should not be forgotten that there were other possible influences. As we have seen, the fluidity of first and second intentions is clearly apparent in Lullism, that other Franciscan system of logic.[97] It is also evident among the medieval speculative grammarians or *modistae*, whose argument for a direct parallelism between ontological modes of being (*modi essendi*), cognitive modes of understanding (*modi intelligendi*), and linguistic modes of signifying (*modi significandi*) displays many affinities with Richardson's and Ames' own approach to logic and language.[98] A much closer parallel with the Cambridge Ramists, perhaps even closer than Scotus himself, is found in Walter Burley the fourteenth-century English Franciscan logician, who held that second intentions are actually inherent in things themselves, such that they become parts of extra-mental reality.[99] Indeed, going beyond this, Burley and his follower John Wyclif also espoused a definite propositional Realism, affirming the propositional structure of reality itself—a view we have already seen to have important precedent in Lull as well as in Rimini's *complexe significabile*. The Richardsonian view of propositions and syllogisms as somehow existing outside the mind clearly reflects this important Augustinian and Franciscan trend of the Late Middle Ages.[100]

---

[94] Richardson, *Logicians School-Master*, 57–59. For Scotus' view see Knudsen, "Intentions and Impositions", 485–86.
[95] Richardson, *Logicians School-Master*, 57–59.
[96] Ames, *Theses Logicae*, 22.
[97] Johnston, *Spiritual Logic*, 4–6, 16–18, 46–52.
[98] See Ria van der Lecq, "*Modistae*", in *Encyclopedia of Medieval Philosophy*, ed. Henrik Lagerlund (Dordrecht: Springer, 2010). Richardson, *Logicians School-Master*, 90–92, 94, 95, 146, 154 employs the language of modes to his treatment of Ramist arguments. See also Ames, *PTT*, 277 and Richardson, *Grammatical Notes*, 8, in *Logicians School-Master*.
[99] Knudsen, "Intentions and Impositions", 494–95.
[100] Richardson, *Logicians School-Master*, 29.

Indeed, positing such a connection is by no means far-fetched, for not only was Agricolan and Ramist logic permeated by a definite topical Scotism and nascent propositional Realism, as we have seen, but also the logic taught at Cambridge in the early sixteenth century was profoundly influenced by the English Realism of Burley, Wyclif, and their followers. We may see this from the 1535 statutes responsible for the sea-change in the university curriculum which specifically legislated against the "ashy and frivolous questions and the obscure glosses of Scotus, Burley, Anthony Trombeta, Bricot, Bruliferius and others of these mealy men".[101] Yet while the statutes were undoubtedly effective, Realist and Scotistic logic remained accessible at Cambridge, perhaps to an extent which we have not realized hitherto.[102] Moreover, as Kantik Ghosh has argued, Wyclif's own Realist and scriptural logic penetrated much more deeply into the popular movement of Lollardy than has previously been realized.[103] The Reformation revival in Wyclif studies likely influenced English theology more profoundly than has hitherto been suspected. In fact, in our case there is no need to speculate on this, for there is good evidence that seventeenth-century Ramists *were* interested in Wyclif's philosophical theology, with one even connecting Wyclif and Ramus in a line of Neo-Platonic Reformers of the Church.[104]

Ultimately, then, Richardson and Ames should be seen as standing shoulder-to-shoulder with Burley and Wyclif in a lineage of Augustinian, Realist, and Scotist reform.[105] In a sense, however, the precise channels of influence do not matter, for they could easily find in Augustine's own works this understanding of reality as spiritually charged and resonating with the voice of God. In a famous passage in his *Confessions*, cited in this respect by one of their Ramist contemporaries, Augustine holds a dialogue with the whole of creation, questioning it about God.[106] For Augustine, and especially for his medieval disciples such as Hugh of St Victor and Bonaventure, nature was vocal and propositional; it was a book to be read with the eyes of faith, in which every creature

---

[101] Cited from Jardine, "Place", 51 n. 44: "*plus quam cimmeris et frivolis quaestiunculis caecisque et obscuris glossematis Scoti Burlei Anthonii Trombetae Bricoti Bruliferii et aliorum eius farinae hominum*".

[102] For the importance of these logical currents at Cambridge before the Reformation see E. J. Ashworth, "The 'Libelli Sophistarum' and the Use of Medieval Logic Texts at Oxford and Cambridge in the Early Sixteenth Century", *Vivarium* 17 (1979): 134–58 and Damian Riehl Leader, *A History of the University of Cambridge: Volume 1, The University to 1546* (Cambridge: Cambridge University Press, 1988), 133.

[103] Kantik Ghosh, "Logic and Lollardy", *Medium Aevum* 76 (2007): 251–67.

[104] See Trinity College Dublin, MSS 334 and 775 for James Ussher's Ramist reflections. See also Richard Baxter, *The Reduction of a Digressor* (London, 1654), 34 and Gale, *Court of the Gentiles*, "Preface".

[105] Scotus' formal distinction played a vital role in structuring Wyclif's account of propositional Realism, allowing him to uphold the one-many structure of reality and a Realist account of predication. See further Conti, "Wyclif's Logic and Metaphysics", 70–72.

[106] Augustine, *Confessions*, 10.6.8–10; cf. Johann Heinrich Alsted, *Theologia Naturalis Exhibens Augustissimam Naturae Scholam* (Frankfurt, 1615), II.234–35.

was a word or sentence speaking of the glory of God.[107] It was the genius of these Ramists, even going beyond that of their late medieval predecessors, to take up this Augustinian, and indeed biblical, understanding, and transform it into a systematic and encyclopaedic account of the entire field of knowledge and reality.

### 4.3.3. Divine Ideas and Emanation

One of the chief characteristics of Cambridge Ramism is the connection it poses between the dynamic structure of human thought, the metaphysical composition of reality, and the transcendent pattern of divine understanding. As Richardson neatly expressed this, "truth is first in God, then secondly, all things are so far forth true, as they answer to the idea in God".[108] What therefore might be called the fundamental presupposition of Richardson's and Ames' logic is that in the process of perceiving and understanding the world around us our thought comes to mirror the internal structure and relations of what we perceive and understand. There is therefore a precise conformity, or isomorphism, between the human mind and reality. Taking up an important Platonic streak in Ramus himself, Ames and Richardson held that the theological ground of this Realism and exemplarism was the doctrine of the divine ideas, and significantly they extrapolated this into a complex philosophy of logic and its relation to the other arts and sciences—the *technologia* or encyclopaedia. As we shall see below, this also impinges closely on their understanding of the relation between logic and theology. Here we shall focus on Ames' doctrine of the divine ideas, which has recently been the topic of some discussion, returning briefly to Richardson's account towards the end of the chapter.[109]

Following both a biblical and a Neo-Platonic precedent, Ames takes up the notion of God as a divine artist skilfully fashioning his creation. Thus just as the craftsman looks to an idea in the mind and conforms his action to it, so God may be conceived of as "pre-existent idea" and "exemplar cause of all things to be effected".[110] Such an understanding is clearly reminiscent of Aquinas, Scotus, and

---

[107] For an account of the Augustinian tradition of the "books of God" and its reception in a medieval and early modern milieu see Pavlas, "The Book Metaphor Triadized", 384–416. For Augustine's influence on late medieval propositional Realism see Laurent Cesalli, "Intentionality and Truth-Making: Augustine's Influence on Burley and Wyclif's Propositional Semantics", *Vivarium* 45 (2007): 283–97.

[108] Richardson, *Logicians School-Master*, 261.

[109] Compare Richard A. Muller, "Calvinist Thomism Revisited: William Ames (1576–1633) and the Divine Ideas", in *From Rome to Zurich, between Ignatius and Vermigli: Essays in Honor of John Patrick Donnelly*, ed. Gary Jenkins, W. J. Torrance Kirby, and Kathleen Comerford (Leiden: Brill, 2017), 103–20 and Philip Fisk, *Jonathan Edwards' Turn from the Classic-Reformed Tradition of Freedom of the Will* (Göttingen: Vandenhoeck & Ruprecht, 2016), 167–89.

[110] William Ames, *Medulla S.S. Theologiae* (Amsterdam, 1659), 1.7.13. For the background to Ames' craftsman analogy and his wider understanding see Ames, *Technometria*, 1, in *Philosophemata*.

Bonaventure, as well as a host of other scholastics. While Ames' tendency to speak of the divine "idea" might be seen with Henri Krop as evincing a Nominalist direction to his thought, it better reflects that dynamic tension between "idea" and "ideas" to be found in thirteenth-century scholasticism.[111] Against a Nominalist tendency to relegate divine ideas to their instantiation in the created order, Ames strongly emphasized that "all things are prior in the divine mind than in themselves".[112] Indeed, buttressing Ames' Realism is his implied claim that ideas of both "universal and singular things" are to be found in God.[113]

In explaining how the simple divine essence can serve as an "exemplar cause" for a multiplicity of creatures, Ames deploys a variety of strategies drawn from his scholastic sources. The first of these concerns the connection between ideas and imitability. Thus Ames claims that the "idea of all things is the divine essence as it is understandable by God himself as imitable by creatures".[114] The multiplicity of divine ideas therefore reflects the manifold ways in which the divine essence is capable of being imitated by creatures. As Muller argues, there are clear and important parallels to be seen here with Aquinas.[115] Yet while the notion of divine ideas as conceptual "relations of imitability" is most famously associated with Aquinas, it was by no means unique to him. Indeed, Scotus described it as the consensus view of his own day.[116] It was, for example, prominent in Bonaventure—whose account of the divine ideas resonates with Ames[117]—and even Scotus, despite his critique of the mainstream view, affirmed that "it is certain that in God there are distinct relations—as distinct ideas—for knowing distinct knowables".[118]

Scotus' own preference was to describe ideas, under the inspiration of Plato, as "quiddities known to the divine mind". He held that the "intelligible world and the idea in the divine mind is nothing but the sensible world outside as it is objectively in the divine mind in cognised being (*in esse cognito*)".[119] This brings us

---

[111] Henri Krop, "Philosophy and the Synod of Dordt: Aristotelianism, Humanism and the Case against Arminianism", in *Revisiting the Synod of Dordt (1618–1619)*, ed. Aza Goudriaan and Fred van Lieburg (Leiden: Brill, 2011), 70, 75. It should be noted that Krop's association of Ames with Nominalism is not with respect to the divine ideas per se. For the dynamic tension of idea and ideas see Timothy Noone, "Aquinas on Divine Ideas: Scotus's Evaluation", *Franciscan Studies* 56 (1998): 307–24 and Carl Vater, "Divine Ideas: 1250–1325" (PhD Dissertation, The Catholic University of America, 2017), 80–88.

[112] Ames, *Medulla*, 1.7.14–15. For the Nominalist critique of divine ideas see Maarten Hoenen, *Marsilius of Inghen: Divine Knowledge in Late Medieval Thought* (Leiden: Brill, 1993), 135–41.

[113] Ames, *Medulla*, 1.7.25.

[114] Ames, *Medulla*, 1.7.14.

[115] Muller, "Calvinist Thomism Revisited", 111–14.

[116] Scotus, *Rep. 1A*, d. 36 pars. 1 q. 1–2 n. 35.

[117] Both Bonaventure and Ames distinguish between the divine ideas considered *secundum rem* and *secundum rationem*. See Ames, *Medulla*, 1.7.19 and Vater, "Divine Ideas", 80–93. Notably, in his commentary on Hebrews, Aquinas made an identical claim (Gregory Doolan, *Aquinas on the Divine Ideas as Exemplar Causes* [Washington, DC: Catholic University of America Press, 2008], 118 n. 90).

[118] Scotus, *Rep. 1A*, d. 36 pars. 1 q. 1–2 n. 27, 31; cf. Noone, "Aquinas on Divine Ideas", 314–15.

[119] Scotus, *Rep. 1A*, d. 36 pars. 1 q. 1–2 n. 74–75.

to Ames' second scholastic strategy, which is the account he gives of intelligible being. For, as both Muller and Philip Fisk have noted,[120] Ames draws on marked Scotistic terminology in his claim that "before creation... no creatures have real being (*esse reale*), either of existence, or of essence, although they have cognised being (*esse cognitum*) from eternity in the divine knowledge".[121] Following Scotus, Ames clearly sought to preserve the divine simplicity by affirming only the intelligible—and not real—being of the multiplicity of ideas in God.[122] For both theologians this served as an important defence of the doctrine of creation *ex nihilo*, foreclosing any Platonic arguments for the co-eternity of creatures with God by squarely identifying the divine ideas with thoughts in the mind of God.[123] Indeed, for Ames, "creatures, as they are conceived in the divine mind, are the idea of that nature which they have in themselves".[124] Buttressing this broader Scotist metaphysical approach was Ames' denial of a real distinction between the essence and existence of creatures, revealing his clear affinities with a Franciscan and Scotist—rather than Thomist—model of participation.[125]

Furthering this Christian and Franciscan reconfiguring of Platonism, and establishing an important voluntaristic and covenantal turn in his method, was Ames' account of the relation of the divine ideas to the divine will. Following Scotus, Ames held that as the ideas are considered before the divine decree they represent the quiddity, or essence, of individual things and their "possible existence", and as considered after the divine decree their actual existence to be realized in time.[126] In this way the decision of the divine will plays a crucial role in the constitution of the divine ideas—something insightfully recognized by both Muller and Fisk.[127] Indeed, citing both Scotus and "our Bradwardine", the fourteenth-century English Augustinian, Ames clearly affirms the Scotist view of synchronic contingency underpinning this, structuring the divine understanding and willing according to a "sequence" of different logical instants of nature.[128] Nevertheless, rather like John Davenant, his associate at the Synod

---

[120] Muller, "Calvinist Thomism Revisited", 112–13; Fisk, *Jonathan Edwards' Turn*, 173–74.
[121] Ames, *Medulla*, 1.8.8. Ames also refers to *esse intelligible* in *Technometria*, 1.
[122] Hoenen, *Marsilius*, 130–31.
[123] Ames, *Medulla*, 1.8.8. Ames' description here matches precisely Hoenen's summary of Scotus' doctrine of *esse cognitum* (*Marsilius*, 130–32). See also Vater, "Divine Ideas", 297–301, 310.
[124] Ames, *Medulla*, 1.7.14.
[125] Ames, *Theses Logicae*, 27. Such a denial is implicit but Ames clearly affirms a (formal) modal distinction between the essence and existence of creatures.
[126] Ames, *Medulla*, 1.7.23.
[127] Muller, "Calvinist Thomism Revisited", 113–15; Fisk, *Jonathan Edwards' Turn*, 173–74. Fisk makes a direct connection with Scotus' account of "neutral truth". Such voluntarism is also evident in Ames, *Medulla*, 1.7.38, for he is clear that the divine will does not "presuppose the goodness of the object, but by willing places and makes it"; cf. John Duns Scotus, *Duns Scotus on the Will and Morality*, ed. Alan B. Wolter (Washington, DC: Catholic University of America Press, 1997), 201.
[128] William Ames, *Bellarminus Enervatus* (London, 1632), III.282–83. For Ames' approbation of Bradwardine see III.257. For Scotus' account of synchronic contingency and its wider significance see Van Asselt et al., *Reformed Thought on Freedom*.

of Dordt, Ames also tempers his Scotism somewhat, holding that these "signs, or instants, or prior or posterior moments, do not agree to divine acts in themselves, but only according to our mode of understanding".[129]

Ames' third and final scholastic strategy concerns the kind of distinctions he is willing to admit within the Godhead in characterizing the divine ideas. Following Aquinas, Ames strongly affirms the divine simplicity, holding that we ascribe to God a plurality of divine names and attributes since the divine essence "is not able to be sufficiently comprehended by us through one act" and so is explained by us "as if manifold".[130] Yet complicating this straightforward Thomistic picture is Ames' subsequent statement that "the divine attributes are in God, not only virtually, and eminently, but also formally (*formaliter*), although not in that mode, by which qualities are in creatures".[131] Clarifying this, Ames distinguishes the divine essence as relating to the "first being" of God, holding that the divine attributes "are in God as if in second being (*secundo esse*), because they are not of the formal reason of divine essence, for we are able to conceive God to be, before we are able to conceive him to be just and good".[132] For this reason he also holds that the divine attributes are distinguished "not only by reason reasoning (*ratione ratiocinante*) (as it is called), but also by reason reasoned (*ratione ratiocinata*), so that the foundation of the distinction is in God himself".[133]

Ames' distinction of first and second being is rooted in Scotus, who held that from this first entity [the divine essence] . . . emanate all other features in an orderly manner"—first the divine attributes, then the divine persons and then the entire created order.[134] In arguing that the divine attributes are not of the same "formal reason" as the divine essence he also clearly differs from Aquinas.[135] Indeed, Ames is explicit that the *ratio* of the divine will is not the same as the *ratio*

---

[129] Ames, *Bellarminus Enervatus*, III.279–80; cf. John Davenant, *De Praedestinatione et Reprobatione in Dissertationes Duae* (Cambridge, 1650), 108–11. For more on Davenant's Nominalist critique of Scotus see Burton, *Hallowing of Logic*, 286–89. This may also reflect the argument of Muller, *Divine Will* which sees a certain amount of blending of Thomist and Scotist views of contingency.

[130] Ames, *Medulla*, 1.4.18; cf. Aquinas, *ST*, 1a 13.4, 6.

[131] Ames, *Medulla*, 1.4.26: "*Attributa divina insunt Deo, non tantum virtualiter et eminenter, sed etiam formaliter, quamvis non eo modo, quo qualitates insunt creaturis*".

[132] Ames, *Medulla*, 1.4.27: "*Deo insunt quasi in esse secundo, quia non sunt de formali ratione essentiae divinae, concipimus enim Deum esse antequam concipere possumus, eum esse justum et bonum*". This text only appears in full in the 1659 *novissima* edition, but the basic idea seems unchanged from earlier editions.

[133] Ames, *Medulla*, 1.4.28.

[134] John Duns Scotus, *God and Creatures: The Quodlibetal Questions*, ed. Felix Alluntis and Allan Wolter (Princeton, NJ: Princeton University Press, 2015), q. 5 art. 2 n. 55 (p. 127). Although Muller, "Calvinist Thomism Revisited", 113 is right to note that language of emanation is somewhat muted in Ames, he does claim that in God the "ideas of all perfections . . . come forth (*proveniunt*) from divine active virtue" (*Medulla*, 1.4.25; 1.7.20).

[135] See Aquinas, *ST*, 1a 13.5.

of divine knowledge and divine power, and, like Scotus, he grounds this distinction in the immanent being of God.[136]

Ames' terminology of "reason reasoned" derived from the Thomist tradition and he was likely attracted to it due to the elegant way it indicated the ground of all such distinctions in God without threatening the divine simplicity.[137] Yet Ames also followed both Francisco Suárez and a number of prominent seventeenth-century Reformed theologians in giving this well-known Thomist distinction a marked Scotist twist, virtually equating it with Scotus' formal distinction.[138] Moreover, if Ames allowed a formal distinction, or better a formal non-identity, between the divine attributes, it is likely that he would also admit one between the divine ideas. For it was common in scholastic understanding to posit a narrower distinction between the divine essence and attributes than between the divine essence and ideas.[139] Nevertheless, what is most important is that like both Aquinas and Scotus, Ames held that the multiplicity of divine ideas in God is the ground for the real multiplicity in creatures—and not vice-versa.[140]

Overall, Ames' discussion of the divine ideas clearly marks a rapprochement—or, better, convergence—between a Thomist and Scotist approach.[141] In this sense, Ames' precise use of conceptualities drawn from *both* Aquinas and Scotus serves both to establish the Realist base of his exemplarism and to give careful expression to the relation of divine transcendence and immanence which runs through his theology. Like Bonaventure and Scotus, he seems especially concerned to fuse two very different paradigms of the divine understanding: an Augustinian one which tends to characterize the divine ideas as eternal reasons pre-existing in the divine simplicity, and a Dionysian one which emphasizes the emanation of the divine ideas, comparing them to light radiating from the divine essence. After all, we should remember that Scotus' notion of the formal distinction was first expressed within the Neo-Platonic framework of the

---

[136] Ames, *Medulla*, 1.7.47.

[137] Muller, *PRRD*, 3.291; "Calvinist Thomism Revisited", 109.

[138] See Alexei Chernyakov, *The Ontology of Time: Being and Time in the Philosophies of Aristotle, Husserl and Heidegger* (Dordrecht: Springer, 2002), 86; Amandus Polanus von Polansdorf, *Syntagma Logicum Arisotelico-Ramaeum ad Usum Imprimis Theologicum Accommodatum* (Basel, 1605), 155–56 and Andreas J. Beck, "Gisbertus Voetius (1589–1676): Basic Features of His Doctrine of God", in *Reformation and Scholasticism*, ed. Asselt and Dekker, 220. Interestingly, Beck points out that Voetius has borrowed Suárez's terminology here. It is also worth remembering that in later works, notably the *Reportatio*, Scotus himself pulled back from the language of formal distinction within God, preferring to speak of a formal non-identity. Indeed, Scotus was just as emphatic as Ames or Aquinas that in God there was a perfect coinciding of all divine attributes as one divine reality (Hoenen, *Marsilius*, 42–45). Ames' use of such terminology also likely indicates a desire to harmonize a Thomist and Scotist account of the divine attributes. See further Muller, *PRRD*, 3.291; "Calvinist Thomism Revisited", 109.

[139] Doolan, *Aquinas on the Divine Ideas*, 90.

[140] See Doolan, *Aquinas on the Divine Ideas*, 116–17 and Hoenen, *Marsilius*, 128–30.

[141] It is notable that Noone, "Aquinas on Divine Ideas", 307–13 emphasizes important common ground between Aquinas' and Scotus' account.

metaphysics of light in order to express God's "unitive containment" of all creaturely perfections.[142]

## 4.4. Exemplarism and Encyclopaedism

If the Realist and exemplaristic logic of these Cambridge Ramists was expressed according to the precise idiom of Aquinas and Scotus, it was undoubtedly also animated by the spirit of Bonaventure's quest for a Christian philosophy. For, like Bonaventure, they recognized an intimate connection between the human arts and sciences and the ideal pattern of the divine mind, developing an important encyclopaedic framework of the unity of all knowledge in God. Fundamental to this was the integration of all knowledge and praxis in the unity of the divine "art". In positioning Richardsonian Ramism as a sharp break from the medieval scholastic tradition, with its divide between contemplative and practical knowledge, Adams has therefore neglected to consider the impact of Franciscan encyclopaedism and practical theology on Ames' and Richardson's "philosophy of art".[143] Before we can see this connection, however, we need to have a clearer understanding of their view of art, in both its divine and human aspects.

Axiomatic to the Cambridge Ramists is their view that the arts have their beginning and end in God their "Alpha and Omega".[144] According to them, God's simple understanding can be expressed in terms of multiple different aspects—the Aristotelian genera of intelligence, science, wisdom, prudence, and art.[145] Of these, art marks both a culmination and summation of all the other modes of divine understanding. It is dependent on them, but also expresses and communicates them in actuality.[146] Fundamental to these Ramists' understanding of art is thus its teleological structure. Encoded in every art, including the divine art, is therefore its end or purpose—referred to by Ames and Richardson, following Ramus, as its "*eupraxia*" or "well-doing".[147] In these terms, Ames defined art succinctly as "the idea of *eupraxia* delineated methodically by catholic rules"—a definition which clearly needs some unpacking.

Art as "*idea eupraxias*" is essentially an idea directed to an end or purpose.[148] In God and in his divine action the idea of this *eupraxia* exists as an "act uniquely one and most simple". However, in God's workmanship—created beings—the

---

[142] See Aertsen, "Being and One", 25.
[143] See Adams, "Richardson's Puritan Theory of Discourse", 260–61 and "Richardson's Philosophy of Art", 227–47.
[144] Richardson, *Logicians School-Master*, 15.
[145] Ames, *Medulla*, 1.7.29.
[146] Ames, *PTT*, 180.
[147] Richardson, *Logicians School-Master*, 5, 16; Ames, *Technometria*, 1–7.
[148] Ames, *Technometria*, 1–2.

one light of divine knowledge and *eupraxia* becomes refracted into multiple different arts. In Platonic fashion, the arts may therefore be regarded as radiations or emanations of the single divine art, like rays of the Sun leading back to a single, unified source. It is as multiplied and divided that man's reason, the eye of his mind, apprehends these different arts and puts them into practice.[149] At the same time, as reflections, or refractions, of the divine ideas, the arts also exhibit their own internal structure which ultimately mirrors that to be found within God himself[150]—they are truly "blueprints of reality".

For Ames, art has a fourfold existence and a fourfold expression: in idea, in the act exercised, in the work completed, and in the image expressed. While he certainly holds that "the idea of art is first, perfectly, and eminently in First Being, from which all other things emanate", he also affirms that it exists partly in the rational creature, "to whom God has both given an eye to perceive it and also has communicated the idea itself proportionally to the rational creature's condition through sense, observation, and experience".[151] Significantly, this twofold human idea mirrors the late medieval, Scotistic, distinction between intuitive cognition as the direct and immediate apprehension of reality by the "eye of the mind" and abstractive cognition as the processing and refining of knowledge from the senses.[152] At the same time, it is also redolent of Bonaventure's understanding of contuition—the co-intuition of reality through the human mind's participation in God—a process which importantly involves the recognition of the ideal pattern of the divine mind in its created instantiations.[153] Continuing this dual divine-human track, Ames holds that the second category of "act exercised" can either refer to God's creative manifesting of the divine ideas or human imitation of divine creativity. Likewise, the third category of "work completed" can refer either to "created things themselves" or to human artefacts. Finally, the fourth category of "image" is either the "likeness which exists ... in the speculation of a rational creature" or "its delineation, which is put in a book, determining from most perfectly arranged precepts the *eupraxia* of the particular thing".[154]

---

[149] Ames, *Technometria*, 3; Richardson, *Logicians School-Master*, 16. See also Ames, *PTT*, 181.
[150] Ames, *Medulla*, 1.7.22 remarks on the interconnected structure of divine ideas according to prior and posterior. This, of course, has to be interpreted in light of what was said above.
[151] Ames, *PTT*, 180 (trans. Gibbs).
[152] Compare Ames, *PTT*, 277–79 with *PTT*, 180. In *PTT*, 279 (trans. Gibbs) Ames holds that the perception of spiritual things requires the "actual presence of such things, or at least a spiritual representation of them". For this distinction in Scotus see Tachau, *Vision and Certitude*, 68–85.
[153] See, for example, Bonaventure of Bagnoregio, *The Major Legend of St Francis*, in *Francis of Assisi: Early Documents. Vol. 2: The Founder*, ed. Regis Armstrong and Wayne Hellmann (New York: New City Press, 2000), 596–97. For a helpful discussion of contuition see Leonard Bowman, "Bonaventure's 'Contuition' and Heidegger's 'Thinking': Some Parallels", *Franciscan Studies* 37 (1977): 18–31. Bowman makes clear that this intuition is connected to the perception of a reality in relation to its exemplary causes, but is not a form of "ontologism", and so preserves the transcendence of God.
[154] Ames, *PTT*, 180–81 (trans. Gibbs).

The delineation of art clearly corresponds to its logical and systematic expression according to Ramist principles, and the catholic, or universal, rules governing this are simply Ramus' laws of truth, wisdom and justice, reflecting their most true, just and wise source in God.[155] Likewise the two reciprocal processes of human intellect—analysis and genesis—embodied in invention and judgement, are understood by Ames as fundamental to the way in which humans come to apprehend the unity and distinction of the arts.[156] Ames is insistent that God knows all things in their intelligible structure through genesis and not through analysis.[157] Humans come to mirror this first by gathering the image "from the artificial thing through its analysis into first principles" and then by converting this into an "idea, which also portrays a similar structure, which is called genesis".[158] The whole system of propositional truth expressed in human art, and embedded in reality, is thus a created reflection of the simplicity of the divine essence.

According to both Ames and Richardson, the arts are divided according to their use or *eupraxia*. The general arts are those whose use founds that of all the others. These correspond to the liberal arts of logic, grammar, and rhetoric—the trivium of the scholastics' arts course. The primary art is logic, succinctly defined as "to dispose well the reasons of things well found".[159] The use of this founds all the others, and without logic all of the other arts could not exist. Following logic we have grammar and rhetoric, which are also essential to the other more specialized arts which come after them. These take up the truths of logic and communicate them from man to man—something we touched on above in our discussion of *logismos* and *eponymia*. The special arts—mathematics, physics, and theology—are so called because their use is more restricted and not universally communicated. Importantly, these also relate to the intrinsic structure of reality, which was held by these Ramists to consist of quantity from the material cause, nature from the formal cause, and end from the final cause. Thus the art relating to quantity is mathematics, to nature is physics, and to end is theology.[160]

These six arts together make up the basic pattern of the encyclopaedia or *pansophia*.[161] In Richardson's poetic image, the arts are like ordered links in a

---

[155] Ames, *Technometria*, 7, 34; Richardson, *Logicians School-Master*, 16.
[156] Ames, *Technometria*, 3–4.
[157] Ames, *Medulla*, 1.7.22.
[158] Ames, *PTT*, 181.
[159] Ames, *Technometria*, 4.
[160] Ames, *Technometria*, 5–6, 10–11, 18–19.
[161] Ames, *Technometria*, 52–62 offers an expanded encyclopaedia arranged around this sixfold pattern. The expanded edition of Richardson's *Logicians School-Master* was the nucleus of an unfinished encyclopaedia. A manuscript of Richardson's encyclopaedia is also to be found in Trinity College Dublin, MS 711. Ames' use of the term *pansophia* may suggest a connection with Comenius. Certainly, we will see in Chapter 9 that Comenius was also significantly indebted to Bonaventure for the structure of his pansophic works.

chain, arranged according to use, with their beginning and end in God's own knowledge of himself—a powerful reminder of Ramus' "golden chain" reaching down from heaven to earth.[162] If these are arranged in the wrong order, or a link of the chain is broken or left out, then the circle of knowledge will be incomplete.[163] As communications of divine knowledge, the arts are intended to lead to the perfection of man. Each art is designed by God and intended to perfect a particular aspect, or faculty, of human life. As Ames says,

> These six arts perfect the whole of man; [perfecting] the intellect by logic, the will by theology and by the rest—grammar, rhetoric, mathematics and physics—precisely directing his locomotive power to its own *eupraxia*.[164]

While theology is the most specialized of all the arts, Ames is insistent that it is preeminent in dignity. It concerns that "universal goodness, namely the glory of God, which is looked at in all things and to which all things look". All the other arts are thus directed towards theology as the supreme "art of living well", and so must be "reduced to the contemplation and worship of God with the greatest piety".[165] In this way, theology is truly the crown of the Ramist encyclopaedia.

Such a vision resonates profoundly with Perkins' own desire for a Christian philosophy. In his *Commentary on Hebrews 11* Perkins urged "students in human learning" to "have care to join faith and knowledge of religion" in order to attain to the "deepness and perfection" of philosophy.[166] Significantly he held that the template for such a "sound philosophy" was to be found in Scripture. Echoing Augustine in *De Doctrina Christiana* he thus claimed:[167]

> For if we yield that rhetoric is good and lawful and practiced in the Scripture, then it must needs follow that it is there practiced in the best manner. For shall the divinity there taught be the soundest? The history there reported the truest? The conclusions of philosophy, astronomy, geometry, arithmetic, cosmography, and physic there delivered, the surest? The music there practiced, the exactest? The logic there practiced, the sharpest? The laws there enacted, the justest? And shall not the rhetoric there practiced be the purest? ... Let them study God's

---

[162] Ramus, *Animadversiones*, 2r–3v.
[163] Ames, *Technometria*, 23; Richardson, *Logicians School-Master*, 17–18.
[164] Ames, *Technometria*, 22: "Hae sex artes totum hominem perficiunt; Logica Intellectum; Theologia voluntatem; reliquis, Grammatica, Rhetorica, Mathesi, Physica, Locomotivam eius in εὐπραξίαις suis ad amussim dirigentibus". See also Sprunger, *Learned Doctor*, 119.
[165] Ames, *Technometria*, 10–11, 23. Interestingly, Ames cites Marsilio Ficino's *Theologia Platonica* for this point, confirming his broader Neo-Platonic orientation (Marsilio Ficino, *Theologia Platonica de Immortalitate Animorum Duo de Viginti Libris* (Paris, 1559), "*Proemium*").
[166] William Perkins, *Commentary on Hebrews 11*, v. 3 (*Works*, 3.21).
[167] Perkins, *Commentary on Hebrews 11*, v. 3 (*Works*, 3.21–22).

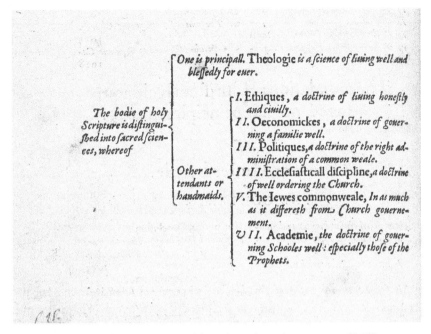

Figure 4.1 Ramist chart of the sacred disciplines from the opening of William Perkins, *A Golden Chaine* (London, 1600). Reproduced by kind permission of the Syndics of Cambridge University Library.

books, and there they shall find not only divinity but knowledge and learning of all sorts.[168]

Buttressing this Perkins offered his own evangelical version of the *prisca philosophia* developed by Ficino and the Florentine Platonists, tracing logic and other sciences back though Cicero and Plato to Solomon, Noah, Abraham, and even Adam.[169] In his *Golden Chaine* Perkins offered a condensed Ramist and encyclopaedic analysis of the Bible, prefacing the work with a chart showing the way in which the "body of Holy Scripture is distinguished into sacred sciences" including theology, ethics, oeconomics, politics, ecclesiastical discipline, the Jewish commonwealth, prophecy, and academics (Figure 4.1).[170] While his understanding of other sciences as "handmaids" resonates with the famous opening

---

[168] Perkins, *Commentary on Hebrews 11*, v. 12 (*Works*, 3.188).
[169] William Perkins, *A Short Treatise That Fully Explains Dickson's Wicked System of Artificial Memory* (*Works*, 6.508); cf. Ramus, *Scholae in Liberales Artes*, col. 312. See Bruyère, *Méthode et dialectique* and Walker, *The Ancient Theology*.
[170] Perkins, *Golden Chain* (*Works*, 6.9, 11).

| Bonaventure | | Ames |
|---|---|---|
| Light of Sensitive Cognition | Senses and Sensible Figures | |
| Light of Mechanical Art | Mechanical Arts | |
| Light of Rational Philosophy | Logic | Logic |
| | Grammar | Grammar |
| | Rhetoric | Rhetoric |
| Light of Natural Philosophy | Mathematics | Mathematics |
| | Physics | Physics |
| | Metaphysics | |
| Light of Moral Philosophy | Ethics | |
| | Oeconomics | |
| | Politics | |
| Light of Scripture | Theology | Theology |

**Figure 4.2** Table comparing Ames' sixfold encyclopaedism with Bonaventure's account of the sixfold light in *De Reductione Artium*. Ames, *Technometria*, 52–62 elaborates on the basic sixfold pattern to encompass the higher faculties and mechanical arts as well.

of Aquinas' *Summa*, his desire to derive philosophical sciences from Scripture fits much closer into an Augustinian and Franciscan paradigm of Christian philosophy, harmonizing well with his Ramist and Scotistic vision of theology as a practical science.[171]

What is implicit in Perkins becomes fully explicit in Ames, who follows Bonaventure in effecting his own reduction of all the arts to theology. For Ames the "comprehension of all these arts by which things emanate from First Being and finally return to that being is called encyclopaedia".[172] In this we are reminded of the Franciscan's famous dictum in his *Hexaemeron* that the "sum total of our metaphysics" is "emanation, exemplarity, and consumation",[173] and even more his insistence in the *De Reductione* that the Christian encyclopaedia should follow this triadic pattern. The *De Reductione* is very likely also the pattern for Ames' fourfold and sixfold divisions of art. For Bonaventure likewise holds that the divine light of art descends according to a fourfold progression, but that it is best expressed according to a sixfold encyclopaedic scheme in which theology (the knowledge of Scripture) is the culmination. While the two schemes are not identical—in part because Ames absorbs both moral philosophy and metaphysics into theology—the structural similarities are striking (Figure 4.2).[174] Indeed, the Richardsonian comparison of God and the encyclopaedia to

---

[171] It should be noted that Perkins never says this classification of "sacred sciences" is exhaustive and his *Commentary on Hebrews* would suggest the inclusion of other sciences. For the Ramist and Scotistic dimension of practical theology see Muller, *PRRD*, 1.324–54.

[172] Ames, *PTT*, 182 (trans. Gibbs).

[173] Cited from Ilia Delio, "Theology, Metaphysics and the Centrality of Christ", *Theological Studies* 68.2 (2007): 267.

[174] Bonaventure, *Reduction*, n. 1, 6–7 (*BOO*, V.319, 321–22).

mathematical point and circle also resonates with Bonaventure's Neo-Platonic understanding of the emanation of the sixfold "circle" of disciplines from God.[175]

Significantly, Ames' inaugural oration at Franeker also offers a powerful adumbration of Bonaventure's Christological and illuminationist framework of knowledge. Here, following a well-trodden Ramist path, he focusses on the Urim and Thummim as "oracles" of the true God.[176] These, he suggests, represent the "truth of righteousness and doctrine"—the principles of faith and observance which are the twin pillars of all of theology.[177] Displaying a Neo-Platonic, even Cabalistic, understanding, he describes them as "flames and illuminations" and "simple sincerities and perfections". Their twin light radiates out from Christ the "Sun of Righteousness", in whom perfect knowledge and activity are united, illuminating the elect. This "one light of truth" is also expressed in the two luminaries of Scripture and philosophy, which Ames compares to the Sun and Moon. The reflected light of philosophy provides us with light for our path, but it is only in Scripture that "the Sun by its own full splendour ... rules the course of our life to its very end, and leads to eternal happiness". Christians are therefore called "sons of this double light", and it would be hard to find a more appropriate expression of Bonaventure's own scriptural exemplarism.[178] Moreover, if we are justified in reading a Ramist reference in the Urim and Thummim, then it is apparent that logic too must share in this double light, a topic to which we will now turn at some length.

## 4.5. Archetype, Ectype, and the Logic of Scripture

For Ames it was quite natural to trace this Bonaventuran intuition concerning Scripture as the exemplaristic foundation of all knowledge in terms of the technical distinction between archetypal and ectypal theology. Forged in the crucible of heated scholastic debates in the thirteenth and fourteenth centuries, by early modern times this distinction had become used to express the relation between God's infinite, archetypal knowledge of himself and our finite, ectypal knowledge of him mediated through Scripture and Christ. Birthed in a Ramist and Scotistic context, as we will see in the next chapter, this could be used to express both the way in which Scripture and theology mirrored or exemplified God's

---

[175] Yates, *Modell*, "*Celeberrimae apud Cantabrigienses Academiae*"; cf. Bonaventure, *Reduction*, n. 7 (*BOO*, V.322). It also has something of a Cusan feel to it.
[176] See, for example, Beurhaus, *Disputationes Scholasticae*, "*Praefatio ad Lectorem*".
[177] See Ames, *Medulla*, 1.2.2.
[178] Ames, *PTT*, 346–52 (trans. Gibbs).

self-understanding and the infinite gulf between divine and human knowledge bridged only through God's willed self-communication.[179]

Particularly innovative in our Ramists, although with deep late medieval roots, was the way in which logic itself became incorporated within this overarching archetypal-ectypal framework and then expressed according to a scriptural mode.[180] Recently, Baird Tipson has argued powerfully for the grounding of human logic in divine logic in the Richardsonian tradition—something which much of this chapter bears out. For Tipson, however, the archetypal logic that the Ramists drew upon—their eternal "Rule"—was ultimately to eclipse Scripture in their theology and hermeneutics, leading the Ramists to privilege "the logic of theology over biblical narrative".[181] By contrast, our reading of the Ramist use of the archetype-ectype distinction will suggest much more of a coordination—even integration—of logic and Scripture.

For Ames the archetype is God's eternal wisdom as "creator and governor" of all things, the ectype is our limited apprehension of this, and what he calls the mediating type is creation itself. "In the beginning", Ames says, "this type of created things was perfectly referring all things to man as constituted in his state of integrity". Human processes of reasoning were unimpaired and all things were "easily clear" to him. While man did not understand everything in one intuition like God, but still required syllogistical judgement, this was easy for him and did not require unpleasant effort. Reason taught him to see God as revealed in the whole of creation.[182] Sadly, such a harmonious relationship was shattered by the Fall, which darkened human reason, leaving it seriously impaired, especially in its knowledge of goodness and divine things.[183] Instead of the principles of knowledge being easily accessible to us, "unwearied analysis" was now required to penetrate to the interior of being.[184] Yet God did not leave humanity in this miserable state. Instead, out of his great kindness and wisdom, he substituted the Scriptures for what was now deficient in the type of created things, revealing "most perfectly the principles of goodness, that is, of honesty, piety, justice and equity".[185]

---

[179] See Muller, *PRRD*, 1.225–38 and Willem J. van Asselt, "The Fundamental Meaning of Theology: Archetypal and Ectypal Theology in Seventeenth-Century Reformed Thought", *Westminster Theological Journal* 64.2 (2002): 319–35.

[180] Nathaniel Gray Sutanto, "Two Theological Accounts of Logic: Theistic Conceptual Realism and a Reformed Archetype-Ectype Model", *International Journal for the Philosophy of Religion* 79 (2016): 239–60 builds on early modern Reformed theology to construct a notion of archetypal and ectypal logic. This has some important resonances with our discussion, but the parallels are not exact. In particular, while Sutanto speaks of a "created logic", our reading suggests a "revealed logic". Sutanto also does not discuss either the late medieval precedent for this concept or its Ramist manifestation.

[181] Tipson, *Hartford Puritanism*, 212–17.

[182] Ames, *Technometria*, 11; cf. Richardson, *Logicians School-Master*, 36–37, 293–94.

[183] Ames, *Technometria*, 11.

[184] Ames, *Technometria*, 11–12.

[185] Ames, *Technometria*, 11.

For Ames, Scripture is thus a more perfect, unflawed type of God's self-revelation, bridging the chasm that opened up between Creator and creatures after the Fall. Significantly, Scripture provides us with true knowledge not only of God but also of the arts. Indeed, Ames holds that following the Fall the mediation of Word and Spirit has become "greatly and absolutely necessary" for discovering these principles.[186] The implication is that without Scripture we cannot gain a proper grasp of logic and all the other arts. Conversely, Ames is just as insistent that logic is necessary to come to a proper understanding even of Scripture's special principles. He therefore holds that it is not possible to come to an intimate and perfect understanding of the principles of goodness revealed in Scripture unless one has been "made dextrous by the analysis of the Holy Scriptures themselves, with the eyes of the mind opened simultaneously by the Holy Spirit". For this reason he claims that "the analysis of Holy Scripture is perfected by the precepts of logic rightly applied".[187]

Clearly evident in Ames is a mutuality between Scripture and logic. While each has its clearly defined domain, with neither subsumed under the other, they also overlap in important ways. Following Piscator, the English Ramists were careful to integrate Scripture into their logic as infallible, divine testimony.[188] Indeed, such a view of Scripture as divine speech or testimony fitted naturally into the vocal world of the Ramists, in which language became encoded in being itself. Expressing this nexus of Scripture, creation, and logic, Richardson held that "neither is there any divine testimony, but if we look after it, we shall see it in the thing".[189] In such terms, Ramism becomes both revealed logic and divine rhetoric.

*Pace* Tipson, the Cambridge Ramists were also careful to integrate logic into the very nature of Scripture itself. In a fascinating discourse on the light of nature and grace, Ames spoke of the "leading" of "effervescent light" as

> nothing else but that logic, together with the grammar and rhetoric, by which the mysteries of salvation in the Scriptures are transmitted to us, and which we regard as so clear and evident in all matters which are absolutely necessary, so that in all the majesty of things, nothing more illustrious can even be conceived, much less experienced.

Coupled with this objective clarity, or illumination, of Scripture was the disposing light of grace elevating the mind to receive it.[190] He therefore emphasized to his

---

[186] Ames, *Technometria*, 11–12.
[187] Ames, *Technometria*, 11–12.
[188] Richardson, *Logicians School-Master*, 237.
[189] Richardson, *Logicians School-Master*, 237.
[190] Ames, *PTT*, 280 (trans. Gibbs).

students the need to "study the Scriptures diligently . . . to study to understand them logically and clearly".[191]

The Ramists were convinced that the Spirit worked in a methodical manner in all things. Thus Richardson traces the physical order within nature, in which everything occupies its proper place, directly to the work of the Spirit of God, who governs all things according to "the rule of method continually".[192] Perkins too justified the "lawfulness of the art of logic" by appeal to the Holy Spirit.[193] In a similar manner another Cambridge Ramist, Richard Bernard, traced the methodical arrangement of Scripture to the inspiration of the Spirit, saying in his popular handbook for preachers,

> By Logicke we see the method of the Spirit, we behold the arguments, the coherence and the scope; by it we collect doctrines, confirme them, enlarge the proofes, gather thence consequently apt uses and urge them by reasons upon the hearers.

The role of logic is therefore to reveal the "method of the Spirit" contained in the Word. In this way for Bernard, just as for Ames, logic could be regarded as "an especiall handmaid by the assistance of Gods Spirit", necessary for understanding any text of Scripture.[194] In other English Ramists such as Dudley Fenner and Thomas Granger this is taken even further, with the whole panoply of Ramist arguments copiously illustrated from Scripture.[195] Indeed, following Piscator, Perkins affirmed not only that the Bible had an intricate logical structure but that the entire "sum of the Scripture" could be expressed in a single Ramist syllogism.[196]

Evident in many Ramist texts is therefore an intimate connection between logic and the Word and Spirit, both on the global level of the archetype-ectype schema and on the individual level of the illumination of the believer's heart. Ramism thus presupposed an intimate relation between the "two books" of nature and Scripture, as complementary modes of divine revelation.[197] Only through real encounter with the world around us and with the text of Scripture

---

[191] Ames, *PTT*, 363 (trans. Gibbs).
[192] Richardson, *Logicians School-Master*, 336–37. The examples he gives are both taken from natural philosophy: the hierarchical arrangement of the elements and the magnetic properties of the lode-stone.
[193] William Perkins, *Exposition upon the First Three Chapters of Revelation* (*Works*, 4.410).
[194] Richard Bernard, *The Faithfull Shepheard* (London, 1607), 25. Bernard also jointly wrote another book called *Davids Musick* (London, 1616), in which he gives a logical exposition of the Psalms complete with Ramist diagrams.
[195] See Thomas Granger, *Syntagma Logicum or the Divine Logike* (London, 1620) and Fenner, *The Artes of Logike and Rethorike*, I c. 2.
[196] Perkins, *Art of Prophesying*, c. 3 (*Works*, 10.292); cf. Piscator, *Commentarii*, 3.
[197] Ames, *Technometria*, 19.

are we able to derive any logical insights; moreover, the deeper this encounter, the closer our logic will come to conform to reality. Behind this claim, of course, lies the Ramist understanding that all human arts, including logic, are simply an imitation of the order that God has imposed on nature.[198] In fact, Richardson notably buttresses his metaphysical Realism with a direct appeal to Scripture and especially God's creation of all things "after their own kind".[199] In this we are reminded not only of Bonaventure, who described Scripture in exemplaristic terms as a "noble mirror . . . designed to reflect the whole complex of created reality" and encompassing the "breadth and length and height and depth of the entire universe", but also of Wyclif, whose propositional Realism extended into a detailed elaboration of a Realist "logic of Scripture" grounded on the divine ideas.[200]

## 4.6. Counter-Logic and Metaphysics

In espousing this Augustinian and Realist paradigm of a logic of Scripture, it was quite natural for Ames to oppose the pretensions of a philosophical system which had been developed in isolation from revelation. We may see this especially from Ames' *Disputatio Theologica adversus Metaphysicam*, which represents a full-frontal attack on the scholastic disciplines of metaphysics and natural theology, particularly as represented by Aristotle, "the pope of metaphysics", and Suárez, "the patriarch of the neoterics".[201] Ames' objections to metaphysics can be summed up in three main points. Firstly, he argues that metaphysics does not respect the integrity of reality. It is a "hallucination of the mind" in which one simple being is falsely seen as many. In particular, he held that metaphysicians found a real specific difference of science on a mere "respect of reason", something he says Scotus rightly forbade.[202] Metaphysicians therefore carve up being without respect to its intrinsic formal structure, meaning that philosophy loses its secure grounding in reality.

Secondly, and even more seriously, Ames argues that metaphysics attempts to usurp theology's own task and set up a system of natural theology independently of Scripture. Particularly odious to Ames is Suárez's claim that the contemplation of God, in which man's natural beatitude consists, is both the proper act

---

[198] Richardson, *Logicians School-Master*, 28–30.
[199] Richardson, *Logicians School-Master*, 21–22, 49, 55–57, 81, 121–25, 152, 205, 212–15.
[200] See Bonaventure, *Breviloquium*, "Prologue" 3-4 (pp. 3-4; BOO, V.201-2) and John Wyclif, *Trialogus*, ed. and trans. Stephen E. Lahey (Cambridge: Cambridge University Press, 2012), III.31 (pp. 190-94). For Wyclif's logic of Scripture and its Realist and exemplaristic character, see especially Levy, *John Wyclif*, 81–122.
[201] William Ames, *Disputatio Theologica adversus Metaphysicam*, in *Philosophemata*, 46, 51.
[202] Ames, *Disputatio Theologica*, 45–46, 48–49.

and final end of metaphysics.[203] Indeed, elsewhere, in his theological disputation against ethics, Ames outright denies the second scholastic distinction between natural and supernatural beatitude.[204] Without grace the rational contemplation of God avails nothing, for the devil himself is the "greatest metaphysician".[205] This leads into Ames' final critique of metaphysics—that it is of no practical use. Citing Scotus' position, which he calls "worthy of every approbation", he argues that there can be no speculative science of God. Indeed, Ames rejects entirely the Thomistic distinction between speculative and practical knowledge, arguing in typical Ramist fashion that all knowledge must be oriented towards praxis. To Ames' mind, the metaphysical habit of asking speculative questions about God has not led to true piety but rather to pride and presumption.[206]

For Ames, then, metaphysics is simply an "imaginary discipline". Like Ramus, he held that it is not metaphysics that is the science of "being *qua* being" but rather logic. Having stated this bold claim, Ames proceeds to show how the so-called transcendental "affections of being"—unity, truth, and goodness—which were a major plank of scholastic metaphysics, fall under the domain of Ramist logic, and are comprehended in the invention and judgement of arguments.[207] Ames also attacks the Aristotelian account of the predicaments. Noting the traditional debate about whether the predicaments fall under logic or metaphysics, he argues that they must instead be apportioned into logic, physics, and mathematics, once again pulling the rug out from under the metaphysical discussion of being.[208]

While Ames is unusual in the vehemence of his attacks against scholastic metaphysics, his view is nevertheless indicative of two major reasons why Ramism proved attractive to many Reformed theologians: its metaphysical Realism and its orientation towards practical use. Whereas metaphysics only concerned itself with the shadows of things, logic considered the things themselves, preserving the formal integrity of their being. In doing so it pointed the way towards the use of all things in cultivating the right worship of God.[209] Indeed, in Ames' pure Ramist reform of philosophy, exemplaristic metaphysics became fused with the logic of Scripture in a manner paralleling rather remarkably the Augustinian and Realist syntheses of the Late Middle Ages.

---

[203] Ames, *Disputatio Theologica*, 47–48.
[204] Ames, *PTT*, 174.
[205] Ames, *Disputatio Theologica*, 47.
[206] Ames, *Disputatio Theologica*, 50–51; cf. Muller, *PRRD*, 1.340–54. For parallels with Scotus see Scotus, *Will and Morality*, 127–35.
[207] Ames, *Disputatio Theologica*, 52–56.
[208] Ames, *Disputatio Theologica*, 57.
[209] Ames, *Disputatio Theologica*, 50; *Technometria*, 10–11, 23.

## 4.7. Towards the Logic of Faith

In seeking to relate logic to God, it was of course necessary to clarify the question of how the being of creatures related to the being of God. As Muller has convincingly argued, many early modern Reformed theologians engaged with a Thomistic, analogical understanding of being.[210] Ames too was clearly influenced by the scholastic *analogia entis*, although his departure from Thomas' metaphysics of participation—something he notably shared with many of his Reformed contemporaries—should caution us about assimilating his account too closely to Aquinas.[211] While, as we will see, a number of Ramists edged closer to a univocal notion of being, we do not find any evidence in Ames for this Scotistic turn. Indeed, he is perhaps closer to those Reformed theologians who tended to associate the notion of univocity with their opponents, arguing that it threatened to place God and creatures on the same ontological plane.[212] One can very well see, for example, that this might have been a complaint of Ames against Suárez, particularly in his attempt to embrace both God and creatures under a common metaphysics of being. Overall, Ames' reading of analogy may therefore come closest to Bonaventure, who combined analogical exemplarism and a nascent understanding of the formal distinction with a marked departure from metaphysical univocity.[213]

In Richardson we find an even clearer statement of this apophatic Ramism, which balances his ontological account of truth with an assertion of the absolute transcendence of God. We remarked above that while Ames affirms a real multiplicity of ideas in the mind of God, Richardson speaks only of a singular "idea" in God.[214] In this, he seems to locate created multiplicity in the emanation, or refraction—he can use both terms—of the unique and simple divine idea into the created realm of time and space—a paradoxical Nominalistic trend which resurfaces in a number of his followers despite his own avowed Realism.[215]

---

[210] Muller, "Not Scotist", 127–50.
[211] Ames, *Medulla*, 1.4.30 affirms that the divine attributes are analogical in creatures. However, Ames, *Theses Logicae*, 27 complicates this Thomist picture.
[212] Gisbertus Voetius, *Selectarum Disputationum Theologicarum* (Utrecht, 1648), I.1 associates univocity with Socinianism. However, Beck, "Voetius", 235–40 argues persuasively that Voetius' rejection of a real, metaphysical univocity is consistent with his espousal of a Scotist, logical univocity.
[213] Schumacher, *Divine Illumination*, 121–53 and Cullen, *Bonaventure*, 66–67. Schumacher argues that Bonaventure adopts a form of univocity. However, it is clear from Cullen that this must be understood as a logical and not metaphysical univocity as Bonaventure espouses a wider theory of analogy.
[214] This is also evident from Yates, *Modell*, 103–6 which speaks of the "ideaa", "platforme", or "plot" of all things. John Yates, *Gods Arraignement of Hypocrites* (Cambridge, 1615), does mention God's "ideaas" but describes these as "Gods plots, which he hath formed and fashioned in himself", suggesting that these ideas are not God's own being or "idaea".
[215] Yates, *Modell*, 38 may well be attacking Scotus in saying "it would present him for a furious and raving Bedlam, that should once formalize God to his own fancies". Yates, *Gods Arraignement*, 75–76 does, however, call Scotus a "great doctour".

Significantly, Richardson's account of being also shows a similar radical disjunction between the created and uncreated spheres. We may see this from the influential preface to his *Logicians School-Master*, in which he poses an important distinction between the necessary, self-existent being of God and the derived, utterly dependent being of creatures.[216] For Richardson, this entails that God must be beyond our logic. Although God is greatly intelligible, we can have no science of him, since human science relies on causal knowledge. Likewise, we can have no art concerning God, for every art requires a final cause. Moreover, since every art is an eternal rule corresponding to the divine idea, it follows that in order to have an art concerning God we must postulate a prior being in whom inheres an idea according to which God is made and governed—a contradiction in terms. It follows that God is beyond our reason and our logic and even beyond our speech as exceeding our grammar and rhetoric. Indeed, echoing Pseudo-Dionysius, Richardson can argue that God is being beyond being itself.[217]

In this, while drawing on Aquinas, Richardson seems to also press beyond him, towards a more fundamental disjunction between divine and human logic.[218] For although the scholastic tradition contained many affirmations that God is beyond our reason, this did not prevent medieval theologians from developing a science of God grounded on the canons of logic.[219] Even Scotus, who resolutely affirmed that there could be no proportion between the finite and infinite, took great pains to defend the treatment of the Triune mystery of God according to the syllogistic rules of Aristotelian logic.[220] Rather, the strict assertion of a gulf between human and divine logic runs counter to high scholasticism and fits more within the context of the Late Middle Ages, when confidence in Aristotle's logic had begun to ebb.[221] Inverting Piscator's attack on Buscher, it also conforms closely to that Lutheran emphasis on the divine transcendence of logic which flourished among Melanchthon and the Philippo-Ramists.

In light of this, it would be helpful to know precisely what Richardson understood by his concept of God being beyond our logic, but unfortunately the *Logicians School-Master* offers only scattered clues. Richardson clearly believed that as hyper-logical God is beyond every conceivable form of logical expression. This applies to the Ramists as much as scholastics, since cause, effect, subject, adjunct, and all other arguments are only "liable to all our logick".[222] Indeed, for Richardson, the logic "that brings us to the first cause, doth but shew him as

---

[216] Richardson, *Logicians School-Master*, 1–4.
[217] Richardson, *Logicians School-Master*, 4–7; Yates, *Modell*, 38; cf. Pseudo-Dionysius, *Divine Names*, 5.1, in *The Complete Works*, ed. Paul Rorem and trans. Colm Luibheid (London: SPCK, 1987).
[218] Aquinas, *ST*, 1a 13.3.
[219] Aquinas, *ST*, 1a 1.2; 13.3.
[220] Gelber, "Logic and the Trinity", 60–102.
[221] See Gelber, "Logic and the Trinity", 163ff.
[222] Richardson, *Logicians School-Master*, 7, 205.

he argueth, not as he is in his being".[223] In Nominalist fashion, this seems to assume two different theological domains: one referring to God in himself and the other to God as he argues, the former hyper-logical and the latter in some way susceptible to our logic.[224] Drawing directly on Ramus' exegesis of Exodus 33, Ames too affirms that what God is, none can perfectly define, but that hath the logicke of God himselfe". The best we can do is an "imperfect description which commeth nearest to unfold Gods nature", which, as the *Medulla* makes clear, is best captured in the Ramist pattern of arguments and dichotomous division.[225]

While Ames affirmed a formal distinction (or at least formal non-identity) between the divine attributes and divine ideas, this did not serve to bring God under the purview of human logic, or render him any more comprehensible. Indeed, he would have likely sympathized with Ockham who held that the formal distinction was as much a mystery as God himself.[226] In this context, it is particularly striking that Richardson should affirm the breakdown of the syllogistic rule that "things which agree in a third agree among themselves" in certain contexts.[227] Frustratingly, we cannot be sure of the situation, or situations, in which Richardson believed this logical rule to fail, but both late medieval and early modern precedent suggests that one of the prime candidates would surely be with reference to the Trinity.[228] Many also believed that the hypostatic union of the divine and human natures in Christ transcended ordinary logic.[229] This is a matter which Ames considers in his *Medulla*, endeavouring to express it according to the Ramist arguments of subject, adjunct, and relate, and noting that "wee endeavour to describe this union, by many logicall wayes, because it cannot be sufficiently explained by one".[230] Yet this remains shrouded in mystery, always surpassing our attempts to logically express it according to human terms and notions.

Notably, in Richardson's and Ames' later followers adherence to the late medieval logic of faith becomes fully explicit. Thus George Lawson is plain in affirming that God cannot be defined according to the rules of Logick".[231] For Lawson, this is seen especially in relation to the supreme mystery of the Trinity, and he

---

[223] Richardson, *Logicians School-Master*, 47, 83. Yates, *Modell*, 24–25 argues for the need to describe God according to his "owne logicke".
[224] I am grateful to Dolf te Velde for discussion of this point.
[225] Ames, *Marrow*, 13 (*Medulla*, 1.4.32); cf. Ramus, *Commentariorum*, 15. See further *Medulla*, 1.4.1–17.
[226] See Allan Wolter, "The Formal Distinction", in *John Duns Scotus, 1265-1965* (Washington, DC: Catholic University of America Press, 1965), 45.
[227] Richardson, *Logicians School-Master*, 293.
[228] Shank, "*Unless You Believe*", 57–86.
[229] See Robert Holcot, *In Quatuor Libros Sententiarium Quaestiones* (Frankfurt: Minerva, 1967), 1 q. 5 ad. 5 and Baxter, *Methodus*, I.93. For more on the logic of faith see Shank, "*Unless You Believe*", and Gelber, "Logic and the Trinity", 265–72.
[230] Ames, *Marrow*, 82 (*Medulla*, 1.18.18).
[231] George Lawson, *Theo-Politica* (London, 1659), 20.

therefore holds that "the predications and expressions used in the Scripture concerning God the Father, Son, and Holy Ghost, transcend the Rules of Humane Logick, Grammar, Rhetorick".[232] Instead, Lawson holds that we must draw a new logic from Scripture:

> The word of God therefore is the rule of our understanding, and directing it in the knowledge of his essence, is our supernaturall logick, and the attributes are our divine topicks. For the logick which we now have composed by man, serves only for a rule in the understanding of things created: we must have a far higher and more excellent logick, to understand the being of our God.[233]

In espousing such a view Lawson was clearly indebted to Pierre d'Ailly, the "great Cardinal of Cambray", who was one of his favourite medieval theologians.[234] With the Dominican Robert Holcot, d'Ailly was one of the most important late medieval exponents of the logic of faith, serving as the touchstone for the entire tradition in Luther's 1517 *Disputation against Scholastic Theology*.[235] It is therefore of enormous significance to find Richard Baxter, Lawson's friend and fellow Ramist, drawing explicitly on Holcot's account of the *logica fidei* in his own assertion of the need for a supernatural, scriptural logic transcending the logic of Aristotle and the scholastics.[236] Ramism thus served as a "logic of faith", an ectypal reflection of the archetypal logic found in God. Elegantly summed up by Richardson, its ultimate purpose was to "see Gods Logick in the things".[237]

## 4.8. Living to God

Ultimately, for these Cambridge Ramists, logic must be understood as a mode of the self-revelation of God. The Ramist aspiration was to learn to read the wisdom of God in things.[238] Through the encyclopaedia they hoped to reconstruct the pattern of the arts as given by God. There was therefore in pure Ramism, as we have seen, a strong drive towards a pristine, original logic—a logic of Scripture— and not the flawed logic of Aristotle, with its detachment from ontological and spiritual reality. As Granger put this, "The main end, and height of logicke is

---

[232] Lawson, *Theo-Politica*, 32.
[233] Lawson, *Theo-Politica*, 19–20.
[234] Lawson, *Theo-Politica*, 18.
[235] For d'Ailly's logic of faith see Steven E. Ozment, "Mysticism, Nominalism and Dissent", in *Pursuit of Holiness*, ed. Trinkaus and Oberman, 92. For Luther's critique of it see *Disputation against Scholastic Theology*, 12.
[236] Richard Baxter, *Methodus Theologiae Christianae* (London, 1681), I.93.
[237] Richardson, *Logicians School-Master*, 37.
[238] Richardson, *Logicians School-Master*, 37, 48.

science, that is, the simple apprehension of truths as they are in God, and were from God in Adam".[239] In a very real sense logic, as aided by the "supernatural canons" of Word and Spirit, was therefore intended to reverse the noetic effects of the Fall and to teach man to again refer all things in creation to the worship of God.[240]

Significantly, one of the chief ways in which this scriptural logic became expressed was through covenant, and it is notable that British Ramists were early pioneers of Reformed federal theology. As Torrance Kirby and Robert Wainwright have demonstrated, the "Zurich connection" stretches right back to Henrician and Edwardian evangelicalism, placing covenant theology at the heart of the emerging English Reformation.[241] This was even more true in Scotland where the influence of Zwingli, Bullinger, and Calvin was transmitted early through George Wishart, John Knox, and Andrew Melville, and fused with a political tradition of covenanting reaching back to Scotus and the fourteenth-century Scottish Franciscans.[242]

The late sixteenth- and early seventeenth-century saw a new wave of Continental influence in the works of Olevian, Piscator, and the Herborn School which were eagerly read across Britain. In the Scottish Ramist Robert Rollock and the English Ramists Fenner, Perkins, and Ames covenant theology achieved a new level of depth and systematic expression. This was only aided by the institutionalization and confessionalization of Ramism in the Puritan colleges of Cambridge, the newly founded Trinity College Dublin, and the Scottish universities, leading to generations of Reformed students being educated in the new Ramist and federal methods.[243] Through a flood of Ramist sermons, biblical commentaries, devotional treatises, catechisms, and casuistic works, this movement deeply touched the lives of many ordinary Christians.[244]

Significantly, as the printing of Rollock's works in Herborn and Geneva and the widespread diffusion of Perkins' works across Continental Europe indicate,

---

[239] Granger, *Syntagma Logicum*, 2.
[240] Granger, *Syntagma Logicum*, 343–45.
[241] See W. J. Torrance Kirby, *The Zurich Connection and Tudor Political Theology* (Leiden: Brill, 2007) and Robert J. D. Wainwright, *Early Reformation Covenant Theology: English Reception of Swiss Reformed Thought, 1520-1555* (Phillipsburg, NJ: P&R Publishing, 2020).
[242] See David G. Mullan, "Federal Theology from the Reformation to c. 1677", in *The History of Scottish Theology, Volume I: Celtic Origins to Reformed Orthodoxy*, ed. David Fergusson and Mark W. Elliott (Oxford: Oxford University Press, 2019), 225–36; James H. Burns, *The True Law of Kingship: Concepts of Monarchy in Early-Modern Scotland* (Oxford: Clarendon Press, 1996); and Alexander Broadie, "The Declaration of Arbroath in the Shadow of Scotus", in *Scotland and Arbroath 1320-2020: 700 Years of Fighting for Freedom, Sovereignty and Independence*, ed. Klaus Peter Müller (Frankfurt am Main: Peter Lang, 2020), 75–89.
[243] See Boran, "Ramism in Trinity College, Dublin", 177–99 and Reid, *Humanism and Calvinism*, 77ff.
[244] For popular Ramist piety and devotion see extensively Miller, *New England Mind* and McKim, *Ramism*.

this federal Ramism also had a major impact on the whole Reformed world.[245] The influence of Perkins and Ames in Puritan England and New England cannot be exaggerated, but less known is the impact that both had on Dutch Reformed theology and piety. Together they were a principal inspiration for the *Nadere Reformatie*, the Dutch movement of further reformation, and exercised a major influence on predestinarian and covenantal theology in the lead-up to and aftermath of the Synod of Dordt, with Ames' work becoming regarded as a providential "gift from England".[246] Across Germany and the Netherlands, British practical divinity became regarded as the gold standard of Reformed piety to be aspired to and emulated. Indeed, this new methodological and covenantal theology exercised an incalculable impact on the wider transformation of Reformed Church and society.

Key to its success was its expression of what we might call a new "covenantal exemplarism". For the British Ramists, developing an important emphasis of the Herborn School, covenant represented a temporal unfolding of the eternal divine decrees. It was thus susceptible to a logical as much as a biblical expression, especially within the paradigm of the Ramist logic of faith. Key to this was the Trinitarian correlation of the inward being of God with his outward working, harmonizing all of history in light of the divine revelation and infusing the present with eternal purpose. Through covenant the sweeping narrative of salvation revealed its unity in the mind of God and on the pages of Scripture, fulfilling the Reformation dream of a biblical theology and tapping into a much older Franciscan conceptuality. With its scriptural and exemplaristic orientation, Ramism came to be seen by many as the perfect vehicle for its realization.

We may see this from Perkins' *A Golden Chaine*, which carries a Ramist allusion in its very title. Indeed, like Ramus, Perkins also believed method to be a golden chain, holding that "by grasping it an infinite series of items can be so bound together that one item easily follows upon another".[247] Yet in seeking to offer a logical analysis of the biblical "order of causes of salvation and damnation" according to an intricate pattern of branching dichotomies, Perkins reconfigured this popular Neo-Platonic and Ramist motif in a markedly covenantal and

---

[245] For Perkins see Hans Schneider (ed.), *Bibliographie zur Geschichte des Pietismus. Band 2: A Catalog of British Devotional and Religious Books in German Translation from the Reformation to 1750* (Berlin: De Gruyter, 1996), 322–35. For the Continental printing of Robert Rollock see the Universal Short Title Catalogue (https://www.ustc.ac.uk/; accessed 18/12/2021).

[246] For the English and American influence see Miller, *The New England Mind* and Sprunger, *Learned Doctor*. For the Dutch influence see Arie de Reuver, *Sweet Communion: Trajectories of Spirituality from the Middle Ages through the Further Reformation*, trans. James A. De Jong (Grand Rapids, MI: Baker Academic, 2007) and Yagi, *Gift*.

[247] William Perkins, *A Handbook on Memory*, c. 4 (*Works*, 6.533).

voluntaristic fashion,[248] In this way, he proved instrumental in the early modern reforging of the great chain of being.

Perkins' own desire, drawing on Zanchi, was to trace the "patterns" of predestination in the human soul back to their origin in the mind of God.[249] Not only the Bible but also the elect soul could be seen as a mirror of the divine nature, so that by "beholding of these forms and impressions in ourselves, we shall easily be brought to the knowledge of those patterns (as it were), which are in the Lord Himself".[250] Perkins' theology thus hinged on a vital correlation between the inner being of God and his outward works, especially as they became impressed on the human soul. In articulating this, he notably drew on an important current of Franciscan and Scotist thought, continuing and deepening the important logical turn of the Herborn School and reinforcing the exemplaristic character of his method.

For Perkins, anticipating the explicit formulation of the covenant of redemption in the seventeenth century, the roots of the covenant lie in the delight taken by the persons of the Trinity in each other and the divine decrees.[251] The eternal self-motion of the Trinity becomes manifest in the three attributes of Power, Wisdom and Will, which, following a distinctive Franciscan tendency, he tends to identify with the three persons of Father, Son, and Holy Spirit.[252] In this light, his implicit logical ordering of the divine decrees according to the unfolding of these three attributes has a definite Trinitarian stamp.[253] As has therefore rightly been said, "it is impossible to understand predestination without realizing that God's decrees flow from the inner life of the triune God".[254]

Elsewhere Perkins makes fully explicit his debt to Scotism by expressing his approval of Francis of Meyronnes' elaboration of predestination according to different logical "signs" or instants of nature.[255] Likewise, both he and Rollock follow a definite Franciscan and Scotist trajectory in their "Christological

---

[248] For Perkins' voluntarist shift see Richard A. Muller, *Grace and Freedom: William Perkins and the Early Modern Reformed Understanding of Free Choice and Divine Grace* (New York: Oxford University Press, 2020), 8–9, 19, 25–30. This is not to discount an important Thomist influence as Muller argues.

[249] William Perkins, *The Whole Treatise of the Cases of Conscience*, "A Brief Discourse Taken Out of the Writings of Hier. Zanchius" (*Works*, 8.620).

[250] William Perkins, *Commentary on Galatians 1–5* (*Works*, 2.18) and *Whole Treatise*, "Brief Discourse" (*Works*, 8.620–21).

[251] William Perkins, *An Exposition of the Creed* (*Works*, 5.50). For detailed discussion of the Trinitarian covenant of redemption see Fesko, *Covenant of Redemption*.

[252] Perkins, *Exposition of the Creed* (*Works*, 5.24–27, 52). See Aquinas, *ST*, 1a q. 18. For Franciscan dynamism see Sylwanowicz, *Contingent Causality*, 103–20.

[253] Perkins, *Golden Chain*, c. 6 (*Works* 6.23–24).

[254] Joel R. Beeke and Greg A. Salazar, "Preface to Volume 6 of William Perkins's *Works*", in Perkins, *Works*, 6.xix.

[255] William Perkins, *A Christian and Plain Treatise of the Manner and Order of Predestination* (*Works*, 6.320). Muller, *Grace and Freedom*, 57, 147 also notes his connection to the instants of nature framework but not the specific Scotist character of this.

supralapsarianism".[256] We may see this especially in Rollock who offered a markedly Christocentric account of the divine decree, following Scotus in prioritizing the decree of Incarnation over that of Creation and the Fall:

> The first decree of Gods free grace, was concerning the incarnation of his Sonne, and the glorifying of him at the appointed time, unto the praise of his grace. . . . The second decree proceeding from grace, was concerning the first creation of man after his owne image: then after the Fall, concerning his restoring by his Sonne Jesus, I trust, unto the image of his Sonne: that is to say, by calling, justifying, and glorying of man to the glory of Christ, and to the praise of his own grace in his appointed time.[257]

Conforming to a Scotist ordering of intention and execution, Perkins himself is clear in arguing that creation and fall must both be seen as means to achieve God's end of glorying himself in Christ.[258]

For Perkins covenant must be understood as the pivot between the "eternal foundation of election" in Christ and the "outward means of the same". Covenant itself he defines as God's "contract with man concerning the obtaining of life eternal upon a certain condition". It is expressed in terms of both "God's promise to man" by which he "binds Himself to man to be his God"—a clear application of the late medieval dialectic of divine absolute and ordained power—and "man's promise to God" to devote himself to God and perform the conditions of the covenant.[259] Following Rollock, he dichotomized covenant into a pre-Fall covenant of works and a post-Fall covenant of grace, thus placing all of salvation history within an overarching federal framework. Following the Scotist order of intention and execution, the covenant of works must be seen as the means towards the fulfilment of the covenant of grace and the glorifying of Christ and the Trinity.[260] At the heart of covenant theology was the Cross, and Perkins' belief was that all three divine persons are "appeased" through Christ's sacrifice, demonstrating again the Trinitarian and Christocentric dynamic of covenant.[261]

---

[256] See Brannon Ellis, "The Eternal Decree in the Incarnate Son: Robert Rollock on the Relationship between Christ and Election", in *Reformed Orthodoxy in Scotland*, ed. Denlinger, 45–65 and Beeke and Salazar, "Preface to Volume 6", ixviii–xix. Ellis does not pick up the Scotist resonance of this but Denlinger, *Omnes in Adam*, 74–76, 223–25 highlights Rollock's Scotist background. For the Franciscan and Scotist doctrine of the absolute primacy of Christ see Dominic Unger, "Franciscan Christology: Absolute and Universal Primacy of Christ", *Franciscan Studies* 2.4 (1942): 428–75. I am very grateful to Richard Muller for this reference.
[257] Robert Rollock, *A Treatise of Gods Effectual Calling* (London, 1603), c. 38 (p. 231).
[258] Perkins, *Golden Chain*, c. 7 (*Works*, 6.26–27). For the Scotist dimensions of this reasoning see Burton, *Hallowing of Logic*, 285–95.
[259] Perkins, *Golden Chain*, c. 19 (*Works*, 6.65).
[260] Perkins, *Golden Chain*, c. 19, 31 (*Works*, 6.65–66, 153).
[261] Perkins, *Golden Chain*, c. 18 (*Works*, 6.61).

Perkins' systematizing of theology came to full fruition in Ames' *Medulla*, which offers a comprehensive Ramist and federal treatment of theology. As Perry Miller argued, Ames must be regarded as the "chief architect" of seventeenth-century federal theology, and Jan van Vliet has recently demonstrated his immense influence on the development of Reformed method and system.[262] While the Ramist structure of Perkins' *Golden Chaine* was only implicit, in Ames' *Medulla* it became fully explicit, as evidenced by the meticulous Ramist chart prefaced to the work and encompassing every head of theological doctrine.[263]

Like Perkins, Ames places the Trinity at the heart of covenant theology.[264] Through God's working "all in all" his Triune impress becomes manifest in all his actions.[265] This is encompassed especially in the natural ordering of his power, understanding, and will, which establishes the covenantal dialectic of absolute and ordained power which runs through his theology.[266] As Takayuki Yagi has convincingly demonstrated, this logical ordering within the being of God and its correlative unfolding into creation is buttressed by explicit appeal to Scotus' instants of nature.[267] Teaching explicitly a pre-temporal covenant of redemption between the Father and the Son—something only ever implicit in Perkins[268]—this unfolds through the agency of the Holy Spirit into the two covenants of works and grace, binding together all of human history from Eden to the eschatological consummation of all things.[269]

Patterned after revelation, the theology of Perkins, Ames, and the Richardsonian Ramists constantly witnessed to the simultaneity of transcendence and immanence. The Neo-Platonic pattern of emanation, exemplarity, and consumption we detected in Ames' encyclopaedism was significantly replicated in his theology, where it dovetailed neatly with his federal theology. Reflecting and exemplifying its divine source, theology itself was to be considered as living, active, and transformative. For Perkins it was the "science of living blessedly for ever", and for Ames it was the "doctrine of living to God... proceeding in a speciall manner from God, treating of God, and divine matters, and tending and leading man to God". It was not only a "speaking of God" but a "living to God" and a "working to God".[270] Ultimately, therefore,

---

[262] Van Vliet, *Reformed System*, 29.
[263] See the chart prefacing Ames, *Marrow*.
[264] Van Vliet, *Reformed System*, 30–31.
[265] Ames, *Medulla*, 1.6.1–31.
[266] Ames, *Medulla*, 1.6.4–8, 18–20.
[267] Yagi, *Gift*, 63–72.
[268] Van Vliet, *Reformed System*, 31 suggests this is not found in Perkins but this may be to miss his incipient Trinitarian covenantal structure clearly taken up by Ames in the *Medulla*.
[269] For a detailed account of Ames' covenant theology and its link to the Trinity see Van Vliet, *Reformed System*, 27–58.
[270] Perkins, *Golden Chain*, c. 1 (*Works*, 6.11) and Ames, *Marrow*, 1, 3–4 (*Medulla*, 1.1.1, 13).

these Puritan Ramists saw theology, and indeed the whole of Christian life, as an invitation to participation in the Trinity. Ramist theology was thus inescapably experiential, and this is indeed one of its most striking and distinctive features—theology is not only to be contemplated but rather it is to be continually lived and enacted.

# 5
# Catholic Symphony
## Scaliger, Polanus, and the Reconfiguring of Ramism

In an important encomium to logic written towards the end of the sixteenth century, Amandus Polanus von Polansdorf, the leading Reformed theologian of the University of Basel, drew on an impressive chorus of ancient philosophers, patristic and medieval theologians, and Protestant theologians to evidence logic's divine character and contemporary utility.[1] One of the most prominent of these voices was Melanchthon, and Polanus shared fully his view that dialectic should be done to the glory of God and the benefit of the Church. For him, it was not merely an instrumental tool but a fundamental aspect of the reform programme that Melanchthon had initiated in Germany and which he and others were now seeking to continue in Basel and other Reformed schools and universities.[2] Indeed, taking up the claims of the Wittenberg Reformer, he referred to logic as nothing less than the "bond of concord" itself, a key to reuniting a Church and society profoundly fractured by the Reformation.[3]

In Polanus' day such unity was sadly lacking. A Philippo-Ramist himself who sought to combine the best of Melanchthon's and Ramus' methodologies, he yet recognized a deep and growing split between two different "families of philosophers"—one following Aristotle, the "Prince of Gentile Philosophers", and the other following Ramus, the "Christian philosopher and hieromartyr".[4] Indeed, at the time Polanus was writing, Ramism was beginning to face increasing attack from both a resurgent Protestant scholasticism and an elitist humanism, which together conspired to shut Ramist methodology out of many of the leading universities of Europe.

For many scholastics, Ramus' contempt for Aristotle, his oversimplification of logic, and his hostility to metaphysics all served to discredit him.[5] As Hotson has shown, the reaction of the humanists was, if anything, even stronger. From

---

[1] Polanus, *Syntagma Logicum*.
[2] For the reform of the Basel schools and continuity with Melanchthon see Amy Nelson Burnett, *Teaching the Reformation: Ministers and Their Message in Basel, 1529–1629* (Oxford: Oxford University Press, 2006), 111–26.
[3] Polanus, *Syntagma Logicum*, "*Epistola Dedicatoria*".
[4] Polanus, *Syntagma Logicum*, "*Epistola Dedicatoria*".
[5] Pozzo, "Ramus' Metaphysics", 92–106.

across Europe leading humanists closed ranks against Ramus, proclaiming Ramism and Ramist compendia to be detrimental to the achievement of true erudition, especially the advanced philological and historical scholarship characteristic of seventeenth-century "high humanism".[6] The elitist attitude characteristic of many humanists was well expressed in the celebrated tag of the leading Dutch scholar Justus Lipsius, pointedly chosen by Ong as the frontispiece for his own work: "No one will be great who thinks Ramus is great".[7] In Hotson's striking assessment, "humanism . . . had spawned something which now jeopardised humanism itself".[8]

Yet, despite this double onslaught, Ramism continued to ride high, not only flourishing in many schools and academies but also well and truly capturing the undergraduate market for textbooks even in such hostile environments as Leiden and Heidelberg.[9] Also by no means all humanists or scholastics shared this hostile attitude. A case in point is Polanus' own Basel, where, as we will see, Ramism became established to an impressive degree, informing humanist scholarship and scholastic discourse alike.[10] Likewise, the pressing need of leading Reformed philosophers to come to terms with Ramus' legacy, suggests the seriousness with which they approached his thought. Indeed, the methodological revolution that Ramus had initiated was scarcely one that could be ignored by Protestant thinkers, and Ramism thus came to play a major role in shaping the new systematic and practical orientation of Reformed scholasticism.[11]

The enormous impact of Ramism on early modern Reformed system has been skilfully charted by Muller, who argues that the prevailing topical framework of Reformed theology proved easily capable of absorbing both Ramist and scholastic elements.[12] In this sense, it has been wrong to pit Ramism against Reformed scholasticism as Moltmann and others have done.[13] For, as we saw above, both were part of a wider movement of systematization and confessionalization. Just like other Reformed theologians, Ramists could often draw on Aristotelian and scholastic patterns of argumentation and seamlessly integrate them into their own methodological framework.[14] Of course, as Muller himself points out, this is not to suggest method was a neutral category, divorced from philosophical and

---

[6] Hotson, *Commonplace Learning*, 52–68.
[7] Cited from Hotson, *Commonplace Learning*, 56. See the frontispiece of Ong, *Ramus, Method, and the Decay of Dialogue*.
[8] Hotson, *Commonplace Learning*, 57; cf. Grafton and Jardine, *Humanism*, 161–200.
[9] Hotson, *Commonplace Learning*, 51–68.
[10] Rother, "Ramus and Ramism", 9–37.
[11] Muller, *PRRD*, 1.112–13, 181–84, 353.
[12] Muller, *PRRD*, 1.52–81; *The Unaccommodated Calvin*, 101–17.
[13] Muller, *PRRD*, 1.183–84.
[14] Muller, *PRRD*, 1.181–84.

theological content.[15] Rather, method was often highly contested in early modernity, capable of profoundly shaping philosophical and theological system.

In this chapter we will seek to chart the beginnings of one of the most important of these conflicts, determinative for the entire seventeenth-century tradition of Ramism and universal reform. This is the dispute over the status of logic and metaphysics which erupted in the late sixteenth century and came to engulf much of the Ramist tradition. While Melanchthon had sought to excise metaphysics from the university curriculum, the later sixteenth century witnessed a veritable metaphysical renaissance in German universities.[16] One of the most significant figures within this revival was the celebrated Catholic scholastic philosopher Julius Caesar Scaliger, whose 1557 *Exotericae Exercitationes* became one of the most popular of all German physics textbooks. Scaliger had been a fierce critic of Ramus' displacing of metaphysics from the curriculum, and the inclusion of him in German curricula, alongside other Aristotelian and scholastic philosophers, signalled the beginning of a sea-change from the purer Philippism and Ramism of an earlier generation.[17]

Beginning from Scaliger's Franciscan-inspired logic and metaphysics, this chapter shows how his Scotistic Realism and nascent Trinitarian and transcendental metaphysics were enthusiastically taken up by Reformed thinkers. It also demonstrates the absorption of Scaliger's metaphysics into Ramism through Goclenius and Polanus. Paradoxically, it was thus the Scaligeran critique of Ramism which served to reinforce the definite Scotist tendencies evident in Piscator and other early German Ramists. Ludger Honnefelder has argued persuasively for a Scotist and transcendental turn in early modern metaphysics.[18] Although among the Reformed this must clearly be balanced with a broader eclectic and harmonizing reception of scholastic and second scholastic metaphysics—including prominent Thomistic currents—this chapter bears him out, while pointing to a neglected Scaligeran and Ramist impulse behind this turn.[19]

The chapter also shows how the metaphysical turn within the Ramist movement combined with a wider Franciscan drive towards scriptural exemplarism and Christian philosophy characteristic of Bonaventure. Recent discussion and

---

[15] For discussion of scholasticism and method see Muller, *PRRD*, 1.34–37. Muller, *After Calvin*, 26–30 does tend to suggest a neutral meaning of scholasticism, but more recently, Richard Muller, *Calvin and the Reformed Tradition: On the Work of Christ and the Order of Salvation* (Grand Rapids, MI: Baker Academic, 2012), argues for a complex interrelationship between method and content.

[16] Lohr, "Metaphysics", 620–38.

[17] For the popularity of Scaliger's textbooks see Kuni Sakamoto, *Julius Caesar Scaliger, Renaissance Reformer of Aristotelianism: A Study of His Exotericae Exercitationes* (Leiden: Brill, 2016), 7, 87.

[18] Honnefelder, *Scientia transcendens*.

[19] For the important Thomist elements of this see Svensson and VanDrunen (eds.), *Aquinas Among the Protestants*; Ballor, Gaetano, and Sytsma (eds.), *Beyond Dordt and "De Auxiliis"*; and Muller, "Not Scotist", 127–50.

debate on Reformed scholasticism has tended to bypass Bonaventure's influence, but this chapter shows the important presence of a Reformed Bonaventuranism. We have already seen this in Ames but in both Polanus and his contemporary Stephanus Szegedinus this reaches a new zenith. Together Scaliger, Polanus, and Szegedinus thus mark the beginnings of a new harnessing of Ramism, Franciscanism, and Trinitarian metaphysics with profound consequences for the seventeenth-century movement of encyclopaedism and universal reform.

## 5.1. Scaliger's Franciscan Logic and Metaphysics

Julius Caesar Scaliger, the self-styled Prince della Scala, was a flamboyant and mysterious figure who came to exercise a vital influence on the philosophy of the sixteenth century. Born in 1484 in Padua as the son of an illuminator, and not a Veronese Prince as he claimed, he appears to have grown up in Venice and spent some time in a Franciscan monastery, where by his own claim he made an intense study of the works of Duns Scotus.[20] Certainly we know he enrolled at the University of Padua, where he received his doctorate in arts in 1519 and was also offered the chair of logic. His contribution of a poem to the 1516 edition of Antonio de Fantis' *Tabulae Scoticae Subtilitatis* reveals that he was intimately connected to Scotist circles in Padua.[21] Scaliger had also trained as a physician at Padua, and this secured him an important post in France, where he married a French noblewoman and lived the life of a wealthy gentleman intellectual. Later in life Scaliger became sympathetic to the Huguenot cause and also came into contact with Ramism.[22]

While a noted humanist who wrote elegant works on the Latin language and poetry, Scaliger's international reputation as a philosopher was secured by his aforementioned *Exercitationes*, which he wrote against the *De Subtilitate* of the controversial Renaissance physician Girolamo Cardano.[23] In this work Scaliger was especially concerned to defend the "divine" Aristotle against the attacks of Renaissance Neo-Platonists.[24] Following the precedent of Trebizond and the Fabrists, he sought to elevate Aristotle, and not Plato, as the zenith of

---

[20] Sakomoto, *Scaliger*, 3; Paul Lawrence Rose, "Scaliger (Bordonius), Julius Caesar", in *Complete Dictionary of Scientific Biography*, ed. Marshall de Bruhl, 27 vols. (Detroit, MI: Charles Scribner's Sons, 2008), 12.134. For a comprehensive discussion of Scaliger's family background and true identity see Myriam Billanovich, "Benedetto Bordon e Giulio Cesare Scaligero", *Italia Medioevale e Humanistica* 11 (1968): 187–256.
[21] Kristian Jensen, *Rhetorical Philosophy and Philosophical Grammar: Julius Caesar Scaliger's Theory of Language* (Munich: Fink, 1990), 16–18; Sakamoto, *Scaliger*, 168–70.
[22] Rose, "Scaliger", 12.135–36; Jensen, *Rhetorical Philosophy*, 101.
[23] Sakamoto, *Scaliger*, 4–5.
[24] Kuni Sakamoto, "Creation, the Trinity and *Prisca Theologia* in Julius Caesar Scaliger", *Journal of the Warburg and Courtauld Institutes* 73 (2010): 196–97, 202.

the *prisca theologia*, arguing for his insight into the fundamental Christian doctrines of creation and the Trinity.[25] Yet, like Lefèvre, he tacitly offered a selective and Neo-Platonized reading of Aristotle, which in its concern to integrate Aristotelian philosophy and Christian theology went well beyond Aquinas and the Thomists.[26] Overall, the *Exercitationes* therefore espouses a highly eclectic Christian Aristotelianism which, as Kuni Sakamoto has argued, manifests a definite Franciscan and Trinitarian approach to reality.[27] Indeed, it might even be said that against the subtlety of Cardano he ranged the thought of the Subtle Doctor himself.[28]

The relation between words, concepts, and things was one of Scaliger's abiding concerns. As a humanist who desired to establish a new science of grammar and language, words and their meaning were naturally of fundamental importance to him. Scaliger was deeply familiar with scholastic debates over the relation of terms and universals, and, as Kristian Jensen has argued, was particularly drawn to the speculative grammar of the medieval *modistae*, and their drive to map human language onto the metaphysical structure of reality.[29] We find this same broadly Realist orientation in Scaliger's wider discussion of truth. Drawing on a common Aristotelian theme, Scaliger held that truth is the "adequation of notions, which are in the intellect, with things". He insisted that truth was not to be found in the understanding of either singular terms or propositions but rather in the correspondence of the mental and spoken proposition with external reality.[30]

In this, like his Ramist contemporaries, Scaliger seems to espouse a version of the theory of *complexe significabile*, which we have already seen to be current in late medieval Augustinian and Franciscan circles. This is scarcely surprising, for both Gregory of Rimini and Paul of Venice were extensively studied in Padua during his student days. His teacher Marcantonio Zimara was thoroughly familiar with Rimini, expounding his views in his *De Primo Cognito*, a work which Jensen has significantly identified as an important influence on Scaliger's own epistemology.[31] For Rimini, the *complexe significabile* had been important in

---

[25] Sakamoto, "Creation", 199–207.
[26] Ivor Leclerc, *The Philosophy of Nature* (Washington, DC: Catholic University of America Press, 1986), 51 places Scaliger in the stream of Christian Neo-Platonism.
[27] Sakamoto, *Scaliger*, 3, 22–24, 33–37, 170; "Creation", 201–3. Sakamoto notes a probable link to the Scotist Antonio Trombetta and a definite link to Antonio de Fantis, Trombetta's Paduan disciple.
[28] For contemporary views of Scaliger's Scotism see Johann Heinrich Alsted, *Systema Mnemonicum Duplex* (Frankfurt, 1610), II.72.
[29] Julius Caesar Scaliger, *De Causis Linguae Latinae Libri Tredecim* (Lyon, 1540), I.i (pp. 1–3); cf. Jensen, *Rhetorical Philosophy*, 104–9. For more on the *modistae* see L. G. Kelly, *The Mirror of Grammar: Theology, Philosophy and the* Modistae (Amsterdam: John Benjamins, 2002).
[30] Julius Caesar Scaliger, *Iulii Caesaris Scaligeri Exotericarum Exercitationum Liber Quintus Decimus, De Subtilitate ad Hieronymum Cardanum* [hereafter *Exercitationes*] (Paris, 1557), ex. 307.9 (pp. 395r–v); Jensen, *Rhetorical Philosophy*, 105.
[31] Baschera, *Tugend und Rechtfertigung*, 93; Jensen, *Rhetorical Philosophy*, 138–40.

shaping a new Augustinian and Aristotelian philosophy alive to the subtlety and complexity of reality. It allowed him to argue for the exemplaristic correspondence between reality and the divine mind without committing him to a Platonic or Scotistic Realism.[32] Scaliger too likely found it attractive for his own Christian Aristotelianism, since it allowed him to preserve an essentially Realist account of truth while at the same time disconnecting this from a Platonic account of ideas which he found to be highly problematic.[33]

Probing further we find that Scaliger himself espoused a definitely Scotistic account of universals as well as an Aristotelian theory of abstractive cognition.[34] Yet perhaps due to the influence of Rimini's Nominalism, he often sought to combine a Realist understanding of the relation between thought and reality with a Nominalistic emphasis on the mind as the ground of its own conceptual expression, and as an active sculptor or shaper of its own reality.[35] While affirming the real existence of universals, he insists with the wider scholastic tradition that they are always to be found existing in individuals.[36] Following a Scotist line of argumentation, evident in Zimara, Scaliger held that individuals, and not universals, were the first object of cognition.[37] Scaliger also followed a Scotist trend in maintaining that form itself (and not quantified matter as in Aquinas) is the individuating principle. Confirming this Scotist orientation is his view of individuals and universals as formally distinct (*ex natura rei*), and his explicit espousal of Scotist formalities.[38] Yet, in line with his wider epistemology, he gave this something of a Nominalist twist offering an account of these formalities as "different concepts based on the same things".[39] In choosing to express Scotist concepts in a Nominalist fashion, Scaliger was not at all unusual. For since Scotus' own day there had been heated debates over the ontological status of formalities, and by the seventeenth century it was not uncommon to express Scotus' purely intrinsic distinction in terms of its extrinsic apprehension.[40]

---

[32] Rimini, *Lectura*, Prol. q. 1 art. 1 (I.1–12). For the mixed Augustinian and Aristotelian character of Rimini's thought see Bermon, *L'assentiment et son objet*, 113, 117–37, 276–80.
[33] Scaliger, *Exercitationes*, ex. 6.4 (pp. 12v–13r); cf. Sakamoto, *Scaliger*, 44, 47, 67.
[34] Scaliger, *Exercitationes*, ex. 307.7, 21 (pp. 394r–v, 405v–407r).
[35] Jensen, *Rhetorical Philosophy*, 134–44.
[36] Scaliger, *Exercitationes*, ex. 307.22 (pp. 407r–408r).
[37] Scaliger, *Exercitationes*, ex. 307.18, 21 (p. 402v, 405v–407r); cf. Baschera, *Tugend und Rechtfertigung*, 32–33.
[38] Scaliger, *Exercitationes*, ex. 5.6; 61.1; 307.15, 17; 346 (pp. 8r, 91r 399v–400r, 401v–402r, 456r–v).
[39] Jensen, *Rhetorical Philosophy*, 134–44.
[40] Stephen Dumont, "Duns Scotus's Parisian Question on the Formal Distinction", *Vivarium* 43.1 (2005): 7–62 makes clear that this debate began in Scotus' own lifetime. For the tendency to view Scotus' formal distinction according to its external apprehension see S. Y. Watson, "A Problem for Realism: Our Multiple Concepts of Individual Things and the Solution of Duns Scotus", in *John Duns Scotus, 1265-1965*, ed. Bernadino Bonansea and John Ryan (Washington, DC: Catholic University of America Press, 1965), 64–69, 75–81.

Importantly we find that Scaliger's Scotism extended beyond his Realism into a broader Trinitarian account of metaphysics. We see hints of this in his important paralleling of the powers of the soul with unity, truth, and goodness as the transcendentals of being. In sharp contrast to Aquinas, Scaliger denied that the powers of the soul could be considered as really distinct either from the soul itself or from each other. Like Scotus, he also viewed both the powers of the soul and transcendentals as formally distinct.[41] For Scotus and other Franciscans this marked part of a broader attempt to develop a Trinitarian metaphysics of being, going beyond the Thomistic demarcation of philosophy and theology.[42] While Scaliger does not make such a move explicit, it connects into his remarkable attempt, as the culmination of the *Exercitationes*, to offer a comprehensive Trinitarian view of reality.

Demonstrating a striking resemblance to both Pico and Cusa, Scaliger offers an innovative ninefold division of reality grounded in the Trinity. Drawing explicitly on Neo-Pythagorean and Neo-Platonist sources, he argues both that the "novenary is the most perfect and sum of all which confines and contains all others" and that the "Trinity is the root of the novenary".[43] Unfolding from the Trinity, Scaliger recognizes a ninefold hierarchy of the universe, evident in the nine orders of angels but also in the further threefold division of creation into souls, inanimates, and principles. Scaliger suggests that each of these has a further ninefold expansion, which he illustrates from his nine metaphysical principles of rest, motion, harmony, accident, privation, end, efficient, form, and prime matter.[44] Scaliger's triadic metaphysics has a definite Franciscan character, and it is notable that he appeals directly to Lull and the Cabalists, as well as Aristotle and the Neo-Platonists, in his understanding of God.[45] Indeed, like Lull, Scaliger clearly seems to recognize the fecundity of God's attributes of Power, Wisdom, and Goodness as patterning the dynamic Trinitarian structure of the whole of reality.[46] In this he followed in an important late medieval and Renaissance trajectory of seeking to assimilate Scotist, Lullist and indeed mathematical conceptualities within a dynamic Trinitarian framework.[47]

---

[41] Scaliger, *Exercitationes*, ex. 5.6; 307.15 (pp. 8r, 399v–400r); cf. John Duns Scotus, *Quaestiones in Librum Secundum Sententiarum*, 2 d. 16, n. 17–22, in *Joannis Duns Scoti Doctoris Subtilis, Ordinis Minorum, Opera Omnia*, ed. Ludovic Vivès (Paris, 1891), XIII.43–47.

[42] Aertsen, *Medieval Philosophy*, 345–46 makes clear that the association of the Trinity and the transcendentals is a hallmark of Franciscan thought, although also to be found in Dominicans like Meister Eckhart. Leo Elders, *The Metaphysics of Being of St Thomas Aquinas in a Historical Perspective* (Leiden: Brill, 1993), 60 notes that Aquinas usually resists the parallel between the Trinity and the transcendentals.

[43] Scaliger, *Exercitationes*, ex. 365.1 (p. 471v).

[44] Scaliger, *Exercitationes*, ex. 365.1 (pp. 471r–472r).

[45] Scaliger, *Exercitationes*, ex. 365.1 (p. 472v).

[46] Scaliger, *Exercitationes*, ex. 365.7 (pp. 474v–475r).

[47] See Victor, "Revival of Lullism", 517–20; Oosterhoff, *Making Mathematical Culture*, 27–55.

## 5.2. Goclenius and Reformed Metaphysics

Scaliger's *Exercitationes* offered a nuanced and sophisticated Christian Aristotelianism and Scotism which proved highly attractive to Protestant scholastics in offering the new outlines of a Christian, and even Trinitarian, metaphysics. Yet what is striking is how attractive this synthesis also proved to many early modern Ramists. At first sight, such a conjunction would not be at all expected. For not only was Scaliger implacably opposed to Ramus' methodology, but his own son, Joseph Justus Scaliger, later became one of the leading humanist opponents of Ramism, successfully defending the elitist curriculum at Leiden from any Ramist incursions.[48] That the older Scaliger was able to appeal to Ramists at all had much to do with Rudolph Goclenius the Elder, one of the most celebrated philosophers of his age. For Goclenius himself had a Ramist background and thus, despite being a champion of scholastic metaphysics, incorporated important aspects of Ramism into his developing philosophy. His own 1599 *Analyses* of the *Exercitationes* thus opened the way to an important rapprochement between Scaligeran scholasticism and Ramism.[49]

Scaliger's own views on Ramism are clear in a letter to the rabidly anti-Ramist Jacob Carpentarius in which he claimed that Ramus had "never perceived the true method of demonstrating". In seeking to follow the "order of nature" in all things, Scaliger held that Ramus had failed to recognize the crucial distinction between the metaphysical order of things and its varied logical apprehension by the human mind.[50] Scaliger's emphasis on the subjective dimension of logic meant that he strongly denied the Ramist view that logic contemplates "being as being", regarding this as the province of metaphysics alone. The role of dialectic as an art was simply to fabricate instruments for "modes of teaching", namely proposition, division, definition, and demonstration. Logic was thus not a universal science but an instrumental discipline.[51]

In his *Analyses* Goclenius took up Scaliger's views on dialectic, attacking Ramus' views on the identity of logic and metaphysics.[52] Goclenius was in no doubt that metaphysics, not logic, is the "Prince of Sciences", providing the principles of all the particular arts and sciences.[53] Departing from the Ramists, he held that the subject of logic was second intentions, which he understood as

---

[48] Jensen, *Rhetorical Philosophy*, 101; Hotson, *Commonplace Learning*, 57–58.
[49] Hotson, *Commonplace Learning*, 72, 125. See also Jakub Freudenthal, "Goclenius, Rudolf, 1547–1628", in *Allgemeine Deutsche Biographie* 9 (1879): 308–12 (https://www.deutsche-biographie.de/).
[50] Letter of Julius Caesar Scaliger cited in Jacobus Carpentarius, *Ad Expositionem Disputationis de Methodo* (Paris, 1564), fol. 9r; cf. Jensen, *Rhetorical Philosophy*, 101.
[51] Scaliger, *Exercitationes*, ex. 1.3 (pp. 2v–3v).
[52] Rudolph Goclenius, *Analyses in Exercitationes Aliquot Julii Caesaris Scaligeri* (Marburg, 1599), 94.
[53] Goclenius, *Analyses*, 15–16.

concepts representing concepts, and not first intentions.[54] Yet while Goclenius sought to preserve Scaliger's emphasis on metaphysics, he also gave more space to logic as a universal discipline. In doing so, he clearly sought to reconcile the two philosophical systems, accommodating the Ramist pattern of invention, judgement, and method within Scaliger's more sophisticated Aristotelian treatment of logic.[55] In this, he paved the way for an important integration of Ramist and Scaligeran logic.

We may see this in Goclenius' own logical works which he copiously illustrated with Ramistic charts. Particularly striking in this regard is a Ramist chart he provided illustrating his own Aristotelian understanding of the order of the disciplines, encompassing within a broadly dichotomous structure the theoretical disciplines of metaphysics, physics, and mathematics; the practical disciplines of ethics and politics; and the poetical, or logical, disciplines of dialectic, rhetoric, and grammar.[56] Indeed, while clearly indebted to Scaliger and other contemporary Aristotelians, Goclenius' own treatment of logical invention has a definite Ramist structure, following almost exactly the sequence of arguments laid down in Ramus' own dialectical works.[57] Like Piscator and other Ramists, Goclenius was particularly concerned to integrate logic, as a "ray of divine wisdom", not only into his philosophy but also into his theology and analysis of Scripture.[58]

Like Ramus, Goclenius was deeply attracted to a Platonic understanding of dialectic, and at times could even speak of this as embracing both logic and metaphysics within its scope.[59] Crucially, he recognized the treatment of identity and distinction as pertaining to both, offering a "metaphysico-logical" disputation on this topic conforming to a tightly ordered sequence of Ramist dichotomies.[60] The intersection of Goclenius' logic and metaphysics is also clear from his celebrated *Lexicon Philosophicum* of 1613, in which he sought to provide a comprehensive philosophical dictionary. While ordered alphabetically according to different philosophical topics, the work is replete with Ramist charts and

---

[54] Goclenius, *Analyses*, 13–15.
[55] Goclenius, *Analyses*, 24–26. Here Goclenius also endorses Scaliger's complex account of truth as a via media between Nominalism and the simplistic Realism of the pure Ramists.
[56] Rudolph Goclenius, *Institutionium Logicarum de Inventione, Liber Unus* (Marburg, 1598), 17. Notably the inspiration for this came from the Aristotelian Jacopo Zabarella.
[57] Goclenius, *Institutionum Logicarum*, 22, 29 draws on Scaliger for the definition of logic as an instrumental discipline. At the same time, the work clearly follows a Ramist order in moving through cause, effect, subject, adjunct, diverse, relates, etc. and concluding with testimony.
[58] Goclenius, *Institutionum Logicarum*, 1–16. This quote can be found on p. 6 where Goclenius denies that the "logic of God has nothing in common with our logic".
[59] Rudolph Goclenius, *Problematum Logicorum Pars I* (Marburg, 1591), 11–14. Notably, Goclenius' discussion here takes its lead from the dispute between Ramus and Carpentarius over the nature of dialectic.
[60] Rudolph Goclenius, *Disputatio Philosophica-Duplex Metaphysico-Logica de Identitate et Distinctione* (Marburg, 1604). This also broadly follows a Ramist sequence of arguments.

"uses". One striking example of this is Goclenius' use of a Ramist chart to illustrate Scaliger's own division of being (Figure 5.1), but similar charts can be found scattered throughout the work.[61] In this, as Hotson suggests, Ramism played an important role in the elaboration of early modern ontology as an ordered and structured system of thought.[62]

While highly eclectic in character, Goclenius' metaphysics also had a definite Scotist impulse. In this he followed Scaliger, whom he regarded as an important exponent of Scotist ideas.[63] Thus we find Goclenius treating metaphysics as a transcendental science and arguing for a formal distinction between being and the transcendentals. In common with many other Reformed, he also denied Aquinas' understanding of a real distinction between essence and existence in creatures, following Scotus and other late medieval philosophers in affirming only a modal or formal distinction.[64] For Aquinas, this distinction had been crucial in sharply distinguishing the infinite, Triune being of God from the finite, participated being of his creatures. In rejecting this notion, Goclenius affirms an important parallel between divine and creaturely being, far more congenial to a developed Trinitarian metaphysics.[65]

Although Goclenius' understanding of metaphysics as the science of "being common to both God and creatures" likely derives from the fifteenth-century Thomist Paulo Soncinas,[66] in light of his wider account of being and the transcendentals it also conveys at least a whiff of Scotus' notion of *ens commune*. Jensen has suggested that Scaliger's own account of *ens commune* evidences a tentative move towards a Scotist, univocal understanding of being, and we find some evidence of this in Goclenius as well.[67] Thus his account of "Analogy" in his *Lexicon* draws an important distinction between a nominal and a real account of analogy.[68] As Sebastian Rehnman argues, in this he seems to affirm something

---

[61] Rudolph Goclenius, *Lexicon Philosophicum* (Frankfurt, 1613), 150.

[62] Hotson, *Reformation of Common Learning*, 172–74.

[63] Guido Giglioni, "Philosophy", in *The Oxford Handbook of Neo-Latin*, ed. Stefan Tilg and Sarah Knight (Oxford: Oxford University Press, 2015), 257–58; cf. Goclenius, *Lexicon*, 19.

[64] Rudolph Goclenius, *Isagoge in Peripateticorum et Scholasticorum Primam Philosophiam* (Frankfurt, 1598), 25–29; *Lexicon*, 196–98. Goclenius holds that the transcendentals differ not really but by reason, but his account of this is drawn from Scaliger. He also affirms that things can be one in reality but multiple in definition, giving Scaliger's Scotistic example of the formal distinction between the powers in the soul. For Scotus' account of essence-existence see King, "Scotus on Metaphysics", 54–56.

[65] For Aquinas' metaphysics of participation and real distinction between essence and existence see Wippel, *Metaphysical Thought*, 94–131. For his sharp distinction between the Trinitarian being of God and his creation see Gilles Emery OP, *The Trinitarian Theology of St Thomas Aquinas*, trans. Francesca Aran Murphy (Oxford: Oxford University Press, 2010), 23–26.

[66] Paolo Soncinas, *Pauli Soncinatis Ordinis Praedicatorum Quaestiones Metaphysicales Acutissime* (Lyon, 1586), fol. 14b. I am greatly indebted to Richard Muller for this reference.

[67] Jensen, *Rhetorical Philosophy*, 169–70; cf. Scaliger, *De Causis*, IV.xci (pp. 167–68). See Goclenius, *Analyses*, 94.

[68] Goclenius, *Lexicon*, 96.

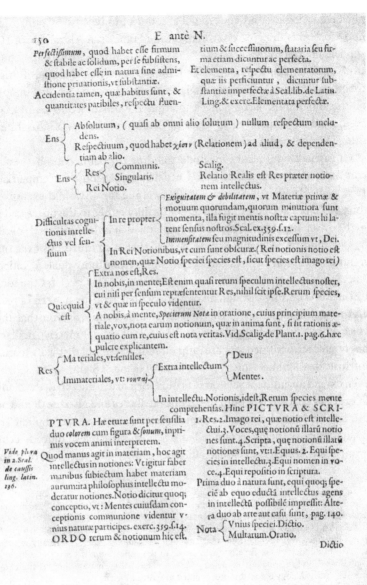

**Figure 5.1** Ramist chart of Julius Caesar Scaliger's division of being from Rudolph Goclenius, *Lexicon Philosophicum* (Frankfurt, 1613), 150. Reproduced by kind permission of the Bibliothèque Nationale de France.

like Scotus' logical and conceptual account of univocity.[69] Confirming this we find Goclenius drawing elsewhere on the Franciscan Alexander of Hales in an explicit attempt to reconcile the Scotist view of univocity with the Thomist doctrine of the analogy of being.[70] In Ramus too we found a hint of this univocal treatment of being, and intriguingly Goclenius draws on Simon Simonius' attack on the anti-Ramist Jacob Schegk to argue the broad Scotist point that being is predicated as "something superior to God" but in terms of causation is something far inferior to him.[71]

Of marked significance for understanding the connection between Ramism and scholasticism in Goclenius is his strikingly Scotistic exemplarism. In the *Lexicon* he drew explicitly on Scotus to argue for a twofold exemplarism and thus a twofold account of truth as conformity either to the uncreated exemplar in the divine mind or the created exemplar which is the "universal species caused by the thing".[72] Following Scotus, he held that such universals exist outside the mind as common natures formally distinct from individuals.[73] Indeed, in his "metaphysico-logical" disputation Goclenius clearly correlates the identity and distinction running through all of being with a Scotistic pattern of real, formal, and modal distinctions.[74] This serves as added confirmation that the Ramist charts that he provides to illustrate the *Lexicon* are not merely ancillary aids, as has often been assumed, but are rather intended exemplaristically to map out the intrinsic distinctions which structure all of being.[75] Significantly, Goclenius can even extend an eminent version of Scotus' formal distinction to the being of God, in order to characterize both the divine attributes and also the divine persons of the Trinity.[76] Like Scaliger, Goclenius therefore espouses an implicit Trinitarian metaphysics of being grounded on Scotist principles. Indeed, echoing the Franciscans, he refers to God as efficient, formal, and final cause of all things and

---

[69] Sebastian Rehnman, "The Doctrine of God in Reformed Orthodoxy", in *A Companion to Reformed Orthodoxy*, ed. Herman Selderhuis (Leiden: Brill, 2013), 363 n. 45.

[70] Rudolph Goclenius, *Conciliator Philosophicus* (Kassel, 1609), 14–16. Schumacher, *Early Franciscan Theology*, 134–35 notes that although the *Summa Halensis* formally rejects univocity, its account of analogy "is already much closer to the conception of univocity advocated by later Franciscans". Smith, "Analogy of Being", 633–73 makes clear that arguing for the compability of univocity with analogy is a Scotist move rooted in Scotus himself.

[71] Goclenius, *Conciliator Philosophicus*, 13; cf. Simon Simonius, *Antischegkianorum liber unus* (Basel, 1570), 60.

[72] Goclenius, *Lexicon*, 196. See Roger Ariew, *Descartes among the Scholastics* (Leiden: Brill, 2011), 109.

[73] Goclenius, *Lexicon*, 551–52, 594, 596; cf. Scotus, *Ord.* 1 d. 8 p. 1 q. 3 n. 106–7 (Vatican, IV.201–2).

[74] Goclenius, *Disputatio Philosophica-Duplex*. Notably, Goclenius draws on Scaliger to argue for a Scotistic principle of individuation.

[75] Peter Dear, "Reason and Common Culture in Early Modern Natural Philosophy: Variations on an Epistemic Theme", in *Conflicting Values of Inquiry: Ideologies of Epistemology in Early Modern Europe*, ed. Tamás Demeter, Kathryn Murphy, and Claus Zittel (Leiden: Brill, 2015), 20 notes the presence of Ramist charts in the *Lexicon* but downplays their significance.

[76] Goclenius, *Lexicon*, 551–52.

holds that all things participate in the "Aristotelian triad" of beginning, middle, and end.[77]

Through his influential *Lexicon*, which served as the standard philosophical dictionary for much of the seventeenth century, Goclenius' transcendental metaphysics, with its important Scotist accents, had a wide diffusion in early modern thought, coming to profoundly shape the emerging science of ontology—the discipline which he effectively founded. While Goclenius certainly marks a radical departure from Ramus in his enthusiastic endorsement of metaphysics, his own attempts to map out his ontology according to Ramist principles suggest that the divorce between Ramist method and scholasticism has here been considerably exaggerated. Indeed, Goclenius' intimate connection with the German Ramist movement ensured the enthusiastic reception of his Scotist metaphysics among the methodological pioneers of the seventeenth century, as well as further attempts to integrate it with Ramist method building on his own *Isagoge* and *Lexicon*.[78]

## 5.3. Polanus' Symphonic Method of Theology

### 5.3.1. Franciscan Realism and Logic

As one of the early Ramist pioneers, following in Goclenius' footsteps, Polanus too was deeply influenced by Scaliger.[79] His own attempt to combine Ramism with Scaligeran scholasticism followed closely the contours of his education. Born in Silesia in 1563, he received his early education in Philippism at the gymnasium in Breslau. Following a brief period of university study at Tübingen, where he was exposed to both the Aristotelian philosophy of Schegk and the Mosaic philosophy of Daneau, he swiftly moved on to Basel, where he was taken under the wing of Johann Jakob Grynaeus, the leading light of the theological school, whose son-in-law he later became.[80] It was here that Polanus changed from being a convinced Aristotelian to an ardent Ramist. Like Piscator, Polanus later spoke of this as his conversion, remarking that it was through "divine providence" that he was first introduced to Ramism in the Basel schools.[81]

The University of Basel itself had been founded in the wake of the great fifteenth-century Council, which had itself served as an important gathering

---

[77] Goclenius, *Lexicon*, 1140.
[78] For Goclenius' intimate connections to the German Ramist movement see Hotson, *Commonplace Learning*, 72, 104, 116, 125, 131.
[79] Polanus, *Syntagma Logicum*, "Epistola Dedicatoria" cites Goclenius as an influence.
[80] Burnett, *Teaching the Reformation*, 139–42; Max Eugene Deal, "The Meaning and Method of Systematic Theology in Amandus Polanus" (PhD Dissertation, University of Edinburgh, 1980), 1–3.
[81] Polanus, *Syntagma Logicum*, "Epistola Dedicatoria".

point for humanist scholars.[82] In the late fifteenth and sixteenth centuries Basel was known for its allegiance to the *via antiqua* and, as the young Zwingli discovered, had a flourishing Scotist tradition.[83] However, if anything, Basel was even more well known for its links to humanist erudition, as witnessed in Zwingli's teacher Thomas Wyttenbach and the great Erasmus himself, for whom the city served as an important haven when much of Christendom had abandoned him.[84] In Polanus' own day the university was dominated by the Grynaeus dynasty he married into, above all Simon Grynaeus, the friend of Erasmus and Melanchthon and erudite mathematician famed for his editions of Plato's *Opera* and Euclid's *Elements*.[85]

As a fertile ground for the study of Realism and Christian Platonism, it is perhaps no surprise that Ramism early took root here. While Heidelberg and other German universities were to shun Ramus, Basel welcomed him with open arms, granting him an entree into Swiss humanist and reforming circles. Ramus wrote his *Basileia* to celebrate this connection and the advice of Protestant theologians from Basel and Zurich profoundly shaped his *Commentariorum*, which was largely written in Basel.[86] A number of Basel humanists also became deeply committed to Ramism including Thomas Platter, the head of the Latin school; Theodore Zwinger, the Professor of Greek and Ramus' own former pupil; and Johann Thomas Freige, the leading early systematizer of Ramism. Indeed, through Zwinger's *Theatrum Vitae* and Freige's *Paedagogus*, Basel became a pioneering centre of Ramist encyclopaedism.[87] Previously the domain of scholasticism, university theses became dominated by Ramism. By the early seventeenth century even the Professor of the *Organon* at Basel was teaching Aristotle through the lens of Ramus' methodological humanism.[88]

When Polanus returned to Basel as Professor of Old Testament in 1596, following time spent among the Bohemian Brethren as tutor and schoolmaster, he was determined to continue and expand this flourishing Ramist tradition. While hitherto Ramism had been largely confined to the Latin school and Faculty of Arts, Polanus sought to introduce it as a mainstay of biblical and theological studies. As Amy Nelson Burnett suggests, it was through this appointment that "Ramist method gained a firm foothold in Basel's theology faculty".[89] Although

---

[82] Hans Rudolph Guggisberg, *Basel in the Sixteenth Century: Aspects of the City Republic* (Eugene, OR: Wipf & Stock, 2010), 3–24 and Overfield, *Humanism*, 61.
[83] Kärkkäinen, "Philosophy", 192.
[84] Guggisberg, *Basel*, 41–68.
[85] For Grynaeus' connections to Erasmus and mathematics see Richard J. Oosterhoff, "The Fabrist Origins of Erasmian Science: Mathematical Erudition in Erasmus' Basel", *Journal of Interdisciplinary History of Ideas* 3.6 (2014): 1–37.
[86] Rother, "Ramus and Ramism", 9–11.
[87] Rother, "Ramus and Ramism", 10, 14–20.
[88] Rother, "Ramus and Ramism", 25–31.
[89] Burnett, *Teaching the Reformation*, 140.

a convinced Aristotelian, Johann Jakob had been pioneering in his application of logic to biblical exegesis and had proven surprisingly open to Ramus' methodological innovations. Following in his footsteps, as well as those of Piscator at Herborn, his son-in-law now proceeded to initiate a "revolution in theological method" at Basel.[90] Polanus held that Ramist dialectic was vital for properly understanding the Bible and learning skills in the logical, exegetical, and systematic treatment of Scripture. His own biblical commentaries and sermons follow a definite Ramist pattern.[91] It was also for his students that Polanus wrote his major logical treatise, the *Syntagma Logicum Aristotelico-Ramaeum* of 1605. As the title proclaimed, this was "especially accommodated for theological use" and became a standard introduction to Ramist logic.[92]

Polanus' logic was explicitly intended as an "Aristotelian-Ramist" logic. As Byung Soo Han has suggested, Polanus did not "dismiss Melanchthon's supposedly speculative Aristotelian teaching method when he was actively assuming Ramus' praxis-centred philosophy".[93] Rather, following his characteristic "symphonic" approach, his *Syntagma Logicum* drew on a whole range of voices, including Ramists, Renaissance humanists, and strident Aristotelians like Schegk and Scaliger. Significantly, this openness extended to late medieval scholastics, and Polanus cites Scotus, Ockham, and the German Nominalist Gabriel Biel as some of his most important medieval interlocutors. His evident interest in late medieval scholasticism, reflected also in his theological works, therefore provides the wider context for his own reception of Scaliger's ideas.[94]

Signalling his Ramist approach from the beginning, Polanus held that both terms and things could be seen as the subject of logic—a marked departure from Peter of Spain's view of logic as a purely rational "science of speech" (*scientia sermocinalis*).[95] In arguing this, Polanus cited Scaliger's claim that the use of terms is necessary to come to the perception of things. Like Scaliger, he drew on Plato's argument in the *Cratylus* that words are useful both for teaching things and as "symbols of things".[96] Unlike Scaliger, however, Polanus held that logic could concern both first intentions, like "man" or "animal", and second intentions, like "subject" or "predicate".[97] In this, we already see a clear affinity

---

[90] Burnett, *Teaching the Reformation*, 133–36.
[91] Burnett, *Teaching the Reformation*, 140–41.
[92] Polanus, *Syntagma Logicum*.
[93] Byung Soo Han, *Symphonia Catholica: The Merger of Patristic and Contemporary Sources in the Theological Method of Amandus Polanus (1561-1610)* (Göttingen: Vandenhoeck & Ruprecht, 2015), 51.
[94] Polanus, *Syntamga Logicum*, "*Epistola Dedicatoria*".
[95] Polanus, *Syntagma Logicum*, 4. For Peter of Spain's treatment of logic as effectively a *scientia sermocinalis* and the continuation of this tradition into early modernity see Ashworth, *Language and Logic*, 38.
[96] Polanus, *Syntagma Logicum*, 4–5; cf. Scaliger, *Exercitationes*, ex. 1 (p. 1r).
[97] Polanus, *Syntagma Logicum*, 9–10.

with the late medieval Realist attempt, reflected also in Ramism and Lullism, to found a logic of first intentions.

Polanus' Platonic view of language opened him up to a strongly Realist account of the relation between words and things. This is seen especially in his discussion of a "universal thing"—nomenclature also found prominently in Scaliger[98]—as something existing in many things and therefore capable of being predicated of all of them. Leaving no doubt whatsoever of his Realist understanding of universals, he remarks that "universals or predicables are not terms but things outside the intellect", citing in support Scaliger's *Exercitationes*.[99] Following Scaliger, Polanus holds that as far as things have an "essence which is apt by its own nature to be predicated of many they are universal things and constitute a species" but "as far as they subsist in singulars or are individuals existing by act they are singular things".[100]

In holding that common natures have real being, Polanus follows the moderate Realism of Scotus. In holding that singular and universal "differ by reason and not really" he makes clear that he understands by this Scotus' formal distinction in which things can be "distinguished by definition even though they are one and the same thing".[101] Elsewhere he also cites with approbation Scaliger's two paradigm examples of this: the distinction between the soul and its powers and the distinction between being and its transcendental affections.[102] Notably, following discussion in Ockham and Biel, Polanus also extends his account of the formal distinction to the Trinity. Going beyond Scaliger, Polanus emphasizes much more the intrinsic character of this distinction and not just its conceptual apprehension by the mind.[103]

Significantly, Polanus also takes up this Scotist and Realist interpretation into a broader Ramist logical framework of invention and disposition. Indeed, Polanus offers his own account of Ramus' category of argument in terms of an explanation of either the simple themes of *res* or *vox* or their complex combinations. In this, as in Piscator and indeed as in Ramus and Agricola themselves, arguments become not simply the rhetorical places (*loci*) of Cicero or Quintilian, but also real, metaphysical features of things in themselves and of things in their interrelation to each other and to the human mind.[104] Like Scaliger, Polanus seems to have subscribed to a definite propositional Realism. However, echoing Goclenius' exemplaristic account of truth, he also held that terms could be true in themselves.[105] In fact, taking this further, Polanus claimed that names and things are

[98] Scaliger, *Exercitationes*, ex. 307.7 (pp. 394r–v).
[99] Polanus, *Syntagma Logicum*, 18.
[100] Polanus, *Syntagma Logicum*, 21–22.
[101] Polanus, *Syntagma Logicum*, 155–56.
[102] Polanus, *Syntagma Logicum*, 87, 156.
[103] Polanus, *Syntagma Logicum*, 156.
[104] Polanus, *Syntagma Logicum*, 3–6.
[105] Amandus Polanus von Polansdorf, *Logicae Libri Duo* (Basel, 1599), 3.

the two "ideas of truth".[106] In this, as we will see, Polanus' Ramism and Scotism paved the way for an important convergence of logic and theology.

## 5.3.2. Symphonic Theology

Polanus' *Syntagma Theologiae* of 1609 was one of the most impressive and comprehensive Ramist works of theology ever to be written, and a landmark of early modern Reformed systematics. As its title proclaimed, the work was "conformed according to the laws of methodical order". While, unlike his earlier 1590 *Partitiones Theologiae*, the ten-volume *Syntagma Theologiae* contained no Ramist charts, it was structured according to an elaborate series of branching dichotomies and bore witness throughout to Ramist patterns of argumentation.[107] In composing a theological system, Polanus was clearly inspired by his Heidelberg professors Franciscus Junius and Georg Sohn, both of whom had Ramist connections,[108] but especially by Piscator, whose attempt to compile a methodically-organized set of biblical *loci communes* paved the way for his own endeavour.[109]

Reaching back beyond Piscator, it is clear that Polanus was also inspired by Ramus' own *De Religione Christiana* as well as the tradition of Renaissance Neo-Platonism that preceded him. For like Ramus and the Fabrists his desire was to bridge the gap between the new evangelicalism and Protestantism of the sixteenth century and older currents of reform going back to the Middle Ages and early Church. What Polanus desired to achieve therefore was a "Catholic Symphony"—the title he gave his earlier methodically-arranged *florilegium* of sources—and so Polanus set himself to gather patristic, medieval, and Protestant theologians into a unified methodical harmony.[110] Of the great scholastics, Polanus had a special affection for Aquinas, Scotus, and Bonaventure, all of whom came to profoundly shape his exemplaristic theology.[111] Yet while undoubtedly eclectic and harmonizing in his use of sources, his understanding of

---

[106] Polanus, *Syntagma Logicum*, 4.

[107] For the Ramist character of these see Burnett, *Teaching the Reformation*, 140–42.

[108] For Junius' Ramist background see Franciscus Junius, *"For My Worthy Freind Mr. Franciscus Junius": An Edition of the Correspondence of Francis Junius F.F. (1591–1677)*, ed. Sophia van Romburgh (Leiden: Brill, 2004), 94. For Sohn's Ramist background see Georg Sohn, *Methodus Theologiae*, in *Operum Georgii Sohnii Sacrae Theologiae Doctoris*, 3 vols. (Herborn, 1591–92), 1.87ff, which is structured according to a chain of Ramist dichotomies and was clearly popular in Herborn.

[109] Polanus, *Syntagma Logicum*, "Epistola Dedicatoria".

[110] Han, *Symphonia Catholica*, 69–124, 183–93; cf. Amandus Polanus von Polansdorf, *Syntagma Theologiae Christianae* [hereafter *STC*], 2 vols. (Hanau, 1609), "*Epistola Dedicatoria*".

[111] Amandus Polanus von Polansdorf, *Symphonia Catholica seu Consensus Catholicus et Orthodoxus* (Basel, 1607), 89–90; *STC*, 1.10, 78–79.

theology is shaped by a clear Franciscan and Scotist imperative.[112] This not only neatly dovetails with his Realist and Scotist logic, but also comes to inform a pioneering Reformed appropriation of Bonaventure's Trinitarian and Scriptural exemplarism as well as his Christian philosophy.

Following a long Franciscan and Neo-Platonic tradition, Polanus seeks to express all of theology within a dynamic framework of emanation, exemplarism, and consummation. The Trinity is thus the *Summum Bonum* from which all things originate, in which all things participate, and to which all things return.[113] From the opening invocation to the Trinity, and to Christ the "treasure-house" of all wisdom, the whole of his *Syntagma Theologiae* follows a marked Trinitarian trajectory.[114] Indeed, for Polanus, the goal and purpose of all theology is nothing less than the glory of the Triune God and happiness, or beatitude, which consists alone in communion with the Father, Son, and Holy Spirit—the fruition of the Trinity and the Franciscan beatific embrace.[115]

Polanus' whole theology is predicated on the self-communicative nature of the divine goodness.[116] In Neo-Platonic fashion he can even compare this relation to the unfolding of number from unity.[117] Drawing directly on Plato, Polanus delights in the understanding of God as the "idea of the good" or the "good itself". Like Goclenius, whose "Platonic annotations" on the highest good he tacitly draws on, he describes God as "the one ineffable principle of all things, from which and to which one are all things . . . beauty itself, the first beauty, the ocean of beauty". God is therefore the exemplar cause of all reality and, as the "idea of the good", contains in his divine mind the idea of all created things, the "eternal exemplar forms".[118]

Following Aquinas, Polanus espouses an analogical understanding of the relation between God and creation. He also rejects emphatically the Scotist understanding of the formal distinction *ex natura rei* between either the divine attributes and essence or the divine ideas and essence.[119] Defusing a Nominalist understanding of the divine ideas as "creatures themselves cognised by God", he argues that they are rather "objective reasons", namely the "divine essence itself conceived by God as imitable by creatures".[120] While he stops short of espousing

---

[112] For the Scotist dimensions of Polanus' thought see Tipton, "Defining 'Our Theology'", 291–313; and Deal, "Meaning and Method", 12, 26–28, 108, 121.
[113] Polanus, *STC*, 1.15–20.
[114] Polanus, *STC*, "*Epistola Dedicatoria*", 1.1.
[115] Polanus, *STC*, "*Epistola Dedicatoria*".
[116] Polanus, *STC*, 1.20–21, 1038–39.
[117] Polanus, *STC*, 1.1724.
[118] Polanus, *STC*, 1.20; cf. Rudolph Goclenius, *Exercitationes Ethicae* (Marburg, 1592), Disputatio XXXI, pp. 207–8. Goclenius appears to be summarizing key ideas from Plato's *Parmenides* and *Symposium*.
[119] Polanus, *STC*, 1.880–81, 1723–24. Polanus makes it clear that the divine ideas in God are not really distinct from God and are of "one reason". For Aquinas' account of analogy see *ST*, 1a q. 13.
[120] Polanus, *STC*, 1.1725.

an explicit Trinitarian exemplarism, likely due to his Thomistic desire to safeguard the revealed nature of the Trinity,[121] he does recognize an important imprint of the Trinity on the human soul and on being and the transcendentals. Indeed, drawing on Scaliger, he clearly characterizes all of these according to Scotus' formal distinction or "distinction by definition".[122] In this, in a manner redolent of the Richardsonian Ramists, we see a definite blending of Thomistic and Scotistic models of exemplarism, establishing an important pattern which runs through the whole of his theology.

Polanus' blended exemplarism is evident above all in his vital distinction between archetypal and ectypal theology. His own account of this derived from that of his teacher Junius but indicated explicitly the medieval, Scotistic, source of this distinction.[123] It became foundational to the later Reformed tradition and likely also exercised an important influence on the contemporary formulations of Ames and the Richardsonian Ramists, revealing once again the intertwining of the different Ramist streams.

An important context for understanding Polanus' treatment of the archetype-ectype distinction is his wider exemplaristic account of truth, which in Ramist fashion he distinguishes into the truth which is in God himself, the truth which is in things, the truth which is in the human mind, and the truth which is expressed in words. Following Scotus, Polanus holds that the Trinity is the first truth on which all other truth depends.[124] This is evident in the reciprocity of being and truth within God, as well as in his role as the "first, highest and greatest truth, and immutable archetype, exemplar and idea of all created truths which are outside him".[125] It is also evident in all God's works and words, from the internal emanation of the Trinity and the eternal establishing of the divine decrees, through their execution in space and time, to the uttering of his words in Scripture.[126] It is due to these "three modes" of divine truth that "the effect of the truth of God is every created truth". Indeed, as we have seen with other Ramists, truth is revealed to be ultimately nothing other than the conformity of things to their "first and uncreated truth, or idea, in the divine mind".[127]

Polanus' exemplaristic account of truth thus already assumes an exemplaristic coordination of the divine mind, created reality, the human mind, and Scripture. It was entirely natural for him to argue that this truth becomes expressed and

---

[121] Polanus, *STC*, 1.70–73.
[122] Polanus, *Syntagma Logicum*, 159.
[123] Tipton, "Defining 'Our Theology'", 301; Van Asselt, "Fundamental Meaning", 322. For Junius' account of this see Franciscus Junius, *A Treatise on True Theology with the Life of Franciscus Junius*, trans. David C. Noe (Grand Rapids, MI: Reformation Heritage Books, 2014), 107–21.
[124] Polanus, *STC*, 1.92; cf. Scotus, *Ord.* "*Prologus*" p. 5 q. 1–2 n. 314–22 (Vatican, I.207–10).
[125] Polanus, *STC*, 1.1174.
[126] Polanus, *STC*, 1.1173–76.
[127] Polanus, *STC*, 1.1176–78.

analysed to the established pattern of Ramist arguments—effects, adjuncts, dissentanies, comparates, and uses.[128] The pattern of theology established in the divine mind and embodied in the divine decrees and their execution thus becomes expressed through a Ramist system attentive to the logical—and indeed covenantal—unfolding of Scripture. Indeed, this is precisely the insight which underlies Polanus' distinction between archetypal theology as the hidden and infinite theology of God's own mind and ectypal theology as its finite and revealed expression.[129]

Polanus expresses his distinction between archetypal and ectypal theology in a definite Neo-Platonic context. Not only does he derive the terms archetype and ectype themselves from the Christian Platonism of the Church Fathers, citing Philo, Clement, Theodore, and Basil as well as the New Testament books of Colossians and Hebrews in support,[130] but he also relates them to a Platonic account of "ideation"—the participation of a created form in its divine exemplar:

> Archetypal theology is the first idea of theology, from which ectypal theology is ideated (as that term is used) and expressed. For just as essential truth and goodness in God is the archetype and first idea of truth and goodness, from which every created truth and good is ideated, [so] archetypal theology is the exemplar and ectypal theology is the exemplified (*exemplum*) which agrees with the exemplar.... Ectypal theology in itself is the whole wisdom of divine things communicable with rational creatures, in this and in the future life, by the mode of God communicating them.[131]

To put it simply, ectypal theology is the ideal copy of God's own infinite and archetypal knowledge of himself.

Significantly, the *Syntagma Theologiae* reveals a number of important medieval sources for both Polanus' distinction between archetypal and ectypal theology. One of the most important of these was Aquinas, and Polanus eagerly took up his argument that theology is a subaltern science which derives its principles not from the light of natural reason but from the superior science of God

---

[128] Polanus, STC, 1.1177–83.2.
[129] Polanus, STC, 1.9–14. For the covenantal dimension of Polanus' system see Robert Letham, "Amandus Polanus: A Neglected Theologian?", *The Sixteenth Century Journal* 21.3 (1990): 463–76.
[130] Polanus, STC, 1.10–12.
[131] Polanus, STC, 1.13: "*Theologia archetypa est prima idea Theologiae, a qua ideatur (ut hac voce utar) et exprimitur Theologia ectypa: sicut veritas et bonitas essentialis in Deo est archetypa et prima idea veri et boni, a qua omne creatrum verum et bonum ideatur. Theologia archetypa est exemplar: ectypa est exemplum quod exemplari convenire.... Theologia ectypa in se, est tota sapientia rerum divinarum cum creaturis rationalibus communicabilis, in hac et in futura vita, pro modo Dei illam communicantis*".

and the blessed, apprehended by the light of divine revelation and faith.[132] Of even greater importance than Aquinas, however, as Stephen Tipton has astutely recognized, was Scotus.[133] For, drawing explicitly on the Prologue to Scotus' *Ordinatio* as well as the *Aureum Rosarium* of the fifteenth-century Hungarian Scotist Pelbartus of Temesvár, he sources his account of archetypal and ectypal theology directly in the Subtle Doctor's crucial disjunction between "theology in itself" (*theologia in se*) and "our theology" (*theologia nostra*).[134]

For Scotus, this distinction expressed the radical disjunction between God's infinite, uncreated knowledge of himself and our created, finite, and revealed knowledge of him. Indeed, while Scotus clearly conceived this relation exemplaristically, his decisive emphasis on the determination of the divine will was important in tempering and reconfiguring a Neo-Platonic framework of participation.[135] Like Scotus, as Willem van Asselt has rightly emphasized, Polanus was keen to emphasize that ectypal theology was a free, willed communication of God and not a necessary emanation or overflow of his being.[136] Yet, like Scotus too, he was insistent that ectypal theology reflects the archetypal being and knowledge of God as its exemplar. Importantly, it is also this Scotist distinction which gives that marked covenantal orientation to Polanus' theology which has been noted by Robert Letham.[137] For conditioning theology as God's willed, self-communication, means that human relation to God is covenantal in character. Indeed, following Scotus, we might say that Polanus employs both exemplarism and covenant as the two axes along which the immanent being of the Trinity unfolds into its economic manifestation in time and space.

Following a broader Franciscan trajectory, Polanus also connects his Scotist account of the archetypal-ectypal distinction into an explicitly Christological and Trinitarian treatment of theology. Thus Pelbartus' definition from Alexander of Hales of "our theology" as "the knowledge of God and his essence transmitted to our mind through Christ and terminated in God" has a definite parallel with Polanus' own understanding of our theology as the "wisdom of divine things" communicated by Christ and the Holy Spirit for the glory of God and our salvation.[138] Even more significantly, it becomes clear from

---

[132] Polanus, *STC*, 1.10, 76–79; cf. Aquinas, *ST*, 1a q. 1 art. 2.
[133] Tipton, "Defining 'Our Theology'", 300–1.
[134] Polanus, *STC*, 1.10; cf. Pelbartus of Temesvár, *Aureum Sacrae Theologiae Rosarium* (Venice, 1586), 7v; Scotus, *Ord.* "Prologus" p. 3 q. 1–3 n. 141 (Vatican, I.95–96). See also Muller, *PRRD*, 1.227–28.
[135] See Scotus, *Ord.* "Prologus" p. 3 q. 1–3 n. 141–50 (Vatican, I.95–114) makes clear both a participative and volitional dimension of *theologia nostra* in its reflection of *theologia in se*.
[136] Van Asselt, "Fundamental Meaning", 328–30.
[137] Letham, "Polanus", 466–71.
[138] Polanus, *STC*, 1.10, 63–64, 67; cf. Pelbartus, *Aureum Rosarium*, 7v.

Pelbartus that Polanus' concern to root our ectypal theology in Christ, as it flows down from the head to the members of his mystical body, answers to a broader Franciscan template.[139] Characteristically Franciscan and Scotist is his understanding that the blessed vision will be an intuitive knowledge of God mediated through Christ.[140] Indeed, for Polanus, following explicitly in the footsteps of Scotus, theology was emphatically to be understood as a practical science in which the most sublime mysteries of Christ and the Trinity are to be understood as eminently "practical truths" oriented continually towards the love of God.[141]

Scotus and Alexander of Hales were by no means the only Franciscan sources available for Polanus in elaborating his understanding of archetypal and ectypal theology. Indeed, in the implicit scriptural and Trinitarian exemplarism underlying this distinction, he arguably comes even closer to Bonaventure. The term "exemplary theology" which Polanus took over from Junius to refer to this relation of ideation is certainly redolent of Bonaventure. Likewise, Polanus shares fully in Bonaventure's characteristic understanding that the world was created according to, and thus patterned upon, a "certain supreme archetypal divine art".[142] We can have no doubt that Polanus knew Bonaventure directly, for he cites his *Breviloquium* in his *Symphonia Catholica* to demonstrate his Trinitarian and illuminative understanding of Scripture.[143] Indeed, Han's perceptive identification of the striking parallel between Polanus' and Jan Hus' doctrine of the Trinity and Scripture as the *principium* of all things makes perfect sense if we take into account their common debt to Bonaventure's understanding of Scripture as having its origin "from an inflowing of the Most Blessed Trinity".[144] Polanus' symphonic understanding of Scripture as a "panharmony" manifesting the "perpetual and most sweet consent" of all of its diverse parts also carries important echoes of Bonaventure,[145] as well as connecting into his Cabalistic, even Lullist, understanding of the Hebraic divine names in Scripture as encoding an explicit Trinitarian and Christological doctrine.[146]

---

[139] Polanus, *STC*, 1.62–70. We find the same concern in Pelbartus, *Aureum Rosarium*, 7v–8r although the emphasis here is perhaps more on Christ's divine than human intellect. Also significant is Pelbartus' Scotistic distinction of archetypal theology into necessary and contingent aspects.

[140] Polanus, *STC*, 1.63–65. Polanus' definition of intuitive and abstractive cognition clearly derives from Scotus. See Scotus, *Ord.* 2 d. 3 p. 2 q. 2 n. 318–21 (Vatican, VII.552–53); cf. Tachau, *Vision and Certitude*, 68–85.

[141] Polanus, *STC*, 1.92; cf. Scotus, *Ord.* "Prologus" p. 5 q. 1–2 n. 314–22 (Vatican, I.207–10).

[142] Polanus, *STC*, 1.1018; cf. Bonaventure, *Breviloquium*, "Prologue" 3.2 (p. 12; *BOO*, V.205).

[143] Polanus, *Symphonia Catholica*, 89–90; cf. Bonaventure, *Breviloquium*, 5.7.5 (p. 198).

[144] Han, *Symphonia Catholica*, 89–90; cf. Bonaventure, *Breviloquium*, "Prologue" (pp. 1–2; *BOO*, V.201–2); Jan Hus, *Super IV Sententiarum*, ed. V. Flajšhans (Prague: Jaroslav Bursík, 1904), "Incepcio" 1–4 (pp. 3–5). See also Polanus, *STC*, "*Epistola Dedicatoria*".

[145] Polanus, *STC*, 1.155; Bonaventure, *Breviloquium*, "Prologue" 3.2 (p. 12; *BOO*, V.205).

[146] Polanus, *STC*, 1.887–88. Polanus was clearly indebted to Pico and Reuchlin for this understanding.

### 5.3.3. Shadows of Divine Logic

Notably, Polanus' Scriptural exemplarism carried through into a definite commitment to a Bonaventuran model of Christian philosophy. The parallel between Polanus and Bonaventure's *De Reductione* has been touched on by Han, but the connection of this to a wider, Ramist and Neo-Platonic, tradition has not been noted.[147] For Polanus, drawing on Aquinas, theology is to be understood as the "queen" of the sciences, and all the other arts and sciences are thus to be considered its "handmaids". Pressing beyond Aquinas, however, he argues that the principles of all the arts and sciences are contained within theology. As divine wisdom, it embraces within itself completely all the properties of intelligence, science, art, and prudence, whether natural or transcending nature. Theology is therefore the "most certain and ample index of all the theoretical and practical sciences"—the "genuine mother" of all the sciences as well as their queen.[148]

While Polanus stops short of arguing that theology proves the principles of other sciences, he does maintain that theology is to judge them. In this sense, as Han rightly notes, all of philosophy must be conditioned by theology.[149] Indeed, as we have seen, such a stance is already evident in his sharp dichotomizing of the pagan philosophy of the Aristotelians and the Christian philosophy of the Ramists.[150] Drawing on the overarching Ramist distinction of theology into faith and good works, Polanus therefore concludes that

> Theology contains under itself philosophy, and thence it is clear is wider than philosophy. For theology is not only to reason concerning God in himself and his essence and attributes, nor only of the most excellent work of God, the redemption and instauration of the human race, nor only even of invisible works created by him, namely the heavenly habitation and angels: but truly also of his visible works, which are called by physics natural and corporeal, and to track down, understand and contemplate their nature, principles, properties and use, as teaches the first and second [chapter] of Genesis, the book of Job, the Psalter, the Prophets and Apostles. Where better, more truly and certainly are ethics and politics handled than in Holy Scripture.[151]

---

[147] Han, *Symphonia Catholica*, 115, 121.
[148] Polanus, *STC*, 1.83–86.
[149] Han, *Symphonia Catholica*, 105–25.
[150] Polanus, *Syntagma Logicum*, "*Epistola Dedicatoria*".
[151] Polanus, *STC*, 1.843–44: "*Theologia sub se contineat Philosophiam, ac proinde latius pateat quam Philosophia. Nam Theologia est non tantum de Deo in se, deq. eius essentia atque attributis disserere, nec solum de praestantissimo Deo opere, redemtione et instauratione humani gernis, nec solum etiam de invisibilibus ab ipso conditis operibus, caelesti nimirum habitaculo et Angelis: verum etiam visibilia eius opera, quae Physica naturalique corpora vocantur; eorumque naturam, principia, vires et usum indagare, cognoscere et contemplari, ut docet caput primum et secundum Geneseos, liber Jobi, Psalterium, Prophetae et Apostoli. Ethica, Philosophia et Oeconomica ubi melius, verius, certius traduntur, quam in Scriptura Sacra*".

Affirming the encyclopaedic character of his theology, Polanus holds that this scriptural philosophy is something he intends to cover in the rest of the *Syntagma Theologiae*. Indeed, the work contains within it a lengthy hexameral treatment of natural philosophy according to the Book of Genesis, likely reflecting the contemporary scriptural philosophy of Melanchthon and Daneau, but also drawing on a Trinitarian and exemplaristic understanding characteristic of the medieval Augustinians and Franciscans.[152]

For Polanus, it is axiomatic that all men know God to exist through a "touch of divinity" before the use of their reason. In this Neo-Platonic understanding, God becomes in some way the hidden presupposition of all our understanding, the lodestone of all our knowledge. As Polanus makes clear, this ontological perspective marks an explicit departure from Aquinas.[153] By contrast, it shows definite affinities with Scotus and even more so with Bonaventure's understanding of the being of God as the first object of our understanding, just as the Trinity is the "first truth".[154] There can be no doubt that Polanus understood God as the "archetype of our rational nature".[155] Like Ames, he clearly draws logic into the dynamic tension of the archetype–ectype relationship.[156] We may see this from the *Syntagma Theologiae* where, in a quote familiar to us already from Ramus' *De Religione Christiana*, he argues that "God is not able to be defined", as "for perfectly defining God it would be necessary to have the logic of God himself".[157] The same theme is taken up right at the beginning of his *Syntagma Logicum*, where he draws on Scotus' Prologue to the *Ordinatio*—the source of many of his rich reflections on the nature of theology—to argue that "God does not reason ... nor discourse ... but knows all things in one simple intelligence, the cognition of which we follow in a certain shadow by understanding of definitions".[158] For Polanus, as a Ramist and Christian Platonist, human logic is ultimately but the shadow of divine logic.

---

[152] Polanus, *STC*, 1.843–44. For Melanchthon, Danaeus and the wider movement of Mosaic philosophy see Blair, "Mosaic Physics".

[153] Rinse H. Reeling Brouwer, "The Conversation between Karl Barth and Amandus Polanus on the Question of the Reality of Human Speaking of the Simplicity and the Multiplicity in God", in *The Reality of Faith in Theology: Studies on Karl Barth Princeton-Kampen Consultation 2005*, ed. Bruce L. McCormack and G. W. Neven (Oxford; Peter Lang, 2007), 56 n. 16 notes the Platonic character of this immediate knowledge of God and its probable link with Calvin's *sensus divinitatis*.

[154] Bonaventure, *Itinerarium*, 3.3 (*BOO*, V.304).

[155] Polanus, *STC*, 1.11.

[156] This tends to corroborate Sutanto, "Two Theological Accounts of Logic", 239–60 which offers a theoretical treatment of the archetypal-ectypal distinction with some striking similarities to these early modern Ramists.

[157] Polanus, *STC*, 1.857; cf. Ramus, *Commentariorum*, 15.

[158] Polanus, *Syntagma Logicum*, 2: "Neque enim Deus ratiocinatur ... non discurrit ... sed una simplici intelligentia omnia cognoscit, cuius cognitionis umbram aliquam assequimur intellectione definitionum". See Scotus, *Ord.* "*Prologus*" p. 3 q. 1–3 n. 158 (Vatican, I.105–6).

## 5.4. Szegedinus' Trinitarian Method of Theology

### 5.4.1. Analogical and Participationist Vision of Reality

While today much less well known than Polanus, Istvan Kis of Szeged, or Stephanus Szegedinus, to give him his Latin moniker, was one of the most innovative systematic theologians of the sixteenth century. For he was not only a major Hungarian Reformer, later becoming a Bishop of the Hungarian Reformed Church, but also a stalwart champion of Trinitarian orthodoxy. The pupil of both Luther and Melanchthon, he became the friend and correspondent of Reformed luminaries such as Theodore Beza and Johann Jakob Grynaeus.[159] Indeed, the 1585 posthumous printing in Basel of Szegedinus' *magnum opus*, the *Theologiae Sincerae Loci Communes*, which was orchestrated by Grynaeus, connects him directly to Polanus.[160] Composed of hundreds of pages of interconnected branching charts, the *Loci Communes* was both an important precursor to Polanus' *Syntagma Theologiae* and a landmark of Reformed method in its own right.[161] Going beyond Polanus, it is also a pioneering work of Trinitarian method, combining the dialectical approaches of the sixteenth century with the Franciscan Neo-Platonism of Bonaventure in a remarkable and fruitful synthesis pregnant with encyclopaedic potential.

The roots of Szegedinus' innovative method can be located in the Renaissance humanism and Philippism he learned at the Universities of Cracow, Vienna, and Wittenberg. Certainly, Szegedinus' biographer, his devoted student Matthaeus Scaricza, saw his thought as simply a continuation of that Renaissance flowering of German humanism evident in Conrad Celtis, Johannes Reuchlin, and Melanchthon himself the "light of Germany".[162] From Scaricza we know that Szegedinus was taught both the *Loci Communes* and dialectic by Melanchthon himself. His teaching of Melanchthon's *Loci Communes* in tabular format as early as 1546, at a time when Ramus was still largely unknown, is striking.[163] For it serves as an important reminder that branching charts were not unique to Ramism but were rather a part of a wider Renaissance dialectical culture.[164]

Szegedinus' theology was profoundly shaped by his controversy against the Anti-Trinitarians. In his *Assertio Vera de Trinitate*, published in 1571 with

---

[159] For Szegedinus' life and significance see Matthaeus Scaricza, "*Stephani Szegedini Vita*", in Stephanus Szegedinus, *Theologiae Sincerae Loci Communes de Deo et Homine* (Basel, 1585).
[160] Johann Jakob Grynaeus, "*Praefatio*", in Szegedinus, *Loci Communes*.
[161] Muller, *PRRD*, 1.112 refers to this as "perhaps the first major thoroughly Ramist model found in a Reformed dogmatics of the era".
[162] Scaricza, "*Vita*".
[163] Scaricza, "*Vita*".
[164] See, for example, Heinrich F. Plett, *Rhetoric and Renaissance Culture* (Berlin: De Gruyter, 2004), 22, 36 who notes Petrus Mosellanus' popular *tabulae* of Melanchthon's works which preceded Ramus. See also Oosterhoff, *Making Mathematical Culture*, 118–20 for prominent Fabrist examples.

a warm dedicatory epistle by Beza, Szegedinus set himself against the "delirious opinions" of the Spanish Anti-Trinitarian Michael Servetus and his Transylvanian followers Giorgio Biandrata and Ferenc Dávid.[165] Servetus had famously denied the eternal generation of the Son, holding that the Word of God was not a distinct person in the Godhead but rather an "ideal reason" or "exemplar of a future man".[166] Similarly, he also reduced the Holy Spirit to a mode of divine operation. Effectively Servetus collapsed the Trinity into either the eternal understanding and will of God or the temporal execution of his decrees. Certainly, he denied any notion of real distinction within the Godhead.[167]

While Platonic in tone, Servetus' doctrine is often seen as having important roots in the Nominalist tradition, as evidenced by his appropriation of theologians such as Ockham, Holcot, and Rimini. In particular, he interpreted the late medieval struggle to accommodate Aristotelian logic to the Trinity as evidence for the doctrine's fundamental irrationality—a radical divergence from both Reformed scholastic logic and the Ramist logic of faith.[168] Servetus also extrapolated Nominalist claims for the univocity of being into a generalized theory of language in which terms were held to signify identically with respect to God and creatures. In this, all the subtleties of the Scotistic discussion of univocity have been largely discarded, and the metaphysical distinction between created and uncreated entirely flattened.[169]

Having sat at the feet of both Luther and Melanchthon, Szegedinus was deeply familiar with Nominalist logic. Indeed, his own mature theology is definitely coloured by Nominalistic emphases.[170] Despite this, however, he criticizes the Servetians heavily for their equating of divine and human terms. As he says, "we use human terms of God but all these must be understood far otherwise than [in] human matters".[171] Espousing both an analogical and apophatic approach,

---

[165] Stephanus Szegedinus, *Assertio Vera de Trinitate* (Geneva, 1576).

[166] Szegedinus, *Assertio*, 75; cf. Michael Servetus, "On the Errors of the Trinity", in *The Two Treatises on the Trinity*, trans. Earl Morse Wilbur (Eugene, OR: Wipf & Stock, 2013), 27, 33, 45, 75–79, 125–27, 140, 171–77.

[167] Szegedinus, *Assertio*, 34–38, 53–54, 111–12; cf. Servetus, "On the Errors of the Trinity", 33–35, 55–57, 93–95, 132, 178–81.

[168] Servetus, "On the Errors of the Trinity", 38–39, 49–53, 63–67. Intriguingly on p. 167 Servetus endorses a "heavenly philosophy". For the connection between late medieval Nominalism and early modern Anti-Trinitarianism see Russell L. Friedman, *Medieval Trinitarian Thought from Aquinas to Ockham* (Cambridge: Cambridge University Press, 2010), 186 and Roland Bainton, "Michael Servetus and the Trinitarian Speculation of the Middle Ages", in *Autour de Michel Servet et de Sebastien Castellion*, ed. Bruno Becker (Haarlem: Tjenk Willink, 1953), 29–46.

[169] Servetus, "On the Errors of the Trinity", 35–38 offers what is effectively a univocal discussion of oneness. For contemporary associations of Anti-Trinitarianism with univocity see Voetius, *Selectarum Disputationum Theologicarum*, I.1.

[170] Szegedinus, *Loci Communes*, 23, 27–28, 41–42, 71–72. This is seen in his emphasis on God's absolute power and his omnipotent will, his covenantal action, and the radical disjunction between divine and human justice.

[171] Szegedinus, *Assertio*, 79.

Szegedinus held that the Servetians had missed the fundamental Christian metaphysics of participation.[172] Responding to Servetus' claim that generation or procession implied some kind of division in the divine nature, Szegedinus argued that incorporeal nature should not be subjected to corporeal laws.[173] In buttressing this argument, he significantly drew on the Neo-Platonic metaphysics of light to argue that just as the Sun emits rays of light but remains undiminished and undivided in itself, so the Father can eternally generate the Word, or Son, without diminishing or dividing his substance. The emanation of light therefore serves him as an important model, or analogy, of the Trinity, as it had done for Melanchthon, Bonaventure, and many others before him.[174]

### 5.4.2. Journeying into God

Turning to the *Loci communes* we find that what served Szegedinus as a model in the *Assertio* has now become the centrepiece of a more ambitious, constructive endeavour. Following a strongly Reformed epistemology, Szegedinus held that reason was blind with respect to the Godhead.[175] Yet at the same time he manifested a deep attraction to the Augustinian doctrine of the *vestigia Trinitatis*, expressing his desire to trace the divine footsteps throughout the realm of nature, the human mind and the structure of theology itself.[176] In particular, Szegedinus held that, as illumined by faith, the human intellect was able to discern an important Trinitarian structure to the created order, mirroring its divine original. Furthermore, this can serve as an important aid to doctrinal construction, helping to elucidate the inner mysteries of the Godhead.[177]

We may see this from a set of seven tables which Szegedinus described as "concerning the contemplation of God, or the ladder of ascent to God from the journey of the mind of Bonaventure".[178] In these tables Szegedinus set out a comprehensive and encyclopaedic vision of the Trinitarian character of theology drawn principally, as the title of these tables suggests, from Bonaventure's celebrated *Itinerarium*, but judiciously augmented by references to other works of the Seraphic Doctor. Following Bonaventure, Szegedinus divides the ladder of divine ascent into six different rungs, organized into pairs corresponding to the knowledge of God outside, inside, and above us. The first pair concern the *vestigia* of God in creation, the second pair concern the image of God in the

---

[172] Szegedinus, *Assertio*, 79.
[173] Szegedinus, *Assertio*, 46, 66.
[174] Szegedinus, *Assertio*, 25, 49, 53, 74–75.
[175] Szegedinus, *Loci Communes*, 3.
[176] Szegedinus, *Loci Communes*, 1–12.
[177] Szegedinus, *Loci Communes*, 12–13.
[178] Szegedinus, *Loci Communes*, 6–18.

human soul—the natural image and that reformed by grace, and the third and final pair relate to God himself, known in his Unity as Being and in his Trinity as Goodness. Significantly, these six stages also correspond to six kinds of divine illumination, or six modes of cognizing God, through sense, imagination, reason, intellect, intelligence, and mind. The seventh and final stage, described in terms of affectivity or mystical excess, corresponds to union with God and sharing in the divine knowing—which Szegedinus, like Bonaventure, calls contuition. It is a Franciscan mode of deification, a crossing with the Crucified Christ to the bosom of the Father.[179]

Szegedinus' use of Bonaventure frames a scriptural and Trinitarian encyclopaedism, which views all of knowledge as oriented towards its end in God. In this every being is held to mirror the Trinity through participation in the divine attributes of Power, Wisdom, and Goodness, which Szegedinus clearly perceives—in significant tension with Augustine—as existing in Trinitarian relation—the Power of the Father, the begotten Wisdom of the Son, and the binding Goodness, or Love, of the Holy Spirit.[180] Through participation in these, every facet of creation, including all of the various human arts and sciences, come to exemplify a Trinitarian structure and dynamic. Following Bonaventure's discussion in the *Itinerarium* and *De Reductione*, Szegedinus divided his encyclopaedia into a set of three triads of natural, rational, and moral disciplines which he correlated with Power, Wisdom, and Goodness: metaphysics, mathematics, and physics; grammar, dialectic, and rhetoric; ecclesiastics, oeconomics, and politics.[181] Significantly, in representing this Trinitarian division of the trivium and quadrivium, Szegedinus transposed the standard Ramist dichotomy into a new trichotomous logic (Figure 5.2).

For Bonaventure, the encyclopaedic reform of the human faculties represented an important harmony of natural and supernatural illumination. Following his more Reformed epistemology, Szegedinus held that even the natural light of the soul has become extinct and must therefore be renewed by the grace of the "supernatural type".[182] Nevertheless, he is at one with Bonaventure in holding that the Trinitarian structure of the soul, which he holds in Augustinian fashion remembers, knows and loves itself, means that it is open to receive the "irradiations" of wisdom which exist all around it.[183] In fact, Szegedinus significantly chose to express this understanding according to the important Augustinian and Franciscan trope of the "Books of God". Combining discussion

---

[179] Szegedinus, *Loci Communes*, 6–18. For Bonaventure's sixfold scheme of illumination see *Itinerarium*, "Prologus" 3, 1.5 (*BOO*, V.295-97). For his account of contuition see *Itinerarium*, 6.1 (*BOO*, V.310). Szegedinus speaks of contuition at *Loci Communes*, 17.
[180] Szegedinus, *Loci Communes*, 10, 13.
[181] Szegedinus, *Loci Communes*, 10.
[182] Szegedinus, *Loci Communes*, 10.
[183] Szegedinus, *Loci Communes*, 10–12.

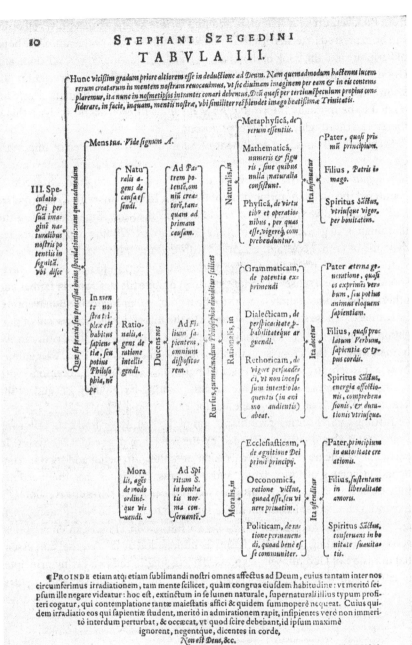

**Figure 5.2** Chart showing triadic treatment of the disciplines in Stephanus Szegedinus, *Theologiae Sincerae Loci Communes de Deo et Homine* (Basel, 1585), Tabula III (p. 10). Reproduced by kind permission of the Syndics of Cambridge University Library.

from Bonaventure's *Breviloquium* and *Itinerarium* he argues that universal order can be expressed in terms of a triad of books—the book of the creature, the book of Scripture and the book of the Church—reflecting divine Power, Wisdom, and Goodness respectively.[184] Seen within this Triune framework of revelation, the knowledge of nature (philosophy) and the knowledge of Scripture is clearly intended to be mutually informing. As Szegedinus himself acknowledges, this is therefore a thoroughly "Christian philosophy".[185]

Szegedinus' Trinitarian treatment of Scripture has a number of important consequences for the relation of exegesis and system. Fusing Bonaventure's *Breviloquium* with the Reformed doctrine of *sola scriptura*, Szegedinus countered the incipient rationalism of the Anti-Trinitarians with a participative and transformative treatment of revelation and theology. Emerging out of the illumination of grace theology becomes structured according to the Trinitarian dynamic of faith, hope, and charity.[186] Through the influx of these theological virtues the soul's spiritual senses are awakened, allowing it to perceive the corresponding spiritual senses of Scripture, which despite the strictures of Luther and others he has no hesitation relating to the medieval *quadriga*. Like Bonaventure, he connected these three spiritual senses to the threefold mystical ascent of purgation, illumination, and perfection and to the indwelling of the Trinity in the human soul.[187] This Franciscan mystical approach deeply impacted Szegedinus' own approach to Scripture. Fascinatingly, like Polanus, it combines with a Cabalistic analysis of the divine names, pointing to the deep imprint of the Trinity and Christ on the language and logic of the Bible.[188]

Turning to Szegedinus' own discussion of the Trinity we find that, following Bonaventure, his doctrine is shaped by the influence of Pseudo-Dionysius. In particular, while he recognizes a Trinitarian pattern in being and its transcendental principles of unity, truth, and goodness, he argues that this becomes fully explicit in the understanding of God as the highest, self-diffusive Good.[189] Expanding his earlier treatment of the Trinity in terms of the Neo-Platonic metaphysics of light, Szegedinus now offers a full-blown Franciscan emanational account. According to this the Trinity is understood as the "eternal and essential diffusion of God himself" expressed according to the two divine principles of nature and will.[190] In this Scotistic schema, the Son represents the natural

---

[184] Szegedinus, *Loci Communes*, 7.
[185] Szegedinus, *Loci Communes*, 18.
[186] Szegedinus, *Loci Communes*, 12.
[187] Szegedinus, *Loci Communes*, 12–13. For the early Reformation critique of the *quadriga* see Muller, *PRRD*, II.66–75. Muller makes clear that aspects of the *quadriga* are certainly present in Luther, but that Calvin marks a more decisive turn away from medieval exegesis.
[188] Szegedinus, *Assertio*, 11–15, 81–82 demonstrates Cabalistic reasoning arguing from the meaning of Hebrew letters to Christ and the Trinity.
[189] Szegedinus, *Loci Communes*, 10–11, 15–16.
[190] Szegedinus, *Loci Communes*, 15–16.

emanation from the Father and Holy Spirit the voluntary emanation—although both are held to be simultaneously necessary and free in character.[191] Inverting Aquinas' model, the emanations themselves become the ground of the identity-in-distinction within the Trinity, structuring the coinherent relations of Father, Son, and Holy Spirit.[192]

Drawing on famous passages of the *Itinerarium* and *Breviloquium*, Szegedinus holds that this entire Trinitarian vision is held together in Christ. It is he who is the highest and lowest, first and last, centre and circumference of all things. Similarly, it is he who is the "mystical book, written inside and outside".[193] It is Christ then who binds together all three books of nature, Scripture, and Church and becomes the key to their interpretation.[194] Crucially, this engages not only the intellect but also the heart. Indeed, knowledge of Christ is affective more than intellective. Dying to oneself the believer is crucified with Christ and makes the mystical transit to union with the Father in the Holy Spirit. In this way the Trinitarian pattern of nature and Scripture becomes fully realized in the life of each individual believer, as well as in the Church, where believers are unified in the love of God and the love of God in each other. Everything therefore finds its ultimate fulfilment in Christ, in whom every treasure of Wisdom is hidden.[195]

## 5.5. Trinitarian and Transcendental Turn

Overall, in Scaliger, Polanus, and Szegedinus we see an important drive towards a new Christian philosophy and the beginning of a Trinitarian and transcendental metaphysics which was to take deep root in the Reformed tradition of the seventeenth century. Such a move was not exclusively Ramist in character—and undoubtedly incorporated elements markedly hostile to Ramism—but it was part of the wider Ramist turn of early modernity. It was also by no means hostile to the developing Reformed scholasticism, belying Moltmann's claims for a radical dichotomy here, but rather came to deeply inform it on multiple levels.[196] It would be mistaken to see it as entirely Franciscan or Scotist in character, for like Richardsonian Ramism it can often blend in important elements of Thomist

---

[191] Szegedinus, *Loci Communes*, 15; cf. Scotus, *Ord.* 1 d. 10 q. 1 n. 6–8 (Vatican, IV.341). See further Sylwanowicz, *Contingent Causality*, 204–12.
[192] Szegedinus, *Loci Communes*, 3–4, 15–16. For the contrast of Dominican and Franciscan models of the Trinity in this regard see Friedman, *Medieval Trinitarian Thought*, 5–49.
[193] Szegedinus, *Loci Communes*, 16
[194] Szegedinus, *Loci Communes*, 6–7.
[195] Szegedinus, *Loci Communes*, 6–7, 16–18.
[196] Moltmann, "Zur Bedeutung", 295–318.

exemplarism and analogical reasoning.[197] Yet in its deepest impulses and its commitment to an exemplaristic philosophy and logic it can clearly be seen as part of that evangelical renewal of method beginning in the thirteenth century, intensifying under the influence of the revived Platonism, Augustinianism, and humanism of the Renaissance and Late Middle Ages, and flourishing anew in the Protestant schools of the sixteenth and seventeenth century. In Szegedinus especially, this Franciscan Reformation of method is taken to new heights, anticipating the Lullist encyclopaedism of the Herborn School and beginning an important movement towards Trinitarian logic, marking out a new direction for the Ramist logic of faith.

---

[197] Szegedinus, *Loci Communes*, 14 affirms an analogical view of being. Given the context this likely fits Bonaventure's view of analogy which Schumacher, *Divine Illumination*, 124–25 locates in proximity to Scotus' account of univocity.

# 6
# Christian Philosophy
## Keckermann, Encyclopaedism, and the Return to Eden

Bartholomäus Keckermann is undoubtedly a towering figure who looms over the entire landscape of early modern method and stands at the origin of that encyclopaedic transformation of philosophy which was to occupy some of the best European minds in the decades surrounding the Thirty Years' War. No one reading his works could have any doubt of his zeal for method, but his commitment, or lack of commitment, to Ramism has long been a major bone of contention among intellectual historians. While Ong followed Keckermann's contemporaries in classifying him as a semi- or Philippo-Ramist, more recent scholarship has tended to dissent from this judgement. Thus Meerhof classes Keckermann along with Ursinus and other Heidelberg philosophers as a prominent Anti-Ramist, and Danilo Facca goes even further along the road to identifying him as a pure Peripatetic, denying any real trace of Ramism in his philosophy.[1]

An important exception to this general trend is Hotson, whose penetrating evaluation of Keckermann's "methodical Peripateticism" has highlighted his careful and sensitive fusion of both Ramist and Aristotelian methods in support of a thoroughgoing encyclopaedism. Perhaps even more significantly, he has also connected this to the broader Ramist aspiration to employ the encyclopaedia for the instauration of the image of God, showing that Keckermann's commitment to Ramism goes beyond any kind of superficial repackaging of Aristotelian content. Within the arc of Hotson's broader reevaluation of Ramism, Keckermann thus marks a key point of transition from the Philippo-Ramism of the sixteenth century to the post-Ramist encyclopaedism of the seventeenth century.[2] At the same time, however, Hotson also sees Keckermann as marking the beginnings of an important departure from a Reformation restraint of reason, displaying a new confidence in humanity and its capacities, not least in his conception of logic as a kind of repristination of man's unfallen nature. Going beyond this, Willem van

---

[1] Ong, *Ramus, Method, and the Decay of Dialogue*, 298–300; Meerhof, "Keckermann", 169–205; Danilo Facca, "Bartholomäus Keckermann (1572–1609): The Theology of the Reformation and the Logic", *Odrodzenie i Reformacja w Polsce* (2013): 201–3. Miller, *New England Mind*, 152, 336–37 also tends to identify Keckermann as an Aristotelian and notes his attack on Ramus.

[2] Hotson, *Commonplace Learning*, 127–65.

Zuylen and others have no qualms in seeing Keckermann as an early herald of the Enlightenment.[3]

This view of Keckermann's incipient rationalism has been strongly contested by Richard Muller, Danilo Facca, and Byung Soo Han, who all, in their different ways, point to important continuities with Reformation and scholastic norms of reason.[4] For Han, Keckermann marks the beginning of a new "academization" of Reformation teaching in which the encyclopaedic elaboration of philosophy cannot be detached from the overarching framework of grace in which it takes place.[5] Yet, while this is a valuable corrective to the excesses of the older scholarship, Hotson is surely right to suggest that Keckermann's remarkably positive view of logic deserves further consideration and contextualisation. Likewise, the extent to which Keckermann sought to uphold a Christian philosophy grounded on exemplaristic, illuminationist, and even Trinitarian presuppositions has scarcely been realized. In this light, his own evident connection to a tradition of Christian reflection reaching back beyond Ramus to an Augustinian and Franciscan tradition of pious philosophy promises to serve as a valuable key for unlocking his complex account of human reason and its capacities.

In this chapter, building on the important insights of Hotson, Muller, and Han, we will consider in depth the shape of Keckermann's methodical Peripateticism and encyclopaedism. While this reveals definite anti-Ramist elements to his thought, it also suggests that his commitment to a Ramist and exemplaristic method goes much deeper than is often realized. Hotson has insightfully suggested the need to view Keckermann's thought in relation to that of Rudolph Goclenius, Otto Casmann, and Clemens Timpler, with all of whom he maintained close connections.[6] In doing so, we find that Keckermann was committed to a Ramist project of Christian and scriptural philosophy with deep Augustinian and Franciscan roots. In this sense, while Keckermann's Aristotelian and broadly Thomistic account of logic can certainly be seen as an important foil to what he would have viewed as the simplistic Scotism of the pure Ramists, he himself turns out to have been engaged in a thoroughgoing, if often implicit, Scotistic and Trinitarian transformation of philosophy. Moreover, in continuity with Bonaventure and other Franciscans, Keckermann could also see the encyclopaedia as mapping out an itinerary for a return to Eden. In this, his therapeutic account of theology and architectonic understanding of politics combine

---

[3] Hotson, *Alsted*, 68–82. For discussion of the rationalist interpretation of Keckermann see Facca, "Keckermann", 184–85, 195–96.

[4] Muller, *After Calvin*, 122–36; Facca, "Keckermann", 198; Byung Soo Han, "The Academization of Reformation Teaching in Johann Heinrich Alsted", in *Church and School in Early Modern Protestantism: Studies in Honor of Richard A. Muller on the Maturation of a Theological Tradition*, ed. Jordan J. Ballor, David Sytsma, and Jason Zuidema (Leiden: Brill, 2013), 283–94.

[5] Han, "Academization", 283–94.

[6] Hotson, *Commonplace Learning*, 131–35.

with his broader encyclopaedism to effect a holistic and far-reaching transformation of Church and society.

## 6.1. Keckermann and German Ramism

Keckermann's entire life and career occurred in the wake of the impressive German Ramist movement and of a profound confessionalization of philosophy and theology taking place in gymnasia, academies, and universities across the Holy Roman Empire. In educational terms, the progress of the Reformed movement had been evident in its distinctive fusion of Philippism and Ramism. It is therefore scarcely surprising that a new, conservative, Gnesio-Lutheran faction should come to vigorously oppose Philippism as a betrayal of Luther's legacy and a form of "Crypto-Calvinism". In this new confessionally charged atmosphere, many Reformed became concerned that both the supposedly simplistic character of Ramist logic and its marginalization of metaphysics would leave their confession badly exposed to attacks by Catholics, Lutherans, and Anti-Trinitarians alike. In response, in a kind of "metaphysical arms-race", the Reformed engagement with scholastic logic and metaphysics, which had begun with Scaliger and Goclenius, began to accelerate dramatically, leading to extensive and surprisingly positive engagement with leading Catholic philosophers, including Ames' bête-noir Suárez.[7]

Nevertheless, as we have seen, the new Protestant scholasticism remained deeply influenced by Ramist systematics, and the publishing history of Ramist works belies any kind of notion of retreat. If anything, the Ramist drive for method and encyclopaedism and its distinctive framing of a Christian philosophy came to dominate more than ever before. Ever a protean movement, as Hotson has rightly suggested, Ramism proved able to adapt, survive, and, in many ways, flourish.[8] German philosophy came to be dominated by a definite eclecticism in which Philippist, Ramist, and Aristotelian currents—and very quickly also Lullist ones—were fused together in various ways.[9] Yet while undoubtedly a valuable heuristic label, the term "post-Ramism" can be misleading if it is interpreted as implying a fundamental departure from Ramus' own methodological aspirations or, especially, his desire to institute a Christian reformation of the entire cycle of disciplines. Rather, it should be seen as a

---

[7] For discussion of the rise of Protestant metaphysics see Lohr, "Metaphysics", 620–38 and Kusukawa, *Transformation*, 201–210.

[8] Hotson, *Commonplace Learning*, 25–37, 101–13, 127–35, 274–77. The ongoing adaptation and transformation of Ramism throughout the seventeenth century is also well-evidenced in Hotson, *Reformation of Common Learning*.

[9] Hotson, *Commonplace Learning*, 124–35.

distinctive methodological and systematic orientation to philosophy in which encyclopaedism carried through into the far-reaching transformation of Church and society.

Keckermann stands at the beginning of this post-Ramist movement and the different stages of its development are clearly mirrored in his formative years of education. His home-town of Danzig (Gdańsk), where he was born in 1572 and received his early education, and to which he later returned to spearhead Reformed confessionalization, was in many ways a microcosm of the intellectual, confessional, and theological tensions so deeply felt across the Empire.[10] For divisions were intensified not only by Danzig's situation as a Protestant German enclave in the Catholic Polish-Lithuanian Commonwealth but by the entrenched division in the city between a Gnesio-Lutheran majority and a Reformed elite who dominated the senate, Church, and schools. During Keckermann's childhood the city was in the throes of what Michael Müller has described as a highly contested "second Reformation".[11] Keckermann and his family belonged to the Reformed minority and he himself was later to become a noted champion of Reformed orthodoxy against the Lutheran "Ubiquitarians".[12]

By the time Keckermann enrolled in the Danzig Gymnasium in 1587, this process of further reformation was already well in train. The Gymnasium was founded on Philippist principles in which philosophical studies were combined with the study of Scripture. In 1580 the new Rector Jakub Fabricius, the "leading theologian of the Prussian Second Reformation", instituted curricular reforms as part of his own aggressive campaign of Reformed confessionalization.[13] In this context, a tempering of Lutheran Philippism with a more Reformed Ramism likely appealed to Fabricius. Like so many other Germans of his day, Keckermann thus received an education which marked him out as a Philippo-Ramist.[14] Indeed, Keckermann's later logical works have nothing but praise for

---

[10] For an account of Keckermann's life and context see Joseph S. Freedman, "The Career and Writings of Bartholomew Keckermann (d. 1609)", *Proceedings of the American Philosophical Society* 141.3 (1997): 305–64 and Hotson, *Commonplace Learning*, 136–65.

[11] Michael Müller, *Zweite Reformation und städtische Autonomie im Königlichen Preussen: Danzig, Elbing und Thorn in der Epoche der Konfessionalisierung (1557–1660)* (Berlin: Akademie Verlag, 1997).

[12] See Hotson, *Commonplace Learning*, 136–37. For an account of the Prussian Reformation see Janusz Małłek, "The Reformation in Poland and Prussia in the Sixteenth Century: Similarities and Differences", in Małłek, *Opera Selecta Vol. II: Poland and Prussia in the Baltic Area from the Sixteenth to the Eighteenth Century* (Toruń: Wydawnictwo Naukowe Uniwersytetu Mikołaja Kopernika, 2013), 179–90 and especially Müller, *Zweite Reformation*, 77ff.

[13] See Sven Tode, "Preaching Calvinism in Lutheran Danzig: Jacob Fabritius on the Pastoral Office", *Nederlands archief voor kerkgeschiedenis* 85 (2005): 242 and also Müller, *Zweite Reformation*, 37–38, 65–150.

[14] Hotson, *Commonplace Learning*, 137; cf. Bartholomäus Keckermann, *Praecognita Logica* (Hanau, 1604), 8–9. Dariusz M. Bryćko, "The Danzig Academic Gymnasium in Seventeenth-Century Poland", in *Church and School*, ed. Ballor, Sytsma, and Zuidema, 341–44 points to tensions between Lutheran and Reformed elements in the gymnasium during the period of confessionalization.

Melanchthon, "the Phoenix of Europe" and the "great light of every doctrine in Germany".[15]

Given his education in Danzig, it was only natural that the young and ambitious Keckermann should proceed to further study at the Universities of Wittenberg and Leipzig in 1590-92.[16] It was at Wittenberg that Keckermann came under the tutelage of Daniel Claepius, his "faithful and first teacher in Aristotelian philosophy", to whom he owed the beginning of his departure from "Ramist errors".[17] It was also here, in the context of growing controversies over Philippism and Crypto-Calvinism, that Keckermann came to first engage with the heated contemporary debates concerning the relation of philosophy and theology.[18]

In 1592 a dynastic change led to the expulsion of Reformed students from the Saxon Lutheran universities, and Keckermann joined the mass exodus to Heidelberg. He came to Heidelberg at the beginning of its golden age, just a few years after it had been reclaimed from the Lutherans for the Reformed Church by Prince Johann Casimir.[19] In the late sixteenth century Heidelberg still prided itself on its long Aristotelian and scholastic heritage, stretching back to its foundation in the fourteenth century, when the university had earned its reputation as a leading centre for the *via moderna*.[20] Melanchthon himself had been a student at Heidelberg and later was asked to reform its curriculum. By the mid-sixteenth century the curriculum followed an uncompromising Philippism.[21] It was therefore no surprise that the Heidelberg professors had given Ramus such a cold welcome to their university, despite the warm personal invitation of the Elector himself.[22] Writing directly to the Elector, Hermann Wittekind, the Rector of the University, cited both Melanchthon and Ramus' Parisian opponent Turnèbe against the French humanist, saying that the authority of Aristotle had stood firm for 2000 years. He was joined in protest by Thomas Erastus and also, as we have seen, by Ursinus, who extolled Aristotle and his "methodical" philosophy as a divine gift.[23] Even after Ramus had been driven out of Heidelberg a concerted anti-Ramist campaign was mounted, with the 1590s seeing the publication of at

---

[15] Keckermann, *Praecognita Logica*, 178. Joseph S. Freedman, "The Life, Significance and Philosophy of Clemens Timpler, 1563/4-1624" (PhD Dissertation, University of Wisconsin-Madison, 1982), 275 notes the contemporary identification of Timpler as a Philippo-Ramist. Meerhof, "Keckermann", 174-75 also notes his strong Philippism.

[16] Freedman, "Career and Writings", 306.

[17] Keckermann, *Praecognita Logica*, 196.

[18] Richard A. Muller, "*Vera Philosophia cum sacra Theologia nusquam pugnat*: Keckermann on Philosophy, Theology and the Problem of Double Truth", *Sixteenth Century Journal* 15.3 (1984): 347-48 and Freedman, "Career and Writings", 306-7.

[19] Freedman, "Life", 39-40.

[20] Overfield, *Humanism*, 55.

[21] Meerhof, "Keckermann", 171-72.

[22] Freedman, "Ramus and the Use of Ramus", 98-99.

[23] Meerhof, "Keckermann", 173-74.

least three different critiques of Ramism, including Ursinus' own.[24] While only one, abridged, edition of Ramus' works seems ever to have been published in Heidelberg, those of Turnèbe went through a veritable boom.[25]

Ursinus' legacy lived on in Keckermann's day and David Pareus was one of his professors, as was Joachim Jungnitz, the editor of Ursinus' logical works and an accomplished Aristotelian logician.[26] It was no surprise therefore that the young Ramist quickly found himself engaging in intensive studies of Aristotle. Indeed, in a kind of inversion of Piscator's experience, he soon experienced a definite conversion from Ramism to Peripateticism, completing the process which had already begun in Wittenberg.[27] As Meerhof suggests, the changed attitude of the Danziger is apparent in an oration *On Aristotle and Peripatetic Philosophy* that he gave at Heidelberg against Ramism.[28] In this he offered an elaborate comparison of Aristotelian and Platonic philosophy in which both Plato and his French disciple Ramus were clearly found wanting. For Keckermann, Plato was an elegant swan, best suited for ornament, while Aristotle was a soaring eagle rising to the heights of philosophical knowledge. Echoing Ursinus, he clearly saw his logic as a divine gift to humanity.[29]

Yet, as Hotson rightly points out, this was not a conversion to the Aristotelianism of either the medieval schools or the Renaissance humanists, but rather to the new methodologically oriented Aristotelianism of Jacopo Zabarella and the Paduan school. Keckermann was fortunate to learn this first-hand from Zabarella's own pupil, the Reformed convert Giulio Pace, whose own pioneering Zabarellan edition was explicitly intended to combat the errors of Ramus.[30] Through Pace's lectures and his reading of others such as Fortunatus Crell, he gained an intimate knowledge of Zabarella's corpus. By the end of the sixteenth century, many German philosophers were caught up in a kind of Zabarellan fever, and Keckermann proved no less susceptible to the sophistication and elegance of the Paduan's method. Indeed, from this point onwards he was always to identify himself as a "methodical Peripatetic".[31]

---

[24] Freedman, "Ramus and the Use of Ramus", 95–96.
[25] Meerhof, "Keckermann", 196 suggests that no editions of Ramus were ever published. Freedman, "Ramus and the Use of Ramus", 98–99 notes an exception to this is an abridged edition of Ramus' *Ciceronianus* published in the 1620s.
[26] Keckermann, *Praecognita Logica*, 187–90 praises both for their Aristotelian teaching and notes his personal connection to them. For Jungnitz's Aristotelianism see Donald Sinnema, "Joachim Jungnitz on the Use of Aristotelian Logic in Theology", in *Späthumanismus und reformierte Konfession*, ed. Strohm, Freedman, and Selderhuis, 127–52.
[27] Keckermann, *Systema Logicae*, "Epistola Dedicatoria"; *Praecognita Logica*, 186–87, 196. Hotson, *Commonplace Learning*, 138 points out that his exposure to Zabarella had already begun at the Lutheran Philippist universities. See also Ian Maclean, *Learning and the Market Place: Essays in the History of the Early Modern Book* (Leiden: Brill, 2009), 40–43.
[28] Meerhof, "Keckermann", 175–77.
[29] Meerhof, "Keckermann", 178.
[30] Maclean, *Learning and the Market Place*, 46.
[31] Hotson, *Commonplace Learning*, 137–42 and Maclean, *Learning and the Market Place*, 39–58.

For Zabarella, as much as for Ramus, it was true that "every science, every art, every discipline is conveyed by some method and cannot endure without method". Like Ramus, he insisted that the study of logic should be reoriented towards method.[32] Unlike Ramus, however, Zabarella sharply distinguished order and method, seeing the latter as an intellectual habit leading to the production of new knowledge rather than a systematic disposition of a subject.[33] Like his fellow Paduan Scaliger, he also opposed strongly the (Ramist) attempt to ground method in the order of being rather than the order of knowing, insisting that both logic and method were entirely instrumental in character and not to be classed as Aristotelian sciences.[34] Compared to Ramus' universal aspirations for logic and method, this was a definite dethroning.

Yet while Zabarellan logic was explicitly promoted in the German context as a rival to Ramism, it would be a mistake to pit the two movements entirely against each other or to suggest that Keckermann's own youthful enthusiasm for Ramus was quenched by his time at Heidelberg. Many of the German proponents of Zabarella were committed to a definite methodological eclecticism, in which Aristotelianism, Ramism and Lullism all jostled for position, and Zabarella's works were clearly marketed to appeal to those already of a Ramist predilection. Indeed, as Ian Maclean suggests, Zabarella's own *Tabula Logicae*, which presents his logic in a series of dichotomous charts, proved very popular in a German context.[35] While excluded from the curriculum, Ramism continued to be studied in private courses at the *Collegium Sapientiae*.[36] Away from the heat of battle, even Ursinus could admit the considerable profit of students studying Ramism, provided they first had a secure grounding in Aristotle.[37] Likewise, Pareus' much vaunted anti-Ramism did not stop his son Johann Philipp from laying out his father's commentary on Romans in a linked series of Ramistic charts.[38] Moreover, by no means all enthusiasts for Zabarella shared Pace's concerns about his work.[39] Thus in his 1609 *Conciliator Philosophicus* Goclenius, undoubtedly the leading German philosopher of his day, drew frequently on Ramus and Zabarella, taking both seriously for their contributions to philosophy.[40]

---

[32] Jacopo Zabarella, *Jacopo Zabarella: On Methods*, ed. and trans. John P. McCaskey, 2 vols. (Cambridge, MA: Harvard University Press, 2013), 1.1 (p. 3).
[33] Zabarella, *On Methods*, 1.2; 1.3 (pp. 7–13, 20–21).
[34] Zabarella, *On Methods*, 1.2; 1.3; 1.6 (pp. 13, 19–21, 29–37).
[35] Maclean, *Learning and the Market Place*, 51.
[36] Freedman, "Ramus and the Use of Ramus", 102–103.
[37] Meerhof, "Keckermann", 178.
[38] David Pareus and Johann Philipp Pareus, *Analysis Logicae Divi Pauli ad Romanos* (Frankfurt, 1609).
[39] Freedman, "Ramus and the Use of Ramus", 95 points out that Pace himself praised Ramus in a letter of 1586.
[40] Goclenius, *Conciliator Philosophicus*, 3, 8, 19, 32, 109, 119, 315, 369.

Despite the claims of Meerhof and Facca to the contrary, Keckermann did not therefore emerge from his years at Heidelberg as an anti-Ramist in the mould of Ursinus or Pareus.[41] Indeed, as Meerhof himself suggests, Keckermann's denunciations of Ramus must be seen as part of a deliberate Aristotelian self-fashioning and self-promotion.[42] Moreover, it seems clear that they must also be seen in the context of the age-old battle between Aristotelianism and Platonism, which at Heidelberg stretched back into the Renaissance and Middle Ages.[43] While prominent anti-Ramist currents can undoubtedly be identified in Keckermann's thought, and were clearly dominant during his Heidelberg years, they must be seen alongside his definite Ramist commitments. In fact, as we will see below, Keckermann shared something of Goclenius' own harmonizing and conciliatory attitude. This should come as no surprise, for another of Keckermann's teachers at Heidelberg was none other than Clemens Timpler, Goclenius' own disciple. The two met at Heidelberg and Timpler, who was later to call Keckermann his "disciple and intimate friend",[44] quickly singled him out for private tuition in logic, even going so far as prepare an "elegant epitome" of the *Organon* and a compendium of logic for him.[45]

As with Keckermann, Timpler's own relation to Ramism has been the subject of much debate.[46] While Timpler's love of metaphysics meant that he could not but be critical of Ramus, his innovative combining of logic and metaphysics on the plane of intelligibility suggests his attempt at a deeper realization of Ramus' own aspirations. For the Ramist notion of logic as the science of being and non-being, could easily be transposed into Timpler's new metaphysics of intelligibility. Indeed, in both Timpler and his disciple Jacob Lorhard, as in Goclenius, the systematizing bent of Ramism clearly lent itself to the elaboration of the new discipline of ontology.[47] In this sense, the ontological revolution of early modernity, which Timpler and Keckermann both participated in enthusiastically, can scarcely be detached from Ramus' own complex legacy. Certainly, Timpler himself had no doubt of Ramus' philosophical significance. In his 1606 *Technologia*,

---

[41] Meerhof, "Keckermann", 169–205; Facca, "Keckermann", 201–3.
[42] Meerhof, "Keckermann", 169–70.
[43] Overfield, *Humanism*, 55–65 notes the fifteenth-century clash of the *via antiqua*, *via moderna*, and emerging humanism. Franz Posset, *Johann Reuchlin (1455–1522): A Theological Biography* (Berlin: De Gruyter, 2015) notes extensively the reception of Reuchlin's Neo-Platonism in Heidelberg.
[44] Freedman, "Life", 138–39.
[45] Freedman, "Life", 47–48, 138–39; cf. Keckermann, *Praecognita Logica*, 196.
[46] Freedman, "Life", 271–75.
[47] Joseph S. Freedman, "Timpler, Clemens", in *Encyclopedia of Renaissance Philosophy*, ed. Marco Sgarbi (Cham: Springer International, 2015) and Ulrik Sandborg-Petersen and Peter Øhrstrøm, "Towards an Implementation of Jacob Lorhard's Ontology as a Digital Resource for Historical and Conceptual Research in Early Seventeenth-Century Thought", in *Text Comparison and Digital Creativity: The Production of Presence and Meaning in Digital Text Scholarship*, ed. Wido van Peursen, Ernst D. Thoutenhoofd, and Adriaan van der Weel (Leiden: Brill, 2010), 63–64. See also Hotson, *Reformation of Common Learning*, 172–74.

which offers an important treatise on the liberal arts, he hailed him as having carried out the first modern "reformation of the liberal arts". Offering a careful and nuanced defence of Ramus' application of his three laws of method to all precepts of art, he attacked the "more rigid Aristotelians" for their restriction of them only to syllogistic discussion,[48] and Zabarella for confusing the "method of inventing the arts" with the method of teaching them. Departing from the Zabarellan multiplication of methods, he maintained with Ramus that all arts could be constituted by a single, unified method.[49] In this Ramistic understanding of method and system, he was to exert a fundamental influence on Keckermann's own encyclopaedism, and thus on the development and evolution of early modern systematics.[50]

## 6.2. Methodical Peripateticism

In contrast to his teacher Timpler, who failed to make a mark in Heidelberg, Keckermann's zeal for Aristotle enabled a swift progression through the academic ranks, allowing him to reach the post of Professor of Hebrew by 1600.[51] Yet, although praised as a theologian, it was as a logician that Keckermann first came to European renown. Often called the first "historian of logic", Keckermann proved tireless in collecting and collating logical manuscripts during his time at Heidelberg.[52] The first fruits of this appeared in his *Praecognita Logica* of 1599. In offering a detailed analysis of the "three coryphaei of logic", Aristotle, Ramus, and Lull[53]—discussion of the last of which we will reserve for the next chapter—and their followers, this prepared the way for his own comprehensive treatment of logical system in the *Systema Logicae* of 1600, which Facca has justly praised as his masterpiece.[54] While by his own rigorous standards his logical oeuvre was not to be complete until the publication of his *Gymnasium Logicum* in 1608, these early works reveal the fundamental shape of his methodical Peripateticism.[55] They also conveniently mark out a distinctive logical phase of his philosophical endeavours before his return to Danzig and the onset of a second, encyclopaedic

---

[48] Clemens Timpler, *Technologia*, in *Metaphysicae Systema Methodicum Libris Quinque* (Hanau, 1616), 16–18.
[49] Timpler, *Technologia*, in *Metaphysicae Systema*, 19.
[50] Freedman, "Life", 330–36; "Timpler, Clemens"; and Hotson, *Commonplace Learning*, 153–68.
[51] Freedman, "Career and Writings", 329.
[52] Freedman, "Career and Writings", 323; Hotson, *Commonplace Learning*, 144–45.
[53] Keckermann, *Praecognita Logica*, 11.
[54] Keckermann, *Praecognita Logica*, 8 implies his system of logic is already largely complete. See Facca, "Keckermann", 193.
[55] Bartholomäus Keckermann, *Gymnasium Logicum* (Hanau, 1608). Keckermann's logical *Praecognita*, *Systema* and *Gymnasia* exemplify the threefold pattern which he sought to apply to all the arts, as we will discuss below.

phase. They reveal a man committed to an Aristotelian and Zabarellan understanding of logic, who is critical of Ramism but also highly receptive to new Ramist views of method and system.

Like his teacher Pace, Keckermann was well aware that he was in the midst of a hostile conflict between Ramists and Aristotelians. The *Praecognita Logica* therefore opens with a discussion concerning the controversies between the two camps. In this he eulogizes Ramus as a "man of exalted genius, singular industry and ardent zeal against the entwined spines of the scholastics and Sorbonnists in philosophy and theology" and, in the opinion of many, a Christian martyr. Yet as much as Keckermann clearly admired Ramus, he openly deplored his attacks on Aristotle: "I love Ramus, I honour him, but I do not wish Aristotle's philosophy to be discarded and Ramus' preferred".[56] These are hardly the words of an anti-Ramist! Indeed, Keckermann goes on to say that there are "many most thoughtful men" among the Ramists greatly displeased by his invectives against Aristotle. Among these he singles out the Dutch philosopher Rudolph Snell as the "Prince of Ramists" who attacked Ramus for failing to flesh out the bare-bone precepts of his art with commentaries. Fascinatingly, Keckermann ranges Snell against the so-called pseudo-Ramists—those who remain wedded to Ramus' earlier anti-Aristotelian tracts—taking up his attack on those who "connect together chains of dichotomies" and "ridicule and despise the Peripatetics from on high".[57]

The rest of the *Praecognita* offers three fundamental critiques of Ramism which build on those of Snell and helpfully reveal the contours of his own methodical Peripateticism.[58] The first was that in seeking to "heal the disciplines" Ramus had only succeeded in mutilating and truncating them further. In particular, he attacked Ramus for cutting off, or cutting short, three mainstays of Aristotelian logic: the Predicaments, the syllogism, and logical sophisms, all of which he treated at length in his own *Systema Logicae*.[59] For Keckermann, the predicaments were the root of all logical definition and division[60] and therefore essential for both logical invention and judgement.[61] In abandoning

---

[56] Keckermann, *Praecognita Logica*, "Ad Logicae Studiosos", 12: "De Petro Ramo ita semper indicavi, ut de viro excelsi ingenii, singularis industriae, et ardentis zeli adversus Scholasticorum et Sorbonistarum in Philosophiam et Logicam saepe intextas spinas ... Ramum amo, colo; sed Aristotelis Philosophiam proculcari nolim, et Rameam praeferri".

[57] Keckermann, *Praecognita Logica*, 14–16.

[58] The discussion in the next paragraphs draws on Simon J. G. Burton, "From Minority Discourse to Universal Method: Polish Chapters in the Evolution of Ramism", in *Protestant Majorities and Minorities in Early Modern Europe: Confessional Boundaries and Contested Identities*, ed. Simon J. G. Burton, Michał Choptiany, and Piotr Wilczek (Göttingen: Vandenhoeck & Ruprecht, 2019), 61–90. I am grateful to the publishers Vandenhoeck & Ruprecht for permission to reuse this material.

[59] Keckermann, *Praecognita Logica*, 12, 251–57. For Keckermann's treatment of these see *Systema Logicae*, 85–119, 399–580.

[60] Bartholomäus Keckermann, *Systema Logicae Tribus Libris Adornatum* (Hanau, 1603), 29–30, 35–36. This is the second edition of the work.

[61] Keckermann, *Systema Logicae*, 1–5, 30.

them, Ramist logic severely handicapped itself. To attempt to replace them with Agricolan *loci* was to no avail, since these are themselves entirely dependent on the predicaments as the "little places and repositories of the universe of things".[62] Likewise, to cut short the syllogism was to remove the central plank of all proof and demonstration. Indeed, Keckermann attacked Ramus in no uncertain terms for attempting to replace Aristotle's sophisticated syllogistic machinery with his own all-encompassing theory of method. While he recognized that the topics or places could be used in logical proof,[63] and in the spirit of Agricola and Ramus even sought to develop his own universal topical method,[64] he nevertheless found Ramus' account of demonstration woefully inadequate.[65] An even graver sin was Ramus' later removal of sophisms, which Keckermann held "miserably mutilated the body of logic and gave occasion to his followers to hack to pieces the minds of its students".[66]

It is no surprise that Keckermann should view Ramus, in compromising Aristotelian accounts of definition and proof, as undermining the ability of logic to function as a technical, scientific discipline, reducing it to a mere "poet's logic".[67] In particular, he found the Ramist reframing of logic in terms of dialectical invention and judgement, itself part of a wider Renaissance "rhetorical turn", deeply problematic. Against both Agricola and Ramus, he argued that invention and judgement should not be treated as two separate, really distinct, parts of logic but rather, in Aristotelian fashion, as two different aspects of "one and the same most simple operation of the mind".[68] Following Aristotle, he distinguished logic according to three different acts of the mind—the apprehension of simple terms, the formation of mental propositions through composition and division, and the syllogistic and methodical connection of different propositions—dividing his own logic accordingly into three books answering to this division.[69] In doing so, Keckermann added that he has "preferred trichotomy to dichotomy", since three is the perfect number. Here we find just a hint, which we shall return to below, of a connection between his trichotomous logic and the Trinity.

Keckermann's second major complaint is that Ramus mixes and confuses the disciplines. In fact, he viewed Ramist logic as a confused jumble of principles taken from grammar, dialectic, rhetoric, physics, and metaphysics.[70] In

---

[62] Keckermann, *Systema Logicae*, 30.
[63] Keckermann, *Systema Logicae*, 529–30.
[64] Keckermann, *Systema Logicae*, 469–71. See also Stefan Heßbrüggen-Walter, "Thinking about Persons: *Loci Personarum* in Humanist Dialectic between Agricola and Keckermann", *History and Philosophy of Logic* 38.1 (2017): 3–4, 10–17.
[65] Keckermann, *Praecognita Logica*, 254–55.
[66] Keckermann, *Praecognita Logica*, 150, 254–55.
[67] Keckermann, *Praecognita Logica*, 148, 217–20.
[68] Keckermann, *Praecognita Logica*, 41–44, 220–26.
[69] Keckermann, *Systema Logicae*, 3–4. His critique of Agricola's and Ramus' assigning of invention to the first part of logic is to be found in Keckermann, *Praecognita Logica*, 220–26.
[70] Keckermann, *Praecognita Logica*, 217–20, 252.

particular, Keckermann was strongly opposed to the Ramist tendency to swallow up other disciplines, especially metaphysics, in logic. While he believed logic, as the "sole mistress of every order", was essential for shaping these disciplines into coherent systems, this did not mean that it should seek to arrogate their roles.[71] Drawing on Scaliger and Zabarella, he argued logic handles being not primarily as metaphysics does as the "science of being *qua* being", but only derivatively and instrumentally as it becomes the subject for logical reasoning. Ranging himself with Zabarella against the entirety of the scholastic tradition, he stoutly maintained that logic was not properly a part of philosophy at all but rather its common instrument.[72]

Like Goclenius, he sought to give precision to this by distinguishing metaphysics and logic as disciplines handling first and second intentions respectively. In this he naturally opposed the Ramist attempt to ground logic on first intentions.[73] Further distinguishing himself from the Scotistic treatment of intentions to be found in many Ramists, he offered an explicitly Thomistic treatment of these, drawn from Aquinas and the fifteenth-century Dominican Girolamo Savonarola. In this view, logical intentions, as the "shadows of things", do not directly represent things themselves, or something inherent in things, but are rather intellectual norms by which we form and order things conceptually.[74] While rooted in reality, logic must be seen as at one further remove from it—contrasting with the stronger Realism of other Ramists.

Departing from his mentor Timpler, Keckermann also emphatically rejected the Ramist claim that there was a single method for treating all arts and sciences.[75] While he affirmed the need to ground logical method in the order of nature,[76] he believed the variety of disciplines was already signalled in the diversity of their second intentions, something which the Ramists completely missed in their attempt to force them all to fit the same logical mould.[77] Instead, Keckermann self-consciously followed Scaliger and Zabarella, "the greatest

---

[71] Keckermann, *Systema Logicae*, 66–69.

[72] Bartholomäus Keckermann, *Praecognitorum Philosophicorum Libri Duo* [hereafter *PP*] (Hanau, 1612), 56–57. William F. Edwards, "The Logic of Jacopo Zabarella (1533–1589)" (PhD Dissertation, Columbia University, 1960), 110–34 notes that Zabarella's instrumental logic is directed against the Scotist view of logic as a science, but Keckermann singles out the Thomists for attack.

[73] Bartholomäus Keckermann, *Scientiae Metaphysicae Compendiosum Systema* (Hanau, 1611), 54–56; cf. Goclenius, *Analyses*, 14–15. Keckermann, *Praecognita Logica* 111, 216–17 attacks those seeking a logic of first intentions or a mixed logic of first and second intentions. A good example of this mixed Ramist logic is found in Polanus, *Syntagma Logicum*, 7–10, 84–86.

[74] Keckermann, *Praecognita Logica*, 257–61; cf. Girolamo Savonarola, *Epitome Universae Philosophiae* (Wittenberg, 1596), 6–7.

[75] Keckermann, *Praecognita Logica*, 149–51.

[76] Keckermann, *Praecognita Logica*, 149–51.

[77] Keckermann, *Praecognita Logica*, 259.

architect of methods", in offering a basic twofold division of method into synthetic and analytic. The synthetic method appropriate for theoretical disciplines was a priori and proceeded from a cause or principle to its effects. By contrast, the analytic method appropriate for practical disciplines followed the order of means and end. Although synthetic method followed Ramus in proceeding from universals to particulars, analytic method inverted the ideal Ramist order in proceeding from particulars to universals.[78] For Keckermann, Ramism's superficial and premature Realism and its monolithic account of method thus forecloses a proper engagement with reality.

Keckermann's third complaint was perhaps the most serious of all. Demonstrating that he had fully imbibed the critique of Ursinus and the Heidelberg anti-Ramists, he held that pure Ramism was inadequate as a theological method.[79] Due to its "truncated" form and antipathy to metaphysics, he saw Ramism as preventing the proper definition of key theological notions essential for the defence of Trinitarian orthodoxy. Indeed, he argued that the Ramist penchant for dichotomies risks reducing the Trinity itself to a series of dualities.[80] In the same way, its watered-down account of demonstration and jettisoning of sophisms rendered it unable to defend Reformed doctrine from sophisticated logical attack. While sharing the Ramist aspiration for a systematic theology, he could still maintain that Ramism's insistence on a one-size-fits-all method was problematic in handling a practical discipline like theology.[81]

For someone who had experienced all the strife of the confessionally divided contexts of Danzig and the Saxon universities, these were clearly serious problems. Yet while undoubtedly major objections, there was no reason why these had to prove devastating. For Keckermann firmly believed, with Snell, that Ramism contained within it the potential to adapt and transform for the better. There can be no doubt that he proved a weighty critic of Ramus' logic, but it is important to understand that he did so as one who loved, and even cherished, his method. Indeed, removed from the comfortable and somewhat cosy context of Heidelberg Aristotelianism, with its all too easy assumptions of superiority, he was soon to find Ramism indispensable in developing a thoroughgoing Christian reform of the disciplines and a far-reaching theological vision of education.[82]

---

[78] Keckermann, *Praecognita Logica*, 150–51; cf. Joseph S. Freedman, *Philosophy and the Arts in Central Europe, 1500–1700: Teachings and Texts at Schools and Universities* (Abingdon: Routledge, 2018), 1581, 1596 and Hotson, *Commonplace Learning*, 144–52. For Zabarella see Gilbert, *Renaissance Concepts*, 167–73.
[79] Hotson, *Commonplace Learning*, 142–43.
[80] Keckermann, *Praecognita Logica*, 135.
[81] Keckermann, *Praecognita Logica*, 149–57.
[82] Hotson, *Commonplace Learning*, 153–68.

## 6.3. Christian Philosophy

In 1602 Keckermann resigned his Professorship of Hebrew at Heidelberg in order to take up the much humbler position of Professor of Philosophy in Danzig. The circumstances surrounding this dramatic move, leading to Keckermann's abandonment of preferment at one of Europe's most prestigious universities, have been the cause of considerable speculation.[83] While they owe much to his own desire to spend more time on philosophical study and be of service to his "fatherland", his move also came in response to an urgent plea from the city council to come back to teach at the ailing Reformed gymnasium, which was increasingly threatened both by Lutheran and Counter-Reformation forces.[84] Charged with this sacred duty, Keckermann lost no time in proceeding to rewrite the entire philosophical curriculum—a monumental task which eventually sent him to an early grave in 1609.[85]

While Keckermann may have airily renounced his Danzig Ramism at Heidelberg as a juvenile disease he had outgrown, it is remarkable how quickly he turned back to the method of his youth on returning to his native city.[86] Determining to cover the whole of philosophy in just three years, beginning with logic and physics in the first year, proceeding to mathematics and metaphysics in the second year and concluding with the practical disciplines of ethics and politics, his hope was that such a swift education would enable the efficient training of the new army of ministers, lawyers, and civil servants necessary to keep the Reformed community in Danzig afloat.[87] Keckermann's decision to return to Danzig and the beginning of a new, encyclopaedic phase in his work must therefore be seen, as Hotson insightfully suggests, in light of a pressing need to defend and advance Reformed confessionalization in beleaguered Royal Prussia.[88] A fundamental aspect of this, as Muller has revealed, were the fierce contemporary debates raging over the place of philosophy in theology, at the heart of which was renewed controversy over the Ramist notion of Christian philosophy.[89]

We have already seen how much of Keckermann's academic formation occurred in the shadow of the conflict between Philippists and Gnesio-Lutherans. In 1598 the ever-simmering tensions erupted once again when Daniel Hofmann, the Lutheran Professor of Theology at Helmstedt, launched a savage attack on philosophy for its corruption of theology, accusing all philosophers of being the

---

[83] Hotson, *Commonplace Learning*, 154.
[84] Hotson, *Commonplace Learning*, 153–54; Freedman, "Career and Writings", 307–9.
[85] Hotson, *Commonplace Learning*, 156–57.
[86] Meerhof, "Keckermann", 170 and Hotson, *Commonplace Learning*, 137–57.
[87] Hotson, *Commonplace Learning*, 137–57.
[88] Hotson, *Commonplace Learning*, 153–57.
[89] Muller, "*Vera Philosophia*", 341–65.

"patriarchs of the heretics".[90] While such attacks were not unknown, Hofmann raised the stakes significantly by enlisting Luther in support of the controversial theory of double truth—that what is true in philosophy can be false in theology, and vice-versa.[91] Far from being a mere jurisdictional dispute between philosophers and theologians, Hofmann's attack struck at the foundations of the entire Protestant scholastic enterprise. It is no surprise that it raised a storm of controversy.

One of the most important responses to Hofmann came from Otto Casmann in his 1601 *Modesta Assertio*.[92] As a prominent Ramist proponent of "Christian philosophy", with close links to Helmstedt, it was natural enough for Casmann to become involved in this *Hofmannstreit*. However, looking closer we find that he had a definite personal stake. For Hofmann had embarrassingly found support for his theory of double truth in Fortunatus Crell, a leading Reformed proponent of Zabarellan logic. While Crell believed that this position actually gave more honour to Scripture, elevating it above the claims of mere human reason,[93] he was hotly opposed by many of his fellow Protestants, including most notably Goclenius and his disciple Casmann, who were deeply worried about this influx of Paduan Averroism into the German Church. In his 1598 *Cosmopoeia*, itself an important exposition of the Mosaic physics, Casmann had mounted an explicit attack on Crell's doctrine of *duplex veritas* and this was certainly known to Hofmann. While Hofmann may well have expected support from the Helmstedt Ramists, who shared his antipathy to Aristotelian logic and philosophy, he thus soon found himself under attack from two of the leading figures in the German Ramist movement.[94]

In this light, as Zornitsa Radeva insightfully suggests, Casmann's *Modesta Assertio* should be seen as effectively a two-pronged attack against Hofmann and Crell, proposing a *via media* between a complete rejection of philosophy and a complete endorsement of its autonomy.[95] Casmann had no hesitation in proclaiming double truth to be diabolical and ardently maintained that there can be no fight, or contradiction, between "healthy philosophy" and theology, since they coincide in proclaiming one and the same truth.[96] Indeed, as rivulets both trace their origin from the fontal plenitude of "omniscient wisdom". For Casmann, this account of philosophy notably had a definite Trinitarian

---

[90] Pietro Daniel Omodeo, "The European Career of a Scottish Mathematician and Physician", in *Duncan Liddel (1561–1613): Networks of Polymathy and the Northern European Renaissance*, ed. Pietro Daniel Omodeo in collaboration with Karin Friedrich (Leiden: Brill, 2016), 82–83.

[91] Zornitsa Radeva, "At the Origins of a Tenacious Narrative: Jacob Thomasius and the History of Double Truth", *Intellectual History Review* 29.3 (2019): 417–38.

[92] Radeva, "Origins", 423.

[93] Radeva, "Origins", 421.

[94] Omodeo, "European Career", 84.

[95] Radeva, "Origins", 423–24.

[96] Otto Casmann, *Philosophiae Christianae et Verae ... Modesta Assertio* (Frankfurt, 1601), 40–41.

dimension to it, since the Logos, in whom "all the treasures of wisdom and knowledge are hidden", is himself the eternal wisdom of the Father and it is the "Spirit of Wisdom" who "works every wisdom in all the wise".[97] While Casmann, like Snell, warned against the danger of pseudo-Ramists in his *Modesta Assertio*, his programme of a methodical Christian philosophy clearly has deep Ramist roots.

As Muller points out, Keckermann cannot have been unaware of these issues.[98] In fact, all the evidence suggests that they touched him to the quick. Despite his personal admiration for Crell, he was deeply concerned about the growing influence of Italian Averroism, expressed above all in Pietro Pomponazzi's attack on the immortality of the soul.[99] The title of Keckermann's celebrated work "true philosophy nowhere fights with holy theology", which is specifically addressed to the "controversy raged by some at this time concerning the fight of philosophy and theology", echoes Casmann's own claim in his *Modesta Assertio*.[100] To an extent that has perhaps not been realized, Casmann's *Modesta Assertio* became a model for Keckermann's own Christian encyclopaedism.

It is also significant that Keckermann's return to Danzig coincided with the height of the Hofmann controversy. Many of the city's ardent Gnesio-Lutheran ministers could be expected to support Hofmann, and Keckermann was soon also forced to justify his own confident philosophical stance to rector Fabricius, who was likely nervous about stoking further conflict.[101] For his part, Keckermann himself was in no doubt that Lutheran theology flew in the face of sound reason and sound philosophy. As early as his *Systema Logicae*, a work which as Facca suggests was profoundly shaped by his conflict with Lutheran "Ubiquitarians",[102] he had already roundly attacked Lutherans for their violation of the principle of non-contradiction, and especially for holding it "nothing absurd that two contradictories are at once true".[103] The controversy about double truth can only have fuelled his deepest suspicions. With the Reformed on the retreat in Danzig, it became more important than ever to articulate and defend a carefully worked out philosophical synthesis.

Keckermann's own response to all these issues and his definitive statement of the relation between philosophy and theology can be found in his 1607 *Praecognita Philosophica*. Intended as the introduction to his entire Danzig encyclopaedic curriculum this was notably published together with his

---

[97] Casmann, *Modesta Assertio*, 46.
[98] Muller, "*Vera Philosophia*", 347–48.
[99] Keckermann, *PP*, 82.
[100] Bartholomäus Keckermann, *Vera Philosophia Cum S. Theologia Nusquam Pugnat*, in *PP*, 181ff. Radeva, "Origins", 429–30 points out that Thomasius later linked Keckermann and Casmann together.
[101] Bryćko, "Danzig Academic Gymnasium", 344.
[102] Facca, "Keckermann", 190–92.
[103] Keckermann, *Systema Logicae*, 359–60.

disputation against double truth. Echoing Casmann, Keckermann held that "philosophy rises from the first wisdom infinite and most perfect, as if a ray from a solar body". This "first wisdom", he adds, "is of God and the divine Spirit".[104] Immediately therefore we find Keckermann's account of philosophy couched in a definite exemplaristic and illuminationist context, as well as an implicit Trinitarian one. In fact, he clearly maintained that philosophy was a singular "gift of God" and so stemmed from his common grace given to all humanity. Ultimately, there could be no such thing as a philosophy independent of God.

For Keckermann, philosophy had an important twofold motivation. Firstly, as we will return to below, it was motivated by a desire to recover the original perfection of humanity lost through the Fall. Secondly, it was motivated by a sense of wonder and delight in the created order and the desire to trace God's footsteps in creation back to his "inestimable power, wisdom and goodness".[105] We thus see his wisdom in the "beautiful order and proportion of things", his power in the creation of all things, and his goodness in that all things have an end and a purpose. In exemplaristic fashion, Keckermann holds that both the universe and the human soul are "most clear" and "most lucid" mirrors in which we see God's "native face".[106] Indeed, for Keckermann, as for Pico, humans must be regarded as the "image and compendium" of the universe, uniquely poised between the physical and spiritual realms.[107] Drawing on an Augustinian and Franciscan model which we will see amplified below, he could even hold that philosophy's scope extended to the Trinity, with human intellect, the soul and its faculties and the nature of solar rays all illustrating this mystery.[108]

For Keckermann, it is clear that God must be considered efficient, exemplar, and final cause of his creation. Drawing on Augustine and Scotus, he defined exemplar as an "idea or form which is imitated by the intention of the agent", whether by God or by man.[109] Notably this exemplarism carried through into an important twofold account of truth as either the "harmony and congruence of the intellect and words with things" or the "harmony and congruence of things themselves with ideas in the divine mind".[110] As a Realist, with a Scotist tinge, he held that individuals have within them a universal nature and that God has distinct ideas of both individuals and universals.[111] Following a definite Ramist and

---

[104] Keckermann, *PP*, 38.
[105] Keckermann, *PP*, 49–53, 77–78.
[106] Keckermann, *PP*, 77–78, 82.
[107] Keckermann, *PP*, 83.
[108] Keckermann, *PP*, 78–79.
[109] Keckermann, *Systema Logicae*, 135–36.
[110] Bartholomäus Keckermann, *Systema S.S. Theologiae Tribus Libris Adornatum* (Hanau, 1610), 119.
[111] Keckermann, *Systema Theologiae*, 136; *Scientiae Metaphysicae*, 45–52; and *Systema Logicae*, 46–49. While Keckermann praises Aquinas' discussion of universals (*Systema Logicae*, 48) his discussion of genus, species, and individual seems to assume a formal distinction (*Systema Logicae*, 257–60) and he seems to reluctantly accept the Scotist term *haecceitas* (*Scientiae Metaphysicae*,

Christian Platonist trajectory, truth becomes the congruence of things, whether simple natures or complex propositions, with ideas in the mind of God.[112]

Ultimately, for Keckermann, philosophy and theology are not independent, or semi-independent, disciplines but are radically entwined. While he greatly admired Aquinas' account of the relation of philosophy and theology set out in the first question of his *Summa Theologiae*,[113] and resisted stoutly the commixing of the disciplines,[114] his conviction that theology is necessary to both emend and complete philosophy pushes beyond this to an Augustinian and Franciscan model of Christian philosophy.[115] Indeed, as Muller suggests, Keckermann's own resolution of the problem of double truth comes close to that of Bonaventure and the English Franciscan John Pecham, a leading opponent of Aquinas.[116] For Keckermann, "true philosophy" and theology are reciprocally connected in precisely the same way as the transcendental affections of being and truth.[117] The truth of philosophy is not only dependent on the being of theology but mutually convertible with it. Of course, this does not mean that philosophy and theology are identical. For they differ in end and purpose, and contrast in philosophy's use of logical instruments compared to theology' reliance in argumentation on the "hyperphysical" force of the Holy Spirit.[118] Nevertheless, Keckermann resists the conclusion that philosophy and theology differ simply in terms of faith and reason, since "philosophy is not only established on human reasons" but also on divine truth.[119]

While Keckermann has not generally been seen as espousing a scriptural philosophy it seems clear that that is exactly what is entailed by his position. In Ramist fashion he construes Scripture as divine testimony, holding that such testimony is the essential truth of God himself and is therefore self-authenticating (*axiopistos*).[120] The same exemplaristic and illuminationistic relation that governs the relation of philosophy and theology also holds between philosophy

---

28–29). Heßbrüggen-Walter, "*Loci Personarum*", 15–16 assumes a more Thomistic framework of individuation in terms of accidents, but for Keckermann existence, the individuating principle, is not accidental to essence (*Scientiae Metaphysicae*, 81–83). Rather, he holds that it is modally distinct (*Systema Logicae*, 277).

[112] Keckermann, *Systema Logicae*, 302–3; *Systema Theologiae*, 119. Meerhof, "Keckermann", 175–78 notes that Keckermann identified Ramus with Plato. While he emphasizes Keckermann's strong preference for Aristotelianism, this need not exclude an important influence of Platonism.
[113] Keckermann, *PP*, 110.
[114] Keckermann, *Praecognita Logica*, 101–2.
[115] Keckermann, *PP*, 103–5. The shift in tone from the *Praecognita Logica* to *Praecognita Philosophica* may mark a shift in attitude.
[116] Muller, *PRRD*, 1.384–85.
[117] Keckermann, *PP*, 106.
[118] Keckermann, *PP*, 106, 122–24.
[119] Keckermann, *PP*, 113.
[120] Keckermann, *Systema Logicae*, 412; *Systema Theologiae*, 120.

and Scripture. Philosophy can thus be grounded on the truth of Scripture as much as the truth of logical argument. In the *Praecognita* Keckermann notes that of all the more recent philosophers the Ramists especially attribute to philosophy "the study of charity, the love of truth, modesty, humility, order, perspicuity, brevity, candour and the study of peace".[121] He also praised the scriptural reformation of the disciplines which had been taking place "in these recent times" in which many matters of philosophy had been emended and illuminated by the Word of God.[122] While Keckermann is not so explicit as Casmann in advocating for a Christian logic or a Christian metaphysics, he clearly belongs to the same Ramist tradition. Notably, as we will now turn to, this same exemplaristic and illuminationist impulse governs his Christian encyclopaedism and carries through into a thoroughgoing, if implicit, Trinitarian reform of philosophy.

## 6.4. Encyclopaedism and Eden

Echoing his teacher Timpler, Keckermann affirmed at the beginning of the *Praecognita Philosophica* that "method is the soul and form of disciplines, without which things do not cohere nor the thoughts of men concerning things".[123] From the beginning his entire encyclopaedic enterprise is therefore framed in the context of method. Transgressing the Zabarellan distinction between order and method, Keckermann effectively identified method as the "orderly union of cohering things represented to the human mind", seeing it as following a broad Ramist sweep from more general to more special.[124] While Zabarella had vocally rejected the notion of method as the ordering or disposition of parts and whole, for Keckermann it was absolutely fundamental.[125] Likewise, while acknowledging the important Zabarellan distinction between method as a system and as a habit, he actually inverted Zabarella's order of priority, identifying method, with Timpler, as a "system of useful precepts" and philosophy as a whole as a "system of ordered liberal arts" or a "system of wisdom".[126]

In the *Praecognita* Keckermann thus stoutly maintained that the way of teaching which forms a method or system as if "in an idea" (i.e. according to the discipline's nature and scope) is "far to be preferred" to that "textual" mode of teaching relying on authors and commentators.[127] Since every truth can be regarded as a "ray of the divine mind coming forth from the Holy Spirit", it

---

[121] Keckermann, *PP*, 103.
[122] Keckermann, *PP*, 103–4.
[123] Keckermann, *PP*, 1.
[124] Keckermann, *PP*, 1–2.
[125] Keckermann, *PP*, 15; cf. Zabarella, *On Methods*, 1.3 (p. 21).
[126] Keckermann, *PP*, 13, 16–17.
[127] Keckermann, *PP*, 134.

follows that method should be seen in Ramist fashion as the concrete embodiment of the idea of a discipline found in the mind of God.[128] In fact, Keckermann clearly assumes an exemplaristic imaging relation even within the different disciplines in the encyclopaedia. Thus "logic has itself to philosophy as an image represented in a mirror to the face which it represents". For logic handles the "images and simulacra of philosophical things as instruments of knowing". Yet logic also has express images of theological things and in some respects is an even more excellent instrument of theology than philosophy.[129] Indeed, realized in encyclopaedic form, the whole of philosophy can be seen as an image of divine truth itself.

Keckermann's systematic and exemplaristic handling of philosophy thus signals his intimate connection to the Ramistic encyclopaedic tradition, especially as embodied in the *Technologia* of his teacher Timpler. For as much as he dissented vocally from Ramus on the application of methods to individual disciplines,[130] his own threefold pattern of *praecognita*, *systemata*, and *gymnasia*—which he employed as a blueprint for philosophy both as a whole and with respect to its individual disciplines—must be seen, as Hotson persuasively argues, as an expansion and modification of Ramus' basic methodical template.[131] Thus *praecognita* provides the necessary principles of a discipline, *systemata* emphasizes their Ramist methodical ordering elaborated according to Aristotelian "canons" and rules, and *gymnasia* corresponds to the Ramist emphasis on the "use" of the discipline.[132] Indeed, the whole programme closely matches Snell's desire to flesh out the basic Ramist system with precepts and commentaries,[133] and it is notable that Keckermann had nothing but praise for those who seek to combine the best of Ramist and Aristotelian principles in order to reach the "solid and full form of philosophy".[134]

Confirming the Ramist nature of Keckermann's encyclopaedia was the possibility of presenting its entire structure in a series of Ramist charts organized methodically according to a pattern of dichotomies. Examples of this are evident in Keckermann's own works but notably it was Goclenius who first "resolved" Keckermann's logic into a system of dichotomous charts. He was soon followed in this endeavour by a major posthumous editing project organized by Johann Heinrich Alsted and carried out by Keckermann's devoted students. As Hotson has shown, it proved remarkably easy for them to combine all his *praecognita*,

[128] Keckermann, *PP*, 113.
[129] Keckermann, *PP*, 111–12.
[130] Keckermann, *PP*, 1–2. In affirming the Aristotelian dimensions of this Keckermann followed the mature Ramus.
[131] Hotson, *Commonplace Learning*, 148–51, 157–65.
[132] Keckermann, *PP*, 134–35, 161–62.
[133] Keckermann, *Praecognita Logica*, 12–15.
[134] Keckermann, *PP*, 161–62.

*systemata*, and *gymnasia* into a single, comprehensive methodical work, which Alsted fittingly titled *Systema Systematum*—a "system of systems". Framed as this was by the *Praecognita Philosophica* the whole encyclopaedia was thus placed in an exemplaristic context of Christian philosophy, as Keckermann had himself intended.[135]

Following Timpler's insight that the perfection of man was the end and goal of philosophy according to which all of its individual disciplines must be oriented, Keckermann sought to organize his encyclopaedia according to the perfecting of different faculties of the soul.[136] According to a Timpleran template he thus defined philosophy as an integral whole consisting of six disciplines, the three theoretical disciplines of metaphysics, physics, and mathematics and the three practical disciplines of ethics, oeconomics, and politics. In these terms, the theoretical sciences of metaphysics, physics, and mathematics were intended for the perfecting of the speculative dimension of the human intellect and the practical disciplines of ethics, oeconomics, and politics for the perfecting of the active dimension of the human intellect and the will. In identifying the practical disciplines as prudences and not sciences, Keckermann departed from Timpler, in favour of Zabarella's sharp twofold distinction between the analytic method appropriate for practical disciplines and the synthetic method appropriate for theoretical disciplines.[137] Once again, Keckermann's methodical Peripateticism effectively blended Ramist and Zabarellan methods to attain his own unique, encyclopaedic, synthesis of philosophy.

Philosophy therefore unites and joins "diverse sciences and prudences in a most sweet harmony of common principles on which all sciences and prudences depend" and is intended for the perfection of the human intellect and will.[138] In this, metaphysics takes first place as both "most common and general" and as postulating the (Ramist) progression from general to special on which all method is grounded.[139] Although relegated to an instrumental role, logic too has a special place, becoming ubiquitous in all philosophical reasoning. For since logical method is the form of all the philosophical disciplines it follows that the whole of philosophy can be described as *logicam utentem*, namely "logic applied to things".[140]

Indeed, logic had a special dignity in restoring the image of God in man, and Keckermann held it to be its "greatest glory" that it should strive to restore the "divine twilight" in us to a "brighter light" and "heal the failing of our mind"

---

[135] Hotson, *Commonplace Learning*, 157–65.
[136] Timpler, *Technologia*, 5–6.
[137] Keckermann, *PP*, 140–41.
[138] Keckermann, *PP*, 15.
[139] Keckermann, *PP*, 139.
[140] Keckermann, *PP*, 58.

so far as it is possible to do in this life.[141] Before the Fall, Keckermann held that human reason had been perfect, containing all the principles of knowledge within itself. It ability to deduce conclusions from general principles almost instantaneously meant that it was able to cover at a stroke all possible knowledge, relating it to God as its ground and origin and directing all human actions to him with effortless ease. Such a perfectly ordered state of affairs was shattered by the Fall, reducing reason from being a Godlike power of universal scope to a pale shadow of itself, and forcing humans to limp through the disciplines from one painful syllogism to another.[142]

It was the encyclopaedia which represented an important attempt to mend the damage occasioned by the Fall. In restoring the instrumental character of reason towards its original perfection, logic also enables the methodical ordering of the theoretical sciences of metaphysics, physics, and mathematics and the practical prudences of ethics, oeconomics, and politics. In doing so, the encyclopaedia impresses habitually on the mind the ideal order that these disciplines have in the mind of God, thus perfecting the human intellect and will in cognition and action and restoring the fractured unity of the soul.[143] Following the Ramist account of the *prisca philosophia*, Keckermann also sought to trace the origin of all the arts and sciences, including logic, back to Noah-Prometheus and the biblical patriarchs, thus reinforcing his understanding of the divine inspiration of the encyclopaedia.[144] Following a long Augustinian and Franciscan tradition, Keckermann's understanding of the divine character of logic and its Adamic origins thus unfolds into a vision of the encyclopaedia as the road back to Eden.[145]

## 6.5. Towards a Trinitarian Philosophy

For Keckermann, there was also an important, if implicit, Trinitarian dimension to this encyclopaedism which harmonized well with the broader Augustinian and Franciscan contours of his Christian philosophy. Since philosophy proceeded as a ray from the divine mind it followed for him that it should come to bear the hallmark of its Trinitarian origin in both its structure and dynamic. We may see this first of all in his threefold understanding of logic in which the mutual interaction of invention and judgement in the rational analysis of discourse can be

---

[141] Cited from Hotson, *Alsted*, 68.
[142] Keckermann, *Praecognita Logica*, 57–59; *Systema Logicae*, 2–3; *Systema Theologiae*, 215–33; cf. Hotson, *Alsted*, 66–82. Cited from Burton, "Minority Discourse", 70.
[143] Keckermann, *PP*, 37–39; cf. Hotson, *Alsted*, 66–82.
[144] Keckermann, *Praecognita Logica*, 77–78.
[145] Keckermann, *Praecognita Logica*, 76–77; *PP*, 40, 113. For Ramus' own comparison between Prometheus and Noah see Bruyère, *Méthode et dialectique*, 196, 290–93.

seen as dimly mirroring the Trinity. Indeed, Keckermann held that reason had a natural openness towards the Trinity. While acknowledging the Trinity to be a mystery above all human understanding, he still held it possible for reason to demonstrate its truth.[146]

Pressing beyond the wall of separation which Aquinas had erected between philosophy and theology, Keckermann's assertion of the demonstrability of the Trinity resembles much more closely the Franciscan and Scotist attempt to derive the Trinity from the infinite and intrinsic perfection of God, or even more the Lullist recourse to "necessary reasons".[147] Significantly, for our understanding of his encyclopaedism, he grounded this claim in the reflexive dynamic of human intellect and will imaging the Trinity. While his specific account of this derived from Aquinas' *Summa Contra Gentiles*, and reflects that earlier, more Neo-Platonic, phase of Aquinas' thought, it becomes expressed within the framework of a Scotistic metaphysics of modes which turns out to underpin his entire Christian philosophy.[148]

In the *Systema Logicae* Keckermann had attacked the Scotists for their subtle distinctions, even going so far as to compare them to the hated Ubiquitarians.[149] However, in his calmer moments he was willing to concede that not only had he profited from Scotus' account of distinctions, but that he even preferred it, in some respects, to that of Aquinas.[150] In particular, although he espoused Aquinas' account of the rational distinction of the divine attributes he drew on Scotus' understanding of the modal distinction, which he significantly classed with the formal distinction as intrinsic, real and *ex natura rei*, to characterize the persons of the Trinity as transcendental, and relational, "modes of existence".[151]

Significantly, Keckermann also drew on this Scotistic modal treatment of the Trinity in his innovative reworking of scholastic metaphysics. Paralleling the

---

[146] Keckermann, *Systema Theologiae*, 16, 33. For a detailed discussion of this see Simon J. G. Burton, "Bartłomiej Keckermann o trynitarnej naturze rozumu: Źródła scholastyczne i ramistyczne" [Bartholomäus Keckermann on the Trinitarian Shape of Reason: Scholastic and Ramist Paradigms] (trans. Michał Choptiany), in *Antytrynitaryzm w Pierwszej Rzeczypospolitej w kontekście europejskim: Źródła—rozwój—oddziaływanie* [Anti-Trinitarianism in the Polish-Lithuanian Republic in a European Context], ed. Michał Choptiany and Piotr Wilczek (Warsaw: Wydawnictwa Uniwersytetu Warszawskiego, 2017), 99–119. The following paragraphs draw on this study with permission.

[147] Muller, *PRRD*, 4.162–64 and Facca, "Keckermann", 195–96.

[148] Compare, for example, Keckermann, *Systema Theologiae*, 24–25 with Thomas Aquinas, *Summa Contra Gentiles*, ed. Joseph Kenny, OP (New York: Hanover House, 1955–57), IV.11.2–5 (https://isidore.co/aquinas/english/ContraGentiles.htm). For Keckermann's Scotist and Trinitarian metaphysics of modes see *Systema Theologiae*, 16–19. Muller, *PRRD*, 4.163 also points to his blending of Thomist and Scotist conceptualities.

[149] Keckermann, *Systema Logicae*, 219. Meerhof, "Keckermann", 184 notes that he "severely censured" Scotus as well as Lull.

[150] Keckermann, *Systema Logicae*, 278–81; *Praecognita Logica*, 105–6.

[151] Keckermann, *Systema Theologiae*, 16–19, 56–61, 90; cf. *Systema Logicae*, 277–82. Like Scotus, Keckermann conceives modes of being by analogy to degrees of intensity of heat and light. See further Scotus, *Ord.* 1 d. 8 p. 1 q. 3 n. 138–40 (Vatican, IV.222–23) and King, "Scotus on Metaphysics", 25–26.

Franciscan emanation model of the Trinity, or indeed the emanation of the soul's powers from its essence, he argued that the transcendental affections of being flow from being itself but yet remain really identical with it, and so are to be understood as intrinsic modes of being.[152] Indeed, Keckermann went even further than this in his Trinitarian reconfiguring of the transcendentals, arguing that just as the divine intellect understands itself eternally as "most perfect being and most true truth" so the will wills itself as "highest and most perfect good".[153] Rooted within the dynamics of God's own uni-triune being, truth and goodness are thus defined ultimately according to their conformity to divine intellect and will.[154]

Keckermann was thus not only an important participant in the early modern transcendental reorientation of metaphysics, whose deep Scotist roots have been exposed by Honnefelder,[155] but was also, following in the wake of Scaliger, Polanus, and Szegedinus, a pioneer in a new Trinitarian understanding of Christian philosophy. Grounded in his Trinitarian and transcendental understanding, Keckermann's Scotistic treatment of modes expanded to structure the whole of his metaphysics. It undoubtedly gave a new sophistication and depth to his exemplaristic treatment of logic and metaphysics and their relation. It also revealed an important Trinitarian coordination of philosophy and theology. For the convertibility of these disciplines is now revealed as having its ground in the Trinity itself. For the being and truth which is the object of the theoretical sciences flows naturally into the goodness which is the object of the practical sciences and thus into theology itself. In perfecting intellect and will in the image of the Trinity, the encyclopaedia not only elevates the mind to knowledge of God but "wonderfully inflames" the will to love him, renewing the soul in the image of the Trinity.[156]

### 6.6. Therapeutic Theology and Architectonic Politics

For Keckermann philosophy and theology were always intended to be united together in the reform of Church and society. Writing in the preface to his *Praecognita*, Georg Pauli, the assistant-rector of the Danzig Gymnasium, thus described the "singular utility" of his encyclopaedic project for Church and

---

[152] Keckermann, *Scientiae Metaphysicae*, 29–36.
[153] Keckermann, *Systema Theologiae*, 28–29.
[154] Keckermann, *Scientiae Metaphysicae*, 32–35.
[155] Ludger Honnefelder, "Metaphysics as a Discipline: From the 'Transcendental Philosophy of the Ancients' to Kant's Notion of Transcendental Philosophy", in *The Medieval Heritage in Early Modern Metaphysics and Modal Theory*, ed. Lauge O. Nielsen, Russell L. Friedman, and Richard Sorabji (Dordrecht: Springer, 2003), 53–74.
[156] Keckermann, *PP*, 80.

commonwealth. As a "ray of divine wisdom and truth" flowing from the "inexhaustible divine ocean of wisdom", philosophy received in the human mind would make the divine image shine anew, conspiring in a "most friendly" manner with theology for the furthering of piety and the benefit of the whole of society.[157] Theology was thus the crown of Keckermann's encyclopaedia.

While seeking to join philosophy and theology in the closest conjunction, Keckermann never lost sight of the fact that philosophy alone, without theology, was utterly insufficient for restoring the human soul. Censuring the Platonic view of philosophy as a "meditation on death", he also rejected utterly Cicero's claim that it is the "medicine of our sins and vices". For Keckermann, at least in the *Praecognita Philosophica*, the instauration of man is the true office of theology not philosophy and comes through the remission of sins and peace of conscience attained by Christ's death on the Cross.[158] While philosophy is important and even necessary for framing theology as a system, it is in no way necessary for Christian faith. With the Apostle Paul then Keckermann can sincerely say, "I desire to know nothing except Jesus Christ and him crucified".[159]

Admittedly, Keckermann's views here appear somewhat in tension with his clear statements elsewhere concerning the capacities of even fallen human reason.[160] In this light, it is notable that the *Praecognita Philosophica* seeks to offer an important double safeguard against encroaching rationalism. Firstly, as an Augustinian, he places the restoration of the image of God not under the common grace or illumination which founds the encyclopaedia but under the special grace of God's unconditional election.[161] Secondly, he insists that all the arts and sciences are ultimately dependent on the guidance of theology to reach their goal of perfecting humanity and renewing the image of God.[162] As Muller suggests, Keckermann is therefore very much in continuity with the Christian humanism of Melanchthon and the early Reformation as well as the revived scholasticism of Reformed orthodoxy.[163] Even more to the point, his Ramistic heritage connects him to a long Augustinian and Franciscan tradition of Christian reflection in which philosophy naturally becomes taken up and transformed by theology.

Given this it is no surprise that Keckermann subscribes to an Augustinian, even Scotistic, view of theology as a practical discipline. Departing from Aquinas

---

[157] Georg Pauli, "*Philosophiae Studiosis S.*", in Keckermann, *PP*.
[158] Keckermann, *PP*, 84.
[159] Keckermann, *PP*, 86–87 citing 1 Corinthians 2:1.
[160] Hotson, *Alsted*, 66–82.
[161] Keckermann, *PP*, 38–39.
[162] Keckermann, *PP*, 6–14 demonstrates the intimate relation of philosophy, theology and prudence. Bartholomäus Keckermann, *Systema Ethicae* (Hanau, 1610), 13–24 shows the continuity between ethical and theological virtue.
[163] Muller, "*Vera Philosophia*", 59–60. Muller notes both the continuity and the sense of development.

and following Scotus and the Augustinian tradition he argues that the end of theology is not the contemplation of God but the enjoyment, or fruition, of God, namely "to be united to God or to adhere to God by love on account of himself".[164] Keckermann's denial that theology was an Aristotelian science also shows definite affinities with Scotus and late medieval scholasticism. In this way, his identification of theology as prudence also reflects the Scotist view of prudence as governing the praxis of the will and its choices, as well as the Thomist view of it as unifying and coordinating all the virtues. Yet it was also highly distinctive and pressed considerably beyond the usual scholastic discourse on theology.[165]

In order to understand why Keckermann identified theology as prudence it is necessary to see his account of theology in the broader context of his encyclopaedism. Given his denial that theology was a science, it made sense for him to identify it as a practical prudence. Keckermann's 1602 *Systema Theologiae* was based on lectures given at Heidelberg and it is therefore unsurprising that he should trace the inspiration for this prudential understanding of theology directly to Ursinus and the Heidelberg Catechism, the latter of which he held to follow the "most correct" method in proceeding from end to means.[166] In particular, he followed an analytic approach in arguing that as the true, divine *therapeia*, it is theology—not philosophy—which provides the means for healing the soul and at the same time directs all these means—including logic and the other disciplines—towards their supreme end of union with Christ" and "participation in the Godhead", seen in "conformity with God in the soul by reason of intellect and will".[167] His account of this in the *Systema* innovatively blends both Ramist and Zabarellan methods in seeking to treat God not in metaphysical terms as an object of contemplation but rather in practical and prudential terms as a goal to be reached and loved. For the image of God cannot be restored by "nude contemplation" but by "theological praxis".[168]

Significantly, the nature of theology as religious prudence is mirrored by the nature of politics as political prudence. For Keckermann, the goals of the two are closely entwined but also sharply distinct. In fact, just as prudential theology plays an important role in governing the other disciplines so too

---

[164] Keckermann, *Systema Theologiae*, 5–6.
[165] Keckermann, *Systema Theologiae*, 1–5. For Keckermann's discussion of the genus of theology in relation to the broader scholastic tradition see Muller, *PRRD*, 1.331–33. For Aquinas and Scotus on prudence see Bonnie D. Kent, *Virtues of the Will: The Transformation of Ethics in the Late Thirteenth Century* (Washington, DC: Catholic University of America Press, 1995) and Thomas M. Osborne Jr., "Thomas and Scotus on Prudence without All The Major Virtues: Imperfect or Merely Partial?", *The Thomist* 74 (2010): 165–88.
[166] Keckermann, *Systema Theologiae*, 1–2, 211–15.
[167] Keckermann, *Systema Theologiae*, 209–15.
[168] Keckermann, *Systema Theologiae*, 2. Facca, "Keckermann", 201–2 notes this blending but identifies it as a mere "concession" to Ramism.

does prudential politics. At the very beginning of his 1607 *Systema Disciplinae Politicae* Keckermann thus affirmed:

> Politics is a certain chief and architectonic discipline whence depends not indeed the things and methods of other disciplines but yet the institution and occasion of teaching and handling, and in which if it errs, the error is at once most widely diffused and conjoined with the greatest danger.[169]

The purpose of politics is to direct society to public happiness.[170] It builds directly on ethics and oeconomics which direct towards individual and domestic happiness respectively. Following Daneau, Keckermann thus assumes an important distinction between civil politics as an "order by which human society is administered and directed towards honesty" and ecclesiastical politics as an "order by which the society (*coetus*) of the Church is directed to the worship of God and salvation of souls".[171]

The term "order" immediately suggests a connection with method and the encyclopaedia. Indeed, Keckermann was clear that the purpose of politics as a methodical discipline is to frame an "idea" of civil or ecclesiastical polity to which individual polities conform to varying degrees.[172] Despite his pragmatism, there can be no doubt that there is an important exemplaristic streak running through his politics.[173] Indeed, as Maxwell Staley suggests, his system of politics represents a definite Ramistic blueprint for a perfect society.[174] For Keckermann, it was axiomatic that the order of Church, school, and society should mirror the order of the philosophical disciplines. What he meant by this is that just as philosophy unites "in most sweet harmony" and dependence diverse sciences and prudences, so civil and ecclesiastical polities should unite diverse members in pursuit of the temporal or eternal good.[175] In effect, it is not only the order of the family or domestic unit which becomes extrapolated onto the whole of society but also the order of the academy itself.[176] The state becomes seen as a school of virtue and, in its most eminent degree, a school of piety. Amid growing

---

[169] Bartholomäus Keckermann, *Systema Disciplinae Politicae* (Hanau, 1607), 4: "*Disciplina Politica est princeps quaedam et architectonica, unde aliarum omnium disciplinarum non quidem res ipsae et methodus, sed institutio tamen et docendi tradendiq. occasio pendet, et in qua si erretur, error statim latissime diffunditur, ac cum maximo periculo coniunctus est*".

[170] Keckermann, *Systema Disciplinae Politicae*, 1.

[171] Keckermann, *Systema Disciplinae Politicae*, 1-3.

[172] Keckermann, *Systema Theologiae*, 383-84.

[173] Keckermann, *Systema Disciplinae Politicae*, 23-24 shows scepticism about achieving the perfect political society.

[174] Maxwell Reed Staley, "A Most Dangerous Science: Discipline and German Political Philosophy, 1600-1648" (PhD Dissertation, University of California, Berkeley, 2018), 21-34.

[175] Keckermann, *PP*, 15; *Systema Disciplinae Politicae*, 382, 514.

[176] Staley, "Dangerous Science", 30-37; cf. Keckermann, *Systema Disciplinae Politicae*, 2.

confessional conflict and strife, Keckermann intended the Danzig Academy, with its integrated philosophical and theological curriculum, to be an embodiment of this ideal Reformed order and a microcosm of the wider reformation that he hoped to institute in Church and society.

Writing in the Danzig context, in which a Protestant minority was under the authority of a Catholic ruler, Keckermann followed the "Two Kingdoms" approach in maintaining a sharp separation between civil and ecclesiastical polity.[177] Unlike his contemporary Althusius, the Herborn Ramist, he did not espouse a strong resistance theory or try to remodel society on the basis of a federal or covenantal structure as a godly Republic.[178] Instead, he held that the most perfect and ideal form of government, representing the highest instantiation of divine rule, was monarchy. While there was doubtless a pragmatic element in this, his main argument for this was metaphysical and idealizing, namely that monarchy represents a Neo-Platonic progression from unity to multiplicity according to which the whole of society becomes conceived (implicitly) as a kind of Ramistic "golden chain".[179] Paralleling Plato's Philosopher King he held that the ideal monarch would be trained in all the arts and sciences in order to govern wisely and prudently and to the best of his ability. For this reason Keckermann prescribes an encyclopaedic curriculum for his monarch and prioritizes the founding of schools, academies, and colleges as necessary to the flourishing of society.[180]

While what Keckermann called "absolute" civil rule required only the inculcation of the moral virtues, he held that its highest degree should also promote the intellectual virtues of contemplation and religion as well.[181] Here Keckermann felt able to draw freely on Althusius' notion of a biblical polity to frame his picture of an ideal Christian society, in which the magistrate exercises his "right of majesty" in both civil and ecclesiastical spheres. Civil polity blends with ecclesiastical polity, just as philosophy becomes taken up by theology, as the monarch directs both Church and society towards eternal happiness.[182] In its highest form,

---

[177] Keckermann, *Systema Disciplinae Politicae*, 12, 24; cf. Staley, "Dangerous Science", 39–41. For the political situation of Danzig at this time see Karin Friedrich, *The Other Prussia: Royal Prussia, Poland and Liberty, 1569–1772* (Cambridge: Cambridge University Press, 2000), 20–121.

[178] Staley, "Dangerous Science", 39 notes his reluctance to affirm the Calvinist resistance theory. On p. 532 he suggests that limited or covenantal monarchy, which was favoured by Althusius, is imperfect. For more on Althusius' politics see Thomas O. Hueglin, *Early Modern Concepts for a Late Modern World: Althusius on Community and Federalism* (Waterloo, Ontario: Wilfrid Laurier University Press, 1999).

[179] Keckermann, *Systema Disciplinae Politicae*, 32–34, 38. Keckermann also drew deeply on Aquinas' *De Regno*. Staley, "Dangerous Science", 34 makes the point that a government "ought to resemble a Ramist tree of knowledge, with all authority flowing progressively outward from a single articulated source" but misses the Neo-Platonic connection to Ramus' doctrine of the golden chain.

[180] Keckermann, *Systema Disciplinae Politicae*, 68–76, 196.

[181] Keckermann, *Systema Disciplinae Politicae*, 24–28.

[182] Keckermann, *Systema Disciplinae Politicae*, 514–20.

within a truly "Reformed polity", the monarch comes to reflect and embody the heavenly rule of Christ in his Church, with the union of individuals under a godly monarch paralleling the union of the elect under Christ the King, knitting all together in the "sweetest harmony and proportion".[183] In the Church, Christ as Head rules through the Holy Spirit bringing all Christians directly under the authority of God and his Word.[184] The Trinitarian pattern of rule of Christ through the Spirit thus becomes stamped on the Church and through the Church on the rest of society. Through the mediation of the encyclopaedia, and especially the architectonic discipline of politics, the union with the Triune God, which is the end and goal of theology, thus becomes transposed onto whole communities and even whole nations.[185] Method becomes the means for effecting a universal transformation and conformation of Church and society into the image of the Triune God.

[183] Keckermann, *Systema Disciplinae Politicae*, 27–28; *Systema Theologiae*, 374–82.
[184] Keckermann, *Systema Theologiae*, 399–402.
[185] Keckermann, *Systema Disciplinae Politicae*, 202 affirms that politics directs the ends of all the other disciplines.

# 7

# Philosophical Panacea

## Alsted, Lullism, and Trinitarian Encyclopaedism

Johann Heinrich Alsted's *Encyclopaedia* of 1630 is rightly seen as one of the landmark achievements of the Ramist age, paving the way for the modern encyclopaedia with its systematic and methodological treatment of all the disciplines. To his son-in-law, Johann Heinrich Bisterfeld, Alsted had opened up a "new world of the muses".[1] A century later the American philosopher Cotton Mather could still call it a "North-West passage to all the sciences".[2] A staple of Reformed academies and libraries from New England to Transylvania, for many early moderns Alsted's work represented the pinnacle of Ramist method. It was quite simply a route to achieve all learning. As the English Puritan Richard Baxter suggested, to have Alsted's *Encyclopaedia* was to have a whole library at one's fingertips.[3]

Alsted's contributions to the Ramist and encyclopaedic traditions have been brilliantly illuminated by Hotson and there can be no doubt that any student of Alsted must walk closely in his footsteps. However, Hotson's Alsted is something of a Janus-faced figure: on the one hand a Ramist encyclopaedist and doyen of Reformed orthodoxy, on the other a Lullist and hermetic philosopher seeking out forbidden knowledge. For Hotson, the divide already opening in Keckermann between Reformed orthodoxy and encyclopaedism, has only widened with Alsted.[4] Indeed, he has little doubt that Alsted has moved away from the pessimistic Calvinist anthropology of his forebears, tacitly replacing it with a new and optimistic anthropology grounded on the heterodox ideals of Renaissance Platonism and hermeticism.[5] The effect of this was to both challenge and erode the Reformation standard of *sola gratia*. For it implies that the instauration of the image of God is not dependent on divine grace alone but on

---

[1] Johann Heinrich Bisterfeld, "*Aliud*", in Johann Heinrich Alsted, *Encyclopaedia Septem Tomis Distincta*, 7 vols. (Herborn, 1630), vol. 1, cited from Hotson, *Alsted*, 199.
[2] Cotton Mather, *Dr Cotton Mather's Student and Preacher* (London, 1781), 36.
[3] Richard Baxter, *A Christian Directory* (London, 1678), 922. For Alsted's English reception see Howard Hotson, "'A Generall Reformation of Common Learning' and Its Reception in the English Speaking World, 1560–1642", *Proceedings of the British Academy* 164 (2010): 193–228.
[4] Hotson, *Alsted*, 66–94, 144–81.
[5] Hotson, *Alsted*, 180 refers to his "pagan quest for human perfection".

an intensive programme of study and self-reform.[6] For Hotson, this was to subtly displace Scripture from the centre of Alsted's theology.[7]

Hotson's thesis of a conflicted Alsted has not gone uncontested. It has been tacitly denied by Richard Muller and called into question by Byung Soo Han. In particular, Han is concerned to contest any interpretation of Alsted which connects the "theological academization" of the seventeenth century with Pelagianism or proto-rationalism.[8] Both Han and Muller marshal important theological arguments. In fact, as with Keckermann, it will become clear that Alsted sought to situate his encyclopaedism squarely within a Reformed context of grace and illumination.[9]

Nevertheless, it does seem right to identify with Hotson a latent ambiguity in Alsted, something of which he was himself, at times, uncomfortably aware. His dramatic deathbed renunciation of his mature work, even placing it under anathema, is only the most vivid reminder of this.[10] Likewise, his intense and enthusiastic engagement with hermetic and even occult thought also marks him out from many within the Reformed mainstream, and it is scarcely surprising that it should have occasioned suspicion and concern.[11] Moreover, while Hotson is clear that Alsted continued to wrestle with these issues throughout his life, seeking to avoid the trap of Pelagianism and reconcile these divergent elements within his Reformed biblical worldview, he raises legitimate doubts as to whether he was ultimately successful.[12]

There can be no question that any interpretation of Alsted must grapple with this evident tension. Yet without seeking to entirely defuse it, this chapter will suggest that Alsted found an important resolution of it in his new and expansive approach to Christian philosophy, with its drive to encompass every method, including the hermetic, under the canopy of divine inspiration and illumination.[13] It will therefore aim above all to see Alsted as a Christian philosopher, according to the title that he both claimed for himself and his student Comenius conferred

---

[6] Hotson, *Alsted*, 75–81.

[7] Hotson, *Alsted*, 138–39, 181 distances Alsted from "biblical fundamentalism" and a "rigidifying Calvinist orthodoxy".

[8] Richard A. Muller, "Was It Really Viral? Natural Theology in the Early Modern Reformed Tradition", in *Crossing Traditions: Essays on the Reformation and Intellectual History in Honour of Irena Backus*, ed. Daniela Solfaroli Camillocci, Maria-Cristina Pitassi, and Arthur A. Huiban (Leiden: Brill, 2017), 521–25 and Han, "Academization", 283–94.

[9] Hotson, *Alsted*, 78–79 does acknowledge the important role of direct inspiration but still tends to see Keckermann and Alsted as having "departed from the first generation of Reformers" in their positive anthropology and their account of the encyclopaedia as a platform for the restoration of the image of God.

[10] Hotson, *Alsted*, 178–80. Alsted even attempted to destroy his own later manuscripts.

[11] Hotson, *Alsted*, 82, 96–143.

[12] For discussion of Alsted's desire to avoid Pelagianism see Hotson, *Alsted*, 73. For his doubts see p. 180.

[13] Hotson, *Alsted*, 78–79, 82 insightfully highlights the important role that divine inspiration plays in Alsted's philosophy.

on him.[14] In doing so, not only will we recontextualize Alsted's intellectual development within a much longer Augustinian and Franciscan tradition, but we will also see how this leads him to a far-reaching project of Trinitarian, biblical, and apocalyptic encyclopaedism. This will reveal Alsted to be in radical continuity with the Ramist programme of Christian philosophy and Trinitarian metaphysics which coincided in Keckermann, but also seeking to deepen this by recourse to Franciscan and Lullist encyclopaedism.

Contrary to Radical Orthodoxy it will argue once again that Scotist ontology could play an important role in instituting a Christian and exemplaristic metaphysics of participation.[15] It will also support the thesis of Lohr, Leinkauf, and Antognazza that Lullist and Trinitarian metaphysics paved the way for the new, dynamic ontology of the Renaissance and Enlightenment.[16] Indeed, Alsted will be seen as an important stage in the progressive mathematization of the encyclopaedia and the development, under Brunian and Cusan auspices, of an innovative new "infinite philosophy". In this sense, while remaining deeply embedded in the Ramist movement, Alsted may also be seen as marking a new departure in the post-Ramist movement towards the pansophic and encyclopaedic projects not only of his own students Comenius and Bisterfeld but also of the great Leibniz himself.[17]

In recent scholarship this Ramist and Alstedian encyclopaedic movement has often been portrayed as outdated and even collapsing under its own weight. Thus Levitin, who himself tends to separate Ramism from the burgeoning early modern culture of erudition, points to Cardinal Borromeo's view at the beginning of the seventeenth century that encyclopaedic learning was an unnecessary and unrealistic goal distracting from mastery of individual disciplines.[18] Likewise, Vera Keller points to the important early modern shift away from a focus on

[14] Alsted, *Encyclopaedia*, "Praefatio"; Jan Amos Comenius, *Naturall Philosophie Reformed by Divine Light* (London, 1651), "Preface"; cf. Hotson, *Alsted*, 138.
[15] For a recent critique of Radical Orthodoxy's view of Scotist ontology and univocity see Horan, *Postmodernity and Univocity*.
[16] Lohr, "Metaphysics", 537–99; Leinkauf, *Einheit, Natur, Geist*, 15–50; and Maria Rosa Antognazza, "Bisterfeld and *Immeatio*: Origins of a Key Concept in the Early Modern Doctrine of Universal Harmony", in *Spätrenaissance Philosophie in Deutschland 1570–1650: Entwürfe zwischen Humanismus und Konfessionalisierung, okkulten Traditionen und Schulmetaphysik*, ed. Martin Mulsow (Tübingen: Max Niemeyer Verlag, 2009), 64–81.
[17] For Alsted's link with Leibniz see Leroy E. Loemker, *Struggle for Synthesis: The Seventeenth Century Background of Leibniz's Synthesis of Order and Freedom* (Cambridge, MA; Harvard University Press, 1972) and Maria Rosa Antognazza and Howard Hotson, *Alsted and Leibniz: On God, the Magistrate, and the Millennium* (Wiesbaden: Harrassowitz, 1999).
[18] Dmitri Levitin, "Introduction: Confessionalisation and Erudition in Early Modern Europe: A Comparative Overview of a Neglected Episode in the History of the Humanities", in *Confessionalisation and Erudition in Early Modern Europe: An Episode in the History of the Humanities*, ed. Nicholas Hardy and Dmitri Levitin (Oxford: Oxford University Press, 2019), 22. On p. 68 he implicitly contrasts Ramism and erudition. Likewise, Levitin, *Ancient Wisdom*, 150 dismisses the "scholarly backwardness" of the Oxford Ramist Theophilus Gale.

encyclopaedic method as the key to all knowledge to a more open-ended, collaborative pursuit of knowledge.[19] Focussing the critique on the Herborn tradition, Sheehan has said that "through Alsted's own corpus ran the bright thread of Peter Ramus' overweening didacticism, a didacticism whose pretension of encompassing the entire corpus of human knowledge was both its attraction and the cause of its ultimate demise".[20] In this sense, he held that encyclopaedism "became, at the same time, the solution to the problem of this multiplicity and an index of the failure of scholars ever to achieve their goals".[21] Hotson too, for all his admiration of the Ramist architectonic of Alsted's *Encyclopaedia*, has told a similar story, recounting his ongoing struggle to contain everything within the compass of one, overarching method and his eventual relinquishing of this in favour of eclectic pluriformity.[22] In this light, Leibniz's subsequent failure to complete the Herborn encyclopaedic project must be seen as a "major watershed in European intellectual history", sounding the effective death knell of the Renaissance encyclopaedia.[23]

That Ramism, like scholasticism and other movements of the time, ultimately failed to contain the divergent forces of early modernity is surely beyond doubt. Yet to view Alstedian encyclopaedism as an essential failure, as Sheehan seems to do, is to miss both its dynamic creative potential and its innovative attempts to come to terms with an ever-growing body of knowledge. Indeed, as much as Alsted and his Ramist contemporaries saw the runaway growth of the disciplines as a definite problem to be overcome, they also gloried in the expanding horizons of human ingenuity. Yet for them this was not a matter of hubris or pride, and certainly not a proto-Enlightenment confidence in the untrammelled powers of human reason, but rather a stance of humble dependence on the illumination and irradiation of the Triune God. In its Realist and Trinitarian dimensions it also sought to give the entire body of human knowledge an unprecedented coherence as part of its programmatic endeavour of reform.

## 7.1. Between Ramism and Lullism

For Alsted, Ramism was very much in his blood. His father Jacob Alsted had been Professor of Logic at Herborn and a close friend of Olevian's and thus had

---

[19] Vera Keller, *Knowledge and the Public Interest, 1575–1725* (Cambridge: Cambridge University Press, 2015), 127–98.
[20] Sheehan, "From Philology to Fossils", 43.
[21] Sheehan, "From Philology to Fossils", 48.
[22] Hotson, *Commonplace Learning*, 254–73.
[23] Hotson, *Reformation of Common Learning*, "Abstract: Chapter 11". See further, pp. 305–405.

been at the epicentre of Reformed confessionalization in Herborn.[24] Through his mother, Rebecca Pincier, he was connected to an impressive network of further reformers, responsible for the "pervasive dissemination" of Agricolan and Ramist logic in Germany and the Netherlands.[25] A number of these, including own Alsted's grandfather, had played a key role in the Reformed and Ramist transformation of the University of Marburg in the early seventeenth century.[26] From the beginning, then, Alsted's intellectual horizon was oriented between the two poles of Herborn and Marburg.[27]

Following in his father's footsteps, Alsted enrolled in the Herborn Academy in 1602. While Ramism was beginning to lose its dominance here, exposing the young student to a renewed scholasticism and a broader conception of method, there can be no doubt it still remained a "sharp sword" in the confessional struggle.[28] Indeed, here he was inducted into the scriptural and encyclopaedic strands which gave Herborn Ramism its distinctive character. Piscator was one of his principal teachers and became a mentor to the young Alsted.[29] His Ramist commentaries on Scripture and his Realist account of logic served as an important impetus to Alsted's own methodological development, and it may have been from him that he caught the first stirrings of Millenarian doctrine.[30] It was at Herborn too that Alsted was first introduced to the encyclopaedia by Matthias Martinius, the Professor of Philosophy. Martinius' own Ramist encyclopaedia, the 1606 *Idea Methodica et Brevis Encyclopaedia*, was an important inspiration for him. Bearing all the hallmarks of Timpler's influence, it pointed to the role of the encyclopaedia in the recovery of the image of God and for the upbuilding of the Christian commonwealth.[31] Elsewhere, Martinius subscribed to a definite, Scotistic, Realism, elevating Ramus as a Christian philosopher and presenting Ramist and Platonic dialectic as an important route of ascent to God.[32]

Even more important than Martinius in shaping Alsted's Ramist encyclopaedism was Keckermann. Indeed, Alsted was always eager to hear news of the great man and his progress with the encyclopaedia. The death of Keckermann was a definite blow to Alsted but also an important opportunity.

---

[24] Howard Hotson, "*Arbor Sanguinis, Arbor Disciplinarum*: The Intellectual Genealogy of Johann Heinrich Alsted—Part I. Alsted's Intellectual Inheritance", *Acta Comeniana* 25 (2011): 50–57.
[25] Hotson, "*Arbor Sanguinis*", 64.
[26] Hotson, *Alsted*, 55–56.
[27] Hotson, *Alsted*, 15–65 expresses this in terms of "Three Varieties of Further Reform".
[28] Menk, *Hohe Schule*, 211–16. Freedman, "Ramus and the Use of Ramus", 101 n. 35 notes that in 1598 Ramist logic was still being taught to the highest classes but by 1611 this had ceased.
[29] Hotson, *Alsted*, 39. One of Alsted's earliest disputations was disputed under him (p. 236).
[30] For Alsted's complex relation to Piscator's Millennialism see Hotson, *Alsted*, 208–13.
[31] Gerhard Menk, "Martinius, Matthias, 1572–1630", in *Neue Deutsche Biographie* 16 (1990): 305–7; cf. Hotson, *Alsted*, 117. Matthias Martinius, *Idea Methodica et Brevis Encyclopaedia* (Herborn, 1606), "*Praefatio*".
[32] Martinius, *Methodus Theologiae*, 140–50.

For he clearly saw himself as inheriting the mantle of Keckermann. His desire was thus both to emulate and surpass him.[33] As Hotson has shown, it was in the editing and shaping of Keckermann's works into the *Systema Systematum* that Alsted really cut his teeth as an encyclopaedist. From Keckermann too, Alsted inherited the vision of the encyclopaedia as a means not only of capturing all of knowledge but of harnessing it for the transformation of individual, Church, and society.[34]

A final important link in the Ramist chain of Alsted's early education was provided by his "most worthy teacher" Polanus.[35] Alsted arrived in Basel in 1607 in the year that Polanus published his *Symphonia Catholica* and while he was still working on his massive *Syntagma Theologiae*.[36] Under Polanus, as we have seen, Ramism played a central role in structuring theological education in Basel, shaping the exegesis, preaching, theology, and polemic of a generation of students.[37] Such an atmosphere was surely congenial to the young Herborner, but Basel Ramism had its own important distinctives. From Polanus, Alsted learned the new "symphonic" approach to theology which informed his own budding eclecticism. Exposure to Polanus also served to reinforce the Franciscan and Scotist Realism he had been taught at Herborn. Finally, the *Syntagma* gave the young Alsted important impetus towards his own Trinitarian systematization of philosophy and theology, which was to bear fruit in both his massive *Methodus Theologiae* and his unfolding encyclopaedic project.[38]

Even before he went to Basel, Alsted was already gravitating towards a different kind of method: the Lullism which flourished at the University of Marburg as part of a wider Neo-Platonic, hermetic, and alchemical programme of further reform. Alsted arrived at Marburg just two years after the Landgrave Moritz of Hesse had wrested the university back from his Lutheran relatives and introduced a far-reaching programme of Reformed confessionalization—events in which Alsted's own relatives played a leading role. Aided by Goclenius, the Landgrave purged the Lutheran faculty, replacing them with leading alchemists and Paracelsian philosophers including Goclenius' own son Rudolph; Alsted's relative Johannes Hartmann, the holder of the first European chair in chemical medicine; and the controversial Swiss Reformed theologian and alchemist Raphael Egli, who became Alsted's friend and mentor at Marburg.[39]

---

[33] Hotson, *Commonplace Learning*, 165–66.
[34] Hotson, *Commonplace Learning*, 161–65.
[35] Alsted, *Systema Mnemonicum*, II.604.
[36] Hotson, *Alsted*, 51–52, 63–64.
[37] Burnett, *Teaching the Reformation*, 136, 142, 150–54.
[38] For discussion of the burgeoning *Methodus Theologiae* project see Muller, "Was It Really Viral?", 521–25.
[39] Hotson, *Alsted*, 59–65.

By the first decade of the seventeenth century Marburg had thus become the leading centre of a new "Reformed hermeticism".[40] Coordinating this, as Bruce Moran suggests, was Moritz's own dream of attaining a "hermetic synthesis in all the arts" including theology itself.[41] While the notion of Reformed hermeticism may seem self-contradictory, even outrageous, there were definite points of contact. One can see how doctrines of grace and predestination might foster a philosophy of the enlightened or elect. Likewise, the distinctive Reformed—and indeed Ramist—account of the *prisca philosophia* and Mosaic philosophy provided a readily available means of integrating all kinds of knowledge, including hermetic, into the stream of divine revelation.[42] Of course, this is not to say that the desire to engage Reformed theology with hermeticism was uncontroversial or unproblematic. There were those who clearly took this much too far, and Alsted may also have been regarded at times as an offender in this regard—at least if his own defensiveness is anything to go by.[43] Yet Reformed views on hermeticism ought perhaps to be seen on a spectrum, and we should be careful of driving too much of a wedge between Reformed hermetics and the Reformed mainstream. Despite their hermetic trappings, alchemy, astrology, Lullism and even Cabalism could all find their place within the Reformed encyclopaedia.[44] Indeed, as the "German Solomon" Moritz's desire was to preside over a biblical renewal of the arts, and for him and his circle alchemy and Paracelsian medicine were to be regarded as sacred endeavours sanctified by God and attuned to their broader Reformed convictions.[45]

It was no surprise therefore that Lullism could prosper in such an environment and become easily integrated into a broader, transformative enterprise in which

---

[40] The term is my own but for aspects of Reformed hermeticism see Wallace, *Shapers*; Walter W. Woodward, *Prospero's America: John Winthrop, Jr., Alchemy, and the Creation of New England Culture* (Chapel Hill NC: University of North Carolina Press, 2010); and William R. Newman, *Gehennical Fire: The Lives of George Starkey, An American Alchemist in the Scientific Revolution* (Cambridge, MA: Harvard University Press, 1994).

[41] Bruce T. Moran, "Court Authority and Chemical Medicine: Moritz of Hessen, Johannes Hartmann, and the Origin of Academic Chemiatria", *Bulletin of the History of Medicine* 63.2 (1989): 233.

[42] Theophilus Gale, *The Court of the Gentiles: or A Discourse Touching the Original of Human Literature both Philologie, and Philosophie, from the Scriptures, and Jewish Church . . . Part II. Of Philosophie* (Oxford, 1670), 12-13. The Oxford Ramist Gale praises Hermes Trismegistus and even identifies him with the patriarch Joseph. However, as Wallace, *Shapers*, 107 points out, this is by no means to say that he is sympathetic with all aspects of hermetic philosophy.

[43] See Hotson, *Alsted*, 60-63, 96-109, 178-80. Two striking cases are Raphael Egli's fall from grace and Alsted's own deathbed renunciation of his mature work.

[44] See, for example, Wallace, *Shapers*; Woodward, *Prospero's America*; and Newman, *Gehennical Fire*, 28-38. Newman points to the important role that alchemy played in the works of Richardson, Ames and the wider Harvard milieu. See also Gale, *The Court of the Gentiles . . . Part II. Of Philosophie*, 29-30, 37. Here the distinction made in Wallace, *Shapers*, 88 between interest in hermeticism and hermetic literature may have some validity, but even this can become blurred.

[45] Timothy Raylor and J. W. Binns, "English Responses to the Death of Moritz the Learned: John Dury, Sir Thomas Roe, and an Unnoted Epicede by William Cartwright", *English Literary Renaissance* 25.2 (1995): 236-38; Moran, "Court Authority and Chemical Medicine", 233, 240.

Ramist encyclopaedism, Aristotelian metaphysics, and alchemy all took their due place. For Lull's Art was of course the epitome of a spiritual logic, and the Renaissance image of Lull himself was that of an adept in alchemy, astrology, and the Cabala. From the late sixteenth century Marburg had important associations with the English Lullist philosophers John Dee and Robert Fludd, the latter of whom has been called "the most important English representative of the school of Nicholas of Cusa".[46] In Alsted's own time the elder Goclenius was said to have "read, re-examined, emended, corrected, and restored with the greatest diligence and the sharpest judgement" the whole of Lull's massive *Ars Magna, Generalis et Ultima*.[47] Alsted's teachers introduced him to the Zetzner edition of Lull's work, which he eagerly read cover-to-cover, as well as to leading Lullist commentators like Cornelius Agrippa, Valerius de Valeriis, Petrus Gregorius Tholozanus, and Cornelius Gemma.[48] It was here also that he came into contact with the work of the Fabrists and especially of Bernardo de Lavinheta, whose Lullist encyclopaedia was to become an important inspiration for his own Trinitarian and apocalyptic encyclopaedism.[49]

Yet for Alsted it was Giordano Bruno, the wandering Dominican friar, who came to epitomize Renaissance Lullism. Through Egli, as Hotson has shown, Alsted had an important entree into the world of Brunian Lullism. For the Swiss theologian not only had met Bruno himself but also had received from him an important manuscript which he later bequeathed to Alsted.[50] In Bruno's Lullist works Alsted discovered a dynamic, Neo-Platonic view of the world which he found highly attractive. While Bruno is famous for the infinite cosmology he developed under the influence of the "deeper and divine" works of Nicholas of Cusa and Copernicus, it was significantly his understanding of the infinite potentiality of the human mind which came first.[51]

Axiomatic to Bruno was the Cusan understanding that the human mind by taking on the pattern of the entire universe also comes to mirror the dynamic creativity of the divine mind. For Bruno, method became an embodiment of this principle and the Lullist wheels in their unfettered multiplication and

---

[46] See Moran, "Court Authority and Chemical Medicine", 32 and Raylor and Binns, "English Responses", 237–38. For Fludd's Cusan connection see Wilhelm Schmidt-Biggemann, "Robert Fludd's Kabbalistic Cosmos", in *Platonism at the Origins of Modernity: Studies on Platonism and Early Modern Philosophy*, ed. Douglas Hedley and Sarah Hutton (Dordrecht: Springer, 2008), 76.
[47] Hotson, *Alsted*, 57.
[48] Hotson, *Alsted*, 44–45.
[49] Hotson, *Alsted*, 91–92 affirms the importance of Lavinheta for Alsted's early development.
[50] Hotson, *Alsted*, 59–65.
[51] For Bruno's approbation of Cusanus see Giordano Bruno, *Four Works on Llull*, trans. Scott Gosnell (USA: Huggin, Munninn & Co, 2015), 82. For his development of Cusan cosmology see Hilary Gatti, *Giordano Bruno and Renaissance Science* (Ithaca, NY: Cornell University Press, 1999), 118–20. Hotson, *Alsted*, 92 points out that, unlike Bruno, Alsted remained a conservative in terms of cosmology. However, on p. 171 he points out how attractive Bruno's notion of the infinity of the human mind was to Alsted.

combination were intended to reflect the infinite dynamism and creativity of both the divine and human minds.[52] Before he fled his convent in Naples, Bruno had been famous as an exponent of the Dominican art of memory, and so it was only natural that he should later integrate this with his Lullist encyclopaedic interests. By placing the traditional images of the Dominican art on Lullist wheels he was able to outline an impressive mnemonic encyclopaedia.[53] Indeed, for Bruno, Lullism was very much a universal logic and metaphysics, enabling its practitioner to range the entire ladder of being and ultimately to ascend to God in a kind of mystical deification.[54]

While Alsted's Lullist turn has often been seen as a departure from his Herborn roots—the beginnings of a new pansophic and post-Ramist movement—it is important to realize that he was neither the first nor the last of those schooled in Ramism to feel the deep tug of attraction to the Lullist methodology. For below the surface the two movements shared a common purpose and a common framework. Indeed, as Anita Traninger has insightfully pointed out, the Renaissance Lullism that Alsted and his contemporaries were familiar with was a method that had already gone through an important rhetorical transformation, bringing it into ever closer proximity with Ramism.[55] From the start Ramism and Lullism were competing and converging methodologies, and Ramist responses to Lullism ranged across the spectrum from the downright hostility of Perkins and Keckermann, through Pace's attempt to purify Lullism of its hermetic associations, to the hermetic Lullism of the Marburg reform.[56]

It should also, of course, not be forgotten that Ramism first developed in the context of a mystical milieu in which Lullist and Neo-Platonic ideas had made deep inroads. Its subsequent development into Philippo-Ramist encyclopaedism only served to heighten these mathematical and exemplaristic connections. The two movements therefore shared far deeper affinities than their shared topical framework, which Alsted, as an enthusiast of the Fabrist reform, was well-placed to recognize. Entwined from the beginning, it was only natural that Ramism and Lullism would encounter each other again, and that when they did so their latent mathematical and mystical bond would also begin to resurface. For Alsted, who made it his life's work to marry the two, this was truly a match made in heaven.

---

[52] See Alessandro G. Farinella and Carole Preston, "Giordano Bruno, Neoplatonism and the Wheel of Memory in 'De Umbris Idearum'", *Renaissance Quarterly* 55.2 (2002): 596–624.
[53] Yates, *Art of Memory*, 175–227; cf. Giordano Bruno, *De Umbris Idearum* (Paris, 1582).
[54] Bruno, *Four Works on Llull*, 81–84, 161; cf. Farinella and Preston, "Bruno", 596–624.
[55] Anita Traninger, "The Secret of Success: Ramism and Lullism as Contending Methods", in *Ramus, Pedagogy and the Liberal Arts*, ed. Reid and Wilson, 113–31.
[56] For Perkins' opposition to Brunian Lullism see Yates, *Art of Memory*, 260–78. For Pace's purification of Lullism see Giulio Pace, *Iul. Pacii Artis Lullianae Emendatae Libri IV* (Valentia, 1618).

## 7.2. The Quest for a Lullist Key

From the beginning Alsted's fascination with Lullism was associated with the early modern quest for a *clavis universalis*—a key to all knowledge.[57] We may see this already from his massive *Systema Mnemonicum Duplex* of 1610, his own early attempt to frame a mnemonic encyclopaedia. The fruit of many years' labour, Alsted had trawled the libraries of Europe to find medieval and Renaissance manuscripts on the art of memory.[58] While intended as a posthumous fulfilment of Keckermann's desire to write a mnemonic system, Alsted's final synthesis combining the traditional Dominican art of memory with Ramist, Lullist, and Cabalistic memory aids was a far cry from anything the Danziger would ever have written and clearly bore the imprint of Alsted's Marburg years.[59]

For Alsted, the art of memory had a divine origin (*ortu*), for memory itself was a singular gift of God.[60] While he admired the streamlined and elegant logical structure of the Ramist art of memory, he was especially attracted to the vivid images of the Dominican art and the dynamic, combinatorial potential of the Lullist Art.[61] Drawing on Aquinas he held that the highest and most spiritual intentions were best conveyed in corporeal similitudes, and believed, contrary to Keckermann, that such images were important in motivating an ascent from individuals to universals.[62] Indeed, the theme of ascent forms the backbone of the *Systema* allowing Alsted to harmonize a medley of Aristotelian, Platonic, Ramist, and Lullist-Cabalistic memory arts.[63] While Hotson is right to stress the miscellaneous, even unsystematic, character of the work, it is also important to mark the profound connections he sought to map out (quite literally) between the different methods (Figure 7.1).[64] Nor should we miss the fact that Alsted self-consciously grounds his mnemonic pedagogy and encyclopaedism in an Augustinian and Reformed affective spirituality in which all study is carried out by God's grace and for his glory.[65]

Preceding the *Systema Mnemonicum* and, in a sense, preparing the way for it was Alsted's *Clavis Artis Lullianae* of 1609, the work in which he offers

---

[57] Rossi, *Logic and the Art of Memory*, 130–32.
[58] Hotson, *Alsted*, 85.
[59] Hotson, *Alsted*, 85–87.
[60] Alsted, *Systema Mnemonicum*, "*Epistola Dedicatoria*".
[61] Alsted, *Systema Mnemonicum*, I.1–7, 389; cf. Rossi, *Logic and the Art of Memory*, 130–33.
[62] Hotson, *Alsted*, 85. For Alsted's own account of sense cognition, singulars, and universals see *Systema Mnemonicum*, I.343–44.
[63] Alsted, *Systema Mnemonicum*, I.191–99, 373, 379.
[64] Hotson, *Alsted*, 86–87. For the mapping of this see, for example, Alsted, *Systema Mnemonicum*, I.378 which contains a Ramist chart of Cabalistic notions of ascent.
[65] See Alsted, *Systema Mnemonicum*, II.463–84 where he connects the art of memory to piety and the reading of Scripture drawing on medieval and Reformed authorities such as Augustine, Bernard of Clairvaux, Ursinus, and Perkins.

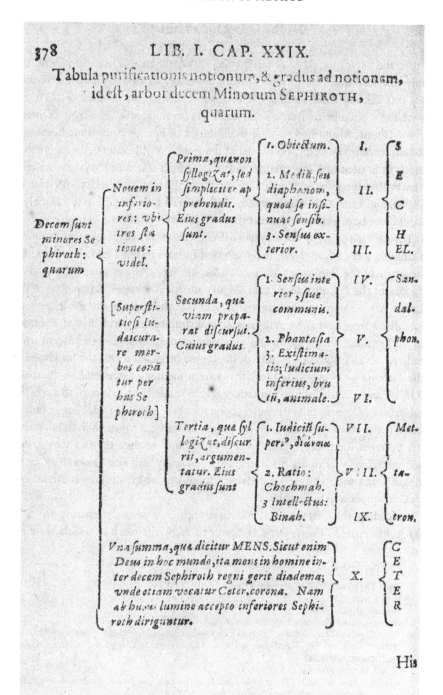

**Figure 7.1** Ramist chart of Cabalistic notions of ascent from Johann Heinrich Alsted, *Systema Mnemonicum Duplex* (Frankfurt, 1610), I.378. Reproduced by kind permission of the Bibliothèque Nationale de France.

his most comprehensive discussion of the Lullian Art. Written at the very beginning of his Herborn career it is clearly intended as both an apologetic for Lullism and a demonstration of its value for the philosophical and theological schools. It marks an ambitious attempt of the young Alsted sought to fashion a new, Reformed Lullism, attentive to the method and dynamics of Scripture and capable of instituting the "compendiary way" that he and other universal reformers dreamed of.[66] Rather, like Pace, whose work on Lullism he was later to recommend, Alsted sought to clear up the confused chaos of previous Lullist commentaries and provide a methodical route through the Lullist *loci*—just as Ramus and other innovators had done previously in their own transformation of the topical tradition.[67]

For Alsted, like many before him, the chief attraction of Lullism was its claim to represent a "universal art". By constantly revolving the Lullian circles to match different subjects with different absolute and respective predicates and questions, he held that it was possible to discourse across a whole universe of being and thought.[68] Yet for its detractors such as Keckermann, such fluidity, far from being a strength, was actually a great weakness. Viewing Lullism as a chaotic and confused system, he roundly condemned it for its indiscriminate mixing of terms taken from logic, metaphysics, physics, mathematics, and ethics. As with Ramism, he also attacked its desire to be a logic of first intentions. For him, the confusion was only compounded by the Lullist revolving of circles, in which a single letter could represent a whole range of terms.[69]

Given Keckermann's prominence, as well as his own profound debt to him, it was necessary for Alsted to confront such objections head-on in the *Clavis*.[70] His response—reminiscent of that of Lull centuries earlier—was to seek to show a parallel between Lullism and other accepted methods. To Keckermann's accusation that Lullism was a logic of first intentions, he pointed out that a similar charge could be levelled against Keckermann's own understanding of the predicaments as "dispositions of things" or the Ramist understanding of arguments.[71] Like Lull, Alsted recognized an important distinction between the way terms function in the Art and the way they signify in different disciplines.[72] His own position, following the Scotism of Bruno, Lavinheta, and Valerius, was that logical terms are second intentions bound intimately to first intentions.[73]

---

[66] Alsted, *Clavis*, "Praefatio".
[67] Alsted, *Clavis*, "Praefatio"; Pace, *Artis Lullianae Emendatae*, "Praefatio".
[68] Alsted, *Clavis*, 91.
[69] Keckermann, *Praecognita Logica*, 206–12; Alsted, *Clavis*, 19–20.
[70] Hotson, *Alsted*, 87–90.
[71] Alsted, *Clavis*, 20–21.
[72] Alsted, *Clavis*, 20–21, 128; cf. Johnston, *Spiritual Logic*, 46–47.
[73] Alsted, *Clavis*, 117, 127; *Systema Mnemonicum*, I.169. For the Scotism of these figures see Bruno, *Four Works on Llull*, 154; Lavinheta, *Opera*, 52–55; and Valerius de Valeriis, *Aureum Sane Opus* (Augsburg, 1589), 17, 30–32.

While Keckermann had attacked Lull's confusing use of circles, Alsted defended teaching by "concamerations, revolutions and involutions of letters" as "the most suitable of all" for it informs both intellect and memory directly with the things themselves. In fact, he held that the Lullist combination of letters marked an elegant means of condensing and systematizing Keckermann's own methodological Peripateticism.[74] In reflecting discourse itself, Alsted held, like Bruno and the enigmatic Croatian Lullist Paul Scalich, that the combinatorial character of the Lullist circles can be mapped directly onto Aristotle's three operations of the mind, with each circle representing different "places of invention".[75]

Alsted's own distinctive adaptation of Lullism employs five different circles.[76] Following Agrippa's precedent, and departing from Lull and Bruno, these combine the circle of subjects (S) and the circle of accidents (I) in combinatorial fashion to generate all of being. These are then combined with two further circles of the absolute (A) and respective (T) predicates, which, following Lavinheta, are taken to represent the divine attributes and their diffusion into created reality. Finally, the last circle (Q) contains the Lullist questions and serves as both "key of invention" and "instrument of disposition" (Figures 7.2.a–e).[77] It was this that gave Alsted's logic its important moralizing and spiritualizing dimension, allowing all things to be related to their end in God.

Essential to the interaction of all the circles, as it also was to Lull, is the fact that the pattern of predication closely corresponds to the metaphysical structure of the universe itself. Alsted knew Lull's important work on "hunting the middle" and shared his view that the relation between subject and predicate in a proposition expressed their metaphysical relation. The truth of a proposition becomes grounded in its exemplaristic correspondence to the structure of reality—the metaphysical concordance, or discord, between subject and predicate.[78] Drawing on both Lull and Bruno, Alsted thus held that all of reality is arranged as a Neo-Platonic ladder of being ranging from the most universal to the most special. This is mapped out in predicative terms by figure T, which can be used for ascending and descending this ladder.[79] Following a Ramist pattern, Alsted distinguished between a synthetic mode of Lullism which could be used to invent, depend, and multiply propositions—thus fulfilling the Renaissance dream of *copia*—and an analytic mode of Lullism in which propositions were

---

[74] Alsted, *Clavis*, 21.
[75] Alsted, *Clavis*, 20–24. For the topical character of Alsted's Lullism as a grounds of reconciling it with Aristotelianism and Ramism see *Systema Mnemonicum*, II.602–5.
[76] Alsted, *Clavis*, 25.
[77] Alsted, *Clavis*, 24–48. For the moralizing character of Lullist logic see Johnston, *Spiritual Logic*, 5–6, 16–18.
[78] Alsted, *Systema Mnemonicum*, II.605; *Clavis*, 42–44, 102–8. For Lull's bond between logic and metaphysics Bonner, *Art and Logic*, 195–206.
[79] Alsted, *Clavis*, 39–45.

PHILOSOPHICAL PANACEA 255

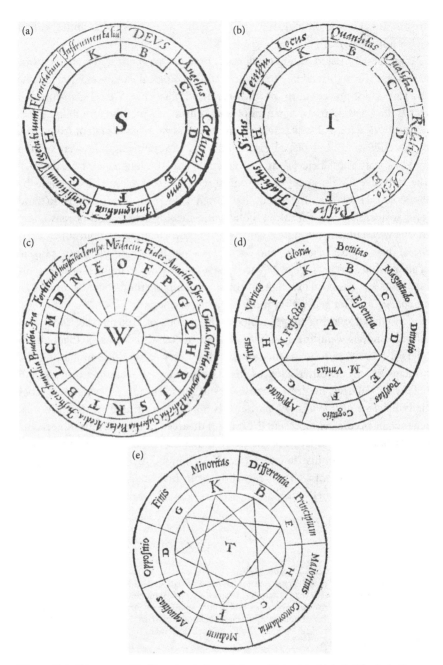

**Figure 7.2** Diagram of Lullist wheels from Johann Heinrich Alsted, *Clavis Artis Lullianae* (Strasbourg, 1609), 25–28, 39. Reproduced by kind permission of the Bibliothèque Nationale de France.

broken down into their logical parts. For both, circle Q served as an important key to unlock all truth.[80]

Importantly, Alsted sought to illustrate both the synthetic and analytic mode of Lullism through recourse to biblical and theological examples.[81] In this, he had important precedent in fifteenth-century Lullists like Wessel Gansfort and Denys the Carthusian, who had employed Lullism as a method for biblical meditation.[82] Viewing Lull as a "divine man" who had received his talent from God, he saw Lullism in a Cabalistic light, holding that the divine dignities were written into not only the fabric of the universe but also the language of Scripture.[83] The extensive development of the logical machinery of analysis and genesis by Piscator and other Ramists meant that Alsted had a ready-made pattern to hand for transforming Lullism into a biblical and theological method of reasoning. In this way, Lullism could be used to analyse the meaning of biblical passages, reveal their logical structure, and construct a multiplicity of syllogisms capable of addressing any theological debate.[84] Finally, following an important late medieval tradition, Alsted also sought to show how Lull's method could be used as an *ars concionandi* for generating and structuring sermons.[85]

As well as exploring the theological dimensions of Lullism, the *Clavis* also offers a condensed outline of a Lullist encyclopaedia. Alsted believed that Lullism offers a "true and solid science concerning every knowable", containing the principles of all the other sciences, just as particulars are found in universals.[86] Following Valerius, he drew extensively on Lull's "Hundred Forms" and especially his *Tree of Sciences*, which he calls his "divine summa". In this arboreal schema the predicates represent the roots of the trees and the various subjects the trunks, branches, and fruits of the trees so that the "whole multitude of being" can be expressed in just fourteen trees.[87] Strikingly, Alsted illustrates each of these trees with Ramist charts, revealing again his conviction of Ramism and Lullism as kindred methods.[88]

---

[80] Alsted, *Clavis*, 48, 80–86, 91–92.
[81] See, for example, Alsted, *Clavis*, 66, 92–93.
[82] For the late medieval and Renaissance integration of Lullism and scriptural piety see Emery, *Renaissance Dialectic*, 26–60. Kent Emery Jr., "Denys the Carthusian and the Invention of Preaching Materials", 406–7 and "Twofold Wisdom and Contemplation in Denys of Ryckel (Dionysius Cartusiensis, 1402–1471)", 129 both in *Monastic, Scholastic and Mystical Theologies from the Later Middle Ages* (Aldershot: Ashgate Variorum, 1996) hint at Denys' interest in Lullist, concordant methodology for biblical studies.
[83] Alsted, *Clavis*, 21, 126.
[84] Alsted, *Clavis*, 93–114, 150–54.
[85] Alsted, *Clavis*, 111–15. This anticipates the developed Lullist *Ars Concionandi* of his pupil Bisterfeld as we will see in the next chapter.
[86] Alsted, *Clavis*, 49, 79.
[87] Alsted, *Clavis*, 126–34.
[88] Alsted, *Clavis*, 132.

A much more ambitious attempt to combine Ramist and Lullist encyclopaedism can be found in the *Panacea Philosophica* of 1610. In this bold work, following the medieval alchemists, Alsted sought a philosophical panacea, or universal medicine, capable of curing the sickness which the intellect labours under in its "cognition of things, words and modes", and thus of restoring the perfection of the human mind, will and speech.[89] Notably, Alsted locates this panacea in Keckermann's own fourfold method of *lexica, praecognita, systemata*, and *gymnasia*.[90] Going beyond Keckermann, however, Alsted placed the Lullist art which he so despised as the foundation of the entire encyclopaedia. For he envisaged placing Lull's subjects, predicates, and questions in a single large folio volume as a "universal library of common places". Constructed as a theological encyclopaedia this could be used to refer everything to God whose attributes he describes as "scattered through singular disciplines".[91] Within such a schema Lullism constitutes the divine ground of the encyclopaedia, Keckermannian Ramism its methodological unfolding, and the *technologia* of Timpler enables the perfecting of every faculty of the human soul, mapping out a ground-plan for the instauration of the image of God.[92]

## 7.3. Harmonic Philosophy and *Mathesis Universalis*

Following the *Panacea* Alsted began to explore further the encyclopaedic and combinatorial potential of the Lullist Art, reaching towards what he called a new infinite, or harmonic, philosophy established on mathematical grounds. Significantly, such a move coincided with his own attempt to develop a *mathesis universalis*. Conceived at first simply as a "general mathematics", Alsted's later Lullist works reveal his desire to press beyond this towards a comprehensive mathematical treatment of all of reality.[93] Alsted's mathematical encyclopaedism has been neglected, but it connects him not only to the new mathematical spirit of his own age, anticipating Descartes and Leibniz, but also to a long tradition with deep roots in the Lullist and Cusan traditions.[94]

We may discern the beginnings of this mathematical turn in his 1610 *Criticus*, which offers an "infinite harmony of Aristotelian, Ramist and Lullist philosophy".

---

[89] Johann Heinrich Alsted, *Panacea Philosophica* (Herborn, 1610), 10–12. For the wider importance of the *Panacea* in this regard and its alchemical connections see Hotson, *Alsted*, 90–94.
[90] Alsted, *Panacea*, 6, 12.
[91] Alsted, *Panacea*, 16–17.
[92] Alsted, *Panacea*, 9–13, 18–19.
[93] For Alsted's early approach to *mathesis universalis* as "general mathematics" see Johann Heinrich Alsted, *Methodus Admirandorum Mathematicorum* (Herborn, 1613).
[94] Loemker, *Struggle for Synthesis*, 109 notes briefly Alsted's attempt to advance mathematics as a philosophical tool but suggests he was hampered by his lack of mathematical ability.

For, going beyond the *Panacea*, this offers the outline of a new philosophy in which logic, metaphysics, and mathematics all converge on a common theological centre—the divine infinity.[95] Confronting the fragmentation of philosophy into competing schools, Alsted traced the contemporary clash of methods back to the late medieval *Wegestreit*, and the bitter, internecine disputes between Realists and Nominalists.[96] While Alsted's solution to this has rightly been labelled eclecticism, it is better understood in his own terms as a harmonic or conciliatory philosophy.[97] For his eclecticism is grounded in the realization of a higher unity to which all the philosophical *viae* (note the term) lead as paths to a single goal. Alsted's optimistic hope was to combine the most "compendiary" ways of Aristotelianism, Ramism, and Lullism into a "threefold harmony", thus laying the foundation for the invention of a new "infinite philosophy".[98]

Alsted's desire to harmonize so many opposing schools of thought echoes Pico della Mirandola, a philosopher whom he called the "Prince of Erudition".[99] For Pico, in confronting at much closer proximity the chaos of the medieval schools, likewise appealed to a higher unity, which for him attained its ultimate expression in Christ and the Cabala.[100] It bears an even closer resemblance to another towering figure of the fifteenth century, namely Nicholas of Cusa. Whether or not Alsted knew his works directly, he would have certainly known them indirectly through Bruno, the Fabrists, and indeed Pico himself.[101] Certainly, he shared Cusa's conviction that a Lullist and mathematical method was the best approach to infinite truth. While the infinite cannot be realized in nature, it can be realized in mathesis, allowing the mind to extend reasoning to its infinite limit and serving as the template for an infinite philosophy.[102]

[95] Johann Heinrich Alsted, *Criticus de Infinito Harmonico*, in *Panacea*, 42–44.
[96] Alsted, *Criticus*, 42–43.
[97] Hotson, *Commonplace Learning*, 225–27 notes Alsted's eclecticism, its Renaissance roots and its new systematic expression.
[98] Alsted, *Criticus*, 42–44. Mercer, *Leibniz's Metaphysics*, 37–76 affirms the Neo-Platonic roots of early modern German eclecticism.
[99] Johann Heinrich Alsted, *Metaphysica, Tribus Libris Tractata* (Herborn, 1616), 63.
[100] See Pico, *Syncretism in the West*, 53–56, 211–49 and Pico, *Oration on the Dignity of Man*, ed. Borghesi, Papio, and Riva, 203–5, 261–65.
[101] Anita Traninger, *Mühelose Wissenschaft: Lullismus und Rhetorik in den deutschsprachigen Ländern der frühen Neuzeit* (Munich: Fink, 2001), pp. 169–71 points to Cusan affinities in Alsted. For the wider link of Alsted and the Herborn circle to the Fabrists see Antognazza, "Bisterfeld and *Immeatio*", 64–81. For an important example of Pico's dependence on Cusa compare the detailed account of the three worlds and the metaphysics of light in Cusa, *De Conjecturis*, 1.12.61–13.69 (*NCOO*, III.63–69) with Giovanni Pico della Mirandola, *Heptaplus*, in *Opera Omnia Ioannis Pici Mirandulae* (Basel, 1557), 5–6. Francisco Bastitta Harriet, "Giovanni Pico, a Reader of Cusanus? The *Imago Mundi* in *De Conjecturis* and *Heptaplus*" (conference paper given at Renaissance Society of America Virtual 2021) has recently argued for the same parallel and I am very grateful to him for discussion of this point.
[102] Alsted, *Criticus*, 58–59 argues that mathematics and the Lullist method of the infinite circle allows an ascent from sensibles to intelligibles unifying logic, grammar, and metaphysics. It also identifies mathematics in Cusan fashion as a kind of game of the mind. For Cusan links see Charles Lohr, "Mathematics and the Divine: Ramon Lull" and Jean-Michel Counet, "Mathematics and

Alsted defines his desired infinite harmony as the "method of treating one and the same thing by infinite modes".[103] Applying the combinatorics of the Lullist circles to the universal art of logic and to metaphysics as the "highest science" enables a method of infinite discourse in which infinite things can be said about infinite subjects.[104] Signalling more clearly his desire to institute Lullism as a divine logic, he also seeks to integrate testimony within this mathematical schema.[105] Significantly, Alsted presents a valuable "epitome of the infinite or circular harmony" in terms of the convertibility of circle, square, and triangle. Following an important fifteenth-century Lullist trend of geometrical method, he thus triangulates the circle of divine attributes with the respective principles governing their diffusion into the created order and the logical square of relations.[106] For Alsted, following Bonaventure, Cusa, and Ramus, God was to be understood as an "infinite circle whose centre is everywhere and circumference nowhere".[107] Mathematical symbolism thus points towards not only the harmony of different methods but also their unified ground and dynamic convertibility in the infinite being of God himself.

Following hot on the heels of the *Criticus* was the *Trigae Canonicae* of 1612, which yoked together the art of memory, Lullist logic, and Lullist rhetoric within a three-horsed chariot whose wheels were the combinatorial wheels of the Lullist Art itself.[108] Without a hint of the reservation found in the *Clavis*, Alsted represents Lull's Art as a divinely inspired method. Drawing on the Neo-Platonic metaphysics of light, in which God is the intelligible Sun and universals the intelligible rays streaming from him, he held that the "star" of Lull's intellect was particularly receptive to divine illumination. In a manner reminiscent of the Albertist or Cusan mystical tradition, it was thus the direct intuition of this divine light which allowed him to develop his universal art, the practitioners of which may ascend on high like contemplative eagles to gaze upon the divine Sun.[109]

---

the Divine in Nicholas of Cusa", both in *Mathematics and the Divine: A Historical Study*, ed. Luc Bergmans and Teun Keutsier (Amsterdam: Elsevier, 2005), 213–28 and 273–90 respectively.

[103] Alsted, *Criticus*, 45.
[104] Alsted, *Criticus*, 45–58.
[105] Alsted, *Criticus*, 48.
[106] Alsted, *Criticus*, 58–59. This is developed extensively in Johann Heinrich Alsted, *Trigae Canonicae* (Frankfurt, 1612). For fifteenth-century precedents in Heimeric de Campo and Cusa see Florian Hamann, *Das Siegel der Ewigheit: Universalwissenschaft und Konziliarismus bei Heymericus de Campo* (Münster: Aschendorff Verlag, 2006), 65–97, 129–42, 230–57.
[107] Johann Heinrich Alsted, *Loci Communes Theologici Perpetuis Similitudinibus Illustrati* (Frankfurt, 1630), 18. Hotson, *Alsted*, 199 cites this dictum but does not draw the link with Cusa or Ramus.
[108] Alsted, *Trigae Canonicae*, "*Epistola Dedicatoria*".
[109] Alsted, *Trigae Canonicae*, 48–51. Alsted notably emphasizes the proximity of Lullist and mathematical methods. For the Dionysian metaphysics of light in Albertism and Cusa see Jorge M. Machetta, "Die Präsenz Alberts des Großen im Denken des Nikolaus von Kues", in *Nikolaus von Kues*

The *Trigae* also reveals Alsted's fascination with the connections between mathematical mnemonics, Lullism, and theology. From Lavinheta, Alsted gained an understanding of mathematics as a transcendental science capable of motivating an ascent beyond images into the realm of intelligibles.[110] Through a careful mathematical arrangement of images according to their "natural coherence", he believed it would be possible to establish a comprehensive "universal encyclopaaedia" on mnemonic principles and even a new kind of systematic theology.[111] Much later, in his 1630 *Loci Communes Illustrati*, Alsted returned to this idea, presenting the whole body of theology in terms of an interconnected logical chain of images. While Alsted knew he would face the censure of the "Genevans" for doing so, he himself believed he was tapping into a profoundly biblical method, seen above all in the parables of Christ.[112] Complementing the Dominican mnemonic focus on images, the work is itself saturated with reference to the Neo-Platonic and Franciscan metaphysics of light and serves once again to show the integral link of Alsted's mnemonics to his quest for a Christian philosophy.[113]

Finally, undoubtedly the most important theological development in the *Trigae* was Alsted's reintegration of Lull's Trinitarian method into the framework of the encyclopaedia. We may see this first of all in Alsted's reincorporation of Lull's correlatives—notably absent in earlier works—as three coessential principles "by which all things are proved", making clear their connection to the intrinsic moments of activity—namely passive power, active power, and act—which Lull held to mirror the Trinity.[114] Even more significant is Alsted's account of the "immeation" (*immeatio*) of logical terms, subjects, and even entire disciplines. Rooted in the Fabrists, as Antognazza has shown, immeation referred either to the coinherence and convertibility of the Lullist absolute principles, as they "penetrate and immeate themselves in turn", or to the perichoresis of the divine persons themselves.[115] For Alsted, it offered an implicit Trinitarian framework for logic reminiscent of both Lull and Cusa.[116] Even more striking is Alsted's connection of immeation to Bruno's mysterious "Proteas" seal, which in

---

in der Geschichte des Platonismus, ed. Harald Schwaetzer and Henrieke Stahl (Regensburg: Roderer, 2007), 135–66.

[110] Lavinheta, *Opera*, 237ff. offered Alsted a sophisticated Lullist mathematics.
[111] Alsted, *Trigae Canonicae*, 18.
[112] Alsted, *Loci Communes Illustrati*, "*Praefatio*".
[113] Alsted, *Loci Communes Illustrati*, 1–7, 17–19. Alsted draws prominently on the Augustinian and Franciscan model of the books of nature and Scripture here.
[114] Alsted, *Trigae Canonicae*, 56–57; cf. Johnston, *Spiritual Logic*, 18–20.
[115] Johann Heinrich Alsted, *Methodus Theologiae in VI Libros Tributa* (Hanau, 1634), 208; *Trigae Canonicae*, 63. For links with the Fabrists see Antognazza, "Bisterfeld and *Immeatio*", 62–63.
[116] Alsted, *Trigae Canonicae*, 56–57, 66. Alsted's discussion of the second figure includes reference to the distinctive Lullist method of proof *per aequiparantiam*, which Johnston, *Spiritual Logic*, 114–17 describes as founding a kind of Trinitarian logic.

Cusan fashion enabled "all things to be said of all things", revealing the harmonious and encyclopaedic connection of all of reality.[117]

The *Trigae* marks the early zenith of Alsted's Lullist career, and in its own way is surely as important as the *Panacea* for understanding of his thought. While Hotson has brilliantly illuminated Alsted's use of Lullism as an "alchemical logic" its relation to his new mathematical project of encyclopaedism has largely gone unnoticed.[118] Significantly, this also serves to illustrate another important bond between Ramist and Lullist encyclopaedism. For Alsted's system of universal mathematics was heavily indebted to Ramus as well as Ramist mathematicians such as Buscher, Reisner, and Keckermann himself.[119] Ultimately, Alsted's own Lullist interests must be seen in light not only of hermetic interests but also of a broader Philippo-Ramist encyclopaedism by now deeply entrenched within Reformed pedagogy. Mapped out in an incipient fashion in the *Trigae* itself, in years to come his budding spiritual logic was to flower into a new Trinitarian method of encyclopaedic scope.

## 7.4. Towards a Triune Universal Method

Alsted's early works demonstrate his concern for a spiritual logic, but do little to map out the contours of his new scriptural and Trinitarian encyclopaedism. In this respect, his *Theologia Naturalis* of 1615 is both an important and programmatic work. For not only was this a key component of his massive multi-volume *Methodus Theologiae* but also it functioned as a crucial linchpin between his theological and encyclopaedic projects. For Hotson, both the comprehensive scope of the *Theologia Naturalis*, nearly unrivalled in contemporary German works, and the suspicion and downright hostility that it met are evidence that Alsted has by no means abandoned his "liberal anthropology".[120] By contrast, Muller and especially Han have tended to see Alsted as in fundamental continuity with the wider Reformed tradition.[121]

There can be no doubt that Alsted is daringly expansive in his natural theology. However, he also grounds this on a definite Reformed epistemology, following Calvin and Melanchthon in holding that there are divine sparks, or seeds, of reason within humanity which can be kindled and inflamed by grace.[122] In

---

[117] Alsted, *Trigae Canonicae*, 104–5. For Bruno's Proteas and other seals see Yates, *Art of Memory*, 239–59. For the Cusan connection see *De docta ignorantia*, 2.5.117–22 (*NCOO*, I.76–78).
[118] Hotson, *Alsted*, 82–89. Hotson certainly acknowledges Alsted's mathematical method in terms of his Lullist combinatorics (pp. 163–70) but does not dwell on it.
[119] Alsted, *Methodus Admirandorum Mathematicorum*, 19.
[120] Hotson, *Alsted*, 123–24.
[121] Muller, "Was It Really Viral?", 521–25 and Han, "Academization", 283–94.
[122] Alsted, *Theologia Naturalis*, I.3, 15. For the Augustinian and Stoic doctrine of seminal reasons in Reformation natural theology see Beck, "Melanchthonian Thought".

Thomistic fashion he holds that "grace amends nature and nature commends grace", although with the late medieval Augustinians he insists that natural knowledge is only efficacious in the elect through the "special help" of God's grace.[123] Unlike Keckermann—and in this respect at least he is undoubtedly less and not more "liberal" than him—he therefore rejects all a priori demonstrations of the Trinity.[124] For Alsted, the mystery of Christ and the Trinity clearly exceeds natural reason, although it in no way conflicts with it.[125] In this, his approach in the *Theologia Naturalis* clearly belongs within the wider ambit of the Reformed tradition as Muller outlines it.[126]

Nevertheless, and this is an important clue to the capaciousness of his discussion when compared with his contemporaries, Alsted is clear that declaring arguments can be provided for all the articles of faith even if demonstrative arguments cannot. Following Aquinas' *Summa Contra Gentiles*, Lull's rational apologetic and Philippe Duplessis-Mornay's *De la verité de la religion chrestienne* he can thus argue that the mystery of the Trinity has "certain images" in the book of nature—a radical reinterpretation of Lull's necessary reasons, but one that gave them much more traction in the Reformed tradition.[127] Drawing on the late medieval Nominalistic device of *in puris naturalibus*, Alsted also makes an important distinction between his own "naked" approach to natural theology according to pure reason alone and other "clothed" approaches which consider nature in relation to the realm of grace.[128] In this respect, Christian philosophy is the clothed, or graced, form of natural theology, which mediates between theology and naked philosophy.[129]

Alsted is adamant that natural theology, like Scripture itself, is a mode of divine revelation and not reducible to metaphysics. Illustrating this he draws on the important Augustinian and Franciscan motif of the books of God. While the notion of the "Two Books" was all but ubiquitous at this time, with an important presence in Reformed Confessions, Alsted's innovative account of the "fivefold book" of God—encompassing the book of divine decrees, the book of Scripture, the book of human deeds, the book of life and the book of nature—has undoubted medieval roots, deriving from Hugh of St Victor, as well as from

---

[123] Alsted, *Theologia Naturalis*, I.3–5. For a comparison of the Thomist and late medieval Augustinian doctrine of grace see Denis R. Janz, *Luther and Late Medieval Thomism: A Study in Theological Anthropology* (Waterloo: Wilfred Laurier University Press, 1983), 60–91.
[124] Alsted, *Theologia Naturalis*, I.12–15.
[125] Alsted, *Theologia Naturalis*, I.12–13.
[126] Muller, "Was It Really Viral?", 507–21.
[127] Alsted, *Theologia Naturalis*, I.13–14.
[128] Alsted, *Theologia Naturalis*, I.2–3. For the Nominalist device of "*in puris naturalibus*" see Heiko A. Oberman, *The Harvest of Medieval Theology: Gabriel Biel and Late Medieval Nominalism* (Grand Rapids, MI: Baker Academic, 2000), 47–50.
[129] Muller, "Was It Really Viral?", 524.

Bonaventure, whose *Hexaemeron* he knew well.[130] In particular, it has a pronounced Realist, exemplaristic and above all encyclopaedic element to it, highly redolent of both these medieval thinkers.[131]

For Alsted, the entire structure of the book of nature reflects the intrinsic metaphysical pattern of the universe. Its division thus mirrors the division of creatures into genera and species, with every creature marking a folio in the book of nature. The whole book of nature can also be read encyclopaedically, with each discipline a "representative world".[132] This can be seen graphically in the Ramist charts that structure the work, pointing to the way in which the encyclopaedia is to be understood both as a transcript of the universe and of the mind of God.[133] Echoing the *Panacea* Alsted holds that the "fame of God is scattered (*sparsa*) through the arts".[134] In Lullist fashion the goal of the encyclopaedia is to trace out the "conveniences and differences" which pattern all of creation.[135]

Alsted's Realism, exemplarism, and tempered Lullism thus serve to reinforce the intimate correspondence between the book of nature and the book of Scripture, as well as between philosophy and theology. Indeed, as in Richardson and Ames, the latter of whom had some contact with Alsted's work, the encyclopaedia actually becomes included in the ectypal knowledge of God and elevated into a mode of theology and devotion. Following a medieval, Franciscan model which we have seen in other Ramists, theology and the encyclopaedia become mutually informing. Indeed, according to this exemplaristic template, Scripture itself becomes a fountainhead of both theology and the encyclopaedia, launching a new project of biblical encyclopaedism. Alsted can thus speak passionately in the preface to the work of his desire to give his readers a sacred angelology, astronomy, anthropology, oeconomics, scholastics, politics, and ecclesiastics, not to mention a sacred meteorology, metallography, piscology, ornithology, and more.[136]

This reading of the *Theologia Naturalis* as a kind of prototype for a biblical encyclopaedia is confirmed in the expansive second-part of the work, in which

---

[130] Alsted, *Theologia Naturalis*, I.11–12, II.234–49; cf. Hugh of St Victor, *De Sacramentis Christianae Fidei*, 1.6.5 (*PL* 176.266B–267C); Bonaventure, *Breviloquium*, II.11.2 (p. 94; *BOO*, V.229). See further Johann Heinrich Alsted, *Compendium Theologicum* (Hanau, 1624), 14–20, 82–84. Hotson, *Alsted*, 124 notes that Bonaventure's *Hexaemeron* was a work he recommended highly. For further discussion of the book metaphor in the medieval and Renaissance tradition see Pavlas, "The Book Metaphor Triadized", 384–416.

[131] For the books of God in Victorine and Franciscan theology see Boyd Taylor Coolman, *The Theology of Hugh of St Victor: An Interpretation* (Cambridge: Cambridge University Press, 2013), 131–33 and Bonaventure, *Breviloquium*, II.11.2 (p. 94; *BOO*, V.229).

[132] Alsted, *Theologia Naturalis*, II.233–34.

[133] See, for example, Alsted, *Theologia Naturalis*, II.231.

[134] Johann Heinrich Alsted, *Triumphus Bibliorum Sacrorum seu Encyclopaedia Biblica* (Frankfurt, 1625), 22 and *Encyclopaedia*, 1.78.

[135] Alsted, *Theologia Naturalis*, I.31–32.

[136] Alsted, *Theologia Naturalis*, "Praefatio".

he treats each of these sacred disciplines. On the face of it his method is purely Ramistic, and we have already mentioned the Ramist charts that structure the work, but on closer inspection it becomes clear that his Ramism is incorporated within a dynamic, Trinitarian framework. Rather like Szegedinus, this becomes evident in his important use of triadic charts.[137] Drawing on Hugh of St Victor's *De Arca Noe Morali*, Alsted speaks of every creature as a threefold "voice of God". Caught up in the Augustinian Trinitarian nexus of giver, receiver, and gift, each creature reflects the Trinity and serves the threefold purpose of helping us to worship God, know ourselves, and love our neighbour.[138] Building on this, Alsted proposes a "golden rule" for reading the book of nature, namely that each page of it—each creature—must be treated according to a sevenfold pattern. Theoretically it must be read according to both its nature and history, while practically it must be read according to its own voice, God's voice within it, and the threefold division of human duties to God, self, and neighbour. While this admittedly seems somewhat forced, it bears a clear resemblance not only to the Victorines but also especially to Bonaventure's *Itinerarium Mentis in Deum* with its distinctive interweaving of triads and septads in the mystical ascent to the Triune God.[139]

Highlighting this new Trinitarian reading of the book of nature we also find Alsted speaking quite openly of his desire for what he calls a "Triune universal philosophy and theology". Modifying his earlier discussion he now describes Scripture, nature, and conscience as a universal, threefold book of God:

> All mysteries of God and secrets of nature, which indeed God wants us to know, every reason of morality and of just laws, all knowledge of past, present and future things, wells up, flows out and flows into us by right of creation and redemption from this threefold font; and are revealed to us and handed down, I say, from the biblical book of Holy Scripture, from the macrocosmic [book] and microcosmic [book].[140]

It is this triune book read in a triune manner which becomes the basis for the desired Triune universal method. Presented in terms of a ninefold unfolding into

---

[137] Alsted, *Theologia Naturalis*, II.243.
[138] Alsted, *Theologia Naturalis*, II.234–41; cf. Hugh of St Victor, *De Arca Noe Morali Libri IV*, 2.3–4 (*PL*, 176 col. 637A–638D).
[139] Alsted, *Theologia Naturalis*, II.241–48; cf. Hugh of St Victor, *De Arca Noe Morali Libri IV*, 2.3–4 (*PL*, 176 col. 637A–638D) and Bonaventure, *Itinerarium*, 1.6, 10–14; 2.10, 12; 3.5–7 (*BOO*, V.297–99, 302–3, 305–6).
[140] Alsted, *Theologia Naturalis*, II.242: "*Omnia siquidem Dei mysteria, naturaeq., secreta, quae quidem ille nos scire vult, omnis morum et legum iustarum ratio, omnis praeteritorum, praesentium et futurom notitia ex triplici hoc fonte scaturiunt, emanant, et derivantur in nos iure creationis et redemtionis; ex libro inquam Sacrae Scripturae Biblico, Macrocosmico, et Microcosmico, nobis revelantur et traduntur*".

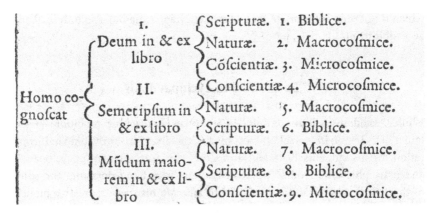

**Figure 7.3** Triadic chart of Triune universal philosophy from Johann Heinrich Alsted, *Theologia Naturalis Exhibens Augustissimam Naturae Scholam* (Frankfurt, 1615), II.243. Reproduced by kind permission of the Bibliothèque Nationale de France.

a triad of triads, man comes to know God, himself and the world biblically, macrocosmically, and microcosmically (Figure 7.3). The Trinity thus becomes the exemplaristic ground of all being and knowing, leading us finally to the divine good of the vision, cognition, union, and fruition of God.[141]

In this, once again, Alsted can be seen to share deep affinities whose *Breviloquium*, along with his *Itinerarium*, stands out as his most important methodological model. For it is in this work that the Seraphic Doctor offers a Trinitarian and exemplaristic coordination of the different books of God, treating Scripture as a "certain noble mirror" and method as the harmonizing of Scripture, macrocosm, and microcosm.[142] For Alsted, this Triune, universal method is also the "true Cabal". It gives access to the voice of God which is "in all, through all, concerning all, to all, speaking to us always and everywhere either biblically or macrocosmically or microcosmically".[143] In knowing things "biblically, macrocosmically and microcosmically" it gives a "circular and therefore perfect cognition" of all things in God.[144] Here, the triune interaction of the three books, and especially their mutual penetration and informing of each other, reflects not only a Bonaventuran pattern of contuition but also a profoundly Lullist dynamic. In this sense we might speak of a kind of sublimation of Franciscan, Cabalistic, and Lullist methods into a new Triune methodology

[141] Alsted, *Theologia Naturalis*, II.242–43.
[142] Bonaventure, *Breviloquium*, "Prologue" (pp. 2, 4, 9, 16; BOO, V.201–2, 203–4, 206).
[143] Alsted, *Theologia Naturalis*, II.242.
[144] Alsted, *Theologia Naturalis*, II.243.

which is not only appropriate for a sacred encyclopaedia but also universal and accessible to all.

## 7.5. Biblical Encyclopaedism

While Alsted himself never fulfilled his own far-reaching ambitions to attain a new Triune universal philosophy and theology, this proved a vital inspiration for his students Bisterfeld and Comenius in their own encyclopaedic and pansophic endeavours. Nevertheless, far from lying dormant, the spirit of this Triune universal method came to animate his own impressive biblical encyclopaedia, the *Triumphus Bibliorum Sacrorum* of 1625. The nature and purpose of Alsted's scriptural encyclopaedism has been the subject of much discussion, with both Sheehan and Jan Čížek seeing it as a failed endeavour and little more than a superficial veneer for his secular encyclopaedism.[145] By contrast, Hotson acknowledges the *Triumphus* as one of Alsted's "most famous and significant works", only opposing the idea that the work can be seen as a "retreat from eclecticism into biblical fundamentalism". Notably, he blames Comenius for starting the trend of misinterpreting the work as a purely biblical—rather than biblically-grounded—encyclopaedia.[146]

Certainly, it is clear, as Hotson rightly points out, that Alsted did not wish to argue that Scripture was the *sole* norm of philosophy.[147] Likewise, we should also be careful to distinguish his wider enterprise of Christian philosophy from the rather more specific approach of the *Triumphus*.[148] Yet as the fruit of more than a year of intense meditation on Scripture and the Cross of Christ,[149] every page of the *Triumphus* breathes out not only a deep love for and devotion to the Bible, but also a conviction of its central importance to the philosophical project. Affirming the centrality of the Bible for the encyclopaedia, Alsted affirms that "in the codex of the holy scriptures, as though in some cornucopia, are contained the seeds of the whole of philosophy".[150] Scripture must therefore certainly be seen as bearing a programmatic relation to Alsted's own encyclopaedism, even if not always a determinative one.

Precisely what this means is spelled out clearly in the rest of the work. Drawing on the *De Fonte Lucis* of Denys the Carthusian, he describes the encyclopaedia as

---

[145] Sheehan, "From Philology to Fossils", 41–60 and Jan Čížek, "The 'Physica Mosaica' of Johann Heinrich Alsted", *Teorie Vědy/Theory of Science* 42.1 (2020): 117–39.
[146] Hotson, *Alsted*, 140–42.
[147] Hotson, *Alsted*, 140–41 rightly emphasizes this point.
[148] See the definite contrast between the discussion of Christian and scriptural philosophy in Hotson, *Alsted*, 110 and 140–42.
[149] Hotson, *Alsted*, 142.
[150] Alsted, *Triumphus*, "*Praefatio*".

structuring a threefold path of ascent to God, an itinerary through the mystical stages of purgation, illumination, and union.[151] In triadic fashion he recognizes three degrees of principles governing the encyclopaedia and harmonizing the lights of nature and grace: infused, innate, and acquired. The highest, infused principles contained in Scripture govern and inform all the principles below them, including those innate principles which are the "seeds" of philosophy.[152] Scripture is seen as both generative of all the principles of the arts and sciences, like a "cornucopia" or an "inexhaustible fount", and regulative of them, as their "touchstone" or "canon".[153]

Scripture also becomes central to the methodological construction of the encyclopaedia, with the *Triumphus* expressing the desire to unfold the whole Bible into a system of commonplaces.[154] More specifically, Alsted's purpose is to draw out of Scripture all material relating to the arts and sciences and then arrange this "by a certain method into chapters and systems of faculties and disciplines, or parts of systems, or finally combinations of various systems".[155] Indeed, he believed that Scripture contained "sacred predicaments" and thus was not only pregnant with its own logic but also capable of revealing universal tables showing all the conveniences and differences of things and functioning as Ramistic commonplaces to which anything in the world can be referred.[156]

We also find important hints in the *Triumphus* that Alsted hoped to express his new biblical conception of the encyclopaedia in a Lullist and combinatorial manner. His affirmation that the seeds of philosophy have been strewn through the Bible and book of nature is redolent of the *Panacea*.[157] Even more significant is his view of the different divisions of the encyclopaedia as "disciplinary circles" which can be combined together in combinatorial fashion. In these terms, Alsted's insistence that Scripture is the centre of every (didactic) doctrine, and the centre of every truth,[158] begins to take on a new and deeper significance. We see a similar pattern in the combination of the various "rays" of intelligence, synteresis, wisdom, science, prudence, and art through which all the faculties are illuminated. In fact, Alsted can go further, seeing the whole encyclopaedia as a combination of lights governed by the canon that "whatever is more intelligible or loveable is to be preferred". In this sense not only does Scripture form

---

[151] Alsted, *Triumphus*, 4.
[152] Alsted, *Triumphus*, 1–7.
[153] Alsted, *Triumphus*, "*Mens Authoris*"; "*Praefatio*".
[154] Alsted, *Triumphus*, "*Mens Authoris*"; cf. Hotson, *Alsted*, 137.
[155] Alsted, *Triumphus*, "*Praefatio*",
[156] Alsted, *Triumphus*, 592–97.
[157] Alsted, *Triumphus*, "*Praefatio*"; 22.
[158] Alsted, *Triumphus*, 26.

the centre and circumference of every discipline, but also it is a Lullist principle which governs the combinatorial construction of the entire encyclopaedia.[159]

For Alsted, the entire enterprise of "sacred" or "Christian philosophy" is thus the centring of truth on Scripture. In light of the *Theologia Naturalis* this all makes perfect sense.[160] For the "Triune universal philosophy and theology" which he sought there likewise assumed an intimate compenetration of the books of nature and Scripture, something which Alsted expresses in the *Triumphus* in terms of the coalescing of innumerable rays of the light of nature and grace. In fact, the triad of Scripture, reason, and experience that Alsted continually recurs to in the *Triumphus* clearly echoes the Triune book of the *Theologia Naturalis*, with reason relating to the microcosm and experience to the macrocosm.[161] For Alsted, all of philosophy should conform to the Triune God. As he boldly expresses this, the doctrine of the Trinity is the "foundation of every solid wisdom", such that every wisdom outside of this dogma is "pure foolish stupidity". Abandoning something of the caution of the *Theologia Naturalis*, and his other earlier theological works, Alsted even goes on to claim that the "trace (*vestigium*) of unity and trinity" may be seen "in the whole of nature by the eyes of the mind", so that if we "run through all and singular creatures we will see unity not to be without trinity, nor trinity without unity".[162]

## 7.6. Scriptural and Scotist Metaphysics

We may gain some insight about what Alsted meant by this both from the "Sacred Metaphysics" of the *Triumphus* and from his earlier *Metaphysica*. For in both of these we find him seeking to develop his Trinitarian metaphysics in the wake of Scaliger and the wider Scotist turn of early modernity. Alsted had the greatest admiration for Scaliger, whom he called the "most subtle of all mortals", and also recognized his profound debt to Scotus.[163] Such Scotist influences were further reinforced by his engagement with Keckermann and Polanus, but even more so by his intensive study of Lavinheta and Valerius. For both encyclopaedists are prime exemplars of that prevailing fifteenth- and sixteenth-century tendency to

---

[159] Alsted, *Triumphus*, 7–10. For the Lullist character of such "necessary reasons" see Johnston, *Spiritual Logic*, 76–93.
[160] For Alsted's identification of this as a Christian philosophy see *Triumphus*, 24–26.
[161] Alsted, *Triumphus*, 5.
[162] Alsted, *Triumphus*, 54: "*qui vestigium unitatis et trinitatis in tota natura oculis mentis se ingerere animadverunt. Percurre omnes et singulas creaturas, videbis unitatem non esse sine trinitate, neque trinitatem sine unitate*".
[163] Alsted, *Systema Mnemonicum*, II.72, 117. Alsted refers to Scaliger's view of Scotus as the "polisher of truth".

read Lull through a Scotist prism.[164] In particular, their thought assumes an innovative coordination of the Trinity, divine attributes, and divine ideas within the ambit of Scotus' formal distinction, according to which all of being becomes a dynamic reflection of the unity-in-distinction of the Trinity.[165]

For Alsted, as for these Lullists, all of reality may be said to emanate from the Trinity. Following a Scotistic paradigm he distinguishes two different "moments of nature" within God: his essence and his life.[166] For Scotus, we will recall, the framework of moments of nature was used to characterize the inner emanation within God of divine attributes, persons, and ideas from the divine essence. It was grounded on a metaphysics of synchronic contingency, in which an instant of time or the single "instant" of eternity could be analysed into different logical instants.[167] Just the same is true of Alsted, who draws explicitly on both Scaliger and Scotus in explaining his understanding of moments of nature and contingency.[168] For he too distinguishes the essence (first moment) from the divine life "flowing from the divine essence" (second moment) and subsequently dividing into the twin channels of the principal divine attributes of power, intellect and will (absolute) and the divine persons of Father, Son, and Holy Spirit (respective).[169]

Referencing the Neo-Platonic metaphysics of light, Alsted compares the emanation of the divine persons, and indeed the divine ideas, to rays flowing from the Sun.[170] While Alsted speaks of a modal distinction of the persons he is clear that this is *ex natura rei* and must be understood in close proximity to Scotus' formal distinction.[171] Notably, in his treatment of both the divine attributes and divine ideas, Alsted shows a deep concern to reconcile Thomist and Scotist understandings, holding that these are only rationally distinct from the divine essence itself but become formally distinct as they emanate from it.[172] Yet in identifying these as inner emanations within God distinguished according to various logical instants of nature he follows a definite Scotist trajectory.

Equally Franciscan and Scotist is Alsted's extensive comparison of the relation of divine essence and persons in the Trinity to that of universals and particulars.

---

[164] See Rafael Ramis Barceló, "En torno al Escoto-Lulismo de Pere Dagui", *Medievalia* 16 (2013): 235–64; Victor, "Revival of Lullism", 517–20; and Meier-Oeser, "Von der Koinzidenz zur *coincidentia oppositorum*", 325–30.

[165] See Lavinheta, *Opera*, 40–54, 62–63, 443–53 and Valerius, *Aureum Sane Opus*, 17.

[166] Alsted, *Methodus*, 54.

[167] Scotus, *God and Creatures*, q. 5 art. 2 n. 55 (p. 127). For the link between emanation and Scotus' contingency metaphysics see Sylwanowicz, *Contingent Causality*, 123–92.

[168] Alsted, *Metaphysica*, 43, 231–32 cites Scotus and Scaliger on both these points.

[169] Alsted, *Methodus*, 54–55.

[170] Johann Heinrich Alsted, *Theologia Scholastica Didactica* (Hanau, 1618), 124; *Methodus*, 213.

[171] Alsted, *Methodus*, 203–4, 207–8; *Metaphysica*, 248 identifies the distinction between the persons as modal, real, and rational.

[172] Alsted, *Methodus*, 213.

In his *Triumphus* he is explicit in correlating the two moments of existence within God with the divine essence and persons according to the model of universal and particulars.[173] What this implies, as indeed he makes fully explicit, is an intimate connection between the Trinitarian emanation of persons, the divine ideas, and their created instantiations, whether universal or particular. Alsted can thus distinguish the "absolute archetype" of the divine essence itself from the "relative archetype" as the "essence of divine idea which God conceives from eternity inside himself, as ... the exemplar of things proceeding outside God in time".[174]

For Alsted, the Trinity thus becomes the dynamic pattern of all creation. In particular, he weaves together the Trinity, the threefold causality of God, the three principal attributes and the transcendentals in a complex pattern. Drawing on Pico, Alsted thus relates God as efficient, exemplary, and final cause of all creation to being, truth, and goodness respectively.[175] In a number of places he can also parallel the Trinity to the transcendentals of being as well as the principal attributes of Power, Wisdom, and Love, which he insists are "insculpted" in all creatures. Indeed, Alsted can even maintain, against the mainstream of the Augustinian tradition, that Power is in the Father, Wisdom in the Son, and Love in the Holy Spirit.[176] In this he follows the early Scotus and a number of medieval Scotists in offering an absolute treatment of the persons.[177]

Unsurprisingly, Alsted's treatment of the transcendentals also follows a markedly Scotist trajectory. He thus identifies the transcendentals as intrinsic modes of being which are "unitively contained in being", really identical with it but formally distinct, just as intellect and will relate to the soul. Here, not only the comparison between the transcendentals and the powers of the soul but also the Dionysian concept of "unitive containment" derives directly from Scotus.[178] Significantly, Alsted's threefold division of the transcendentals in the

---

[173] Alsted, *Theologia Scholastica*, 57–60; *Triumphus*, 28–30. Compare with Alsted, *Methodus*, 208 where he disavows this analogy due to the immeation of persons. For the Scotist nature of this see Richard Cross, "Duns Scotus on Divine Substance and the Trinity", *Medieval Philosophy and Theology* 11.2 (2003): 185. On pp. 181–83 he notes that this was a view specifically rejected by Aquinas and Augustine but shared with the Cappadocians.

[174] Alsted, *Triumphus*, 29.

[175] Alsted, *Metaphysica*, 63–64.

[176] Alsted, *Methodus*, 65–67; *Metaphysica*, 248–49.

[177] For Scotus and the wider context of this see Russell L. Friedman, *Intellectual Traditions at the Medieval University: The Use of Philosophical Psychology in Trinitarian Theology among the Franciscans and Dominicans, 1250–1350*, 2 vols. (Leiden: Brill, 2013), 345–75. See also Scotus, *Ord.* 1 d. 26 q. 1 n. 70–71 (Vatican, VI.29).

[178] Alsted, *Metaphysica*, 60; *Encyclopaedia*, 3.579–80, 603–4; cf. John Duns Scotus, *Quaestiones in Librum Secundum*, 2 d. 16, n. 17–22, in John Duns Scotus, *Joannis Duns Scoti Doctoris Subtilis, Ordinis Minorum, Opera Omnia*, ed. Ludovic Vivès, 26 vols. (Paris, 1891), 13.43–47. Alsted, *Systema Mnemonicum*, I.319 affirms explicitly that he follows a Scotist, and indeed Scaligeran, account of the powers of the soul. Alsted here offers a detailed account of his understanding of the formal distinction *ex natura rei* which both draws on and modifies Pedro da Fonseca, *Comentariorum P. Fonsecae D. Theologi Societatis Iesu, In Libros Metaphysicorum Aristotelis Stagiritae Tomus Primus* (Lyon, 1585), 587–88, 600–602.

*Triumphus*—into being, moments of being, and modes of being—finds its direct parallel in God himself. Indeed, as becomes clear in the *Triumphus*, the relation of creaturely essence and existence (as first and second moments of being) mirrors the dynamic unity-in-distinction of the Trinity.[179] In Scotist fashion universals and particulars are thus understood to be formally distinct, and Alsted is explicit in his espousal of Scotus' *haecceitas* as the principle of individuation.[180] Indeed, Alsted's important treatment of Scotus' formal distinction in both his Mosaic physics and *Triumphus* confirms that this is at the heart of his Christian philosophy.[181] While Alsted's earlier works explicitly repudiated Scotus' univocity of being, his later works follow Goclenius in contrasting a logical order in which being is "prior" to God and a metaphysical order in which being is "posterior" to God.[182] In this, following Lavinheta and other Scotists, he perhaps seeks to blend something of a univocal and analogical treatment of being.[183]

Drawing on a Franciscan and Neo-Platonic trope Alsted describes metaphysics as the centre of the entire circle of disciplines. In this context the different encyclopaedic arts and sciences can all be compared to radial lines emanating from and converging on their metaphysical centre. Metaphysics is the Sun of the philosophical heaven, logic its Moon, and all the other disciplines like bright stars irradiated by its light.[184] Centred on metaphysics all disciplines may thus be considered as founded exemplaristically on the transcendentals and thus the Trinity. The whole of creation becomes a Trinitarian and analogical ladder of being which the soul ranges up and down according to a distinctive threefold motion. The first motion, from the intellect, is the descent from the most general principles of metaphysics to the particular conclusions of other disciplines. This is followed by an ascent through the senses from singulars to universals. Finally, there is circular motion, the most perfect of all, which is the full conversion of the ascent and descent into the rational discourse of the mind.[185]

Returning to the *Triumphus* what we find therefore is a biblical encyclopaedia expounded according to a definite Franciscan and Lullist template. Like Bonaventure, Alsted clearly conceives the encyclopaedia as a circle of lights

---

[179] Alsted, *Triumphus*, 27–37.
[180] Alsted, *Metaphysica*, 250.
[181] Johann Heinrich Alsted, *Systema Physicae Harmonicae* (Herborn, 1612), 20; *Metaphysica*, 250; *Triumphus*, 44–45. The *Triumphus* expresses this in terms of a real, modal distinction as opposed to a pure distinction of reason.
[182] Alsted, *Theologia Naturalis*, I.31–32 explicitly repudiates Scotus' univocity of being in favour of a Thomist, analogical understanding of being. Alsted, *Encyclopaedia*, 3.574 affirms that being is prior to God in the order of predication.
[183] Alsted, *Encyclopaedia*, 3.574 suggests that being is said of God univocally and of creatures analogically. Lavinheta, *Opera*, 448–49 argues explicitly for the compability of analogy with the univocity of being. From Smith, "Analogy of Being", 633–73 it is clear that this is the common position of the Scotist school.
[184] Alsted, *Metaphysica*, "Praefatio".
[185] Alsted, *Metaphysica*, "Praefatio".

centred on, and indeed emanating from, Scripture. In Lullist fashion he goes on to describe this as a series of combinatorial circles centred on Scripture and paralleling the dynamic circular motion of the divine and human minds. Finally, as in Bonaventure, the encyclopaedia must be understood as grounded on a dynamic correlation of the Trinity and the transcendentals of being. In this the encyclopaedia itself comes to mirror the emanation and return of all things to the Triune God.[186]

## 7.7. Trinitarian and Apocalyptic Encyclopaedism

Alsted wrote his *Triumphus* in the midst of some of the darkest days of the Thirty Years' War. Convinced that he was living in the last age of the world, which would usher in the Millennial reign of the saints on earth, he sought to show in a "Sacred Chronology" included within the work how the entire history—and future—of the Church was recapitulated in the Book of Revelation. For Alsted, the breaking of the seven seals saw the expansion of the Church in its first centuries and the triumph of Christian Empire. This was followed by the seven trumpets proclaiming the twin evils of the rise of the Papal Monarchy and the spread of Islam. The last of these had sounded in the days of Petrarch, Wyclif, and Hus heralding a new age of reform. The first bowl of God's wrath had coincided with the spread of the Protestant Gospel, and Alsted himself was now living in the time of the third bowl in which bloody war was being poured out on the Earth. All that remained before the Millennium was the conversion of the Jews and the defeat of the Papal Antichrist.[187]

For Alsted, the encyclopaedia was thus a reading not only of the book of nature or book of Scripture, open for all to see, but also of the hidden book of divine providence. It became a key to unlock the threefold book of God.[188] Notably, Hotson traces the roots of this apocalyptic conception all the way back to Alsted's student days, and especially to the confluence of astrological and hermetic currents which shaped the Marburg reform.[189] Yet while he is undoubtedly right to argue that Alsted's encyclopaedism and apocalyptic were entwined from the beginning, there remains a need to see their developing bond in the context of Alsted's own lifelong search for a Christian philosophy. In doing so, we will see

---

[186] Alsted, *Triumphus* 1–40; cf. Bonaventure, *Itinerarium*, 13.5–7 and *De Reductione*, 4, 6–7 (*BOO*, V.305–6, 321–22).

[187] Alsted, *Triumphus*, 493–95.

[188] Alsted, *Theologia Naturalis*, I.11–12 linked the fivefold book of God to the hidden decrees of the divine will.

[189] Howard Hotson, *Paradise Postponed: Johann Heinrich Alsted and the Birth of Calvinist Millenarianism* (Dordrecht: Springer, 2000), 33–84.

that his encyclopaedism was shaped by a powerful biblical and Trinitarian vision of reform rooted in Franciscan eschatology.

Retracing our steps to Alsted's formative years we already find evidence of an important Franciscan matrix for his encyclopaedic and apocalyptic thought in his Lavinheta edition of 1612. For Hotson, this work represents both the "deepest penetration of Alsted's early published works into the murky world of Renaissance occultism" and a milestone in the development of his hermetic eschatology.[190] In the *Trigae* Alsted had already experimented with using Lullist wheels to represent at a "single glance" the revolution of the ages from the world's creation to its final days.[191] In Lavinheta's encyclopaedia this is taken a step further by assimilating Lull's combinatorial wheels to the revolutions of the planets in the heavens.[192] In this way, Lavinheta's harnessing of alchemical medicine with Lullist astrological wheels in order to develop a universal panacea for all human ills is seen by Hotson as the epitome of Marburg hermeticism, with its drive for human deification.[193]

Yet, without in any way discounting these hermetic affinities, on closer inspection a rather different picture begins to reveal itself. For as a Fabrist, Lavinheta belonged to a movement of Christocentric and evangelical reform and his encyclopaedia must be seen in this late medieval, devotional context.[194] Following Bonaventure, Christ is seen as the centre of every discipline in the encyclopaedia, the point to which they all return as lines converging on the middle of a circle.[195] Crucially this Christological emphasis carries over into the discussion of both astrology and alchemy. For Lavinheta, the revolution of the heavens emanates from the love of God as Prime Mover and is directed towards "attaining an end in the most glorious body of Christ".[196] Likewise, the discussion of alchemical medicine, drawn from Lull and the fourteenth-century Spiritual Franciscans Arnold de Villanova and John de Rupescissa, is prefaced by a prayer placing all healing under the canopy of Christ's redemption and reflecting an important patristic and medieval tradition of Christ as the "double medicine" for body and soul.[197] Indeed, the quest for the quintessence becomes viewed as a gracious anticipation of eschatological redemption.[198] Zachary Matus insists that Franciscan alchemy of the fourteenth century was shaped far more by a

---

[190] Hotson, *Alsted*, 90; *Paradise Postponed*, 79–80.
[191] Alsted, *Trigae Canonicae*, 169–71; cf. Hotson, *Paradise Postponed*, 77–78.
[192] Hotson, *Paradise Postponed*, 79–80.
[193] Hotson, *Alsted*, 91–94.
[194] For Lavinheta's connection to the Fabrists see Victor, "Revival of Lullism", 533.
[195] Lavinheta, *Opera*, 658.
[196] Lavinheta, *Opera*, 78. This is also seen in pp. 324–34 where astrology is integrated into the Calendar of Saints of the Catholic Church.
[197] Lavinheta, *Opera*, 348–49, 428.
[198] Lavinheta, *Opera*, 348–49.

Christian Edenic paradigm than a hermetic one, and this still seems equally true of Lavinheta himself.[199]

We have touched above on the broad Franciscan dimensions of the Marburg reform. What is striking is that Alsted was well aware of this himself. In his *Encyclopaedia* he pointed out that the Paracelsians were not original at all but drew their "every doctrine" from the chemical works of Lull, Villanova, Rupescissa, Isaac Holland, Abbot Trithemius, and others. As if to reinforce the point, Alsted adds that "very many" of the more recent chemists have also been monks.[200] For those who might be worried about Paracelsus' orthodoxy, Alsted thus deftly resituates alchemy as a truly Christian philosophy. Indeed, for Alsted, Villanova was not only a pioneer of alchemy but also a "witness of the truth" who had stood up against the Papal Antichrist. Belonging to the same age as Wyclif, Hus, and Savonarola, he too could be seen as one of the heralds of the seventh trumpet.[201]

Alsted's recognition of this link was astute. For Franciscan alchemy was intimately connected to universal reform through its espousal of the controversial eschatology of Abbot Joachim of Fiore. Correlating the unfolding of the ages with the persons of the Trinity, this led to expectation of a dawning Third Age of the Holy Spirit. For Roger Bacon, this fed into his vision of a renewed Papal Church spearheaded by the Franciscan Order. For Villanova and Rupescissa, living in the wake of the Spiritual Franciscan Movement, the coming confrontation with the Papal Antichrist was utmost in their minds. For these Franciscan alchemists the production of the elixir of life and transmuted gold were to be seen as important spiritual weapons and part of a wider quest to institute a scriptural philosophy.[202] In Rupescissa, these views further crystallized into a Millenarian understanding which anticipated the imminent rule of the saints, the conversion of the Jews, and the establishing of a perfect Church on earth.[203]

Alsted's enlisting of Villanova as a forerunner of the Reformation and his commitment to an alchemical reform movement rooted in Franciscan ideals raises the question of his own links to medieval Millenarianism. Following the Lutheran Reformation there was a resurgence of interest in Joachimite prophecy in Germany and there can be no doubt, as Hotson hints, that Alsted belongs to this wider Joachimite movement.[204] Alsted knew Joachim's works and cited

---

[199] Zachary Matus, *Franciscans and the Elixir of Life: Religion and Science in the Later Middle Ages* (Philadelphia: University of Pennsylvania Press, 2007), 104–110.

[200] Alsted, *Encyclopaedia*, 2.2010. The same point about the lack of originality of the Paracelsians is made by Daniel Sennertus, *Chymistry Made Easy and Useful* (London, 1662), 19, who notes that it would be unnecessary to have Paracelsus' works if those of Isaac Holland were extant.

[201] Johann Heinrich Alsted, *Thesaurus Chronologiae* (Herborn, 1624), 235.

[202] Matus, *Franciscans and the Elixir of Life*, 95–96.

[203] Leah DeVun, *Prophecy, Alchemy, and the End of Time: John Rupescissa in the Late Middle Ages* (New York: Columbia University Press, 2009), 37–44.

[204] Howard Hotson, "Outsiders, Dissenters and Competing Visions of Reform", in *The Oxford Handbook of the Protestant Reformations*, ed. Ulinka Rublack (Oxford: Oxford University Press,

his commentary on Revelation for the important view that the Church itself would be the seat of Antichrist.[205] He was also deeply influenced by the eschatological calculations made by Villanova and Rupescissa, and taken up wholesale by Lutheran Reformers, and used these to offer his own prediction that the Millennium would begin in 1694.[206] As the *Triumphus* reveals, he was plainly committed to a historical concordism with profound roots in a Joachimite and Franciscan view of history. In such a context, Alsted's frequent references to the triadic pattern of the Kingdoms of Nature, Grace, and Glory is redolent of Joachim's own Trinitarian and concordant eschatology.[207]

From the beginning Franciscan and Joachimite eschatology were thus an important seedbed for Alsted's apocalypticism. It was no surprise that in this fertile soil other apocalyptic and Millenarian impulses began to germinate and flower. In an age of increasing confessional conflict, in which the threat of war loomed ever larger, many began to look not only to the Bible but also to the heavens for signs disclosing God's purposes. The appearance of a new star in 1603, coinciding with a rare "great conjunction" of Jupiter and Saturn, fuelled enormous apocalyptic speculation, causing many to look for Christ's Second Advent.[208] Caught up in the excitement, as Hotson has convincingly shown, Alsted eagerly turned to the works of the Silesian astrologer Johannes Dobricius and Hungarian-Slavic philosopher Stephanus Pannonius for illumination. Drawing on Dobricius' astrology and Pannonius' "circle of the works and judgement of God", he was moved to prophesy a new "reformation of the Church" and a "universal alteration of the world" which would culminate in the Hungarian lands with great revival, and presage the mass conversion of the Jews, ushering in the events of the end times.[209]

So confident in this prediction was Alsted that he even included a version of it in the prefatory remarks to his *Cursus* of 1620, his first encyclopaedia.[210] By this time the Thirty Years' War was well underway, heightening the atmosphere of eschatological expectation still further. At first, Alsted shared in the enthusiasm, but, as Hotson has shown, the catastrophic defeats of Protestant forces in Bohemia, the Rhineland, and Palatinate, which touched him personally in the destructive occupation of Herborn in 1625–26, caused him to rethink

---

2016), 311; Leigh T. I. Penman, *Hope and Heresy: The Problem of Chiliasm in Lutheran Confessional Culture, 1570–1630* (Dordrecht: Springer, 2019), 3.

[205] Hotson, *Paradise Postponed*, 7 n. 23; cf. Johann Heinrich Alsted, *Paratitla Theologica* (Frankfurt, 1626), 16–17; *Compendium Theologicum*, 83.
[206] Hotson, *Paradise Postponed*, 95–100.
[207] Alsted, *Triumphus*, 466–67. Alsted, *Methodus*, 46 expresses all of theology programmatically in terms of the threefold Kingdom of Nature, Grace, and Glory.
[208] Hotson, *Alsted*, 187.
[209] Hotson, *Alsted*, 189–91, 194–98; *Paradise Postponed*, 41–44.
[210] Hotson, *Alsted*, 190 n. 41; *Paradise Postponed*, 46–53, 62–75.

his eschatology, and posit a deferred Millennium.[211] Drawing extensively on Piscator's own unpublished Millenarian writings, Alsted was moved to publish his own eschatology in his celebrated *Diatribe de Mille Annis Apocalyptis*, a work specifically intended for the comfort of distraught German Protestants.[212] In this work, Alsted integrated his earlier Joachimite and Rupescissan speculation with the astrological schemes of Pannonius and Dobricius and the intricate biblical exegesis of Piscator, to formulate a new Millenarianism for his own troubled age.[213]

In 1628, just a year after the publication of the *Diatribe*, Alsted was recruited, along with Piscator's son Ludwig and his own son-in-law Johann Heinrich Bisterfeld, by the Transylvanian Prince Gábor Bethlen to teach in his newly founded academy of Gyulafehérvár. While the opportunity to escape an uncertain future in war-torn Herborn surely factored into this decision, Hotson and Graeme Murdock both point to eschatological motives.[214] For it was precisely the nature of Transylvania as a Reformed principality defying the Catholic and Muslim rule which made it so attractive a move. The fact that its Prince was a key ally of the Palatinate and a close relative of the Swedish King Gustavus Adolphus, hailed by many as the saviour of Protestant Europe, only compounded this.[215] For it had been Alsted's own apocalyptic writings which had first led Gustavus to take up the prophetic mantle of the "Lion of the North" who would devour the Catholic Antichrist.[216] In the wake of Gustavus' stunning victories in Germany, hopes for a new Swedish–Transylvanian alliance were still riding high. For Alsted, awaiting the final unfolding of the eschatological drama in Hungary and the East, and hoping for a resurgence in Protestant fortunes, the opportunity to be at the heart of this was too good to pass up.[217]

For his part, Bethlen must have welcomed a Millenarian vision which cast him in an almost Messianic role. His own "Calvinization" of Transylvania was a model example of the further reformation pursued in the German principalities allied to his house, and the 1622 statutes of his new academy at Gyulafehérvár were modelled on those of Heidelberg and Herborn.[218] His attraction to a Ramist

---

[211] Hotson, *Alsted*, 206–8.
[212] Hotson, *Alsted*, 208–14; *Paradise Postponed*, 109–20; cf. Johann Heinrich Alsted, *Diatribe de Mille Annis Apocalypticis* (Frankfurt, 1627), "*Christiano Lectori*".
[213] Hotson, *Alsted*, 182–222; *Paradise Postponed*, 121–53. Hotson locates the sources of the *Diatribe* in Herborn Millenarianism and Marburg hermeticism especially.
[214] Hotson, *Alsted*, 198; Graeme Murdock, *Calvinism on the Frontier, 1600–1660: International Calvinism and the Reformed Church in Hungary and Transylvania* (Oxford: Clarendon Press, 2000), 267–70.
[215] For a wider discussion of Transylvania, eschatology, and the Thirty Years' War see Murdock, *Calvinism*, 258–89.
[216] Hotson, *Alsted*, 193–94; *Paradise Postponed*, 74–75.
[217] Hotson, *Alsted*, 196–98; *Paradise Postponed*, 74–75.
[218] Murdock, *Calvinism*, 81–82.

and encyclopaedic curriculum was one of his main reasons for recruiting Alsted and his two companions to spearhead reform in Transylvania, and he gave the Herborners complete freedom in its implementation.[219] From the beginning of Alsted's Transylvanian sojourn we thus see a new harnessing of encyclopaedism and apocalypticism for the reform of Church and society. Although Bethlen did not live to see it, it was nothing but appropriate that Alsted should choose to dedicate his long-awaited encyclopaedia to his new Prince and patron.[220]

For Alsted, the encyclopaedia is intended for the "glory of the divine name and the salvation of the Church and commonwealth". Its purpose is that the students of the academy can find in one methodically ordered book what has taken him many years and much labour to draw out of hundreds of authors.[221] Echoing Keckermann, Alsted draws the tightest connection between the order manifest in the whole universe, "as if its soul"; the order in the mystical body of the Church; the order which binds the family together; and the order manifest in the school. Through its Ramist charts the encyclopaedia is intended to imprint this order on the memory and thus on the human soul itself.[222] Its supreme end and goal is the imitation of God and nature, and the encyclopaedia becomes a divine instrument for the holistic transformation of individual, Church, and society.[223]

The opening words of the *Encyclopaedia* indicate that this exemplarism is to be seen in a Trinitarian, illuminationist, and therapeutic context. For the supreme dedicatee of the *Encyclopaedia* is not Gábor but the Trinity, without whose "light and divinity (*numine*) there is nothing in man", and certainly no health or salvation.[224] Schools therefore are to be seen as temples of God and the philosophy instituted in them is explicitly a Christian philosophy.[225] Such a programme could be traced back to Clement and Augustine,[226] and Alsted also saw an important realization of it in Gianfrancesco Pico della Mirandola, who placed the beginning and end of all knowledge in the "divine philosophy" of Scripture, directing the encyclopaedia to the knowledge and love of God.[227] Echoing Bonaventure, he can thus speak of all the disciplines descending from God as illuminations from the "Father of lights".[228]

---

[219] Murdock, *Calvinism*, 79–80.
[220] Alsted, *Encyclopaedia*, "*Dedicatio*".
[221] Alsted, *Encyclopaedia*, "*Dedicatio*".
[222] Alsted, *Encyclopaedia*, 1.1.
[223] Alsted, *Encyclopaedia*, 1.49–50.
[224] Alsted, *Encyclopaedia*, "*Deo Uno et Trino*".
[225] Alsted, *Encyclopaedia*, "*Deo Uno et Trino*"; "*Praefatio*".
[226] Alsted, *Triumphus*, 24–26; Jan Amos Comenius, *The Great Didactic*, trans. M. W. Keatinge (London: Adam and Charles Black, 1907), 25.18 (p. 241); and *Naturall Philosophie Reformed*, "Preface".
[227] Alsted, *Encyclopaedia*, 1.73; cf. Gianfrancesco Pico della Mirandola, *De Studio Divina et Humana Philosophia* (Halle, 1702), "*Prooemium*". While Alsted does not cite this passage directly his scriptural approach shows a definite correspondence with the younger Pico.
[228] Alsted, *Encyclopaedia*, 1.74.

Reinforcing this understanding is Alsted's explicit treatment of the relationship between Scripture, the divine ideas, and the encyclopaedia. Placing these in intimate relationship, he holds that both the "divinely expressed" light of Scripture and the natural light of principles impressed on human minds are informed by God's own eternal and immutable reason.[229] Echoing Aquinas he can compare this to human participation in the eternal law of God, and even place both Scripture and the encyclopaedia in a hierarchical framework of subaltern sciences dependent on the supreme science of God himself.[230] Yet this Thomistic paradigm is itself included in an overarching Augustinian and Franciscan framework of scriptural and Triune exemplarism. For, as Alsted explains, "these three principles, eternal in the mind of God, revealed in Scripture, indited in our minds, these three, I say, are in a certain manner one; since the eternal reason is one, which ingenerates the natural law and infuses the divine law".[231]

It follows that, much like in Lavinheta, the whole *Encyclopaedia* can be seen as having an implicit Trinitarian structure and dynamic. As Hotson has pointed out, we may see this from Alsted's espousal of a tripartite model of the encyclopaedia in which logic, ethics, and physics are clearly intended to perfect the soul in the image of the Trinity.[232] The three parts of the encyclopaedia thus become three degrees by which we approach to the likeness of God, logic leading to the illumination of the soul, ethics to its purification, and natural philosophy to its ascent. Notably, Alsted derived such an understanding from Augustine and the Neo-Platonists in their account of the "threefold ascent to the intelligible world". Yet his connection of the tripartite structure of philosophy to the transcendentals of unity, truth, and goodness hints at a connection to Bonaventure as well.[233] Indeed, Alsted's own discussion shows a marked triadism anticipating his student Comenius.[234] Summing this up he holds that the "threefold bond" of his philosophy is the true Homeric chain binding earth and heaven.[235]

In fact, looking closely we find that this Trinitarian pattern at the heart of the encyclopaedia itself, evident especially in its implicit Lullist structure. Thus the exposition of the Lullist "cyclognomic" art serves as a template or blueprint for "recasting the whole encyclopaedia into a combinatorial mould"—something we will see in the next chapter that Alsted was pursuing ardently in his

---

[229] Alsted, *Encyclopaedia*, 1.76.
[230] Alsted, *Encyclopaedia*, 1.76–77; cf. Aquinas, *ST*, 1a q. 1 art. 2.
[231] Alsted, *Encyclopaedia*, 1.76: "*Haec enim tria principia aeternum in mente Dei, revelatum in Scriptura, et mentibus nostris inditum, haec, inquam, tria sunt quodammodo unum; cum aeterna ratio una sit, quae et naturalem ingenerat, et divinam infundit legem*".
[232] Hotson, "Instauration", 13–14.
[233] Alsted, *Encyclopaedia*, 1.68–69.
[234] Hotson, "Instauration", 13–14 makes a similar point but without discussing the full extent of this triadism.
[235] Alsted, *Encyclopaedia*, I.75.

final years in Transylvania.[236] This is also evident in Alsted's claim that the encyclopaedia constitutes a "philosophical chariot with four wheels". For while the wheels correspond to the Keckermannian fourfold pattern of *praecognita*, *technologia*, *archelogia*, and *didactica*, Alsted makes plain that these are to be understood according to their Lullist combinatorial interaction.[237] Going beyond this, he is also explicit that Lull's correlatives as "three coessential principles ... agree to all created things" and thus can be extended to cover every term in the encyclopaedia.[238] Originating in God and returning to him, the whole encyclopaedia implicitly comes to bear his Trinitarian stamp.

Finally, we may also discern an important Trinitarian shape to Alsted's *Encyclopaedia* in its threefold exemplaristic coordination of God, the universe, and history. For, as Hotson points out, Alsted intended his encyclopaedia to mirror the pattern of the cosmos with its various parts corresponding to the planets and celestial spheres in their circular revolutions—the Sun of metaphysics, the Moon of logic, and so forth. The encyclopaedia thus constitutes a "new world" in itself, as well as being integrally connected to the ongoing revolutions of the ages.[239] The link back to Lavinheta is clear here, but what has not been noticed is an implicit link to a Trinitarian unfolding of history. For we must remember that Alsted opened the whole work with a dedication to the Triune Creator, Redeemer, and Sanctifier of all things and also makes clear that it pertains to the different Kingdoms of Nature, Grace, and Glory.[240] Mirroring the mind of God, the encyclopaedia thus comes to capture the progression of the ages, connecting past, present, and future in both its quest for an Edenic state of perfection and its anticipation of an eschatological state of glory.

[236] Hotson, *Alsted*, 163–70.
[237] Alsted, *Encyclopaedia*, "*Praefatio*".
[238] Alsted, *Encyclopaedia*, I.78.
[239] Hotson, *Paradise Postponed*, 77–82; cf. Alsted, *Encyclopaedia*, "*Introitus in Philologiam*" and "*Praefatio in Philosophiam Theoreticam*" (II.132; III.572).
[240] Alsted, *Encyclopaedia*, "*Dedicatio*".

# 8
# Universal Harmony
## Bisterfeld, Immeation, and Mystical Transformation

When Alsted died in 1638, his student and son-in-law Johann Heinrich Bisterfeld was already well-known across Europe as a gifted philosopher and theologian. Building on Alsted's legacy, his work engaged creatively with the thought of such leading lights as Bacon, Campanella, and Descartes, and was later to captivate the young Leibniz, paving the way for his own metaphysical and epistemological breakthroughs.[1] Seen from within the Ramist tradition, his writings represent the fruition of Alsted's project for a Trinitarian reformation of the whole of philosophy, marking the "summit of the Herborn encyclopaedic tradition".[2]

From the beginning Bisterfeld's rising star had been bound to that of Alsted. Indeed, he presents himself as merely a humble "foot-follower" to his "revered father-in-law".[3] However, only in recent years has it become clear just how apt such a description truly is. In his pioneering work on Alsted, Hotson pointed to important evidence suggesting that Alsted's mature manuscripts, dramatically rescued from his attempt to destroy them on his death-bed, served as the nucleus—if not much more—of many of Bisterfeld's own later publications in his own name.[4] Recently, through the painstaking researches of Márton Szentpéteri, this suspicion has been spectacularly confirmed by the discovery of a series of manuscripts, including a notebook from one of Alsted's students containing a treatise entitled *Manuductio Excellentissimi Johannis Henrici Alstedii*. What is most significant is that nearly all the works in the *Manuductio* later reappear, in more developed form, as works published under Bisterfeld's name.[5] What this

---

[1] See Martin Mulsow, "*Sociabilitas*: Zu einem Kontext der Campanella-Rezeption im 17. Jahrhundert", *Bruniana & Campanelliana* 1.1/2 (1995): 205–32; Maria Rosa Antognazza, "*Immeatio* and *Emperichoresis*: The Theological Roots of Harmony in Bisterfeld and Leibniz", in *The Young Leibniz and His Philosophy, 1646–1676*, ed. Stuart Brown (Dordrecht: Springer, 1999), 41–64; "*Debilissimae Entitates*? Bisterfeld and Leibniz's Ontology of Relations", *The Leibniz Review* 11 (2001): 1–22; and Loemker, *Struggle for Synthesis*, 143–44, 190–93.

[2] Hotson, *Reformation of Common Learning*, 349.

[3] Johann Heinrich Bisterfeld, *De Uno Deo, Patre, Filio, ac Spiritu Sancto, Mysterium Pietatis* (Amsterdam, 1659), "*Christiano Lectori Salutem*".

[4] For the dramatic narrative of Alsted's deathbed repudiation of his mature work and the fortune of his manuscripts see Hotson, *Reformation of Common Learning*, 346–52 and *Alsted*, 177–80.

[5] Hotson, *Reformation of Common Learning*, 349. For a detailed account of this see pp. 347–52. Hotson's account draws on Márton Szentpéteri, *Egyetemes tudomány Erdélyben—Johann Heinrich*

means, as Hotson insightfully points out, is that Bisterfeld's works can no longer be seen as the "product of one fertile mind working alone in Transylvania".[6] Rather, they now appear to be the product of a collaborative venture in which Alsted's and Bisterfeld's own contributions have become fused into one.[7]

In this chapter we will focus on Bisterfeld's Trinitarian method of immeation and the way he developed it into a comprehensive Trinitarian and biblical encyclopaedism and applied it to the holistic reform of Church and society. As Hotson and Szentpéteri have demonstrated, much of this was dependent on Alsted.[8] Indeed, Antognazza has argued powerfully that Bisterfeld's key notion of immeation was itself profoundly indebted to Alsted and his investigations into the Fabrist circle.[9] In the same Trinitarian vein, Martin Mulsow has pointed to the importance of Campanellan sociability in shaping both his metaphysics and his politics.[10] Taking up and extending these theses we will seek to show a pervasive Lullist-Cusan influence on Bisterfeld, manifest not only in his Trinitarian dynamics but also in his new mathematical orientation towards philosophy. Above all, we will trace his development of the programme of Triune universal method laid down by Alsted and his attempt to formulate a new Christian philosophy on a grander scale than anything achieved in his father-in-law's published works.

In particular, this chapter will develop Antognazza's illuminating approach to Bisterfeld in seeking to show even more fully the Fabrist and evangelical origins of his Christian reform project. In this he intended not only to complete the Ramist tradition from within, but also, following an important late medieval trajectory, to bridge the divide which had opened up in the Lullist tradition between logic and the Bible. In doing so, Bisterfeld ultimately sought to repristinate the Franciscan vision of a scriptural philosophy and theology within a new paradigm of Christocentric reform. Following his Herborn heritage, Bisterfeld's Ramism became closely entwined with his federal theology, reinforcing a Franciscan and covenantal view of reality.

We will do this first by showing how Bisterfeld's thought was rooted not only in his Herborn upbringing but also especially in the powerful combination of

*Alsted és a herborni hagyomány* [Universal Learning in Tranyslvania: Johann Heinrich Alsted and the Herborn Tradition] (Budapest: Universitas, 2008).

[6] Hotson, *Reformation of Common Learning*, 350.
[7] Hotson, *Reformation of Common Learning*, 351 summarizes what is currently known about Bisterfeld's dependence on Alsted's manuscripts. Further work will need to be done to fully disentangle their separate contributions, although it should also be remembered that the two worked extremely closely together. In what follows I will refer to Bisterfeld's works as his own, albeit with the understanding they may derive originally either from Alsted or from their joint ventures.
[8] Hotson, *Reformation of Common Learning*, 346–52 and Márton Szentpéteri, "The Mystery of Piety Revealed and Defended: A Sequel to Johann Heinrich Bisterfeld's De Uno Deo?", *Acta Comeniana* 26 (2012): 89–98.
[9] Antognazza, "Bisterfeld and *Immeatio*", 57–84.
[10] Mulsow, "*Sociabilitas*", 218–32.

Trinitarian, encyclopaedic, and apocalyptic thought which shaped Transylvanian reform. Examining his logic and metaphysics will complement this by offering an in-depth account of his understanding of the immeation of mind, language, and reality and its Trinitarian foundation. This will then lead into a detailed account of his Trinitarian and combinatorial encyclopaedism. It will also reveal that Bisterfeld's encyclopaedic project was closely tied to meditation on Scripture and the mystical ascent to God and will consider his important development of a new theological logic. Finally, we will see how all these influences carried forward into a pioneering Trinitarian account of universal society, which echoed Cusa and late medieval reformers even as it anticipated Leibniz.

## 8.1. Bisterfeld's Formation

Like Alsted, Bisterfeld was a product of Herborn and its Ramist heritage. His father Johann was a noted Ramist, who in 1597 had published a commentary on Ramus' rhetoric. Educated at Herborn himself, he had briefly been a professor there before taking up a position as Court Chaplain and Professor of Theology at Siegen.[11] Johann's prominence is attested to by the fact that he was invited to join Alsted as one of the Nassau representatives at the Synod of Dordt, where he died suddenly in January 1619, the year that his son enrolled at Herborn.[12] From the beginning, perhaps, Alsted was therefore something of a father figure to the younger Bisterfeld, although that relationship was not to be formally sealed until his marriage to Alsted's daughter Anna in 1629, just before they left together for Transylvania.[13]

Certainly there can be no doubt that Bisterfeld imbibed the Philippo-Ramism of Herborn from Alsted and his other professors. Its influence is fully evident in his own logical writings, and was also attested to by the first editor of his works.[14] From Alsted he also took a suspicion of pure Ramism, above all for its rejection of metaphysics, and an enthusiasm for Keckermann's methodological

---

[11] See "Bisterfeld, Johannes", in *Deutsche Biographie* (https://www.deutsche-biographie.de/).

[12] Hotson, *Alsted*, 114 and Donald Sinnema, Christian Moser, and Herman J. Selderhuis (eds.), *Acta et Documenta Synodi Nationalis Dordrechtanae (1618-1619). Acta of the Synod of Dordt* (Göttingen: Vandenhoeck & Ruprecht, 2015), LXXXVI. The younger Bisterfeld was also present briefly at the Synod and likely met Alsted there (p. 493).

[13] For details of Bisterfeld's life see Noémi Viskolcz, *Johann Heinrich Bisterfeld (1605-1655) Bibliográfia, A Bisterfeld-Könyvtár* (Budapest and Szeged: Országos Széchenyi Könyvtár, 2003), "Biográfiai táblázat" and Seivert, "Bisterfeld, Johann Heinrich", in *Allgemeine Deutsche Biographie* 2 (1875): 682–83 (https://www.deutsche-biographie.de/). It seems clear that Bisterfeld was married to Alsted's daughter before their move to Transylvania. In his poem *"Aliud"* prefaced to the 1630 *Encyclopaedia* he notes Alsted's parental kindness to him.

[14] Adriaan Heereboord, *"Lectori"*, in Johann Heinrich Bisterfeld, *Elementorum Logicorum Libri Tres* (Leiden, 1657).

Peripateticism.[15] Many of Bisterfeld's own works often follow a tight Ramist structure and, like those of Keckermann and Alsted, were intended to be laid out in Ramist charts and memorized. Indeed, it is even said that Bisterfeld himself memorized the whole encyclopaedia using Ramist techniques.[16] His own *Isagoge Encyclopaedica* certainly demonstrates his abiding appreciation for Alsted's Ramist systematization of knowledge.[17]

Bisterfeld was even more strongly influenced by Alsted's Brunian Lullism, and it is surely here, in his combinatorial writings, that the voice of the later Alsted can most clearly be heard. Scanning the shelves of Bisterfeld's library we find that Lull's works feature prominently and that, like Alsted, he doubtless read them in light of their perceived alchemical and cabalistic affinities.[18] Certainly his profound interest in mathematics and combinatorics earned him the reputation in Transylvania of being a magician and a "necromantic philosopher"—despite his emphatic rejection of magic as demonic.[19] Even before Alsted's death, Bisterfeld seems to have acquired a reputation as a Lullist adept. Indeed, he was actually conducting private lessons on Lullism and the Cabala when he received the tragic news of his mentor's demise.[20] His skills were also sought out by Samuel Hartlib and his circle, who clearly regarded him as *the* expert on Lullism and the one most capable of realizing its encyclopaedic potential as an *ars universalis*.[21]

By his own confession Alsted's encyclopaedism opened up a "new world" for Bisterfeld, yet very soon he was enthusiastically discovering his own intellectual worlds.[22] In 1623 Bisterfeld left the war-torn Palatinate and proceeded on the conventional tour around the best Reformed colleges and universities. His first port of call was Switzerland and a year spent in Basel and Geneva from 1623 to 1624 was important in nurturing his biblical and theological convictions. In Basel he was privileged to study Hebrew under Johannes Buxtorf, the leading

---

[15] Bisterfeld was to later say he would rather that his own logic were burned than it replace Keckermann's in the Transylvanian schools (Murdock, *Calvinism*, 97).

[16] Hotson, *Reformation of Common Learning*, 343–44. Bisterfeld apparently memorized Alsted's *Cursus*.

[17] Johann Heinrich Bisterfeld, *Isagoge Encyclopaedica seu de Primis Encyclopaediae Principiis* (Basel, 1661), 1–14 follows closely the structure of Alsted's own encyclopaedic works.

[18] Viskolcz, *Bibliográfia*, 56–57, 74–77 records ownership of works by Lull, Roger Bacon, Rupescissa, Isaac Holland, Bruno, Paracelsus, Fludd, and others.

[19] Seivert, "Bisterfeld, Johann Heinrich". For his rejection of magic see Johann Heinrich Bisterfeld, *Logica*, in *Bisterfeldius Redivivus seu Operum Joh. Henrici Bisterfeldi Magni Theologi ac Philosophi, Posthumorum*, ed. Adriaan Heereboord, 2 vols. (The Hague, 1661) [hereafter *BR*], 2.221.

[20] Hotson, *Alsted*, 160, 180.

[21] Samuel Hartlib, "*Ephemerides* 1648, Part 1", 31/22/12A; "*Ephemerides* 1657, Part 2", 29/6/14B. For Bisterfeld's connections with the Hartlib circle see Noémi Viskolcz, "Johann Heinrich Bisterfeld. Ein Professor als Vermittler zwischen West und Ost an der siebenbürgischen Akademie in Weissenburg, 1630–1655", in *Calvin und Reformiertentum in Ungarn und Siebenbürgen: Helvetisches Bekenntnis, Ethnie und Politik vom 16. Jahrhundert bis 1918*, ed. Márta Fata and Anton Schindling (Münster: Aschendorff, 2011), 204–11 and Hotson, *Reformation of Common Learning*, 206–10, 219, 415.

[22] Bisterfeld, "*Aliud*".

Hebraist of his age and a renowned expert on the Jewish and Christian Cabala. In 1625 he moved on to Oxford, and it was here that he forged his links with the English Puritans and Baconians of the Hartlib circle. In later years Bisterfeld was to prove a defender of Puritan principles, and there can be no doubt that he shared the fervour of the Hartlib circle for universal reform.[23]

Of equally lasting significance were the close ties between Bisterfeld and the Dutch Reformed world. In this respect the importance of the three years that he spent in Leiden between 1626 and 1628 can scarcely be emphasized enough.[24] In the decade of the 1620s the Netherlands continued to experience the after-effects of the Remonstrant controversy. Leiden, as Arminius' own university, had been at the very heart of the storm, but since the Synod of Dordt had become known as a bastion of Reformed orthodoxy. It was the home of the celebrated *Synopsis Purioris Theologiae*, published just the year before Bisterfeld's arrival, and two of his Leiden professors, Johannes Polyander and Andreas Rivetus, had been its chief compilers.[25] Indeed, Bisterfeld became close friends with Rivetus, corresponding with him for many years, and wrote his *Phosphorus Catholicus* for Rivetus' son Frederick as an aid for his studies.[26] From a disputation of 1627 on faith, presided over by Polyander, it is clear that he imbibed to the full the anti-Pelagian theology of the *Synopsis* with its strong emphasis on grace and predestination.[27]

In later years Bisterfeld became involved in another dispute which rocked the Dutch Reformed world, namely the Cartesian controversy. Here, Bisterfeld proved closest to those Reformed theologians who sought to make an alliance with Cartesianism and to incorporate it into their own philosophical and dogmatic systems.[28] Adriaan Heereboord, the Dutch Ramist and Cartesian, was a great admirer of Bisterfeld and became the editor of his posthumous works, the two tomes of the *Bisterfeldius Redivivus* of 1661. Indeed, Heereboord was a great admirer of Bisterfeld's panharmony, which he sought to institute in his own

---

[23] Viskolcz, "Biográfiai táblázat"; L. Makkai, "The Hungarian Puritans and the English Revolution", *Acta Historica Academiae Scientiarum Hungaricae* 5.1/2 (1958): 20–35.

[24] Viskolcz, "Biográfiai táblázat".

[25] For Leiden and the Remonstrant controversy see Aza Goudriaan and F. A. van Lieburg (eds.), *Revisiting the Synod of Dordt (1618–1619)* (Leiden: Brill, 2011).

[26] The title page of Johann Heinrich Bisterfeld, *Phosphorus Catholicus seu Artis Meditandi Epitome* (Breda, 1649) records that both the *Phosphorus* and the appended "*Consilium de studiis feliciter instituendis*" were originally written for Frederick Rivetus. For Bisterfeld's correspondence with Andreas Rivetus see University of Leiden, MS BPL 285: A, 64r–76r.

[27] Johann Heinrich Bisterfeld, *Disputatio Theologica de Fide* (Leiden, 1627) in Merton College MS 75.F.1(3). This is bound in a book belonging to Griffin Higgs, a Fellow of Merton and Chaplain to the Queen of Bohemia.

[28] For the Dutch Cartesian disputes see Theo Verbeek, *Descartes and the Dutch: Early Reactions to Cartesian Philosophy, 1637–1650* (Carbondale IL: Southern Illinois University Press, 1992) and Goudriaan, *Reformed Orthodoxy and Philosophy*. For Bisterfeld's interest in Descartes see Viskolcz, *Bibliográfia*, 78.

philosophy.[29] Even more significantly, Bisterfeld also attracted the attention of no less a figure than Marin Mersenne, the French Minim Friar who was at the forefront of the European reception of Descartes. The two became correspondents and engaged in eager discussion of harmony and the possibility of attaining a universal language.[30]

Yet while Bisterfeld shared important affinities with Cartesianism, as was evident to Hartlib, who classed him with Descartes as an exponent of a priori philosophy,[31] there are also significant differences. Indeed, as Mulsow and others have recognized, Bisterfeld's Trinitarian apriorism ultimately shared much more in common with the Italian Renaissance philosopher Tommaso Campanella, with its important connection to a long heritage of Augustinian, Lullist, and Cusan epistemology and metaphysics.[32] Like Bruno, Campanella was a renegade Dominican friar, who was imprisoned in Naples for many years and hounded for his radical reforming and apocalyptic views. He was also one of the most important proponents of the new natural philosophy of Telesio and Patrizzi.[33] However, his primary importance lay much more in his innovative but controversial metaphysics. For Campanella was an exponent of a sophisticated Trinitarian philosophy of pansensism which Bisterfeld, together with the wider Herborn circle, found highly attractive.[34]

Following an important Platonic and Pythagorean tradition, Campanella came to believe that God had impressed on the universe an inchoate sensitivity, which served to bind all creatures together in unity and harmony and to express their participation in divine Wisdom itself.[35] Such a perspective carried over into a thoroughgoing ontological revisionism well-evidenced by his Trinitarian metaphysics of the primalities.[36] Inspired by the Victorines and wider currents in the twelfth-century Renaissance, as well as surely by his youthful devouring of the works of Lull and Cusa, Campanella argued that being itself was structured

---

[29] Adriaan Heereboord, *Meletemata Philosophica* (Amsterdam, 1665), II.334–36; cf. Hotson, *Reformation of Common Learning*, 125–44, 347–52.

[30] Viskolcz, *Bibliográfia*, 24. For Bisterfeld's relation to Mersenne see Petr Pavlas, "The Search for a Final Language: Comenius's Linguistic Eschatology", *Erudition and the Republic of Letters* 5 (2020): 207–28.

[31] Samuel Hartlib, *Ephemerides* 1639, part 1 (Hartlib Papers 30/4/3A, available at www.dhi.ac.uk/hartlib).

[32] Mulsow, "*Sociabilitas*", 218–32.

[33] John M. Headley, *Tommaso Campanella and the Transformation of the World* (Princeton, NJ: Princeton University Press, 2019), 9–138, 152–86 and Germana Ernst, *Tommaso Campanella: The Book and the Body of Nature*, trans. David L. Marshall (Dordrecht: Springer, 2010), 85–104.

[34] Hotson, *Alsted*, 119, 151.

[35] Tommaso Campanella, *Atheismus Triumphatus* (Rome, 1631), 4–6, 16–19. For Campanella's pansensism and its wider context see David Skrbina, *Panpsychism in the West* (Cambridge, MA: MIT Press, 2017), 93–120.

[36] For an account of Campanella's Trinitarian reformation of philosophy see Bernardino Bonansea, *Tommaso Campanella: Renaissance Pioneer of Modern Thought* (Washington, DC: Catholic University of America Press, 1969), 138–64.

intrinsically and dynamically according to three primalities of Power, Wisdom, and Goodness whose mutual "toticipation" precisely mirrored and was grounded in the relations of the three persons of the Trinity.[37] While Campanella did his best to assimilate this view to Thomist orthodoxy, there can be little doubt that his primalitarian metaphysics also has profound links to the emanational metaphysics of Bonaventure, Scotus, and Lull.[38] Indeed, Campanella's *Metaphysics* shows a notable desire to harmonize the Thomist and Scotist schools.[39]

Overall, Bisterfeld's formation was shaped by a powerful current of German eclecticism which went back through Alsted, Keckermann, Goclenius, and Reuchlin to the Italian Renaissance Neo-Platonism of which Cusa had been so important a progenitor and Campanella proved so signal an heir.[40] In his thought, as in Alsted's, Ramism and Lullism could come together due to a common Neo-Platonic, exemplaristic, and mathematical framework. Such a synthesis was robust and proved more than capable of absorbing other influences. Indeed, in Timpler and others, Ramism had already become launched on a metaphysical trajectory of intelligibility which, in important respects, converged on the new Cartesianism.[41] In Bisterfeld, we see the Ramist and Cartesian emphasis on intelligibility taken up and transposed into a powerful Trinitarian and combinatorial metaphysics.

## 8.2. Trinitarian, Encyclopaedic, and Apocalyptic Reform

While Bisterfeld's intellectual formation took place in Herborn, England, and the Netherlands, it was in Transylvania that his thought truly began to flower. Indeed, as Murdock, Szentpéteri, and Noémi Viskolcz have all made clear, the Transylvanian context is vital for understanding Bisterfeld.[42] All his major works were written in Transylvania and shaped by the intellectual and theological landscape of that Reformed Principality, even as they themselves came to profoundly

---

[37] Bonansea, *Campanella*, 138–64. For the Victorine sources of Campanella's primalitarian metaphysics see Tommaso Campanella, *De Sancta Monotriade: Theologicorum Liber II*, trans. Romano Amerio (Rome: Centro Internazionale di Studi Umanistici, 1958), 14–22. For his engagement with Lull and Cusa see Frederick C. Copleston, *A History of Philosophy: Volume III: Ockham to Suárez* (Mahwah, NJ: Paulist Press, 1953), 256 and Bonansea, *Campanella*, 8–11, 18–20, 25.

[38] Campanella, *De Sancta Monotriade*, 12–16, 18, 20, 26. Bonansea, *Campanella*, 112–13, 139–41, 149 highlights some of these Franciscan and Scotist connections, including adherence to a logical doctrine of univocity of being and the formal distinction. Copleston, *History*, 256 notes his close affinity with Bonaventure.

[39] Bonansea, *Campanella*, 139–41.

[40] For this German Neo-Platonic eclecticism see Mercer, *Leibniz's Metaphysics*, 37–76.

[41] Hotson, *Reformation of Common Learning*, 61–200. Gellera, "Univocity of Being", 417–46 traces a Scotistic trajectory through Timpler and Clauberg to Cartesianism.

[42] Murdock, *Calvinism*, 77–109; Viskolcz, "Bisterfeld", 201–14; and Szentpéteri, "Mystery of Piety Revealed", 89–98.

shape it. Indeed, to a much greater extent than the younger Piscator or Alsted, Bisterfeld became closely integrated into the Transylvanian Church and society, becoming a close advisor to the Rákóczi Princes, a tutor to their children and a diplomat on the international Reformed stage.[43] Yet his most important role, and the reason he had first been encouraged to go to Transylvania,[44] was, of course, as a pioneer of educational reform, and together with Alsted, and later Comenius, Bisterfeld sought to institute an ambitious programme of Trinitarian, encyclopaedic, and apocalyptic reform.

Even before the arrival of the Herborners the Ramist confessionalization of Transylvania had already begun in earnest, with the founding of flagship colleges in Gyulafehérvár, Sárospatak, and Kolozsvár, as well as the establishing of a whole network of Reformed schools in towns and villages across the land.[45] Through the influence of Alsted's friend Albert Szenczi Molnár and others the prevailing Philippism was already beginning to be displaced by a resurgent Ramism.[46] With the advent of the Herborn trio this Ramist takeover not only gathered pace but also began to take an important new direction. As Murdock suggests, the most obvious dimension of this was the comprehensive encyclopaedic reform of Transylvanian schools and academies, in a manner going well beyond Molnár's initial forays.[47] Yet of equal significance is the close entwining of education and piety conforming to the wider Ramist pattern of Christian philosophy and especially appropriate for both the many ministers training in the Transylvanian academies and the young noblemen and courtiers who would take a leading role in governing the Reformed Principality.

We find a blueprint for this in the reforms recommended by the Herborners and instituted in Gyulafehérvár in 1630 by Prince György I Rákóczi. Signalling a definite exemplarism, these were said to be according to "that idea which is expressed in the most celebrated schools of Germany and France".[48] The theological orientation of the programme is evident in the focus on biblical languages, as well as the prominent role of the Heidelberg Catechism. Complementing this was a comprehensive programme of philosophical education. Teaching was divided between Alsted, Piscator, and Bisterfeld respectively and occupied an intensive three-year curriculum, reminiscent of that of Keckermann at Danzig.[49] Curriculum changes were supported by a spate of new textbooks written by the

---

[43] For discussion of this see Viskolcz, "Bisterfeld", 201–14 and Murdock, *Calvinism*, 274–89.
[44] Hotson, *Alsted*, 231 points out that Bisterfeld needed to be strongly encouraged by Alsted.
[45] Murdock, *Calvinism*, 78–80.
[46] Gábor Kecskeméti, "Hungarian and Transylvanian Ramism", in *The European Contexts of Ramism*, ed. Sarah Knight and Emma Annette Wilson (Turnhout: Brepols, 2019), 294–302.
[47] Murdock, *Calvinism*, 77–109.
[48] *Magyar Történelmi Tár* (Budapest, 1884), 199. I am very grateful to Zsombor Tóth for providing me with scans of this work.
[49] Murdock, *Calvinism*, 93–94; *Magyar Történelmi Tár*, 199–201.

Herborners and issuing from the Transylvanian presses. Piscator's new rhetorical treatise and Bisterfeld's logic textbook, complete with copious Ramist charts, proved especially popular, becoming a staple of Transylvanian schooling for decades afterwards.[50] For advanced Transylvanian students, Alsted's own *Encyclopaedia* became the crown of this renewed curriculum.[51] The goal of such an encyclopaedic education, as we learn from the graduation disputation of Prince Zsigmond, the brother of the reigning Rákóczi Prince, was a return to the state of an original, Edenic integrity.[52]

While Herborn Ramism quickly took root in Transylvania, fostering a new encyclopaedic fervour, it soon encountered an important rival: the pure Ramism of Ames brought back by the many Hungarian students studying in Franeker and England.[53] For those desiring further reform, Ames' fusion of Presbyterian and Puritan principles and his Christian encyclopaedism and scriptural logic all proved deeply attractive. From 1639 onwards the College of Sárospatak became the epicentre of this new Transylvanian "Puritanism" under the leadership of its new Rector János Tolnai Dali, who had studied with Ames in Franeker. Tolnai lost no time in replacing Keckermann's textbooks with Ramus' logic, banning the teaching of metaphysics and ethics and grounding all theological teaching on Ames' *Medulla*.[54] Together with other key figures of this wider "Amesian Renaissance", including János Apaczai Csere, the celebrated Hungarian encyclopaedist, Tolnai promoted a far-reaching vision of Christian philosophy and further reform.[55]

The radical curriculum innovations of Tolnai, combined with his ardent promotion of a Puritan and Presbyterian programme for the "entire reformation" of Transylvanian Church and society, raised a storm of protest. While Prince György II Rákóczi and Bishop István Geleji Katona were ardently opposed to the reforms, the Puritans soon found powerful defenders in György's brother Prince Zsigmond and his mother, Princess Zsuzsanna.[56] With this damaging split in the Rákóczi family, Bisterfeld quickly found himself torn between competing loyalties. On the one hand, he could not but be suspicious of a system

---

[50] Murdock, *Calvinism*, 95; Gábor Kecskeméti, "The Reception of Ramist Rhetoric in Hungary and Transylvania: Possibilities and Achievements", in *Ramus, Pedagogy and the Liberal Arts*, ed. Reid and Wilson, 220–22; and "Ramism", 302–5.

[51] Murdock, *Calvinism*, 96–97.

[52] Zsigmond Rákóczi, "*Oratio Valedictoria*", in *Pallas Dacica* (Alba Julia, 1650), 101; Murdock, *Calvinism*, 92–93.

[53] Kecskeméti, "Ramism", 300–306; Murdock, *Calvinism*, 49–62.

[54] Kecskeméti, "Ramism", 307–8. For a discussion of the distinctive character of Transylvanian Puritanism see Zsombor Tóth, "The Importance of Being (In)Tolerant: The Strange Case of Transylvanian Puritanism", in *Reformed Majorities in Early Modern Europe*, ed. Herman J. Selderhuis and J. Marius J. Lange van Ravenswaay (Göttingen: Vandenhoeck & Ruprecht, 2015), 89–110.

[55] Cited from Murdock, *Calvinism*, 104. See Makkai, "Hungarian Puritans", 13–45.

[56] Tóth, "Transylvanian Puritanism", 95–98.

of philosophy which abandoned metaphysics and ethics. He was also adamantly opposed to replacing Keckermann's logic with his own, holding that his logic was intended as a gateway to the Danziger's more complex system.[57] On the other hand, he was himself a Presbyterian and the Puritan reforms were zealously promoted by many of his own former students, including Tolnai, Csere, and Prince Zsigmond himself.[58] Although nervous of pure Ramism he was also a dedicatee of Csere's *Magyar Encyclopaedia* and an ardent proponent of Christian philosophy.[59] While it may be going too far to call Bisterfeld the "spiritual mentor" and inspiration of the Hungarian Puritans, there can be no doubt that he was sympathetic to many of their aims.[60]

While the warring parties in the Transylvanian religious disputes became bitterly divided over Ramism and Christian philosophy, they were completely united in maintaining that a key purpose of the new encyclopaedic curriculum was to defend and promote Trinitarian orthodoxy. Such a need was all the more pressing in a Principality which had for a long time been a major centre of Socinianism and Anti-Trinitarianism, and in which Anti-Trinitarian doctrine had often served to foster radical, apocalyptic programmes of further reform rivalling those of the Calvinists themselves.[61] From Szegedinus onwards, Hungarian Reformed theologians had thus devoted themselves to offering sophisticated defences of Trinitarian orthodoxy. The Rákóczis also saw it as their sacred duty to promote the defence of Trinitarian orthodoxy and to eradicate Anti-Trinitarianism, and both Alsted and Bisterfeld were committed to this goal.[62] Indeed, from their perspective, Transylvania was, of course, on the front lines of the eschatological battlefield and their hope was to initiate a new biblical reformation in which not only Socinians and Anti-Trinitarians, but also Jews and Muslims, would come to acknowledge the glory of Trinitarian doctrine, thus triggering a revival which would spread like wildfire through Christendom and herald the dawn of the Millennium.[63]

We may see such a desire from Alsted's posthumous *Prodromus religionis triumphantis* of 1640, his massive work of Trinitarian and Christological

---

[57] Kecskeméti, "Ramism", 307–8.
[58] Murdock, *Calvinism*, 96; Makkai, "Hungarian Puritans", 20–21.
[59] Makkai, "Hungarian Puritans", 21; Murdock, *Calvinism*, 92–93, 104. For Bisterfeld's endorsement of Christian philosophy see *Mysterium Pietatis*, 529.
[60] Makkai, "Hungarian Puritans", 21.
[61] Borbála Lovas, "On the Margins of the Reformation: The 'Local' and the 'International' in György Enyedi's Manuscript Sermons and Printed Works", in *Protestant Majorities and Minorities*, ed. Burton, Choptiany, and Wilczek, 241–42.
[62] Lovas, "On the Margins", 233–34; Hotson, *Alsted*, 131–33.
[63] Hotson, *Alsted*, 134–35. For Bisterfeld's Millenarianism see Martin Mulsow, "Who Was the Author of the *Clavis Apocalyptica* of 1651? Millenarianism and Prophecy between Silesian Mysticism and the Hartlib Circle", in *Millenarianism and Messianism in Early Modern European Culture. Volume IV: Continental Millenarians, Protestants, Catholics, Heretics*, ed. John Christian Laursen and Richard H. Popkin (Dordrecht: Springer, 2001), 57–75 and Hotson, *Paradise Postponed*, 69 n. 92.

apologetic enthusiastically endorsed by the Rákóczi dynasty as advancing their own plans of Reformed confessionalization. For the very title of this—"the forerunner of triumphant religion"—signals his eschatological goals.[64] It is also apparent in Bisterfeld's own 1639 *Mysterium Pietatis*, a runaway success and the work which established his reputation on the international stage as a leading Reformed theologian.[65] It is most evident, however, in Alsted's plans for a "reformation of philosophy" crowned by a projected *Encyclopaedia Digne Restituta*.[66] Sadly such a work has not come down to us, but an important clue to its character is provided by Alsted's *Veraedus* published as a second edition in Gyulafehérvár in 1637.[67] For this work presented a full-outline of his intended reformation of philosophy:

> 1. Lexica and Grammar, 2. Rhetoric, 3. Logic, 4. Oratory and Poetry, 5. The four Praecognita to be prefaced to all faculties and disciplines, 6. Metaphysics, 7. Pneumatics, 8. Physics, 9. Mathematical disciplines, 10. Practical Philosophy, 11. Theology, 12. Law and Medicine, 13. Criticus, 14. Chronology, 15. The whole Encyclopaedia according to the Sacred Scriptures, 16. The Lullian Art, 17. Hieroglyphics, 18. Doctrine of handling copia of words and things, 19. Ancient Philology, 20. Sacred Philology proper to the New Testament, 21. Sacred Onatomology, 22. Latin version of the Bible, 23. Kabbalah, 24. Alchemy, 25. Conclusions of John Pico Mirandola, 26. Mythology, 27. Exercise of all disciplines, 28. Mathematico-chronological calculus from the mind of Capelli.[68]

Drawing on the evidence of this contents page, Hotson has persuasively argued Alsted's intent to reconfigure his entire *Encyclopaedia* in Lullist and combinatorial fashion. Following the template of the "cyclognomica" he envisages doing this by placing all the common terms of the encyclopaedia on the circumference of a "most general circle" and then combining this with "general terms"

---

[64] Johann Heinrich Alsted, *Prodromus Triumphantis Religionis* (Alba-Julia, 1635); cf. Hotson, *Alsted*, 131–33.
[65] Hotson, *Alsted*, 176–77. For Bisterfeld's Trinitarian apologetic see Szentpéteri, "Mystery of Piety Revealed", 89–98.
[66] Hotson, *Alsted*, 173–78.
[67] I am very grateful to Petr Pavlas for providing me with a copy of this rare work.
[68] Johann Heinrich Alsted, *Veraedus* (Alba Julia, 1637), 5–6: "*De Reformatione 1. Lexica et Grammaticae 2. Rhetoricae 3. Logices 4. Oratoria et Poetica 5. quatuor Praecognitorum, quae omnibus facultatibus et disciplinis sunt praemittenda 6. Metaphysices 7. Pneumatica 8. Physices 9. disciplinarum mathematicarum 10. Philisophiae practicae 11. Theologiae 12. Jurisprudentiae et Medicinae 13. Critices 14. Chronologiae 15. universae Encyclopaediae secundum Scripturas sacras 16. artis Lullianae 17. Hieroglyphicae 18. doctrinae tradentis copiam verborum et rerum 19. Philologiae antiquariae 20. Philologiae sacrae novi testamenti propria 21. Onomatologiae sacrae 22. Latinae versionis Bibliorum 23. Kabbalae 24. Alchymiae 25. Conclusionum Joannis Pici Mirandulae 26. Mythologiae 27. exercitationis omnium disciplinarum 28. calculi mathematico–chronologici ex mente Capelli*".

taken from individual disciplines as well as "most special circles" constituting their different aspects. By placing any topic at the centre of all these circles it thus becomes possible to give a simple and elegant encyclopaedic treatment of the whole of reality.[69]

For Hotson, the *Veraedus* constitutes clear evidence of Alsted's open return, after a long hiatus, to the hermetic interests of his youth.[70] For our purposes, however, what is most striking is the fact that at the heart of Alsted's desired "reformation of philosophy" is clearly an intensive programme of scriptural encyclopaedism grounded on the mystical and Christocentric method of Pico— seen as one of the great forerunners of the Reformation whose praise could be found on the lips of the most orthodox of divines.[71] In fact, looking more closely, the *Veraedus* can be seen to offer a template for an integrated biblical encyclopaedia centred on Christ and bound to the wheel of history. For Alsted makes use of his Lullist combinatorial wheels to generate an "infinite" discourse on the Kingship of Christ, extending this Christological and cyclognomic discourse to the rest of the encyclopaedia. Recalling the *Trigae* he makes use of a set of historical circles to illustrate the series of the "years of the world and Christ", revealing the different epochs of the world and the coming dawn of Christ's Millennial Kingdom.[72] Since, for Alsted, the revolutions of the Lullist wheels mirrored the inner dynamic of the Trinity itself, the work thus perfectly captures the Trinitarian, combinatorial, and apocalyptic dimensions of Alsted's Transylvanian reform as they were soon to be taken up by Bisterfeld himself.

## 8.3. Trinitarian and Transcendental Metaphysics

Bisterfeld's metaphysics continues and radically intensifies the Trinitarian and transcendental turn evident in Szegedinus, Keckermann, and Alsted. While the dynamic and correlative structure of Alsted's metaphysics was left rather implicit in his published works, in Bisterfeld it becomes completely explicit. Without doubt this is due to his increased engagement with Franciscan and Lullist encyclopaedism and in this way Bisterfeld can clearly be seen as moving on that same trajectory mapped out by Alsted in the *Veraedus* and *Reformatio Philosophiae*. At the same time, Bisterfeld's metaphysics shows the profound imprint of Campanella's Trinitarian account of the primalities and pansensism. It does so, moreover, at a time when Descartes was challenging the fundamental

---

[69] Alsted, *Veraedus*, 6–7; cf. Hotson, *Alsted*, 164–79.
[70] Hotson, *Alsted*, 173–78.
[71] For Reformed praise of Pico see, for example, John Stoughton, *Felicitas Ultimi Saeculi* (London, 1640), 5.
[72] Alsted, *Veraedus*, 9–24.

presuppositions and structure of the whole of Western ontology. Bisterfeld's response to this is to construct his own Christian metaphysics of intelligibility on Ramist, Lullist, and Campanellan foundations.

For Bisterfeld, metaphysics is the "mother, nourisher and mistress of all the disciplines".[73] Employing the Lullist image of the tree of sciences, he holds that metaphysics provides the root and trunk, whereas all the other disciplines are the branches.[74] Against Ames and his Transylvanian followers he is clear in arguing for the integrity of metaphysics as a distinct discipline. Assigning logic an instrumental role, he argues that metaphysics is grounded on the innate "first notions" of the human mind, while logic is constituted by "second notions" derived from the experience of bodies and spirits. While allowing for a definite demarcation of the two disciplines, such a view also enables a cross-fertilization of metaphysics with logic and other disciplines.[75] Indeed, the intimate bond assumed between metaphysics and politics provides a direct connection between Bisterfeld's philosophy and the reform of Church and society.[76]

Bisterfeld's concern to unite mind and reality into a new metaphysical synthesis is seen right from the start of his *Seminarium Primae Philosophiae*, posthumously published in 1657. Invoking "panharmony" he argues that metaphysics should concern "things cognised, minds cognising and human cognitions".[77] Since metaphysics concerns first notions its starting point is the intelligible principles which are held to govern all of reality. For Bisterfeld the study of being cannot therefore be isolated from the study of the human mind and its cognition; the three are inextricably bound together. Contra Aristotle, we may infer from his discussion that the proper subject of metaphysics is not "being *qua* being" but rather being as it is intelligible. In this, he is clearly influenced by Timpler's reorientation of metaphysics away from the substantiality towards the intelligibility of being.[78]

In handling the intelligible principles which govern and structure all reality, Bisterfeld argues that metaphysics simply unfolds these innate notions as the "seeds of every human cognition"—hence the name *Seminarium*. Its fundamental purpose is to reveal the intelligible unity underlying the multiplicity of created being.[79] In this way, metaphysics also corresponds to a definite mathematical pattern and Bisterfeld is clear that the first notions of metaphysics should be joined together in a "mathematical and geometrical manner" as Pythagoras himself had sought to do. By following the natural sequence of numbers we are

---

[73] Johann Heinrich Bisterfeld, *Philosophiae Primae Seminarium* (Leiden, 1657), 8.
[74] Bisterfeld, *Logica*, in *BR*, 2.326–32.
[75] Johann Heinrich Bisterfeld, *Sciagraphia Analyseos*, in *BR*, 1.201–2; *Logica*, in *BR*, 1.19.
[76] Johann Heinrich Bisterfeld, *Artificium Definiendi Catholicum*, in *BR*, 1.48.
[77] Bisterfeld, *Seminarium*, 1–2.
[78] Timpler, *Metaphysicae Systema*, 6–8.
[79] Bisterfeld, *Seminarium*, 2, 25.

thus able to construct an ordered sequence of axioms.[80] Bisterfeld's metaphysics of intelligibility thus points beyond Timpler towards an explicitly Neo-Platonic and Neo-Pythagorean understanding of reality, strongly reminiscent of Cusa and his followers. Much like the young Alsted, but ultimately in a far more thoroughgoing manner, Bisterfeld seeks to bind together metaphysics, logic, and mathematics into a single coherent expression of reality.

Fundamental to all metaphysics, as what he calls the "mother of first axioms or dignities" is the notion of being itself. It is this which is both "first fount" and "highest apex" of the ontological and epistemological ladder of creation.[81] Most likely drawing on Descartes, Bisterfeld holds that being is "clear and evident *per se*" and "known by the sole attention and reflection of the mind".[82] Unlike Descartes, however, Bisterfeld's own prioritizing of intelligibility does not lead to him developing his metaphysics as a kind of pure thought-experiment. Rather, in Lullist and Cusan fashion, he is always concerned to match the dynamic unfolding of the human mind to the structure of external reality itself.[83] While, as we shall see, his Realism is more muted than that of other Ramists, he nevertheless avoids falling into the trap of Cartesian Nominalism. Indeed, Bisterfeld follows a definite Scotistic and Suarezian trajectory, in arguing that we come to know being through multiple inadequate concepts which are "fundamentally and materially the same" but formally distinct from each other.[84] Such a view also parallels Campanella's "ideal distinction", which Bonansea has argued closely corresponds to Scotus' formal distinction, while placing the emphasis on its conceptual apprehension by the mind.[85] In both cases Scotist metaphysics is taken up and transformed according to a Nominalist or, as Antognazza suggests, conceptualist framework, allowing Bisterfeld to pick out the intrinsic structure of reality without fragmenting it.[86]

As Antognazza insightfully suggests, Bisterfeld's account of metaphysics includes both static and dynamic elements.[87] Concerned to avoid giving an abstract, detached, self-contained notion of being, he emphasizes the intrinsic, dynamic, and relational structure of being—the "sociability" which Mulsow has argued lies at the heart of his metaphysics.[88] It is axiomatic to him that "no being

---

[80] Bisterfeld, *Seminarium*, 25–26.
[81] Bisterfeld, *Seminarium*, 25.
[82] Bisterfeld, *Seminarium*, 24.
[83] Bisterfeld, *Logica*, in *BR*, 1.22, 58, 163, 172. On p. 334 of this work Bisterfeld makes clear that cognition always proceeds from enfolded to unfolded.
[84] Bisterfeld, *Seminarium*, 23. For the Scotistic and Suarezian account of inadequate concepts see Burton, *Hallowing of Logic*, 118–26.
[85] Bonansea, *Campanella*, 149; cf. Tommaso Campanella, *Universalis Philosophiae, seu Metaphysicarum Rerum* (Paris, 1638), 1.2.3.9, 2.6.11.10; *Monotriade*, 130, 132.
[86] Antognazza, "*Debilissimae Entitates?*", 9–10.
[87] Antognazza, "*Debilissimae Entitates?*", 7.
[88] Mulsow, "*Sociabilitas*", 218–32.

is solitary but every being is symbiotic or pertains to society".[89] God himself constitutes an internal society in the Trinity and his own sociality of being is both ground and model for the "nexus, order and panharmony" of his creation. There is thus an "ineffable commerce" and an "infinite union and communion" among all beings grounded on the Trinity. In deriving from and exemplifying God, every being includes an "intrinsic and essential respect" to him.[90] Invoking something like the principle of plenitude, Bisterfeld holds that there is no vacuum in nature but that "all things narrowly cohere", such that there is a Ramistic "golden chain" of being stretching down from God to all creatures.[91]

Departing from a Thomistic paradigm, Bisterfeld denies any real distinction between essence and existence (or what he calls consistence). For to hold such would clearly undercut the dynamic and interconnected character of his metaphysics and especially the parallelism he wishes to establish between the Trinity and creation. Instead, he follows a late medieval Scotistic trend in holding to a formal, or rational, distinction between the two.[92] Indeed, according to a definite Franciscan trajectory, Bisterfeld clearly reconceives being within a dynamic, emanational framework. All the attributes of being flow from being and its principles and so are proportional to them.[93] No longer can fundamental attributes such as quantity and quality, act and passion, or even relation be seen as accidental to being, rather they become "fluid modifications of being" mapping out both its intrinsic structure and its ever-changing flux.[94] Structuring all of Bisterfeld's metaphysics is thus an account of the dynamic and cyclical motion of being expressed in terms of the Neo-Platonic triad of emanation, manation, and remanation.[95]

Emanating from being are not only its general attributes but also the special attributes of the transcendentals of unity, truth, and goodness. If the general attributes correspond to the essence and attributes of God—a comparison which Bisterfeld makes quite explicit[96]—then these special attributes are an important analogue of the Trinity.[97] In characterizing the transcendentals as emanations of being and in connecting them to the Trinity we may see a clear Franciscan imprint on Bisterfeld's Trinitarian metaphysics.[98] Bisterfeld thus holds that these

---

[89] Bisterfeld, *Seminarium*, 35–36.
[90] Bisterfeld, *Seminarium*, 32–36.
[91] Bisterfeld, *Seminarium*, 36.
[92] Bisterfeld, *Seminarium*, 166. Bisterfeld does suggest in a reconciling spirit that many controversies about this are merely "verbal".
[93] Bisterfeld, *Seminarium*, 41–46.
[94] Bisterfeld, *Seminarium*, 43–45.
[95] Bisterfeld, *Seminarium*, 60.
[96] Bisterfeld, *Seminarium*, 46–52.
[97] Bisterfeld, *Seminarium*, 70–81.
[98] Bisterfeld, *Seminarium*, 52–53.

are fundamentally the same as being but formally differing from it as "diverse inadequate concepts",[99] and insists on their convertibility with being itself.[100] It seems clear that he means something like Scotus' own formal distinction, albeit interpreted once again in a Nominalistic or even Thomistic manner.[101]

While the basic structure and dynamic of Bisterfeld's account of the transcendentals conforms to a broad Scotistic paradigm, his detailed discussion of them reveals a daring attempt to assimilate them with Campanella's primalities of being. Unity is thus not only that which is "undivided in itself . . . and divided from others" but also the "congruence of being with itself".[102] Expressed as Power, the first primality, such unity is not sterile but has a "wonderful fecundity" or inner dynamism, such that all things can be seen to emanate from and return to it.[103] In expressing the inner sociability of the universe, unity also stands at the origin of Bisterfeld's Trinitarian conception of immeation.[104] Following the same pattern both truth and goodness may be defined not extrinsically, as the congruence of being with intellect and will, but intrinsically as the self-congruence of being to its own essence and consistence. In such terms, truth clearly corresponds to the Campanellan primality of Wisdom and Goodness to the primality of Love.[105]

Espousing Campanella's panpsychism, Bisterfeld endows being with a universal self-perception and self-appetite, analogous to intellect and will. These primitive notions of "perceptibility" or "appetibility" are not only more general and higher than the notion of intelligibility, but, like unity, are also capable of being unfolded into a Trinitarian and correlative pattern.[106] Internally every being can thus be held to mirror the Trinity, with its generation of a congruous similitude of itself expressing its truth and its desire for union with its own likeness its goodness.[107] Anticipating a central theme of Leibniz's *Monadology* every being comes to reflect not only the Trinity but also the whole universe in itself.[108]

---

[99] Bisterfeld, *Seminarium*, 23.
[100] Bisterfeld, *Seminarium*, 107.
[101] Bisterfeld, *Seminarium*, 202–4. Bisterfeld here assimilates the intermediate modal, formal, and *ex natura rei* distinctions to the Thomist division between the real and rational distinction.
[102] Bisterfeld, *Seminarium*, 53, 61–62.
[103] Bisterfeld, *Seminarium*, 73–74.
[104] Bisterfeld, *Seminarium*, 52–57.
[105] Bisterfeld, *Seminarium*, 81–87, 103–11.
[106] Bisterfeld, *Seminarium*, 82, 86, 104–5.
[107] Bisterfeld, *Seminarium*, 73, 84–85, 105.
[108] Gottfried Wilhelm von Leibniz, *Leibniz's Monadology: A New Translation and Guide*, ed. and trans. Lloyd Strickland (Edinburgh: Edinburgh University Press, 2014), 56 (p. 119).

## 8.4. Neo-Platonic and Mathematical Logic

The main tenet of Bisterfeld's logic is that it should mirror the intelligible structure and dynamic of reality. Structurally, his logic conforms closely to a Ramist pattern, as Heereboord himself remarked on in the preface to the *Ars Logica*.[109] It therefore follows a basic division into invention and judgement, rather than being patterned on the Aristotelian threefold operation of the mind.[110] However, in superimposing this Ramist structure onto a dynamic account of cognition as moving from enfolding to unfolding his logic begins to take on a definite Neo-Platonic shape. In this "innatist" understanding of logic we should certainly discern the influence of Philippism, as Heereboord hints,[111] but even more that of Cusanus. Indeed, pervading his logic, just as it does his metaphysics, is a Lullist and Trinitarian dynamic. For Bisterfeld, this is all captured in the notion of immeation which proves as central to his logic as his metaphysics.[112] Where the early Alsted had hinted at the way of combining Ramist and Lullist logic in his *Clavis* and *Panacea*, Bisterfeld follows through with a comprehensive logical fusion, which is ultimately nothing less than a kind of immeation of the Ramist and Lullist systems.

For Bisterfeld logic is the "art of arts and instrument of instruments".[113] While he denies the Ramist claim for logic's primacy—an honour he gives to metaphysics instead—he by no means denies its universal scope and importance. Due to its instrumental character, Bisterfeld is clear that logic primarily concerns second notions,[114] and "ought not to define or distribute things themselves or first notions", for to do so would be to usurp the place of metaphysics.[115] In his *Seminarium* Bisterfeld also professed his marked distaste for the "thorny and otiose disputations of the schools concerning universals". Following an important late medieval trajectory, he insisted that "whatever exists in nature is in truth singular". Universals are therefore "beings of reason" obtained by the intellect comparing things among themselves in order to express their "convenience and difference". However, they are not "ficta" but have a foundation in reality and also reflect divine ideas in the mind of God.[116] In such an account we may clearly see the influence of Bisterfeld's Philippism creeping back into his Ramism, something which accounts nicely for that distinctive fusion of Nominalist and

---

[109] Heereboord, "*Lectori*".
[110] Bisterfeld, *Logica*, in *BR*, 2.1, 224–25. Bisterfeld's logic closely follows a Ramist order throughout.
[111] Heereboord, "*Lectori*".
[112] Bisterfeld, *Logica*, in *BR*, 2.17–19.
[113] Bisterfeld, *Logica*, in *BR*, 2.332.
[114] Bisterfeld, *Sciagraphia Analyseos*, in *BR*, 1.205.
[115] Bisterfeld, *Logica*, in *BR*, 2.331.
[116] Bisterfeld, *Seminarium*, 201–4.

Augustinian/Neo-Platonic conceptualities which Antognazza has highlighted as running through his work.[117]

In order to penetrate and explore what Bisterfeld calls the "immense abyss of things and disciplines", he holds that it is necessary for the mind to fashion "spiritual instruments". These include universals and other logical instruments as "images of things and norms of the mind" which serve to reveal the proportion between mind and reality.[118] Significantly, Bisterfeld compares the action of the mind in constructing such instruments to that of a "skilled mathematician" or geometer. Logic itself is thus a "most accurate iconography of the world" and he notes that Germans especially have sought to express this in mathematical terms.[119] Bisterfeld's account clearly resonates with the mathematical emphases of the German Philippo-Ramist school. It is also redolent of Ramus' understanding of dialectic as a "map of the mind".[120] However, it resembles especially Cusa's understanding of the mind as a mathematical map-maker, creating its own conceptual worlds in imitation of both God and nature.[121] As ectypal rather than archetypal in character, logic becomes a mathematical reflection of reality in all its myriad diversity.[122]

Confirming this connection is Bisterfeld's remarkable assertion, which stands very much as the gateway to his whole logic, that there is an "infinite immeation of logical instruments".[123] Logical immeation is premised on both real and mental immeation, and indeed stands as their very bond.[124] Logic therefore expresses the infinite connectivity of things, an insight which goes well beyond Ramism and clearly resonates with the combinatorial world of Lullism.[125] Even more explicitly than the published Alsted, Bisterfeld roots immeation in the perichoresis of the divine persons in the Trinity, which he views as the "fount of every created convenience and difference".[126] In its mirroring of the dynamic, interconnected structure of reality logic thus takes on a Trinitarian and correlative character, binding God, reality, and the mind together according to a distinctive Lullist harmony.[127]

Crucially, it is this immeation of logical instruments which becomes the foundation of logical invention, allowing logic to reflect the dynamic movement of

---

[117] Antognazza, "*Debilissimae Entitates*?" 9–10.
[118] Bisterfeld, *Logica*, in *BR*, 2.13.
[119] Bisterfeld, *Logica*, in *BR*, 2.13–14.
[120] See Ong, *Ramus, Method, and the Decay of Dialogue*, 190.
[121] Nicholas of Cusa, *Compendium*, 8.22–23 (*NCOO*, XI/3.17–19).
[122] Bisterfeld, *Logica*, in *BR*, 2.15–16.
[123] Bisterfeld, *Logica*, in *BR*, 2.17.
[124] Bisterfeld, *Logica*, in *BR*, 2.19.
[125] Bisterfeld, *Logica*, in *BR*, 2.19.
[126] Bisterfeld, *Logica*, in *BR*, 2.18. See further Antognazza, "Bisterfeld and *Immeatio*", 57–84.
[127] Antognazza, "Bisterfeld and *Immeatio*", 62–63. Antognazza focusses on the metaphysical and not logical implications of the Fabrist account of *immeatio*.

cognition as it proceeds from enfolding to unfolding.[128] In Neo-Platonic fashion Bisterfeld thus placed the theme as the centre of our reasoning and all the logical arguments it generated at its circumference. He therefore made extensive use of Lullist combinatorial wheels as a means of generating Ramist tables or "places of invention".[129] The fertile notion of immeation thus provided Bisterfeld the long-sought key to reconcile the Ramist and Lullist systems by innovatively tapping into their common topical and combinatorial heritage. By treating Ramist arguments effectively as spokes on the Lullist wheel, he developed a way of combining every argument with every other argument and also with every rung on the metaphysical ladder of being.[130] Following Agricola and Ramus, grounding logic on the combination of terms—and specifically the necessity or contingency of their metaphysical connection—also broke down the sharp Aristotelian boundary between apodictic and dialectic, fulfilling the Renaissance dream of attaining a universal topical logic.[131]

Bisterfeld's treatment of the second division of logic—disposition and judgement—follows a markedly similar pattern, treating judgement as simply the unfolding of invention.[132] Once again logical analysis thus becomes grounded on the metaphysical combination of terms and the network of convenience and difference which connects them.[133] Following the distinctive propositional Realism of the Ramist and Lullist traditions, he thus grounds truth exemplaristically on the correspondence of simple terms, propositions, and even syllogisms to reality.[134] Judgement thus involves a combinatorial, even mathematical, analysis of propositions and their relation to each other. Indeed, Bisterfeld explicitly reconceives Ramus' three laws of truth, justice, and wisdom as operating according to combinatorial and geometrical principles[135] Similarly, he also identifies the two fundamental laws governing the syllogism—the principle of non-contradiction and the principle that things which agree in a third agree among themselves—as being both logical and mathematical in character. In these terms, logic is ultimately the "measuring, numbering and weighing" of syllogisms.[136]

---

[128] Bisterfeld, *Logica*, in *BR*, 2.21–22, 334. The comparison with a seed reflects Nicholas of Cusa, *De Conjecturis*, 2.7.108–111 (*NCOO*, III.105–8). Also *Mysterium Pietatis*, 501 suggests that movement from confused to distinction cognition is a kind of unfolding of a seed.
[129] Bisterfeld, *Logica*, in *BR*, 2.65–66; *Artificium Definiendi Catholicum*, in *BR*, 1.12–18. See also Johann Heinrich Bisterfeld, *Ars Combinatoria*, in *BR*, 2.34–36.
[130] Bisterfeld, *Seminarium*, 37.
[131] Bisterfeld, *Logica*, in *BR*, 2.22.
[132] Bisterfeld, *Logica*, in *BR*, 2.39, 56–58, 225.
[133] Bisterfeld, *Logica*, in *BR*, 2.224–27.
[134] Bisterfeld, *Logica*, in *BR*, 2.229, 236, 267.
[135] Bisterfeld, *Logica*, in *BR*, 2.238–41.
[136] Bisterfeld, *Seminarium*, 79–80.

In Bisterfeld's culminating treatment of method, the mathematical dimension of his logic becomes fully evident. While his passion for immeation can lead him to extravagantly claim that there are multiple—even infinite—methods,[137] he generally affirms a unique template of method in terms of a movement from most general to most special.[138] In this way he preserves a Ramist focus, while at the same time emphasizing the dynamic multiplicity of method. Expressed mathematically, method can be seen as a series of concentric circles rippling from a centre,[139] or an infinite series of numbers generated from unity and its combinations.[140] The "panharmony and symmetry of all things" thus flows from method and its realization of the mathematical, as well as logical and metaphysical, ordering of reality.[141] Connecting panharmonically the unity and multiplicity of all being and thought, Bisterfeld's mathematical and metaphysical logic thus comes to profoundly mirror the Trinitarian immeation running through all of reality.[142]

In intimately linking the numerical unfolding of unity, the metaphysical propagation of being and the fertile combinatorics of method in a dynamic Trinitarian framework, we see Bisterfeld once again attempting that fusion of mathesis, metaphysics, and logic which Ramus had sought for so eagerly in his early works and which Alsted sought once again in the seventeenth century with renewed vigour. This is a quest, as we have seen, which had its origins not only in the Fabrists, and their innovative account of immeation, but also in Cusa and the fifteenth-century resurgence of Neo-Platonism, Neo-Pythagoreanism, and Lullism.[143] Indeed, Bisterfeld's own achievement of a mathematical and Trinitarian logic places him, like Alsted, squarely within an evangelical tradition in which logic and all the arts are carried out for the glory of God, paving the way for his own innovative and transformative Christian encyclopaedism.

## 8.5. Encyclopaedism, Meditation, and Ascent

From Cusa to Comenius, and beyond, the search for the *clavis universalis*—or *topica universalis*—was one which animated late medieval and early modern encyclopaedism.[144] As the pupil of Alsted, and the son of a Ramist father,

---

[137] Bisterfeld, *Sciagraphia Analyseos*, in *BR*, 1.211.
[138] Bisterfeld, *Logica*, in *BR*, 2.321.
[139] Bisterfeld, *Logica*, in *BR*, 2.318–19.
[140] Bisterfeld, *Logica*, in *BR*, 2.192.
[141] Bisterfeld, *Logica*, in *BR*, 2.319.
[142] Johann Heinrich Bisterfeld, *Alphabetum Philosophicum*, in *BR*, 1.58–62.
[143] See Albertson, *Mathematical Theologies*.
[144] See Rossi, *Logic and the Art of Memory* and Wilhelm Schmidt-Biggemann, *Topica Universalis: Eine Modellgeschichte humanistischer und barocker Wissenschaft* (Hamburg: Meiner, 1983).

Bisterfeld, no less than others, was profoundly motivated by the desire to uncover a universal key of reality. Indeed, he clearly thought that he had already found this in his Trinitarian notion of immeation. Writing in his logic, Bisterfeld thus made the striking claim that the "immeation of arguments is the key of the universal topic". In this, "metaphysics is the root of all disciplines, grammar the key, logic the judge and rhetoric the ornamenter".[145] For Bisterfeld, immeation is thus the "doorway of all genesis and analysis and the key throughout the universal encyclopaedia".[146]

For Bisterfeld, the ultimate origins of the encyclopaedia are to be traced back to the Triune God as the "fount of all wisdom".[147] He is the principal efficient cause of the encyclopaedia and the encyclopaedia exists ultimately for his glory. In this way the whole encyclopaedia manifests the by-now familiar triadic pattern of emanation, manation, and remanation to God.[148] It is thus through the encyclopaedia as a means of grace that fallen man is caught up and borne aloft again to God. Indeed, just as in the Franciscan tradition, the encyclopaedia represents nothing less than a kind of Jacob's ladder to God. It both ascends and descends the rungs of the metaphysical hierarchy, revealing the Trinitarian pattern of unity-in-multiplicity which runs through all of reality.[149] Yet in representing nothing less than the immeation of being, mind, and language the encyclopaedia is by no means a static object of knowledge, but rather inexorably draws one to participate in its unfolding reality.[150] It thus exists both for the perfecting of the individual human soul and, as we shall come to see by the end of this chapter, the perfecting of human society as a whole. In principle, its horizons are limitless, and it might therefore be seen not only as an attempt to recapture the lost glories of fallen humanity but also as an attempt to anticipate the future glories of eschatological transformation.

Overflowing from the Triune being of God, the encyclopaedia has three principal founts, from which all the branching tributaries of its different disciplines take their origin. These are the founts of sense experience, right reason, and Scripture, thoroughly familiar to us as the pattern of Alsted's Triune universal method and mature *Encyclopaedia*. Right from the start, therefore, Bisterfeld seeks to integrate Scripture into his encyclopaedism. In fact, he goes further, insisting that no encyclopaedic endeavour detached from the Bible can truly be valid, for a supernatural norm is always necessary to correct the deficiencies of fallen sense and reason.[151] Developing this Trinitarian pattern, Bisterfeld holds

---

[145] Bisterfeld, *Logica*, in BR, 2.325–56.
[146] Bisterfeld, *Seminarium*, 80.
[147] Bisterfeld, *Isagoge*, 11.
[148] Johann Heinrich Bisterfeld, *Consilium de Studiis Foeliciter Instituendis*, in *Phosphorus Catholicus*, 32; *Seminarium*, 58–60.
[149] For the theme of ascent and descent see Bisterfeld, *Isagoge*, 14 and *Logica*, in BR, 2.191–92.
[150] Bisterfeld, *Phosphorus Catholicus*, 19 refers to meditation as the "marriage of mind and being".
[151] Bisterfeld, *Isagoge*, 19–24.

that all the principles, or axioms, derived from each of these three founts must display the three "affections" of truth, clarity, and harmony. Truth expresses their immutable consent with the nature of things, clarity the immediacy of assent—thus short-circuiting the Cartesian cycle of doubt, and harmony their mutual connection and immeation. Importantly, this threefold affection of every axiom represents a natural fit or correspondence with the Trinitarian structure and dynamic of the human soul, especially as seen in the interaction of its three faculties of intellect, will, and executive power.[152]

The pattern of the encyclopaedia thus closely corresponds with, indeed mirrors, the immeation which Bisterfeld believes to be at the heart of reality.[153] Following in the Ramist encyclopaedic tradition he holds that this pattern can be represented either externally as a system of precepts or internally as a habit of the mind.[154] In line with his Trinitarian method, Bisterfeld follows an unfolding threefold division of these into theoretical, practical, and poetic disciplines. Theoretical disciplines expressed as metaphysics, physics, and mathematics are oriented to cognized truth and perfect the intellectual habits of wisdom and intelligence. Practical disciplines expressed as history, ethics, and symbiotics are oriented to good actions and perfect the intellectual habit of prudence. Finally, poetic disciplines expressed as logic, rhetoric, poetry, semantics, mnemonics, and also the mechanical arts are oriented to artificial action and perfect the intellectual habit of art. The higher disciplines of law, medicine, and theology derive from these and share in their nature.[155]

In the Ramist encyclopaedic tradition, methodological arrangement assures a neat division of the disciplines and a kind of parcelling out of habits to different faculties. While Bisterfeld's encyclopaedia is certainly structured according to a Ramist notion of method, moving progressively from general to special, in line with his Lullist understanding he does not view the disciplines as in any way self-contained.[156] In a manner reminiscent of Alsted's *Triumphus*, he thus speaks of the combination of different habits. Indeed, in what seems a striking reference to the Neo-Platonic metaphysics of light, he compares each habit to a different colour, so that their combination can be seen as making up a whole rainbow. It is this "combined habit of the intellect" which is to be called the encyclopaedia.[157] Going beyond even this combinatorial approach, Bisterfeld also speaks quite freely of a Trinitarian immeation of the different disciplines, such that the precepts of every discipline must always be understood in a threefold manner,

---

[152] Bisterfeld, *Isagoge*, 15–21.
[153] Bisterfeld, *Consilium*, 32–34.
[154] Bisterfeld, *Isagoge*, 8.
[155] Bisterfeld, *Logica*, in *BR*, 2.8–9; *Isagoge*, 38–65.
[156] Bisterfeld, *Consilium*, 35.
[157] Bisterfeld, *Isagoge*, 33; *Phosphorus Catholicus*, 22.

namely theoretically (*esse*), practically (*debere*), and poetically (*posse*).[158] In this, he clearly recognizes a natural fit and correspondence between the Trinitarian structure of the mind, world, and encyclopaedia, such that "by an innate impulse the intellect is drawn to truth in a thing, the will to goodness, and the executive power to the possible". In this Bisterfeld reflects not only Campanella but also a "certain of the scholastics"—most likely Bonaventure, for whom the divine attributes of Power, Wisdom, and Love structured the entire encyclopaedia in Trinitarian fashion.[159]

From the *Isagoge* the Trinitarian and transformative dimension of the encyclopaedia has become clear, but it is in his *Phosphorus Catholicus* that we come to see the full extent of this. While the goal of the *Phosphorus Catholicus* is not primarily to set out the encyclopaedia but rather to teach the *ars meditandi*, it places meditation within an explicitly encyclopaedic context. In doing so, it illustrates the intimate link between encyclopaedism, mystical ascent, and transformation. Meditation is defined by Bisterfeld very simply as the "marriage of mind and being". In more technical terms, he holds that it produces within the human intellect a "vital and representative assimilation" of the thing meditated on. Every thought or meditation is thus a "union" or "assimilation".[160] While this clearly resembles the Aristotelian notion of the conformity of the mind to its object, we have already seen enough of Bisterfeld's epistemology to know that he goes far beyond this. Instead, he emphasizes with Cusa the dynamic nature of all thought, as a "living" or "vital" assimilation to reality. Meditation thus receives sensible, intelligible, and supernatural rays of light and combines them together into a dynamic, shifting tapestry of thought reflecting the "panharmony" of all reality.[161] The encyclopaedia represents the culmination of this by providing "living pictures" of all the disciplines, and indeed of the entire universe.[162]

In the *Phosphorus Catholicus* the goal of encyclopaedic meditation thus becomes the exploring of an ever-expanding horizon of knowledge. According to Bisterfeld, combination or immeation is a process which has no limits, giving rise to an "infinite progression". Meditation is thus a way of preparing "infinite methods of reasoning".[163] It gives rise to the "harmonic studies" that he recommended to the young Rivetus and all his students, in which "infinite fruits are joined to infinite modes" through an "eternal marriage" of all the disciplines.[164] For Bisterfeld, the encyclopaedia is thus an attempt to grasp the infinite connectivity of being, mind, and language, a purpose which might

---

[158] Bisterfeld, *Logica*, in BR, 2.8–9.
[159] Bisterfeld, *Logica*, in BR, 2.44–45.
[160] Bisterfeld, *Phosphorus Catholicus*, 19–20.
[161] Bisterfeld, *Phosphorus Catholicus*, 19–24.
[162] Bisterfeld, *Artificium Definiendi Catholicum*, in BR, 1.2.
[163] Bisterfeld, *Phosphorus Catholicus*, 10.
[164] Bisterfeld, *Consilium*, 35.

seem futile if it were not for the immense dignity of the human soul. We may see this from one of the most remarkable passages of his entire corpus in which he remarks that the intellect by its very nature is able to "become all things" and so can be regarded as being of "nearly infinite capacity". By knowing God as "highest and infinite being" and the first object of its cognition, it thus equivalently (*aequipollenter*) knows all things.[165] Under grace, and combined with the supernatural light of Scripture, encyclopaedic meditation thus becomes an instrument not only for restoring the Trinitarian image of God in the soul but for perfecting and consummating intimate union with God, the only one who can ever satisfy the infinite desire of the human soul.

## 8.6. Scriptural Method and the *Ars Concionandi*

Alsted's Triune universal method sought to map out the connections between Scripture, the world of nature and the human mind. Yet despite the promise of this, and the monumental achievement of his *Triumphus*, he never fulfilled his ambition to provide a comprehensive, methodological treatment of the Bible. While the *Clavis* had hinted at the potential of Lullism to unlock the infinite riches of Scripture, it seems to have been only in his final years that Alsted returned to this project. It fell to Bisterfeld therefore, as Alsted's successor, to achieve that vital marriage of Ramist and Lullist biblical method which he had striven for and on which his whole project of Christian encyclopaedism ultimately depended.

Significantly, the roots of Bisterfeld's scriptural method can be traced right back to his early years at Gyulafehérvár, and connect to his complex engagement with the legacy of Ames' Ramism. Despite his qualms over Ames' method, Bisterfeld maintained close links with his followers and was intimately involved in their attempts to foster a new scriptural logic. This is evident in the 1633 *Technologia Theologia* of his friend Caspar Streso, a Dutch Ramist and pupil of Ames who sought to extend his work using new Alstedian and Baconian methods. Streso was a pioneer in biblical method and his *Technologia* attracted widespread interest across Europe, especially from the Hartlib circle.[166] Yet what is fascinating is that his *Technologia* includes an extensive treatise of Bisterfeld himself on biblical concordance, significantly dating from within Alsted's own lifetime.[167]

---

[165] Bisterfeld, *Phosphorus Catholicus*, 11.
[166] See Keller, *Knowledge and the Public Interest*, 171–72 and Hotson, *Reformation of Common Learning*, 190–91, 206–07, 216, 221–23, 280, 295.
[167] See Caspar Streso, *Technologia Theologica* (Leiden, 1633), 175ff. Streso acknowledges explicitly that he has included this discussion of biblical invention from Bisterfeld but not without "additions

In this, we clearly see an attempt to combine a logical and rhetorical approach to Scripture, according to the canons of Ramist invention, with a "universal art" of meditating on Scripture grounded explicitly on the Lullian art.[168] Employing a method of tables and combinations the work dedicates itself to uncovering what we might call the inner "mutuality"—he uses the Lullist terminology of convenience and concordance—of the biblical text.[169] From Streso's *Technologia* we therefore have evidence that by the early 1630s Bisterfeld was seeking to develop a new method of scriptural invention for use in theology. This likely indicates his role as co-architect of Alsted's own mature project of biblical encyclopaedism. It also provides a programmatic outline for his own later, much more ambitious, endeavours to marry his scriptural and Trinitarian methods.

The contours of Bisterfeld's mature methodology become clear from his *De Divina Scripturae Sacrae Eminentia* and *Ars Concionandi*, works published in Leiden in 1654, just a year before his death, and intended to offer an induction into the encyclopaedic meditation on Scripture and the composition of biblical sermons. From the beginning the *De Divina Eminentia* offers what amounts to a thoroughly Trinitarian and Christological reading of Scripture. According to Bisterfeld, the Bible reflects throughout the Trinitarian character of its author.[170] It is Scripture, as the "most absolute mirror and compendium of the light of grace", and not reason or the light of nature which truly reveals the Trinity.[171] Expressing most fully the Trinitarian pattern of immeation, the whole Bible is understood as "panharmonic, one system and one continuous chain ... given from one author, namely from Christ, according to one idea, because of one end, according to his instinct and for his glory".[172]

Conceived as a Ramist chain extending from Christ in heaven down to earth, the entire Scripture is clearly structured according to a divine logic, as well as being the exemplaristic realization of a divine idea. Coupled with this, the notion of the Bible as a "panharmony" or "universal symphony", in which every part is connected to every other, clearly resonates with Polanus, from whom it likely derives.[173] In this we surely also see the influence of Bonaventure for whom, we will remember, the Bible reflected the whole of the universe. In fact, like Polanus,

---

of his own hand". Hotson, *Reformation of Common Learning*, 207 points to Hartlib's interest in this work.

[168] Streso, *Technologia*, 175–79.
[169] Streso, *Technologia*, 182, 192.
[170] Johann Heinrich Bisterfeld, *Scripturae Sacrae, Divina Eminentia et Efficientia* (Leiden, 1654), "Judicioso, Suaeque Salutis Cupido, Lectori Salutem", 3, 12.
[171] Bisterfeld, *Mysterium Pietatis*, "Synopsis".
[172] Bisterfeld, *Divina Eminentia*, 99–100: "Sacra Scriptura est panharmonica, unum systema, unaque continua catena; quippe ab uno authore, juxta unam ideam, ob unum finem, nempe a Christo, juxta eius instinctum, ad eius gloriam data". See also *Mysterium Pietatis*, "Synopsis".
[173] Bisterfeld, *Divina Eminentia*, 100.

Bisterfeld is clearly invested in a Franciscan Christocentric and encyclopaedic view of reality. Affirming the intimate connection between the Bible and the encyclopaedia, he explains that this is because Jesus Christ is the centre of the universe of nature as well as Scripture, therefore Scripture uses the whole of nature for representing him".[174] Indeed, not only is Christ the centre of Scripture but the whole of Scripture can be said to have a Christological shape and dynamic. Christ is both the "nucleus of Scripture" and the "Spirit of the whole Scripture", and the purpose of Scripture is itself to effect union and reunion with him.[175] He is thus the key to unlocking the Bible, as well as the "adequate scope, object or theme and exemplar of the whole Scripture ... and of its all and singular parts, even the least".[176]

Implicit in the *De Divina Eminentia* is therefore an understanding of Christ as both centre and circumference of Scripture. The Bible is not structured simply as a chain of Ramist arguments, as Piscator or Ames might have claimed, but rather as a series of concentric circles radiating out from Christ. Since Christ is the scope not only of the whole of Scripture but also of its very smallest parts, it follows that he is ultimately at the centre of every biblical text. It further follows that every text can be related to every other through a process of immeation.[177] Going beyond Bonaventure, and pointing towards Lullist combinatorics, the horizon of scriptural analysis and application is revealed as unbounded, even infinite, as befitting a book breathed out by an infinite God.

For Bisterfeld, this was reflected not only in the logic of Scripture but also in its language. This was especially evident in the Hebrew of the Old Testament which he believed to be "holy" and "Edenic" in character.[178] Due to the "higher and more common signification" of Hebrew roots he held them to be particularly suitable for expressing the "seeds of first philosophy". Following the precedent of fifteenth-century Lullists and Cabalists like Pico and Cusa, he also held that the "profundity" of the Hebrew language is especially suited for expressing the immeation and combination of terms—most likely a reference to the way in which innumerable Hebrew roots can be formed through the combining of sets of three letters.[179] This reached its zenith in *"Elohim"*, the Hebrew term for God, which he held to perfectly represent the unity-in-multiplicity of the Trinity.[180]

---

[174] Bisterfeld, *Divina Eminentia*, 83.
[175] Bisterfeld, *Divina Eminentia*, "Lectori", 3.
[176] Bisterfeld, *Divina Eminentia*, 98.
[177] Johann Heinrich Bisterfeld, *Ars Concionandi*, in *Divina Eminentia*, 101; *Divina Eminentia*, 83.
[178] Bisterfeld, *Artificium Definiendi Catholicum*, in *BR*, 1.46.
[179] Bisterfeld, *Artificium Catholicum Definiendi*, in *BR*, 1.20. For the fifteenth–century Christian Cabala see Wilhelm Schmidt-Biggemann, "Einleitung: Johannes Reuchlin und die Anfänge der christlichen Kabbala", in *Christliche Kabbala*, ed. Wilhelm Schmidt–Biggemann (Ostfildern: Jan Thorbecke Verlag, 2003), 9–48. Schmidt-Biggemann emphasizes its roots in Cusa and Pico.
[180] Bisterfeld, *Mysterium Pietatis*, 514–15.

Ultimately, the highest exemplar of the Trinitarian immeation of mind, language, and reality is thus to be found in the text of the Bible itself.

For Bisterfeld, it is axiomatic that both ordinary preaching and more sophisticated theological analysis ultimately mark a response to the language and logic of Scripture. As a compact handbook for the making of sermons (*conciones*) Bisterfeld's *Ars Concionandi* seeks to mine the inexhaustible riches of the Scriptures for the benefit of the Church and of individual believers. As a work of "sacred oratory" it is directed to the "glory of God, the building up of the Church and the salvation of the faithful".[181] Its purpose is to teach preachers how to use logic and rhetoric to unlock the riches of the biblical text, and the message of the whole work is that this happens when the structure and dynamic of the sermon corresponds to the structure and dynamic of the biblical text inflaming the affections of both the preacher and his hearers. Expressing this threefold correspondence or *trigum*—a term which resonates with Alsted's *Trigae*—sermons must be pious according to fount, scope, and mode.[182] As "sacred persuasion" they should express the congruity of Scripture to the intellect, will, and executive power of man. Their role is thus transformative, to perfect humanity in the image of the Triune God.[183]

Given his understanding of the intimate relation between the Bible and the encyclopaedia, it comes as no surprise that Bisterfeld held the best way to achieve this was to apply his Ramist and Lullist machinery of analysis to the text of Scripture itself. It is for this reason that the preacher must be educated not only in Scripture but, as far as possible, encyclopaedically in all the liberal arts.[184] Such training is necessary as Bisterfeld holds that sermons must be written according to a threefold pattern of invention, disposition, and elocution. Invention is the "excogitation of matter" for the sermon and follows a Ramist and Lullist pattern of analysing the "conveniences and differences" of any biblical text by making use of encyclopaedic tables of commonplaces. It generates a *copia* of arguments by "running through the circles" of logic, the encyclopaedia, and the "four states of human life"—innocent, fallen, redeemed, and glorified—as well as Lull's fecund questions. The entire process of invention can thus be seen as the progressive unfolding of a sermon from its biblical centre.[185]

Once the sermon theme and the arguments which unfold it have been selected it is then necessary for the preacher to dispose the invented material into a coherent and logically-ordered sermon. According to Bisterfeld, disposition is the "soul of the sermon".[186] Unsurprisingly, method plays a central role for him in

---

[181] Bisterfeld, *Ars Concionandi*, 3.
[182] Bisterfeld, *Ars Concionandi*, 3.
[183] Bisterfeld, *Ars Concionandi*, 4 citing 2 Timothy 3:16.
[184] Bisterfeld, *Ars Concionandi*, 6.
[185] Bisterfeld, *Ars Concionandi*, 10–25.
[186] Bisterfeld, *Ars Concionandi*, 36.

the ordering of invented material into a connected set of propositions. In particular, he holds that the structure of the sermon should always respond to the "anatomy of the text" and the "symmetry of its parts", for in this way it can be better remembered.[187] Beyond this he also recommends the "exchange" (*cambium*) of methods, namely the handling of one thing by a method proportional to another thing.[188] Indeed, Bisterfeld holds that the principle of immeation can be used as a tool for the "infinite multiplication" of sermons, so that a preacher could in principle preach an infinite series of sermons on a single scriptural theme.[189] In this way Bisterfeld's *ars concionandi* represents an attempt to unfold the biblical text within a limitless horizon of interpretation and application.

For Bisterfeld, a sermon was above all a mode of spiritual communication. The framing of a sermon must therefore take into account not only the structure and dynamic of the biblical text but the way it impacts the souls of its hearers. Not only disposition, then, but also "affect" represents the soul of the sermon. Vital to achieving that threefold correspondence of text, preacher, and listener discussed above, is therefore the matching of what he calls the "circle of the sermon"—a term which covers seemingly every facet of the sermon's *inventio, dispositio*, and *elocutio*—with the "circle of affects".[190] For this allows the preacher to match their theme to the affect they wish to inculcate in their congregation and to express this through the vehicle of their sermon. A properly-constructed sermon has a particular power to move the affections of a congregation, not only explaining the meaning of the biblical text to the understanding, but also applying it to the will and enacting it by means of the executive power of the soul.[191] In essence, a sermon thus seeks to match the Trinitarian pattern of Scripture to the Trinitarian pattern of the human soul, illuminating the understanding, inflaming the will with ardent affections, and granting facility to holy actions.

Throughout Bisterfeld's *Ars Concionandi* we see that "homology" of being, mind, and language which Mark Johnston views as being the very essence of Lull's "evangelical rhetoric".[192] Bisterfeld's use of the combinatorial wheels of Lull's art as a means of generating sermons undoubtedly has its origins in Lull himself. It is also evident in fifteenth-century followers of Lull, such as Denys and Gansfort, who sought to use the art and other mnemonic aids as a tool both for inventing sermons and for structured scriptural meditation, by ascending and descending the "ladder of conveniences and differences".[193] For Lull too,

[187] Bisterfeld, *Ars Concionandi*, 35–43.
[188] Bisterfeld, *Ars Concionandi*, 44.
[189] Bisterfeld, *Ars Concionandi*, 75.
[190] Bisterfeld, *Ars Concionandi*, 31–35.
[191] Bisterfeld, *Ars Concionandi*, 4, 21, 35.
[192] Johnston, *Evangelical Rhetoric*, 33–34, 94.
[193] See, for example, Wessel Gansfort, *Scala Meditationis*, in *Opera Omnia* (Groningen, 1614), 275–94. For Denys' more implicit use of this methodology see Emery, "Invention", 406–7 and "Twofold Wisdom", 129.

the language of Scripture had an intrinsic Trinitarian and correlative structure to which any sermon must respond.[194] Notably, a similar understanding is evident in Bonaventure and the eponymous Franciscan *Ars Concionandi* which both hold that the speech of Scripture participates in a Trinitarian and affective dynamic, making use of "artificial divisions" and "subtle distinctions" to enable divine illumination to touch and transform the heart.[195]

Ultimately, Bisterfeld's own *Ars Concionandi* must therefore be seen as a fusion of the Ramist scriptural logic of Piscator and Ames with a Franciscan and Lullist understanding of the "panharmony" of the Bible. Mirroring the infinity of Scripture itself, his combinatorial method provides a means by which the Trinitarian and affective dynamic of Scripture could come to shape the whole of the Christian life. It is best seen not in light of early modern hermeticism but rather of a rich pattern of methodological devotion stretching back beyond the Reformation to the Middle Ages. Like the Franciscan pioneers of the *ars concionandi* in the thirteenth and fourteenth centuries, it offered Bisterfeld a means of systematizing his affective, Christocentric preaching, honing the art of sermonizing as a powerful tool for mission, evangelism, and the reform of the Church.[196]

## 8.7. Theological Logic

Bisterfeld's scriptural and encyclopaedic method reveals his conviction that a Trinitarian pattern can be traced through all of Scripture as well as nature. While we have already seen an important link between Ramism and an incipient Trinitarian method, Bisterfeld's startling claim that Trinitarian immeation represents the *sole* key to *all* understanding, marked a dramatic raising of the epistemological, metaphysical, and theological stakes. For although Keckermann and Alsted had increasingly advocated for a Trinitarian reformation of knowledge, neither had gone so far as to make this the article on which all philosophy stands or falls. Yet for Bisterfeld this was clearly the case, as we may see from an important passage of his *Seminarium*:

> The panharmony of all things is founded on the Holy Trinity . . . the fount, norm and end of all order. With this acknowledged and understood the whole

---

[194] Johnston, *Evangelical Rhetoric*, 169–70, 174–75, 178. Johnston does not note explicitly the Trinitarian pattern but this is clear from the correspondence with matter, form, and end.
[195] Bonaventure, *Breviloquium*, "Prologue"; *De Reductione* (*BOO*, V.321–24); Pseudo-Bonaventure, *Ars Concionandi* (*BOO*, IX.15, 20). The Franciscan *Ars Concionandi* has a threefold structure and notes the importance of threefold division.
[196] Johnston, *Evangelical Rhetoric*, 159; Pseudo-Bonaventure, *Ars Concionandi* (*BOO*, IX.15, 20).

of nature and Scripture is pure light but with it ignored or denied it is horrendous darkness and chaos.[197]

In holding such a view, which can best be seen as both a radicalization and intensification of a Franciscan ideal of Christian philosophy, Bisterfeld was immediately forced to confront two weighty objections. The first, from the Reformed side, concerned the utter incommensurability of reason and the mystery of the Trinity. The second, from the Anti-Trinitarian side, concerned the supposed irrationality of Trinitarian doctrine. In confronting these objections in his Trinitarian apologetic we find Bisterfeld mapping out a new approach to theological logic, which seeks to preserve this delicate balance of reason and mystery within the horizon of an implicit logic of faith.[198]

Writing in the *Mysterium Pietatis*, Bisterfeld claims not only that belief in the Trinity is essential for salvation, but also that denial of the Trinity is the source of all errors in religion.[199] Standing in a long medieval tradition much of this work is therefore devoted to an extended discussion of Christological and Trinitarian paralogisms, exposing the logical fallacies of his opponents in their understanding of Scripture.[200] Bisterfeld's chief objection to the Anti-Trinitarians is that they seek to treat "divine and infinite" matters in the same way as "human and finite" things. They therefore miss the "immense gap between the divine and human" in Scripture, not realizing that the "finite is in no way able to comprehend the infinite".[201]

Yet while Bisterfeld insists that reason can never comprehend the mystery of the Trinity, it is central to his case against the Anti-Trinitarians that it should be able to demonstrate its coherence and rationality.[202] While he is adamant that for one essence to be identically common to three persons is a "privilege proper to infinite nature", he holds that reason is able to recognize instances where something which is singular and utterly indivisible can be common to diverse things.[203] Fascinatingly, he illustrates this with the mathematical example

---

[197] Bisterfeld, *Seminarium*, 132: "*omnium rerum panharmonia fundari in Sacro–Sancta Trinitate, ipsamque esse omnis ordinis fontem, normam et finem. Ipsa cognita et agnita, universa natura et Scriptura, mera lux est: ignorata, vel negata, nil nisi tenebrae et horrendum chaos*".
[198] For Bisterfeld's delicate balance between these extremes see *Mysterium Pietatis*, "*Synopsis*", n. 22. For the wider context of both currents see Maria Rosa Antognazza, *Leibniz on the Trinity and Incarnation: Reason and Revelation in the Seventeenth Century* (New Haven, CT: Yale University Press, 2008) and Ulrich L. Lehner, "The Trinity in the Early Modern Era (c.1550–1770)", in *The Oxford Handbook of the Trinity*, ed. Gilles Emery and Matthew Levering (Oxford: Oxford University Press, 2012), 240–49.
[199] Bisterfeld, *Mysterium Pietatis*, "*Synopsis*", n. 52.
[200] Bisterfeld, *Mysterium Pietatis*, "*Synopsis*", n. 34–52. For late medieval discussion of paralogisms see Shank, "*Unless You Believe*", 57–86.
[201] Bisterfeld, *Mysterium Pietatis*, 503.
[202] Bisterfeld, *Mysterium Pietatis*, "*Synopsis*", n. 8, 10, 22.
[203] Bisterfeld, *Mysterium Pietatis*, "*Synopsis*", n. 10.

of a single indivisible point which is able to be both in a globe and the plane which it touches.[204] In pointing to a kind of coincidence of a point, line, and plane, Bisterfeld's understanding clearly resonates with the Cusan and Neo-Pythagorean tradition.[205]

By his later works Bisterfeld's views on the theological use of logic became expressed as something of a *via media* between two opposite extremes. One extreme, which is clearly that of the Anti-Trinitarians themselves, is of those who "feign that every use of logic, even in the highest mysteries of nature and Scripture, is analogous or univocal and adequate". For this "crass error" is not only a-theological but a-philosophical, and leads those who hold this principle to deny the divine eternity, to teach that God is composite and above all to deny the Trinity.[206] Here we clearly see Bisterfeld attacking the Nominalistic reasoning of the Anti-Trinitarians with its attempts to place the being of God on the same univocal plane as the being of creatures. In the decades after Szegedinus the philosophical gulf between Reformed theologians and Anti-Trinitarians in Hungary and Transylvania had only widened further. Indeed, György Enyedi, one of Bisterfeld's chief opponents in the *Mysterium Pietatis*, made extensive use of Nominalist arguments in his attempt to deconstruct the Trinity. In responding to him and others, Bisterfeld sought to remind them of the pitfalls of using human logic to grasp the divine mystery.[207]

Yet Bisterfeld's insistence on the utter transcendence of God did not mean he lurched to the opposite extreme of those he called the "irrational theologians", who "deny the use of right reason in divine mysteries". These he depicted as saying, when led by their opponents to contradictions, that "although it is against right reason, yet it is not against Scripture".[208] Bisterfeld likely has in mind here the ongoing dispute over double truth, as well as the wider Lutheran affirmation of the coincidence of opposites. Indeed, unlike his colleague and friend Comenius, this is one place where Bisterfeld—like Leibniz after him—very definitely parts company with Cusanus.[209] For Bisterfeld, the Trinity is the supreme instantiation of the principle of non-contradiction and thus the foundation of all logical and syllogistic reasoning. In his logic he therefore cautioned strongly against making the principle of immeation, so potent in Christological

---

[204] Bisterfeld, *Mysterium Pietatis*, 522.
[205] Nicholas of Cusa, *De Ludo Globi*, 1.9-11 (*NCOO*, IX.10-14).
[206] Bisterfeld, *Logica*, in *BR*, 2.27.
[207] See Jószef Simon, "Aristotelismus, Nominalismus und Trinitätskritik: Die philosophischen Grundzüge der Explicationes Locorum Veteris et Novi Testamenti von György Enyedi (1555-1597)", in *Radikale Reformation: Die Unitarier in Siebenbürgen*, ed. Ulrich A. Wien, Juliane Brandt, and András F. Balogh (Cologne, Böhlau Verlag, 2013), 227-40. On pp. 233-34 Simon emphasizes his reliance on Ockham's terminist analysis.
[208] Bisterfeld, *Logica*, in *BR*, 2.27.
[209] For Leibniz's denial of the coincidence of opposites Antognazza, *Leibniz on the Trinity*, 69-70, 103, 162-63. For Comenius' Cusan appropriation of this principle see Chapter 9 in this volume.

and Trinitarian reasoning, a pretext for seeking to conciliate contradictories or things truly incompossible.[210] For Bisterfeld, such a view of the coincidence of opposites risked undermining completely the rationality of the Christian faith.

Recurring throughout Bisterfeld's discussion of the Trinity in *Mysterium Pietatis* we find again and again the contrast between fallen reason and right reason. Fallen reason is that which attempts to apply its own finite norms to the nature of the Trinity, ultimately reducing God to a mere projection of itself. By contrast, right reason is reason that has been healed and elevated by its encounter with Scripture, and illuminated by the "new Sun" of faith.[211] In this, Bisterfeld clearly holds, there is an important sense in which logic itself must be transformed through its encounter with the Triune God. As he neatly put this, "although we do not repudiate right reason in the least, yet it is most iniquitous and most alien from right reason to subject the divine essence fully to these same rules by which it is customary to explain the essence of created things".[212]

Charting his own *via media*, Bisterfeld held that when confronted with the transcendent mystery of God "right reason corrects itself" recognizing that infinite being cannot be treated in the same manner as finite being.[213] He therefore argued for the need for a special "theological logic" to treat the nature of God, which would respect the infinite incommensurability between the finite and infinite.[214] Providing an illustration of this he argued that the fundamental syllogistic rule that "things which are the same of one to a third, are the same among themselves" is only true of the Trinity according to the stricter reading that things are true "in the same mode". By modifying the principle in this way, to refer to reciprocal and non-reciprocal modes of identity, Bisterfeld is able to preserve the distinction between essence and persons in the Godhead, and thus defuse the syllogisms of the Anti-Trinitarians.[215] Yet, as the rest of the *Mysterium Pietatis* makes clear, this is a modification, or refinement, which only truly makes sense in the light of Scripture. Tacitly, but plainly, therefore Bisterfeld advances a new logic of Scripture, in continuity with the wider Ramist movement and even more so with that late medieval doctrine of the logic of faith birthed in the Franciscan schools.[216] However, whether such a logic can properly be called supernatural, as Holcot and others would claim, must remain something of an open question in Bisterfeld's case.

For by the time he wrote his later works, Bisterfeld seems to have changed his mind about the possibility of reason proving the Trinity. In Lullist fashion

---

[210] Bisterfeld, *Logica*, in BR, 2.55.
[211] Bisterfeld, *Mysterium Pietatis*, 503–4.
[212] Bisterfeld, *Mysterium Pietatis*, 505.
[213] Bisterfeld, *Mysterium Pietatis*, 504.
[214] Bisterfeld, *Sciagraphia Analyseos*, in BR, 1.209.
[215] Bisterfeld, *Mysterium Pietatis*, "Synopsis", n. 11–12.
[216] Shank, *"Unless You Believe"*, 57–86.

he holds that a "ternary of persons" can now be demonstrated "as if *a priori* or *a posteriori*".[217] Key to this change is his remarkable conviction that in the state of innocence reason was "not only able to know the mystery of the Trinity, but that this was its "first and natural object"—a view which goes well beyond even Bonaventure's doctrine of the being of God as the first object of the human intellect.[218] Given that the human mind is a kind of infinity it does not make sense to him anymore to emphasize the radical disjunction between reason and the Trinity. Of course, we are no longer in the state of innocence so divine revelation must now supply the defect of human ignorance and sinfulness, but in doing so "reason by a reflex act is able to invent arguments demonstrating this mystery". The error of the scholastics therefore is to think that all cognition of the Trinity must be supernatural and to deny that the highest human perfection—namely union with God—is natural.[219] The quest to understand the Trinity is also a quest to understand oneself. Ultimately, the logic of faith proves connatural to the human soul.

## 8.8. Trinity, Symbiotics, and Society

For Bisterfeld, it is axiomatic that "the panharmony of all things is founded on the Holy Trinity as the "fount, norm and end of all order".[220] Trinitarian order is thus the "soul of the world ... of the kingdom of nature, grace and glory, of every society divine, angelic and human, and thence of domestic, scholastic, political and ecclesiastical society, and is finally the soul of the whole encyclopaedia".[221] Bisterfeld's Trinitarian account of society is to be found in his *Sciagraphia Symbioticae* and must be seen as the culmination of his far-reaching vision of universal reform.[222] In particular, it connects the Trinitarian reform of the individual at the heart of his scriptural and encyclopaedic enterprises, to the Trinitarian reform of human society.

Symbiotics is to be understood as "prudence concerning society"—a definition which echoes that to be found in the "sacred politics" of Alsted's *Triumphus*.[223]

---

[217] Bisterfeld, *Sciagraphia Symbioticae*, in BR, 1.127.
[218] Bisterfeld, *Sciagraphia Symbioticae*, in BR, 1.126; cf. Bonaventure, *Itinerarium*, 3.3 (BOO, V.304).
[219] Bisterfeld, *Sciagraphia Symbioticae*, in BR, 1.126.
[220] Bisterfeld, *Seminarium*, 132.
[221] Bisterfeld, *Seminarium*, 130: "*Ordo est, anima mundi. Mundi, inquam, generalissime assumpti. Nimirum, ordo est anima, regni naturae, gratiae, et gloriae; est anima omnis societatis divinae, angelicae et humanae; ac proinde domesticae, scholasticae, politicae et ecclesiasticae: est denique anima, universae encyclopaediae, singularumque eius partium*".
[222] Szentpéteri, "Mystery of Piety Revealed", 89–98 offers the intriguing argument that the *Sciagraphica Symbioticae* incorporates all we have of the announced sequel to the *Mysterium Pietatis*.
[223] Bisterfeld, *Sciagraphia Symbioticae*, in BR, 1.3. Alsted, *Triumphus*, 198 defines this as "prudence of rightly constituting and administering the polity or republic".

As a discipline it is closely akin to metaphysics, and the *Sciagraphia* reminds us that metaphysical terms are the "first roots" of symbiotic terms.[224] The term itself derived from Aristotle, but Bisterfeld's use of it to designate the entire discipline of politics is distinctive and connects him to an important early modern tradition of Political Ramism, evident in Keckermann and Alsted but reaching its apogee in Althusius and his *Politica Methodice Digesta*. Such a tradition was of course thoroughly familiar to Bisterfeld from his time at Herborn. In order to understand his political system it is thus important to understand something more of its character.[225]

We have already touched upon Althusius' significance in previous chapters. Written in the context of the Dutch Revolt his *Politica* is often discussed in terms of its contribution to Calvinist resistance theory.[226] As such the work clearly had a particular valence in Transylvania in serving to justify that Principality's own revolt against Habsburg overlordship. It is thus scarcely surprising that it finds a prominent place in Csere's *Magyar Encyclopaedia* with its abiding concern for political and social reform.[227] Even more significant, however, is Althusius' distinctive fusing of the Herborn Ramist and federal traditions into a new methodologically-freighted conception of politics. True to its title the *Politica* presents a tightly-woven Ramist synthesis of politics understood as the "art of consociating".[228] For Althusius, as for Keckermann, it is clear that society in conforming to this logical pattern embodies a divine concord and harmony. At the same time, this exemplaristic pattern is combined with a covenantal pattern of society reflecting both late medieval Conciliarist and early modern Reformed emphases.[229] In such an understanding all human authority must be understood as limited and conditioned by law and covenant, deflating prominent early modern theories of absolute rule to be found in Jean Bodin and William Barclay.[230]

In contrast, to the top-down Neo-Platonic models of society so often used to justify political absolutism, Althusius presupposes a bottom-up account of the origins of political authority grounded on freedom and consent.[231] This

---

[224] Bisterfeld, *Sciagraphia Symbioticae*, in *BR*, 1.3.
[225] For discussion of Althusius' connection to Herborn Ramism see Menk, *Hohe Schule*, 39–40, 257–65.
[226] See Hueglin, *Early Modern Concepts*, 29–70.
[227] Makkai, "Hungarian Puritans", 37–38.
[228] Johannes Althusius, *Politica: An Abridged Translation of Politics Methodically Set Forth and Illustrated with Sacred and Profane Examples*, trans. Frederick S. Carney (Indianapolis, IN: Liberty Fund, 1995), 3–4, 17–18. Althusius' discussion of method as the "fountain and nursery of memory and intelligence" (p. 4) is found in the 1603 preface to the first edition.
[229] Althusius, *Politica*, 26–28, 114, 118.
[230] Althusius, *Politica*, 87–88, 113 attacks Bodin's absolutism holding that all power is conditioned by law. Hueglin, *Early Modern Concepts*, 73–82 contrasts Bodin's Ramist vertical view of "hierarchical determinism" with Althusius' equally Ramist view of horizontal communication and consociation.
[231] For the contrast between these two modes of politics in a medieval context see Ozment, *Age of Reform*, 135–81.

receives its supreme expression in covenant, with its codification of mutual rights and responsibilities. Althusius is therefore explicit in holding that every political society must be freely constituted (and if necessary freely dissoluble), founded on a covenant between ruler and ruled, and governed by representative assemblies.[232] Built up in combinatorial fashion through the consociation of individuals into larger and larger group—families, colleges, villages, towns, cities, provinces, kingdoms, and empires—Althusius thus conceives society as a complex and interconnected hierarchy of federal units.[233] Precisely the same is true of the Church which he holds is formed through the combination of individual congregations into presbyteries, synods, dioceses, and arch-dioceses constituted under the absolute rule of Christ as universal head.[234] Going beyond Keckermann, Althusius espouses an explicitly Christian politics, insisting that the law of God, and specifically the Decalogue, must be the foundation of all human law. At the same time, in line with his Herborn Scotism, he is clear in grounding all law on the will of God.[235]

For Bisterfeld, such a synthesis was highly attractive and on closer inspection it is clear that the *Politica* is in the background of much of his discussion. Like Althusius, he thus structures the entire *Sciagraphia* according to a Ramist analysis of "consociation", showing how politics may be expressed methodically in terms of different relational configurations and combinations.[236] Inevitably, however, such a combinatorial understanding quickly becomes reconceived by Bisterfeld in light of his own distinctive metaphysical and Trinitarian understanding of sociability. In effect, what the *Sciagraphia* offers is therefore a Trinitarian transposition of Althusius' federalism. In this, as we shall see, he draws deeply on a Lullist and Cusan account of concordance, as well as an exemplaristic account of dominion reminiscent of late medieval Augustinian Realism.

Axiomatic to Bisterfeld's metaphysics, we will recall, is the claim that "no being is solitary". Every being is therefore symbiotic and "pertains to society".[237] Symbiotics thus seeks to analyse the convenience—or habitude—that connects all beings, and especially all intelligent beings, together.[238] For Bisterfeld, God as Trinity represents not only a "society of persons" but *the* archetypal "society of persons".[239] Following the pattern of the divine archetype, Bisterfeld holds that human society "arises from a congruous union and communion of persons".

---

[232] Althusius, *Politica*, 55, 60, 88, 106, 111.
[233] Althusius, *Politica*, 27–66 encompasses the family, college, city, and province and ascending federal units.
[234] Althusius, *Politica*, 56, 58, 75, 144, 159–75.
[235] Althusius, *Politica*, 139–42.
[236] Bisterfeld, *Sciagraphia Symbioticae*, in BR, 1.16ff.
[237] Bisterfeld, *Seminarium*, 35–36.
[238] Bisterfeld, *Sciagraphia Symbioticae*, in BR, 1.17.
[239] Bisterfeld, *Sciagraphia Symbioticae*, in BR, 1.81.

Reflecting his Lullist methodology he argues that every society is characterized by a set of conveniences and differences between persons. Society can therefore be described as both in terms of "concordant discord" and "discordant concord".[240]

Like Ramus, it seems likely that he took this notion from Cusa. In fact, such a connection would scarcely be surprising here, for, as Nicholas Aroney has convincingly argued, Cusa must undoubtedly be seen as at the fountainhead of early modern Althusian federalism.[241] For not only does Cusa's *De Concordantia Catholica* present a fusion of top-down Neo-Platonic accounts of authority with a bottom-up covenantal emphasis on freedom and consent but he also reconceives both Church and society as a hierarchy of interlocking synodical, and federal, units.[242] Indeed, the account that Cusa offers in book three of the *De Concordantia Catholica* of the reform of the Holy Roman Empire through the institution of a chain of representative assemblies can be seen as a prototype for a very similar discussion in Althusius' *Politica*.[243] While Cusa does not extend this into an explicit Trinitarian account of federalism, there can be no doubt that his influential reconceiving of the Boethian notion of *concordia discors* within a dynamic Lullist and relational framework paved the way for such a transposition.[244]

In light of this it is striking that Bisterfeld also understands society in terms of a network of Trinitarian relations between persons understood as Trinitarian agents. All symbiotic actions and passions are thus to be considered in proportion to human intellect, will, and executive power, and it is from this Trinitarian interaction that fundamental political notions of right (*ius*) or power (*potestas*) arise. Through a further threefold expansion this can be considered as freedom (*potestas sui ipsius*) in relation to persons, dominion (*dominium*) in relation to things, and duty (*officium*) in relation to actions.[245] In this way, the entire moral and political field comes to mirror a Trinitarian pattern.

The purpose of symbiotics is certainly to analyse such political configurations but even more to identify those symbiotic means which are ideal, i.e. those which most perfectly mirror the Trinity. Importantly, he traces such means back to human affections and virtues, such as love, joy, wisdom, prudence, etc. Viewing these as analogical to the divine attributes, he reconceives them as Lullist dignities diffused through all of society. In Lullist-style he therefore provides axioms to govern their use, such as "whatever is, is good", "good agrees with good",

---

[240] Bisterfeld, *Sciagraphia Symbioticae*, in *BR*, 1.4.
[241] Nicholas Aroney, "Before Federalism? Thomas Aquinas, Jean Quidort and Nicolas Cusanus", in *The Ashgate Research Companion to Federalism*, ed. Ann Ward and Lee Ward (Aldershot: Ashgate, 2009), 31–48.
[242] Cusa, *Catholic Concordance*, 2.18.164–66, 19.167–68 (pp. 124–28).
[243] Cusa, *Catholic Concordance*, 3.12.376–79 (pp. 248–50); cf. Aroney, "Before Federalism?", 31–48.
[244] Cusa, *Catholic Concordance*, 1.1.6–2.12 (pp. 6–10).
[245] Bisterfeld, *Sciagraphia Symbioticae*, in *BR*, 1.6–8, 23.

"every good is communicative of itself", and "a greater good is to be preferred to a lesser". Clearly structuring idealizing reasons in relation to society, the affections also reveal Bisterfeld's understanding of the good of society as intended to be multiplicative and self-communicative, such that society itself can be called a "panharmony of goods".[246]

Following Althusius, Bisterfeld holds that society is intended to be a harmony governed by *ius* or law, which he defines as the "norm of symbiotic actions and passions".[247] In other words, it reflects an ideal state of relations between individuals, a notably organic and social understanding. Law thus binds society together harmoniously and so it is no surprise that Bisterfeld further categorizes symbiotic means in terms of union and communion. Reflecting the "ineffable immeation of things" union and communion must be seen as reciprocal to each other, such that "every union is on account of communion and every communion flows from union".[248] Society is thus expressed according to the dynamic ebb and flow of union and communion. Expressed in Lullist correlative terms, both union and communion can be seen to follow a Trinitarian dynamic of symbiotic action, passion, and their conjunction.[249] Indeed, such a triadic expansion gives Bisterfeld's symbiotics a branching Trinitarian structure blending Ramist and Lullist conceptualities, Bisterfeld's account of union and communion quickly becomes very complex. Yet it may be amply summed up in his account of dominion and covenant and their dynamic mutuality.

For Bisterfeld it is axiomatic that all dominion is grounded ultimately in the dominion of God himself. Since God most perfectly possesses himself in the Trinity, he must be seen as the fount and exemplar of all dominion, having absolute dominion over all things.[250] Indeed, properly speaking only God can exercise dominion in this way. Human dominion over the created order is thus derivative and grounded on the fact that God created all things for the sake of humanity.[251] Such an exemplaristic grounding of dominion has important parallels with Augustinian Realists such as Wyclif and Hus. Indeed, Bisterfeld shares to the full their conviction that political dominion is an ectypal reflection of the archetypal dominion of God himself.[252] Like them, he also indexes dominion directly to predestination, holding that "all things completely occurring in the whole society, as much as according to essence as according to mode or degree,

---

[246] Bisterfeld, *Sciagraphia Symbioticae*, in BR, 1.16–18.
[247] Bisterfeld, *Sciagraphia Symbioticae*, in BR, 1.19; cf. Althusius, *Politica*, 55, 86–88.
[248] Bisterfeld, *Sciagraphia Symbioticae*, in BR, 1.25.
[249] Bisterfeld, *Sciagraphia Symbioticae*, in BR, 1.25–27.
[250] Bisterfeld, *Sciagraphia Symbioticae*, in BR, 1.141–42.
[251] Bisterfeld, *Sciagraphia Symbioticae*, in BR, 1.138–39.
[252] For a discussion of Wyclif's Realist and Neo-Platonic notion of dominium see Stephen E. Lahey, *Philosophy and Politics in the Thought of John Wyclif* (Cambridge: Cambridge University Press, 2003).

are most perfectly preordained from eternity". The execution of the divine decree in space and time is thus said to mirror its eternal exemplar.[253] For Bisterfeld, this notion of the irresistible divine will does not remove creaturely freedom but establishes it: "for God determines creatures in order that (*ut*) they determine themselves".[254]

Yet while deeply influenced by currents of Augustinian Realism, it is apparent that Bisterfeld did not espouse the doctrine of the dominion of grace characteristic of the Wyclifite and Hussite movement.[255] Thus, his account of dominion, or rule, is clearly grounded in the natural order of creation, rather than in any supernatural communication of grace. Even more pertinently, although he does hold that human dominion is an instrument of divine dominion, he never seeks to restrict the exercise of this to those in a state of grace, rather grounding it on freedom and consent.[256] Following a clear Reformed and Ramist trajectory, the supreme expression of this is found in covenant as expressing mutual relationship, and Bisterfeld holds that the whole of society is built on a covenantal foundation.[257] In such terms, covenantal dominion involves the "concordance of the will of the inferior with the superior", and becomes expressed in different modes of government such as monarchy, aristocracy, and democracy.[258] Significantly, the ideal political system marks the conjunction of the highest liberty and most perfect unity characteristic of the Trinity.[259] In Bisterfeld, as in Cusanus, we thus see a Trinitarian and hierarchical unfolding of dominion expressed above all in relations of consent and concordance.

For Bisterfeld, the final goal and purpose of all these symbiotic means of union and communion is beatitude. It is this that the whole treatise of the *Sciagraphia* is continually straining towards. Having traced the emanation and outflow of divine dominion through all the ranks of human society, beatitude turns us full circle in the remanation back to God.[260] It thus expresses nothing less than the eschatological horizon of his Trinitarian and idealist reform. In its highest expression this beatitude is nothing other than the "most congruous manifestation of the divine glory", as the "highest and most universal measure" of the divine society of God and humanity. It is expressed supremely in God's glorying and rejoicing in his own infinite perfection, but is also expressed in terms of God's "most free communication" of his glory to his creatures, and especially to humanity.[261] This human beatitude is the final perfection of human nature. It

---

[253] Bisterfeld, *Sciagraphia Symbioticae*, in BR, 1.140–41.
[254] Bisterfeld, *Sciagraphia Symbioticae*, in BR, 1.112.
[255] For an account of dominion of grace see Lahey, *Philosophy and Politics*, 68–108.
[256] Bisterfeld, *Sciagraphia Symbioticae*, in BR, 1.141.
[257] Bisterfeld, *Sciagraphia Symbioticae*, in BR, 1.43.
[258] Bisterfeld, *Sciagraphia Symbioticae*, in BR, 1.53–55.
[259] Bisterfeld, *Sciagraphia Symbioticae*, in BR, 1.57.
[260] Bisterfeld, *Sciagraphia Symbioticae*, in BR, 1.5.
[261] Bisterfeld, *Sciagraphia Symbioticae*, in BR, 1.117–18, 138.

perfects the intellect through wisdom, the will through rectitude and liberty, and executive power through sufficiency. Indeed, it not only restores the Triune image of God in the individual soul but effectively restores the lost dominion of humanity over the whole of creation.[262]

Significantly, Bisterfeld sees not divine dominion but divine covenant as the mode by which this glory is communicated.[263] For covenant, with its implicit Trinitarian structure of mutuality and consent, he holds to be most appropriate for expressing the relation between God and humanity. Moreover, as covenant both answers to and mirrors predestination, it places this relationship within a broader eschatological horizon of transformation. Finally, covenant is also supremely appropriate for expressing the social reality of the people of God and their beatitude. In this the whole society of the blessed, whether human or angelic, can be considered as united into one mystical body, in which every part is in harmony both with every other and with the whole.[264] For the message of the *Sciagraphia* is that reform of the individual cannot take place apart from the reform of society, and ultimately the reform of the universe itself—that greatest instauration which God alone can bring about. With every being reflecting every other, as if a living mirror of infinity itself, the whole universe thus comes to be seen as a kind of Trinitarian, pre-established harmony.[265] In this the glory of the Trinity shines out over all creation and is manifested supremely in the harmonious union and communion of God and humanity. It is nothing less than the instantiation of the heavenly society of the Trinity on Earth.

---

[262] Bisterfeld, *Sciagraphia Symbioticae*, in BR, 1.14–15.
[263] Bisterfeld, *Sciagraphia Symbioticae*, in BR, 1.139.
[264] Bisterfeld, *Sciagraphia Symbioticae*, in BR, 1.138–42.
[265] For parallels with Leibniz's famous doctrine of pre-established harmony see *Monadology*, 56, 59, 78–80, 87–88 (pp. 119, 123, 143–45, 153–54). For the connection between Bisterfeld and Leibniz here see Antognazza, "*Immeatio* and *Emperichoresis*", 141–64.

# 9
# Pansophia
Comenius and the Quest for Human Omniscience

For Jan Amos Comenius, the last Bishop of the Unity of the Brethren Church, the legacy of the Late Middle Ages was still very much alive in his own day. As part of a Church which traced its origins back to the Bohemian Reformation of the fifteenth century, the Brethren could proudly claim to be the first in Europe to rekindle the light of the Gospel after it had been snuffed out by centuries of papal oppression.[1] Comenius saw himself and his flock as spiritual descendants of Jan Hus and heirs to his Realist reform. For readers of his *History of the Bohemian Brethren* it was natural to connect the Hussite heritage of the Unity, their role as an "exemplar" for all other Churches and Comenius' own project of pansophia and universal reform.[2] What Wyclif and Hus had begun, and Luther and Calvin had continued, Comenius hoped to bring to completion by ushering in a "perfect and universal reformation".[3]

The claim that Comenius' thought can only truly be understood in light of the philosophical and theological breakthroughs of the fifteenth century is by no means a new one. It was put forward vigorously by the great Czech scholar Jan Patočka, who traced a direct connection between Comenius and Cusa. For Patočka, Cusa's dynamic Trinitarian and Christocentric understanding of reality offered Comenius an escape from the confines of Aristotelian scholasticism and a path towards realizing that unity of philosophy and theology which was to become the ultimate goal of his pansophia.[4] His speculation that Cusa's thought might have been the seed from which all of Comenius' thought unfolded,[5] is one

---

[1] For an account of the Hussite roots of the Unity of the Brethren see Craig Atwood, *The Theology of the Czech Brethren from Hus to Comenius* (University Park: Pennsylvania State University Press, 2009).

[2] See the title-page of Jan Amos Comenius, *Historia Fratrum Bohemorum* (Halle, 1702). Joshua Tymarchus, "To the Reader", in Jan Amos Comenius, *An Exhortation of the Churches of Bohemia to the Church of England* (London, 1661) significantly refers to this as a "A Copy of a real Reformation".

[3] Daniel Neval, "An Approach to the Legacy of Comenius' Theology", *The Bohemian Reformation and Religious Practice* 3 (2000): 215; cf. Comenius, *Panorthosia*, 23.2–3 in *Consultatio*, II.330–31.

[4] See Jan Patočka, "Comenius und Cusanus", in Jan Patočka, *Andere Wege in die Moderne: Studien zur europäischen Ideengeschichte von der Renaissance bis zur Romantik*, ed. Ludger Hagedorn (Würzburg: Königshausen & Neumann, 2006), 237–43 and "*Centrum Securitatis* und Cusanus", in Jan Patočka, *Andere Wege in die Moderne*, 245–56.

[5] Patočka, "Comenius und Cusanus", 238–40.

that other scholars such as Jaromír Červenka, Klaus Schaller, Pavel Floss, Simon Kuchlbauer, and Petr Pavlas have subsequently borne out.[6]

Yet surprisingly Comenius' wider inheritance from the Middle Ages still remains largely unknown. Astonishingly Daniel Neval's study remains the only detailed account of Comenius' Hussite roots.[7] Likewise, the profound influence of Bonaventure and Lull on his pansophia—a major theme of this chapter—have barely been touched on.[8] While Leinkauf and Antognazza have insightfully connected the wider movement of universal reform to the dynamism of the Christian Neo-Platonism and Lullism of preceding centuries, the deep origins of Comenius' pansophic reform in the Augustinian and Franciscan Realism of the Middle Ages still remain to be probed.[9]

By contrast, Comenius' status as one of the leading universal reformers of the seventeenth century is now well attested. Following the pioneering work of Dagmar Čapková, Milada Blekastad, George Turnbull, Charles Webster, Howard Hotson, Vladimír Urbánek, and numerous Czech scholars, Comenius' intimate links to a network of further reformers spanning the whole of Christendom have very become clear.[10] Paramount among these connections were those to the Hartlib circle of universal reformers. Comenius' intellectual debts to Francis Bacon, Tommaso Campanella, and Francesco Patrizi have also all been

---

[6] Jaromír Červenka, *Die Naturphilosophie des Johann Amos Comenius* (Prague: Academia, 1970); Klaus Schaller, "Sein und Bewegung in den Frühschriften Komenskys", *Zeitschrift für philosophische Forschung* 23.1 (1969): 36–46; Pavel Floss, "Cusanus und Comenius", *Mitteilungen und Forschungsbeiträge der Cusanus-Gesellschaft* 10 (1973): 172–90; *The Philosophy of Nicholas of Cusa: An Introduction into His Thinking* (Basel: Schwabe Verlag, 2020), 323–44; Simon Kuchlbauer, *Johann Amos Comenius' antisozinianische Schriften: Entwurf eines integrativen Konzepts von Aufklärung* (Dresden: Thelem, 2011), 61–89, 197–221; Pavlas, "The Book Metaphor Triadized"; Simon J. G. Burton, "'Squaring the Circle': Cusan Metaphysics and the Pansophic Vision of Jan Amos Comenius", both in *Nicholas of Cusa and the Making of the Early Modern World*, ed. Burton, Hollmann, and Parker, 384–416, 417–49; and Simon J. G. Burton, "Contested Legacies of the Late Middle Ages: Reason, Mystery and Participation in Jan Amos Comenius and Richard Baxter", *Acta Comeniana* 30 (2016): 119–49.

[7] Daniel Neval, *Die Macht Gottes zum Heil: Das Bibelverständnis von Johann Amos Comenius in einer Zeit der Kriese und des Umbruchs* (Zürich: Evangelisches Verlagshaus, 2006). Atwood, *Theology of the Czech Brethren* also places Comenius in a Hussite trajectory.

[8] Erwin Schadel, *Sehendes Herz (Cor Oculatum)—Zu einem Emblem des späten Comenius* (Frankfurt am Main: Peter Lang, 2003), 55–78 highlights important parallels between Bonaventure and Comenius. Recent work by Tomáš Havelka, "The Metaphorical Layer in Comenius' *The Labyrinth of the World and the Paradise of the Heart*" (Conference paper given at "Between the Labyrinth and the Way of Light: Early Modern Metaphors of Knowledge and Johannes Amos Comenius", Institute of Philosophy, Czech Academy of Sciences, Prague, September 2021) reveals the early impress of Lullism on Comenius' thought. I am very grateful for permission from Tomáš Havelka to use this paper.

[9] See Thomas Leinkauf, *Mundus Combinatus: Studien zur Struktur der barocken Universalwissenschaft am Beispiel Athanasius Kirchers SJ (1602–1680)* (Berlin: Akademie Verlag, 1993); Antognazza, "*Immeatio* and *Emperichoresis*", 41–64; and "Bisterfeld and *Immeatio*", 64–81.

[10] The literature is extensive, but for a helpful overview see Dagmar Čapková, "The Comenian Group in England and Comenius' Idea of Universal Reform", *Acta Comeniana* 25 (1969): 25–34 and Hotson, *Reformation of Common Learning*, 203–304.

extensively explored.[11] More recently Hotson's studies have begun to uncover the "Ramist roots" of Comenius' pansophia, revealing his intimate connections to Alsted, Bisterfeld, and the encyclopaedism of the Herborn circle.[12]

Focussing on Comenius' pansophia this chapter will seek to reconnect the universal reformation of the seventeenth century to its late medieval roots. It will begin by considering the hinterland of his pansophia in the diverse influences that shaped it, showing how influences from Ramism and Lullism combined with those from Bacon and Campanella into a Trinitarian programme of reform. Equally important was Comenius' early enthusiasm for Rosicrucianism which gave his reform a definite Millenarian impulse. For while often seen in light of its hermetic and occult dimensions, this too had a vital Franciscan and Joachimite dimension and must be seen in relation to the perennial quest for a truly Christian philosophy.

From here we will see how Comenius' pansophia first took shape as a project of Augustinian and Franciscan encyclopaedism before coming, under Cusa's influence, to embody a mystical coincidence of opposites against the encroaching rationalism of his age. All these influences came to an important culmination in Comenius' attempt to construct a Trinitarian and combinatorial method on Ramist, Lullist, and Cusan foundations, revealing the pansophia as nothing less than the fulfilment of the late medieval quest for a logic of faith. Finally, Comenius' pansophia came to fruition in an ambitious project of universal reform profoundly indebted to Cusa and Campanella and seeking to fulfil Ramus' idealistic dream of the renewal of Christendom and the total transformation of Church, academy, and society.

## 9.1. Ramist and Lullist Formation

Comenius was born in 1592 near the Hungarian border in Southern Moravia to a family who were devout members of the Bohemian Brethren. While his

---

[11] See Jan Čížek, *The Conception of Man in the Works of John Amos Comenius* (Frankfurt am Main: Peter Lang, 2016); "Comenius' Pansophia in the Context of Renaissance Neo-Platonism", in *Platonism and Its Legacy: Selected Papers from the Fifteenth Annual Conference of the International Society for Neoplatonic Studies 2017 Olomouc*, ed. John F. Finamore and Tomáš Nejeschleba (Lydney: The Prometheus Trust, 2019), 357–68; "Patricius—Alstedius—Comenius. A Few Remarks on Patricius' Reception in Early Modern Central Europe", in *Francesco Patrizi: Philosopher of the Renaissance*, ed. Paul Richard Blum and Tomáš Nejeschleba (Olomouc: University of Olomouc Press, 2014), 372–84; Petr Pavlas, "The Book of the Mind: The Shift towards the Subject in Patrizi and Comenius", in *Francesco Patrizi*, ed. Blum and Nejeschleba, 343–59; and Matteo Raffaelli, *Macht, Weisheit, Liebe: Campanella und Comenius als Vordenker einer friedvoll globalisierten Weltgemeinschaft* (Frankfurt am Main: Lang, 2009).

[12] Howard Hotson, "The Ramist Roots of Comenian Pansophia", in *Ramus, Pedagogy and the Liberal Arts*, ed. Reid and Wilson, 227–52 and *Reformation of Common Learning*, 224–301.

parents died when he was young, his guardians arranged that he should receive the best education available both at the local school at Strážnice and from the age of sixteen at the Brethren School at Přerov.[13] From his earliest education Comenius was thus taught the scriptural principles of the Hussite Reformation, as well as the piety of the modern devotion, which had Prague as its "second centre", learning to dedicate all his learning to the glory of God and the imitation of Christ.[14] Such influences were only reinforced by the Ramism he learned from his teacher Thomas Dubinus, who had been one of Martinius' prize students at Herborn.[15] Indeed, Ramism was a major influence on the curriculum at Přerov, and Comenius was likely taught from Johann Bisterfeld's popular editions of Ramus' dialectic and Talon's rhetoric.[16]

From Přerov he proceeded to Herborn, following in the footsteps of many of his own countrymen.[17] He matriculated at Herborn in 1611 at a time when the academy was at the zenith of its influence. While Martinius had already left by the time he arrived, the influence of his Ramist encyclopaedism lived on, and his *Idea Methodica* must have been an early inspiration for the young Moravian. Alsted too was already making his mark and beginning to write the groundbreaking works on method and reform which would establish his Europe-wide reputation. He was quickly to become Comenius' mentor and inspiration. Along with Alsted, Comenius' other teachers Heinrich Gutberleth, Ravensperger, and the great Piscator, who had a particularly high regard for him, ensured that he received a Ramist education in the best Herborn encyclopaedic tradition.[18]

Following his education at Herborn and Heidelberg, Comenius returned to teach at his old school at Přerov, where he spent two years before his ordination into the Unity of the Brethren. Here we see the first fruits of his Herborn education in his remarkable efforts to compose a Latin textbook, Czech-Latin dictionary and the first parts of his massive Czech *Encyclopaedia Universitatis Rerum*.[19] Scholars are accustomed to neatly separate out the early pedagogical phase of Comenius' thought from the later encyclopaedic and pansophic phases, but his Přerov works suggest that this can be something of an artificial distinction.[20] Certainly his desire for an all-encompassing Christian method

---

[13] Daniel Murphy, *Comenius: A Critical Assessment of His Life and Work* (Dublin: Irish Academic Press, 1995), 8–9.
[14] Mikuláš Teich, *Bohemia in History* (Cambridge: Cambridge University Press, 2004), 68.
[15] Gerhard Menk, "Johann Amos Comenius und die Hohe Schule Herborn", *Acta Comeniana* 8 (1989): 42.
[16] Hotson, "Ramist Roots", 250; *Reformation of Common Learning*, 246.
[17] Murphy, *Comenius*, 10; Hotson, "Ramist Roots", 250; and *Reformation of Common Learning*, 246.
[18] Menk, "Comenius", 41–47; Howard Hotson, "Irenicism and Dogmatics in the Confessional Age: Pareus and Comenius in Heidelberg, 1614", *Journal of Ecclesiastical History* 46.3 (1995): 440–41.
[19] Murphy, *Comenius*, 11.
[20] For a detailed categorization of the stages of the pansophia see Jan Čížek, "From Pansophia to Panorthosia: The Evolution of Comenius' Pansophic Conception", *Erudition and the Republic of*

can be traced very early in his works and, as Hotson has insightfully suggested, his pansophic works have definite Ramist origins. We find it especially in his pedagogical works and his desire to teach everything to everyone in every way, and thus to initiate a new transformative programme of education capable of renewing the image of God in humanity.[21]

Yet while the influence of Ramism on Comenius ran deep, he soon became dissatisfied with Ramist encyclopaedism. In particular, he held that contemporary encyclopaedists were too limited in their aspirations. Alsted had held that the ectypal encyclopaedia should mirror the archetypal pansophia of God as closely as possible, and nothing less than "human omniscience" became Comenius' own goal.[22] Comenius also complained about the static character of contemporary encyclopaedias compared to the dynamic pansophic method he hoped to institute:

> The most exact Encyclopaedias, or sums of Art, which I could ever lay my eyes upon, seemed to me like a chaine neatly framed of many linkes, but nothing compared to a perpetuall mover, so artificially made with wheeles, that it turnes it selfe: or like a pile of wood, very neatly laid in order, with great care, and diligence, but nothing like unto a tree arising from its living roots, which by its inbred vertue spreads it selfe into boughs, and leaves, and yeeldeth fruit.[23]

For Comenius, the Ramist encyclopaedias, composed like so many links in a chain were clearly inadequate. While they offered an accurate picture of reality, they lacked the dynamism and vitality, the "inbred vertue", necessary for a true encyclopaedia.

Comenius' conception of his pansophia as a living tree of knowledge is a clear reference to Lull's *arbor scientiae*, and as Tomáš Havelka has argued registers early in his works.[24] Likewise, his comparison of the neat ordering of the Ramist system with the rotating wheels of his pansophia is surely intended to evoke the dynamism of the Lullist combinatorial method. Comenius' commitment to Lull is hardly surprising in one educated by Alsted, and his own arrival at Herborn coincided with the publication of both the *Clavis Artis Lullianae* and the *Panacea Philosophica*, which was dedicated to Comenius' own patron Karl

---

Letters 4.2 (2019): 199–227. Hotson, "Ramist Roots", 233 points out a definite proximity between his encyclopaedic phase and early pansophic phase.

[21] Hotson, "Ramist Roots", 227–52; "Instauration", 1–21; and *Reformation of Common Learning*, 224–46.
[22] Hotson, "Ramist Roots", 233; *Reformation of Common Learning*, 225–29.
[23] Jan Amos Comenius, *A Reformation of Schooles Designed in Two Excellent Treatises* (London, 1642), 24.
[24] Havelka, "Metaphorical Layer".

von Žerotín.²⁵ For an astute pupil like Comenius, the implicit Lullist dynamism of his great *Encyclopaedia* would have been obvious, and through Bisterfeld he must have known of the Trinitarian and combinatorial direction in which Alsted's thought was moving. Indeed, Alsted's Triune universal philosophy and theology surely constitutes one of the most important early models for the pansophia, and Comenius' own early and enthusiastic reception of Alsted's biblical encyclopaedism indicates just how much an impression this left on him.²⁶ Alsted's desire for a new method capable of integrating an encyclopaedic discussion of Scripture, nature, and reason in a new Trinitarian synthesis is reflected in the pansophia right from the beginning. While Alsted did not pursue this again until much later in life, the junior Herborner eagerly took up his Triune method, with its clear Franciscan and Lullist overtones, in the hope of reuniting a sundered philosophy and theology.

Yet while indebted to Alsted's Lullist sources such as Agrippa, Trithemius, and Gemma, Comenius' attention to other Lullists like Ramon de Sebonde, concerning whom he was later to complain his Herborn teachers had never mentioned, and the Capuchin encyclopaedist Yves of Paris signal his definite independence of Alsted.²⁷ Indeed, Comenius was so enthralled by Sebonde when he discovered his *Theologia Naturalis* that he produced his own annotated edition of this massive work in his *Oculus Fidei* of 1661. While he came to Sebonde relatively late, Kuchlbauer has argued convincingly that the fifteenth-century Lullist must be seen, together with his contemporary Cusa, as a decisive influence on the pansophia.²⁸ Indeed, it is clear that, for Comenius, Sebonde's Lullist pattern of argumentation represented a new mathematical approach to theology which he hoped to institute as a panacea against the rationalism of his age.²⁹ Frank Manuel claimed that the "distant origins" of Comenius' pansophia could be found in Lull, but his mature works suggest that this influence was anything but distant.³⁰

---

²⁵ Menk, "Comenius", 47–49; Howard Hotson, "Johann Heinrich Alsted's Relations with Silesia, Bohemia and Moravia: Patronage, Piety and Pansophia", *Acta Comeniana* 14 (2000): 13–36; and *Alsted*, 47–48.
²⁶ Hotson, *Alsted*, 101.
²⁷ Jan Amos Comenius, *Oculus Fidei* (Amsterdam, 1661), "*Praefatio*" and *Pansophia*, in *Consultatio*, I.203.
²⁸ Kuchlbauer, *Comenius' antisozinianische Schriften*, 222–51.
²⁹ Comenius, *Oculus Fidei*, "*Epistola*"; "*Praefatio*". For more on Comenius's relation to Sebonde see Pavlas, "Book Metaphor Triadized", 384–416 and Amedeo Molnár, "Comenius' *Theologia Naturalis*", *Communio Viatorum* 8.1 (1965): 53–64. Comenius doubtless saw this mathematical approach in Sebonde's combination of Anselmic "necessary reasons" and Lullist demonstrations.
³⁰ Frank E. Manuel and Fritzie P. Manuel, *Utopian Thought in the Western World* (Cambridge, MA: Harvard Belknap Press, 2009), 207. Rossi, *Logic and the Art of Memory*, 136 suggests that although Comenius was highly critical of his Lullist predecessors his own thought shared considerable "common ground" with them.

## 9.2. Baconian and Campanellan Influence

While Comenius' desire to institute the encyclopaedia as a living tree is undoubtedly redolent of Lullism, it was, in fact, an aspiration lifted straight from the pages of the celebrated *Advancement of Learning* of the Elizabethan philosopher Francis Bacon.[31] Comenius' debt to Bacon is well known and has been the topic of a great deal of discussion.[32] Together with Campanella, he saw Bacon as a new Hercules cleaning out the Augean stables of Aristotelian philosophy.[33] The two could thus be seen as pioneers of a new philosophy of "sense and Scripture" to be opposed to an inward-looking, speculative scholasticism divorced from nature.[34] Comenius' juxtaposing of Bacon with Campanella is significant but was scarcely unusual at the time. Leibniz was later to connect the two enthusiastically, holding that while Descartes and Hobbes "grovel upon the earth", Bacon and Campanella "soar to the heavens". Comenius' own perspective on their profound affinity was undoubtedly shaped by Tobias Adami, the editor of Campanella's works, who portrayed both as deriving their philosophy directly from the "book of nature".[35]

We know from a letter to his Polish patron Count Rafał Leszczyński that Comenius discovered the works of Bacon and Campanella as early as 1627.[36] By this time his project for a Czech encyclopaedia was well in hand, but he had not yet turned his attention to the development of the pansophia. Despite his near simultaneous discovery of both philosophers, Comenius' engagement with Campanella seems to have come first, and he was always to read Bacon through something of a Campanellan lens. Right from the start Comenius was attracted, like Bisterfeld, to Campanella's Trinitarian metaphysics of the primalities. The deep imprint of Campanella's primalities on the pansophia has been revealed by Matteo Raffaelli and will be returned to below.[37] In many ways, Campanella's philosophy therefore proved a natural fit with Alsted's own programme to institute a Triune universal philosophy in Brunian fashion. However, like Bisterfeld, Comenius went considerably beyond Alsted in his interest in Campanella's pansensism. For him this became an important way of overcoming the matter-form dualism of contemporary scholasticism and natural philosophy in order

---

[31] Francis Bacon, *The Twoo Bookes of Francis Bacon: Of the Proficience and Advancement of Learning, Divine and Humane* (London, 1605), 62; cf. Keller, *Knowledge and the Public Interest*, 141.

[32] For a comprehensive discussion see Jan Čížek, "Jan Amos Comenius and Francis Bacon: Two Early Modern Paths to the Restoration of Knowledge", *Acta Comeniana* 31 (2017): 9–22.

[33] Comenius, *Naturall Philosophie Reformed*, "Preface".

[34] Comenius, *Naturall Philosophie Reformed*, "Preface" and "Prolegomena".

[35] Macvey Napier, "Remarks, Illustrative of the Scope and Influence of the Philosophical Writings of Lord Bacon", *Transactions of the Royal Society of Edinburgh* 8 (1818): 422. For his citation of Adami see Comenius, *Naturall Philosophie Reformed*, "Preface".

[36] Čížek, "Jan Amos Comenius and Francis Bacon", 11.

[37] Raffaelli, *Macht, Weisheit, Liebe*, 79ff.

to affirm the dynamic and active imprint of the Trinity even within material reality.[38]

Although Comenius was never to lose his enthusiasm for Campanella, he quickly came to find him wanting methodologically. Comenius was unhappy not only with Campanella's enthusiasm for Galileo—to the end he proved a resolute anti-Copernican[39]—but also with his insistence in grounding his natural philosophy on two opposing principles. For Comenius, this could only be a betrayal of the triadism which Campanella had so promisingly treated in his metaphysics. By contrast, he viewed Bacon's *Great Instauration* as the "most bright beam of a new age of philosophers arising". He particularly welcomed his method of induction as a new "key of nature". He also soon came to realize that Bacon could be used to correct the errors he had found in Campanella, not least the drifting of his philosophical principles from a secure mooring in Scripture.[40]

Comenius' heralding of Bacon as a scriptural philosopher has been granted with some bewilderment by scholars. Indeed, Ann Blair has argued, with some justification, that Comenius' own desire to unify philosophy and theology flew in the face of Bacon's own project for the advancement of learning.[41] Yet, while Bacon certainly warned against the undue mixing of philosophy and theology,[42] his works also bear witness to their mutual interaction and even mutual shaping. For Bacon, all of reality can be understood in Neo-Platonic fashion as emanating from unity into multiplicity.[43] In his *Advancement of Learning* he identified a "double emanation" of God's power and wisdom, the one giving rise to the "subsistence of the mater" and the other "the beauty of the fourme".[44] Elsewhere in the same work he coupled this with another pairing of divine power and will. Bacon's purpose in doing so was to affirm the traditional framework of the Two Books: the Scriptures revealing the will of God and creation his power (and wisdom).[45]

For Bacon, the motif of the Two Books could be used to offer an innovative correlation of philosophy and theology. Despite Rossi's protests, he clearly develops this according to an exemplaristic template, affirming the impress of the

---

[38] Comenius, *Naturall Philosophie Reformed*, 20–27 offers a triadic treatment of physics in terms of matter, light, and spirit. For Comenius' Trinitarian pansensism see Guido Giglioni, "The Darkness of Matter and the Light of Nature: Notions of Matter in Bacon and Comenius and their Theological Implications", *Acta Comeniana* 17 (2003): 9–31.

[39] See, for example, Jan Amos Comenius, *Pansophiae Prodromus* (Leiden, 1644), 28.

[40] Comenius, *Naturall Philosophie Reformed*, "Preface".

[41] Blair, "Mosaic Physics", 41–42. Čížek, "Jan Amos Comenius and Francis Bacon", 15–16, 20 does highlight the differences like Blair, but also acknowledges an important shared theological motivation.

[42] Bacon, *Advancement*, 23–25.

[43] Bacon, *Advancement*, 27–28.

[44] Bacon, *Advancement*, 27.

[45] Bacon, *Advancement*, 6, 31.

divine ideas as "authentic seals that the Creator has stamped upon his creation".[46] Affirming that God was the Sun of the mind he also sought to bind the "truth of being" and the "truth of knowing" tightly together within an illuminationist epistemological framework.[47] Philosophy, like theology, is thus grounded on God and reflects his nature and character. Indeed, despite his contempt for those who seek to erect an entire system of philosophy from Scripture, Bacon can still affirm that Scripture contains "much aspersion of Philosophie".[48] In fact, the *Advancement* even goes so far as to speak of the knowledge of creation as a "key" to opening our understanding of the Bible in order to conceive the "true sence" of Scripture according to "general notions of reason".[49] Bacon's own desire to organize his *Instauratio Magna* into six parts reflecting the six days of creation suggests a likely debt not only to Guillaume du Bartas, the Huguenot poet and Ramist, but also to older Augustinian and Franciscan models.[50]

Bacon's ambitious attempt to found a new Organon was also something deeply attractive to Comenius, marking as it did a bold, frontal attack on the prevailing Aristotelian and scholastic philosophy of his day. The *Novum Organum* of 1620 makes clear his conviction that Aristotelian syllogistic logic was utterly inadequate for that investigation of nature which Bacon takes to be the foundation of all true philosophy.[51] For Bacon, the scholastics are to be compared to spiders spinning out webs of ideas from their own minds without any reference to the world around them.[52] He is especially critical of their leaping from nature straight to the most general axioms and first principles, ignoring all the steps in between.[53] Against the Aristotelians his own method of induction was intended to supply a new natural logic.

While in places Bacon could be highly critical of Ramists and Lullists for their "over-early and peremptorie reduction of knowledge into Arts and Methods", in one place even denouncing Ramism and Lullism as "methods of imposture", Rossi is nonetheless right to argue for the profound influence of both on his

---

[46] Francis Bacon, *Oxford Francis Bacon XI: The Instauratio Magna Part II: Novum Organum and Associated Texts*, ed. Graham Rees and Maria Wakely (Oxford: Oxford University Press, 2004), 1.124 (pp. 186–87); Paolo Rossi, *Francis Bacon: From Magic to Science*, trans. Sacha Rabinovitch (London: Routledge, 2009), 55–56, 148–51 detaches Bacon from a Neo-Platonic, hierarchical view of the world while acknowledging its lingering influence upon him.

[47] Bacon, *Advancement*, 6, 21, 39–40. See also Caleb Kobosh, "Francis Bacon and Human Flourishing: Instauration, Induction and Christian Charity" (MTh Dissertation, University of Edinburgh, 2019).

[48] Bacon, *Advancement*, 29.

[49] Bacon, *Advancement*, 31.

[50] See Jürgen Klein and Guido Giglioni, "Francis Bacon", *Stanford Encyclopedia of Philosophy* (https://plato.stanford.edu/entries/francis-bacon/, accessed 29/12/2021).

[51] Bacon, *Novum Organum*, 1.12–19 (pp. 69–70); cf. Michel Malherbe, "Bacon's Method of Science", in *The Cambridge Companion to Bacon*, edited by Markku Peltonen (Cambridge: Cambridge University Press, 2012), 79–82.

[52] Bacon, *Advancement*, 19–21.

[53] Bacon, *Novum Organum*, 1.104–5 (pp. 160–63); cf. Malherbe, "Bacon's Method", 76–79.

developing methodology.[54] For Bacon's search for a new art of invention could hardly have made sense outside the context of the early modern methodological ferment. Not only did he tacitly transpose Ramus' celebrated three laws of method onto his new inductive method, but his dynamic and generative method of invention—often regarded as an innovative hallmark of his thought—owed much to the Lullist and Agricolan development of a combinatorial, and indeed inductive, procedure for uncovering the middle terms of syllogisms as the natural bond of subject and predicate.[55] Moreover, Bacon's desire to turn from the idols of philosophy to the ideas of the divine mind clearly resonates with contemporary Ramists.[56] For he too spoke of the need to "seek the dignitie of knowledge in the Archi-type or first platforme".[57] Following Perkins he reconfigured Ramus' "Golden Chayne" in a markedly voluntarist fashion.[58] Like Ramus, and indeed Bonaventure, he held that the mind was an "enchanted mirror" in continual need of polishing.[59] Affirming the dynamic parallel of divine and human creativity, he sought to transcend tired debates between Realists and Nominalists.[60]

For Bacon, as for Ramus and indeed Cusa, method should thus be seen as a "map of the mind".[61] In both his *Advancement* and *Novum Organum* he memorably extrapolated this two-dimensional image into three dimensions. In these terms Bacon's own hope was to institute the encyclopaedia as a "small Globe of the Intellectuall world".[62] Significantly, the *Advancement* presents the entire encyclopaedia in Bonaventuran fashion as a hierarchy of lights flowing down from God the Father of lights.[63] While Bacon once again bifurcated theology and philosophy according to the lights of revelation and reason, his whole scheme

[54] See Bacon, *Advancement*, 24, 65–66 and Ong, "English Ramism", 171. Rossi, *Francis Bacon*, 135–51 explores important parallels with Ramism. In *Logic and the Art of Memory*, 103–11 he notes deep affinities with Lullism, suggesting that Bacon's critique was directed more against its magical and occultic connections than its encyclopaedic potential as a *scientia universalis*.

[55] Malherbe, "Bacon's Method", 78, 81. See Bacon, *Advancement*, 64–65 for his approbation of Ramus' three laws and his clear focus on method. For Lull's combinatorial procedure of invention see Bonner, *Art and Logic*, 219–20.

[56] Bacon, *Novum Organum*, 1.124 (pp. 186–87).

[57] Bacon, *Advancement*, 27,

[58] Bacon, *Advancement*, 22–23; cf. Perkins, *Golden Chaine*.

[59] Rossi, *Francis Bacon*, 148; cf. Bacon, *Advancement*, 46. See also Bonaventure, *Itinerarium*, "Prologue", 4 (*BOO*, V.296).

[60] Bacon, *Novum Organum*, 1.70 (pp. 112–13). Antonio Pérez-Ramos, "Bacon's Forms and the Maker's Knowledge Tradition", in *The Cambridge Companion to Bacon*, 113 links Bacon to a Renaissance understanding of maker's knowledge going back to Ramus and Cusa. Fundamental to this was the dynamic parallel of divine and human creativity, which attained a classic expression in Cusa, *Idiota de Mente*, 4.74–79 (*NCOO*, V.113–20) as we have seen. In Nominalist fashion Bacon apparently denies the existence of universals, while at the same time affirming a Franciscan-Lullist understanding of the combinatorial plurality of forms in the "alphabet" of nature and their eternal and immutable nature as divine ideas. See *Novum Organum*, 1.121, 124; 2.2, 9, 17 (pp. 181–83, 186–87, 200–203, 214–15, 254–56).

[61] Bacon, *Advancement*, 65, 93.

[62] Bacon, *Advancement*, 118; *Novum Organum*, 1.84 (p. 133).

[63] Bacon, *Advancement*, 6, 20–21, 109; cf. Bonaventure, *Reduction*, n. 1–4 (*BOO*, V.319–20).

assumes an overlap and harmonization of the two lights.[64] For Bacon, reason and revelation not only have their own provinces but must also both become mutually informing. He thus spoke of both a "divine philosophy" and even a "divine Dialectique". This he believed would not only bypass the "vanity of the schools" but would also be capable of resolving contradictions and thus ending the controversies that had torn the Church apart.[65] Following in the footsteps of contemporary English Ramists, Bacon thus sought to institute a new spiritual logic for divinity in place of the Aristotelian logic taught in the schools.[66]

Continuing his Franciscan and illuminative paradigm of knowledge, Bacon also recognized an important triadic division of the encyclopaedia into history, poetry, and philosophy each of which he intended for the perfecting of a different faculty of the soul in the image of God.[67] In fact, Bacon continues this loose triadic structure throughout his whole encyclopaedia, correlating it in one place with three rays of light—the direct ray of sense, the reflected ray of reason, and the refracted ray of revelation.[68] For Bacon, this triadic structure also corresponded with a "triple Character" which he believed to be evident in all things—the power of God, the difference of nature, and the use of man—leading Aderemi Artis to speak of the "Trinitarian roots" of his pragmatism.[69] It revealed especially the imprint of God's "speciall attributes" of Power, Wisdom, and Love on all things and thus the dynamic impress of the Trinity.[70]

For Bacon, revealing a definite affinity with Bonaventure, the purpose of the encyclopaedia is to lay a "foundation in the human understanding for a holy temple after the model of the world".[71] It therefore unites all the "Notions and conceptions" of the sciences.[72] It is axiomatic that the highest good is communicative and he sees this as applying to both religion and philosophy. What this means is that the whole encyclopaedia is geared in Ramist fashion to "use", and the knowledge gained by the intellect is intended to lead to the action of the human will. Charity which comes through participation in God is thus the end

---

[64] Bacon, *Advancement*, 20–21.
[65] Bacon, *Advancement*, 21, 24, 110–11.
[66] Bacon, *Advancement*, 112–13 offers a discussion of "Methodical" approaches to divinity.
[67] Bacon, *Advancement*, 7.
[68] Bacon, *Advancement*, 35–36.
[69] Bacon, *Advancement*, 21; cf. Aderemi Artis, "Trinitarian Roots of Francis Bacon's Pragmatism", *Heythrop Journal* 60.2 (2019): 197–204.
[70] Bacon, *Advancement*, 117.
[71] Bacon, *Novum Organum*, 1.120 (pp. 179–81). This is not necessarily to claim the direct influence of Bonaventure, as there are a variety of channels by which this kind of Franciscan, Neo-Platonic understanding could have reached Bacon, including Lullism and hermeticism. Interestingly, Michael McCanles, "The New Science and the *Via Negativa*: A Mystical Source for Baconian Empiricism", in *Francis Bacon and the Refiguring of Early Modern Thought: Essays to Commemorate The Advancement of Learning (1605–2005)*, ed. Julie Robin Solomon and Catherine Gimelli Martin (London: Routledge, 2017), Chapter 3 also draws parallels between Bacon and Bonaventure.
[72] Bacon, *Advancement*, 28.

and goal of the encyclopaedia.[73] Comenius was not mistaken therefore to recognize in Bacon the paradigm of a new type of Christian philosophy, grounded on a Trinitarian and encyclopaedic in-duction into nature and sharing the Neo-Platonic and exemplaristic heritage of Ramism and Lullism.

## 9.3. Millennialism and the Rosicrucian Furore

From early on, Comenius' encyclopaedic endeavours became entwined with a pronounced Franciscan and Joachimite apocalypticism. The Millennialism of his teachers Piscator and Alsted exerted a profound influence on him, and it should not be forgotten that it was during his time at Herborn that Alsted's edition of Lavinheta's encyclopaedia was published, with its heady mix of Franciscan alchemy, astrology, and apocalypticism.[74] During his time at Heidelberg Comenius was undoubtedly exposed to the growing Millennialist fervour surrounding the Palatinate dynasty, with its Joachimite and hermetic overtones. It was Comenius' friend Christoph Kotter who kept alive the hope that the "Lion of Midnight" would rise again. Comenius not only personally conveyed these prophecies to Elector Frederick in exile but also later played a major role in stoking the eschatological fervour surrounding the hope of a Protestant resurgence under a new alliance of the Palatinate, Sweden, and Transylvania.[75]

Through his contact with the Hartlib circle and others, Comenius was clearly fascinated by the utopian ideals of Bacon and Campanella. Bacon's dream of a "Great Instauration" had already connected the unlimited expansion of human "epistemic empire" and dominion to a new flourishing of encyclopaedism to take place in the end times.[76] His *New Atlantis* of 1627 vividly imagined a utopian Christian society in which such an encyclopaedic mastery of knowledge and extension of dominion had already been achieved.[77] This fusion of encyclopaedism and apocalypticism was even more evident in Campanella's 1623 *City of the Sun*. For the organization of the city reflects not only Campanella's Trinitarian primalities of Power, Wisdom, and Love, but also all the different arts and

---

[73] Bacon, *Advancement*, 69, 72, 81.
[74] Hotson, *Alsted*, 182–222; *Paradise Postponed*, 15–26, 143, 160.
[75] Frances Yates, *The Rosicrucian Enlightenment* (London: Routledge, 1999), 156–61; Murdock, *Calvinism*, 274–89. For a critique of Yates see Donald R. Dickson, *The Tessera of Antilia: Utopian Brotherhoods and Secret Societies in the Early Seventeenth Century* (Leiden: Brill, 1998), 20 and Brian Vickers, "Frances Yates and the Writing of History", *Journal of Modern History* 51.2 (1979): 287–316.
[76] Bacon, *Advancement*, 15; cf. Keller, *Knowledge and the Public Interest*, 127–66.
[77] Francis Bacon, *New Atlantis*, in *The Works of Francis Bacon. Volume 3: Philosophical Works 3*, ed. James Spedding, Robert Leslie Ellis, and Douglas Denon Heath (Cambridge: Cambridge University Press, 2013), 135–39, 145–47, 156–66. For Millenarian dimensions of this work see Travis DeCook, "Francis Bacon's 'Jewish Dreams': The Specter of the Millennium in New Atlantis", *Studies in Philology* 110.1 (2013): 115–31.

sciences.[78] For Campanella the new age of invention and discovery pointed towards the imminent advent of a new, universal religion, which he linked to the Spanish monarchy and the expansion into the New World.[79] Campanella's ideal city was well known to Comenius and anticipated features of his own *Labyrinth of the World*.[80]

Comenius himself saw his own Hussite Church of the Unity of the Brethren as heirs of the radical Taborites of the fifteenth century with their biblical and eschatological desire to realize heaven on earth.[81] It was only natural therefore that he should gravitate to the Lutheran apocalyptic thinkers who sought to link Luther and Hus together in an eschatological narrative of reform stretching back to the Middle Ages.[82] The origins of this project went back to Luther himself, who not only famously declared that "we are all Hussites now" but also came to believe Hus had prophesied his Reformation.[83] It gained a significant boost with the circulation of works such as the *Horologium Hussianum*, an apocalyptic work which purported to be written by Hus and promised that the seventeenth century would see the emergence of a new Christian world order.[84]

The new Lutheran apocalypticism was profoundly influenced by Joachimite eschatology. Its Trinitarian division of time proved particularly appealing, with the age of Father and Son corresponding to the Law and Gospel and fuelling the expectation of the dawning of a new age of the Holy Spirit. A number of Joachim's works were reprinted in the first decades of the Reformation and had a wide diffusion.[85] In Andreas Osiander's 1544 *Conjecturae de Ultimibus Temporibus*

---

[78] Tommaso Campanella, *City of the Sun*, in *Ideal Commonwealths: Comprising More's Utopia, Bacon's New Atlantis, Campanella's City of the Sun and Harrington's Oceana*, ed. Henry Morley (New York: Colonial Press, 1901), 171–79.

[79] Campanella, *City of the Sun*, 159, 161, 174, 179. For Campanella's apocalyptic hopes see Manuel and Manuel, *Utopian Thought*, 261–88.

[80] Jan Amos Comenius, *Triertium Catholicum*, ed. George Klima and L. Zelenka Lerando (Prague: Sokol-Packard, 1922), 16 (pp. 102–3) cites this work. Yates, *Rosicrucian Enlightenment*, 161 points to the parallels between Comenius' *Labyrinth* and Campanella's *City of the Sun*. The *Labyrinth* went through a period of later editing so there may be an even stronger dependence here. I am very grateful to Vladimír Urbánek for discussion of this point.

[81] Comenius, *Exhortation*, "Dedicatory Address", n. 12–23 links the history of the Bohemian Churches directly to the contemporary struggle against Antichrist.

[82] Penman, *Hope and Heresy*, 3–5.

[83] From Luther's letter to Georg Spalatin, in Martin Luther, "Luther an Spalatin", in Martin Luther, *D. Martin Luthers Werke: Abteilung 4 Briefwechsel*, 18 vols. (Weimar, 1883–2009), 2.42. For Luther's prophetic connection with Hus see Robert W. Scribner, *Popular Culture and Popular Movements in Reformation Germany* (London: Hambledon, 1987), 309 and Susan E. Schreiner, *Are You Alone Wise? The Search for Certainty in the Early Modern Era* (Oxford: Oxford University Press, 2011), 137–39. Comenius, *Exhortation*, 44 makes direct reference to Hus' purported prophecy that "To day you rost the Goose [Huss among the Bohemians signifies a Goose] but there shall come a Swan [Luther] which you shall not be able to rost".

[84] Penman, *Hope and Heresy*, 41.

[85] For Joachimite influence in the Augustinian Friars and the German Reformation see Marjorie Reeves, *The Influence of Prophecy in the Later Middle Ages: A Study in Joachimism* (Oxford: Clarendon Press, 1969), 251–73, 453ff. and Penman, *Hope and Heresy*, 3–5, 13–15. Penman does not make the connection with the Law and Gospel here. See also Robin Bruce Barnes, *Prophecy and*

mainstream Lutheranism acquired a popular eschatology deeply influenced by Joachimite and Cusan eschatology.[86] In such an account the Hussite cleansing of the Church and the Church's subsequent crucifixion under papal oppression had preceded the glorious Lutheran Resurrection of the Church. For Osiander, Luther could even be seen as the Angelic Pope, prophesied centuries earlier by Franciscans, who had come to reform the world in the last times.[87] Exactly the same motif is evident in the influential 1614 *Signa Temporum* of Christoph Besold, the leading Tübingen philosopher, in which Joachim, Rupescissa, Hus, Luther, and even Ramus are taken up into a sweeping narrative of eschatological reform.[88]

Although Osiander might have been optimistic about the progress of the Lutheran Reformation, for Besold's generation this ascension was something many Lutherans still awaited with prayers and tears. For by the seventeenth century Lutheranism had entered into a profound "crisis of piety".[89] The rise of Lutheran orthodoxy, the threat of Catholic and Reformed expansion, and growing confessionalization led many to tire of what they contemptuously called the *Mauernkirchen*—the Church of walls—and yearn for a new spiritual Church to take root in human hearts. The attack on the *Mauernkirche* was first made by the Radical Reformer Paracelsus, whose extraordinary appropriation of Franciscan Trinitarian and Mariological speculation fused with a mystical and eschatological expectation of humanity's return to an Edenic state through Christ.[90] Despite its heretical overtones, Paracelsus' teaching proved attractive to pastors like Johann Arndt, who innovatively combined Paracelsian, Franciscan, and Rhineland sources in elaborating the new Lutheran piety.[91] Paracelsian ideas also had a prominent influence on the Lutheran mystic Jakob Boehme and

---

*Gnosis: Apocalypticism in the Wake of the Lutheran Reformation* (Stanford, CA: Stanford University Press, 1988), 22–30, 56, 76–77, 116.

[86] See Barnes, *Prophecy and Gnosis*, 56 for the Joachimite influence. Hotson, *Paradise Postponed*, 20 n. 67 notes that Osiander's apocalyptic calculations derive from Nicholas of Cusa's *Conjectura de Ultimibus Diebus*. The similarity in the titles is also striking.
[87] Penman, *Hope and Heresy*, 4–5.
[88] Christoph Besold, *Signa Temporum* (Tübingen, 1614), 10, 18–19, 22–30.
[89] See Penman, *Hope and Heresy*, 1–35.
[90] Penman, *Hope and Heresy*, 7–11. For Paracelsus' theology and its Franciscan dimensions see Urs Leo Gantenbein, "The Virgin Mary and the Universal Reformation of Paracelsus", *Daphnis* 48 (2020): 4–37; Dane T. Daniel, "Paracelsus' *Astronomia Magna* (1537/38): Bible-Based Science and the Religious Roots of the Scientific Revolution" (PhD Dissertation, Indiana University, 2003), 16–18, 23; and DeVun, *Prophecy*, 3, 60, 159, 163. Paracelsus drew deeply on Rupescissa's Franciscan alchemy.
[91] Penman, *Hope and Heresy*, 24–7. For Arndt's engagement with Paracelsianism and medieval mysticism see Thomas Illg, "Johann Arndt", in *Protestants and Mysticism in Reformation Europe*, ed. Ronald K. Rittgers and Vincent Evener (Leiden: Brill, 2019), 309–27 and Douglas H. Shantz, *An Introduction to German Pietism: Protestant Renewal at the Dawn of Modern Europe* (Baltimore, MD: Johns Hopkins University Press, 2013), 28.

his circle.[92] Through Kotter and others Boehme's work was certainly known to Comenius, who appreciated its Trinitarian mysticism if not its controversial theodicy.[93]

The profound confluence of the new Lutheran apocalypticism with mysticism and encyclopaedism can clearly be seen in the Rosicrucian manifestos composed by the Paracelsian Tobias Hess and his younger friend and collaborator Johann Valentin Andreae. Both Hess and Andreae belonged to Besold's circle in Tübingen, with Andreae later praising Besold as one who was a master of every science and "had evolved all divine and human things".[94] The central endeavour of the Tübingen group was the search for a new Christian philosophy expressing the harmony and correspondence of the book of God's Word and the book of his works.[95] It was this interest which gave rise to the Rosicrucian tracts centring on the persona of Christian Rosencreutz, a fictional German knight alleged to have founded a new religious order dedicated to the renewal of the world. Rosencreutz was the creation of the youthful Andreae in his *Chymische Hochzeit*, and as "Brother CRC" came to play a starring role in the foundational Rosicrucian treatises of the *Fama Fraternitatis* of 1614 and the *Confessio Fraternitatis* of 1615. According to Donald Dickson, Rosencreutz's name "rose-cross" drew on the heraldic symbolism of Andreae's own family coat of arms, which was itself modelled on Luther's and reflected the symbolic "union of the Lutheran reformation and Christian hermeticism".[96]

The tracts told how Christian Rosencreutz, filled with a burning desire to travel to the Holy Land, had journeyed to Arabia, where he learned a new method revealing the harmony and concord of the universe. Drawing on Christian principles, Rosencreutz was able to improve on this even further and on returning to Germany founded a new and secret fraternity dedicated to achieving a universal reform. This would meet every year at the house of the Holy Spirit and from here the brothers would go out into the world to teach and heal others and to await the dawn of the sixth age.[97] According to the *Fama* the order had continued into the seventeenth century and the recent discovery of Rosencreutz's hidden tomb and the appearance of new stars in the heavens signalled that that time of "general reformation" had now arrived. Indeed, in its intricate geometrical arrangement

---

[92] See Urs Leo Gantenbein, "The New Adam: Jacob Böhme and the Theology of Paracelsus (1493/94–1541)", in *Jacob Böhme and His World*, ed. Bo Andersson, Lucinda Martin, Leigh T. I. Penman, and Andrew Weeks (Leiden: Brill, 2019), 166–96.

[93] Comenius, *Pansophia*, in *Consultatio*, I.247. For Comenius' links with Boehme's circle see Leigh T. I. Penman, "Jacob Böhme and His Networks", in *Jacob Böhme and His World*, ed. Andersson, Martin, Penman, and Weeks, 106–14.

[94] Donald R. Dickson, "Johann Valentin Andreae's Utopian Brotherhoods", *Renaissance Quarterly* 49.4 (1996): 760–73; Jan Valentin Andreae, *Mythologiae Christianae* (Strasbourg, 1618), 8.

[95] Dickson, "Utopian Brotherhoods", 770.

[96] Dickson, "Utopian Brotherhoods", 763–64, 787–88.

[97] *Fama Fraternitatis*, trans. Benjamin Rowe (https://order.rosy-cross.org/fama-fraternitatis).

this tomb itself functioned as an encyclopaedic model of the entire universe to be interpreted by Rosencreutz's own book containing all his art and secrets.[98] Armed with this knowledge the fraternity was now finally ready to reveal itself to anyone who was worthy, and with their vast intellectual, spiritual, and material wealth—attained by turning base metals into gold—and their ability to prolong life, to inaugurate a new Lutheran world order which would see the purifying of the Holy Roman Empire, the overthrow of the papacy, the second coming of Christ, and the return of humanity to a state of perfection.[99] By means of a "magic writing" and a new language the fraternity had even been able to overcome the curse of Babel. As the *Confessio* put it, "God hath certainly and most assuredly concluded to send and grant to the world before her end, which presently thereupon shall ensue, such a truth, light, life, and glory, as the first man Adam had, which he lost in Paradise".[100]

The Rosicrucian reformation of method drew on many sources from the Christian and hermetic tradition of which Bacon, Campanella, and Paracelsus are undoubtedly among the most prominent.[101] However, what is most notable, and too little noticed, is the way in which the whole Rosicrucian agenda is profoundly shaped by Franciscan and Lullist priorities.[102] With his birth in 1378, the year of the Great Schism, and death in 1484, the year of Luther's birth, Rosencreutz was clearly intended to epitomize the whole sweep of late medieval and Renaissance reform with its eschatological promise finally coming to fruition in the Reformation.[103] His own personal motto—"the highest wisdom is to know nothing"—is intended to evoke Franciscan and Cusan learned ignorance.[104] Rosencreutz's unconsumed body is reminiscent of a saint and his possession of a *Vitam* and *Itinerarium*, his Christian encyclopaedism, his brilliance in mathematics, science, and alchemy and his far-flung journeys make him seem a kind of composite of the entire Franciscan intellectual and spiritual tradition.[105]

---

[98] *Fama Fraternitatis*.
[99] *Fama Fraternitatis*; *Confessio Fraternitatis*, trans. Benjamin Rowe (https://order.rosy-cross.org/confessio-fraternitatis).
[100] *Confessio Fraternitatis*.
[101] Paracelsus is named explicitly in the *Fama Fraternitatis*.
[102] Although see Lyke de Vries, "The Rosicrucian Reformation: Prophecy and Reform at Play in the Rosicrucian Manifestos", *Daphnis* 48 (2020): 270–95 for a valuable account of the "general reformation" the Rosicrucians hoped to bring about and its link to Spiritual Franciscan and Joachimite ideals. See also the expansion of these arguments in Lyke de Vries, *Reformation, Revolution, Renovation: The Roots and Reception of the Rosicrucian Call for General Reform* (Leiden: Brill, 2022).
[103] *Confessio Fraternitatis*.
[104] Jan Valentin Andreae, *The Chymical Wedding of Christian Rosenkreutz*, 86 (https://order.rosy-cross.org/sites/default/files/docs/Chymical%20Wedding.pdf; translation derived from the English edition of 1690). The date of 1459 is a link with Cusa as well.
[105] See especially *Fama Fraternitatis*. Comparisons to Francis, Bonaventure, Bacon, Lull, and Rupescissa could easily be made. De Vries, "Rosicrucian Reformation" also makes the connection between Rupescissa and the Franciscan "reform of knowledge".

In Bonaventuran fashion the new philosophy is grounded on the Bible and traces the "characters and letters" of God written in the book of his Word and of his works.[106] Its astrological, mathematical, and alchemical character and its claim to represent a *prisca theologia* going back to Solomon, Moses, and Adam himself vividly recall Bacon and Rupescissa.[107] The Arabic style of the method and the fact it offers "true and infallible axiomata" out of all faculties, sciences, and arts directed like a globe or circle to the "only middle point or centre" make it seem like an extrapolation of Lullism into three dimensions.[108] Indeed, it is clear that Christ is this centre, for the motto of the Rosicrucians is "Jesus is all things to me" and their philosophy is intended to be nothing less than an image of Christ himself. Its fulfilment is thus in an all-embracing Trinitarian mysticism: "In God we are born, in Jesus we die, and in the Spirit we will live again".[109]

By his own testimony Comenius came into contact with the *Fama Fraternitatis* in 1612 likely during his time as a student at Herborn. This was two years before its publication and suggests that Comenius had access to one of the many circulating manuscript copies of the *Fama*.[110] For the young Bohemian, recently inducted to the world of Ramist and Lullist encyclopaedism, the idea of a "perfect philosophy" capable of "raising the wisdom of man to that degree what it had in paradise" must have been near intoxicating.[111] Like their progenitor Andreae, Comenius quickly gave up on the Rosicrucians, disgusted by their materialism and lust for alchemical gold. Yet, like Andreae, he proved reluctant to give up the Rosicrucian dream, despite his own disillusion with it.[112] As he said:

> If dear God would allow the light within us to kindle and from here go forth into the wide world . . . for founding a new truly catholic, philadelphic church—would not the Fraternity of the Rose Cross be the spectacle of the wisdom of God, whose prelude was half a century before? Whose first fulfilment occurred in the Unity of Czech Brethren, which God brought to light through the cross.[113]

---

[106] *Confessio Fraternitatis*.
[107] *Fama Fraternitatis*.
[108] *Fama Fraternitatis*.
[109] *Confessio Fraternitatis*.
[110] For an account of this see Yates, *Rosicrucian Enlightenment*, 161–70, and Hotson, *Alsted*, 103, 105.
[111] Jan Amos Comenius, *The Labyrinth of the World and Paradise of the Heart*, trans. Matthew Spinka (Ann Arbor MI: University of Michigan Press, 1972), 13.1–2 (https://czech.mml.ox.ac.uk/labyrint).
[112] Dickson, *Tessera*, 160–62; Jan Valentin Andreae, *Christianopolis: An Ideal State of the Seventeenth Century*, trans. Felix Emil Held (New York: Oxford University Press, 1916), 138.
[113] Cited from Dickson, *Tessera*, 162.

For Comenius, the true Rosicrucians, the real heirs of Christian Rosencreutz, were his own Hussite forebears and those who followed in their footsteps in working for a Christian renewal of the world. In the years after the manifestos, the Rosicrucian desire for a Christian philosophy would come to early flower in Comenius' pansophia, in which we shall find evident the same vital blend of Franciscan, Lullist, and Cusan inspirations.

## 9.4. Augustinian and Franciscan Encyclopaedism

From the beginning Comenius' pansophic project was deeply influenced by currents of Augustinian and Franciscan encyclopaedism. The Hussite movement had, of course, long been shaped by Realism and Neo-Platonism and the ideal of a scriptural philosophy. It also espoused a clear understanding of the whole universe as a mirror of the Trinity, including supremely the human soul as reformed by the theological virtues of faith, hope, and charity. While the Unity of the Brethren movement sought to turn away from scholastic theology back to the simplicity of the Gospel, it still retained many of these Hussite distinctives, especially the Trinitarian imprint. Indeed, as Neval has argued, the influence of the Unity of the Brethren on Comenius' philosophy and his developing pansophic project was deep and pervasive.[114]

Similar influences were communicated to Comenius from another very different source, the *Speculum Intellectuale* of Ulrich Pinder, which he first read around 1621.[115] Published in 1510 this was a *florilegium* of Cusan writings and the primary, if not only, known source for Comenius' engagement with the fifteenth-century Cardinal. Yet although much of the text of the *Speculum Intellectuale* was drawn from Cusanus, the work also showed the deep influence of Bonaventure, and like the *Itinerarium* is structured as a mystical ascent from the footsteps of the Trinity in the created order, through the human mind as the image of God to Christ and the Trinity.[116] Arranged as a kind of Christological "hall of mirrors" the supreme goal of the *Speculum Intellectuale* is the centring of all reality in Christ. In combining and synthesizing Bonaventuran and Cusan

---

[114] Neval, *Die Macht Gottes zum Heil*, 103–27.

[115] Jan Amos Comenius, *De Iterato Sociniano Irenico Iterata ad Christianos Admonitio* (Amsterdam, 1661), 117–18.

[116] Ulrich Pinder, *Speculum Intellectuale Felicitatis Humanae* (Nuremberg, 1510), Xv, XVIIv-r, LXXVv-LXXVIr. For more on Pinder see Catrien Santing, "Through the Looking Glass of Ulrich Pinder: The Impact of Humanism on the Career of a Nuremberg Town Physician around 1500", in *Medieval and Renaissance Humanism: Rhetoric, Representation and Reform*, ed. Stephen Gersh and Bert Roest (Leiden: Brill, 2003), 203–25. For Cusan connections see Ewald Lassnig, "Dürers 'MELENCOLIA-I' und die Erkenntnistheorie bei Ulrich Pinder", *Wiener Jahrbuch für Kunstgeschichte* 57 (2008): 51–95.

influences into one it thus became an important prototype for Comenius' own pansophic method.[117]

From Comenius' earliest works we can see his desire for a Christian, and indeed scriptural, reformation of philosophy along Augustinian and Franciscan lines. In his spiritual classic, the *Labyrinth of the World and Paradise of the Heart* of 1623, he sharply contrasts the darkness of worldly philosophy with the divine illumination of Christian philosophy. The work culminates with Christ's promise to the weary pilgrim to give him "one book in which are deposited all the liberal arts", and Comenius shows how the Bible grounds all disciplines, with grammar consisting in the contemplation of God's words, dialectic in faith, rhetoric in prayer, mathematics in the counting of blessings and natural philosophy in examining God's works.[118]

We find a similar theme in Comenius' early educational treatise *The Great Didactic*, written in the middle of the 1630s, which holds that Scripture is to be the "Alpha and Omega of Christian schools" and that "God's Book should rank before all other books".[119] In this work the entire purpose of education is seen to be conformity to Christ and the Trinity as the "absolute ideal of all perfection".[120] Its goal is already that of the later pansophia—to bring people as close as possible to the archetype of God's own omniscience.[121] In Franciscan fashion the whole world, understood as the mirror of the Trinity, becomes our school, preparing us for the heavenly university.[122] Taking up explicitly Augustine's call for a Christian philosophy, Comenius holds once again that the Bible itself must become our philosophy and logic.[123] In doing so, he places himself in the trajectory of "many recent writers" who have returned to this understanding "that the foundations of all the sciences and philosophic arts are contained in Scripture" which he says both teaches of things "invisible and eternal" and "unfolds the laws of nature and art"—in saying which he surely has Alsted and the Ramists in mind.[124]

In the *Synopsis of Natural Philosophy Reformed by Divine Light* of 1633, the work which hails Bacon, Campanella, and Alsted as pioneers of a new Christian philosophy, we find Comenius' first detailed programme for a scriptural and Trinitarian reform of all knowledge. Inspired by the hexameral works of Bonaventure, which were known to him at least through Alsted, and the Augustinian Neo-Platonist Giles of Rome, this takes up extensively the

---

[117] Pinder, *Speculum Intellectuale*, XXXIIIr–v.
[118] Comenius, *Labyrinth of the World*, 36.3–4; 38.1–2; 39.5.
[119] Comenius, *Great Didactic*, 25.20 (p. 203). Comenius, *Pansophiae Prodromus*, 52 speaks much more positively of pagan books and their use in the pansophia.
[120] Comenius, *Great Didactic*, 10.15–16 (p. 74).
[121] Comenius, *Great Didactic*, "Greeting to the Reader", 4.5–6; 5.4 (pp. 5, 37, 41).
[122] Comenius, *Great Didactic*, 3.3; 24.3 (pp. 33–34, 218).
[123] Comenius, *Great Didactic*, 25.18 (p. 241).
[124] Comenius, *Great Didactic*, 25.18 (p. 241).

Trinitarian metaphysics of light beloved by the Franciscans, tracing the impress of God's Power, Wisdom, and Love on the agency of matter, light, and spirit.[125] A distinctive feature of this work is Comenius' triadic treatment of natural philosophy, and his division of everything into a sevenfold hierarchical ascent, before making a "mysticall eighth" with God who is "above all, without all, and beneath all".[126] Taking up another sevenfold pattern, Comenius also follows Bonaventure in paralleling six stages of ascent to God both to the six days of creation and the six steps of Solomon's throne,[127] as well as in his desire to see the manifestation of the divine light in every level of being.[128] In fact, Comenius' own prayer for his work could have been taken straight from the lips of the Seraphic Doctor: to see God's external light shining on all creatures, his internal light informing them, and in both to glimpse his eternal and uncreated light.[129]

While the *Synopsis* adumbrates many of the themes of the developed pansophia—in Comenius' own terms marking an early confluence of its diverse "streams"[130]—it is particularly significant for its methodological reflections. In offering the "lineament of a new Christian philosophy" Comenius urges the "harmonicall reduction" of all things to sense, reason and Scripture—its three fundamental principles. As inspiration for this he cites Campanella and his interpreter Adami.[131] Comenius found both Campanella's Trinitarian metaphysics and his pansensism deeply attractive, for they affirmed his view of the visible creation as a theatre of God's glory. It is no surprise therefore to find Campanella at the origins of his own triadic approach to philosophy.[132] Comenius is clear that all three of these sources must be mutually informing to avoid falling into any error or superstition. As he succinctly put it, revelation grants belief, reason understanding, and sense certainty. At the same time, he undoubtedly gave priority to Scripture, holding that we must begin in sense, move on to reason, and conclude in revelation.[133]

The Augustinian tone of the *Great Didactic* and *Synopsis* is notably reprised in the 1639 *Pansophiae Prodromus*, the work that introduced the pansophia on a European stage. Citing Augustine, Comenius holds that "only Christianity is

---

[125] Comenius, *Naturall Philosophiae Reformed*, 8–37. For Comenius' citation of Giles of Rome see Jan Amos Comenius, *Pansophiae Christianae Liber III*, Canon 21, in Jan Amos Comenius, *Dílo Jana Amose Komenského*, ed. Antonín Škarka (Prague: Academia, 1969–) [hereafter *DJAK*], 14.64).

[126] Comenius, *Naturall Philosophie Reformed*, "Preface", 238–42.

[127] Comenius, *Naturall Philosophie Reformed*, 240–41; cf. Bonaventure, *Itinerarium*, 1.5 (*BOO*, V.297).

[128] Comenius, *Naturall Philosophie Reformed*, "Preface"; cf. Bonaventure, *Reduction*, n. 2–6 (pp. 37–45; *BOO*, V.319–22). The "Prayer" at the end of Comenius' preface is especially striking in this regard.

[129] Comenius, *Naturall Philosophie Reformed*, "Preface".

[130] Comenius, *Naturall Philosophie Reformed*, "Preface".

[131] Comenius, *Naturall Philosophie Reformed*, "Preface".

[132] Comenius, *Naturall Philosophie Reformed*, "Preface".

[133] Comenius, *Naturall Philosophie Reformed*, "Preface".

the true philosophy". Indeed, he goes further equating his new pansophia with the endeavour of Christian philosophy itself.[134] In this work Comenius attacks in no uncertain terms the contemporary trend to separate philosophy and theology from each other, ranging Christian philosophy and the "divine philosophy of Plato" against Aristotle and contemporary scholasticism.[135] In place of the labyrinthine confusion of methods and approaches, Comenius seeks to institute his own unique method of pansophia—"the full wisdom embracing all things within itself and everywhere cohering with itself".[136]

Pansophia thus ensures that the whole of philosophy becomes a "living image of things" and that the soul becomes the "image of the pansophia of God".[137] Yet to those concerned that pansophia seeks to elevate humanity beyond its status, Comenius insists that the omniscience that is sought is actually the true way to "holy ignorance". For it shows us that our knowledge is "nothing but a shadow compared to eternal truth".[138] Comenius' explicit source for this "holy" or "learned" ignorance was Augustine,[139] but there can be little doubt that the notion was already also familiar to him from Cusa through his reading of Pinder.[140] His paradoxical equating of pansophia with learned ignorance certainly added a new and important dimension to his Augustinian understanding of Christian philosophy which we will return to below.

From his earliest works Comenius had emphasized the importance of a Realist approach to method.[141] Continuing this trajectory, the *Pansophiae Prodromus* offers renewed attention to the coordination of words, things, and ideas. While critical of the Ramists for their neglect of metaphysics, he fully shared their concern that method "is not proportioned well enough either to things or the human mind", recognizing the need for an ideal grounding of method itself.[142] As he put this, "there cannot be a method parallel to things unless the things are reduced to harmony in the intellect as much as they have it themselves and connect to themselves outside the intellect".[143] For Comenius, such a Realist and exemplaristic method represented the true fulfilment of Baconian induction, "leading the mind into" (*in-ducere*) the ideal structure of reality.[144]

Reflecting a definite Augustinian and Franciscan understanding, the *Pansophiae Prodromus* also affirms an intimate, encyclopaedic parallel between

---

[134] Comenius, *Pansophiae Prodromus*, 94.
[135] Comenius, *Pansophiae Prodromus*, 27–28.
[136] Comenius, *Pansophiae Prodromus*, 6–7.
[137] Comenius, *Pansophiae Prodromus*, 7, 35–40.
[138] Comenius, *Pansophiae Prodromus*, 95.
[139] Comenius, *Pansophiae Christianae Liber III*, Canon 32 (*DJAK*, 14.73).
[140] See Pinder, *Speculum Intellectuale*, XIXr.
[141] Comenius, *Great Didactic*, 16.15 (p. 115).
[142] Comenius, *Pansophiae Prodromus*, 23–24.
[143] Comenius, *Pansophiae Prodromus*, 30.
[144] Comenius, *Pansophiae Prodromus*, 61–62.

Scripture and exemplarism. Its stated goal is thus to gather the "dispersed rays of truth" into one so that "in sensuals, intellectuals and in revelation one and the same symmetry appears" and the "clear Sun of Truth" can scatter the "infinite clouds of opinion".[145] As Comenius put this elsewhere, even more emphatically, Scripture is the "ray of omniscience". Just as the world is the "system of systems"—a definite Alstedian notion—in which all things are enfolded, so Scripture is the "book of books" in which all things are unfolded.[146] Axiomatic to the *Pansophiae Prodromus* is therefore the understanding that all method must reflect the harmony—or system—of ideas contained eminently in the mind of God and reflected in nature, the human mind and Scripture. In exemplaristic fashion method mirrors this divine art and is patterned upon it. Indeed, echoing the *Itinerarium*, the pansophia can be compared to a heavenly temple adorning our mind, the "image of the heavenly Jerusalem", and the dwelling place of divine Wisdom itself.[147]

Indeed, the theme of the pansophic Temple touched on in the *Pansophiae Prodromus* becomes central to the later *Pansophiae Diatyposis* of 1645, which offers a detailed ground-plan of this Temple and its different courts and components, recalling the elaborate allegorical and mystical works of Bonaventure's beloved Victorines.[148] Here the progression through the three courts to reach the sanctuary clearly mirrors Bonaventure's outer, inner, and transcendent light, which we have already seen adumbrated in the closing prayer of the *Synopsis*. Pansophia "resolves" all things into the glory of God "of whom, by whom and in whom are all things." It teaches us to recognize him in all things and put everything to us for his glory. Just as in the *Itinerarium* it reaches its summit with the mystical vision of God in the Holy of Holies and the passing over from the world to the Crucified Christ—the central theme of Comenius' earlier *Labyrinth of the World*.[149]

---

[145] Comenius, *Pansophiae Prodromus*, 29.

[146] Jan Amos Comenius, *Pansophiae Seminarium*, s. 52, 58 (*DJAK*, 14.26, 30–31). Comenius here draws on the Cusan terminology of enfold and unfold, which will become so important in his later pansophia. See also Hotson, *Reformation of Common Learning*, 259–60.

[147] Comenius, *Pansophiae Prodromus*, 37, 65–66; cf. Bonaventure, *Itinerarium*, 4.2, 8 (*BOO*, V.306, 308).

[148] Jan Amos Comenius, *Pansophiae Diatyposis* (Amsterdam, 1645), "*Orthographica*" (pp. 90ff.). See also Jan Amos Comenius, *Patterne of Universall Knowledge* (London, 1651), 99ff. This is an English edition and translation of the work prepared by the Hartlib circle. Comenius, *Pansophia*, in *Consultatio*, I.202 connects the mathematical dimensions of Noah's Ark and Solomon's and Ezekiel's Temple to his Trinitarian scheme of number, measure and weight. For parallels with the Victorines see Conrad Rudolph, *The Mystic Ark: Hugh of Saint Victor, Art, and Thought in the Twelfth Century* (Cambridge: Cambridge University Press, 2014) and Walter Cahn, "Architecture and Exegesis: Richard of St.-Victor's Ezekiel Commentary and Its Illustrations", *The Art Bulletin* 76.1 (1994): 53–68.

[149] Comenius, *Patterne*, 101–4; cf. Bonaventure, *Itinerarium*, 7.6 (*BOO*, V.313).

While Comenius' scriptural exemplarism is thoroughly redolent of Bonaventure, his view of method as a kind of logic of divine ideas betrays a definite Hussite and Ramist influence.[150] As the "art of arts" and "science of sciences" pansophic method is clearly intended as a replacement of Aristotelian logic. Its goal is to offer an "accurate anatomy of the universe showing all the branches of all things".[151] Like Keckermann's *Systema Systematum* or Alsted's *Encyclopaedia*, the pansophia was capable of being represented by Ramist charts. As Hotson has pointed out, pansophia, following Ramist method, moves from general to particular through a pattern of definition, division, and canons.[152] For Comenius, the blueprint of the new pansophic temple was very clearly a Ramist one.

The same intriguing convergence of Franciscan and Ramist motifs can also be found in the new Trinitarian method advocated in the *Pansophiae Prodromus*. Notably, Comenius described the origin of this method in fervent terms appropriate to a religious conversion:

> One thing is singular, and even wonderfull in our Method, that all the chiefest divisions of things are made by a Trichotomie, which I protest I sought not by an superstitious affectation, but that it offered itselfe freely unto mee in things of greatest moment, even from the first attributes of things (One, True, Good) that I was for a while at a stand, being amazed with the newnesse of the thing. But being erected in expectation by those examples that I first lighted on, I began to try it other where, and found it everywhere to proceed. Therefore not daring to oppose the truth of things, which represented itselfe so in a threefold mystery, but rather heartily embracing so great an harmony of the sacred Ternary, I prosecuted it in other things also.... Let therefore this Christian pansophy, unfolding the Ternary mysteries be sacred unto that eternal Trinity, JEHOVAH, God only wise, Almighty, most good, and ever to be worshipped.[153]

Bacon had earlier critiqued the Ramist dichotomy as too restrictive and Comenius is clearly following in his wake.[154] His new trichotomous and Trinitarian logic at once reflects and transcends Ramism itself.

Comenius' coordination of the transcendental affections with the Trinity is highly suggestive of Franciscan influence. Indeed, Matthias Scherbaum has rightly noted a definite Scotistic dimension to his view of the transcendentals as

---

[150] For the Wyclifite and Hussite logic of divine ideas see Levy, *Wyclif*, 81–121. For the Ramist logic of divine ideas see Chapter 4.
[151] Comenius, *Pansophiae Prodromus*, 52, 76.
[152] Comenius, *Pansophiae Prodromus*, 77; cf. Hotson, "Ramist Roots", 246 and *Reformation of Common Learning*, 238–46.
[153] Comenius, *Reformation*, 51–52. See also *Pansophiae Prodromus*, 92–93.
[154] For Bacon's critique of this see Comenius, *Triertium Catholicum*, 8 (pp. 57–58).

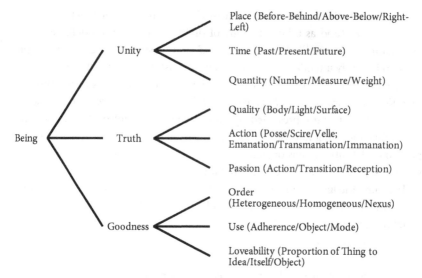

**Figure 9.1** Chart showing Comenius' triadic treatment of the transcendentals from Jan Amos Comenius, *De Christianorum Uno Deo, Patre, Filio, Spiritu S⁰* (Amsterdam, 1659), 25.8–23 (pp. 32–39).

intrinsic perfections or modes of being.[155] As Patočka and Pavlas have argued, it also clearly reflects the triadism of Cusa himself.[156] Indeed, drawing on the Lullist-Cusan account of correlatives, Comenius could unfold the transcendental triad into a whole series of further triads encompassing the ninefold order of place, time, quantity, quality, action, passion, order, use, and amiability (Figure 9.1).[157] Comenius could thus insist in Franciscan fashion that "every creature is a certain wonderful image of the Trinity of the Creator".[158] Indeed, for Comenius, space, time, and even the ideal realm of thought come to take on a distinctive Trinitarian structure and dynamic, as we shall return to again below.[159]

---

[155] Matthias Scherbaum, *Der Metaphysikbegriff des Johann Amos Comenius: Das Projekt der Pansophie im Spannungsbogen von "Realismus", Heilsgeschichte und Pan-Paideia* (Oberhaid: Utopica, 2008), 154.

[156] Petr Pavlas, "Jan Patočka's *Transcendentalia and Categories* on Jan Amos Comenius' Triadic System and Its Cusan Inspiration", *Acta Comeniana* 30 (2016): 187–211.

[157] Jan Amos Comenius, *De Christianorum Uno Deo, Patre, Filio, Spiritu S⁰* (Amsterdam, 1659), 25.8–23 (pp. 32–39).

[158] Comenius, *Pansophia*, in *Consultatio*, I.398; cf. Pinder, *Speculum Intellectuale*, XIIIr–v which cites Cusa, *De Beryllo*, 32–34 (*NCOO*, XI/1.35–38). Patočka, "Comenius und Cusanus", 239 also suggests a connection between Comenius's application of the triad of transcendentals and Cusa.

[159] Comenius, *De Christianorum Uno Deo*, 25.8–23 (pp. 32–39).

## 9.5. Pansophia, Anti-Socinianism, and the Coincidence of Opposites

Evident in Comenius' pansophic works is thus a profound engagement with Augustinian and Franciscan encyclopaedism. Pansophia strives for a universal system of Christian philosophy grounded on a Realist logic of the divine ideas.[160] Yet, taken alone, it is clear that the divine ideas could never be enough for Comenius. For the framework of the divine ideas reflected that static paradigm of encyclopaedism from which he was so desperately trying to break free. It thus melded uneasily with that Trinitarian and Lullist dynamism which had already begun to infuse other aspects of his pansophia. It is significant then that Comenius in his later works began to explore the possibilities of Cusa's coincidence of opposites for reconceiving the entire enterprise of the pansophia as a mystical participation in the divine omniscience. In this sense, we may therefore speak of a very definite Cusan turn in Comenius' pansophia.

As Patočka has demonstrated, the definite impress of Cusa's thought, and especially his coincidence of opposites, can be found from the earliest of Comenius' writings. Cusa's Christocentrism proved deeply attractive to the young Comenius, offering him a much-needed "centre of security" amid the turmoil in Church and state, especially in the wake of the disastrous defeat of the Czech Protestants at the Battle of the White Mountain in 1620.[161] In his *Labyrinth* we thus find a playful and ironic juxtaposition of a false, worldly coincidence of opposites with the true coincidence of opposites glimpsed through the spectacles of Scripture. Implicit in the work is a movement from the circumference of the world—which falsely appears as having its own autonomous centre—to Christ the true centre of all things.[162] Notably, this is a theme taken up in the eponymous *Centrum Securitatis*, which traces the motion of all things, including his own bewildered mind, back to their true and eternal centre in God.[163] Recalling the Neo-Pythagorean trope beloved of Ramus and Cusa, Comenius is explicit in identifying God as a "circle whose centre is everywhere and circumference truly nowhere".[164]

While Comenius' *Pansophiae Prodromus* does not engage with the coincidence of opposites, remaining in an Augustinian-scholastic realm in which the light of divine ideas becomes manifest in the clarity of the Aristotelian principle

---

[160] This section and the following section draws extensively on material from Burton, "Squaring the Circle", 428–49 including reproducing a number of paragraphs verbatim. This is by the kind permission of the publisher Brill.
[161] Patočka, "*Centrum Securitatis* und Cusanus", 245–56.
[162] Comenius, *Labyrinth of the World*, 5.5, 50.4.
[163] Jan Amos Comenius, *Centrum Securitatis*, "Praefatio" (*DJAK*, 3.478–80).
[164] Comenius, *Centrum Securitatis*, "Praefatio" (*DJAK*, 3.478).

of non-contradiction,[165] signs of a change come with his *Pansophiae Diatyposis* of 1643. For in this work we find Comenius reconceiving the ideas in terms of a definite Cusan dynamic of enfolding and unfolding.[166] He also explicitly identifies the purpose of the pansophia as being the reduction of "contraries into identity".[167] Echoing Cusa, the form of pansophia is described as the "consonance and consent of all things to all things". In doing so, it seeks to reconcile "the extreames and opposites" of things bringing them to agreement in their common centre in God where there is "no dissonance". This entails that "the most contradictions and controversies may be decided by neither or both"—a phrase that Comenius later used to describe the coincidence of opposites.[168]

Reinforcing this connection is Comenius's fascinating comparison of pansophia to the squaring of the circle. Here he remarks that just as the square is counted by geometers the measure of all figures, so the quadrangular method of pansophia—so-called as it offers a comprehensive account of all things through the medium of four different questions—is the "measure of all methods".[169] For Comenius, the figure of the square symbolized an axiomatic approach to reality while the figure of a circle symbolized the plenitude of things (the encyclopaedia).[170] In matching axioms to plenitude, squaring the circle was therefore a fitting image for his universal method of pansophia. Yet at the same time in expressing the coincidence of straight and curved lines, squaring the circle can also be seen as a kind of shorthand for the coincidence of opposites itself.[171] In this we are reminded especially of Cusa, for whom the quest to square the circle represented the quest for the coincidence of opposites and ultimately for God himself.[172]

For Comenius it was Christ who is the "bond of eternity and time" and who "alone joins all opposites in himself" and in this Christological reading of the coincidence of opposites we find another clear connection to Cusa.[173] Indeed, as becomes clear from his later Anti-Socinian works, Comenius came to view Christ as the true paradigm of the coincidence of opposites. We see this especially

---

[165] Comenius, *Pansophiae Prodromus*, 29. Comenius's resolution of these tensions in his Cusan dialectic of divine Idea and ideas is discussed below.

[166] Giglioni, "The Darkness of Matter and the Light of Nature", 21.

[167] Comenius, *Pansophiae Diatyposis*, 14, 65 (pp. 13–14, 80). It must be admitted that Comenius's discussion here, as in *Pansophiae Prodromus*, is not always free from ambiguity.

[168] Comenius, *Patterne*, 6–7; *Pansophiae Diatyposis*, 14 (pp. 13–14).

[169] Comenius, *Patterne*, 112–13; *Pansophiae Diatyposis*, "Delineatio", 39 (p. 134).

[170] Comenius, *Pansophia*, in *Consultatio*, I.528.

[171] This is particularly clear in Jan Amos Comenius, *De Irenico Irenicorum* (Amsterdam, 1660), 44–45 but see also *Pansophia*, in *Consultatio*, I.661.

[172] Burton, "Squaring the Circle", 417–49; cf. Harries, *Infinity and Perspective*, 63. For an extensive discussion of squaring the circle in Cusa see Jean-Michel Counet, *Mathématiques et Dialectique chez Nicolas de Cuse* (Paris: Vrin, 2000), 257–94.

[173] Jan Amos Comenius, *Lexicon Reale Pansophicum*, in *Consultatio*, II.482; cf. Bonaventure, *Itinerarium*, 5.8 (*BOO*, V.310); Cusa, *De Docta Ignorantia*, 1.2.5 (*NCOO*, I.7).

from his conflict with the Polish Anti-Trinitarian Daniel Zwicker, which as Kuchlbauer has demonstrated had a major influence on the development of the pansophia.[174] Comenius clearly saw Zwicker as representing the influx of a new and dangerous rationalism, tracing his errors to the "serpentine" principle that in matters of faith we begin not from God and the divine testimony of Scripture but from "our own dictates of reason".[175] For him, Zwicker embodies this new "sceptical" and "diabolical" theology, above all in his attempt to use the Aristotelian principle of non-contradiction to provide an "irrefutable" argument against the divinity of Christ, by showing that two disparates—the divine and human nature—cannot belong to the same subject at the same time. In violating this, the orthodox doctrine of the two natures of Christ, and thus also of the Trinity itself, could only be viewed as a logical contradiction of the worst order.[176]

In arguing this, Comenius held that Zwicker is trying to tear Christ down from his throne with syllogisms. Like Wyclif and Hus centuries earlier, he responded to this by arming himself with the weapons of a new heavenly logic. Drawing explicitly on Pinder's *Speculum* and its Cusan geometrical illustrations of the coincidence of opposites, Comenius argued that "all proportions and improportions of finites to each other are thus absorbed by infinity, so that there first and last, maximum and minimum, highest and lowest, straight and curved, mobile and immobile coincide" (Figure 9.2).[177] Echoing Luther's famous claim that the mysteries of the Christian faith transcend all syllogistic arguments,[178] he thus pointed Zwicker to the crucial distinction between a logic of finite and infinite quantities:

> Contraries and contradictories are never able to be said concerning the same thing according to Aristotelian logic, which contains rules made only about finite beings, distinguished from themselves by specific forms. But the more divine logic, contemplating the affections of infinite being, and pronouncing according to them, joins even the most distant and diametrical opposites, because it sees all things to coincide there.[179]

---

[174] Kuchlbauer, *Comenius' antisozinianische Schriften*, 89ff.
[175] Comenius, *De Irenico Irenicorum*, 23.
[176] Comenius, *De Irenico Irenicorum*, 189; Daniel Zwicker, *Irenicum Irenicorum* (Amsterdam, 1658), 5–12.
[177] Comenius, *De Irenico Irenicorum*, 44–45, 73; *De Iterato Sociniano*, 117–19; cf. Pinder, *Speculum Intellectuale*, XXIIv, XXXIv.
[178] Luther, *Disputation on the Word Made Flesh* (*WA*, 39.2, pp. 4–5).
[179] Comenius, *De Irenico Irenicorum*, 72: "*Contraria et contradictoria de eadem re nunquam dici posse, iuxta logicam Aristotelicam: quae regulas tantum de entibus finitis, formis specificis a se disterminatis, factas continet. Divinior autem logica, entis infiniti affectiones contemplans, et secundum eas pronuntians, etiam distantissima, et diametraliter opposita, jungit, quia ibi omnia coincidere videt*" (author's own translation).

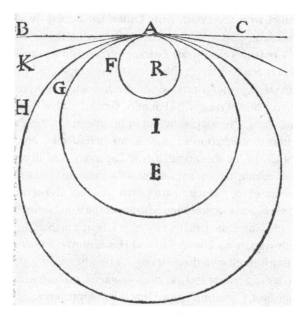

**Figure 9.2** Cusan geometrical illustration of the coincidence of opposites derived from Ulrich Pinder, *Speculum Intellectuale Felicitatis Humanae* (Nuremberg, 1510), XXIIv in Jan Amos Comenius, *De Irenico Irenicorum* (Amsterdam, 1660), 73. Reproduced by kind permission of the Bibliothèque Nationale de France.

For Comenius, this logic of "transnaturals and eternals" therefore pointed to the coincidence of divine and human in Christ. Significantly, this represented not only a mathematical turn in his thought, but an important scriptural move. Where the Socinians rely on "Scripture illuminated by reason" they should rely on "reason illuminated by Scripture".[180] Logic must therefore be taken up and transformed by Scripture.

Comenius' mature pansophia was written in the wake of his polemic with Zwicker and takes up the coincidence of opposites as the centrepiece of his new pansophic vision. The essence of the pansophia, as we have seen, was the understanding of the Trinity as the dynamic archetype of all reality. Following a Franciscan paradigm, he thus paralleled the inner emanation of the Trinity with the outer emanation of creation. All of reality is therefore a correlative unfolding of the Triune being of God into space and time. Elsewhere Comenius expressed this in a new dialectic of Idea and ideas, holding that God as eternal Idea expresses himself in multiple created ideas which can be considered a kind of mean between Creator and creation. These he described as "a certain channel,

---

[180] Comenus, *De Irenico Irenicorum*, 30–31.

through which the infinite begins to contract itself into the form of some finite, but in an immutable fashion", citing a "certain philosopher" as saying that the "ideas of things are in God as triangles or other figures are made from a circle". In eternity God is therefore to be considered as an infinite circle or line who produces a creature through contracting himself into finite lines and figures.[181]

Such a view is clearly Cusan and only truly makes sense in light of the coincidence of opposites. Indeed, reading between the lines, it becomes clear that Comenius' novel equation of the divine Idea with the pure possibility of the divine essence reflects the fifteenth-century theologian's own radical break from the constraint of the scholastic metaphysics of pure actuality. For following Cusa's *De possest*, the work he cites prominently against Zwicker, Comenius identified God as pure possibility.[182] In such terms, creation becomes a "commotion from the centre of omnipotence" in which infinite rest and motion coincide,[183] an unfolding of the absolute possibility of God's own Triune being:

> The mind from itself, through itself and in itself existing is God, eternal thought, speech and act. (For whence would these three be in created minds, if not rivulets flowing from their eternal font?). By thinking inside himself whatever he was able to, was knowing and was willing to be thought, he found the possible world and foresaw all things which were able to be with order and truth. By speaking with himself (eternal Wisdom with eternal Power and Love) concerning these things he created the eternal laws of things, or the ideal world. By acting outside himself whatever he was able to act he produced the real world separately existing.[184]

Here the possible world correlates with the divine possibility, the ideal world with the divine knowing and the real world with the divine will. The divine ideas thus become expressed in the world according to the familiar Trinitarian pattern of power, knowledge, and will. Whereas in scholastic thought and much of Platonism the ideas tend to be conceived more or less as static exemplars, for Comenius they become fruitful and dynamic forms with their own intrinsic dynamism and potentiality.

---

[181] Comenius, *Pansophia*, in *Consultatio*, 1.202.
[182] Nicholas of Cusa, *Trialogus de possest*, 14–17 (NCOO, XI/2.17–22).
[183] Comenius, *Pansophia*, in *Consultatio*, I.246.
[184] Comenius, *Pansophia*, in *Consultatio*, I.219: "*Mens a seipso, per seipsum, in seipso existens, Deus est, aeternum Cogitans, aeternum Loquens et Agens. (Unde enim tria illa in nobis creatis Mentibus essent, si non rivuli a suo aeterno fonte fluerunt?). Cogitando enim intra Seipsum quicquid cogitari poterat, sciebat, volebat, invenit Mundum Possibilem, praevisa scilicet omnia quae esse poterant cum Ordine et Veritate sua. Loquendo autem de his cum seipso (Sapientia aeterna cum Potentia et Amore aeterno) condidit Rerum leges aeternas, sive Mundum Idealem. Agendo vero extra se quicquid agi potuit, produxit Mundum Realem seorsim existentem*".

Earlier Comenius had made this claim of the transcendentals in support of a comprehensive Trinitarian metaphysics, but Cusa now offered him a way to extrapolate his exemplarism from the realm of being to the realm of pure possibility and of pure ideality. This marks a step beyond even the *Diatyposis*, and it is notable that it is only now that he makes the explicit identification of the method of neither and both with the coincidence of opposites.[185] In doing so, he also offered a new insight into pansophia as the squaring of the circle. For Comenius, like Cusa, knowledge is ultimately asymptotic. It can always be more precise, in the same way that a polygon can always approach infinitely closer to the limit of a circle. For it is only the infinite, transcendent understanding of God that can grasp the coincidence of the eternal circle of his own essence with every finite and transitory figure.[186] In attempting to imitate this divine squaring of the circle the practitioner of pansophia attains an omniscience which is paradoxically also nulliscience, bringing it about that the more he sees the more he realizes his ignorance.[187] With the heart fixed on God, moved out of the circumference of things he always finds himself in God the centre.[188] Following the pilgrim trail of Cusa's "learned ignorance", pansophia is thus, at its core, the contemplation of the all in the "all in all".[189]

### 9.6. *Mathesis Universalis*

In Comenius' later works his pansophic enterprise began to converge more and more with his desire to attain to *mathesis universalis*. This mathematical turn in Comenius' thought is certainly prominent in his final *Pansophia*, the very first lines of which urge a mathematical reduction of all things in imitation of God himself,[190] but it arguably came to fruition in an important pair of works, the *Ianua Rerum Reserata* and *Triertium Catholicum*, written right at the end of his life. For in these works we find Comenius striving to offer a mathematical account of the whole of reality, rivalling that espoused by contemporary champions of the new philosophy and science. While Comenius welcomed the wider early modern desire for a mathematization of knowledge, he was also deeply concerned about the growing tendency to detach mathematics from its transcendent ground in the mind of God. In response to the growing threat of rationalism, Comenius self-consciously turned back to an older Neo-Platonic

---

[185] Comenius, *Pansophia*, in *Consultatio*, I.481.
[186] Cf. Cusa, *De docta ignorantia*, 1.3.10 (*NCOO*, I.9).
[187] Comenius, *Patterne*, 64.
[188] Comenius, *Patterne*, 8.
[189] Comenius, *Patterne*, 106. Its aim is to contemplate "God in the creatures and the creatures in God".
[190] Comenius, *Pansophia*, in *Consultatio*, I.179.

and Neo-Pythagorean understanding of mathematics which could be found in Augustine, Bonaventure, and Cusa, as well as finding inspiration in the dynamic, combinatorial account of reality offered by the Lullists.

From early on Comenius had spoken of his desire to give mathematical expression to the whole sphere of knowledge, describing *mathesis* as containing the principles of all other disciplines and as a "philosopher's stone" of the mind.[191] In his *Pansophiae Diatyposis* this became an attempt to realize a universal *mathesis* in which every idea encodes mathematical certainty.[192] However, it was not until the *Ianua Rerum* that Comenius provided the framework for a comprehensive mathematical metaphysics. Following in Timpler's and Bisterfeld's trajectory, Comenius defines metaphysics in his *Ianua Rerum Reserata* of 1670 as the "science of ideas and possible worlds". Metaphysics therefore finds its proximate origin in the sphere of the human mind as containing within itself (potentially) the infinite possibilities of all things—an understanding already redolent of Cusa.[193]

Following in Cusa's footsteps the main goal of the *Ianua Rerum* is to offer a direct correlation between mathematical, ideal and metaphysical structures. Comenius thus holds that what is thinkable (*cogitabile*)—i.e. that which correlates with every possible numerical combination in the realm of pure thought—precedes the realm of being itself.[194] In line with his Trinitarian understanding Comenius sees the ternary, which he elsewhere calls the "eternal root of eternal harmony in our things and our concepts",[195] as the root of all numbers. For even unity has a trinitarian dynamic. From the ternary, in which he says all contraries are resolved, he thus holds that all numbers may be understood to unfold in progression, but, like Cusa, he gives special place to the perfect numbers of seven and ten as well as to the number four.[196] In seeking to break down numbers themselves into combinations of ternaries, we may clearly see how Comenius expresses the unfolding of differentiated multiplicity from the enfolded Trinitarian dynamics of unity.

In his *Triertium Catholicum*, which was significantly finished in the same year as the *Ianua Rerum*, Comenius sought to extend his new mathematical

---

[191] Jan Amos Comenius, *Geometria*, "Proemium" (*DJAK*, 12.13). See also Jan Amos Comenius, *J. A. Comenii Physicae ad Lumen Divinum Reformatae Synopsis* (Leipzig, 1633), "Praefatio" and *De Christianorum Uno Deo*, 25.1–30 (pp. 30–41).

[192] Comenius, *Pansophiae Diatyposis*, "Delineatio", 63–64 (pp. 168–70); cf. Alsted, *Encyclopaedia*, 1.4 (p. 55).

[193] Jan Amos Comenius, *Ianua Rerum Reserata*, "Praefatio", c. 1–4 (*DJAK*, 18.153–73); cf. Cusa, *Idiota de mente*, 9.125; 11.135 (*NCOO*, V.178, 188–89).

[194] Comenius, *Ianua Rerum*, c. 10, 11 (*DJAK*, 18.182–85).

[195] Jan Amos Comenius, *Panaugia*, 10.24 (*DJAK*, 19/1.234).

[196] Comenius, *Ianua Rerum*, c. 32 (*DJAK*, 18.212–14); cf. Cusa, *De Conjecturis*, 1.2.7–3.11 (*NCOO*, III.11–17). Both Cusa and Comenius give special priority to the numbers 1, 4, 7, and 10 in the unfolding of reality. This can be most clearly seen by comparing Comenius's account of number with Cusa's diagram of the unfolding of number in *De Conjecturis*, 3.11 (*NCOO*, III.17), as well as with his *De Ludo Globi*, 2.107–9 (*NCOO*, IX.133–36).

metaphysics into a mathematical logic. In the preface to this work, which he dedicated to the Amsterdam Senate as part of his wider efforts to promote universal reform, Comenius pointedly remarked that "we do not yet have a perfect logic". Such a logic, he held, would attain "the faith of Plato" that "the truth is not able to be contradicted"—a hint towards its ideal as well as apodictic character.[197] Despite his evident debt to Ramism, Comenius was rather critical of the *loci* employed by many contemporary logicians describing these as "very sterile".[198] Over the years he had also tempered somewhat his early enthusiasm for Baconian logic. While taking seriously Bacon's injunction to polish the "mirror of the mind", he now sought a new logic which would be "so ample and lucid a mirror of the mind, as the mind itself is the ample and lucid mirror of things".[199]

Comenius' *Triertium* had as its ultimate goal the triune unification of thought, speech, and action.[200] It was thus the fulfilment of his quest for a truly trinitarian logic, as well as an ambitious attempt to reconstruct the pansophia from the ground up, by uniting the trivium and quadrivium into a single synthesis.[201] Comenius held that the "eternal archetype" for his logic was to be found in God himself who first thought, then spoke, then acted, bringing all things into being according to his "ideas foreseen from eternity". Notably, he also held that this dynamic unity of thinking, speaking, and acting was also characteristic of the unfallen Adam.[202] The express purpose of the *Triertium* is therefore to aid us in imitating God the "highest artificer" and Adam the original logician.[203] In this twofold horizon of perfectibility we have a clear link back through Cusa and others to the Franciscan Reformation of method.

Signalling his debt to Ramus, but at the same time transposing his logic onto a new metaphysical plane of intelligibility, Comenius held that logic was the "art of thinking well".[204] Following Keckermann, he construed logical invention, judgement, and method as three dynamically interrelated aspects of a single act of reasoning.[205] Indeed, for Comenius this logical circle of invention, method, and judgement reflected a definite trinitarian pattern, which he compared to the Augustinian and scriptural triad of number, measure, and weight.[206] Invoking Augustine, Comenius therefore held that just as "thoughts are nothing but the numbering, measuring and weighing of things" so logic is "nothing but the

---

[197] Comenius, *Triertium Catholicum*, "Dedicatio", 5–6 (pp. 9–10).
[198] Comenius, *Triertium Catholicum*, "Dedicatio", 6 (p. 10).
[199] Comenius, *Triertium Catholicum*, "Dedicatio", 7 (p. 11).
[200] Comenius, *Triertium Catholicum*, "Dedicatio", 2; 1.9–10 (pp. 9, 18).
[201] Comenius, *Triertium Catholicum*, 13.1–5 (pp. 92–93).
[202] Comenius, *Triertium Catholicum*, 1.14–15 (p. 19).
[203] Comenius, *Triertium Catholicum*, 4.1–4 (p. 38).
[204] Comenius, *Triertium Catholicum*, 2.1 (p. 20).
[205] Comenius, *Triertium Catholicum*, 3.1–47 (pp. 27–38); cf. Keckermann, *Praecognita Logica*, 220–26.
[206] Comenius, *Triertium Catholicum*, 3.1–22 (pp. 27–32); cf. Alsted, *Metaphysica*, "Praefatio", 4–8.

numbering, measuring and weighing of thoughts".[207] Cementing the intimate mathematical bond between logic and metaphysics is the fact that the places (*loci*) which logical invention draws on are nothing other than the ninefold, trinitarian unfolding of the three transcendentals of unity, truth, and goodness. In a bold bid to unite Aristotelian, Ramist, and Lullist logic, Comenius refers to these nine categories as his "own predicaments".[208] Logic, as the *mathesis* of thought, is thus derivative of and flows out of metaphysics, as the *mathesis* of things.

While Comenius had castigated the Ramists, and especially Ames, in the *Ianua Rerum* for their neglect of metaphysics,[209] his own logic is clearly metaphysical in character. As Hotson suggests, it follows a broad Ramist pattern of definition and division.[210] Definition is grounded in Comenius' own predicaments and is therefore implicitly mathematical and Trinitarian.[211] The same is true of logical division which must respect the mathematical and metaphysical structure of reality. Thus dichotomy is retained for logical opposition, trichotomy relates to the "essential parts of things", tetrachotomy explains things returning into the world, heptachotomy expresses the "full gradation of things", and decachotomy their "most solemn" numerical division. As we would expect, trichotomy is especially important due to its reflection of the mystery of the Trinity.[212] To definition and division Comenius also added comparison, thus giving a clearer triadic shape to his logic. Reflecting both a Ramist and Lullist paradigm, comparison was intended to show the convenience and difference of things. The possibility of comparing one thing with any other could thus be considered a "universal key of cognition".[213]

Reinforcing this connection, Comenius offered both a Realist and combinatorial account of predication according to the combining—or copulating—of notions, and grounded on his own predicaments as an "alphabet of things".[214] Truth is thus found not only in the conformity of a notion to a thing—something to be verified pansophically through the canons of sense, reason, and testimony—but also in the conformity of propositions and syllogisms to extra-mental reality.[215] In Ramist and Lullist fashion predication therefore maps directly onto

---

[207] Comenius, *Triertium Catholicum*, 3.9 (p. 29): "*Unde apparet (NB) sicuti cogitationes humanae nihil sunt nisi numeratio, mensuratio, ponderatioque rerum: ita logicam nihil esse nisi numerationem, mensurationem, ponderationemque cogitationum. Et per consequens (NB) logicam nihil esse, nisi mathesin, applicatam cogitationibus: grammaticam, nihil nisi mathesin applicatam sermonibus: pragmaticam, nihil nisi mathesin applicatam actionibus*".
[208] Comenius, *Triertium Catholicum*, 8.7 (p. 53).
[209] Comenius, *Ianua Rerum*, "Praefatio" (*DJAK*, 18.154).
[210] Hotson, "Ramist Roots", 246 and *Reformation of Common Learning*, 238–46.
[211] Comenius, *Triertium Catholicum*, 8 (p. 53).
[212] Comenius, *Triertium Catholicum*, 8 (pp. 56–58).
[213] Comenius, *Triertium Catholicum*, 8 (pp. 59–60).
[214] Comenius, *Triertium Catholicum*, 8 (pp. 67–68).
[215] Comenius, *Triertium Catholicum*, 9–11 (pp. 61–81).

the metaphysical structure of reality.[216] Propositions as "tri-notions" consist of subject, predicate, and copula and are analysed according to their transcendental relation to unity, truth, and goodness.[217] Similarly, the syllogism also consists of three terms—major, minor, and conclusion—and three propositions which coalesce into one. Both notions and syllogisms also mirror a sevenfold stage of becoming, since the "wisdom of God diffuses all things" in a perfect, sevenfold manner.[218] Logic thus represents a dynamic, Trinitarian unfolding of the mind's potentiality, and even truth itself proves ultimately susceptible to a Trinitarian analysis, as the interplay of the object with sense and intellect.[219]

Comenius' attempt to offer a Trinitarian and combinatorial account of logic in the *Triertium* was undoubtedly influenced by Bisterfeld, his colleague and rival in the Transylvanian schools.[220] Echoing the *Phosphorus Catholicus* he held that logic follows the "immeations or enfoldings of things".[221] Following Alsted and Bisterfeld, Comenius held that all method, and especially pansophic method, must have the "reason of a circle", unfolding everything which is enfolded in the essence of things themselves.[222] Such a method he called *logica cyclognomica*, drawing on the terminology of Gemma's *De arte cyclognomica*. He held that it had been pioneered by Lull and Trithemius, but not with the "facility, plenitude and certitude" which they had hoped for, and subsequently developed by others such as Agrippa, van Helmont, and Gemma himself. It offers an "abyss of meditation" by placing the subject in the centre of a circle which sends out rays to the whole universe of things. Since every being is the "image of the universe"—a Cusan principle[223]—every concept can be connected to every other concept. This can be regulated by the *loci* of invention which function as an alphabet which one can run through, giving rise to an infinite set of combinations. In these terms, Comenius' own predicaments come to fulfil in one the role of Lull's absolute, respective, and correlative principles. Furthermore, by combining this circular method of the *Triertium* with the metaphysical "ladder of being" set out in the

---

[216] Comenius, *Triertium Catholicum*, 9 (p. 68).
[217] Comenius, *Triertium Catholicum*, 10 (p. 70).
[218] Comenius, *Triertium Catholicum*, 11 (pp. 75–76).
[219] Comenius, *Triertium Catholicum*, 8 (p. 61).
[220] Comenius, *Triertium Catholicum*, 8 (pp. 67–68). Comenius, *Ianua Rerum*, "Praefatio" (DJAK, 18.154) cites Bisterfeld as an inspiration for his metaphysical turn.
[221] Comenius, *Triertium Catholicum*, 15.9 (p. 100).
[222] Comenius, *Triertium Catholicum*, 3.1–22 (pp. 27–32); cf. Alsted, *Metaphysica*, "Praefatio", 4–8. Comenius could even parallel the movement of a circle from centre to circumference to the unfolding of unity into the threefold and sevenfold patterns characteristic of his mature logic and metaphysics (*Lexicon Reale Pansophicum*, in *Consultatio*, II.483).
[223] See Cusa, *De Docta Ignorantia*, 2.5.117–22 (NCOO, I.76–78).

*Ianua Rerum* we can encompass every term in the "orb" of things and the "circumvolution" of understanding.[224]

For Comenius, pansophia was characterized by a "trine celerity, elegance and solidity".[225] It thus combined the best of Aristotelian, Ramist, and Lullist methodologies.[226] As rapid or cyclognomic it offered a means of discoursing on all things. As solid it is apodictic representing the epitome of that Ramist "golden chain" in which all things are bound together by indissoluble bonds according to their essential order.[227] Finally, as elegant or symbolic it offered a key for understanding all metaphorical and parabolic thought and supremely that of Scripture itself. Intriguingly, Comenius compared his new *logica elegans* to the parabolic method of Campanella's *City of the Sun*, Bacon's *New Atlantis*, and Andreae's *Golden Mythology*. However, its ultimate expression is found in Christ himself, whose parables reveal a wisdom hidden from the foundation of the world. Comenius' ambitious goal was to render this symbolic logic fully demonstrative by reducing all metaphors to combinations of ideas. It thus represented the final stage of the mathesis of thought and Comenius even dreamed of developing a whole system of theology on this basis.[228]

In what may well be an echo of Wyclif and Hus, Comenius held that such a symbolic logic of ideas would represent the true "logic of Christ" to be contrasted with the "arms of the human logic" with which we have hitherto fought.[229] Here, once again, we have a reminder of that vital disjunction between natural and supernatural logic sourced in late medieval reflection but characteristic of the wider Ramist movement. Indeed, for Comenius it is notable that the whole of the *Triertium Catholicum* could be seen as embodying a kind of "learned ignorance".[230] While, in offering a logic intended for the created order, the *Triertium* stops short of affirming the coincidence of opposites, it nevertheless seeks to reconcile all opposites within the ambit of a higher unity.[231] In its dynamic, Trinitarian character as well as its quest to achieve a "biblical omniscience", the "divine method" of the *Triertium* can thus be seen not only as the supreme fulfilment of Comenius' quest for a trichotomous logic but as a clear reflection of that "transnatural and eternal" logic of God's own Triune being.[232]

---

[224] Comenius, *Triertium Catholicum*, 12, 13.1 (pp. 91–92).
[225] Comenius, *Triertium Catholicum*, 14 (p. 95).
[226] Comenius, *Triertium Catholicum*, 18.4 (p. 117).
[227] Comenius, *Triertium Catholicum*, 14 (p. 96).
[228] Comenius, *Triertium Catholicum*, 16 (pp. 102–7).
[229] Comenius, *Triertium Catholicum*, 16 (p. 107). For the Wyclifite account of the spiritual logic of Christ see Levy, *Wyclif*, 81–122.
[230] Comenius, *Triertium Catholicum*, 5.7–8 (pp. 40–41).
[231] Comenius, *Triertium Catholicum*, 10, 17 (pp. 71–72, 113).
[232] Comenius, *Triertium Catholicum*, 18 (p. 122); cf. *De Irenico Irenicorum*, 30–31.

## 9.7. *Consultatio Catholica*

Comenius' final pansophia is contained in his *Consultatio Catholica*, which offers a comprehensive programme for the universal reform of Church and society. While previous works had offered little more than an outline of the pansophia, the *Consultatio* marked an impressive attempt to erect the pansophic temple itself. Significantly, the work is divided into seven books: the *Panegersia*, the *Panaugia*, the *Pansophia*, the *Pampaedia*, the *Panglottia*, the *Panorthosia*, and the *Pannuthesia*. Enfolded within the opening and closing exhortations (the *Panegersia* and *Pannuthesia*), it offered an account of the universal light (*Panaugia*) by which all things are known, the universal wisdom (*Pansophia*) in which all things are comprehended, the universal system of education (*Pampaedia*) by which all things are taught, the universal language (*Panglottia*) through which all things must be expounded and the universal reform (*Panorthosia*) to be accomplished in the last days. While the work was never completed and, apart from the *Panegersia*, never even saw the light of day until its rediscovery centuries later, it undoubtedly marks both the summation and consummation of Comenius' life's work.[233]

True to its name the *Consultatio Catholica* sought to initiate a "universal consultation" for the reform of all human affairs.[234] In the wake of the confessional and political strife of his age, Comenius held out the vision of a Church and society reunited in praise of Christ and the Triune God. Inspired by the hope of the imminent Millenniall dawn of Christ's Kingdom he foresaw not only the recovery of Christendom but also its expansion by peaceful mission to embrace every nation, culture, language, and religion, so that the whole earth might be filled with the glory of God.[235] Tracing a trajectory from Babel to Zion, the fundamental theme of the work, sounded out in the *Panegersia* as a call to "universal awakening", is that "we must return to unity from the multiplicity into which we have fallen".[236] In Cusan fashion it therefore sought to reconcile all human divisions and contradictions—whether philosophical, political, or religious in character—in the God in whom all opposites coincide.[237]

The *Consultatio* is shaped throughout by the Franciscan and Joachimite Edenic paradigm that Comenius found so attractive in the Rosicrucians.

---

[233] For an account of Comenius' *Consultatio* and its rediscovery see Dagmar Čapková, "Comenius and His Ideals: Escape from the Labyrinth", in *Samuel Hartlib and Universal Reformation: Studies in Intellectual Communication*, ed. Mark Greengrass, Michael Leslie, and Timothy Raylor (Cambridge: Cambridge University Press, 1994), 75–92.

[234] Jan Amos Comenius, *Panegersia*, 3.1–20, in *Consultatio*, I.48–49.

[235] Comenius, *Panorthosia*, 2.1–54; 18, in *Consultatio*, II.215–30, 309–10.

[236] Comenius, *Panegersia*, 9.6, in *Consultatio*, I.77: "*Redeundum nobis esse a Multiplicitate, in quam dilapsi sumus, ad Unitatem*". For the prominent motif of the turn from Babel to Zion see Comenius, *Panorthosia*, 1.23–24, in *Consultatio*, II.214–15.

[237] Comenius, *Pansophia*, in *Consultatio*, I.246–47.

Following the Hussite idealism of his own Unity of the Brethren, the true heirs of the Rosicrucians, it thus sought to realize the pattern of God's universal ideas on Earth.[238] Crucially, the whole work is dedicated to the Ramist, Lullist, and Baconian theme of the transformation of the human soul into the "living image of the living God".[239] The instauration of the image of God in the individual thus becomes the template for the universal reform of the whole human race. Indeed, the implicit Ramist groundplan of the entire work serves to focus and channel this comprehensive encyclopaedic and pansophic programme, binding together the theory and praxis of universal reform into a distinctive Trinitarian synthesis.[240]

Coming before the *Pansophia* the *Panaugia* is devoted to the theme of the universal light necessary for every reform endeavour. Taking inspiration from Pinder's *Speculum* it provides an impressive Franciscan and Cusan "intellectual optics".[241] Picking up important themes of the early pansophic works, especially the *Seminarium*, the work thus traces a detailed correlation between three lights—the eternal, external, and internal; three mirrors—the world, the mind, and Scripture; and three eyes—sense, reason, and faith.[242] For Comenius, as we saw in the *Triertium*, the mind is to be understood as a mathematical mirror. Through combining the direct rays of sense, the reflected rays of its own "inborn ideas and instincts" and the refracted rays of Scripture—a threefold paradigm deriving directly from Bacon—the mind comes to understand the intelligible numbers, weights, and measurements according to which God has created all things.[243] Further, it becomes perfected in the image of the Trinity, reflecting more and more clearly in itself the Power, Wisdom, and Love of God.[244] The goal of all this is to purify the eye of the soul—as the "most exact image of God's eye within us"—enabling it to see God, itself and the world more clearly.[245]

Following the pattern of the Franciscan metaphysics of light expounded in the *Panaugia* the *Pansophia* traces out a path of emanation, exemplarism, and consummation. Its express purpose is thus to achieve a Bonaventuran-type *reductio* in which the multiplicity of the world, including all its arts and sciences, is brought back to the unity of God himself. Just as God is one so nature is one and must be expressed in one system. We therefore, imitating God, must reduce

---

[238] Comenius, *Panegersia*, 9.14–15, in *Consultatio*, I.78–79.

[239] Comenius, *Panegersia*, 4.7, in *Consultatio* I.50: "*Imago viva vivi DEI*".

[240] See, for example, the Ramist chart in Comenius, *Panegersia*, "*Tabella Synoptica*", in *Consultatio*, I.43.

[241] See further Simon J. G. Burton, "Pansophic Mirrors of the Soul: Comenius, Pinder and the Transformation of Cusan Optics", *Acta Comeniana* 34 (2020): 9–49.

[242] Jan Amos Comenius, *Panaugia*, 2.1–16; 4.1–16, in *Consultatio*, I.102–3, 107–9.

[243] Comenius, *Panaugia*, 8.1–6, in *Consultatio*, I.123–24; cf. Bacon, *Advancement*, 35.

[244] Comenius, *Panaugia*, 5.9–12, in *Consultatio*, I.110–11. The Trinitarian reference is only implicit here.

[245] Comenius, *Panaugia*, 8.5, in *Consultatio*, I.123: "*Oculi divini expressissimam in nobis imaginem*".

(*reduci*) the "threefold fount of light, with its rivulets" to unity—by which he means the three Baconian lights of sense, reason, and faith discussed exhaustively in the *Panaugia*.[246]

The Trinitarian impulse in combining the three lights is evident and ensures that the whole of the pansophia comes to share in the structure and dynamic of the Trinity itself. Already in the *Diatyposis* Comenius had spoken of the threefold division of the pansophia expanding out into a pattern of seven books. Deftly combining Ramist, Lullist, and Baconian motifs into one, he had there spoken of this as being like a living tree of all the sciences, with its roots consisting of the *praecognita*, its trunk of metaphysics or pansophia itself, its branches of natural, artificial, and spiritual disciplines, its vital sap that of eternity itself flowing through the whole tree, and its fruits the use of true knowledge for this and the future life.[247]

In the *Pansophia* we notably find this same, distinctive interweaving of triads and septads. Indeed, just as in the *Synopsis*, the whole work is grounded on a progression—or unfolding—of the Triune being of God into the sevenfold structure of the world.[248] Pansophia thus becomes a universal "ladder of things".[249] Developing the pattern of the *Diatyposis*, and grounding it much more explicitly in the Trinitarian metaphysics of light, Comenius divided his final *Pansophia* into seven books—thus mirroring the pattern of the *Consultatio* as a whole. Significantly, all of these flow out of the possible world (*Mundus possibilis*), or "pure possibility", of God's own Trinitarian being:

1. Ideal or Archetypal World (*Mundus idealis seu archetypus*)
2. Intelligible-Angelic World (*Mundus intelligibilis angelicus*)
3. Material or Corporeal World (*Mundus materialis seu corporeus*)
4. Artificial World (*Mundus artificialis*)
5. Moral World (*Mundus moralis*)
6. Spiritual World (*Mundus spiritualis*)
7. Eternal World (*Mundus aeternus*)[250]

Reinforcing his exemplarism, the Trinitarian pattern of the possible world, shaped by the dynamic of Power, Wisdom, and Love, becomes impressed on the ideal or archetypal world in the mind of God, becoming impressed on all finite being through the transcendentals of unity, truth, and goodness.[251] Fully

---

[246] Comenius, *Pansophia*, in *Consultatio*, I.182.
[247] Comenius, *Patterne*, 101.
[248] Comenius, *Pansophia*, in *Consultatio*, I.182.
[249] Comenius, *Pansophia*, in *Consultatio*, I.192.
[250] For this sevenfold division see Burton, "Pansophic Mirrors", 43. Some of the discussion in this section parallels that in the article.
[251] Comenius, *Pansophia*, in *Consultatio*, I. 219–21, 242–43.

in evidence here is the Ramist pattern of archetype and ectype, albeit transposed into a dynamic Trinitarian motif of enfolding and unfolding.

From here the *Pansophia* traces a trajectory of emanation and return as the Triune being of God becomes mirrored in every level of creation. It is clear that the intelligible world of the angels must participate in the same Trinitarian structure and dynamic as the possible and archetypal worlds. Indeed, Comenius' Trinitarian treatment of the angels connects him to a long Dionysian and Franciscan tradition.[252] Likewise, Comenius' account of the material world is largely a reprisal of the hexameral physics he had expounded in the *Synopsis* and explores the triune interaction of the three principles of matter, light, and spirit in all creation.[253] The triad of material, artificial, and spiritual worlds was prefigured in the *Diatyposis* and offers a comprehensive investigation of the human world and its encyclopaedic structure, culminating in that union with God which is the summit of the pansophic enterprise.[254] In this way the *Pansophia* comes to closely reflect Pinder and Bonaventure, mapping out a sevenfold itinerary for Comenius' own journey into God.

Superimposed on this basic structure is a dynamic parallel between the infinite creativity of the divine and human minds. For Comenius is clear that the "trine world of God"—ideal, intelligible, and material—becomes mirrored inversely in the "trine artificial world"—artificial, moral, and spiritual—of the human soul, with both conjoined in eternity.[255] Comenius had expounded his understanding of the "boundless" nature of the human mind as early as his *Great Didactic*.[256] Defined simply as a "systematic coordination of thoughts", he was clear that the *Mundus possibilis* of the divine mind was also participated in and reflected by the human mind.[257] Guido Giglioni and Jan Čížek have rightly identified Comenius' understanding that the human mind has the ability to create "new worlds" of its own as one of the most important and innovative features of his thought, prefiguring the Enlightenment with its emphasis on human freedom and creativity.[258] Yet such an insight is clearly grounded in the Sebondian and Cusan understanding, also prominent in Ramus we will recall, of the mind as the living image of God capable of conforming itself more and more to its divine archetype. As a mathematical mirror the mind reduces all of reality to number, weight and measure in imitation of God himself.[259]

---

[252] Comenius, *Pansophia*, in *Consultatio*, I.273ff. For Trinitarian treatments of the angels in the Middle Ages see Bonaventure, *Itinerarium*, 4.4 (*BOO*, V.307) and Cusa, *Catholic Concordance*, 1.2.11–12 (pp.9–10; *NCOO*, XIV.35–36).
[253] Comenius, *Pansophia*, in *Consultatio*, I.305ff.
[254] Comenius, *Pansophia*, in *Consultatio* I.421–22, 742–43. See also Comenius, *Patterne*, 8, 106.
[255] Comenius, *Pansophia*, in *Consultatio* I.421–22.
[256] Comenius, *Great Didactic*, 5.4 (p. 42).
[257] Comenius, *Pansophia*, in *Consultatio*, I.199.
[258] Giglioni, "The Darkness of Matter and the Light of Nature", 21; Čížek, "Comenius' Pansophia", 361–63.
[259] Comenius, *Pansophia*, in *Consultatio*, I.179.

Following the *Pansophia* the rest of the *Consultatio* moves out from the transformation of the individual to encompass within its scope the universal reform of the entire human race. This is the culminating theme of the *Panorthosia*, which also embraced within itself the programme of universal education espoused by the *Pampaedia* and the quest for a universal language expressed in the *Panglottia*.[260] In itself the *Panorthosia* marked the fruit of years of irenic and ecumenical endeavours and its genesis was closely bound to the Hartlib circle, the promoters of Comenius' pansophia.[261] For our purposes, what is more important is its clear expression of the Ramist and Cusan ideals which underpinned the entire programme of universal reform, seen especially in its concrete embodying of a Trinitarian and covenantal pattern of Church and society.

Patterned after a Ramist, exemplaristic template, the entire *Panorthosia* is grounded on a quest for the "idea of God".[262] Comenius' conviction was that the best model of reform must be that following God's own "method".[263] As inspiration for this he significantly cites Sebonde, along with the *Theologia Deutsch*, the late medieval mystical treatise beloved by Luther and other Reformers.[264] Such a desire also surely reflected his own Hussite heritage, as well as what Karl Barth rightly identified as the scriptural Platonism of the Protestant Reformers.[265] Nevertheless, Comenius was adamant on the need to go beyond previous Reformers saying:

> We want a complete reformation of the Churches, for a such reformation has not yet occurred. There have been some attempts during the last centuries to reform the Christian Church, but these have only been particular and various for diverse occasions, without a universal idea or without the aim of having one.... Up until now all the past attempts at reformation of the Church (by Wyclif, Hus, Luther, Zwingli, Calvin, Mennon, Socinius, and also sometimes by the pope himself) have been like the first act of the healing of the blind man by Christ. It is now time to demand a perfect and universal reformation, which corresponds to the second act of Christ, through which the blind man received back such clear sight, that he could see everything perfectly.[266]

---

[260] Comenius, *Panorthosia*, "Introitus", in *Consultatio*, II.207–8.
[261] Čapková, "Comenian Group", 25–34.
[262] Comenius, *Panorthosia*, 10.2; 13, in *Consultatio*, II.269–70, 290.
[263] Comenius, *Panorthosia*, 2.9, in *Consultatio*, II.217.
[264] Comenius, *Panorthosia*, 13, in *Consultatio*, II.290. For the role of the *Theologia Deutsch* in the Reformation see Vincent Evener, *Enemies of the Cross: Suffering, Truth and Mysticism in the Early Reformation* (Oxford: Oxford University Press, 2021).
[265] Karl Barth, *The Theology of the Reformed Confessions 1923* (Louisville, KY: Westminster John Knox Press, 2005), 45–46.
[266] Comenius, *Panorthosia*, 23.2–3, in *Consultatio*, II.330. Translation from Neval, "Legacy".

For Comenius, the aim of the *Consultatio Catholica*—and thus of the entire pansophia—was nothing less than to complete the Reformation and usher in the Millennium itself.

Comenius' idealism is thus far from static but takes on a new dynamic character. Ramus too had been attuned to the successive rise and eclipse of reform movements.[267] Yet Comenius goes beyond this in his conviction of the Trinitarian progression of the whole of human history towards its eschatological climax. Such a conviction was undoubtedly fostered by Alsted and the Rosicrucians but was explicitly inspired by Jacopo Brocardo, the Reformed Joachimite prophet.[268] Following Brocardo, Comenius held that history unfolds in Trinitarian fashion as the age of the Father, the age of the Son, and the age of the Holy Spirit "now upon us", when Christ's Kingdom on Earth will come and universal peace will reign.[269] Notably, he expressed this with Joachim and the Franciscans according to a Trinitarian concordance between the three ages of the Church and the seven ages, or millennia, of human history.[270] Believing himself to be living on the very cusp of the seventh millennium, Comenius eagerly expected the fulfilment of that "golden age" promised by the "holy prophets" and a procession of Christian Platonists and mystics. Marking a return to Eden and a "new Pentecost", he held it would coincide with the global expansion of the Church and its establishing as a "School of God", a "Kingdom of Christ", and a "Temple of God"—a universal state with a universal religion and a universal language.[271]

Heralding the dawn of the Millennium would be the calling of a "world assembly" or "ecumenical council" to carry out the long-awaited universal reform of all things and establish the light, peace, and salvation of all humanity.[272] Its purpose would be nothing less than "the restoration of the human race to the state for which it was destined in the Garden of Eden, if we had not fallen from it".[273] Such a council he held would establish the universal language and the universal, pansophic, pattern of education, establishing a new Trinitarian harmony of Scripture, nature, and reason.[274] Comenius' hope for such a world council was

---

[267] Ramus, *Prooemium Mathematicum*, 2.

[268] Comenius, *Panorthosia*, 25.10, in *Consultatio*, II.362. For Comenius' citation of Brocardo see *Panorthosia*, 25.9, in *Consultatio*, II.362. For the important role of Brocardo in the transmission of Joachimite thought see Hotson, *Reformation of Common Learning*, 189 and *Paradise Postponed*, 147, 161–62.

[269] Comenius, *Panorthosia*, 24; 25.10, in *Consultatio*, II.349–50, 362.

[270] Comenius, *Panorthosia*, 2.29–33, in *Consultatio*, II.224–25. For the Trinitarian character of Joachimite eschatology see Marjorie Reeves, "The Abbot Joachim's Sense of History", in *The Prophetic Sense of History in Medieval and Renaissance Europe* (Aldershot: Ashgate, 1998), 782–96.

[271] Jan Amos Comenius, *Panglottia*, 6.8; 10.17, in *Consultatio*, II.166, 187; *Panorthosia*, 1.20–21; 2.22–39; 2.54; 5.21; 18.16, in *Consultatio*, II.214, 221–27, 230, 245–46, 308–10. For Baconian parallels see Charles Webster, *The Great Instauration: Science, Medicine and Reform 1626-1660* (London: Duckworth, 1975), 18.

[272] Comenius, *Panorthosia*, 25.1–2, in *Consultatio*, II.360.

[273] Comenius, *Panorthosia*, 5.21, in *Consultatio*, II.245 (trans. Dobbie).

[274] Comenius, *Panglottia*, 6.7, in *Consultatio*, II.165–66; *Panorthosia*, 25, in *Consultatio*, II.367–71.

inspired by Brocardo and by Joachimite expectations of a new outpouring of the Holy Spirit.[275] It also reflected fifteenth-century Conciliarism and especially Pico's desire for a universal council for the reform of philosophy and theology.[276] Yet it answers most closely to Campanella's striking utopian and eschatological vision in his *City of the Sun* and to Cusa's *De Concordantia Catholica* and *De Pace Fidei*, which set out the Trinitarian concordance of Church and society and the vision of a heavenly council of peace for the unification of all religions respectively.[277]

For Comenius, as for Cusa, concord—or concordance—becomes expressed supremely in the Trinity.[278] Following explicitly the pattern of Campanella's *City of the Sun*, he posits an important correspondence between the political, philosophical, and religious structure of society and the Triune primalities of Power, Wisdom, and Love respectively. Mirroring the coinherence of the primalities, each of these spheres must be seen as mutually conditioned by the others, such that politics, philosophy and religion all express the intimate relation of Power, Wisdom, and Love.[279] Following Cusa's vision in his *Catholic Concordance*, and recalling vividly Bisterfeld's "symbiotics", this Trinitarian and Conciliar pattern becomes multiplied at every level of society, encompassing countries, provinces, cities, towns, and villages in its scope.[280] Church and society thus become regulated by a complex, interconnected hierarchy of synods in which authority, freedom, and consent become combined into a new Trinitarian synthesis[281].

---

[275] Comenius, *Panorthosia*, 25.9–10, in *Consultatio*, II.362.

[276] Comenius, *Panorthosia*, 25.1, 8, in *Consultatio*, II.360, 362; cf. Farmer, "Introductory Monograph", 30–45.

[277] While the influence of Campanella on the *Consultatio Catholica* is clear and has been explored at great length by Matteo Raffaelli in *Macht, Weisheit, Liebe*, the direct influence of Cusa in this regard must remain a matter of some speculation. For although there can be no doubt of the profound influence of Cusa on Comenius' pansophia, it is unclear whether he knew his ecclesiological and eschatological works directly. For these are not included in Pinder's anthology, his only certain Cusan source. Nevertheless, Comenius' familiarity with authors such as Andreas Osiander and Guillaume Postel means that he could have easily picked up these Cusan influences at second-hand. For Comenius' familiarity with these theologians see *Panorthosia*, 8.49, in *Consultatio*, II.260–61 and "Letter of Jan Amos Comenius to Samuel Hartlib, 25th May 1646" (Hartlib Papers 7/73/5B; accessible at https://www.dhi.ac.uk/hartlib/). See further Simon J. G. Burton, "Jan Amos Comenius' Trinitarian and Conciliar Vision of a United Europe: Christ as the Universal 'Centre of Security'", *Reformation and Renaissance Review* 19.2 (2017): 113–14.

[278] See Cusa, *Catholic Concordance*, 1.1.4–10.48 (pp. 5–33). The discussion in the next three paragraphs closely follows that to be found in Burton, "Comenius' Trinitarian and Conciliar Vision", 116–17.

[279] Comenius, *Panorthosia*, 1.2–3, 14–15; 2.38; 10.42–45, in *Consultatio*, II.211, 213, 226, 278. In *Panorthosia*, 2.38, in *Consultatio*, II.226 Comenius cites Campanella explicitly as inspiration for his political theology.

[280] Comenius, *Panorthosia*, 25.4, in *Consultatio*, II.361; cf. Cusa, *Catholic Concordance*, 3.25.469–81, 33.510–13, 35.519–38.551 (pp. 283–86, 296–97, 299–308; NCOO, XIV.420–26, 439–40, 442–53).

[281] For Cusa's Trinitarian fusion of freedom and consent see Cusa, *Catholic Concordance*, 2.19 (pp. 127–28).

Like Cusa, Comenius saw this system of government as combining the best of human government and subordinating this to the rule of Christ. In particular he describes it as "government on the lines of a monarchy, tempered by an aristocracy which should resolve into democracy".[282] Advocating a purely spiritual Church, along Hussite lines, Comenius could yet imagine a hierarchical Church ruled over by an Arch-Patriarch, or even Pope, under the supremacy of Scripture.[283] Comenius' Trinitarian account of the new universal religion was also profoundly indebted to the Hussites. As Neval has convincingly shown, it thus follows the Brethren's characteristic threefold pattern of essentials, ministerials, and accessories.[284] Derived from the "idea of God" as the "best method of practising Religion", Comenius found the essentials in faith, hope, and love as mirroring the Trinity and perfecting the image of God in the human soul.[285]

Notably, such a pattern represented for Comenius not only a Trinitarian but also an ideal, mathematical ordering of Church and society. In this we return full circle back to Ramus' own brave attempts to reform the fracturing Christendom of his own day. Like Ramus and Lefèvre, Comenius thus took up Cusa's coincidence of opposites—which he here refers to as his "method of neither and both"—as a means of reconciling all Christian—indeed, perhaps ultimately, all religious—differences and disputes.[286] Without abandoning the distinctives of the Christian faith, he clearly hoped and dreamed of the possibility—very like Cusa in *De Pace Fidei*—that one day all doctrinal oppositions could be seen to coincide in God.

For Comenius, the supreme exemplar of the coincidence of opposites, as we have seen, was Christ himself. Fundamental to the new universal religion was thus its Christocentric character. As he expressed this in his *Unum Necessarium*, "because the whole world has strayed away from its center, GOD, and going around the circumferences of things it now wanders through labyrinths without exit", it is only through Christ uniting Creator and created that we can return to God.[287] The same theme recurs in his *Panorthosia*: "this and only this, will be the perfect fundamental basis for the perfect Reform of himself and his affairs, to

---

[282] Comenius, *Panorthosia*, 23, in *Consultatio*, II.347 (trans. Dobbie). See also Francis Oakley, *The Conciliarist Tradition: Constitutionalism in the Catholic Church 1300-1870* (Oxford: Oxford University Press, 2008), 68-70. While Oakley notes that Cusa distanced himself from mixed monarchy, he still drew on some of its essential characteristics.

[283] Comenius, *Panorthosia*, 23, in *Consultatio*, II.347.

[284] Neval, *Die Macht Gottes zum Heil*, 103-23.

[285] Comenius, *Panorthosia*, 13, in *Consultatio*, II.290-91.

[286] For the reconciling role of the coincidence of opposites in Cusa and Pico see Joshua Hollmann, *The Religious Concordance: Nicholas of Cusa and Christian-Muslim Dialogue* (Leiden: Brill, 2017) and Pico, *Syncretism in the West*, 402-3.

[287] Jan Amos Comenius, *Unum Necessarium, The One Thing Necessary*, trans. Vernon H. Nelson, 8.2 (I.66) (accessed from www.MoravianArchives.org).

leave the perimeter and the side-tracks of things and return to God, who is their sole and central basis". For it is God who is the "centre where unity, peace and perfection lie", and all other goods are but "rivulets flowing forth from that fountain of the highest Good".[288]

For Comenius, the final goal of the pansophia was thus the re-centring of all reality in Christ and the Trinity. In his vision of a renewed Christendom we therefore find the supreme realization of the Franciscan Trinitarian and Christocentric reform in early modernity. We also find the culmination not only of Herborn Ramism but of the entire Ramist movement. For the pansophia must clearly be seen as the realization of that supreme Ramist endeavour to attain a new, encyclopaedic, Christian philosophy for the comprehensive transformation of Church and society. In its unwavering desire for the remaking of the world in the image of God, it reveals the living spirit which animated the Reformation of method, from the Franciscans of the Middle Ages, through Cusa and the Fabrists, to Ramus and the universal reformers of Comenius' own age. Right at the heart of this was the conviction that all things should come to mirror the glory of the Triune God.

---

[288] Comenius, *Panorthosia*, 7.11, 13, in *Consultatio*, II.250 (trans. Dobbie).

# Bibliography

## Manuscripts

Bisterfeld, Johann Heinrich, and Andreas Rivetus. Correspondence of Johann Heinrich Bisterfeld and Andreas Rivetus. University of Leiden, MS BPL 285: A, 64r–76r.

Hartlib, Samuel, et al. The Hartlib Papers. Sheffield University Library, MS 61. www.dhi.ac.uk/hartlib.

Ussher, James, et al. Ussher Manuscripts. Trinity College Dublin, MS 334 and 775.

## Primary Sources

Agricola, Rudolph. *De Inventione Dialectica*. Cologne, 1527. [DID]

Alan of Lille. *The Complaint of Nature*. Translated by Douglas M. Moffat. New York, 1908. https://sourcebooks.fordham.edu/basis/alain-deplanctu.asp.

Alsted, Johann Heinrich. *Clavis Artis Lullianae et Verae Logicae Duos in Libellos Tributa*. Strasbourg, 1609.

Alsted, Johann Heinrich. *Compendium Theologicum*. Hanau, 1624.

Alsted, Johann Heinrich. *Criticus de Infinito Harmonico*. In Alsted, *Panacea*.

Alsted, Johann Heinrich. *Diatribe de Mille Annis Apocalypticis*. Frankfurt, 1627.

Alsted, Johann Heinrich. *Encyclopaedia Septem Tomis Distincta*. 7 vols. Herborn, 1630.

Alsted, Johann Heinrich. *Loci Communes Theologici Perpetuis Similitudinibus Illustrati*. Frankfurt, 1630.

Alsted, Johann Heinrich. *Metaphysica, Tribus Libris Tractata*. Herborn, 1616.

Alsted, Johann Heinrich. *Methodus Admirandorum Mathematicorum*. Herborn, 1613.

Alsted, Johann Heinrich. *Methodus Theologiae in VI Libros Tributa*. Hanau, 1634.

Alsted, Johann Heinrich. *Panacea Philosophica*. Herborn, 1610.

Alsted, Johann Heinrich. *Paratitla Theologica*. Frankfurt, 1626.

Alsted, Johann Heinrich. *Prodromus Triumphantis Religionis*. Alba-Julia, 1635.

Alsted, Johann Heinrich. *Systema Mnemonicum Duplex*. Frankfurt, 1610.

Alsted, Johann Heinrich. *Systema Physicae Harmonicae*. Herborn, 1612.

Alsted, Johann Heinrich. *Theologia Naturalis Exhibens Augustissimam Naturae Scholam*. Frankfurt, 1615.

Alsted, Johann Heinrich. *Theologia Scholastica Didactica*. Hanau, 1618.

Alsted, Johann Heinrich. *Thesaurus Chronologiae*. Herborn, 1624.

Alsted, Johann Heinrich. *Trigae Canonicae*. Frankfurt, 1612.

Alsted, Johann Heinrich. *Triumphus Bibliorum Sacrorum seu Encyclopaedia Biblica*. Frankfurt, 1625.

Alsted, Johann Heinrich. *Veraedus*. Alba Julia, 1637.

Althusius, Johannes. *Politica: An Abridged Translation of Politics Methodically Set Forth and Illustrated with Sacred and Profane Examples*. Translated by Frederick S. Carney. Indianapolis, IN: Liberty Fund, 1995.

## BIBLIOGRAPHY

Ames, William. *Bellarminus Enervatus*. London, 1632.
Ames, William. *Demonstratio Logicae Verae*. In Ames, *Philosophemata*.
Ames, William. *Disputatio Theologica adversus Metaphysicam*. In Ames, *Philosophemata*.
Ames, William. *Guilielmi Amesii Magni Theologi ac Philosophi Acutissimi Philosophemata*. Cambridge, 1646.
Ames, William. *The Marrow of Sacred Divinity Drawne Out of the Holy Scriptures*. London, 1642.
Ames, William. *Medulla S.S. Theologiae*. Amsterdam, 1659.
Ames, William. *The Philosophical and Theological Treatises of William Ames*. Edited by Lee Gibbs. Lewiston, NY: Edwin Mellen Press, 2013. [*PTT*]
Ames, William. *Technometria*. In Ames, *Philosophemata*.
Ames, William. *Theses Logicae*. In Ames, *Philosophemata*.
Andreae, Jan Valentin. *Christianopolis: An Ideal State of the Seventeenth Century*. Translated by Felix Emil Held. New York: Oxford University Press, 1916.
Andreae, Jan Valentin. *The Chymical Wedding of Christian Rosenkreutz*. English translation: 1690. https://order.rosy-cross.org/sites/default/files/docs/Chymical%20Wedding.pdf.
Andreae, Jan Valentin. *Mythologiae Christianae*. Strasbourg, 1618.
Aquinas, Thomas. *De Regno*. Edited by Joseph Kenny, OP. https://isidore.co/aquinas/english/DeRegno.htm.
Aquinas, Thomas. *De Veritate*. Edited by Joseph Kenny, OP. https://isidore.co/aquinas/QDdeVer.htm.
Aquinas, Thomas. *Summa Contra Gentiles*. Edited by Joseph Kenny, OP. https://isidore.co/aquinas/english/ContraGentiles.htm.
Aquinas, Thomas. *Summa Theologiae. Blackfriars English Translation*. 60 vols. London/New York: McGraw-Hill, 1964–1976. [*ST*]
Aristotle. *Metaphysics*. In *The Complete Works of Aristotle: The Revised Oxford Translation*, edited by Jonathan Barnes, II.313–489. 2 vols. Princeton, NJ: Princeton University Press, 1984.
Aristotle. *Topics*. In *The Complete Works of Aristotle: The Revised Oxford Translation*, edited by Jonathan Barnes, I.167–277. 2 vols. Princeton, NJ: Princeton University Press, 1984.
Augustine of Hippo. *Augustinus: De Musica*. Edited by Martin Jacobson. Berlin: De Gruyter, 2017.
Augustine of Hippo. *Confessions*. Translated by R. S. Pine-Coffin. London: Penguin, 1961.
Augustine of Hippo. *De Civitate Dei Contra Paganos Libri Viginti Duo*. In Migne, *PL*, 41 col. 13–803.
Augustine of Hippo. *Eighty-Three Different Questions*. Translated by David L. Mosher. Washington, DC: Catholic University of America Press, 2002.
Augustine of Hippo. *Enarrationes in Psalmos*. In Migne, *PL*, 36 col. 67–1027.
Augustine of Hippo. *On Christian Teaching*. Translated by R. P. H. Green. Oxford: Oxford University Press, 2008.
Augustine of Hippo. *On Genesis*. Translated by Edmund Hill, OP. Hyde Park, NY: New City Press, 2006.
Augustine of Hippo. *On Order: St Augustine's Cassiciacum Dialogues*. Translated by Michael P. Foley. New Haven, CT: Yale University Press, 2021.
Augustine of Hippo. *The Literal Meaning of Genesis*. In Augustine, *On Genesis*, 168–506.

Augustine of Hippo. *The Trinity: De Trinitate*. Translated by Edmund Hill, OP. Hyde Park, NY: New City Press, 1991.
Augustine of Hippo. *Unfinished Literal Commentary on Genesis*. In *On Genesis*, 114–51.
Bacon, Francis. *New Atlantis*. In Francis Bacon, *The Works of Francis Bacon. Volume 3: Philosophical Works 3*, edited by James Spedding, Robert Leslie Ellis, and Douglas Denon Heath. Cambridge: Cambridge University Press, 2013.
Bacon, Francis. *Oxford Francis Bacon XI: The Instauratio Magna Part II: Novum Organum and Associated Texts*. Edited by Graham Rees and Maria Wakely. Oxford: Oxford University Press, 2004.
Bacon, Francis. *The Twoo Bookes of Francis Bacon: Of the Proficience and Advancement of Learning, Divine and Humane*. London, 1605.
Bacon, Roger. *The Opus Maius of Roger Bacon*. Edited by John Henry Bridges. 2 vols. Oxford: Clarendon Press, 1897.
Banosius, Theophilus. *Petri Rami Vita*. In Petrus Ramus, *Commentariorum de Religione Christiana Libri Quattuor*. Frankfurt, 1576.
Baxter, Richard. *A Christian Directory*. London, 1678.
Baxter, Richard. *Methodus Theologiae Christianae*. London, 1681.
Baxter, Richard. *The Reduction of a Digressor*. London, 1654.
Baxter, Richard. *Richard Baxter's Catholick Theologie*. London, 1675.
Baxter, Richard. *A Treatise of Knowledge and Love Compared*. London, 1689.
Bernard, Richard. *Davids Musick*. London, 1616.
Bernard, Richard. *The Faithfull Shepheard*. London, 1607.
Besold, Christoph. *Signa Temporum*. Tübingen, 1614.
Beurhaus, Friedrich. *Defensio P. Rami Dialecticae*. Erfurt, 1588.
Beurhaus, Friedrich. *De P. Rami Dialecticae Praecipius Capitibus Disputationes Scholasticae*. Dortmund, 1581.
Beurhaus, Friedrich. *De Sacro Sancta Trinitate, seu, De Tribus Deitatis Personis Disputatio Theologica*. Dortmund, 1608?.
Beurhaus, Friedrich. *Disputatio Theologica et ex Parte Physica*. Dortmund, 1608.
Beurhaus, Friedrich. *P. Rami Dialecticae Libri Duo et His e Regione Comparati Philippi Melanchthonis*. Frankfurt, 1588.
Bilsten, Johannes. *Syntagma Philippo-Rameum Artium Liberalium*. Basel, 1596.
Bisterfeld, Johann Heinrich. "*Aliud*". In Alsted, *Encyclopaedia*, vol. 1.
Bisterfeld, Johann Heinrich. *Alphabetum Philosophicum*. In Bisterfeld, *BR*.
Bisterfeld, Johann Heinrich. *Ars Combinatoria*. In Bisterfeld, *BR*.
Bisterfeld, Johann Heinrich. *Ars Concionandi*. In Bisterfeld, *Divina Eminentia*.
Bisterfeld, Johann Heinrich. *Artificium Definiendi Catholicum*. In Bisterfeld, *BR*.
Bisterfeld, Johann Heinrich. *Bisterfeldius Redivivus seu Operum Joh. Henrici Bisterfeldi Magni Theologi ac Philosophi, Posthumorum*. Edited by Adriaan Heereboord. 2 vols. The Hague, 1661. [*BR*]
Bisterfeld, Johann Heinrich. *Consilium de Studiis Foeliciter Instituendis*. In Bisterfeld, *Phosphorus Catholicus*.
Bisterfeld, Johann Heinrich. *De Uno Deo, Patre, Filio, ac Spiritu Sancto, Mysterium Pietatis*. Amsterdam, 1659.
Bisterfeld, Johann Heinrich. *Disputatio Theologica de Fide*. Leiden, 1627.
Bisterfeld, Johann Heinrich. *Isagoge Encyclopaedica seu de Primis Encyclopaediae Principiis*. Basel, 1661.
Bisterfeld, Johann Heinrich. *Logica*. In Bisterfeld, *BR*.

Bisterfeld, Johann Heinrich. *Philosophiae Primae Seminarium*. Leiden, 1657.
Bisterfeld, Johann Heinrich. *Phosphorus Catholicus seu Artis Meditandi Epitome*. Breda, 1649.
Bisterfeld, Johann Heinrich. *Sciagraphia Analyseos*. In Bisterfeld, *BR*.
Bisterfeld, Johann Heinrich. *Scripturae Sacrae, Divina Eminentia et Efficientia*. Leiden, 1654.
Boethius. *De Topicis Differentiis*. Translated by Eleonore Stump. Ithaca, NY: Cornell University Press, 2018.
Bonaventure of Bagnoregio. *Breviloquium*. Edited and translated by Dominic V. Monti. Saint Bonaventure, NY: Franciscan Institute Press, 2005.
Bonaventure of Bagnoregio. *Breviloquium*. In Bonaventure, *BOO*, V.199–291.
Bonaventure of Bagnoregio. "*Christus Unus Omnium Magister*". In Bonaventure, *BOO*, V.567–74.
Bonaventure of Bagnoregio. *Collationes in Hexaemeron*. In Bonaventure, *BOO*, V.327–454.
Bonaventure of Bagnoregio. *Doctoris Seraphici S. Bonaventurae Opera Omnia*. 10 vols. Quaracchi, 1882. [*BOO*]
Bonaventure of Bagnoregio. *Itinerarium*. In Bonaventure, *BOO*, V.293–316.
Bonaventure of Bagnoregio. *Legenda Sancti Francisci*. In Bonaventure, *BOO*, VIII.504–64.
Bonaventure of Bagnoregio. *The Major Legend of St Francis*. In *Francis of Assisi: Early Documents. Vol. 2: The Founder*, edited by Regis Armstrong and Wayne Hellmann, 525–684. New York: New City Press, 2000.
Bonaventure of Bagnoregio. *Opusculum de Reductione Artium ad Theologiam*. In Bonaventure, *BOO*, V.319–25.
Bonaventure of Bagnoregio. *Quaestiones Disputatae de Scientia Christi*. In Bonaventure, *BOO*, V.1–43.
Bonaventure of Bagnoregio. *St Bonaventure's Life of Our Lord and Saviour Jesus Christ*. New York: P. J. Kenedy and Sons, 1881.
Bonaventure of Bagnoregio. *St Bonaventure's On the Reduction of Arts to Theology*. St Bonaventure, NY: Franciscan Institute, 1996.
Bovelles, Charles de. *Ars Oppositorum*. In Bovelles, *Que Hoc Volumine Continetur*.
Bovelles, Charles de. *Liber de Sapiente*. In Bovelles, *Que Hoc Volumine Continetur*.
Bovelles, Charles de. *Que Hoc Volumine Continetur: Liber de Intellectu, Liber de Sensu, Liber de Nichilo, Ars Oppositorum, Liber de Generatione, Liber de Sapiente, Liber de Duodecim Numeris, Epistole Complures*. Paris, 1511.
Bruno, Giordano. *De Umbris Idearum*. Paris, 1582.
Bruno, Giordano. *Four Works on Llull*. Translated by Scott Gosnell. USA: Hugginn, Munninn & Co, 2015.
Bullinger, Heinrich. *Ratio Studiorum*. In *De Ratione Studiorum Opuscula Aurea*, Edited by Johann Heinrich Heidegger. Zurich, 1670.
Buscher, Heizo. *Arithmeticae Libri Duo Logica Methodo Conformati et Conscripti*. Hamburg, 1597.
Buscher, Heizo. *De Ratione Solvendi Sophismata Solide et Perspicue ex P. Rami Dialectica Deducta et Explicata Libri Duo*. Lemgo, 1593.
Buscher, Heizo. *Harmoniae Logicae Philipporamae Libri Duo*. Lemgo, 1597.
Calvin, John. *Institutes of the Christian Religion*. Translated by Henry Beveridge. Grand Rapids, Michigan: Eerdmans, 1989.
Campanella, Tommaso. *Atheismus Triumphatus*. Rome, 1631.

Campanella, Tommaso. *City of the Sun*. In *Ideal Commonwealths: Comprising More's Utopia, Bacon's New Atlantis, Campanella's City of the Sun and Harrington's Oceana*, edited by Henry Morley. New York: Colonial Press, 1901.
Campanella, Tommaso. *De Sancta Monotriade: Theologicorum Liber II*. Translated by Romano Amerio. Rome: Centro Internazionale di Studi Umanistici, 1958.
Campanella, Tommaso. *Universalis Philosophiae, seu Metaphysicarum Rerum*. Paris, 1638.
Carpentarius, Jacobus. *Ad Expositionem Disputationis de Methodo*. Paris, 1564.
Casmann, Otto. *Philosophiae Christianae et Verae . . . Modesta Assertio*. Frankfurt, 1601.
Cicero. *De Inventione*. In Cicero, *De Inventione, De Optimo Genere Oratorum, Topica*, translated by H. M. Hubbell, 1–345. Cambridge, MA: Harvard University Press, 1956.
Cicero. *Topica*. In Cicero, *De Inventione, De Optimo Genere Oratorum, Topica*, translated by H. M. Hubbell, 382–459. Cambridge, MA: Harvard University Press, 1956.
Clauberg, Johannes. *Joh. Claubergii Logica Vetus et Nova*. Amsterdam, 1658.
Comenius, Jan Amos. *A Reformation of Schooles Designed in Two Excellent Treatises*. London, 1642.
Comenius, Jan Amos. *An Exhortation of the Churches of Bohemia to the Church of England*. London, 1661.
Comenius, Jan Amos. *Centrum Securitatis*. In Comenius, *DJAK*, 3.
Comenius, Jan Amos. *De Christianorum Uno Deo, Patre, Filio, Spiritu S⁰*. Amsterdam, 1659.
Comenius, Jan Amos. *De Irenico Irenicorum*. Amsterdam, 1660.
Comenius, Jan Amos. *De Iterato Sociniano Irenico Iterata ad Christianos Admonitio*. Amsterdam, 1661.
Comenius, Jan Amos. *De Rerum Humanarum Emendatione Consultatio Catholica*. Edited by Otokar Chlup, Jaromír Červenka, and Vlasta T. Miškovská-Kozáková. 2 vols. Prague, 1966.
Comenius, Jan Amos. *Dílo Jana Amose Komenského*. Edited by Antonín Škarka. Prague: Academia, 1969-. [*DJAK*]
Comenius, Jan Amos. *Geometria*. In Comenius, *DJAK*, 12.
Comenius, Jan Amos. *The Great Didactic*. Translated by M. W. Keatinge. London: Adam and Charles Black, 1907.
Comenius, Jan Amos. *Historia Fratrum Bohemorum*. Halle, 1702.
Comenius, Jan Amos. *Ianua Rerum Reserata*. In Comenius, *DJAK*, 18.
Comenius, Jan Amos. *J. A. Comenii Physicae ad Lumen Divinum Reformatae Synopsis*. Leipzig, 1633.
Comenius, Jan Amos. *The Labyrinth of the World and Paradise of the Heart*. Translated by Matthew Spinka. Ann Arbor, MI: University of Michigan Press, 1972. https://czech.mml.ox.ac.uk/labyrint.
Comenius, Jan Amos. *Lexicon Reale Pansophicum*. In Comenius, *Consultatio*, II.
Comenius, Jan Amos. *Naturall Philosophie Reformed by Divine Light*. London, 1651.
Comenius, Jan Amos. *Oculus Fidei*. Amsterdam, 1661.
Comenius, Jan Amos. *Panaugia*. In Comenius, *DJAK*, 19/1.
Comenius, Jan Amos. *Panorthosia*. In Comenius, *Consultatio*, II.
Comenius, Jan Amos. *Panorthosia or Universal Reform*. Translated by A. M. O. Dobbie. 2 vols. Sheffield: Sheffield Academic Press, 1993–95.
Comenius, Jan Amos. *Pansophia*. In Comenius, *Consultatio*, I.
Comenius, Jan Amos. *Pansophiae Christianae Liber III*. In Comenius, *DJAK*, 14.
Comenius, Jan Amos. *Pansophiae Diatyposis*. Amsterdam, 1645.
Comenius, Jan Amos. *Pansophiae Prodromus*. Leiden, 1644.

Comenius, Jan Amos. *Pansophiae Seminarium*. In Comenius, *DJAK*, 14.
Comenius, Jan Amos. *Patterne of Universall Knowledge*. London, 1651.
Comenius, Jan Amos. *Triertium Catholicum*. Edited by George Klima and L. Zelenka Lerando. Prague: Sokol-Packard, 1922.
Comenius, Jan Amos. *Unum Necessarium: The One Thing Necessary*. Translated by Vernon H. Nelson. www.MoravianArchives.org.
*Confessio Fraternitatis*. Translated by Benjamin Rowe. https://order.rosy-cross.org/confessio-fraternitatis.
Cusa, Nicholas of. *Compendium*. In Cusa, *NCOO*, XI/3.3–36.
Cusa, Nicholas of. *Conjectura de Ultimibus Diebus*. In Cusa, *NCOO*, IV.91–100.
Cusa, Nicholas of. *De Aequalitate*. In Cusa, *NCOO*, X/1.1–49.
Cusa, Nicholas of. *De Beryllo*. In Cusa, *NCOO*, XI/1.1–85.
Cusa, Nicholas of. *De Conjecturis*. In Cusa, *NCOO*, III.1–183.
Cusa, Nicholas of. *De Docta Ignorantia*. In Cusa, *NCOO*, I.1–164.
Cusa, Nicholas of. *De Ludo Globi*. In Cusa, *NCOO*, IX.1–149.
Cusa, Nicholas of. *De Venatione Sapientiae*. In Cusa, *NCOO*, XII.3–113.
Cusa, Nicholas of. *Haec Accurata Recognitio Trium Voluminum Operum Clariss. P. Nicolai Cusae Card*. Edited by Jacques Lefèvre d'Étaples. Paris, 1514.
Cusa, Nicholas of. *Idiota de Mente*. In Cusa, *NCOO*, V.81–218.
Cusa, Nicholas of. *Idiota de Sapientia*. In Cusa, *NCOO*, V.3–80.
Cusa. Nicholas of. *Nicolai de Cusa Opera Omnia*. Edited by Raymond Klibansky et al. Hamburg: Felix Meiner, 1932. [NCOO]
Cusa. Nicholas of. *The Catholic Concordance*. Edited and translated by Paul E. Sigmund. Cambridge: Cambridge University Press, 2003.
Cusa, Nicholas of. *Trialogus de Possest*. In Cusa, *NCOO*, XI/2.3–87.
Daneau, Lambert. *In Petri Lombardi Episcopi Parisiensis Librum Primum Sententiarium Commentarius*. Geneva, 1580.
Davenant, John. *De Praedestinatione et Reprobatione in Dissertationes Duae*. Cambridge, 1650.
Dante Alighieri. *The Comedy of Dante Alighieri The Florentine: Cantica III Paradise (Il Paradiso)*. Translated by Dorothy L. Sayers and Barbara Reynolds. London: Penguin, 2004.
Dee, John. "To the Unfained Lovers of Truthe". In Euclid, *The Elements of Geometrie of the Most Aunciente Philosopher Euclide of Megara*. Translated by H. Billingsley. London, 1570.
Digby, Everard. *De Duplici Methodo Libri Duo Unicam P. Rami Methodum Refutantes*. London, 1580.
*Fama Fraternitatis*. Translated by Benjamin Rowe. https://order.rosy-cross.org/fama-fraternitatis.
Fenner, Dudley. *The Arts of Logike and Rethorike Plainlie Set Forth in the English Tounge*. Middelburg, 1584.
Ficino, Marsilio. *De Religione Christiana*. Paris, 1559.
Ficino, Marsilio. *Epistolae*. Florence, 1494.
Ficino, Marsilio. *Theologia Platonica de Immortalitate Animorum Duo de Viginti Libris*. Paris, 1559.
Fonseca, Pedro da. *Comentariorum P. Fonsecae D. Theologi Societatis Iesu, in Libros Metaphysicorum Aristotelis Stagiritae Tomus Primus*. Lyon, 1585.
Freige, Johann Thomas. *P. Rami Professio Regia*. Basel, 1576.

Frisius, Paul. *Comparationum Dialecticarum Libri Tres*. Frankfurt, 1590.
Fuller, Thomas. *The Holy State*. Cambridge, 1642.
Gale, Theophilus. *The Court of the Gentiles: Or a Discourse Touching the Original of Human Literature Both Philologie, and Philosophie, from the Scriptures, and Jewish Church . . . Part II. Of Philosophie*. Oxford, 1670.
Gale, Theophilus. *The Court of the Gentiles: Part IV: Of Reformed Philosophie: Wherein Plato's Moral and Metaphysic or Prime Philosophie is Reduced to an Useful Forme and Method*. London, 1677.
Gansfort, Wessel. *Scala Meditationis*. In Wessel Gansfort, *Opera Omnia*. Groningen, 1614.
Goclenius, Rudolph. *Analyses in Exercitationes Aliquot Julii Caesaris Scaligeri*. Marburg, 1599.
Goclenius, Rudolph. *Collegium Philosophico-Theologicum*. Marburg, 1610.
Goclenius, Rudolph. *Conciliator Philosophicus*. Kassel, 1609.
Goclenius, Rudolph. *Disputatio Philosophica-Duplex Metaphysico-Logica de Identitate et Distinctione*. Marburg, 1604.
Goclenius, Rudolph. *Exercitationes Ethicae*. Marburg, 1592.
Goclenius, Rudolph. *Institutionium Logicarum de Inventione, Liber Unus*. Marburg, 1598.
Goclenius, Rudolph. *Isagoge in Peripateticorum et Scholasticorum Primam Philosophiam*. Frankfurt, 1598.
Goclenius, Rudolph. *Lexicon Philosophicum*. Frankfurt, 1613.
Goclenius, Rudolph. *Problematum Logicorum Pars I*. Marburg, 1591.
Granger, Thomas. *Syntagma Logicum or the Divine Logike*. London, 1620.
Grosseteste, Robert. *On the Six Days of Creation*. Translated by C. F. J. Martin. Oxford: Oxford University Press, 1999.
Grosseteste, Robert. "Robert Grosseteste's *On Light*: An English Translation", translated by Neil Lewis. In *Robert Grosseteste and His Intellectual Milieu: New Editions and Studies*, edited by John Flood, James R. Ginther, and Joseph W. Goering, 239–47. Toronto: Pontifical Institute of Medieval Studies, 2013.
Grynaeus, Johann Jakob. "*Praefatio*". In Szegedinus, *Loci Communes*.
Heereboord, Adriaan. "*Lectori*". In Johann Heinrich Bisterfeld, *Elementorum Logicorum Libri Tres*. Leiden, 1657.
Heereboord, Adriaan. *Meletemata Philosophica*. Amsterdam, 1665.
Holcot, Robert. *In Quatuor Libros Sententiarium Quaestiones*. Frankfurt: Minerva, 1967.
Holdsworth, Richard. "Directions for a Student in the Universitie". In Harris Francis Fletcher, *The Intellectual Development of John Milton: Volume II, The Cambridge University Period, 1625–32*, 623–64. Urbana: University of Illinois Press, 1981.
Hugh of St Victor. *De Arca Noe Morali Libri IV*. In Migne, *PL*, 176 col. 617–680D.
Hugh of St Victor. *De Sacramentis Christianae Fidei*. In Migne, *PL*, 176 col. 173–618B.
Hugh of St Victor. *The Didascalion of Hugh of St Victor: A Medieval Guide to the Arts*. Translated by Jerome Taylor. New York: Columbia University Press, 1961.
Hus, Jan. *Super IV Sententiarum*. Edited by V. Flajšhans. Prague: Jaroslav Bursík, 1904.
Hyperius, Andreas. *De Formandis Concionibus Sacris*. Basel, 1573.
Hyperius, Andreas. *Methodi Theologiae Libri Tres*. Basel, 1567.
Junius, Franciscus. *A Treatise on True Theology with the Life of Franciscus Junius*. Translated by David C. Noe. Grand Rapids, MI: Reformation Heritage Books, 2014.
Junius, Franciscus. "*For My Worthy Freind Mr. Franciscus Junius*": *An Edition of the Correspondence of Francis Junius F.F. (1591–1677)*. Edited by Sophia van Romburgh. Leiden: Brill, 2004.

Keckermann, Bartholomäus. *Gymnasium Logicum.* Hanau, 1608.
Keckermann, Bartholomäus. *Praecognita Logica.* Hanau, 1604.
Keckermann, Bartholomäus. *Praecognitorum Philosophicorum Libri Duo.* Hanau, 1612. [*PP*]
Keckermann, Bartholomäus. *Scientiae Metaphysicae Compendiosum Systema.* Hanau, 1611.
Keckermann, Bartholomäus. *Systema Disciplinae Politicae.* Hanau, 1607.
Keckermann, Bartholomäus. *Systema Ethicae.* Hanau, 1610.
Keckermann, Bartholomäus. *Systema Logicae Tribus Libris Adornatum.* Hanau, 1603.
Keckermann, Bartholomäus. *Systema S.S. Theologiae Tribus Libris Adornatum.* Hanau, 1610.
Keckermann, Bartholomäus. *Vera Philosophia Cum S. Theologia Nusquam Pugnat.* In Keckermann, *PP*, 181-200.
Lavinheta, Bernardo de. *Opera Omnia.* Edited by Johann Heinrich Alsted. Cologne, 1612.
Lawson, George. *Theo-Politica.* London, 1659.
Lefèvre d'Étaples, Jacques. *Introductio in Metaphysicorum Libros Aristotelis.* Paris, 1493.
Lefèvre d'Étaples, Jacques. *The Prefatory Epistles of Jacques Lefèvre d'Étaples and Related Texts.* Edited by Eugene F. Rice Jr. New York: Columbia University Press, 1972.
Leibniz, Gottfried Wilhelm von. *Leibniz's Monadology: A New Translation and Guide.* Edited and translated by Lloyd Strickland. Edinburgh: Edinburgh University Press, 2014.
Leigh, Edward. *A Treatise of Religion and Learning and of Religious and Learned Men.* London, 1656.
Lull, Ramon. *Arbor Scientiae.* In Lull, *ROL*, 24.4-26.1390.
Lull, Ramon. *Ars Brevis.* In Bonner and Bonner, *DI*, 297-364.
Lull, Ramon. *Ars Generalis Ultima.* In Lull, *ROL*, 14.5-527.
Lull, Ramon. *Liber de Demonstratione per Aequiparantiam.* In Lull, *ROL*, 9.216-31.
Lull, Ramon. *Liber de Fine.* In Lull, *ROL*, 9.250-291.
Lull, Ramon. *Raimundi Lulli Opera Latina.* Edited by Friedrich Stegmüller et al. Turnhout: Brepols, 1975. [*ROL*]
Lull, Ramon. *The Book of the Gentile and the Three Wise Men.* In Bonner and Bonner, *DI*, 85-171.
Lull, Ramon. *Vita.* In Lull, *ROL*, 8.272-309.
Luther, Martin. *D. Martin Luthers Werke: Abteilung 1 Schriften.* 72 vols. Weimar, 1883-2009. [*WA*]
Luther, Martin. *D. Martin Luthers Werke: Abteilung 4 Briefwechsel.* 18 vols. Weimar, 1883-2009.
Luther, Martin. "Die Disputation de Sententia: Verbum Caro Factum Est". In Luther, *WA*, 39/II.1-33.
Luther, Martin. *Disputation against Scholastic Theology.* In *Martin Luther's Works, Vol. 31: Career of the Reformer I*, edited by Harold J. Grimm and Helmut T. Lehmann, 3-16. Philadelphia, PA: Muhlenberg Press, 1957.
Luther, Martin. "Luther an Spalatin". In Luther, *WA Br.*, 2.40-42.
*Magyar Történelmi Tár.* Budapest, 1884.
Martinius, Matthias. *Christianae Doctrinae Summa Capita.* Herborn, 1603.
Martinius, Matthias. *Methodus Theologiae.* In *Christianae Doctrinae Summa Capita.* Herborn, 1603.
Martinius, Matthias. *Idea Methodica et Brevis Encyclopaedia.* Herborn, 1606.

Mather, Cotton. *Dr Cotton Mather's Student and Preacher*. London, 1781.
Mather, Increase. "To the Reader". In James Fitch, *The First Principles of the Doctrine of Christ*. Boston, 1679.
McIlmaine, Roland. *The Logike of the Most Excellent Philosopher P. Ramus Martyr*. London, 1574.
Melanchthon, Philipp. *De Anima*. Leiden, 1542.
Melanchthon, Philipp. *Erotemata Dialectices*. Wittenberg, 1555.
Melanchthon, Philipp. *Loci Communes 1521*. In *Corpus Reformatorum, Volume 21*, edited by Heinrich Ernest Bindseil, col. 81-230. Brunswick: C. A. Schwetschke et Filium, 1854.
Melanchthon, Philipp. *Melanchthon: Orations on Philosophy and Education*. Edited by Sachiko Kusukawa and translated by Christine F. Salazar. Cambridge: Cambridge University Press, 1999.
Migne, Jacques-Paul, ed. *Patrologia Latina Cursus Completus*, 221 Vols. Paris, 1844-55. [*PL*]
More, Henry. *Enchiridion Metaphysicum*. London, 1671.
Nancel, Nicholas. "Nicolaus Nancelius, '*Petri Rami Vita*'. Edited with an English Translation", translated by Peter Sharratt. *Humanistica Lovaniensia* 24 (1975): 161-277.
Olevian, Caspar. *De Inventione Dialecticae Liber e Praelectionibus Gasparis Oleviani Excerpti*. Geneva, 1583.
Olevian, Caspar. *De Substantia Foederis Gratuiti inter Deum et Electos*. Geneva, 1585.
Olevian, Caspar. *An Exposition of the Symbole of the Apostles*. Translated by John Fielde. London, 1581.
Olevian, Caspar. *In Epistolam D. Pauli Apostoli ad Romanos Notae*. Geneva, 1584.
Pace, Giulio. *Iul. Pacii Artis Lullianae Emendatae Libri IV*. Valentia, 1618.
Pareus, David, and Johann Philipp Pareus. *Analysis Logicae Divi Pauli ad Romanos*. Frankfurt, 1609.
Pauli, Georg. "*Philosophiae Studiosis S.*". In Keckermann, *PP*.
Pelbartus of Temesvár. *Aureum Sacrae Theologiae Rosarium*. Venice, 1586.
Perkins, William. *Antidicsonus Cuiusdam Cantabrigiensis G. P.* London, 1584.
Perkins, William. *The Art of Prophesying*. In Perkins, *Works*, 10.281-356.
Perkins, William. *A Christian and Plain Treatise of the Manner and Order of Predestination*. In Perkins, *Works*, 6.273-381.
Perkins, William. *Commentary on Galatians 1-5*. In Perkins, *Works*, 2.1-394.
Perkins, William. *Commentary on Hebrews 11*. In Perkins, *Works*, 3.1-397.
Perkins, William. *An Exposition of the Creed*. In Perkins, *Works*, 5.1-416.
Perkins, William. *Exposition upon the First Three Chapters of Revelation*. In Perkins, *Works*, 4.287-626.
Perkins, William. *A Friendly Admonition to Alexander Dickson*. In Perkins, *Works*, 6.541-58.
Perkins, William. *A Golden Chain*. In Perkins, *Works*, 6.1-272.
Perkins, William. *A Handbook on Memory*. In Perkins, *Works*, 6.527-40.
Perkins, William. *The Problem of Forged Catholicism*. In Perkins, *Works*, 7.171-410.
Perkins, William. *A Short Treatise That Fully Explains Dickson's Wicked System of Artificial Memory*. In Perkins, *Works*, 6.507-21.
Perkins, William. *The Whole Treatise of the Cases of Conscience*. In Perkins, *Works*, 8.615-37.
Perkins, William. *The Works of William Perkins*. Edited by Joel R. Beeke and Derek W. H. Thomas. 10 vols. Grand Rapids, MI: Reformation Heritage Books, 2014-20.

Pico della Mirandola, Gianfrancesco. *De Studio Divina et Humana Philosophia.* Halle, 1702.
Pico della Mirandola, Giovanni. *Heptaplus.* In *Opera Omnia Ioannis Pici Mirandulae.* Basel, 1557.
Pico della Mirandola, Giovanni. *Oration on the Dignity of Man.* Translated by A. Robert Caponigri. Chicago, IL: Gateway, 1956.
Pico della Mirandola, Giovanni. *Oration on the Dignity of Man: A New Translation and Commentary.* Edited and translated by Francesco Borghesi, Michael Papio, and Massimo Riva. Cambridge: Cambridge University Press, 2012.
Pico della Mirandola, Giovanni. *Syncretism in the West: Pico's 900 Theses (1486): The Evolution of Traditional Religious and Philosophical Systems: With Text, Translation and Commentary.* Edited and translated by S. A. Farmer. Tempe, AZ: Medieval & Renaissance Texts and Studies, 1998.
Pinder, Ulrich. *Speculum Intellectuale Felicitatis Humanae.* Nuremberg, 1510.
Piscator, Johannes. *Admonitio Johannis Piscatoris de Exercitationibus Heizonis Buscheri.* Herborn, 1594.
Piscator, Johannes. *Analysis Logica Epistola Horatii Omnium.* Speyer, 1595.
Piscator, Johannes. *Analysis Logica Epistolae Pauli ad Romanos.* Herborn, 1595.
Piscator, Johannes. *Animadversiones Ioan. Piscatoris. Arg. In Dialecticam P. Rami.* 2nd ed. Frankfurt, 1582.
Piscator, Johannes. *Aphorismi Doctrinae Christianae ex Institutione Calvini Excerpti.* Herborn, 1589.
Piscator, Johannes. *Commentarii in Omnes Libros Novi Testamenti.* Herborn, 1638.
Piscator, Johannes. *Exercitationum Logicarum Libri II.* 1585.
Piscator, Johannes. *Hypotyposis S.S. Theologiae ad Leges Methodi qua Popularis qua Scholasticae Delineata et Conformata.* Herborn, 1611.
Piscator, Johannes. *Kurzer Bericht vom Leben und Sterben Herrn Gasparis Oleviani.* Herborn, 1587.
Piscator, Johannes. *Leges Scholae Herbornensis.* Neustadt, 1585.
Piscator, Johannes. *Responsio.* In Temple, *Epistola.*
Piscator, Johannes. *Responsio Johannis Piscatoris ad Elenchos Heizonis Buscheri.* Herborn, 1593.
Piscator, Johannes. *Volumen Thesium Theologicarum.* Herborn, 1596.
Plato. *Parmenides.* In Plato, *Plato: Complete Works,* edited by Cooper, 359–97.
Plato. *Philebus.* In Plato, *Plato: Complete Works,* edited by Cooper, 398–456.
Plato. *Plato: Complete Works.* Edited by John M. Cooper. Cambridge: Hackett, 1997.
Plato. *Republic.* In Plato, *Plato: Complete Works,* edited by Cooper, 971–1223.
Polanus von Polansdorf, Amandus. *Logicae Libri Duo.* Basel, 1599.
Polanus von Polansdorf, Amandus. *Symphonia Catholica seu Consensus Catholicus et Orthodoxus.* Basel, 1607.
Polanus von Polansdorf, Amandus. *Syntagma Logicum Arisotelico-Ramaeum ad Usum Imprimis Theologicum Accommodatum.* Basel, 1605.
Polanus von Polansdorf, Amandus. *Syntagma Theologiae Christianae.* 2 vols. Hanau, 1609. [STC]
Pseudo-Bonaventure. *Ars Concionandi.* In Bonaventure, *BOO,* IX.8–21.
Pseudo-Dionysius. *Divine Names.* In Pseudo-Dionysius, *Pseudo-Dionysius: The Complete Works,* edited by Paul Rorem and translated by Colm Luibheid, 49–131. London: SPCK, 1987.

Rada, Johannes de. *Controversiae Theologicae*. Cologne, 1620.
Rákóczi, Zsigmond. "*Oratio Valedictoria*". In *Pallas Dacica*, edited by Johann Heinrich Bisterfeld. Alba Julia, 1650.
Ramus, Petrus. *Algebra*. Paris, 1560.
Ramus, Petrus. *Arguments in Rhetoric against Quintilian: Translation and Text of Peter Ramus's Rhetoricae Distinctiones in Quintilianum*. Edited by James J. Murphy and translated by Carole Newlands. Carbondale: Southern Illinois University Press, 2010.
Ramus, Petrus. *Aristotelicae Animadversiones*. Paris, 1543; facsimile edition Stuttgart: Friedrich Frommann Verlag, 1964.
Ramus, Petrus. *Commentariorum de Religione Christiana Libri Quattuor*. Frankfurt, 1576.
Ramus, Petrus. *De Religione Christiana*. Frankfurt, 1583.
Ramus, Petrus. *Dialecticae Libri Duo*. Edited by Sebastian Lalla and Karlheinz Hülser. Paris, 1572; Stuttgart: Frommann-Holzboog, 2011. [*DLD* 1572]
Ramus, Petrus. *Dialectique de Pierre de la Ramee*. Paris, 1555.
Ramus, Petrus. *Institutiones Dialecticae*. Paris, 1543; facsimile edition Stuttgart: Friedrich Frommann Verlag, 1964.
Ramus, Petrus. *Liber de Moribus Veterum Gallorum*. Frankfurt, 1584.
Ramus, Petrus. *The Logike of the Most Excellent Philosopher P. Ramus Martyr*. London, 1581.
Ramus, Petrus. *Oratio de Studiis Philosophiae et Eloquentiae Conjungendis*. In Ramus, *Collectaneae*.
Ramus, Petrus. *Oratio Pro Philosophica Parisiensis*. In Ramus, *P. Rami Scholae in Liberales Artes*.
Ramus, Petrus. *P. Rami Dialectica, Audomari Talaei Praelectionibus Illustrata*. Cologne, 1573. [*DC*]
Ramus, Petrus. *P. Rami Dialecticae Libri Duo*. Cologne, 1566. [*DLD* 1566]
Ramus, Petrus. *P. Rami Professoris Regii Prooemium Mathematicum*. Paris, 1567.
Ramus, Petrus. *P. Rami Professoris Regii Scholarum Metaphysicarum*. Paris, 1566.
Ramus, Petrus. *P. Rami Scholae in Liberales Artes*. Basel, 1578.
Ramus, Petrus. *P. Rami Scholarum Dialecticarum*. Frankfurt, 1594.
Ramus, Petrus. *Peter Ramus's Attack on Cicero: Text and Translation of Ramus's Brutinae Quaestiones*. Edited by James J. Murphy and translated by Carole Newlands. Portland, OR: Hermagoras Press, 1992.
Ramus, Petrus. *Petri Rami Mathematicae Praefationes: Prima*. In Ramus, *Collectaneae*.
Ramus, Petrus. *Petri Rami Professoris Regii, et Audomari Talaei Collectaneae*. Paris, 1577.
Ramus, Petrus. *Petri Rami Scholarum Mathematicarum Libri Unus et Triginta*. Frankfurt, 1599.
Ramus, Petrus. *Prooemium Reformandae Parisiensis Academiae*. In Ramus, *Collectaneae*.
Ramus, Petrus. *Scipionis Somnium*. Paris, 1550.
Ravensperger, Hermann. *Gemma Theologica Hoc est Brevis et Facilis Locorum S.S. Theologiae Communium Institutio*. Herborn, 1611.
Rhenanus, Beatus. *Briefwechsel des Beatus Rhenanus*. Edited by Adalbert Horawitz and Karl Hartfelder. Nieuwkoop: B. de Graaf, 1966.
Richardson, Alexander. *The Logicians School-Master: or, A Comment upon Ramus Logick*. London, 1657.
Rimini, Gregory of. *Gregorii Ariminensis OESA Lectura Super Primum et Secundum Sententiarium*. Edited by A. Damasus Trapp, OSA, and Venicio Marcolino. 6 vols. Berlin: Walter de Gruyter, 1981.

Rollock, Robert. *A Treatise of Gods Effectual Calling*. London, 1603.
Rutherford, Samuel. *The Covenant of Life Opened*. Edinburgh, 1655.
Rutherford, Samuel. *The Due Right of Presbyteries*. London, 1644.
Savonarola, Girolamo. *Epitome Universae Philosophiae*. Wittenberg, 1596.
Scaliger, Julius Caesar. *De Causis Linguae Latinae Libri Tredecim*. Lyon, 1540.
Scaliger, Julius Caesar. *Iulii Caesaris Scaligeri Exotericarum Exercitationium Liber Quintus Decimus, De Subtilitate ad Hieronymum Cardanum*. Paris, 1557. [*Exercitationes*]
Scaricza, Matthaeus. "*Stephani Szegedini Vita*". In Szegedinus, *Loci Communes*.
Scotus, John Duns. *Duns Scotus on the Will and Morality*. Edited by Alan B. Wolter. Washington, DC: Catholic University of America Press, 1997.
Scotus, John Duns. *The Examined Report of the Paris Lecture: Reportatio 1A*. Edited by Allan B. Wolter, OFM, and Oleg V. Bychkov. St. Bonaventure, NY: Franciscan Institute, 2004. [*Rep. 1A*]
Scotus, John Duns. *God and Creatures: The Quodlibetal Questions*. Edited by Felix Alluntis and Allan Wolter. Princeton, NJ: Princeton University Press, 2015.
Scotus, John Duns. *Opera Omnia*. Edited by Charles Balić et al. Rome: Typis Polyglottis Vaticanis, 1950-. [Vatican]
Scotus, John Duns. *Ordinatio*. In Vatican, I–XIV. [*Ord.*]
Scotus, John Duns. *Philosophical Writings: A Selection*. Translated by Allan Wolter, OFM. Indianapolis, IN: Hackett Publishing Company, 1987.
Scotus, John Duns. *Quaestiones in Librum Secundum Sententiarum*. In Scotus, *Joannis Duns Scoti Doctoris Subtilis, Ordinis Minorum, Opera Omnia*. Edited by Ludovic Vivès. 26 vols, vol. 11–13. Paris, 1891.
Scotus, John Duns. "Six Questions on Individuation". *In Five Texts*, edited by Spade, 57–113.
Scribonius, Wilhelm Adolf. *Triumphus Logicae Rameae*. Basel, 1587.
Sebonde, Ramon de. *Theologia Naturalis*. Venice, 1581.
Sennertus, Daniel. *Chymistry Made Easy and Useful*. London, 1662.
Servetus, Michael. "On the Errors of the Trinity". In Michael Servetus, *The Two Treatises on the Trinity*, 1–184. Translated by Earl Morse Wilbur. Eugene, OR: Wipf & Stock, 2013.
Simonius, Simon. *Antischegkianorum Liber Unus*. Basel, 1570.
Sohn, Georg. *Methodus Theologiae*. In *Operum Georgii Sohnii Sacrae Theologiae Doctoris*, I.87–289. 3 vols. Herborn, 1591–92.
Spade, Paul Vincent, ed. *Five Texts on the Mediaeval Problem of Universals: Porphyry, Boethius, Abelard, Duns Scotus, Ockham*. Indianapolis, IN: Hackett Publishing Company, 1994.
Stoughton, John. *Felicitas Ultimi Saeculi*. London, 1640.
Sturm, Johannes. *Partitionum Dialectiarum Libri IIII*. Strasbourg, 1566.
Streso, Caspar. *Technologia Theologica*. Leiden, 1633.
Szegedinus, Stephanus. *Assertio Vera de Trinitate*. Geneva, 1576.
Szegedinus, Stephanus. *Theologiae Sincerae Loci Communes de Deo et Homine*. Basel, 1585.
Temple, William. *Francisci Mildapetti Navarenni ad Everardum Digbeium*. London, 1580.
Temple, William. *Gulielmi Tempelli Philosophi Cantabrigiensis Epistola de Dialectica P. Rami*. London, 1583.
Timpler, Clemens. *Metaphysicae Systema Methodicum Libris Quinque*. Hanau, 1616.
Timpler, Clemens. *Technologia*. In *Metaphysicae Systema*.

Turretin, Francis. *Institutes of Elenctic Theology: Volume One*. Edited by James T. Dennison Jr. and translated by George Musgrave Giger. Phillipsburg, NJ: Presbyterian and Reformed Publishing Company, 1992.
Tymarchus, Joshua. "To the Reader". In Comenius, *Exhortation*.
Ursinus, Zacharias. *The Commentary of Dr Zacharias Ursinus on the Heidelberg Catechism*. Translated by G. W. Williard. Cincinnati, OH: T. P. Bucher, 1861.
Valerius de Valeriis. *Aureum Sane Opus*. Augsburg, 1589.
Valla, Lorenzo. *Dialectical Disputations*. Edited and translated by Brian P. Copenhaver and Lodi Nauta. Cambridge MA: Harvard University Press, 2012.
Valla, Lorenzo. *Encomium for Thomas Aquinas*. In *Christianity, Latinity and Culture: Two Studies on Lorenzo Valla*, edited and translated by Christopher S. Celenza and Patrick Baker, 297–316. Leiden: Brill, 2013.
Vignon, Eustace. *"Typographus Candidus Lectoribus"*. In Olevian, *De Inventione Dialecticae*.
Voetius, Gisbertus. *Selectarum Disputationum Theologicarum*. Utrecht, 1648.
Walker, George. *A True Relation of the Chiefe Passages betweene Mr. Anthony Wooton, and Mr. George Walker*. London, 1642.
Wyclif, John. *Wyclif: Trialogus*. Translated by Stephen E. Lahey. Cambridge: Cambridge University Press, 2013.
Yates, John. *Gods Arraignement of Hypocrites*. Cambridge, 1615.
Yates, John. *A Modell of Divinitie, Catechistically Composed*. London, 1622.
Zabarella, Jacopo. *Jacopo Zabarella: On Methods*. Edited and translated by John P. McCaskey. 2 vols. Cambridge, MA: Harvard University Press, 2013.
Zwicker, Daniel. *Irenicum Irenicorum*. Amsterdam, 1658.

## Secondary Sources

Adams, John. "Alexander Richardson's Philosophy of Art and the Sources of the Puritan Social Ethic". *Journal of the History of Ideas* 50.2 (1989): 227–47.
Adams, John. "Alexander Richardson's Puritan Theory of Discourse". *Rhetorica* 4.3 (1986): 255–74.
Aertsen, Jan A. "Being and One: The Doctrine of the Convertible Transcendentals in Duns Scotus". In *John Duns Scotus (1265/6-1308): Renewal of Philosophy*, edited by Bos, 13–26.
Aertsen, Jan A. *Medieval Philosophy as Transcendental Thought: From Philip the Chancellor (ca. 1225) to Francisco Suárez*. Leiden: Brill, 2012.
Albertson, David. *Mathematical Theologies: Nicholas of Cusa and the Legacy of Thierry of Chartres*. New York: Oxford University Press, 2014.
Andersson, Bo, Lucinda Martin, Leigh T. I. Penman, and Andrew Weeks, eds. *Jacob Böhme and His World*. Leiden: Brill, 2019.
Anfray, Jean-Pascal. "Scottish Scotism? The Philosophical Theses in the Scottish Universities, 1610–1630". *History of Universities* 29.2 (2017): 96–120.
Antognazza, Maria Rosa. "Bisterfeld and *Immeatio*: Origins of a Key Concept in the Early Modern Doctrine of Universal Harmony". In *Spätrenaissance Philosophie in Deutschland 1570-1650: Entwürfe zwischen Humanismus und Konfessionalisierung, okkulten Traditionen und Schulmetaphysik*, edited by Martin Mulsow, 57–84. Tübingen: Max Niemeyer Verlag, 2009.

Antognazza, Maria Rosa. "*Debilissimae Entitates*? Bisterfeld and Leibniz's Ontology of Relations". *Leibniz Review* 11 (2001): 1–22.
Antognazza, Maria Rosa. "*Immeatio* and *Emperichoresis*: The Theological Roots of Harmony in Bisterfeld and Leibniz". In *The Young Leibniz and His Philosophy, 1646–1676*, edited by Stuart Brown, 41–64. Dordrecht: Springer, 1999.
Antognazza, Maria Rosa. "Leibniz and the Post-Copernican Universe: Koyré Revisited". *Studies in History and Philosophy of Science* 34 (2003): 309–27.
Antognazza, Maria Rosa. *Leibniz on the Trinity and Incarnation: Reason and Revelation in the Seventeenth Century*. New Haven, CT: Yale University Press, 2008.
Antognazza, Maria Rosa, and Howard Hotson. *Alsted and Leibniz: On God, the Magistrate, and the Millennium*. Wiesbaden: Harrassowitz, 1999.
Ariew, Roger. *Descartes among the Scholastics*. Leiden: Brill, 2011.
Aroney, Nicholas. "Before Federalism? Thomas Aquinas, Jean Quidort and Nicolas Cusanus". In *The Ashgate Research Companion to Federalism*, edited by Ann Ward and Lee Ward, 31–48. Aldershot: Ashgate, 2009.
Artis, Aderemi. "Trinitarian Roots of Francis Bacon's Pragmatism". *Heythrop Journal* 60.2 (2019): 197–204.
Ashworth, E. J. *Language and Logic in the Post-Medieval Period*. Dordrecht: Reidel, 2012.
Ashworth, E. J. "The 'Libelli Sophistarum' and the Use of Medieval Logic Texts at Oxford and Cambridge in the Early Sixteenth Century". *Vivarium* 17 (1979): 134–58.
Aspray, Silvianne. *Metaphysics in the Reformation: The Case of Peter Martyr Vermigli*. Oxford: Oxford University Press, 2022.
Asselt, Willem J. van. *The Federal Theology of Johannes Cocceius (1603–1669)*. Leiden: Brill, 2001.
Asselt, Willem J. van. "The Fundamental Meaning of Theology: Archetypal and Ectypal Theology in Seventeenth-Century Reformed Thought". *Westminster Theological Journal* 64.2 (2002): 319–35.
Asselt, Willem J. van, J. Martin Bac, and Roelf T. te Velde, eds. *Reformed Thought on Freedom: The Concept of Free Choice in Early Modern Reformed Theology*. Grand Rapids, MI: Baker Academic, 2010.
Atwood, Craig. *The Theology of the Czech Brethren from Hus to Comenius*. University Park, PA: Pennsylvania State University Press, 2009.
Austin, Amy M., and Mark D. Johnston, eds. *A Companion to Ramon Llull and Lullism*. Leiden: Brill, 2019.
Ayres, Lewis. *Augustine and the Trinity*. Cambridge: Cambridge University Press, 2010.
Bac, J. Martin. *Perfect Will Theology: Divine Agency in Reformed Scholasticism as against Suárez, Episcopius, Descartes and Spinoza*. Leiden: Brill, 2010.
Bainton, Roland. "Michael Servetus and the Trinitarian Speculation of the Middle Ages". In *Autour de Michel Servet et de Sebastien Castellion*, edited by Bruno Becker, 29–46. Haarlem: Tjenk Willink, 1953.
Baker, J. Wayne. *Heinrich Bullinger and the Covenant: The Other Reformed Tradition*. Athens, OH: Ohio University Press, 1980.
Ballor, Jordan J., Matthew T. Gaetano, and David S. Sytsma, eds. *Beyond Dordt and "De Auxiliis": The Dynamics of Protestant and Catholic Soteriology in the Sixteenth and Seventeenth Centuries*. Leiden: Brill, 2019.
Ballor, Jordan J., David Sytsma, and Jason Zuidema, eds. *Church and School in Early Modern Protestantism: Studies in Honor of Richard A. Muller on the Maturation of a Theological Tradition*. Leiden: Brill, 2013.

Barker, William. "Fraunce [France], Abraham (1559?–1592/3?)". *ODNB*.
Barnes, Robin Bruce. *Prophecy and Gnosis: Apocalypticism in the Wake of the Lutheran Reformation*. Stanford, CA: Stanford University Press, 1988.
Baron, Hans. *In Search of Florentine Civic Humanism, Volume 1: Essays on the Transition from Medieval to Modern Thought*. Princeton, NJ: Princeton University Press, 2014.
Barth, Karl. *The Theology of the Reformed Confessions 1923*. Louisville, KY: Westminster John Knox Press, 2005.
Baschera, Luca. *Tugend und Rechtfertigung: Peter Martyr Vermiglis Kommentar zur Nikomachischen Ethik im Spannungsfeld von Philosophie und Theologie*. Zurich: Theologischer Verlag Zürich, 2008.
Bates, Todd. "Fine-Tuning Pini's Reading of Scotus's *Categories*". In *Medieval Commentaries on Aristotle's Categories*, edited by Lloyd A. Newton, 259–76. Leiden: Brill, 2008.
Bauerschmidt, Frederick Christian. *Thomas Aquinas: Faith, Reason and Following Christ*. Oxford: Oxford University Press, 2013.
Beck, Andreas J. "Gisbertus Voetius (1589–1676): Basic Features of His Doctrine of God". In *Reformation and Scholasticism: An Ecumenical Enterprise*, edited by Willem van Asselt and Eef Dekker, 205–26. Grand Rapids, MI: Baker Academic, 2001.
Beck, Andreas J. *Gisbertus Voetius (1589–1676) on God, Freedom, and Contingency: An Early Modern Reformed Voice*. Leiden: Brill, 2021.
Beck, Andreas J. "Melanchthonian Thought in Gisbertus Voetius' Scholastic Doctrine of God". In *Scholasticism Reformed: Essays in Honour of Willem J. van Asselt*, edited by Maarten Wisse, Marcel Sarot, and Willemien Otten, 105–26. Leiden: Brill, 2010.
Bedouelle, Guy. *Lefèvre d'Étaples et l'intelligence des écritures*. Geneva: Droz, 1976.
Bedouelle, Guy. *Le Quincuplex Psalterium de Lefèvre d'Étaples: Un guide de lecture*. Geneva: Droz, 1979.
Beeke, Joel R., and Greg A. Salazar. "Preface to Volume 6 of William Perkins's *Works*". In Perkins, *Works*, 6.xii–xliv.
Bergmans, Luc, and Teun Keutsier, eds. *Mathematics and the Divine: A Historical Study*. Amsterdam: Elsevier, 2005.
Bermon, Pascale. *L'assentiment et son objet chez Grégoire de Rimini*. Paris: Vrin, 2007.
Bierma, Lyle D. "The Covenant Theology of Caspar Olevian". PhD Dissertation, Duke University, 1980.
Bierma, Lyle D. "Theology and Piety in Ursinus' *Summa Theologiae*". In *Church and School*, edited by Ballor, Sytsma, and Zuidema, 295–305.
Bihlmaier, Sandra. *Ars et Methodus: Philipp Melanchthon's Humanist Concept of Philosophy*. Göttingen: Vandenhoeck & Ruprecht, 2018.
Bihlmaier, Sandra. "Platonism in Humanist Logic Textbooks of the Sixteenth Century: Melanchthon, Ramus, and the Philippo-Ramists". *Acta Comeniana* 29 (2015): 7–40.
Billanovich, Myriam. "Benedetto Bordon e Giulio Cesare Scaligero". *Italia Medioevale E Humanistica* 11 (1968): 187–256.
Blair, Ann. "Mosaic Physics and the Search for a Pious Natural Philosophy in the Late Renaissance". *Isis* 91.1 (2000): 32–58.
Blum, Paul Richard, and Tomáš Nejeschleba, eds. *Francesco Patrizi: Philosopher of the Renaissance*. Olomouc: University of Olomouc Press, 2014.
Blumenberg, Hans. *The Legitimacy of the Modern Age*. Translated by Robert M. Wallace. Cambridge, MA: MIT Press, 1983.

Boersma, Hans. *Heavenly Participation: The Weaving of a Sacramental Tapestry*. Grand Rapids, MI: Eerdmans, 2011.
Bolliger, Daniel. *Infiniti Contemplatio: Grundzüge der Scotus- und Scotismusrezeption im Werk Huldrych Zwinglis*. Leiden: Brill, 2003.
Bonansea, Bernardino. *Tommaso Campanella: Renaissance Pioneer of Modern Thought*. Washington, DC: Catholic University of America Press, 1969.
Bonansea, Bernadino, and John Ryan, eds. *John Duns Scotus, 1265–1965*. Washington, DC: Catholic University of America Press, 1965.
Bonner, Anthony. *The Art and Logic of Ramon Llull: A User's Guide*. Leiden: Brill, 2007.
Bonner, Anthony, and Eve Bonner. *Doctor Illuminatus: A Ramon Llull Reader*. Princeton, NJ: Princeton University Press, 1993. [DI]
Boran, Elizabethanne. "Ramism in Trinity College, Dublin, in the Early Seventeenth Century". In *The Influence of Petrus Ramus*, edited by Feingold, Freedman, and Rother, 177–99.
Boran, Elizabethanne. "Temple, Sir William (1554/5–1627)". *ODNB*.
Bos, Egbert, ed. *John Duns Scotus (1265/6–1308): Renewal of Philosophy: Acts of the Third Symposium Organised by the Dutch Society for Medieval Philosophy Medium Aevum (May 23 and 24 1996)*. Amsterdam: Rodopi, 1998.
Bowman, Leonard. "Bonaventure's 'Contuition' and Heidegger's 'Thinking': Some Parallels". *Franciscan Studies* 37 (1977): 18–31.
Bremer, Francis J. *Congregational Communion: Clerical Friendship in the Anglo-American Puritan Community, 1610–1692*. Boston, MA: Northeastern University Press, 1994.
Broadie, Alexander. "The Declaration of Arbroath in the Shadow of Scotus". In *Scotland and Arbroath 1320–2020: 700 Years of Fighting for Freedom, Sovereignty and Independence*, edited by Klaus Peter Müller, 75–89. Frankfurt am Main: Peter Lang, 2020.
Broadie, Alexander. *Introduction to Medieval Logic*. Oxford: Clarendon Press, 1993.
Broadie, Alexander. *The Shadow of Scotus: Philosophy and Faith in Pre-Reformation Scotland*. Edinburgh: T&T Clark, 1995.
Brouwer, Rinse H. Reeling. "The Conversation between Karl Barth and Amandus Polanus on the Question of the Reality of Human Speaking of the Simplicity and the Multiplicity in God". In *The Reality of Faith in Theology: Studies on Karl Barth—Princeton-Kampen Consultation 2005*, edited by Bruce L. McCormack and G. W. Neven, 51–110. Oxford: Peter Lang, 2007.
Brower, Jeffrey E. "Aquinas on the Problem of Universals". *Philosophy and Phenomenological Research* 92.3 (2016): 715–35.
Bruyère, Nelly. *Méthode et dialectique dans l'oeuvre de La Ramée: Renaissance et age classique*. Paris: J. Vrin, 1984.
Bryćko, Dariusz M. "The Danzig Academic Gymnasium in Seventeenth-Century Poland". In *Church and School*, edited by Ballor, Sytsma, and Zuidema, 339–46.
Burnett, Amy Nelson. *Teaching the Reformation: Ministers and Their Message in Basel, 1529–1629*. Oxford: Oxford University Press, 2006.
Burns, James H. *The True Law of Kingship: Concepts of Monarchy in Early-Modern Scotland*. Oxford: Clarendon Press, 1996.
Burton, Simon J. G. "Bartłomiej Keckermann o trynitarnej naturze rozumu: Źródła scholastyczne i ramistyczne" [Bartholomäus Keckermann on the Trinitarian Shape of Reason: Scholastic and Ramist Paradigms], translated by Michał Choptiany. In *Antytrynitaryzm w Pierwszej Rzeczypospolitej w kontekście europejskim: Źródła-rozwój–oddziaływanie* [Anti-Trinitarianism in the Polish-Lithuanian Republic

in a European Context], edited by Michał Choptiany and Piotr Wilczek, 99–119. Warsaw: Wydawnictwa Uniwersytetu Warszawskiego, 2017.
Burton, Simon J. G. "Between Aristotle and Augustine: Peter Martyr Vermigli and the Development of Protestant Ethics". *Studies in Medieval and Renaissance History* 11 (2014): 225–60.
Burton, Simon J. G. "Contested Legacies of the Late Middle Ages: Reason, Mystery and Participation in Jan Amos Comenius and Richard Baxter". *Acta Comeniana* 30 (2016): 119–49.
Burton, Simon J. G. "From Minority Discourse to Universal Method: Polish Chapters in the Evolution of Ramism". In *Protestant Majorities and Minorities*, edited by Burton, Choptiany, and Wilczek, 61–90.
Burton, Simon J. G. *The Hallowing of Logic: The Trinitarian Method of Richard Baxter's Methodus Theologiae*. Leiden: Brill, 2012.
Burton, Simon J. G. "Jan Amos Comenius's Trinitarian and Conciliar Vision of a United Europe: Christ as the Universal 'Centre of Security' ". *Reformation and Renaissance Review* 19.2 (2017): 104–21.
Burton, Simon J. G. "Pansophic Mirrors of the Soul: Comenius, Pinder and the Transformation of Cusan Optics". *Acta Comeniana* 34 (2020): 9–49.
Burton, Simon J. G. "Peter Martyr Vermigli on Grace and Free Choice: Thomist and Augustinian Perspectives". *Reformation and Renaissance Review* 15.1 (2013): 37–52.
Burton, Simon J. G. "Reforging the Great Chain of Being: Ramism Reconsidered". In *Faith Working Through Love: The Theology of William Perkins*, edited by Joel R. Beeke, Matthew N. Payne, and J. Stephen Yuille, 205–27. Grand Rapids, MI: Reformation Heritage Books, 2022.
Burton, Simon J. G. "Samuel Rutherford's Euthyphro Dilemma: A Reformed Perspective on the Scholastic Natural Law Tradition". In *Reformed Orthodoxy in Scotland*, edited by Denlinger, 123–40.
Burton, Simon J. G. "'Squaring the Circle': Cusan Metaphysics and the Pansophic Vision of Jan Amos Comenius". In *Nicholas of Cusa and the Making of the Early Modern World*, edited by Burton, Hollmann, and Parker, 417–49.
Burton, Simon J. G., Michał Choptiany, and Piotr Wilczek, eds. *Protestant Majorities and Minorities in Early Modern Europe: Confessional Boundaries and Contested Identities*. Göttingen: Vandenhoeck & Ruprecht, 2019.
Burton, Simon J. G., Joshua Hollmann, and Eric M. Parker, eds. *Nicholas of Cusa and the Making of the Early Modern World*. Leiden: Brill, 2019.
Bychkov, Oleg. "What Does Beauty Have to Do with the Trinity? From Augustine to Duns Scotus". *Franciscan Studies* 66.1 (2008): 197–212.
Byrne, James Steven. "A Humanist History of Mathematics? Regiomontanus's Paduan Oration in Context". *Journal of the History of Ideas* 67.1 (2006): 41–61.
Cahn, Walter. "Architecture and Exegesis: Richard of St.-Victor's Ezekiel Commentary and Its Illustrations". *Art Bulletin* 76.1 (1994): 53–68.
Camporeale, Salvatore I. *Christianity, Latinity and Culture: Two Studies on Lorenzo Valla*. Edited and translated by Christopher S. Celenza and Patrick Baker. Leiden: Brill, 2013.
Camporeale, Salvatore I. "Lorenzo Valla's *Oratio* on the Pseudo-Donation of Constantine: Dissent and Innovation in Early Renaissance Humanism". *Journal of the History of Ideas* 57.1 (1996): 9–26.
Campos, Heber Carlos de, Jr. "Johannes Piscator's (1546–1625) Interpretation of Calvin's *Institutes*". In *Church and School*, edited by Ballor, Sytsma, and Zuidema, 271–82.

Čapková, Dagmar. "Comenius and His Ideals: Escape from the Labyrinth". In *Samuel Hartlib and Universal Reformation*, edited by Greengrass, Leslie, and Raylor, 75–92.
Čapková, Dagmar. "The Comenian Group in England and Comenius' Idea of Universal Reform". *Acta Comeniana* 25 (1969): 25–34.
Casarella, Peter. *Word as Bread: Language and Theology in Nicholas of Cusa*. Münster: Aschendorff, 2017.
Červenka, Jaromír. *Die Naturphilosophie des Johann Amos Comenius*. Prague: Academia, 1970.
Cesalli, Laurent. "Intentionality and Truth-Making: Augustine's Influence on Burley and Wyclif's Propositional Semantics". *Vivarium* 45 (2007): 283–97.
Cesalli, Laurent. "Le 'pan-propositionnalisme' de Jean Wyclif". *Vivarium* 43.1 (2005): 124–55.
Charlton, Donald Geoffrey. *France: A Companion to French Studies*. London: Methuen, 1983.
Chenu, Marie-Dominique. *Aquinas and His Role in Theology*. Collegeville, MN: Liturgical Press, 2002.
Chenu, Marie-Dominique. *Nature, Man and Society in the Twelfth Century: Essays on New Theological Perspectives in the Latin West*. Toronto: University of Toronto Press, 1997.
Chernyakov, Alexei. *The Ontology of Time: Being and Time in the Philosophies of Aristotle, Husserl and Heidegger*. Dordrecht: Springer, 2002.
Christianson, Gerald, Thomas M. Izbicki, and Christopher M. Bellitto, eds. *The Church, The Councils and Reform: The Legacy of the Fifteenth Century*. Washington, DC: Catholic University of America Press, 2008.
Cifoletti, Giovanna. "From Valla to Viète: The Rhetorical Reform of Logic and Its Use in Early Modern Algebra". *Early Science and Medicine* 11.4 (2006): 390–423.
Čížek, Jan. "Comenius' Pansophia in the Context of Renaissance Neo-Platonism". In *Platonism and Its Legacy: Selected Papers from the Fifteenth Annual Conference of the International Society for Neoplatonic Studies 2017 Olomouc*, edited by John F. Finamore and Tomáš Nejeschleba, 357–68. Lydney: The Prometheus Trust, 2019.
Čížek, Jan. *The Conception of Man in the Works of John Amos Comenius*. Frankfurt am Main: Peter Lang, 2016.
Čížek, Jan. "From Pansophia to Panorthosia: The Evolution of Comenius' Pansophic Conception". *Erudition and the Republic of Letters* 4.2 (2019): 199–227.
Čížek, Jan. "Jan Amos Comenius and Francis Bacon: Two Early Modern Paths to the Restoration of Knowledge". *Acta Comeniana* 31 (2017): 9–22.
Čížek, Jan. "Patricius—Alstedius—Comenius. A Few Remarks on Patricius' Reception in Early Modern Central Europe". In *Francesco Patrizi*, edited by Blum and Nejeschleba, 372–84.
Čížek, Jan. "The 'Physica Mosaica' of Johann Heinrich Alsted". *Teorie Vědy / Theory of Science* 42.1 (2020): 117–39.
Clark, R. Scott. "The Authority of Reason in the Later Reformation: Scholasticism in Caspar Olevian and Antoine de la Faye". In *Protestant Scholasticism: Essays in Reassessment*, edited by Trueman and Clark, 111–26.
Clark, R. Scott. *Caspar Olevian and the Substance of the Covenant: The Double Benefit of Christ*. Grand Rapids, MI: Reformation Heritage Books, 2005.
Cleveland, Christopher. *Thomism in John Owen*. Aldershot: Ashgate, 2013.
Cogan, Marc. "Rodolphus Agricola and the Semantic Revolutions of the History of Invention". *Rhetorica* 2.2 (1984): 163–94.
Collinson, Patrick. "Chaderton, Laurence (1536?–1640)". *ODNB*.

Conti, Alessandro D. "Categories and Universals in the Later Middle Ages". In *Medieval Commentaries on Aristotle's Categories*, edited by Lloyd A. Newton, 369–409. Leiden: Brill, 2008.

Conti, Alessandro D. "Wyclif's Logic and Metaphysics". In *A Companion to John Wyclif: Late Medieval Theologian*, edited by Ian Christopher Levy, 67–125. Leiden: Brill, 2006.

Conybeare, Catherine. "Augustine's Rhetoric in Theory and Practice". In *The Oxford Handbook of Rhetorical Studies*, edited by Michael J. MacDonald, 301–11. Oxford: Oxford University Press, 2017.

Coolman, Boyd Taylor. *The Theology of Hugh of St Victor: An Interpretation*. Cambridge: Cambridge University Press, 2013.

Copleston, Frederick C. *A History of Philosophy: Volume III: Ockham to Suárez*. Mahwah, NJ: Paulist Press, 1953.

Costello, William. *The Scholastic Curriculum at Early Seventeenth-Century Cambridge*. Cambridge, MA: Harvard University Press, 1954.

Counet, Jean-Michel. "Mathematics and the Divine in Nicholas of Cusa". In *Mathematics and the Divine: A Historical Study*, edited by Bergmans and Keutsier, 273–90.

Counet, Jean-Michel. *Mathématiques et dialectique chez Nicolas de Cuse*. Paris: Vrin, 2000.

Courtenay, William J. "Nominalism and Late Medieval Religion". In *Covenant and Causality in Medieval Thought: Studies in Philosophy, Theology and Economic Practice*, edited by William J. Courtenay, 26–59. London: Variorum Reprints, 1984.

Cousins, Ewert H. "The Coincidence of Opposites in the Christology of Saint Bonaventure". *Franciscan Studies* 28 (1968): 27–45.

Cross, Richard. *Christology and Metaphysics in the Seventeenth Century*. Oxford: Oxford University Press, 2022.

Cross, Richard. *Communicatio Idiomatum: Reformation Christological Debates*. Oxford: Oxford University Press, 2019.

Cross, Richard. *Duns Scotus*. Oxford: Oxford University Press, 1999.

Cross, Richard. "Duns Scotus on Divine Substance and the Trinity". *Medieval Philosophy and Theology* 11.2 (2003): 181–201.

Cross, Richard. *Duns Scotus on God*. Aldershot: Ashgate, 2005.

Cross, Richard. "Where Angels Fear to Tread: Duns Scotus and Radical Orthodoxy". *Antonianum* 76 (2001): 7–41.

Crouse, Robert. "*Paucis Mutatis Verbis*: St Augustine's Platonism". In *Augustine and His Critics: Essays in Honour of Gerald Bonner*, edited by Robert Dorado and George Lawless, 37–50. London: Taylor and Francis Library, 2005.

Cullen, Christopher M. *Bonaventure*. New York: Oxford University Press, 2006.

Cuno. "Piscator, Johann". *Allgemeine Deutsche Biographie* 26 (1888): 180–81. https://www.deutsche-biographie.de/.

Daniel, Dane T. "Paracelsus' *Astronomia Magna* (1537/38): Bible-Based Science and the Religious Roots of the Scientific Revolution". PhD Dissertation, Indiana University, 2003.

Daniel, Stephen. *George Berkeley and Early Modern Philosophy*. Oxford: Oxford University Press, 2021.

Dauphinais, Michael, Barry David, and Matthew Levering, eds. *Aquinas the Augustinian*. Washington, DC: Catholic University of America Press, 2007.

Davison, Andrew. *Participation in God: A Study in Christian Doctrine and Metaphysics*. Cambridge: Cambridge University Press, 2019.

Deal, Max Eugene. "The Meaning and Method of Systematic Theology in Amandus Polanus". PhD Dissertation, University of Edinburgh, 1980.
Dear, Peter. "Reason and Common Culture in Early Modern Natural Philosophy: Variations on an Epistemic Theme". In *Conflicting Values of Inquiry: Ideologies of Epistemology in Early Modern Europe*, edited by Tamás Demeter, Kathryn Murphy, and Claus Zittel, 10–38. Leiden: Brill, 2015.
Decaluwe, Michiel, Thomas M. Izbicki, and Gerald Christianson, eds. *A Companion to the Council of Basel*. Leiden: Brill, 2017.
DeCook, Travis. "Francis Bacon's 'Jewish Dreams': The Specter of the Millennium in New Atlantis". *Studies in Philology* 110.1 (2013): 115–31.
Delio, Ilia. "Theology, Metaphysics and the Centrality of Christ". *Theological Studies* 68.2 (2007): 254–73.
Denlinger, Aaron C. *Omnes in Adam ex pacto Dei: Ambrogio Catarino's Doctrine of Covenantal Solidarity and Its Influence on Post-Reformation Reformed Theologians*. Göttingen: Vandenhoeck & Ruprecht, 2011.
Denlinger, Aaron C., ed. *Reformed Orthodoxy in Scotland: Essays on Scottish Theology, 1560–1775*. London: Bloomsbury, 2016.
DeVun, Leah. *Prophecy, Alchemy, and the End of Time: John Rupescissa in the Late Middle Ages*. New York: Columbia University Press, 2009.
Dickson, Donald R. "Johann Valentin Andreae's Utopian Brotherhoods". *Renaissance Quarterly* 49.4 (1996): 760–802.
Dickson, Donald R. *The Tessera of Antilia: Utopian Brotherhoods and Secret Societies in the Early Seventeenth Century*. Leiden: Brill, 1998.
Dod, Bernard G. "*Aristoteles Latinus*". In *The Cambridge History of Later Medieval Philosophy*, edited by Kretzmann, Kenny, Pinborg, and Stump, 43–79.
Dominiak, Paul Anthony. *Richard Hooker: The Architecture of Participation*. London: T&T Clark, 2021.
Dominik, William J., and Jon C. R. Hall, eds. *A Companion to Roman Rhetoric*. Oxford: Blackwell, 2007.
Donnelly, John Patrick. "Calvinist Thomism". *Viator* 7 (1976): 441–55.
Doolan, Gregory. *Aquinas on the Divine Ideas as Exemplar Causes*. Washington, DC: Catholic University of America Press, 2008.
Dumont, Stephen. "Duns Scotus's Parisian Question on the Formal Distinction". *Vivarium* 43.1 (2005): 7–62.
Dupré, Louis K. *Religion and the Rise of Modern Culture*. Notre Dame, IN: University of Notre Dame Press, 2008.
Edwards, William F. "The Logic of Jacopo Zabarella (1533–1589)". PhD Dissertation, Columbia University, 1960.
Eire, Carlos. *War against the Idols: The Reformation of Worship from Erasmus to Calvin*. Cambridge: Cambridge University Press, 1986.
Elders, Leo. *The Metaphysics of Being of St Thomas Aquinas in a Historical Perspective*. Leiden: Brill, 1993.
Ellis, Brannon. "The Eternal Decree in the Incarnate Son: Robert Rollock on the Relationship between Christ and Election". In *Reformed Orthodoxy in Scotland*, edited by Denlinger, 45–65.
Elsmann, Thomas. "The Influence of Ramism on the Academies of Bremen and Danzig: A Comparison". In *The Influence of Petrus Ramus*, edited by Feingold, Freedman, and Rother, 54–67.

Emery, Gilles, OP. *The Trinitarian Theology of St Thomas Aquinas*. Translated by Francesca Aran Murphy. Oxford: Oxford University Press, 2010.

Emery, Kent, Jr. "Denys the Carthusian and the Invention of Preaching Materials". In Emery, *Monastic, Scholastic and Mystical Theologies*, 377–409.

Emery, Kent, Jr. "Introduction". In Emery, *Renaissance Dialectic and Renaissance Piety*, 11–85.

Emery, Kent, Jr. *Monastic, Scholastic and Mystical Theologies from the Later Middle Ages*. Aldershot: Ashgate Variorum, 1996.

Emery, Kent, Jr. *Renaissance Dialectic and Renaissance Piety: Benet of Canfield's Rule of Perfection*. Binghamton, NY: Medieval and Renaissance Texts and Studies, 1987.

Emery, Kent, Jr. "Twofold Wisdom and Contemplation in Denys of Ryckel (Dionysius Cartusiensis, 1402–1471)". In Emery, *Monastic, Scholastic and Mystical Theologies*, 99–134.

English, Edward D., ed. *Reading and Wisdom: The "De Doctrina Christiana" of Augustine in the Middle Ages*. Notre Dame, IN: University of Notre Dame Press, 1995.

Ernst, Germana. *Tommaso Campanella: The Book and the Body of Nature*. Translated by David L. Marshall. Dordrecht: Springer, 2010.

Evans, Gillian. *The Language and Logic of the Bible: The Road to Reformation*. Cambridge: Cambridge University Press, 1985.

Evener, Vincent. *Enemies of the Cross: Suffering, Truth and Mysticism in the Early Reformation*. Oxford: Oxford University Press, 2021.

Even-Ezra, Ayelet. *Lines of Thought: Branching Diagrams and the Medieval Mind*. Chicago, IL: University of Chicago Press, 2021.

Facca, Danilo. "Bartholomäus Keckermann (1572–1609): The Theology of the Reformation and the Logic". *Odrodzenie i Reformacja w Polsce* (2013): 184–204.

Farinella, Alessandro G., and Carole Preston. "Giordano Bruno, Neoplatonism and the Wheel of Memory in '*De Umbris Idearum*'". *Renaissance Quarterly* 55.2 (2002): 596–624.

Farmer, S. A. "Introductory Monograph", in Pico, *Syncretism in the West*, 1–182.

Faye, Emmanuel. "Nicolas de Cues et Charles de Bovelles dans le manuscrit '*Exigua pluvia*' de Beatus Rhenanus". *Archives d'Histoire Doctrinale et Littéraire du Moyen Âge* 65 (1998): 415–50.

Feingold, Mordechai. "English Ramism: A Reinterpretation". In *The Influence of Petrus Ramus*, edited by Feingold, Freedman, and Rother, 127–76.

Feingold, Mordechai. "The Humanities". In *The History of the University of Oxford: Volume IV, Seventeenth-Century Oxford*, edited by Nicholas Tyacke, 211–357. Oxford: Oxford University Press, 1997.

Feingold, Mordechai, Joseph S. Freedman, and Wolfgang Rother, eds. *The Influence of Petrus Ramus: Studies in Sixteenth and Seventeenth Century Philosophy and Sciences*. Basel: Schwabe & Co., 2001.

Fesko, John V. *The Covenant of Redemption: Origins, Development, and Reception*. Göttingen: Vandenhoeck & Ruprecht, 2016.

Fesko, John V. *The Covenant of Works: The Origins, Development, and Reception of the Doctrine*. New York: Oxford University Press, 2020.

Fisk, Philip. *Jonathan Edwards' Turn from the Classic-Reformed Tradition of Freedom of the Will*. Göttingen: Vandenhoeck & Ruprecht, 2016.

Fletcher, Harris Francis. *The Intellectual Development of John Milton: Volume II, The Cambridge University Period, 1625–32*. Urbana, IL: University of Illinois Press, 1981.

Floss, Pavel. "Cusanus und Comenius". *Mitteilungen und Forschungsbeiträge der Cusanus-Gesellschaft* 10 (1973): 172–90.
Floss, Pavel. *The Philosophy of Nicholas of Cusa: An Introduction into His Thinking.* Basel: Schwabe Verlag, 2020.
Frank, Günter. "Melanchthon and the Tradition of Neoplatonism". In *Religious Confessions and the Sciences in the Sixteenth Century*, edited by Jürgen Helm and Annette Winkelmann, 3–18. Leiden: Brill, 2001.
Franklin-Brown, Mary. "Ramon Llull as Encyclopedist". In *A Companion to Ramon Llull and Lullism*, edited by Austin and Johnston, 364–96.
Franklin-Brown, Mary. *Reading the World: Encyclopedic Writing in Scholasticism.* Chicago, IL: University of Chicago Press, 2012.
Freedman, Joseph S. "The Career and Writings of Bartholomew Keckermann (d. 1609)". *Proceedings of the American Philosophical Society* 141.3 (1997): 305–64.
Freedman, Joseph S. "The Life, Significance and Philosophy of Clemens Timpler, 1563/4–1624". PhD Dissertation, University of Wisconsin-Madison, 1982.
Freedman, Joseph S. "Melanchthon's Opinion of Ramus and the Utilization of Their Writings in Central Europe". In *The Influence of Petrus Ramus*, edited by Feingold, Freedman, and Rother, 68–91.
Freedman, Joseph S. *Philosophy and the Arts in Central Europe, 1500–1700: Teachings and Texts at Schools and Universities.* Abingdon: Routledge, 2018.
Freedman, Joseph S. "Ramus and the Use of Ramus at Heidelberg within the Context of Schools and Universities in Central Europe, 1572–1622". In *Späthumanismus und reformierte Konfession*, edited by Strohm, Freedman, and Selderhuis, 93–111.
Freedman, Joseph S. "Timpler, Clemens". In *Encyclopedia of Renaissance Philosophy*, edited by Marco Sgarbi. Cham: Springer International, 2015. Electronic resource. https://doi.org/10.1007/978-3-319-02848-4_279-1.
Freja, Valeria de. "Joachim the Abbot: Monastic Reform and the Foundation of the Florensian Order". In *A Companion to Joachim of Fiore*, edited by Matthias Riedl, 109–43. Leiden: Brill, 2018.
French, Roger, and Andrew Cunningham. *Before Science: The Invention of the Friars' Natural Philosophy.* Abingdon: Routledge, 2016.
Freudenthal, Jakub. "Goclenius, Rudolf, 1547–1628". *Allgemeine Deutsche Biographie* 9 (1879): 308–12. https://www.deutsche-biographie.de/.
Friedman, Russell L. *Intellectual Traditions at the Medieval University: The Use of Philosophical Psychology in Trinitarian Theology among the Franciscans and Dominicans, 1250–1350.* 2 vols. Leiden: Brill, 2013.
Friedman, Russell L. *Medieval Trinitarian Thought from Aquinas to Ockham.* Cambridge: Cambridge University Press, 2010.
Friedrich, Karin. *The Other Prussia: Royal Prussia, Poland and Liberty, 1569–1772.* Cambridge: Cambridge University Press, 2000.
Gantenbein, Urs Leo. "The New Adam: Jacob Böhme and the Theology of Paracelsus (1493/94–1541)". In *Jacob Böhme and His World*, edited by Andersson, Martin, Penman, and Weeks, 166–96.
Gantenbein, Urs Leo. "The Virgin Mary and the Universal Reformation of Paracelsus". *Daphnis* 48 (2020): 4–37.
Garin, Eugenio. *History of Italian Philosophy: Vol. 1.* Translated by Giorgio Pinton. New York: Rodolphi, 2008.

Gatti, Hilary. *Giordano Bruno and Renaissance Science*. Ithaca, NY: Cornell University Press, 1999.

Gelber, Hester Goodenough. "Logic and the Trinity: A Clash of Values in Scholastic Thought, 1300–1335". PhD Dissertation, University of Wisconsin, 1974.

Gellera, Giovanni. "Natural Philosophy in the Graduation Theses of the Scottish Universities in the First Half of the Seventeenth Century". PhD Dissertation, University of Glasgow, 2012.

Gellera, Giovanni. "Reformed Scholastic Philosophy in the Seventeenth-Century Scottish Universities". In *Scottish Philosophy in the Seventeenth Century*, edited by Alexander Broadie, 94–110. Oxford: Oxford University Press, 2020.

Gellera, Giovanni. "Univocity of Being, the *Cogito* and Idealism in Johannes Clauberg (1622–1655). In *Cognitive Issues in the Long Scotist Tradition*, edited by Daniel Heider and Claus A. Andersen, 417–46. Basel: Schwabe-Verlag, 2023.

Genest, Jean-François. *Prédetermination et liberté créée à Oxford au XIVe siècle: Buckingham contre Bradwardine*. Paris: Vrin, 1992.

Ghosh, Kantik. "Logic and Lollardy". *Medium Aevum* 76 (2007): 251–67.

Gibbs, Lee W. "William Ames' Technometry". *Journal of the History of Ideas* 33.4 (1972): 615–24.

Giglioni, Guido. "Philosophy". In *The Oxford Handbook of Neo-Latin*, edited by Stefan Tilg and Sarah Knight, 249–62. Oxford: Oxford University Press, 2015.

Giglioni, Guido. "The Darkness of Matter and the Light of Nature: Notions of Matter in Bacon and Comenius and Their Theological Implications". *Acta Comeniana* 17 (2003): 9–31.

Gilbert, Neal W. *Renaissance Concepts of Method*. New York: Columbia University Press, 1960.

Gillespie, Michael Allen. *The Theological Origins of Modernity*. Chicago, IL: University of Chicago Press, 2008.

Gilson, Etienne. *The Philosophy of St Bonaventure*. London: Sheed & Ward, 1938.

Gordon, Bruce. *Calvin*. New Haven, CT: Yale University Press, 2011.

Goswami, Niranjan. "Refiguring Donne and Spenser: Aspects of Ramist Rhetoric". In *Spenser and Donne: Thinking Poets*, edited by Yulia Ryzhik, Chapter 3. Manchester: Manchester University Press, 2021.

Goudriaan, Aza. *Reformed Orthodoxy and Philosophy, 1625–1750: Gisbertus Voetius, Petrus van Mastricht, and Anthonius Driessen*. Leiden: Brill, 2006.

Goudriaan, Aza, and F. A. van Lieburg, eds. *Revisiting the Synod of Dordt (1618–1619)*. Leiden: Brill, 2011.

Goulding, Robert. *Defending Hypatia: Ramus, Savile, and the Renaissance Rediscovery of Mathematical History*. Dordrecht: Springer, 2010.

Goulding, Robert. "Pythagoras in Paris: Petrus Ramus Imagines the Pre-History of Mathematics". *Configurations* 17 (2009): 51–86.

Grabill, Stephen J. *Rediscovering the Natural Law in Reformed Theological Ethics*. Grand Rapids, MI: William B. Eerdmans, 2006.

Grafton, Anthony, and Lisa Jardine. *From Humanism to the Humanities: Education and the Liberal Arts in Fifteenth- and Sixteenth-Century Europe*. London: Duckworth, 1986.

Grajewksi, Maurice J. *The Formal Distinction of Duns Scotus*. Washington, DC: Catholic University of America Press, 1944.

Greengrass, Mark, Michael Leslie, and Timothy Raylor, eds. *Samuel Hartlib and Universal Reformation: Studies in Intellectual Communication*. Cambridge: Cambridge University Press, 1994.

Gregory, Brad S. *The Unintended Reformation: How a Religious Revolution Secularized Society*. Cambridge, MA: Harvard University Press, 2012.

Guggisberg, Hans Rudolph. *Basel in the Sixteenth Century: Aspects of the City Republic*. Eugene, OR: Wipf & Stock, 2010.

Hall, Roland. "Richardson, Alexander (d. in or before 1621)". *ODNB*.

Hamann, Florian. *Das Siegel der Ewigheit: Universalwissenschaft und Konziliarismus bei Heymericus de Campo*. Münster: Aschendorff Verlag, 2006.

Han, Byung Soo. "The Academization of Reformation Teaching in Johann Heinrich Alsted". In *Church and School*, edited by Ballor, Sytsma, and Zuidema, 283-94.

Han, Byung Soo. *Symphonia Catholica: The Merger of Patristic and Contemporary Sources in the Theological Method of Amandus Polanus (1561-1610)*. Göttingen: Vandenhoeck & Ruprecht, 2015.

Hankins, James. *Plato in the Italian Renaissance*. 2 vols. Leiden: Brill, 1991.

Hardarson, Gunnar. "The Method of Exposition in Brynjolf Sveinsson's 'Commentary' (1640) on the *Dialecticae* of Petrus Ramus". In *Ramus, Pedagogy and the Liberal Arts*, edited by Reid and Wilson, 189-203.

Harries, Karsten. *Infinity and Perspective*. Cambridge, MA: MIT Press, 2001.

Harriet, Francisco Bastitta. "Giovanni Pico, a Reader of Cusanus? The *Imago Mundi* in *De Conjecturis* and *Heptaplus*". Conference paper given at Renaissance Society of America Virtual 2021.

Harrison, Carol. *Rethinking Augustine's Early Theology: An Argument for Continuity*. Oxford: Oxford University Press, 2005.

Harrison, Peter. *The Fall of Man and the Foundations of Science*. Cambridge: Cambridge University Press, 2007.

Havelka, Tomáš. "The Metaphorical Layer in Comenius' *The Labyrinth of the World and the Paradise of the Heart*". Conference paper given at "Between the Labyrinth and the Way of Light: Early Modern Metaphors of Knowledge and Johannes Amos Comenius", Institute of Philosophy, Czech Academy of Sciences, Prague, September 2021.

Havely, Nick R. *Dante and the Franciscans: Poverty and Papacy in the Commedia*. Cambridge: Cambridge University Press, 2009.

Headley, John M. *Tommaso Campanella and the Transformation of the World*. Princeton, NJ: Princeton University Press, 2019.

Heller, Henry. "The Evangelicalism of Lefèvre d'Étaples: 1525". *Studies in the Renaissance* 19 (1972): 42-77.

Henreckson, David P. *The Immortal Commonwealth: Covenant, Community, and Political Resistance in Early Reformed Thought*. Cambridge: Cambridge University Press, 2019.

Herold, Vilém. "Platonic Ideas and 'Hussite Philosophy'". *Bohemian Reformation and Religious Practice* 1 (1994): 13-17.

Heßbrüggen-Walter, Stefan. "Thinking about Persons: *Loci Personarum* in Humanist Dialectic between Agricola and Keckermann". *History and Philosophy of Logic* 38.1 (2017): 1-23.

Hill, Preston. "Feeling Forsaken: Christ's Descent into Hell in the Theology of John Calvin". PhD Dissertation, University of St Andrews, 2021.

Hillgarth, Jocelyn N. *Ramon Lull and Lullism in Fourteenth-Century France*. Oxford: Clarendon Press, 1971.

Hoenen, Maarten. *Marsilius of Inghen: Divine Knowledge in Late Medieval Thought*. Leiden: Brill, 1993.

Hoenen, Maarten. "Scotus and the Scotist School: The Tradition of Scotist Thought in the Medieval and Early Modern Period". In *John Duns Scotus (1265/6–1308): Renewal of Philosophy*, edited by Bos, 197–210.

Hollmann, Joshua. "Nicholas of Cusa and Martin Luther on Christ and the Coincidence of Opposites". In *Nicholas of Cusa and the Making of the Early Modern World*, edited by Burton, Hollmann, and Parker, 153–72.

Hollmann, Joshua. *The Religious Concordance: Nicholas of Cusa and Christian-Muslim Dialogue*. Leiden: Brill, 2017.

Honnefelder, Ludger. "Metaphysics as a Discipline: From the 'Transcendental Philosophy of the Ancients' to Kant's Notion of Transcendental Philosophy". In *The Medieval Heritage in Early Modern Metaphysics and Modal Theory*, edited by Lauge O. Nielsen, Russell L. Friedman, and Richard Sorabji, 53–74. Dordrecht: Springer, 2003.

Honnefelder, Ludger. *Scientia transcendens: Die formale Bestimmung der Seiendheit und Realität in der Metaphysik des Mittelalters und der Neuzeit (Duns Scotus, Suárez, Wolff, Kant, Peirce)*. Hamburg: Felix Meiner, 1990.

Horan, Daniel. *Postmodernity and Univocity: A Critical Account of Radical Orthodoxy and John Duns Scotus*. Minneapolis, MN: Fortress Press, 2014.

Hotson, Howard. "*Arbor Sanguinis, Arbor Disciplinarum*: The Intellectual Genealogy of Johann Heinrich Alsted—Part I. Alsted's Intellectual Inheritance". *Acta Comeniana* 25 (2011): 47–91.

Hotson, Howard. *Commonplace Learning: Ramism and Its German Ramifications, 1543–1630*. Oxford: Oxford University Press, 2007.

Hotson, Howard. "'A Generall Reformation of Common Learning' and Its Reception in the English Speaking World, 1560–1642". *Proceedings of the British Academy* 164 (2010): 193–228.

Hotson, Howard. "The Instauration of the Image of God in Man: Humanist Anthropology, Encyclopaedic Pedagogy, Baconianism and Universal Reform". In *The Practice of Reform in Health, Medicine and Science, 1500–2000: Essays for Charles Webster*, edited by Margaret Pelling and Scott Mandelbrote, 1–21. Aldershot: Ashgate, 2005.

Hotson, Howard. "Irenicism and Dogmatics in the Confessional Age: Pareus and Comenius in Heidelberg, 1614". *Journal of Ecclesiastical History* 46.3 (1995): 432–56.

Hotson, Howard. *Johann Heinrich Alsted, 1588–1638*. Oxford: Oxford University Press, 2000.

Hotson, Howard. "Johann Heinrich Alsted's Relations with Silesia, Bohemia and Moravia: Patronage, Piety and Pansophia". *Acta Comeniana* 14 (2000): 13–36.

Hotson, Howard. "Outsiders, Dissenters and Competing Visions of Reform". In *The Oxford Handbook of the Protestant Reformations*, edited by Ulinka Rublack, 301–28. Oxford: Oxford University Press, 2016.

Hotson, Howard. *Paradise Postponed: Johann Heinrich Alsted and the Birth of Calvinist Millenarianism*. Dordrecht: Springer, 2000.

Hotson, Howard. "The Ramist Roots of Comenian Pansophia". In *Ramus, Pedagogy and the Liberal Arts*, edited by Reid and Wilson, 227–52.

Hotson, Howard. *The Reformation of Common Learning: Post-Ramist Method and the Reception of the New Philosophy, 1618–c. 1670*. Oxford: Oxford University Press, 2020.

Howell, Wilbur Samuel. *Logic and Rhetoric in England, 1500–1700*. Princeton, NJ: Princeton University Press, 1956.

Hueglin, Thomas O. *Early Modern Concepts for a Late Modern World: Althusius on Community and Federalism*. Waterloo, Ontario: Wilfrid Laurier University Press, 1999.
Hughes, Philip Edgcumbe. *Lefèvre: Pioneer of Ecclesiastical Renewal in France*. Grand Rapids, MI: Eerdmans, 1984.
Ibish, Joan. "Emmanuel College: The Founding Generation, with a Biographical Register of Members of the College 1584–1604". PhD Dissertation, Harvard University, 1985.
Illg, Thomas. "Johann Arndt". In *Protestants and Mysticism in Reformation Europe*, edited by Ronald K. Rittgers and Vincent Evener, 309–27. Leiden: Brill, 2019.
Iribarren, Isabel. "Le Paradis retrouvé: L'utopie linguistique de Jean Gerson". *Revue de l'histoire des religions* 231.2 (2014): 223–51.
James, Frank A., III. *Peter Martyr Vermigli and Predestination: The Augustinian Inheritance of an Italian Reformer*. Oxford: Clarendon Press, 1998.
James, Frank A., III. "Peter Martyr Vermigli: At the Crossroads of Late Medieval Scholasticism, Christian Humanism and Resurgent Augustinianism". In *Protestant Scholasticism: Essays in Reassessment*, edited by Trueman and Clark, 62–78.
Janz, Denis R. *Luther and Late Medieval Thomism: A Study in Theological Anthropology*. Waterloo: Wilfred Laurier University Press, 1983.
Jardine, Lisa. "Gabriel Harvey: Exemplary Ramist and Pragmatic Humanist". *Revue des sciences philosophiques et théologiques* 70.1 (1986): 36–48.
Jardine, Lisa. "Humanism and the Sixteenth Century Cambridge Arts Course". *History of Education* 4.1 (1975): 16–31.
Jardine, Lisa. "The Place of Dialectic Teaching in Sixteenth-Century Cambridge". *Studies in the Renaissance* 21 (1974): 31–62.
Jensen, Kristian. *Rhetorical Philosophy and Philosophical Grammar: Julius Caesar Scaliger's Theory of Language*. Munich: Fink, 1990.
Jinkins, Michael. "Perkins, William (1558–1602)". *ODNB*.
Johnston, Mark D. *The Evangelical Rhetoric of Ramon Llull: Lay Learning and Piety in the Christian West around 1300*. New York: Oxford University Press, 1996.
Johnston, Mark D. "The Reception of the Lullian Art, 1450–1530". *Sixteenth Century Journal* 12.1 (1981): 31–48.
Johnston, Mark D. *The Spiritual Logic of Ramon Llull*. Oxford: Clarendon Press, 1987.
Kappes, Christian. "Foreword". In J. Isaac Goff, *Caritas in Primo: A Historical-Theological Study of Bonaventure's Quaestiones Disputatae de Mysterio SS. Trinitatis*, xvii–xxxiii. New Bedford, MA: Academy of the Immaculate, 2015.
Kärkkäinen, Pekka. "Philosophy among and in the Wake of the Reformers: Luther, Melanchthon, Zwingli, and Calvin". In *The Routledge Companion to Sixteenth Century Philosophy*, edited by Henrik Lagerlund and Benjamin Hill, 189–202. New York: Routledge, 2016.
Kearney, Hugh. *Scholars and Gentlemen: Universities and Society in Pre-Industrial Britain, 1500–1700*. London: Faber, 1970.
Kecskeméti, Gábor. "Hungarian and Transylvanian Ramism". In *The European Contexts of Ramism*, edited by Sarah Knight and Emma Annette Wilson, 285–329. Turnhout: Brepols, 2019.
Kecskeméti, Gábor. "The Reception of Ramist Rhetoric in Hungary and Transylvania: Possibilities and Achievements". In *Ramus, Pedagogy and the Liberal Arts*, edited by Reid and Wilson, 205–25.
Keenan, James. "The Casuistry of John Mair, Nominalist Professor of Paris". In *The Context of Casuistry*, edited by Keenan and Shannon, 85–102.

Keenan, James. "William Perkins (1558-1602) and the Birth of British Casuistry". In *The Context of Casuistry*, ed. Keenan and Shannon, 105-30.
Keenan, James, and Thomas Shannon, eds. *The Context of Casuistry*. Washington, DC: Georgetown University Press, 1995.
Keller, Vera. *Knowledge and the Public Interest, 1575-1725*. Cambridge: Cambridge University Press, 2015.
Kelley, Donald. *François Hotman: A Revolutionary's Ordeal*. Princeton, NJ: Princeton University Press, 1973.
Kelly, L. G. *The Mirror of Grammar: Theology, Philosophy and the Modistae*. Amsterdam: John Benjamins, 2002.
Kennedy, George. "The 'Rhetorica' of Guillaume Fichet (1471)". *Rhetorica* 5.4 (1987): 411-18.
Kent, Bonnie D. *Virtues of the Will: The Transformation of Ethics in the Late Thirteenth Century*. Washington, DC: Catholic University of America Press, 1995.
Kessler, Eckhard. "Psychology: The Intellective Soul". In *The Cambridge History of Renaissance Philosophy*, edited by Schmitt, Kessler, and Skinner, 485-534.
King, Peter. "Scotus on Metaphysics". In *The Cambridge Companion to Duns Scotus*, edited by Williams, 15-68.
Kirby, W. J. Torrance. *The Zurich Connection and Tudor Political Theology*. Leiden: Brill, 2007.
Klein, Jürgen, and Guido Giglioni. "Francis Bacon". *Stanford Encyclopedia of Philosophy*. https://plato.stanford.edu/entries/francis-bacon/.
Knudsen, Christian. "Intentions and Impositions". In *The Cambridge History of Later Medieval Philosophy*, edited by Kretzmann, Kenny, Pinborg, and Stump, 479-95.
Knuuttila, Simo. "Time and Creation in Augustine". In *The Cambridge Companion to Augustine*, edited by David Vincent Meconi SJ and Eleonore Stump, 81-97. Cambridge: Cambridge University Press, 2014.
Knuuttila, Simo. "Time and Modality in Scholasticism". In *Reforging the Great Chain of Being: Studies of the History of Modal Theories*, edited by Simo Knuuttila, 163-257. Dordrecht: Reidel, 1981.
Kobosh, Caleb. "Francis Bacon and Human Flourishing: Instauration, Induction and Christian Charity". MTh Dissertation, University of Edinburgh, 2019.
Kretzmann, Norman, Anthony Kenny, Jan Pinborg, and Eleonore Stump, eds. *The Cambridge History of Later Medieval Philosophy*. Cambridge: Cambridge University Press, 2008.
Kristeller, Paul Oskar. *Renaissance Thought and Its Sources*. New York: Columbia University Press, 1979.
Krop, Henri. "Philosophy and the Synod of Dordt: Aristotelianism, Humanism and the Case against Arminianism". In *Revisiting the Synod of Dordt (1618-1619)*, edited by Aza Goudriaan and Fred van Lieburg, 49-80. Leiden: Brill, 2011.
Kuchlbauer, Simon. *Johann Amos Comenius' antisozinianische Schriften: Entwurf eines integrativen Konzepts von Aufklärung*. Dresden: Thelem, 2011.
Kusukawa, Sachiko. *The Transformation of Natural Philosophy: The Case of Philip Melanchthon*. Cambridge: Cambridge University Press, 2009.
Ladner, Gerhart B. *The Idea of Reform: Its Impact on Christian Thought and Action in the Age of the Fathers*. Cambridge, MA: Harvard University Press, 2014.
Lahey, Stephen E. *Philosophy and Politics in the Thought of John Wyclif*. Cambridge: Cambridge University Press, 2003.

Lassnig, Ewald. "Dürers 'MELENCOLIA-I' und die Erkenntnistheorie bei Ulrich Pinder". *Wiener Jahrbuch für Kunstgeschichte* 57 (2008): 51–95.
Leader, Damian Riehl. *A History of the University of Cambridge: Volume 1, The University to 1546*. Cambridge: Cambridge University Press, 1988.
Leclerc, Ivor. *The Philosophy of Nature*. Washington, DC: Catholic University of America Press, 1986.
Lecq, Ria van der. "Modistae". In *Encyclopedia of Medieval Philosophy*, edited by Henrik Lagerlund. Dordrecht: Springer, 2010. Electronic resource. https://doi.org/10.1007/978-1-4020-9729-4_341.
Leedham-Green, Elizabeth. *Books in Cambridge Inventories: Book Lists from Vice-Chancellor's Court Probate Inventories in the Tudor and Stuart Periods*. Cambridge: Cambridge University Press, 1996.
Lehner, Ulrich L. "The Trinity in the Early Modern Era (*c.*1550–1770)". In *The Oxford Handbook of the Trinity*, edited by Gilles Emery and Matthew Levering, 240–53. Oxford: Oxford University Press, 2012.
Leinkauf, Thomas. *Einheit, Natur, Geist: Beiträge zu metaphysischen Grundproblemen in Denken von Gottfried Wilhelm von Leibniz*. Berlin: Trafo, 2012.
Leinkauf, Thomas. *Mundus Combinatus: Studien zur Struktur der barocken Universalwissenschaft am Beispiel Athanasius Kirchers SJ (1602–1680)*. Berlin: Akademie Verlag, 1993.
Leinsle, Ulrich G. *Introduction to Scholastic Theology*. Translated by Michael G. Miller. Washington, DC: Catholic University of America Press, 2010.
Leslie, Andrew. *The Light of Grace: John Owen on the Authority of Scripture and Christian Faith*. Göttingen: Vandenhoeck & Ruprecht, 2015.
Letham, Robert. "Amandus Polanus: A Neglected Theologian?" *Sixteenth Century Journal* 21.3 (1990): 463–76.
Levi, Anthony. "Ficino, Augustine and the Pagans". In *Marsilio Ficino: His Theology, His Philosophy, His Legacy*, edited by Michael J. B. Allen, Martin Davies, and Valery Rees, 99–113. Leiden: Brill, 2002.
Levitin, Dmitri. *Ancient Wisdom in the Age of the New Science: Histories of Philosophy in England, c. 1640–1700*. Cambridge: Cambridge University Press, 2015.
Levitin, Dmitri. "Introduction: Confessionalisation and Erudition in Early Modern Europe: A Comparative Overview of a Neglected Episode in the History of the Humanities". In *Confessionalisation and Erudition in Early Modern Europe: An Episode in the History of the Humanities*, edited by Nicholas Hardy and Dmitri Levitin, 1–94. Oxford: Oxford University Press, 2019.
Levy, Ian Christopher. *John Wyclif: Scriptural Logic, Real Presence, and the Parameters of Orthodoxy*. Milwaukee, WI: Marquette University Press, 2003.
Lewis, John. "Rabelais and the Reception of the 'Art' of Ramón Lull in Early Sixteenth-Century France". *Renaissance Studies* 24.2 (2010): 260–80.
Libera, Alain de. *La querelle des universaux: De Platon à la fin du Moyen Age*. Paris: Points, 2014.
Lindberg, Carter. *The European Reformations*. Oxford: Wiley-Blackwell, 2010.
Lobstein, Paul. *Petrus Ramus als Theologe: Ein Beitrag zur Geschichte der protestantischen Theologie*. Strasbourg, 1878.
Loemker, Leroy E. "Leibniz and the Herborn Encyclopedists". *Journal of the History of Ideas* 22.3 (1961): 323–38.

Loemker, Leroy E. *Struggle for Synthesis: The Seventeenth Century Background of Leibniz's Synthesis of Order and Freedom*. Cambridge, MA; Harvard University Press, 1972.
Lohr, Charles. "Mathematics and the Divine: Ramon Lull". In *Mathematics and the Divine: A Historical Study*, edited by Bergmans and Keutsier, 213–28.
Lohr, Charles. "Metaphysics". In *The Cambridge History of Renaissance Philosophy*, edited by Schmitt, Kessler, and Skinner, 535–638.
Lokaj, Rodney. "Petrarch vs. Gherardo: A Case of Sibling Rivalry inside and outside the Cloister". PhD Dissertation, University of Edinburgh, 2001.
Lovas, Borbála. "On the Margins of the Reformation: The 'Local' and the 'International' in György Enyedi's Manuscript Sermons and Printed Works". In *Protestant Majorities and Minorities*, edited by Burton, Choptiany, and Wilczek, 231–50.
Luis-Martínez, Zenón. "Ramist Dialectic, Poetic Examples, and the Uses of Pastoral in Abraham Fraunce's *The Shepherds' Logic*". *Parergon* 33.3 (2016): 69–95.
Machetta, Jorge M. "Die Präsenz Alberts des Großen im Denken des Nikolaus von Kues". In *Nikolaus von Kues in der Geschichte des Platonismus*, edited by Harald Schwaetzer and Henrieke Stahl, 135–66. Regensburg: Roderer, 2007.
Mack, Peter. "Agricola and the Early Versions of Ramus' Dialectic". In *Autour de Ramus: Texte, théorie, commentaire*, edited by Kees Meerhoff and Jean-Claude Moisan, 17–35. Québec: Nuit Blanche, 1997.
Mack, Peter. *A History of Renaissance Rhetoric 1380–1620*. Oxford: Oxford University Press, 2011.
Mack, Peter. *Renaissance Argument: Valla and Agricola in the Traditions of Rhetoric and Dialectic*. Leiden: Brill, 1993.
Maclean, Ian. *Learning and the Market Place: Essays in the History of the Early Modern Book*. Leiden: Brill, 2009.
Mahnke, Dietrich. *Unendliche Sphäre und Allmittelpunkt: Beiträge zur Genealogie der mathematischen Mystik*. Halle: S. Niemeyer, 1937.
Makkai, L. "The Hungarian Puritans and the English Revolution". *Acta Historica Academiae Scientiarum Hungaricae* 5.1/2 (1958): 13–45.
Malherbe, Michel. "Bacon's Method of Science". In *The Cambridge Companion to Bacon*, edited by Peltonen, 75–98.
Małłek, Janusz. "The Reformation in Poland and Prussia in the Sixteenth Century: Similarities and Differences". In Janusz Małłek, *Opera Selecta Vol. II: Poland and Prussia in the Baltic Area from the Sixteenth to the Eighteenth Century*, 179–90. Toruń: Wydawnictwo Naukowe Uniwersytetu Mikołaja Kopernika, 2013.
Manuel, Frank E., and Fritzie P. Manuel. *Utopian Thought in the Western World*. Cambridge, MA: Harvard Belknap Press, 2009.
Matus, Zachary. *Franciscans and the Elixir of Life: Religion and Science in the Later Middle Ages*. Philadelphia, PA: University of Pennsylvania Press, 2007.
Mayorga, Rosa Maria Perez-Teran. *From Realism to "Realicism": The Metaphysics of Charles Sanders Peirce*. Lanham, MD: Lexington Books, 2009.
Mazzotta, Giuseppe. "Dante's Franciscanism". In *Dante and the Franciscans*, edited by Santa Casciani, 171–98. Leiden: Brill, 2006.
McCanles, Michael. "The New Science and the Via Negativa: A Mystical Source for Baconian Empiricism". In *Francis Bacon and the Refiguring of Early Modern Thought: Essays to Commemorate The Advancement of Learning (1605–2005)*, edited by Julie Robin Solomon and Catherine Gimelli Martin, Chapter 3. London: Routledge, 2017.

McEvoy, James. *The Philosophy of Robert Grosseteste*. Oxford: Clarendon Press, 1986.
McKim, Donald. *Ramism in William Perkins' Theology*. New York: Peter Lang, 1987.
Meerhof, Kees. "Bartholomew Keckermann and the Anti-Ramist Tradition at Heidelberg". In *Späthumanismus und reformierte Konfession*, edited by Strohm, Freedman, and Selderhuis, 93–111.
Meerhoff, Kees. "Beauty and the Beast: Nature, Logic and Literature in Ramus". In *The Influence of Petrus Ramus*, edited by Feingold, Freedman, and Rother, 200–214.
Meier-Oeser, Stephan. *Die Präsenz des Vergessenen: Zur Rezeption der Philosophie des Nicolaus Cusanus vom 15. bis zum 18. Jahrhundert*. Münster: Aschendorff, 1989.
Meier-Oeser, Stephan. "Von der Koinzidenz zur coincidentia oppositorum. Zum philosophiehistorischen Hintergrund des Cusanischen Koinzidenzgedankens". In *Die Philosophie im 14. und 15. Jahrhundert. In Memoriam Konstanty Michalski (1879–1947)*, edited by Olaf Pluta, 321–42. Amsterdam: B. R. Grüner, 1988.
Menk, Gerhard. *Die Hohe Schule Herborn in ihrer Frühzeit (1584–1660): Ein Beitrag zum Hochschulwesen des deutschen Kalvinismus im Zeitalter der Gegenreformation*. Wiesbaden: Historische Kommission für Nassau, 1981.
Menk, Gerhard. "Johann Amos Comenius und die Hohe Schule Herborn". *Acta Comeniana* 8 (1989): 41–60.
Menk, Gerhard. "Martinius, Matthias, 1572–1630". *Neue Deutsche Biographie* 16 (1990): 305–7. www.deutschebiographie.de.
Mercer, Christia. *Leibniz's Metaphysics: Its Origin and Development*. Cambridge: Cambridge University Press, 2001.
Metselaar, Suzanne. "Are the Divine Ideas Involved in Making the Sensible Intelligible? The Role of Knowledge of the Divine in Bonaventure's Theory of Cognition". *Recherches de théologie et philosophie médiévales* 79.2 (2012): 339–72.
Miccoli, Lucia. "Two Thirteenth-Century Theories of Light: Robert Grosseteste and St. Bonaventure". *Semiotica* 136.1 (2001): 69–84.
Milbank, John. *Theology and Social Theory: Beyond Secular Reason*. Oxford: Blackwell, 2006.
Miller, Perry. *The New England Mind: The Seventeenth Century*. Cambridge, MA: Harvard University Press, 1982.
Minnis, Alastair. *From Eden to Eternity: Creations of Paradise in the Later Middle Ages*. Philadelphia, PA: University of Pennsylvania Press, 2016.
Moev, Christian. *The Metaphysics of Dante's Comedy*. New York: Oxford University Press, 2005.
Molnár, Amedeo. "Comenius' Theologia Naturalis". *Communio Viatorum* 8.1 (1965): 53–64.
Moltmann, Jürgen. "Zur Bedeutung des Petrus Ramus für Philosophie und Theologie in Calvinismus". *Zeitschrift für Kirchengeschichte* 68 (1957): 295–318.
Monfasani, John. "Lorenzo Valla and Rudolph Agricola". *Journal of the History of Philosophy* 28.2 (1990): 181–200.
Monfasani, John. "The Theology of Lorenzo Valla". In *Humanism and Early Modern Philosophy*, edited by Jill Kraye and M. W. F. Stone, 1–23. London: Routledge, 2000.
Moran, Bruce T. "Court Authority and Chemical Medicine: Moritz of Hessen, Johannes Hartmann, and the Origin of Academic Chemiatria". *Bulletin of the History of Medicine* 63.2 (1989): 225–46.
Mühling, Andreas. "Anmerkungen zur Theologenausbildung in Herborn". In *The Formation of Clerical and Confessional Identities in Early Modern Europe*, edited by Wim Janse and Barbara Pitkin, 71–87. Leiden: Brill, 2006.

Mullan, David G. "Federal Theology from the Reformation to c. 1677". In *The History of Scottish Theology, Volume I: Celtic Origins to Reformed Orthodoxy*, edited by David Fergusson and Mark W. Elliott, 225–37. Oxford: Oxford University Press, 2019.

Müller, Michael. *Zweite Reformation und städtische Autonomie im Königlichen Preussen: Danzig, Elbing und Thorn in der Epoche der Konfessionalisierung (1557-1660)*. Berlin: Akademie Verlag, 1997.

Muller, Richard A. *After Calvin: Studies in the Development of a Theological Tradition*. Oxford: Oxford University Press, 2003.

Muller, Richard A. *Calvin and the Reformed Tradition: On the Work of Christ and the Order of Salvation*. Grand Rapids, MI: Baker Academic, 2012.

Muller, Richard A. "Calvinist Thomism Revisited: William Ames (1576–1633) and the Divine Ideas". In *From Rome to Zurich, between Ignatius and Vermigli: Essays in Honor of John Patrick Donnelly*, edited by Gary Jenkins, W. J. Torrance Kirby, and Kathleen Comerford, 103–20. Leiden: Brill, 2017.

Muller, Richard A. *Divine Will and Human Choice: Freedom, Contingency, and Necessity in Early Modern Reformed Thought*. Grand Rapids, MI: Baker Academic, 2017.

Muller, Richard A. *Grace and Freedom: William Perkins and the Early Modern Reformed Understanding of Free Choice and Divine Grace*. New York: Oxford University Press, 2020.

Muller, Richard A. "Not Scotist: Understandings of Being, Univocity, and Analogy in Early-Modern Reformed Thought". *Reformation and Renaissance Review* 14.2 (2012): 127–50.

Muller, Richard A. "Perkins' *A Golden Chaine*: Predestinarian System or Schematized Ordo Salutis?" *Sixteenth Century Journal* 9.1 (1978): 68–81.

Muller, Richard A. *Post-Reformation Reformed Dogmatics: The Rise and Development of Reformed Orthodoxy, ca. 1520 to ca. 1725*. 4 vols. Grand Rapids, MI: Baker Academic, 2006. [PRRD]

Muller, Richard A. "Scholasticism in Calvin: A Question of Relation and Disjunction", in *Calvinus Sincerioris Religionis Vindex: Calvin as Protector of the Purer Religion*, edited by Wilhelm Neuser and Brian Armstrong, 247–65. Kirksville, MO: Sixteenth Century Journal Publishers, 1997.

Muller, Richard A. "Scholasticism, Reformation, Orthodoxy, and the Persistence of Christian Aristotelianism". *Trinity Journal* 19.1 (1998): 81–96.

Muller, Richard A. *The Unaccommodated Calvin: Studies in the Foundation of a Theological Tradition*. New York: Oxford University Press, 2001.

Muller, Richard A. "*Vera Philosophia cum sacra Theologia nusquam pugnat*: Keckermann on Philosophy, Theology and the Problem of Double Truth". *Sixteenth Century Journal* 15.3 (1984): 341–65.

Muller, Richard A. "Was It Really Viral? Natural Theology in the Early Modern Reformed Tradition". In *Crossing Traditions: Essays on the Reformation and Intellectual History in Honour of Irena Backus*, edited by Daniela Solfaroli Camillocci, Maria-Cristina Pitassi, and Arthur A. Huiban, 507–31. Leiden: Brill, 2017.

Mulsow, Martin. "*Sociabilitas*: Zu einem Kontext der Campanella-Rezeption im 17. Jahrhundert". *Bruniana & Campanelliana* 1.1/2 (1995): 205–32.

Mulsow, Martin. "Who Was the Author of the *Clavis Apocalyptica* of 1651? Millenarianism and Prophecy between Silesian Mysticism and the Hartlib Circle". In *Millenarianism and Messianism in Early Modern European Culture. Volume IV: Continental Millenarians, Protestants, Catholics, Heretics*, edited by John Christian Laursen and Richard H. Popkin, 57–75. Dordrecht: Springer, 2001.

Murdock, Graeme. *Calvinism on the Frontier, 1600-1660: International Calvinism and the Reformed Church in Hungary and Transylvania*. Oxford: Clarendon Press, 2000.

Murphy, Daniel. *Comenius: A Critical Assessment of His Life and Work*. Dublin: Irish Academic Press, 1995.

Napier, Macvey. "Remarks, Illustrative of the Scope and Influence of the Philosophical Writings of Lord Bacon". *Transactions of the Royal Society of Edinburgh* 8 (1818): 373–425.

Nauta, Lodi. "From Universals to Topics: The Realism of Rudolph Agricola, with an Edition of His Reply to a Critic". *Vivarium* 50.2 (2012): 190–224.

Nauta, Lodi. *In Defense of Common Sense: Lorenzo Valla's Humanist Critique of Scholastic Philosophy*. Cambridge, MA: Harvard University Press, 2009.

Neuser, Wilhelm. "Die Calvinistischen Ramisten". In *Handbuch der Dogmen- und Theologiegeschichte*, edited by Carl Andresen, 2.328–52. 3 vols. Göttingen: Vandenhoeck & Ruprecht, 1980.

Neval, Daniel. "An Approach to the Legacy of Comenius' Theology". *The Bohemian Reformation and Religious Practice* 3 (2000): 215–28.

Neval, Daniel. *Die Macht Gottes zum Heil: Das Bibelverständnis von Johann Amos Comenius in einer Zeit der Kriese und des Umbruchs*. Zürich: Evangelisches Verlagshaus, 2006.

Newman, William R. *Gehennical Fire: The Lives of George Starkey, An American Alchemist in the Scientific Revolution*. Cambridge, MA: Harvard University Press, 1994.

Noone, Timothy. "Aquinas on Divine Ideas: Scotus's Evaluation". *Franciscan Studies* 56 (1998): 307–24.

Noone, Timothy. "Universals and Individuation". In *The Cambridge Companion to Duns Scotus*, edited by Williams, 100–128.

O'Rourke, Fran. *Pseudo-Dionysius and the Metaphysics of Aquinas*. Leiden: Brill, 1992.

Oakley, Francis. *Omnipotence, Covenant and Order: An Excursion in the History of Ideas from Abelard to Leibniz*. Ithaca, NY: Cornell University Press, 1984.

Oberman, Heiko A. *The Dawn of the Reformation: Essays in Late Medieval and Early Reformation Thought*. Edinburgh: T&T Clark, 1986.

Oberman, Heiko A. *The Harvest of Medieval Theology: Gabriel Biel and Late Medieval Nominalism*. Grand Rapids, MI: Baker Academic, 2000.

Oberman, Heiko A. *Initia Calvini: The Matrix of Calvin's Reformation*. Amsterdam: Koninklijke Nederlandse Akademie van Wetenschappen, 1991.

Oberman, Heiko A. "The Shape of Late Medieval Thought: The Birthpangs of the Modern Era". In *Pursuit of Holiness*, edited by Trinkaus and Oberman, 13–33.

Olivieri, Grazia Tonelli. "Ideale Lulliano e Dialettica Ramista: Le 'Dialecticae Institutiones' del 1543". *Annali della Scuola Normale Superiore di Pisa* 22.3 (1992): 885–929.

Omodeo, Pietro Daniel. "The European Career of a Scottish Mathematician and Physician". In *Duncan Liddel (1561-1613): Networks of Polymathy and the Northern European Renaissance*, edited by Pietro Daniel Omodeo in collaboration with Karin Friedrich, 35–90. Leiden: Brill, 2016.

Ong, Walter J. *Ramus and Talon Inventory: A Short-Title Inventory of the Published Works of Peter Ramus, (1515-1572) and of Omer Talon, (ca. 1510-1562)*. Cambridge, MA: Harvard University Press, 1958.

Ong, Walter J. *Ramus, Method, and the Decay of Dialogue: From the Art of Discourse to the Art of Reason*. Chicago, IL: University of Chicago Press, 2004.

Oosterhoff, Richard J. "The Fabrist Origins of Erasmian Science: Mathematical Erudition in Erasmus' Basel". *Journal of Interdisciplinary History of Ideas* 3.6 (2014): 1–37.

Oosterhoff, Richard J. "*Idiotae*, Mathematics and Artisans: The Untutored Mind and the Discovery of Nature in the Fabrist Circle". *Intellectual History Review* 24 (2014): 1–19.

Oosterhoff, Richard J. "Jacques Lefèvre d'Étaples". *Stanford Encyclopedia of Philosophy.* https://plato.stanford.edu/entries/lefevre-etaples/.

Oosterhoff, Richard J. *Making Mathematical Culture: University and Print in the Circle of Lefèvre d'Étaples.* Oxford: Oxford University Press, 2018.

Osborne, Thomas M., Jr. "Thomas and Scotus on Prudence without All the Major Virtues: Imperfect or Merely Partial?" *The Thomist* 74 (2010): 165–88.

Overfield, James. *Humanism and Scholasticism in Late Medieval Germany.* Princeton, NJ: Princeton University Press, 2019.

Ozment, Steven E. *The Age of Reform (1250–1550): An Intellectual and Religious History of Late Medieval and Reformation Europe.* New Haven, CT: Yale University Press, 1980.

Parker, Eric M. "Cambridge Platonism(s): John Sherman and Peter Sterry". In *Revisioning Cambridge Platonism: Sources and Legacy*, edited by Douglas Hedley and David Leech, 31–46. Dordrecht: Springer, 2020.

Pasnau, Robert. "Divine Illumination". *Stanford Encyclopedia of Philosophy.* https://plato.stanford.edu/entries/illumination/.

Patočka, Jan. *Andere Wege in die Moderne: Studien zur europäischen Ideengeschichte von der Renaissance bis zur Romantik.* Edited by Ludger Hagedorn. Würzburg: Königshausen & Neumann, 2006.

Patočka, Jan. "*Centrum Securitatis* und Cusanus". In Patočka, *Andere Wege in die Moderne*, 245–56.

Patočka, Jan. "Comenius und Cusanus". In Patočka, *Andere Wege in die Moderne*, 237–43.

Pavlas, Petr. "The Book Metaphor Triadized: The Layman's Bible and God's Books in Raymond of Sabunde, Nicholas of Cusa and Jan Amos Comenius". In *Nicholas of Cusa and the Making of the Early Modern World*, edited by Burton, Hollmann, and Parker, 384–416.

Pavlas, Petr. "The Book of the Mind: The Shift towards the Subject in Patrizi and Comenius". In *Francesco Patrizi*, edited by Blum and Nejeschleba, 343–59.

Pavlas, Petr. "Jan Patočka's *Transcendentalia and Categories* on Jan Amos Comenius' Triadic System and Its Cusan Inspiration". *Acta Comeniana* 30 (2016): 187–211.

Pavlas, Petr. "The Search for a Final Language: Comenius's Linguistic Eschatology". *Erudition and the Republic of Letters* 5 (2020): 207–28.

Peltonen, Markku, ed. *The Cambridge Companion to Bacon.* Cambridge: Cambridge University Press, 2012.

Penman, Leigh T. I. *Hope and Heresy: The Problem of Chiliasm in Lutheran Confessional Culture, 1570–1630.* Dordrecht: Springer, 2019.

Penman, Leigh T. I. "Jacob Böhme and His Networks". In *Jacob Böhme and His World*, edited by Andersson, Martin, Penman, and Weeks, 98–120.

Pérez-Ramos, Antonio. "Bacon's Forms and the Maker's Knowledge Tradition". In *The Cambridge Companion to Bacon*, edited by Peltonen, 99–120.

Pickstock, Catherine. "Duns Scotus: His Historical and Contemporary Significance". *Modern Theology* 21 (2005): 543–74.

Pickstock, Catherine. "Spacialisation: The Middle of Modernity". In *The Radical Orthodoxy Reader*, edited by John Milbank and Simon Oliver, 154–77. Abingdon: Routledge, 2009.

Pini, Giorgio. "Duns Scotus' Commentary on the Topics: New Light on His Philosophical Teaching". *Archives d'histoire doctrinale et littéraire du moyen âge* 66 (1999): 225–43.

Plasger, Georg. "Covenantal Theology: Risks and Chances of a Controversial Term". In *Covenant: A Vital Element of Reformed Theology: Biblical, Historical and Systematic-Theological Perspectives*, edited by Hans Burger, Gert Kwakkel, and Michael Mulder, 379–92. Leiden: Brill, 2022.

Plett, Heinrich F. *Rhetoric and Renaissance Culture*. Berlin: De Gruyter, 2004.

Pomplun, Trent. "Notes on Scotist Aesthetics in Light of Gilbert Narcisse's 'Les Raisons de Dieu'". *Franciscan Studies* 66.1 (2008): 247–68.

Posset, Franz. *Johann Reuchlin (1455–1522): A Theological Biography*. Berlin: De Gruyter, 2015.

Power, Amanda. *Roger Bacon and the Defence of Christendom*. Cambridge: Cambridge University Press, 2013.

Pozzo, Riccardo. "Logic and Metaphysics in German Philosophy from Melanchthon to Hegel". In *Approaches to Metaphysics*, edited by William Sweet, 61–74. Dordrecht: Springer, 2005.

Pozzo, Riccardo, "Ramus' Metaphysics and Its Criticism by the Helmstedt Aristotelians". In *The Influence of Petrus Ramus*, edited by Feingold, Freedman, and Rother, 92–106.

Raalte, Theodore van. *Antoine de Chandieu: The Silver Horn of Geneva's Reformed Triumvirate*. New York: Oxford University Press, 2018.

Radeva, Zornitsa. "At the Origins of a Tenacious Narrative: Jacob Thomasius and the History of Double Truth". *Intellectual History Review* 29.3 (2019): 417–38.

Raffaelli, Matteo. *Macht, Weisheit, Liebe: Campanella und Comenius als Vordenker einer friedvoll globalisierten Weltgemeinschaft*. Frankfurt am Main: Lang, 2009.

Ramis Barceló, Rafael. "En torno al Escoto-Lulismo de Pere Dagui". *Medievalia* 16 (2013): 235–64.

Ratzinger, Joseph. *The Theology of History in St Bonaventure*. Translated by Zachary Hayes, OFM. Chicago, IL: Franciscan Herald Press, 1971.

Raylor, Timothy, and J. W. Binns. "English Responses to the Death of Moritz the Learned: John Dury, Sir Thomas Roe, and an Unnoted Epicede by William Cartwright". *English Literary Renaissance* 25.2 (1995): 235–47.

Reeves, Marjorie. "The Abbot Joachim's Sense of History". In Marjorie Reeves, *The Prophetic Sense of History in Medieval and Renaissance Europe*, 782–96. Aldershot: Ashgate, 1998.

Reeves, Marjorie. *The Influence of Prophecy in the Later Middle Ages: A Study in Joachimism*. Oxford: Clarendon Press, 1969.

Rehnman, Sebastian. "The Doctrine of God in Reformed Orthodoxy". In *A Companion to Reformed Orthodoxy*, edited by Herman Selderhuis, 351–401. Leiden: Brill, 2013.

Reid, Jonathan. *King's Sister, Queen of Dissent: Marguerite of Navarre (1492–1549) and Her Evangelical Network*. 2 vols. Leiden: Brill, 2009.

Reid, Steven J. *Humanism and Calvinism: Andrew Melville and the Universities of Scotland, 1560–1625*. Farnham: Ashgate, 2011.

Reid, Steven J., and Emma Annette Wilson. *Ramus, Pedagogy and the Liberal Arts: Ramism in Britain and the Wider World*. Aldershot: Ashgate, 2011.

Reiss, Timothy J. "From Trivium to Quadrivium: Ramus, Method and Mathematical Technology". In *The Renaissance Computer: Knowledge Technology in the First Age of Print*, edited by Neil Rhodes and Jonathan Sawday, 43–56. London: Routledge, 2000.

Reiss, Timothy J. *Knowledge, Discovery and Imagination in Early Modern Europe: The Rise of Aesthetic Rationalism*. Cambridge: Cambridge University Press, 1997.
Renaudet, Augustin. *Préréforme et humanisme à Paris pendant les premieres guerres d'Italie (1494–1517)*. Paris: Librairie Ancienne Honoré Champion, 1916.
Reuter, Karl. *Das Grundverständnis der Theologie Calvins*. Neukirchen: Verlag des Erziehungsvereins, 1963.
Reuver, Arie de. *Sweet Communion: Trajectories of Spirituality from the Middle Ages through the Further Reformation*. Translated by James A. De Jong. Grand Rapids, MI: Baker Academic, 2007.
Risse, Wilhelm. *Die Logik der Neuzeit: 1. Band. 1500–1640*. Stuttgart-Bad Canstatt: Friedrich Frommann Verlag, 1964.
Rist, John M. *Augustine: Ancient Thought Baptised*. Cambridge: Cambridge University Press, 1994.
Rorem, Paul. *Pseudo-Dionysius: A Commentary on the Texts and an Introduction to Their Influence*. New York: Oxford University Press, 1993.
Rose, Paul Lawrence. "Scaliger (Bordonius), Julius Caesar". In *Complete Dictionary of Scientific Biography*, edited by Marshall de Bruhl, 12.134–36. 27 vols. Detroit, MI: Charles Scribner's Sons, 2008.
Rossi, Paolo. *Francis Bacon: From Magic to Science*. Translated by Sacha Rabinovitch. London: Routledge, 2009.
Rossi, Paolo. *Logic and the Art of Memory: The Quest for a Universal Language*, translated by Stephan Clucas. London: Athlone Press, 2000.
Rother, Wolfgang. "Ramus and Ramism in Switzerland". In *The Influence of Petrus Ramus*, edited by Feingold, Freedman, and Rother, 9–37.
Rubi, Linda Báez. "Lullism in New Spain". In *A Companion to Ramon Llull and Lullism*, edited by Austin and Johnston, 515–32.
Rubinelli, Sara. *Ars Topica: The Classical Technique of Constructing Arguments from Aristotle to Cicero*. Dordrecht: Springer, 2009.
Rubio, Josep E. "Llull's 'Great Universal Art'". In *A Companion to Ramon Llull and Lullism*, edited by Austin and Johnston, 81–116.
Rudolph, Conrad. *The Mystic Ark: Hugh of Saint Victor, Art, and Thought in the Twelfth Century*. Cambridge: Cambridge University Press, 2014.
Rummel, Erika. *The Confessionalization of Humanism in Reformation Germany*. Oxford: Oxford University Press, 2000.
Saak, Eric Leland. *Luther and the Reformation of the Later Middle Ages*. Cambridge: Cambridge University Press, 2017.
Sakamoto, Kuni. "Creation, the Trinity and *Prisca Theologia* in Julius Caesar Scaliger". *Journal of the Warburg and Courtauld Institutes* 73 (2010): 195–207.
Sakamoto, Kuni. *Julius Caesar Scaliger, Renaissance Reformer of Aristotelianism: A Study of His Exotericae Exercitationes*. Leiden: Brill, 2016.
Sandborg-Petersen, Ulrik, and Peter Øhrstrøm. "Towards an Implementation of Jacob Lorhard's Ontology as a Digital Resource for Historical and Conceptual Research in Early Seventeenth-Century Thought". In *Text Comparison and Digital Creativity: The Production of Presence and Meaning in Digital Text Scholarship*, edited by Wido van Peursen, Ernst D. Thoutenhoofd, and Adriaan van der Weel, 57–75. Leiden: Brill, 2010.
Santing, Catrien. "Through the Looking Glass of Ulrich Pinder: The Impact of Humanism on the Career of a Nuremberg Town Physician around 1500". In *Medieval and*

*Renaissance Humanism: Rhetoric, Representation and Reform*, edited by Stephen Gersh and Bert Roest, 203–25. Leiden: Brill, 2003.

Schadel, Erwin. *Sehendes Herz (Cor Oculatum)—Zu einem Emblem des späten Comenius*. Frankfurt am Main: Peter Lang, 2003.

Schaller, Klaus. "Sein und Bewegung in den Frühschriften Komenskys". *Zeitschrift für philosophische Forschung* 23.1 (1969): 36–46.

Scherbaum, Matthias. *Der Metaphysikbegriff des Johann Amos Comenius: Das Projekt der Pansophie im Spannungsbogen von "Realismus", Heilsgeschichte und Pan-Paideia*. Oberhaid: Utopica, 2008.

Schmidt-Biggemann, Wilhelm. "Einleitung: Johannes Reuchlin und die Anfänge der christlichen Kabbala". In *Christliche Kabbala*, edited by Wilhelm Schmidt-Biggemann, 9–48. Ostfildern: Jan Thorbecke Verlag, 2003.

Schmidt-Biggemann, Wilhelm. "Robert Fludd's Kabbalistic Cosmos". In *Platonism at the Origins of Modernity: Studies on Platonism and Early Modern Philosophy*, edited by Douglas Hedley and Sarah Hutton, 75–92. Dordrecht: Springer, 2008.

Schmidt-Biggemann, Wilhelm. *Topica Universalis: Eine Modellgeschichte humanistischer und barocker Wissenschaft*. Hamburg: Meiner, 1983.

Schmitt, Charles B., Eckhard Kessler, and Quentin Skinner, eds. *The Cambridge History of Renaissance Philosophy*. Cambridge: Cambridge University Press, 2008.

Schneider, Hans, ed. *Bibliographie zur Geschichte des Pietismus. Band 2: A Catalog of British Devotional and Religious Books in German Translation from the Reformation to 1750*. Berlin: De Gruyter, 1996.

Schoeck, R. J. "Agricola and Erasmus: Erasmus' Inheritance of Northern Humanism". In *Rodolphus Agricola Phrisius 1444–1485: Proceedings of the International Conference at the University of Groningen 28–30 October 1585*, edited by Fokke Akkerman and Arjo J. Vanderjagt, 181–88. Leiden: Brill, 1988.

Schreiner, Susan E. *Are You Alone Wise? The Search for Certainty in the Early Modern Era*. Oxford: Oxford University Press, 2011.

Schreiner, Susan E. *The Theater of His Glory: Nature and the Natural Order in the Thought of John Calvin*. Durham, NC: Labyrinth Press, 1991.

Schumacher, Lydia. *Divine Illumination: The History and Future of Augustine's Theory of Knowledge*. Chichester: Wiley-Blackwell, 2011.

Schumacher, Lydia. *Early Franciscan Theology: Between Authority and Innovation*. Cambridge: Cambridge University Press, 2019.

Scott, David Hill. "From Boston to the Baltic: New England, Encyclopedics, and the Hartlib Circle". PhD Dissertation, University of Notre Dame, 2003.

Scribner, Robert W. *Popular Culture and Popular Movements in Reformation Germany*. London; Hambledon, 1987.

Seivert. "Bisterfeld, Johannes". *Allgemeine Deutsche Biographie* 2 (1875): 682–83. https://www.deutsche-biographie.de/.

Sellberg, Erland. "Petrus Ramus". *Stanford Encyclopedia of Philosophy*. 9 May 2006; rev. 2 Oct. 2020. https://plato.stanford.edu/entries/ramus/.

Sgarbi, Marco. *The Italian Mind: Vernacular Logic in Renaissance Italy (1540–1551)*. Leiden: Brill, 2014.

Shank, Michael H. *"Unless You Believe, You Shall Not Understand": Logic, University, and Society in Late Medieval Vienna*. Princeton, NJ: Princeton University Press, 1988.

Shantz, Douglas H. *An Introduction to German Pietism: Protestant Renewal at the Dawn of Modern Europe*. Baltimore, MD: Johns Hopkins University Press, 2013.

Sheehan, Jonathan. "From Philology to Fossils: The Biblical Encyclopedia in Early Modern Europe". *Journal of the History of Ideas* 64.1 (2003): 41–60.
Shields, Christopher. *Aristotle*. London: Routledge, 2014.
Simon, Jószef. "Aristotelismus, Nominalismus und Trinitätskritik. Die philosophischen Grundzüge der Explicationes Locorum Veteris et Novi Testamenti von György Enyedi (1555–1597)". In *Radikale Reformation: Die Unitarier in Siebenbürgen*, edited by Ulrich A. Wien, Juliane Brandt, and András F. Balogh, 227–40. Cologne, Böhlau Verlag, 2013.
Sinnema, Donald. "Antoine de Chandieu's Call for a Scholastic Reformed Theology (1580)". In *Later Calvinism: International Perspectives*, edited by W. Fred Graham, 159–90. Kirksville, MO: Sixteenth Century Journal Publishers, 1994.
Sinnema, Donald. "Joachim Jungnitz on the Use of Aristotelian Logic in Theology". In *Späthumanismus und reformierte Konfession*, edited by Strohm, Freedman, and Selderhuis, 127–52.
Sinnema, Donald, Christian Moser, and Herman J. Selderhuis, eds. *Acta et Documenta Synodi Nationalis Dordrechtanae (1618–1619). Acta of the Synod of Dordt*. Göttingen: Vandenhoeck & Ruprecht, 2015.
Skalnik, James. *Ramus and Reform: University and Church at the End of the Renaissance*. Kirksville, MO: Truman State University Press, 2002.
Skinner, Quentin. "Meaning and Understanding in the History of Ideas". *History and Theory* 8.1 (1969): 3–53.
Skrbina, David. *Panpsychism in the West*. Cambridge, MA: MIT Press, 2017.
Slavinski, Sergiej S. "Polemic and Piety in Francis Cheynell's *The Divine Trinunity* (1650)". PhD Dissertation, University of Edinburgh, 2022.
Slotemaker, John T. "John Calvin's Trinitarian Theology in the 1536 *Institutes*: The Distinction of Persons as a Key to his Theological Sources". In *Philosophy and Theology in the Long Middle Ages: A Tribute to Stephen F. Brown*, edited by Kent Emery, Russell Friedman, and Andreas Speer, 781–810. Leiden: Brill, 2011.
Smith, Garrett R. "The Analogy of Being in the Scotist Tradition". *American Catholic Philosophical Quarterly* 93.4 (2019): 633–73.
Southern, Richard W. *Scholastic Humanism and the Unification of Europe, Volume 1: Foundations*. Oxford: Blackwell, 1995.
Spade, Paul Vincent. *Thoughts, Words and Things: An Introduction to Late Mediaeval Logic and Semantic Theory*. 2007. https://pvspade.com/Logic/docs/thoughts.pdf.
Sprunger, Keith. "Ames, Ramus, and the Method of Puritan Theology". *Harvard Theological Review* 59 (1966): 133–51.
Sprunger, Keith. *The Learned Doctor William Ames: Dutch Backgrounds of English and American Puritanism*. Chicago, IL: University of Chicago Press, 1972.
Staley, Maxwell Reed. "A Most Dangerous Science: Discipline and German Political Philosophy, 1600–1648". PhD Dissertation, University of California, Berkeley, 2018.
Steenberghen, Fernand van. *The Philosophical Movement in the Thirteenth Century*. Edinburgh: Nelson, 1955.
Strehle, Stephen. *Calvinism, Federalism and Scholasticism: A Study of the Reformed Doctrine of the Covenant*. Bern: Peter Lang, 1988.
Strohm, Christoph, Joseph S. Freedman, and Herman Selderhuis, eds. *Späthumanismus und reformierte Konfession. Theologie, Jurisprudenz und Philosophie in Heidelberg an der Wende zum 17.Jh*. Tübingen: Möhr Siebeck, 2006.
Stump, Eleonore. *Dialectic and Its Place in the Development of Medieval Logic*. Ithaca, NY: Cornell University Press, 2020.

Sturdy, Robert C. *Freedom from Fatalism: Samuel Rutherford's (1600-1661) Doctrine of Divine Providence.* Göttingen: Vandenhoeck & Ruprecht, 2021.
Sullivan, Michael B. "The Debate over Spiritual Matter in the Late Thirteenth Century: Gonsalvus Hispanus and the Franciscan Tradition from Bonaventure to Scotus". PhD Dissertation, Catholic University of America, 2010.
Sutanto, Nathaniel Gray. "Two Theological Accounts of Logic: Theistic Conceptual Realism and a Reformed Archetype-Ectype Model". *International Journal for the Philosophy of Religion* 79 (2016): 239-60.
Svensson, Manfred, and David VanDrunen, eds. *Aquinas Among the Protestants.* Hoboken: Wiley, 2017.
Sylwanowicz, Michael. *Contingent Causality and the Foundations of Duns Scotus' Metaphysics.* Leiden: Brill, 1996.
Sytsma, David S. "Calvin, Daneau and the 'Physica Mosaica': Neglected Continuities at the Origins of an Early Modern Tradition". *Church History and Religious Culture* 95.4 (2015): 457-76.
Szentpéteri, Márton. *Egyetemes tudomány Erdélyben—Johann Heinrich Alsted és a herborni hagyomány* [Universal Learning in Tranyslvania: Johann Heinrich Alsted and the Herborn Tradition]. Budapest: Universitas, 2008.
Szentpéteri, Márton. "The Mystery of Piety Revealed and Defended: A Sequel to Johann Heinrich Bisterfeld's *De Uno Deo*?" *Acta Comeniana* 26 (2012): 89-98.
Tachau, Katherine H. *Vision and Certitude in the Age of Ockham: Optics, Epistemology and the Foundations of Semantics, 1250-1345.* Leiden: Brill, 1987.
Taylor, Charles. *A Secular Age.* Cambridge, MA: Harvard University Press, 2007.
Teich, Mikuláš. *Bohemia in History.* Cambridge: Cambridge University Press, 2004.
Tipson, Baird. *Hartford Puritanism: Thomas Hooker, Samuel Stone, and Their Terrifying God.* New York: Oxford University Press, 2015.
Tipson, Baird. "Seeing the World through Ramist Eyes: The Richardsonian Ramism of Thomas Hooker and Samuel Stone". *The Seventeenth Century* 28.3 (2013): 275-92.
Tipton, Stephen. "Defining 'Our Theology'". *Journal of Reformed Theology* 10.4 (2016): 291-313.
Tode, Sven. "Preaching Calvinism in Lutheran Danzig: Jacob Fabritius on the Pastoral Office". *Nederlands archief voor kerkgeschiedenis* 85 (2005): 239-55.
Tóth, Zsombor. "The Importance of Being (In)Tolerant: The Strange Case of Transylvanian Puritanism". In *Reformed Majorities in Early Modern Europe*, edited by Herman J. Selderhuis and J. Marius J. Lange van Ravenswaay, 89-110. Göttingen: Vandenhoeck & Ruprecht, 2015.
Traninger, Anita. *Mühelose Wissenschaft: Lullismus und Rhetorik in den deutschsprachigen Ländern der frühen Neuzeit.* Munich: Fink, 2001.
Traninger, Anita. "The Secret of Success: Ramism and Lullism as Contending Methods". In *Ramus, Pedagogy and the Liberal Arts*, edited by Reid and Wilson, 113-31.
Trinkaus, Charles, and Heiko A. Oberman. *The Pursuit of Holiness in Late Medieval and Renaissance Religion: Papers from the University of Michigan Conference.* Leiden: Brill, 1974.
Trueman, Carl, and R. S. Clark, eds. *Protestant Scholasticism: Essays in Reassessment.* Carlisle: Paternoster, 1999.
Turner, Denys. *Thomas Aquinas: A Portrait.* New Haven, CT: Yale University Press, 2014.
Unger, Dominic. "Franciscan Christology: Absolute and Universal Primacy of Christ". *Franciscan Studies* 2.4 (1942): 428-75.

Vasoli, Cesare. *La dialettica e la retorica dell'umanesimo: "Invenzione" e "metodo" nella cultura del XV e XVI secolo.* Milan: Feltrinelli, 1968.
Vater, Carl. "Divine Ideas: 1250–1325". PhD Dissertation, The Catholic University of America, 2017.
Verbeek, Theo. *Descartes and the Dutch: Early Reactions to Cartesian Philosophy, 1637–1650.* Carbondale, IL: Southern Illinois University Press, 1992.
Vickers, Brian. "Frances Yates and the Writing of History". *Journal of Modern History* 51.2 (1979): 287–316.
Victor, Joseph M. *Charles de Bovelles, 1479–1553: An Intellectual Biography.* Geneva: Droz, 1978.
Victor, Joseph M. "The Revival of Lullism at Paris, 1499–1516". *Renaissance Quarterly* 28.4 (1975): 504–34.
Viskolcz, Noémi. "Johann Heinrich Bisterfeld. Ein Professor als Vermittler zwischen West und Ost an der siebenbürgischen Akademie in Weissenburg, 1630–1655". In *Calvin und Reformiertentum in Ungarn und Siebenbürgen: Helvetisches Bekenntnis, Ethnie und Politik vom 16. Jahrhundert bis 1918*, edited by Márta Fata and Anton Schindling, 201–14. Münster: Aschendorff, 2011.
Viskolcz, Noémi. *Johann Heinrich Bisterfeld (1605–1655) Bibliográfia*, A Bisterfeld-Könyvtár. Budapest and Szeged: Országos Széchenyi Könyvtár, 2003.
Vliet, Jan van. *The Rise of Reformed System: The Intellectual Heritage of William Ames.* Milton Keynes: Paternoster, 2013.
Vos, Antonie. *The Philosophy of John Duns Scotus.* Edinburgh: Edinburgh University Press, 2006.
Vos, Antonie. "Scholasticism and Reformation". In *Reformation and Scholasticism: An Ecumenical Enterprise*, edited by Willem J. van Asselt and Eef Dekker, 99–119. Grand Rapids: Baker, 2001.
de Vries, Lyke. *Reformation, Revolution, Renovation: The Roots and Reception of the Rosicrucian Call for General Reform.* Leiden: Brill, 2022.
Vries, Lyke de. "The Rosicrucian Reformation: Prophecy and Reform at Play in the Rosicrucian Manifestos". *Daphnis* 48 (2020): 270–95.
Wainwright, Michael. *The Rational Shakespeare: Peter Ramus, Edward de Vere, and the Question of Authorship.* Cham: Springer International, 2018.
Wainwright, Robert J. D. *Early Reformation Covenant Theology: English Reception of Swiss Reformed Thought, 1520–1555.* Phillipsburg, NJ: P&R Publishing, 2020.
Walker, D. P. *The Ancient Theology: Studies in Christian Platonism from the Fifteenth to the Eighteenth Century.* London: Duckworth, 1972.
Wallace, Dewey, Jr. *Shapers of English Calvinism, 1660–1714: Variety, Persistence and Transformation.* Oxford: Oxford University Press, 2011.
Walton, Craig. "Ramus and Socrates". *Proceedings of the American Philosophical Society* 114.2 (1970): 119–39.
Ward, Graham. *How the Light Gets In: Ethical Life I.* Oxford: Oxford University Press, 2016.
Watson, S. Y. "A Problem for Realism: Our Multiple Concepts of Individual Things and the Solution of Duns Scotus". In *John Duns Scotus, 1265–1965*, edited by Bonansea and Ryan, 61–82.
Weber, Max. *The Protestant Ethic and the Spirit of Capitalism.* Translated by Stephen Kalberg. Hoboken: Taylor and Francis, 2013.
Webster, Charles. *The Great Instauration: Science, Medicine and Reform 1626–1660.* London: Duckworth, 1975.

Weir, David A. "*Foedus Naturale*: The Origins of Federal Theology in Sixteenth-Century Reformation Thought". PhD Dissertation, University of St Andrews, 1984.
Williams, Thomas. *The Cambridge Companion to Duns Scotus*. Cambridge: Cambridge University Press, 2003.
Wilson, Emma Annette. "Reading the 'Unseemly Logomachy': Ramist Method in Action in Seventeenth-Century English Literature". In *Ramus, Pedagogy and the Liberal Arts*, edited by Reid and Wilson, 69–88.
Wippel, John F. *Metaphysical Themes in Thomas Aquinas II*. Washington, DC: Catholic University of America Press, 2011.
Wippel, John F. *The Metaphysical Thought of Thomas Aquinas: From Finite Being to Uncreated Being*. Washington, DC: Catholic University of America Press, 2000.
Wippel, John F. "Thomas Aquinas and the Condemnation of 1277". *Modern Schoolman* 72.2–3 (1995): 233–72.
Wolter, Allan. "The Formal Distinction". In *John Duns Scotus, 1265–1965*, edited by Bonansea and Ryan, 45–60.
Woodward, Walter W. *Prospero's America: John Winthrop, Jr., Alchemy, and the Creation of New England Culture*. Chapel Hill, NC: University of North Carolina Press, 2010.
Yagi, Takayuki. *A Gift from England: William Ames and His Polemical Discourse against Dutch Arminianism*. Göttingen: Vandenhoeck & Ruprecht, 2020.
Yates, Frances. *The Art of Memory*. London: Pimlico, 2008.
Yates, Frances. *The Rosicrucian Enlightenment*. London: Routledge, 1999.
Zimmermann, Jens. "The Cultural Context for Re-Envisioning Christian Humanism". In *Re-Envisioning Christian Humanism: Education and the Restoration of Humanity*, edited by Jens Zimmermann, 137–60. Oxford: Oxford University Press, 2017.
Zahnd, Ueli. "Calvin, Calvinism, and Medieval Thought". In *The Oxford Handbook of Calvin and Calvinism*, edited by Bruce Gordon and Carl R. Trueman, 26–42. Oxford: Oxford University Press, 2021.
Zahnd, Ueli. "The Early John Calvin and Augustine: Some Reconsiderations". *Studia Patristica* 87 (2017): 181–94.

# Index

*For the benefit of digital users, indexed terms that span two pages (e.g., 52–53) may, on occasion, appear on only one of those pages.*

absolute and ordained power, 178–79, 206n.170
absolute principles. *See* Lullism
abstraction. *See* Cognition: abstractive
academies, 89–91, 106–8, 120, 124, 133–35, 137, 182, 215, 240, 242, 287
academization, 214, 243
accident, 69–70, 126, 151, 187, 229–30n.111, 254, 294
action, 149, 160, 169–70, 234, 294, 297, 301, 315–16, 341–42, 350, 358
actuality, 8–9, 151–52, 156–57, 159
Adam, 13, 93–95, 117–18, 163–64, 174–75, 234, 333–35, 350
Adami, Tobias, 325, 338
Adams, John, 139, 149–50, 159
*ad fontes*, 84–85, 114–15
adjuncts, 25, 65, 68, 101, 126, 152, 172–73, 199–200
affective, 207–8, 211, 251, 306–8, 315–16
Agricola, Rudolph, 24, 27–32, 42, 48–49, 59–60, 62–64, 68–69, 75, 90, 107, 115, 123, 140, 196–97, 222–23, 297–98
Agricolan, 31–34, 43, 48–50, 53–54, 62, 107, 113, 115, 120, 122–23, 140, 150, 153, 222–23, 245–46, 327–28
Agrippa, Cornelius, 248–49, 254, 324, 352–53
Albert the Great, 9n.51, 141
alchemy, 247–49, 257, 261, 273–75, 283, 290, 330, 334–35
  elixir of life, 274
Alexander of Hales, 26–27, 190–92, 201–2
Alsted, Jacob, 121, 245–46
Alsted, Johann Heinrich, 35n.221, 121, 127–28, 135–36, 232–33, 242–93, 296–304, 306, 308, 312–13, 320–26, 330, 337–38, 341, 352–53, 359
Alstedian, 244–45, 303, 339–40
Althusius, Johannes, 122n.107, 135, 240–41, 312–16
Ames, William, 39, 138, 146–80, 183–84, 199, 204, 215, 263, 288, 292, 303, 305, 308, 351

analogy of being, 4–5n.20, 14–15, 37, 40, 65–67, 139, 154, 171, 190–92, 206–7, 211–12, 270–71
analysis, logical, 56–57, 85–87, 105, 120, 123–24, 126–28, 130–32, 134–35, 142, 145, 150, 161, 166–67, 176–77, 189, 234–35, 256, 298–300, 305–6, 314
Andreae, Johann Valentin, 333, 335, 353
angels, 187, 203, 263, 312, 318, 357
Antichrist, 124, 272, 274–76
anti-Ramism, 122, 134–35, 188, 190–92, 213–15, 217–20, 222, 225
Anti-Trinitarianism, 34, 134–35, 205–6, 210, 215, 289, 309–11, 344–45
Antognazza, Maria Rosa, 22, 244, 260–61, 281, 293–94, 296–97, 297n.127, 320
apocalypticism, 3–4, 243–44, 248–49, 272–79, 281–82, 285–91, 330–33. *See also* eschatology; Millenarianism
apodictic, 24, 27, 62–63, 73, 297–98, 349–50, 353
apologetic, 17, 20, 131, 251–53, 262, 289–90, 309
apophatic, 37, 61–62, 171–72, 206–7
Aquinas, Thomas, 8–12, 14–16, 23–24, 35–40, 48, 57–58, 117n.72, 129, 141, 150–52, 154–55, 157–59, 163–64, 171–72, 184–87, 190, 198–201, 203–4, 210–11, 224, 229–30n.111, 230, 235, 237–38, 251, 262, 270n.173, 278
*Arbor Scientiae*. *See* Lullism: *Tree of sciences*
archetype, 74, 101, 109, 111, 116, 139–40, 165–69, 174, 199–202, 204, 269–70, 297, 314–17, 323, 337, 346–47, 350, 356–57
aristocracy, 317–18, 361
Aristotelianism, 1, 3–4, 8–10, 12–13, 18, 20–22, 24–27, 29–34, 37, 40–45, 53–55, 63, 65, 68, 72–73, 75–77, 84, 95, 98–102, 105–7, 109–11, 115–16, 121–23, 126, 138, 141–43, 145–47, 159, 170, 172, 182–86, 188–89, 192–95, 203, 206, 213–23, 225, 227, 232, 237–38, 248–49, 251, 257–58, 296–98, 302, 319–20, 325, 327–29, 341, 343–45, 350–51, 353. *See also* Christian Aristotelianism

Aristotle, 8–11, 24–27, 31, 41–42, 44n.1, 49–51, 54, 62–67, 70–72, 75–77, 83–85, 88, 93, 95, 98–99, 101, 107–9, 114–15, 121–23, 133, 137, 141, 169, 172, 174–75, 181–82, 184–85, 187, 194, 217–19, 221–23, 253–54, 292, 312–13, 338–39
arithmetic, 73, 77–78, 89–90, 104, 111, 162–63
Arminian, 34, 147, 284
Arndt, Johann, 332–33
*ars concionandi*, 256, 303–8
art, 159, 203, 267–68
art of memory, 25, 25n.153, 85–87, 144n.46, 145, 249–51, 259–60
arts and sciences, 7–8, 12, 20, 22, 41–42, 50, 57–59, 72–73, 91, 93–94, 138, 149n.76, 154, 159, 163–64, 174–75, 188–89, 208, 224–25, 234, 237, 239–40, 242, 256, 266–67, 271, 329–31, 335, 337. See also *quadrivium*; *trivium*
astrology, 248–49, 272–76, 330, 335
astronomy, 53n.59, 107–8, 162–63, 263
atomizing, 85–87, 139
Augustine of Hippo, 3–4, 6–12, 14–15, 23–27, 31, 40–42, 50–51, 60–61, 97–99, 102, 131, 153–54, 162, 208, 229–30, 270n.173, 277–78, 337–39, 348–51
Augustinianism, 3–6, 8, 11, 14, 21, 23–24, 26–27, 36–37, 40–42, 46–47, 50–51, 56–57, 60–61, 69–70, 98–99, 125–26, 139, 150–51, 153–54, 156–59, 163–64, 169–70, 185–86, 204, 207–12, 214–15, 229–30, 234–35, 237–38, 243–44, 251, 261–64, 270, 278, 285, 296–97, 314, 316–17, 320–21, 326–27, 336–40, 343–44, 350–51. See also late medieval Augustinianism
*autopistia*, 129, 131–32
Averroism, 10, 23–24, 227–28
axioms, 149–50, 292–93, 300–1, 315–16, 327, 344

Bacon, Francis, 1, 320–21, 325–31, 334–35, 337–38, 341, 349–50, 353, 355
Bacon, Roger, 12–13, 274, 278
Baconianism, 283–84, 303, 339, 349–50, 354–56
Banosius, Theophilus, 92, 95–97
Barking academy, 146–47
Basel, University of, 39, 181–82, 193–95, 247, 283–84
Baxter, Richard, 38–39, 174, 242
beatitude, 165, 169–70, 198, 240–41, 317–18
being, 14–16, 18, 23–24, 40, 63–68, 105, 125–26, 139, 148–50, 152, 155–56, 159–60, 166–67, 169–73, 176–77, 187–93, 196, 198–99, 206, 208, 210–11, 219–21, 223–24, 230, 235–36, 249–50, 253–56, 264–65, 268–72, 285–86, 292–95, 297–300, 302–3, 307–8, 310–11, 314–15, 318, 326–27, 337–38, 341–42, 345, 348–49, 352–53, 356–57
analogy of (*see* analogy of being)
dynamic ontology, 22–24, 29, 51–52, 67–68, 109, 116, 118–19, 139–40, 154, 187, 198, 208, 234–36, 244–45, 249–51, 259, 263–66, 268–72, 278, 285–86, 291–302, 315–16, 319–20, 323, 326–29, 341–44, 346–53, 356–57, 359
essence-existence distinction, 40, 155–56, 190, 270–71, 294
mode of, 152, 235–36, 270–71, 341–42
non-being, 63–67, 125, 148
ontology, 2–3, 14–15, 26–27, 152, 171–72, 174–75, 186, 189–90, 193, 204, 220–21, 244, 285–86, 291–93
transcendental affections of, 14–16, 40, 63–64, 170, 183, 187, 190–93, 196, 198–99, 210–12, 230, 235–36, 270–72, 278, 291–92, 294–95, 341–42, 348, 350–52, 356–57
univocity of (*see* univocity of being)
Bernard, Richard, 168
Besold, Christoph, 331–33
Bethlen, Gábor, Prince, 276–77
Beurhaus, Friedrich, 106–7, 110–13, 134–35, 137–38
Beza, Theodore, 33–34, 81, 112–13n.44, 113, 134, 145–46, 205–6
Bible. *See* Scripture
biblical languages, 88–89, 202, 283–84, 305–6
Biel, Gabriel, 195–96
bifurcation. *See* dichotomy
Bilhmaier, Sandra, 109–10
Bilsten, Johann, 108–11
Bisterfeld, Johann, 282, 321–22
Bisterfeld, Johann Heinrich, 242, 244, 266, 276, 280–318, 320–21, 324–26, 349, 352–53, 360
Blair, Ann, 41–42, 326
Bodin, Jean, 104, 313
Boethius, 8n.42, 25, 27, 57–58, 60, 315
Bohemian Brethren. *See* Unity of the Brethren
Bohemian Reformation, 319
Bonaventure of Bagnoregio, 3, 9n.51, 10–17, 23–27, 30, 40–41, 43, 48, 50–52, 58–59, 61–62, 65–67, 73–74, 88, 98–99, 102, 153–55, 158–60, 164–66, 168–69, 171, 183–84, 197–98, 202–11, 214–15, 230, 259, 262–66, 271–74, 277–78, 285–86, 301–2, 304–5, 307–8, 311–12, 320, 327–30, 335–38, 340–41, 348–49, 355–57

Books of God, 7–8, 55–57, 153–54, 168–69, 208–10, 262–66, 272–73, 326–27, 333
Bourges, University of, 113–14
Bovelles, Charles de, 50–53, 61–62, 68, 70n.162, 73–74, 76–77, 84–85, 92–93, 99n.130
Bradwardine, Thomas, 37, 156–57
Bricot, Thomas, 48, 153
Britain, 105, 137, 175
Brocardo, Jacopo, 359–60
Brulefer, Stephen, 38–39, 48
Bruno, Giordano, 135–36, 145, 244, 249–50, 253–56, 258, 260–61, 283, 285, 325–26
Bruyère, Nelly, 45–46, 99n.130
Bullinger, Heinrich, 31–32, 117, 175
Burley, Walter, 21, 152–54
Buscher, Heizo, 108–12, 133–34, 172, 261

Cabala, 98, 165, 187, 202, 210, 248–49, 251, 256, 258, 265–66, 283–84, 290, 305–6
Caesarius, Johann, 53n.62, 72
Calvin, John, 2, 31–34, 38–39, 42, 79–81, 117, 120, 132, 175, 210n.187, 215, 261–62, 319, 358
Calvinism, 4–5, 113–14, 133, 242–43, 289
Calvinist resistance theory, 240n.178, 313
Calvinist Thomism, 34–35, 37, 40–41
Campanella, Tommaso, 280–81, 285–86, 291–93, 295, 301–2, 320–21, 325–26, 330–31, 334, 337–38, 353, 359–60
Carpentarius, Jacob, 188, 189n.59
Cartesian, 284–86, 293, 300–1. *See also* Descartes, René
Casmann, Otto, 214–15, 227–31
casuistry, 145–48
catechism, 32, 34, 97–98, 120, 175. *See also* Heidelberg Catechism
categories, Aristotelian, 65–68, 115, 126, 132n.157, 170, 222–23, 253–54, 267, 350–51. *See also* accident; action; passion; quality; quantity; relation; substance
Catholic Church, 29–30, 34–36, 88, 91–92, 103, 119, 215–16, 240, 276, 332–33
causation, 8–9, 11, 18, 27–28, 32, 115–16, 125–26, 171–73, 176–77, 190–93, 224–25, 229–30, 270, 300
  efficient cause, 300
  efficient, exemplar, and final cause (*see* triads: efficient, exemplar, and final cause)
  efficient, formal, and final cause (*see* triads: efficient, exemplar, and final cause)
  exemplar cause, 18, 154–55, 198
  final cause, 161, 171–72, 304–5
  formal cause, 161
  material cause, 161
causes, logical, 25, 27–28, 65–70, 115, 151–52, 172–73, 189n.57
Chaderton, Laurence, 142–44
Chandieu, Antoine de la Roche, 33–34, 38–39
charity, 12, 210, 230–31, 329–30, 336, 361
Charles IX, King, 83n.26, 89–90
Charpentier, Jacques, 82–83, 87
Christ, 6–7, 12–13, 39, 51–52, 83–84, 101, 103, 113, 117–18, 131–32, 134, 165–66, 173, 178, 198, 201–2, 207–8, 210–11, 237–38, 240–41, 258, 260–62, 266, 273–74, 291, 304–5, 313–14, 321–22, 332–37, 340, 343–46, 353–54, 358–59, 361–62
Christ's College, Cambridge, 141–44, 147
Christendom, 3–4, 23, 43, 80–81, 90–91, 93–94, 193–94, 289, 320–21, 354, 361–62
Christian Aristotelianism, 8–10, 37, 40–41, 184–86, 188
Christian humanism, 1, 3, 5–6, 22–33, 43, 45–46, 48–50, 53–56, 62–63, 69, 72, 82–85, 88–89, 105–7, 113–15, 123, 139–41, 181–82, 184–85, 188, 193–95, 205, 211–14, 217–18, 237
Christian philosophy, 3–4, 7–10, 14–15, 31, 42, 47–48, 52–53, 88, 139–40, 159, 162–64, 183–84, 197–98, 203, 208–12, 214–16, 226–35, 243–44, 260, 262, 268, 270–74, 277, 287–89, 309, 321, 328–30, 333, 336–39, 343, 362
Christocentric, 100, 177–78, 273–74, 281, 291, 304–5, 308, 319–20, 343, 361–62
Christology, 39, 117–18, 117n.72, 133–34, 165, 177–78, 201–2, 273–74, 289–91, 304–5, 309–11, 336–37, 344–45
Church, 44, 46, 79–81, 89, 91–92, 94–95, 98–99, 103–4, 113–14, 116–19, 137, 139, 143–44, 153, 175–76, 181, 197–98, 205, 208–11, 214–18, 227, 236–37, 239–41, 246–47, 272, 274–77, 281, 286–89, 292, 306, 308, 313–15, 319, 321, 328–29, 331–33, 335, 343, 354, 358–62
Church Fathers, 41–42, 98–99, 117, 181, 197–98, 200, 273–74
Church of England, 137, 143–44
Cicero, 24–25, 62–65, 115, 123, 126–27, 129, 132n.156, 141, 163–64, 196–97, 237
Čížek, Jan, 266, 357
classical texts, 84–85, 99, 105, 120
*clavis universalis*, 251–57, 299–300
Clement of Alexandria, 98–99, 200, 277

cognition, 11, 70, 160, 186, 204, 234, 257, 264–66, 292–93, 296–98, 311–12, 351
 abstractive, 150–51, 160, 186, 202n.140
 first object of, 186, 204, 302–3, 311–12
 intuitive, 15, 70, 150, 160, 166, 201–2, 259
coincidence of opposites, 12–13, 23–24, 29–30, 52–53, 102, 133, 309–11, 321, 343–48, 361–62
coinherence, 210–11, 260–61, 360
Colloquy of Poissy, 80, 91–92
combinatorial, 18–21, 29, 46–47, 51–52, 68–69, 251, 253–54, 257, 259, 267–68, 271–73, 278–79, 281–83, 286, 290–91, 297–99, 301–2, 305, 307–8, 313–14, 321, 323–24, 327–28, 348–49, 351–53
Comenius, Jan Amos, 135–36, 243–44, 266, 278, 286–87, 299–300, 310–11, 319–62
commentaries, biblical, 114, 123, 130–32, 145, 147–48, 162, 175, 194–95, 219, 246, 274–75
commentaries, logical, 8–9, 48–51, 63, 73, 95–103, 114, 123–24, 142–43, 194, 222, 232, 251–53, 282
common nature, 71n.174, 151, 192–93, 196. *See also* Universals
commonplaces (*loci communes*), 31–33, 89, 97, 130, 132, 135, 197, 267, 306
comparisons, 65, 100, 199–200
*complexe significabile*, 21, 69–70, 126, 152, 185–86
concepts, 2–3, 14–15, 20–22, 49, 69, 74–75, 104, 130–31, 152, 155, 172–73, 185–86, 188–92, 196, 224, 293–94, 297, 349, 352–53. *See also* intentions
conceptual worlds, 22, 297
Conciliarism, 313, 359–60
concordance, biblical, 303–4
concordance, metaphysical, 18, 51–52, 68, 87–88, 104, 254–56, 274–75, 314, 317, 359–60
concordant discord (*concordia discors*), 100, 103, 254–56, 315
Condemnations of 1277, 3, 10, 14
confessionalization, 32–33, 43, 46, 112, 119–20, 124, 127–28, 133–35, 175, 182–83, 215–17, 226, 245–47, 287, 289–90, 332–33
congruence. *See* harmony
conscience. *See* casuistry
consent, political, 313–14, 317–18, 360
consentaneous arguments, 27–28, 67–68. *See also* Ramism: Ramist arguments
consociation, 313–14
contemplation, 12, 52–53, 93–94, 110, 159, 162, 169–70, 179–80, 203, 207–8, 237–38, 240–41, 259, 337, 345, 348

contingency, 39–40, 69, 156–57, 269, 297–98
contuition, 160, 207–8, 265–66
convenience and difference. *See* Lullism: convenience and difference
conversion, philosophical, 124, 143–44, 193, 218, 341
conversion, religious, 44, 60–61, 79n.3, 80, 81n.13, 91–92, 98–99, 119–20, 137, 143–44, 272, 274–75, 341
Copernicus, Nicholas, 89–90, 249
Counter-Reformation, 80–81, 226
covenant, 14, 39–40, 106, 116–19, 122, 135, 139–40, 175–79, 201, 313–14, 316–18
covenantal theology. *See* federal theology
covenantal turn, 117, 156–57
creation (created world), 6–7, 14–15, 18, 22, 41–42, 153–55, 166–67, 174–75, 179, 184–85, 187, 198–99, 207–8, 229–30, 263, 270–71, 293–94, 317–18, 326–27, 338, 346–47, 357
creation, act of, 11, 30, 71–72, 93, 98–99, 117, 155–56, 168–69, 177–78, 184–85, 229–30, 264, 273, 326–27, 337–38
Crell, Fortunatus, 218, 227–28
Cross of Christ, 12, 101, 178, 207–8, 211, 237, 266, 340
Cross, Richard, 4–5, 39
Crypto-Calvinism, 215, 217
Cusan, 46–48, 56–57, 59–60, 84–85, 102, 244, 248–50, 257, 259–61, 281, 285, 292–93, 309–10, 314, 321, 331–32, 334, 336–37, 341–45, 347, 352–55, 357–58
cyclognomic (*Cyclognomica*), 352–53

Daneau, Lambert, 35n.221, 193, 204, 239
Danzig (Gdańsk), 216–17, 221–22, 226, 228–29, 240
Danzig gymnasium, 216–17, 225, 236–37, 239–40, 287–88
declaration, logical, 126–27, 262
decline narrative, 4–5, 14, 35–36, 45
Dee, John, 89–90, 248–49
definition, logical, 16, 32–33, 50, 71–74, 151, 188, 196, 198–99, 222–23, 341, 351
definitions, 50, 65, 71–74, 204, 222–23, 341, 351
deification, 61–62, 207–8, 249–50, 273
delineation (of art), 159–61
democracy, 317–18, 361
demonstration, logical, 57–58, 62–63, 71–72, 126–27, 133, 188, 223, 225, 234–35, 261–62, 309–12, 353
Denys the Carthusian, 256, 266–67, 307–8
Descartes, René, 1, 257, 280–81, 284–85, 291–93, 325

descent, logical, 71–72, 109–10, 271
*devotio moderna*, 48–49, 92
dialectic (probable argumentation), 24, 27–28, 62–63, 105
dichotomous charts, 2, 44–45, 56–57, 73–74, 84–85, 95, 150, 219, 232–33. *See also* Ramism: Ramist charts
dichotomy, 51–52, 73–74, 118, 134–35, 145–46, 150, 172–73, 176–78, 189–90, 197, 208, 222–23, 225, 232–33, 341, 351. *See also* dichotomous charts; Ramism: Ramist charts
difference, 25, 27–28, 169
dignity of man, 23–24, 56–58, 302–3
Dionysian, 8–9, 8n.42, 16, 51, 158–59, 270–71, 357. *See also* Pseudo-Dionysius
disenchantment, 4–5, 139–40
disposition. *See* judgement
dissentaneous arguments, 27–28, 67–68. *See also* Ramism: Ramist arguments
distinctions, scholastic, 32–35, 63–64, 67–68, 157–58, 189–90, 192–93, 210–11, 235, 294
  distinction of reason reasoned (*rationis ratiocinatae*), 157–58
  distinction of reason reasoning (*rationis ratiocinans*), 157
  formal distinction, 16–17, 23–24, 26–28, 39–40, 51–52, 74–75, 151, 158–59, 171, 173, 186–87, 190, 192–93, 196, 198–99, 229–30n.111, 235, 268–71, 286n.38, 293–95
  formal eminent distinction, 192–93
  ideal distinction, 293
  intrinsic distinction, 17, 186, 196, 235
  modal distinction, 190, 192–93, 229–30n.111, 235, 269, 295n.101
  rational distinction, 16, 235, 269, 294, 295n.101
  real distinction, 16, 151, 155–56, 187, 190, 192–93, 205–6, 223, 294, 295n.101
divine dialectic. *See* logic of God
divine dignities. *See* Lullism: absolute principles
divine illumination, 2–3, 7–9, 11–12, 14–17, 23–24, 26–27, 40–42, 50–51, 56–57, 60–61, 67, 70, 72–73, 77, 84, 100–1, 108–9, 111, 135, 149, 158–60, 164–65, 167–69, 200–2, 206–10, 214, 228–31, 234–35, 237, 243–45, 259–60, 267–68, 271, 277–78, 302–4, 307–9, 311, 326–27, 329, 335, 337–38, 343–44, 346, 354–56
divine logic. *See* divine dialectic
divine philosophy. *See* Christian philosophy

division, logical, 20, 25, 50, 57, 59–60, 67–68, 71–72, 98, 128–29, 134–35, 150, 172–73, 188, 222–25, 296, 298, 341, 351
divisions, 65, 341, 351
Dobricius, Johannes, 275–76
Dominican, 8–10, 34–37, 174, 224, 249–51, 260, 285
dominion, 314–18, 330–31
Dortmund academy, 106–7, 110, 134–35
double truth, 10, 226–30, 310–11

eclecticism, 24, 34–35, 40, 43, 117, 122, 137–40, 183–85, 190, 197–98, 215–16, 219, 244–45, 247, 257–58, 266, 286
economics, 163–64, 201, 208, 233–34, 239, 263
ectype, 165–69, 199–202, 204, 263, 297, 316–17, 323, 356–57
ecumenism, 103, 358–60
Eden, 3–4, 13, 20, 22, 41–43, 94–95, 179, 214–15, 231–34, 273, 279, 287–88, 305–6, 332–33, 354–55, 359–60
Edwards, Jonathan, 1, 175
effects, 25, 27–28, 65, 68–70, 101, 125–26, 150–52, 172–73, 189n.57, 199–200, 224–25
election. *See* predestination
eloquence, 82–84, 88–89, 130, 149
emanation, 11, 14–15, 18, 29, 51, 59–60, 67–68, 148–49, 157–60, 164–65, 171–72, 199, 201, 206–7, 210–11, 235–36, 264, 269–71, 273–74, 285–86, 294–95, 300–1, 316–18, 326, 328–29, 346–47, 356, 361–62
  emanation and return, 29, 57–61, 164–65, 198, 271–72, 278–79, 295, 317–18, 351, 357, 361–62
  emanation, exemplarism, and consummation (*see* triads: emanation, exemplarism, and consummation)
  emanation, manation, and remanation (*see* triads: emanation, manation, and remanation)
Emery, Kent, 31–32, 46–47, 58–59
Emmanuel College, Cambridge, 141–44
encyclopaedism, 1, 3, 20, 22–24, 46, 49–52, 58–60, 72–74, 77–78, 80–89, 91, 93–97, 99, 105, 135–36, 138, 146–48, 153–54, 159, 161–65, 174–75, 179–80, 194, 203, 207–16, 220–22, 226, 228–51, 256–57, 260–64, 266–69, 271–79, 281–83, 286–88, 290–92, 299–303, 306, 308, 312, 320–23, 328–31, 333–44, 354–55, 357, 362 (*see also* arts and sciences; immeation; method, triune universal; pansophia)
  apocalyptic encyclopaedism, 243–44, 248–49, 272–79, 281–82, 286–87, 291, 330–31, 333

encyclopaedism (cont.)
  Franciscan encyclopaedism, 12–13, 23–24, 58–59, 94, 159, 164–65, 179–80, 205, 207–10, 214–15, 234–35, 243–44, 263–64, 271–74, 277, 300, 304–5, 321, 328–30, 334–42, 362
  Lullist encyclopaedism, 20, 49, 51–52, 95, 135–36, 211–12, 235, 242–44, 248–50, 256–57, 260–61, 267–68, 272–74, 278–79, 283, 290–92, 299–303, 323–26, 329–30, 334–35, 362
  mathematical encyclopaedism, 13, 49, 51–52, 60, 77–78, 80–84, 93–94, 110, 244, 257
  scriptural encyclopaedism, 7–9, 12–13, 20, 93–94, 163–64, 203, 243–44, 263–64, 266–68, 272–74, 278, 281–82, 291–92, 303–6, 308, 323–24, 339–41
  Trinitarian encyclopaedism, 7–8, 20, 43, 51–52, 135–36, 183–84, 234–35, 243–45, 248–49, 260–61, 272–73, 277–79, 281–82, 286–87, 289, 300–3, 308, 312, 323–24, 329–30, 350, 354–57, 359–62 (*see also* immeation; pansophia; method: triune universal)
end. *See* Causation: final cause
enfolding and unfolding, 293n.83, 296–98, 339–40, 343–44, 349, 352–53, 356–57
Enlightenment, 213–14, 244–45, 281, 357
*ens commune*, 190–92
epistemology, 2–3, 40, 70, 185–86, 207–10, 261–62, 285, 302. *See also* cognition; sense
*eponymia*, 149, 161
Erasmus, Desiderius, 29–30, 48–49, 88, 193–94
erudition, 45–46, 139, 142–43, 181–82, 193–94, 244–45, 258
eschatology, 13, 22, 93–94, 179, 272–76, 279, 289–90, 300, 317–18, 330–34, 359–60. *See also* apocalypticism; Millenarianism
Estouteville, Cardinal d', 83, 87–89
eternity. *See* God: divine eternity
ethics, 7–8, 33–34, 37, 39, 60, 87–89, 100–1, 107–8, 145–48, 163–64, 169–70, 189, 203, 226, 233–34, 239, 253, 278, 288–89, 301
Eucharist, 80, 133–34
*eupraxia*, 88–89, 159–62
evangelical, 47–53, 79–81, 87–92, 101, 103, 163–64, 175, 197–98, 211–12, 273–74, 281, 299, 307–8
exegesis, 124, 126–32, 135–36, 144–46, 172–73, 194–95, 210, 247, 275–76
exemplar. *See* Causation: exemplar cause
exemplarism, 2–3, 7–15, 17–18, 21–24, 26–27, 29–30, 37, 39–43, 46–48, 51–52, 55–59, 70, 74–76, 84–85, 93, 101, 104, 109, 122, 128–29, 137–40, 150–51, 154–55, 158–66, 168–71, 176–77, 179–80, 183–86, 192–93, 196–208, 211–12, 214–15, 228–33, 236, 239–40, 244, 249–50, 254–56, 260–66, 269–72, 277, 279, 285–88, 295–98, 301, 304–6, 308, 313–19, 323, 326–30, 336–37, 339–40, 347–52, 355–58, 360–62. *See also* God: divine ideas; God: divine truth; ideas
  scriptural exemplarism, 29–30, 165, 168–69, 177, 183–84, 197–98, 203, 265–66, 278, 304–6, 315–16, 339–41
  Trinitarian exemplarism, 7–8, 17–18, 39–40, 42, 197–99, 202, 204, 207–8, 214, 234–35, 260–61, 264–66, 270–72, 277–78, 285–86, 291, 295, 299, 301, 305–6, 308, 313, 336–37, 356–57, 360–62 (*see also* immeation)
exemplars. *See* ideas

Fabricius, Jakub, 216–17, 228
Fabrist, 46–55, 59, 61–64, 68n.152, 73, 75, 77–88, 92–93, 95n.111, 98–99, 101–2, 104, 184–85, 197–98, 242n.11, 248–50, 258, 260–61, 273–74, 281, 299, 362
Facca, Danilo, 213–14, 220–22, 228
faith, 12, 20, 37, 98, 101, 118, 129–32, 145–46, 153–54, 162, 165, 200–1, 203, 207, 210, 230, 237, 262, 284, 310–11, 336–37, 344–45, 355–56, 361
faith, hope, and charity. *See* triads: faith, hope, and charity
Fall, the, 13, 93–95, 108–9, 116–18, 127–28, 166–67, 174–75, 177–78, 229, 233–34, 300–1, 306, 311, 350, 354, 359–60
Fantis, Antonio de, 184–85
Farel, Guillaume, 79–80, 113
federal politics, 313–15
federal theology, 106, 112–13, 116–19, 135, 139–40, 175–76, 178–80, 240, 281, 313. *See also* covenant
Feingold, Mordechai, 45–46, 139, 141–42
Fenner, Dudley, 119n.86, 143n.39, 145, 168, 175
Ficino, Marsilio, 23–24, 50–51, 84, 163–64
Fine, Oronce, 53, 68n.152, 87
Flood, the, 93–94
Fludd, Robert, 248–49, 283n.18
form. *See* Causation: formal cause
France, 20–21, 42, 46–49, 55, 79–84, 89–91, 109–10, 184, 284–85, 287–88. *See also* Paris, University of
Francis of Assisi, 12, 23
Francis of Meyronnes, 24n.146, 177–78
Franciscan encyclopaedism. *See* encyclopaedism: Franciscan encyclopaedism

Franciscan metaphysics. *See* metaphysics: Franciscan metaphysics
Franciscan reformation of method, 3–4, 17, 42, 46–47, 211–12, 350, 362
Franeker, University of, 147–48, 165, 288–91
freedom, 39–40, 54–55, 102, 313–17, 357, 360
Freige, Johann Thomas, 84–85, 106–7, 194
Frisius, Paul, 108–10
further reformation, 31, 137, 143–44, 175–76, 216–17, 247, 276–77, 288–89

Galen, 71–72
Gansfort, Wessel, 256, 307–8
Gemma, Cornelius, 248–49, 324, 352–53
genesis, logical, 56–57, 85–87, 120, 150, 161, 256, 299–300
Geneva academy, 113, 283–84
Geneva, 33–34, 46, 79–80, 175–76, 260
genus, 21, 25, 51–52, 57, 71–76, 100, 111–12, 126, 133–34, 150–52, 229–30n.111, 263
geometry, 52–53, 59–60, 73, 77–78, 89–90, 104, 109, 111, 162–63, 259, 292–93, 298, 333–34, 345
George of Trebizond, 53n.62, 84, 184–85
Germany, 33–34, 62, 80, 89–90, 105–12, 119–20, 124–25, 133, 137, 175–76, 181, 183, 193–95, 205, 215–21, 227, 245–46, 248, 261, 274–77, 286–88, 297, 333–34
Gerson, Jean, 48–49, 82–83, 88–89
Gnesio-Lutheran, 215–16, 226–28
Goclenius, Rudolph, the Elder, 121, 134–35, 183, 188–93, 196–98, 214–15, 219–21, 224, 227, 232–33, 247–49, 270–71, 286
God
   absolute and ordained power of (*see* absolute and ordained power)
   divine art, 22, 159–62, 164–65, 171–72, 339–40
   divine attributes, 16, 18–20, 119n.88, 157–58, 165n.178, 171n.211, 173–74, 177, 187, 192–93, 198–99, 203, 208, 235, 254, 257, 259, 268–70, 294–95, 301–2, 315–16, 329
   divine decrees, 39, 102, 116–19, 139–40, 156–57, 176–78, 199–200, 205–6, 262–63, 272n.188, 316–17
   divine essence, 155, 157–59, 173–74, 198–99, 201–3, 206–7, 269–70, 294–95, 309–11, 347–48
   divine eternity, 2–4, 11, 18, 39, 55–58, 77, 118–19, 155–56, 176–77, 199, 205–6, 235–36, 269–70, 278, 310, 316–17, 344–47, 349–50, 355–57

divine exemplars (*see* God: divine ideas; *see also* exemplarism)
divine freedom, 22, 39–40, 98–99, 178, 201, 210–11, 317–18
divine goodness, 18, 198, 200, 207–8, 210–11, 229, 235–36, 270, 295
divine ideas, 2–3, 6–9, 11, 14, 16, 18, 21, 27, 30, 57–61, 75–77, 93, 109–10, 139–40, 154–61, 168–69, 171–73, 198–200, 202, 205–6, 229–34, 268–70, 278, 296–97, 304–5, 326–28, 339–41, 343–44, 346–48, 350, 354–58, 361
divine immanence, 158–60, 201
divine infinity, 14–15, 22, 39, 57–59, 65–67, 77, 102, 117, 134, 165–66, 172, 190, 199–200, 235, 249–50, 257–59, 309–12, 317–18, 345–47, 357
divine intellect, 109, 235–36, 269
divine logic (*see* logic of God)
divine love, 117–18, 208, 273–74
divine mind, 6–7, 16, 30, 56–61, 75–77, 98–99, 106, 109, 115–16, 118–19, 139–40, 154–56, 159–60, 171–72, 176–77, 185–86, 192–93, 196–97, 199–200, 204, 206, 229–32, 234–35, 249–50, 262–63, 271–72, 278–79, 296–97, 327–28, 339–40, 347–49, 356–57
divine names, 20, 157, 165n.178, 202, 210
divine omniscience, 227–28, 337, 339–40, 343, 348, 353
divine persons (*see* Trinity)
divine power, 16, 18, 22, 122, 157–58, 178–79, 229, 326, 329 (*see also* absolute and ordained power)
divine power, understanding, and will (*see* triads)
divine power, wisdom, and goodness (*see* triads)
divine power, wisdom, and love (*see* triads)
divine reason, 76–77, 158–59, 204–6, 278
divine simplicity, 16, 37, 155–61, 169, 171–72, 174–75, 204
divine transcendence, 39, 45–46, 131–32, 154, 158–59, 171–72, 176, 310–11, 340, 348–49
divine truth, 7–8, 18, 30, 43, 59–61, 138, 154, 174–75, 199–200, 204, 230–32, 258, 339–40
divine understanding, 138, 154, 156–59, 165–66, 179, 205–6, 348
divine unity, 12, 16, 57–58, 103–4, 207–8, 268–71, 300, 305–6, 317, 353, 355–56, 361–62

God (*cont.*)
  divine will, 14, 18, 93, 102, 116–19, 156–58, 165–66, 177, 179, 201, 205–6, 210–11, 269, 313–14, 316–17, 326, 347
  divine wisdom, 55, 60–61, 92–93, 102, 111, 115, 127–29, 161, 166, 174–75, 189, 200–3, 227–29, 236–37, 268, 300, 326, 335, 339–40, 347, 351–53
  glory of, 18, 42, 116, 138, 143–44, 153–54, 162, 178, 181, 198, 201–2, 251, 277, 299–300, 304, 306, 317–18, 321–22, 338, 340, 354, 362
  righteousness of, 117n.77, 165
  Trinity (*see* Trinity)
golden age, 46, 83–84, 91–92, 98–99, 103, 359
golden chain, 57–58, 87–88, 161–62, 176–77, 240, 293–94, 327–28, 353
goodness, 162, 166–67, 200, 229, 235–36, 295, 301–2. *See also* being: transcendental affections of; triads: unity, truth, and goodness
good works, 145–46, 203
Gospel, 41–42, 79, 92, 272, 319, 331–32, 336
Goulding, Robert, 46–47, 55, 59–60, 80–83, 91, 94–95
grace, 37, 39–41, 100–1, 112, 169–70, 178, 207–10, 214, 242–43, 248, 251, 261–62, 284, 300, 302–3, 317
  common grace, 228–29, 237
  special grace, 237, 261–62
Grafton, Anthony, 45–46
grammar, 72–73, 81–82, 94, 123–24, 142, 149, 152, 161, 167, 171–74, 185, 189, 208, 223–24, 258–59n.102, 299–300, 337
Granger, Thomas, 168, 174–75
Gregory of Rimini, 21, 185–86
Grosseteste, Robert, 11, 14–15
Grynaeus, Johann Jakob, 193, 205
Guise family, 79–81, 83
Guise, Cardinal, 91–92
gymnasia, 106–8, 125, 215. *See also* academies
Gyulafehérvár, 276–77, 287–90, 303

habits, 127–28, 219, 231, 234, 301–2. *See also* art; intelligence; prudence; science; wisdom
*haecceitas*, 24n.146, 229–30n.111, 270–71
Han, Byung Soo, 195, 202–3, 214–15, 243, 261
harmonic philosophy. *See* infinite philosophy
harmony, 3, 7–8, 34–37, 84–85, 100–1, 103–4, 108–9, 115, 139–40, 158n.138, 163–64, 166, 176, 183, 187, 197–98, 202, 208–10, 220, 229–30, 233–35, 239–41, 251, 257–61, 265–67, 284–86, 292–95, 297, 299–306, 308–9, 312–18, 328–29, 333–34, 338–41, 349, 359–60

Hartlib circle, 283–84, 303, 320–21, 330–31, 358
Hartlib, Samuel, 283, 285
Harvey, Gabriel, 142–43
healing, 91, 114–15, 135, 222–23, 233–34, 238, 273–74, 277, 311, 333–34
heaven, 43, 57–58, 60–61, 92–93, 161–62, 278, 304–5, 331, 337, 339–40, 359–60
Hebrew. *See* biblical languages
Heereboord, Adriaan, 284–85, 296
Heidelberg Catechism, 112–14, 238, 287–88
Heidelberg, University of, 107, 113–14, 117–20, 122–23, 182, 194, 197, 213, 217–22, 225–26, 238, 276–77, 322–23, 330
Helmstedt, 226–27
Herborn academy, 106–8, 112, 119–22, 124, 132–33, 135–36, 175–76, 194–95, 240, 245–47, 250–53, 266, 275–77, 281–83, 286–88, 312–14, 321–24, 330, 335
Herborn Ramism. *See* Herborn school
Herborn school, 106, 112, 135–36, 175–77, 211–12, 240, 244–46, 280–82, 285, 288, 313, 320–21, 362
heresy, 44, 88, 92, 133, 226–27, 242–43, 332–33
hermeticism, 242–44, 247–48, 250, 261, 272–74, 291, 308, 321, 330, 333–34
  Reformed hermeticism, 243, 248
hexameral, 11, 41–42, 204, 337–38, 357
history, 92–95, 117, 139–40, 162–63, 176, 178–79, 263–64, 272, 274–75, 279, 291, 301, 319, 329, 359. *See also* eschatology; Joachimite
Hoenen, Maarten, 15, 40
Hofmann, Daniel, 226–28
Holcot, Robert, 174, 206, 311
Holy Roman Empire, 215, 315, 333–34
Holy Spirit, 6–7, 104, 167–68, 179, 201–2, 205–6, 210–11, 227–28, 240–41, 269, 333–35, 359. *See also* Trinity
Honnefelder, Ludger, 183, 236
hope, 12, 210, 336, 361
Hotson, Howard, 2, 45–46, 106–8, 112, 119–21, 123–24, 127–28, 137–38, 141, 181–82, 189–90, 213–16, 218, 226, 232–33, 242–47, 249, 251–53, 261, 266, 272–76, 278–79, 290–91, 320–23, 341, 351
Hugh of St Victor, 11–12, 153–54, 262–64
Huguenot, 1, 79–81, 137, 184, 326–27
humanism, 1, 3, 5–6, 22–33, 43, 45–46, 48–56, 62–63, 69, 72, 82–85, 88–89, 105–7, 113–15, 123, 139–41, 181–82, 184–85, 188, 193–94, 195, 205, 211–14, 217–18, 237

Hungary, 200-1, 205, 275-76, 288-89, 310, 321-22
Hus, Jan, 202, 272, 274, 316-17, 319, 331-32, 345, 353, 358
Hussite, 12-13, 317, 319-22, 331-32, 336, 341, 354-55, 358, 361
Hyperius, Andreas, 31-32

Iconius Egli, Raphael, 135-36, 247, 249
ideas, 2-3, 5-6, 30, 57-60, 64, 74-77, 93, 108-9, 111-12, 138-40, 154-61, 171-73, 192-93, 196-201, 205-6, 229-34, 239-41, 269-70, 287-88, 296-97, 304-5, 315-18, 326-28, 339-42, 346-50, 353-58, 361. *See also* God: divine ideas
identity, 18, 67-68, 75, 158, 188-90, 192-93, 206, 210-11, 235-36, 270-71, 309-11
*Idiota(e)*, 55, 83-84
illumination. *See* divine illumination
image of God, 12, 110, 134-35, 207-8, 213-14, 233-34, 237, 242-43, 246, 257, 302-3, 317-18, 322-23, 329, 336-37, 354-55, 357, 361-62
immanence. *See* God: divine immanence
immeation (*immeatio*), 260-61, 281-82, 295-308, 310-11, 316, 352-53
inadequate concepts, 293-95
Incarnation, 117-18, 177-78
incommensurability, 309, 311
individual, 2-3, 15-16, 21, 27-28, 45-46, 51-52, 69-70, 74-75, 88, 111-12, 134, 148-51, 156-57, 186, 192-93, 196, 229-30, 251, 270-71
individuation, 74, 151, 186, 229-30n.111, 270-71
induction, 326-28, 339
infinite circle, 259, 343
infinite philosophy, 244, 257-61
infinite sphere, 12, 61-62, 102, 211, 348
infinity. *See* God: divine infinity
infinity of the human mind, 249-50, 258, 302-3, 318, 349
innate notions. *See* principles: innate principles
instants of nature, 18, 39-40, 71-72, 118-19, 151, 156-57, 160n.150, 177-79, 260-61, 269-71
instauration of the image of God, 129-30, 213-14, 233-34, 237-38, 242-43, 246, 257, 302-3, 317-18, 322-23, 329-31, 354-55, 361-62
instrument, logical, 27-28, 109-10, 181, 188, 219, 223-24, 230-34, 254, 292, 296-98

intellect, 6-7, 12, 52-53, 59, 92-93, 109, 149-51, 161-62, 185, 196, 207-8, 211, 219, 224, 229-30, 233-36, 238, 240-41, 253-54, 270-71, 295-97, 300-3, 306, 311-12, 315, 317-18, 329-30, 339-40, 351-52. *See also* understanding
intellectual cognition. *See* cognition
intelligence, 159, 203-4, 207-8, 267-68, 301
intentions. *See also* concepts
  first intentions, 20-21, 63-64, 109-10, 141, 152, 188-89, 195-96, 224, 224n.73, 253-54, 292-93, 296-97
  second intentions, 20-21, 63-64, 109-10, 141, 152, 188-89, 195-96, 224-25, 253-54, 292
intuition. *See* Cognition: intuitive
invention, logical, 27, 29-30, 50, 59-60, 64-68, 93, 111-12, 115, 123, 126-29, 135, 149-50, 161, 170, 188-89, 196-97, 222-23, 234-35, 253-54, 257-58, 296-98, 304, 306, 327-28, 350-53
irenicism, 103, 358
Islam, 8n.42, 20, 24n.144, 272, 276, 289
isomorphism, 16, 111-12, 154
Italy, 23-24, 33-34, 48-51, 84, 228, 285-86

Jardine, Lisa, 45, 140
Jensen, Kristian, 185-86, 190-92
Jerusalem, New, 143-44, 339-40, 354
Jewish, 8n.42, 20, 24n.144, 93, 163-64, 272, 274-75, 283-84, 289-90
Joachim of Fiore, 13, 274-75, 331-32, 359
Joachimite, 274-76, 321, 330-32, 354-55, 359-60
Johann VI of Nassau-Dillenberg, Count, 119-21
Johnston, Mark, 17, 21-22, 307-8
judgement, logical, 27, 59-60, 62, 64, 69-70, 72, 77-78, 81-82, 93, 111-12, 115, 123, 135, 145, 149-50, 161, 166, 170, 188-89, 196-97, 222-23, 231, 234-35, 253-54, 296, 298, 306-7, 350-51
Junius, Franciscus, 197, 199, 202
justice, 118-19, 166

Keckermann, Bartholomäus, 127-28, 213-44, 246-47, 250-51, 253-54, 257, 261-62, 268-69, 277-79, 282-83, 286-89, 291-92, 308, 312-14, 341, 350-51
Kingdoms of Nature, Grace and Glory, 274-75, 279, 312
Korbach academy, 106-7, 121
Kotter, Christoph, 330, 332-33
Kuchlbauer, Simon, 319-20, 324, 344-45

ladder of ascent, 12, 51, 58–59, 68, 77, 207–8, 249–50, 254–56, 271, 293, 297–98, 300, 307–8, 352–53, 356
late medieval Augustinianism, 21, 36–37, 40–41, 69–70, 125–26, 152, 170, 185–86, 261–62, 314, 316–17
Latomus, Bartholomew, 48–49, 53–54, 62
Lavinheta, Bernado de, 51–52, 248–49, 253–54, 260, 268–71, 273–74, 278–79, 330
law, 41–42, 91, 118–19, 148, 162–63, 264, 290, 292, 313–14, 316, 331–32
Lawson, George, 173–74
learned ignorance, 101–2, 334, 339, 348, 353
Lefèvre d'Étaples, Jacques, 46–47, 49–54, 59–60, 65, 73, 76–77, 79–80, 84–85, 88–89, 92–93, 100–3, 184–85, 361
Leibniz, Gottfried Wilhelm, 1, 244–45, 257, 280–82, 295, 310–11, 325
Leiden, University of, 182, 188, 284, 304
Leinkauf, Thomas, 22, 244, 320
Levitin, Dmitri, 45–46, 244–45
light. *See* metaphysics: metaphysics of light
light of grace, 167–68, 268, 304
light of nature, 77, 167, 200–1, 208–10, 268–69, 278, 304
light of reason. *See* light of nature
light of Scripture, 278, 302–3, 311
living image, 56–57, 339, 354–55, 357
logical affections (*logismoi*). *See* Ramism: Ramist arguments
logic of being and non-being, 63–67, 125, 148
logic of Christ. *See* logic of Scripture
logic of faith (*logica fidei*), 12–13, 29–30, 101, 130, 133–34, 139, 173–74, 176, 206, 211–12, 309, 311–12, 321, 353
logic of first intentions, 21, 109–10, 195–96, 224n.73, 253–54
logic of God, 65–67, 98, 101, 166, 172, 174, 189n.58, 204, 304–5, 345–46, 353
logic of Scripture, 12–13, 29–31, 98, 127–28, 131–32, 134–36, 153, 168–70, 174–75, 288, 303–6, 308, 311, 353
logic of second intentions, 109–10
logic of transnaturals. *See* logic of God
Lohr, Charles, 18, 22, 244
love, 39–40, 103, 117–18, 201–2, 208–11, 230–31, 236–38, 263–64, 267–68, 277, 315–16, 360–61
Ludwig I of Wittgenstein, Count, 114, 119, 123
Lull, Ramon, 17–24, 65–68, 152, 187, 248–49, 253–56, 260–61, 268–69, 273–74, 285–86, 307–8, 320, 323–24, 352–53

Lullism, 3–6, 17–22, 29, 43, 46–47, 51–53, 56–57, 63–70, 84–85, 121, 135–36, 152, 187, 195–96, 202, 211–12, 215–16, 219, 235, 242–44, 247–61, 263, 265–69, 271–73, 278–79, 281, 283, 285–86, 290–92, 296–99, 301–6, 308, 311–12, 314–16, 320–21, 323–25, 327–30, 334–36, 341–43, 348–56
  absolute principles, 18, 22, 253–54, 260–61, 352–53
  convenience and difference, 51–52, 263, 267, 296–98, 304, 306–8, 314–15, 351
  correlative principles, 18, 20, 22, 51–52, 260–61, 278–79, 291–92, 295, 297, 307–8, 316, 341–42, 346–47, 352–53
  Lull's Art, 17–18, 20, 29, 51–52, 248–49, 251–53, 257, 259, 290, 304, 307–8
  Lullist wheel, 18, 249–50, 259, 273, 278–79, 291, 297–98, 307–8, 323–24
  Reformed Lullism, 247–61, 263, 265–69, 271–73, 278–79, 281, 283, 285–86, 290–92, 296–99, 301–6, 308, 311–12, 314–16
  respective principles, 18, 22, 253–54, 259, 352–53
  *Tree of sciences*, 20, 95, 256, 292, 323–24
Luther, Martin, 2, 29–31, 134, 174, 205–7, 210, 319, 331–34, 345, 358
Lutheranism, 31–32, 34, 41–43, 103, 107–8, 114, 119, 123, 133–35, 172, 215–18, 226–28, 247, 274–75, 310–11, 331–34

Mack, Peter, 27, 68, 75–76
macrocosm, 264–66, 268
magic, 282–83, 328n.54, 333–34
Mair, John, 38–39, 48
manation, 8–9, 294, 300
Marburg, University of, 106–7, 121, 134–35, 245–51, 272–74
Marguerite of Navarre, 61–62, 79, 81n.14
Martinius, Matthias, 246–47, 321–22
mathematical logic, 296–99, 349–50
mathematics, 23, 29–30, 41–42, 46–47, 49, 51–54, 57n.84, 58–62, 68, 73–74, 77–78, 80–91, 93–94, 97–98, 101–2, 104, 109–10, 148, 161–62, 164–65, 170, 187, 189, 193–94, 208, 226, 233–34, 244, 250, 253, 257–61, 281, 283, 286, 290, 292–93, 297–99, 301, 309–10, 324, 334–35, 337, 346, 348–51, 355, 357, 361
*mathesis*, 258, 299, 349–51, 353
*mathesis universalis*, 257–61, 273–74
McKim, Donald, 138, 144
medicine, 71–72, 91, 110, 114–15, 127–28, 148, 237, 247–48, 257, 273–74, 290, 301

meditation, 88, 237, 256, 266, 281–82, 302–4, 307–8, 352–53
Meerhoff, Kees, 62, 105, 213, 218, 220
Melanchthon, Philipp, 24, 29–34, 41–43, 49, 60, 72, 89–90, 97, 106–13, 115, 120–21, 123, 126–27, 133, 140, 172, 181, 183, 193–95, 204–7, 216–18, 237, 261–62
Melville, Andrew, 137, 175
memory, 6–7, 12, 85–87, 145, 150, 251, 253–54, 277
memory, understanding, and will. *See* triads: memory, understanding, and will
Menk, Gerhard, 121
metaphysical logic, 63, 109–11, 299
metaphysical turn, 62–64, 105, 183–84, 352n.220
metaphysics
   Franciscan metaphysics, 14–16, 23, 139–40, 198, 210–11, 260, 285–86, 294–95, 337–38, 355–56
   metaphysics of light, 11–12, 14–16, 23, 51, 67, 148–49, 158–60, 164–65, 206–7, 210–11, 236–37, 258n.101, 259–60, 269, 301–2, 328–29, 337–38, 355–56
   ontology (*see* being: ontology)
   Trinitarian metaphysics (*see* Trinity; Trinitarian metaphysics)
method
   analytic method, 224–25, 233
   synthetic method, 224–25, 233
   three laws of, 108–9, 111–12, 127, 220–21, 298, 327–28
   Triune universal, 261, 264–66, 268, 281, 300–1, 303, 323–26
methodical Peripateticism, 213–15, 218, 221–25, 233
microcosm, 264–66, 268
Mildmay, Sir Walter, 143–44
Millenarianism, 13, 246, 272, 274–77, 289, 291, 321, 330–36, 354, 359–60. *See also* apocalypticism; eschatology
Miller, Perry, 44–47, 138–39, 179
Milton, John, 1, 141–43
mind, 2–3, 7, 12, 15–16, 20–21, 27–28, 30–32, 54–62, 64, 69–70, 77, 93, 103, 109–12, 125, 127–30, 135, 145–46, 148–50, 152, 154–56, 160, 167–68, 186, 188, 199–202, 207–8, 223, 231, 233–34, 236, 249–50, 253–54, 257–58, 268, 271–72, 278, 281–82, 292–93, 296–97, 300–3, 305–8, 311–12, 326–29, 336–37, 339–40, 347, 349–52, 355, 357
mnemonic, 73–74, 84–85, 249–51, 260, 301, 307–8

modern devotion. *See devotio moderna*
*modistae*, 152, 185
Moltmann, Jürgen, 116, 182–83, 211–12
moments of being. *See* instants of nature
monarchy, 240–41, 272, 317–18, 330–31, 361
Moritz of Hesse, Landgrave, 247–48
Mosaic philosophy/theology, 41–42, 98–99, 193, 248
Mosaic physics, 11, 227, 270–71
Moses, 41–42, 44, 88–89, 91, 335
most special species, 75, 111–12, 134
Muller, Richard, 4–5, 31–35, 37, 40–41, 99n.131, 132n.157, 155–57, 171, 182–83, 214–15, 226, 228, 230, 237, 243, 261–62
Mulsow, Martin, 281, 285, 293–94
multiplicity, 12, 23–24, 51–52, 59–60, 67–68, 145–46, 155–56, 158, 171–72, 240, 244–45, 256, 292–93, 299–300, 305–6, 326, 349, 354–56
Murdock, Graeme, 276, 286–87
Muslim. *See* Islam
mystery, 37, 134–35, 172–74, 229, 234–35, 261–62, 309–12, 341, 351
mystical ascent, 12, 23–24, 51, 210–11, 249–50, 263–64, 266–67, 281–82, 302, 336–37
mystical illumination, 210, 266–67
mystical purgation, 210, 266–67
mystical union, 12, 58–59, 207–8, 211, 238, 240–41, 264–67, 293–94, 302–5, 311–12, 318, 357
mysticism, 12, 23–24, 42, 47–53, 58–62, 93, 101, 135, 207–8, 210–11, 249–50, 259, 263–64, 266–67, 281–82, 291, 302, 321, 332–33, 335–38, 340, 343, 358–59

names, 65, 126, 196–97
Nancel, Nicholas, 53–54, 89–90
Nassau, 119, 282
natural dialectic, 54–57, 64, 93, 109, 111–12, 114–16, 148, 327, 353
natural law, 37, 39, 122, 278
naturally prior and posterior. *See* instants of nature
natural logic. *See* natural dialectic
natural middle, 29, 254–56, 327–28
natural philosophy. *See* physics
natural theology, 169–70, 261–66
nature, 54–60, 111, 114–15, 127, 141, 153–54, 168–69, 188, 207–11, 224–25, 258, 262–64, 267–68, 272–75, 277, 279, 293–94, 296–97, 303–5, 308–10, 312, 323–27, 329–30, 337, 339–40, 359–60
Nauta, Lodi, 28, 31–32, 69

414  INDEX

necessary reasons, 20, 235, 262
necessity, 27, 69–70, 72–73, 98–99, 167, 171–72, 201, 210–11, 232, 297–98
Neo-Platonism, 3–9, 8n.42, 10–11, 18, 22, 24, 27, 30–34, 36–37, 40–42, 45–52, 54, 58–59, 67, 70, 72–73, 75–76, 84–85, 100, 106–10, 135–36, 138–39, 141, 148–49, 153–59, 164–65, 176–77, 179–80, 184–85, 187, 194, 197–98, 200–1, 203–7, 210–12, 220, 235, 240, 247, 249–50, 254–56, 259–60, 269, 271, 278, 286, 292–94, 296–99, 301–2, 313–15, 320, 326, 329–30, 336–38, 347–49
    Florentine, 50–51, 84, 163–64
    Renaissance, 23–24, 31, 34–35, 184–85, 197–98, 242–43, 286
Neo-Pythagoreanism, 41–42, 46–47, 54, 59–62, 82–83, 89–91, 135–36, 187, 285–86, 292–93, 299–300, 309–10, 343, 348–49
Netherlands, 119, 147, 175–76, 245–46, 284, 286–87
Neval, Daniel, 320, 336, 361
New England, 105, 139, 147–48, 175–76, 242
New World, 1, 143–44, 330–31
Nicholas of Cusa, 12–13, 22–24, 29–30, 50–65, 89–90, 100–2, 104, 187, 248–50, 258–61, 281–82, 285–86, 292–93, 296–97, 299–300, 302, 305–6, 310–11, 315, 317, 319–21, 324, 328–29, 336–37, 339, 341–45, 347–50, 359–62
Noah, 93–94, 163–64, 234, 340n.148
Nominalism, 2–4, 15, 26n.158, 29–30, 34–35, 37–41, 45–46, 48, 65, 69–70, 74, 85–87, 111–12, 117, 138–39, 150–51, 154–55, 171–73, 186, 195, 198–99, 206–7, 257–58, 262, 293–97, 310, 327–28. *See also* terminism
non-being. *See* being: non-being
number, 7, 12–13, 29, 55, 59–60, 73–74, 77–78, 89–90, 98, 100–2, 110, 114–15, 198, 223, 292–93, 298–99, 349–51, 355, 357
    perfect number, 223, 349
number, measure, and weight. *See* triads: number, measure, and weight

Oberman, Heiko, 15, 38–39
occult, 243, 273, 321, 328n.54. *See also* hermeticism; magic
Ockham, William of, 15, 173, 195–96, 206, 310n.207
Olevian, Caspar, 112–25, 127–28, 132, 135–36, 175, 245–46
omniscience, human, 302–3, 311–12, 318, 323, 337, 339, 343, 348–49, 353, 357

Ong, Walter, 44–46, 65–67, 69–72, 75–77, 81–82, 84–87, 182, 213
Oosterhoff, Richard, 46–47, 49, 51, 55, 77–78, 84–85
opposites, 51–52, 65, 68, 73–74
orator. *See* rhetoric
ordained power. *See* absolute and ordained power
order, 2, 7, 28, 32, 43, 51–52, 60–61, 64, 67–68, 71–73, 89, 97–98, 100, 103, 109–12, 115, 117, 127–30, 139–40, 145, 150, 161–62, 168–69, 176–79, 188–90, 197, 208–10, 219, 223–25, 229–34, 239–40, 270–71, 277, 292–94, 299, 306–9, 312, 317, 323–24, 341–42, 347, 353, 361
orthodoxy, Reformed, 31–34, 216, 237, 242–43, 284
Osiander, Andreas, 331–33, 360n.277
Oxford, University of, 8, 10, 141, 283–84

Pace, Giulio, 218–19, 222, 250–53
Padua, University of, 33–34, 36–37, 90n.76, 184–86, 218–19, 227
pagan philosophy, 7–8, 50–51, 88, 100–1, 127–28, 203. *See also* Aristotelianism; Platonism
Palatinate, 113–14, 119, 275–76, 283–84, 330
panacea, 257–58, 261, 263, 267–68, 273, 296, 323–24
panharmony, 202, 284–85, 292–94, 299, 302, 304–5, 308–9, 312, 315–16
Pannonius, Stephanus, 275–76
pansensism, 285, 291–92, 325–26, 338
pansophia, 161–62, 244, 250, 266, 319–26, 336–60, 362
papacy, 10, 35–36, 91, 272, 274, 319, 331–34, 358, 361
parable, 260, 353
Paracelsianism, 247–48, 274, 332–33
Paracelsus, 274, 283n.18, 332–34
Pareus, David, 218–20
Paris, University of, 8, 10, 20–21, 38–39, 44–45, 47–55, 62, 65, 69–70, 72, 75, 79–84, 87–90, 92, 141, 217–18
participation, 4, 8–9, 14–15, 18, 37, 139, 155–56, 160, 171, 179–80, 200–1, 206–8, 210, 238, 244, 278, 285–86, 329–30, 343
passion, 294, 315–16, 341–42
Patočka, Jan, 319–20, 341–43
Patriarchs, 41–42, 44, 93–94, 234
Paul, the Apostle, 11, 50–51, 102, 237
Pavlas, Petr, 319–20, 341–42
peace, 90, 103–4, 118–19, 230–31, 237, 354, 359–62

Pelagianism, 35–36, 243
  anti-Pelagianism, 37, 284
  modern Pelagianism, 40–41
  semi-Pelagianism, 243
Pelbartus of Temesvár, 200–2
Peripateticism, 213–15, 218, 221–25, 233, 253–54, 282–83
Perkins, William, 144–48, 150–51, 162–65, 168, 175–80, 250, 327–28
persuasion, 24, 128–29, 306
Peter of Spain, 20–21, 125n.121, 195–96
Petrarch, 23, 267–68
Philippism, 31–32, 43, 106–13, 115, 120, 123, 183, 193, 205, 215–18, 226–27, 287, 296–97
Philippo-Ramism, 106–13, 115–16, 120–21, 123, 134–36, 172, 181, 213–14, 216–17, 250, 261, 282–83, 297
philology, 26–27, 181–82, 290
physics, 7–8, 11, 33–34, 60–61, 87–88, 107–8, 124, 148, 161–62, 170, 183, 189, 203–4, 208, 223–24, 226–27, 233–34, 253, 270–71, 278, 285, 290, 301, 325–26, 337–38, 357
Pico della Mirandola, Giovanni, 23–24, 50–51, 57–59, 100, 187, 229, 258, 270, 291, 305–6, 359–60
piety, 10, 35, 83–84, 88–89, 101–3, 119–20, 145, 147, 162, 166, 169–70, 175–76, 214, 236–37, 239–40, 251n.65, 287, 291, 306, 321–22, 332–33
Pinder, Ulrich, 336–37, 339, 345, 355, 357, 360n.277
Piscator, Johannes, 112, 114, 121–38, 142–43, 167–68, 172, 175, 183, 189, 193–98, 218, 246, 256, 275–76, 286–88, 305, 308, 322, 330
Piscator, Ludwig, 276, 286–87
place, 27–28, 65–67, 341–42
Plato, 6–9, 16n.102, 26–27, 42, 44, 50–51, 65–67, 71, 76–77, 83–84, 88–93, 98–99, 107–10, 114–15, 137, 155–56, 163–64, 184–85, 198, 218, 230n.112, 338–39, 349–50
Platonism. *See* Neo-Platonism
poetry, 61–63, 84, 127–28, 141–42, 184–85, 189, 223, 290, 301–2, 329
Polanus von Polansdorf, Amandus, 181–84, 193–97, 203–5, 210–12, 236, 247, 268–69, 304–5
politics, 87–88, 163–64, 189, 203, 208, 214–15, 226, 233–34, 238–41, 263, 281, 292, 312–14, 360
polity, 89, 98, 239–41
Pope. *See* papacy

Porphyrian tree, 71–72, 74
possibility, 8–9, 156–57, 233–35, 310–11, 347–49, 356–57
possible worlds, 347, 349, 356–57
post-Ramist, 137–38, 213–16, 244, 250
power, 70, 162, 260–61, 295, 300–2, 306–8, 315, 317–18, 347, 360
practical divinity, 144, 159, 175–76
pragmatism, 62–63, 80–81, 107–9, 239–40, 329
praxis, 98, 138, 145–46, 159, 169–70, 195, 237–38, 354–55
prayer, 97–98, 273–74, 337–38, 340
predestination, 13, 37, 39–41, 102, 116, 118–19, 165, 175–78, 237, 240–41, 248, 261–62, 284, 316–18
predicables, 115, 196. *See also* difference; genus; individual; Porphyrian tree; species
predicaments. *See* categories, Aristotelian
predication, 21, 29, 40, 69–70, 133–34, 173–74, 190–92, 195–96, 253–56, 327–28, 351–52
Přerov, 183–84
Presbyterianism, 46, 80, 288–89
Presles, College of, 83–84
primalities of being, 285–86, 291–92, 295, 325–26, 330–31, 360. *See also* triads: power, wisdom, and love
primitivism, 92, 94–95
principle of non-contradiction, 12–13, 228, 298, 310–11, 343–45
principles, 92–93, 97, 114–15, 166–67, 187–89, 200–1, 203, 223–24, 232–34, 256, 266–67, 271, 278, 292–94, 300–1, 338, 349. *See also* Lullism
  first principles, 8, 63–64, 109, 161, 327
  innate principles, 30, 111–12, 261–62, 266–68, 292–93, 355
printing, 44–45, 135, 143, 175–76, 205, 331–32
*prisca philosophia*, 83–84, 99, 163–64, 234, 248
*prisca theologia*, 99, 184–85, 335
Prometheus, 92–94, 234
proof, 71, 129n.143, 131–32, 222–23
prophecy, 13, 129, 131–32, 143–44, 163–64, 203, 274–76, 330–32, 359
proposition, 20–21, 26–28, 50, 69–70, 125–27, 149–50, 152–54, 161, 185, 188, 223, 254–56, 298, 306–7, 351–52
propositional Realism, 21, 69–70, 150–54, 168–69, 196–97, 298. *See also* Realism
Protestant scholasticism. *See* scholasticism
providence, 93–94, 116, 175–76, 193, 272–73
prudence, 159, 203, 233–34, 237–40, 267–68, 301, 312–13, 315–16
Pseudo-Dionysius, 11, 23–24, 50–51, 102, 171–72, 210–11. *See also* Dionysian

pure act, 37, 347
pure possibility, 347–48, 356
Puritanism, 105, 137–48, 175–76, 179–80, 242, 283–84, 288–89
Pythagoras, 60, 65–67, 89–91, 114–15, 292–93
Pythagorean sphere. *See* infinite sphere
Pythagorean. *See* Neo-Pythagoreanism

quadrivium, 51, 58–60, 77–78, 208, 350. *See also* arts and sciences
quality, 157, 294, 341–42
quantity, 161, 294, 341–42
quiddity, 76–77, 155–57
Quintilian, 24, 62–64, 77–78, 196–97

Rákóczi dynasty, 286–90
Ramism
  pseudo-Ramist, 222, 227–28
  pure Ramism, 111, 121, 137–38, 170, 174–75, 189n.55, 214–15, 225, 282–83, 288–89
  Ramist arguments, 57–60, 64–70, 74–76, 98, 115, 125–34, 149–52, 168, 170, 172–73, 189, 196–97, 199–200, 243, 253–54, 262, 297–300, 305–7, 310–11 (*see also* adjuncts; Causes; comparisons; definitions; divisions; effects; names; opposites; subjects; testimonies)
  Ramist art, 55–59, 62, 72–73, 77–78, 100–1, 109–11, 127, 148–49, 159–62, 164–65, 168, 171–72, 188, 222
  Ramist chart, 2, 44–45, 56–57, 95, 115, 132, 134–35, 145, 150, 163–64, 179, 189–90, 192–93, 197, 205, 219, 232–33, 256, 263–64, 277, 282–83, 287–88, 341
  Ramist encyclopaedism (*see* encyclopaedism)
  Richardsonian, 146–59, 164–66, 179–80, 198–99, 211–12
Ramus, Peter, 1–5, 24, 29–31, 42–115, 117, 120–21, 123–30, 133–34, 137–39, 141–43, 145, 148–50, 153–54, 159, 161–62, 170, 172–73, 176–77, 181–83, 188–98, 204–5, 214–25, 232, 244–46, 251–53, 259, 261, 282, 288, 297–99, 315, 321–22, 327–29, 331–32, 343, 350–51, 357, 359, 361–62
  martyrdom of, 1, 43–44, 80, 137, 181, 222
rationalism, 4–5, 210, 214, 309–11, 321, 324, 344–45, 348–49
Ravensperger, Hermann, 135, 322
Realism, 2–5, 16–17, 21, 25–29, 31–32, 39–40, 42–43, 46–47, 50–52, 59, 65, 69–70, 74–76, 109–12, 122, 125–29, 133, 137–43, 150–55, 158–59, 168–72, 183, 185–87, 194–97, 224–25, 229–30, 245–47, 257–58, 262–63, 293, 298, 314, 316–17, 319–20, 327–28, 336, 339, 343, 351–52 (*see also* propositional Realism; topical Realism)
reason, 9, 11–12, 23, 37, 52–53, 57–60, 62–63, 70, 100–1, 105, 109, 111, 114–15, 129–30, 133–35, 148–49, 160, 166, 168–72, 195–96, 200–1, 204, 207–8, 213–14, 223–24, 227–28, 230, 233–35, 245, 258, 261–62, 268, 271, 297–98, 300–4, 309–12, 323–24, 326–29, 338, 344–46, 350–52, 355–56, 359–60
redemption, 93, 111, 119n.88, 177, 179, 203, 264, 273–74
reduction (*reductio*), 12, 17, 58–59, 61–62, 139–40, 164–65, 203, 208, 327–28, 348–49, 355–56
Reformation, the, 2–5, 27, 29–32, 35, 42, 80–81, 88, 103, 113–14, 153, 176, 213–14, 237, 242–43, 274–75, 291, 308, 331–33, 358–59
Reformed scholasticism. *See* scholasticism
Regiomontanus, Johannes, 89–90
Reid, Jonathan, 47, 80–81
Reiss, Timothy, 46–47, 77–78
relation, 22, 27–28, 65–70, 72–73, 81–82, 125–26, 129–30, 150, 154–55, 185, 201–2, 235, 254–56, 259, 269–70, 285–86, 293–94, 314–18, 351–52
religion, 4–5, 20, 32, 44, 80–84, 88–91, 103, 124, 137, 162, 240–41, 289–90, 309, 329–31, 354, 359–62
Renaissance, 3–6, 18, 20, 22–25, 31–32, 42, 45–46, 48–49, 56–57, 59–62, 69, 71–74, 83–84, 92–94, 99, 102, 105, 128–29, 150, 184–85, 187, 195, 205, 211–12, 218, 220, 223, 244, 248–50, 254–56, 273, 285, 297–98, 334. *See also* Christian humanism; Neo-Platonism: Renaissance
  Northern, 32–33, 48–49
  Twelfth-century, 8n.42, 99, 285–86
Republic, Christian, 26–27, 240
resistance theory, 240, 313
Reuchlin, Johannes, 205, 220n.43, 286
revelation, 17, 50–51, 94, 100–1, 103, 108–9, 111–12, 116, 131–32, 139, 167–69, 174–76, 179–80, 200–1, 208–10, 248, 262–63, 311–12, 328–29, 338–40. *See also* Scripture
rhetoric, 1, 24–29, 45, 55, 62–64, 68, 71–72, 77–78, 81–84, 94, 97, 105, 113–14, 120, 123–25, 127–29, 133, 139, 142–43, 149, 161–63, 167, 171–74, 189, 196–97, 208, 223–24, 250, 259, 282, 287–88, 290, 299–301, 304, 306–8, 321–22, 337. *See also* Ramism: Ramist arguments; topics (*loci*)

INDEX 417

rhetorical turn, 24, 62–63, 105, 223
Rhineland, 53–54, 72, 106–8, 275–76, 332–33
Richardson, Alexander, 138, 146–59, 161–62, 167–69, 171–74, 263
Richardsonian Ramism. *See* Ramism: Richardsonian
righteousness, 117n.77, 131, 165
rights, 313–15
Risse, Wilhelm, 45, 63–64, 109
Rivetus, Andreas, 284, 302–3
Rollock, Robert, 119n.86, 175–78
Rosencreutz, Christian, 333–34, 336
Rosicrucianism, 321, 333–36, 354–55, 359
Rossi, Paolo, 46–47, 326–28
Rupescissa, John de, 273–76, 283n.18, 331–32, 334n.105, 335

salvation, 94, 116, 126–27, 167, 176–78, 201–2, 239, 277, 306, 309, 359–60
salvation history. *See* history
Savonarola, Girolamo, 224, 274
Scaliger, Julius Caesar, 183–93, 195–99, 211–12, 215, 219, 222–25, 236, 268–69
Schegk, Jacob, 72, 122, 190–93, 195
scholasticism, 1, 3–4, 8, 12–13, 18, 20–21, 24–27, 29–36, 38–41, 43–45, 48–49, 53–55, 62–64, 69, 74, 84, 88–89, 95, 97–99, 105–7, 114–16, 122, 125, 135, 138–41, 145–48, 154–59, 161, 165–66, 169–74, 181–86, 188, 192–93, 195, 197–98, 206, 211–12, 214, 217–18, 222–24, 226–27, 235–38, 245–46, 301–2, 311–12, 319–20, 325–27, 336, 338–39, 343–44, 347. *See also* Aristotelianism; Nominalism; Scotism; Thomism
  Protestant, 4–5, 31, 33–34, 43, 112–13n.44, 181–82, 188, 215–16, 226–27
  Reformed, 5–6, 31–42, 105–7, 114–16, 122, 125, 135, 145–48, 181–84, 188, 192–94, 206, 211–12, 215–16, 237
  second scholasticism, 34, 45, 139, 183
Schöner, Lazarus, 121
science, 8, 20–21, 24, 63–64, 105, 125, 159, 169–72, 185, 188–93, 195–96, 200–3, 219, 223–24, 233–34, 236–40, 267–68, 278
  practical science, 39–40, 100–1, 144–46, 159, 163–64, 169–70, 182, 189, 201–3, 224–25, 233, 236–38, 263–64, 290, 301–2
  theoretical science, 189, 203, 224–25, 233–34, 236, 263–64, 301–2
*scientia sermocinalis*, 20–21, 125, 195–96. *See also* speech
Scotism, 4–5, 15–16, 18, 23–24, 28–29, 31, 34–41, 43, 48, 50–52, 63–65, 70–72, 74–75, 111–12, 117–19, 122, 126, 139–40, 151, 153–60, 163–66, 171, 177–78, 183–88, 190–94, 196–202, 206, 210–12, 214–15, 224, 229–30, 235–36, 244, 246–47, 253–54, 268–72, 285–86, 293–95, 313–14, 341–42
  Reformed Scotism, 31, 34–41, 43, 117–19, 122, 139–40, 165–66, 171, 178, 183, 188, 190–93, 196–202, 211–12, 236–38, 244, 246–47, 268–72, 313–14
  topical Scotism, 75, 153
Scotland, 38–39, 119n.86, 121, 137, 175
Scotus, John Duns, 14–17, 21, 23–24, 26–28, 35–40, 48, 51–52, 65–67, 74–77, 117–19, 150–59, 169–70, 172, 175, 177–79, 184, 186–87, 190–93, 195–202, 204, 229–30, 235, 237–38, 268–71, 285–86, 293–95
Scribonius, Wilhelm Adolf, 124–30
scriptural logic. *See* logic of Scripture
Scripture, 7–8, 12–13, 25, 29–34, 41–42, 88, 93, 98, 100–1, 103, 114, 120, 123–24, 126–34, 139–40, 142–48, 162–70, 173–77, 189, 194–95, 199–200, 202–3, 208–11, 216–17, 227, 230–31, 242–43, 246, 251–53, 256, 262–68, 271–73, 275, 277–78, 281–82, 290–91, 300–11, 323–27, 335, 337–40, 343–46, 353, 355, 359–61. *See also* revelation
Sebonde, Ramon de, 56–57, 324, 358
second coming. *See* eschatology
second reformation. *See* further reformation
seeds of arts and sciences. *See* principles: innate principles
seeds of knowledge. *See* principles: innate principles
Sellberg, Erland, 45–46, 75–76
Semi-Ramist. *See* Philippo-Ramism
sense, 11, 30, 51, 59, 99, 149, 155–56, 160, 207–8, 271–72, 285–86, 300–2, 325, 329, 338–40, 351–52, 355–56
sense, reason, and revelation. *See* triads: sense, reason, and revelation
sensible cognition. *See* cognition; sense
Servetus, Michael, 205–7
Shakespeare, William, 1, 142–43
Sheehan, Jonathan, 45–46, 244–45, 266
Sidney, Philip, 1, 95–97, 142–43
Silesia, 193, 275
singular, 51–52, 57–58, 74–76, 110, 150–51, 154–55, 185, 196, 268, 271, 296–97, 309–10
Skalnik, James, 46, 80–83, 103–4
Snell, Rudolph, 222–23, 225, 227–28, 232
sociability, 281, 293–95, 314

society, 1–2, 4, 20, 31, 43–44, 46, 80–81, 83–84, 104, 110, 139, 175–76, 181, 214–16, 236–37, 239–41, 246–47, 276–77, 281–82, 286–89, 292–94, 300, 312–18, 321, 330–31, 354, 358–62
Socinianism, 171n.212, 289, 346
Solomon, 163–64, 248, 335, 337–38
sophistry, 53, 87, 92, 94–95, 133–34, 147, 222–23, 225
Sorbonne, 51–52, 83, 222
soul, 6–7, 12, 16, 23–24, 29–32, 59–60, 70, 83–87, 93–94, 109–10, 114–15, 135, 144–46, 151, 176–77, 187, 196, 198–99, 207–10, 228–29, 233–38, 257, 270–71, 273–74, 277–78, 300–3, 307, 311–12, 317–18, 329, 336, 339, 354–55, 357, 361
  faculties of the, 6–7, 94, 111, 161–62, 208–10, 229, 233, 257, 267–68, 300–2, 329, 335
  powers of the, 12, 16, 187, 196, 235–36, 270–71
  transformation of the, 23–24, 83–84, 302, 354–55, 358 (*see also* instauration of the image of God)
species, 21, 25, 51–52, 57, 71–76, 126–27, 133–34, 150–51, 192–93, 196, 229–30n.111, 263
speech, 55–56, 61–62, 139, 149, 167, 171–72, 195–96, 257, 307–8, 347, 350. See also *scientia sermocinalis*
spiritual logic, 65–67, 248–49, 261, 328–29
squaring the circle, 23, 52–53, 102, 259, 344, 348
St Bartholomew's Day Massacre, 1, 105
Stoicism, 69–70
Strasbourg, 48–49, 103, 122
Streso, Caspar, 303–4
Sturm, Johannes, 48–49, 53–54, 62, 71–72, 74, 90, 107, 120, 122–23
Suárez, Francisco, 34, 158, 169–71, 215, 293
subjects, 25, 65, 68, 75–76, 126, 352–53
substance, 69–70, 74–77, 126
supernatural logic. See logic of faith (*logica fidei*)
Sweden, 276, 330
Switzerland, 117, 283–84. See also Geneva
syllogism, 8, 12–13, 20–22, 24–27, 48–49, 69–70, 72, 89, 95, 126–28, 134–35, 145–46, 149–50, 152, 166, 168, 172–73, 220–23, 233–34, 256, 298, 310–11, 327–28, 345, 351–52
symbiotics, 293–94, 301, 312–18, 360
symbolic, 7, 70, 74, 79–80, 92–93, 125–26, 195–96, 259, 344, 353
symphonic method, 193, 195, 197–98, 202, 247, 304–5

synchronic contingency, 39–40, 156–57, 269
Synod of Dordt, 147, 156–57, 175–76, 282, 284
system, 1–4, 7–8, 11–13, 25, 29–30, 32–34, 36–37, 40–41, 45, 49, 51, 58–59, 71–74, 77, 98, 105–9, 111–12, 115–20, 123, 132–33, 135, 137–38, 141–48, 152–54, 161, 169–70, 175, 179, 182–83, 188–90, 194–95, 197, 199, 205, 210, 219–25, 231–33, 237, 239–40, 242, 246–47, 251–54, 260–61, 267, 282–85, 288–89, 296–98, 301, 304, 308, 312–13, 317, 323–24, 326–27, 339–41, 343, 353–57, 361
Szegedinus, Stephanus, 183–84, 205–12, 236, 263–64, 289, 291–92, 310
Szentpéteri, Márton, 279, 286–87

tables, logical, 49, 84–85, 146–47, 207–8, 267, 297–98, 304, 306
Talon, Omer, 62n.119, 120, 321–22
Tartaret, Pierre, 48, 51–52
*technologia*, 138, 154, 257, 278–79
temple, pansophic, 339–41, 354, 359
Temple, William, 124–30, 137–38, 142–43
Ten Commandments. See Decalogue
terminism, 50, 53–55. See also Nominalism
terms, logical, 20–22, 24–27, 29, 50, 65–70, 111–12, 125–27, 144, 151–52, 173, 185, 195–97, 200, 206–7, 223, 253–56, 260–61, 278–79, 290–91, 297–98, 305–6, 312–13, 327–28, 351–53
testimonies, 65, 128–32, 167, 230–31, 259, 344–45, 351–52
testimonies, divine, 128–32, 167, 230–31, 259, 344–45, 351–52
testimonies, human, 128–30
therapeutic, 106, 110, 114–16, 118, 135–36, 214–15, 236–41, 277
Thirty Years' War, 213, 272, 275–76
Thomism, 34–41, 74, 122, 139, 151–52, 155–59, 169–71, 183–85, 187, 190–92, 198–99, 211–12, 214–15, 224, 237–38, 261–62, 270, 278, 285–86, 294–95
  Calvinist Thomism, 34–41, 122, 139, 171, 183, 190–92, 198–99, 211–12
Timpler, Clemens, 214–15, 220–22, 224–25, 231–33, 246, 257, 286, 292–93, 349
Tipson, Baird, 166–67
topical Realism, 25, 29, 31–32, 43, 109–10. See also Scotism: topical Scotism
*topica universalis*. See *clavis universalis*
topics (*loci*), 24–34, 49, 64–68, 100, 106, 115, 120, 123, 130, 132, 135, 196–97, 205, 222–23, 251–54, 267, 297–98, 306, 349–53. See also Ramism: Ramist arguments

transcendence. *See* God: divine transcendence
transcendentals. *See* being: transcendental affections of
Transylvania, 206, 242, 276–79, 281–83, 286–89, 291–92, 310, 313, 330, 352–53
tree of knowledge, 20, 240n.179, 323–24
*Tree of Sciences. See* Lullism: *Tree of Sciences*
triads, 11–12, 18, 64, 71–72, 98–99, 164–65, 187, 192–93, 208–10, 232, 234–35, 257–58, 263–68, 270–75, 278–79, 294, 296, 300–2, 306–7, 315–16, 326, 329, 337–38, 341–42, 350–51, 355–57, 361
   divine power, understanding, and will, 177, 179, 269
   divine power, wisdom, and goodness, 42, 187, 207–10, 229, 285–86, 295
   divine power, wisdom, and love, 12, 270, 295, 301–2, 329–31, 337–38, 347, 355–57, 360
   efficient, exemplar, and final cause, 8–9, 192–93, 229–30, 270
   emanation, exemplarism, and consummation, 10, 12, 164–65, 179–80, 198, 355–56
   emanation, manation, and remanation, 8–9, 294–95, 300
   faith, hope, and charity, 12, 210, 336, 361
   intellect, will, and executive power, 300–2, 306, 315, 317–18
   matter, light, and spirit, 326n.38, 337–38, 357
   memory, understanding, and will, 6–7, 12
   number, measure, and weight, 7, 55, 89–90, 298, 340n.148, 350–51, 355, 357
   sense, reason, and revelation, 329, 338, 351–52, 355–56
   unity, truth, and goodness, 14–15, 170, 187, 210–11, 278, 295, 350–52, 356–57
trichotomous logic, 208, 223, 341, 351, 353
trichotomy, 223, 341, 351
Trier, 113–14
Trinitarian encyclopedism. *See* encyclopaedism: Trinitarian encyclopaedism
Trinitarian exemplarism. *See* exemplarism: Trinitarian exemplarism
Trinitarian metaphysics, 9, 11, 16, 18, 183–85, 187–88, 190, 192–93, 211–12, 214–15, 227–31, 235–36, 243–44, 247, 268–71, 278, 285–86, 291–92, 294–96, 300, 314, 319–20, 325–26, 329–31, 337–38, 341–43, 347–51, 356–57. *See also* immeation; primalities of being
Trinitarian method, 9, 22, 98–99, 176, 178, 205–12, 261, 263–66, 301, 304–8, 314–16, 321, 323–24, 341. *See also* method: Triune universal

Trinity, 6–8, 11–12, 14–16, 18, 22, 37, 39–40, 42–43, 98–99, 104, 116, 118–19, 134–35, 157–58, 167–68, 172–74, 176–80, 184–85, 187, 190, 192–93, 196–99, 201–2, 204–11, 223, 225, 227–29, 234–36, 240–41, 245, 260–66, 268–72, 274–75, 277–79, 281, 285–86, 289–91, 293–95, 297, 300–1, 303–6, 308–12, 314–18, 325–26, 329, 331–33, 335–37, 341–47, 351, 353–57, 359–62
Trithemius, Abbot, 274, 324, 352–53
trivium, 51, 60–61, 63, 77–78, 161, 208, 350. *See also* Arts and sciences
truth, 7–11, 14–15, 17, 20–21, 25–27, 30, 42–43, 50–51, 54–55, 59–61, 69–70, 77, 87–88, 98, 100–1, 103, 115, 125–27, 129–30, 135, 145–46, 149–50, 154, 161, 165, 171–72, 174–75, 185–86, 192–93, 196–97, 199–202, 204, 226–32, 234–36, 254–56, 258, 267–68, 295, 298, 300–2, 310–11, 326–27, 333, 339–41, 347, 349–52. *See also* being: transcendental affections of; triads: unity, truth, and goodness
Tübingen, 122, 193, 331–33
Turnèbe, Adrian, 72, 217–18
two books. *See* Books of God

Ubiquitarian, 103, 216, 228, 235. *See also* Lutheranism
understanding, 6–7, 12, 69, 134, 149, 152, 156–57, 174, 204, 234–35, 307, 329–30, 352–53. *See also* intellect
union with Christ. *See* mystical union
unitive containment, 16, 158–59, 270–71
Unity of the Brethren, 194–95, 319, 321–23, 331, 335–36, 354–55, 361
unity, 12, 18, 23–24, 29, 43, 51–53, 57–60, 67–68, 73–75, 103–4, 138, 159, 161, 198, 234, 240, 257–58, 268, 285–86, 292–93, 295, 299–300, 326, 349, 353–56, 361–62. *See also* being: transcendental affections of; triads: unity, truth, and goodness
universal language, 284–85, 354, 358–60
universal method, 20, 51–52, 58–59, 62–63, 77–78, 97, 261–66, 281, 300–1, 303, 344
universal reform, 2–4, 13, 27, 91, 127–28, 135–36, 183–84, 251–53, 274–75, 283–84, 289–91, 312, 319–21, 333–34, 349–50, 354–55, 358–60, 362
universal religion, 330–31, 354, 359–62
universals, 2–3, 15–16, 21, 26–28, 30, 51–52, 70, 74, 75n.198, 109–12, 138, 150–51, 185–86, 192–93, 196, 224–25, 229–30, 251, 254–56, 259, 269–71, 296–97, 328n.60

universal wisdom. *See* pansophia
universe, 25, 42, 57, 61–64, 87–88, 168–69, 187, 222–23, 229, 249–50, 253–56, 263, 277, 279, 285–86, 295, 302, 304–5, 318, 333–34, 336, 341, 352–53
univocity of being, 4–5n.20, 14–15, 17, 23–24, 40, 65–67, 171, 190–92, 206, 270–71, 286n.38, 310
Urim and Thummim, 93, 111, 135, 165
Ursinus, Zacharias, 113–14, 117–19, 133, 213, 217–20, 225, 238, 251n.65
use, 27, 64, 68, 77–78, 85–87, 90, 111, 114–15, 131, 138, 145–46, 148, 161–62, 169–70, 194–96, 199–200, 203, 231, 310, 315–16, 329, 341–42, 356
Utopia, 330–31, 359–60

Valeriis, Valerius de, 248–49, 253–54, 256, 268–69
Valla, Lorenzo, 24, 26–27, 32–33, 50–51, 62, 69
Van Asselt, Willem, 4–5, 39, 201
Vermigli, Peter Martyr, 33–34, 36–37, 39n.245, 103n.159
*vestigia Trinitatis*, 6–7, 9, 12, 14–15, 29, 60–61, 207–8, 268
*via antiqua*, 117, 193–94, 220n.43, *See also* Realism
*via moderna*, 38–39, 117, 217–18, 220n.43, *See also* Nominalism
Victorines, 263–64, 285–86, 340
Vienna, University of, 89–90, 205
Vignon, Eustace, 114–15
Villanova, Arnold de, 273–75

virtue, 37, 85–87, 101, 210, 237–41, 315–16, 336
Voetius, Gisbertus, 38–39, 158n.138, 171n.212
Vos, Antonie, 39

Wainwright, Robert, 175
Walker, George, 146–47
Wars of Religion, 44, 80, 89–91
*Wegestreit*, 34–35, 257–58
Wetterau, 114, 119–20
will, 6–7, 12, 39–40, 162, 233–38, 257, 270–71, 295, 300–2, 306–7, 315, 317–18, 329–30
wisdom, 7, 45–46, 55, 60–61, 72–73, 101–2, 111, 115, 127, 159, 174–75, 198, 203, 208–10, 227–29, 231, 267–68, 301, 315–18, 335, 338–39, 354
Wittenberg, University of, 33–34, 181, 205, 217–18
worship, 58–59, 152, 170, 174–75, 239, 263–64, 341
Wyclif, John, 152–54, 168–69, 272, 274, 316–17, 319, 345, 353, 358
Wyclifite, 12–13, 317

Zabarella, Jacopo, 189n.56, 218–21, 223–25, 231, 233
Zabarellan logic, 218–25, 227, 231, 233, 238
Zanchi, Girolamo, 33–34, 36–37, 42, 145–46, 177
Zimara, Marcantonio, 185–86
Zion. *See* New Jerusalem
Zurich, 103, 117, 175, 194
Zwicker, Daniel, 344–47
Zwingli, Huldrych, 38–39, 117, 134, 175, 193–94, 358